S I X T H   E D I T I O N

OPERATIONS MANAGEMENT
Customer-Focused Principles

Richard J. Schonberger
Schonberger & Associates, Inc., and University of Washington

Edward M. Knod, Jr.
Western Illinois University

Boston, Massachusetts   Burr Ridge, Illinois   Dubuque, Iowa
Madison, Wisconsin   New York, New York   San Francisco, California   St. Louis, Missouri

Irwin/McGraw-Hill

*A Division of The **McGraw·Hill** Companies*

OPERATIONS MANAGEMENT: CUSTOMER-FOCUSED PRINCIPLES

This book is printed on acid-free paper.

Printed in the United States of America
  2 3 4 5 6 7 8 9 0 VH/VH 9 0 9 8 7

ISBN 0-256-19406-8

Publisher: *Tom Casson*
Sponsoring editor: *Colleen A. Tuscher*
Senior developmental editor: *Gail Korosa*
Marketing manager: *Colleen Suljic*
Project supervisor: *Karen M. Smith*
Production supervisor: *Dina L. Genovese*
Designer: *Matthew Baldwin*
Prepress buyer: *Jon Christopher*
Compositor: *Interactive Composition Corporation*
Typeface: *10/12 Times Roman*
Printer: *Von Hoffmann Press, Inc*

Library of Congress Cataloging-in Publication Data

Schonberger, Richard.
    Operations management: customer focused principles / Richard J.
  Schonberger, Edward M. Knod, Jr. —6th ed.
      p.   cm.
    Includes index.
    ISBN 0-256-19406-8. —ISBN 0-256-21533-2 (instructor's
  ed.)
      1. Production management.   I. Knod, Edward M.   II. Title.
  TS155.S3244   1997
  658.5—dc20   96–21354

http://www.mhcollege.com

As world trade and global communication networks draw each of us nearer to everyone else, it sometimes seems that life has become too complicated. Whole industries migrate from country to country, riding the currents of lowest labor costs, best tax deals, hottest markets, and most stable political climates. The fortunes of nations, and nations' labor forces, rise and fall in the wake. Steady hands and reliable management are needed to cope.

In business and nonprofit organizations, we sometimes find the necessary steadiness and reliability in operations—the activities in which people carry out the actual transformations of resources into products and services. Just as often, however, the right ingredients are missing. Those ingredients—the *essentials of effective operations management (OM)*—are the main focus of this book. As a practical matter, however, we also present more traditional, often less effective, practices, simply because they are in use. Special contrast boxes scattered throughout the text suggest which conventional OM concepts still work well and which do not, and why.

Operations Management is intended as an introductory textbook, suitable for majors or non-majors, undergraduate or graduate. In addition, practicing operations managers and associates have found it useful as a general guidebook and basic reference.

Effective operations management begins and ends with the customer. The modern view is that every member of every organization has customers at the next processes, where one's work goes next. We earn our pay, and much of our job-related satisfaction, too, from serving those customers well. That means consistently high and every-improving quality—as judged by the customers.

Consistent with that viewpoint, this book's main themes revolve around 15 principles of customer-focused operations management. Chapter 2 presents the full list of principles, which we reiterate as margin notations next to related discussions throughout the book.

Inasmuch as customers are never satisfied, always expecting a bit better performance from their providers, a continuous-improvement objective cuts across all of the principles. Achieving that objective requires engaging, coordinating, and continually upgrading the operating resources of the organization: data, equipment, tools, space, materials, and, especially, people. Effective OM harnesses the talents of front-line employees, technicians, experts, supervisors, and upper-level managers. Their individual skills—as designers, schedulers, equipment operators, planners, and so on—are important, but that is not enough. Individuals too easily get fixated on their own narrow role, to the neglect of the *whole* product or service and its user, the *final* customer.

Therefore, in this text, we emphasize people operating in teams for improved delivery of goods and services to customers. The full power of this approach requires team membership that crosses organizational and company boundaries, heavy reliance on process data and data analysis, and local responsibility for results. These themes—customer-focused, team-driven, data-based continuous improvement—are centerpieces of the worldwide total quality management (TQM) movement.

With other supplementary study materials or readings, this book could serve as a TQM textbook. Eight chapters—1, 2, 3, 4, 5, 8, 9, and 18—provide a strong TQM foundation. Additional TQM-oriented topics may be found in parts of Chapters 10, 11, 12, 16, and 17.

Part of continuous improvement is preventing things from going wrong, which greatly simplifies operations management. Unexpected stoppages, delays, and slowdowns are avoided, making planning easier and cutting out corrective actions that ripple back through the organization disruptively. The simplification theme, found throughout this book, cuts both ways: Simplify to reduce mistakes. Reduce mistakes to make work life simpler.

This should not imply that OM is itself simple and easy to master. Managing operations, even in small organizations, is complex, because it involves coordination of diverse resources, processes, suppliers, and customer demands.

The relevance of operations management to you may be quite direct. If you are an employee—or even a volunteer in a service capacity—as well as a student, you *are* an operations manager. That is, you have some amount of responsibility for planning and controlling the activities though which you convert resources into goods and services that add value to society. Coupled with a little creativity, you will be able to better manage your personal operations. And in the long run—perhaps throughout your career—principles you first encountered or refined in your study of *Operations Management* may serve you well as your management responsibilities continue to grow.

Acknowledgments

We offer special thanks to a wise group of experts who reviewed our text and manuscript and whose candid advice was mostly incorporated. They include Joseph Biggs, California Polytechnic State University; Ashok Chandrashekar, Oregon State University; Sudhakar Deshmukh, Northwestern University; Shad Dowlatshahi, University of Texas at El Paso; James Gilbert, University of Georgia; Mark Ippolito, Indiana University-Purdue University at Indianapolis; Vaidyanathan Jayaraman, University of Southern Mississippi; Farzad Mahmoodi, Clarkson University; Taeho Park, San Jose State University; Farhad Raiszadeh, The University of Tennessee at Chattanooga; and Edward Walker, University of Georgia.

We once again thank those individuals whose input over the past editions has helped the book evolve to its present form: They include: S. Keith Adams, Iowa State University; Karen Brown, Seattle University; James J. Browne, New York University; James P. Gilbert, University of Georgia; James R. Gross, University of Wisconsin, (Oshkosh); Ray M. Haynes, California Polytechnic State University; John J. Lawrence, The University of Idaho; and Victor E. Sower, Sam Houston State University.

We are appreciative as well of specialized advice and information provided by Joseph Devoss of DeVry Institute of Technology for checking the calculations in the problems. Steve Replogle and Farhad Moeeni, both of Arkansas State University, prepared the Study Guide, and Steve Replogle also provided the PowerPoint Lecture Guide and Transparency Masters.

Finally, we thank our publication team headed by Colleen Tuscher, Sponsoring Editor; Gail Korosa, Sr. Development Editor; Karen Smith, Project Editor; Matt Baldwin, Designer; and Dina Genovese, Production Manager, for their efforts to bring real teamwork into this complex business of transforming ill-formed ideas and rough drafts into a complete learning package.

Richard J. Schonberger
Edward M. Knod, Jr.

Operations are everywhere, harnessing resources to provide a service or produce a product. As such, operations constantly touch your life. At times, you are the passive recipient. At others, you may be an involved customer interacting with the operations processes or part of the process as an employee or manager.

Keep these points in mind as you study operations management (OM), and look for ways to make your customer, employee, or manager role more pleasant and productive. If you do that, you will be right in tune with the story line of this textbook.

Yes, it is a story of a sort—a tale of planning and running the inner workings of an enterprise to suit the needs of its customers. Collaborators in this pursuit are other activity areas such as marketing, accounting, product design, human resources, and information systems. As you study OM, you'll find plenty of tie-ins to these other areas, which you may have studied separately. You will obtain the greatest benefit from these studies if you are able to master the details—the tools and techniques of OM—and at the same time develop a vision of how OM and the other functions form a customer-serving whole.

The lore of OM ranges from the complex to the simple. You may be surprised that the book generally favors simple techniques, which are easiest for people to learn, practice, and believe in. The complexity lies more in sorting out what techniques to use in which situations. It does not help that the operating landscape keeps changing: new technologies, markets on the move, shifting competitive threats, economic and political turbulence.

The OM solutions have their hard side, including mathematical treatments. They also have their soft side, such as guidelines, procedures, flowcharts, and organization into teams.

As you study successive chapters, you will encounter repeating core topics: principles of customer-serving operations management; quality first; quick, flexible responsiveness; and continuous improvement, to name a few. The chapter-to-chapter overlapping of these topics is deliberate in that it parallels practices in well-run organizations. Unlike a prior era, when, say, quality was assigned to a quality control department, today's best practices make such important responsibilities everyone's job. Happily, it is easier to really comprehend a topic that crops up several times in different contexts than in the usual textbook fashion: Hit it hard once and quickly put it out of mind.

Special features designed to provide relevance, interest, and help in your studies include:

- Margin notes that highlight a major point, define a term, or add an insight.
- Other, special margin notes in every chapter that connect a point back to "principles of operations management" from Chapter 1.
- Boxed presentations of real-life applications.
- Photos of successful implementations.
- Videotape series, shown at the discretion of your instructor.
- "Contrast" boxes comparing conventional concepts with newer ideas.

- Examples illustrating complex concepts and calculations.
- End-of-chapter solved problems.
- Key-word listings collected into a glossary at the end of the book.
- A large, thorough index.
- A study guide covering key topics.
- End-of-book exercises that tap relevant materials found on the Internet and the World Wide Web.

Good luck in your OM studies. And please let your instructor know what you like and don't like about the sixth edition. We value your opinion, passed on to us via the instructor. Continuous improvement is our objective, too!

R. J. S.
E. M. K.

CONTENTS

OPERATIONS MANAGEMENT
Customer-Focused Principles

Operator Gnoc Matthews is assembling a Deskjet printer at Hewlett-Packard's Vancouver, Washington, plant. Used with permission.

INTRODUCTION TO OPERATIONS MANAGEMENT

I

"It was such sweet revenge.

"Last year, Hewlett-Packard Co. faced a challenge from NEC Corp. The Japanese giant had plans to attack H-P's hegemony in the burgeoning computer printer market in time-honored Japanese fashion: by undercutting prices with new, better-designed models. Over a decade ago, the tactic helped other Japanese companies grab the lead from H-P in a business it had pioneered, hand-held calculators.

"This time it didn't work. Months before NEC could introduce its inexpensive monochrome inkjet printer, H-P launched an improved color version and slashed prices on its best-selling black-and-white model by 40 percent over six months. NEC withdrew its entry, now overpriced and uncompetitive . . . .

"'We were too late,' says NEC's U.S. marketing director. 'We just didn't have the economies of scale' to be competitive with H-P. H-P is one of the most dramatic of an increasing number of U.S. take-back stories, in technologies including disk drives, cellular phones, pagers, and computer chips.

". . . the H-P story dispels common myths about the relative strengths of the U.S. and Japan, showing how big U.S. companies, under proper leadership, can exploit American creativity while using their huge resources to deploy 'Japanese' tactics. H-P used its financial might to invest heavily in a laboratory breakthrough, then kept market share by enforcing rules that are gospel in Japan: Go for mass markets, cut costs, sustain a rapid fire of product variations and price cuts, and target the enemy." [1]

Hewlett-Packard's achievement is attributable to a combination of world-class practices in operations and in all of the supporting services: design, purchasing, quality, scheduling, and others. This book is all about these kinds of combined efforts—which have spread from top-notch manufacturers to superior service organizations. Chapter 1 explains the setting for operations management; Chapter 2 details the kind of strategy the H-Ps of the world are pursuing; and Chapter 3 introduces quality, the rock upon which strong operations management—and whole companies—are built.

1   OPERATIONS—PRODUCING GOODS AND PROVIDING SERVICES

Chapter Outline

Operations Management
  Transformation
  Operations in the Organization

OM Elements
  Time Line
  Customers and Requirements

Competitiveness
Productivity
OM-Related Measures
Operations Managers

Critical Themes in Operations Management

"Customers Are the Center of Our Universe"

That statement is engraved in the lobby at the Jacksonville, Florida, headquarters of AT&T's Universal Card Services (UCS) Company, a 1992 winner of the Malcolm Baldrige national quality award. UCS has a close partner, Total System Services, Inc. (TSYS), which provides hardware and software support for UCS's credit card operations. Top executives at UCS use a PC-based information system to monitor quality, availability (of hardware to customer service associates), capacity, and inventory. Both partners post daily statistics on accuracy, speed, response time, and customer satisfaction measures throughout their business sites. Average phone response time to customers, for example, is within 2.6 seconds. TSYS keeps its 20 Tandem fault-tolerant processors running 24 hours per day, seven days a week, with 99.5 percent availability.[1]

Surgeons operate on patients in operating rooms. Machinists set milling machines to operate on metal castings, shaving millimeters off surfaces so they match with other parts. At United Parcel Service, operations means the actual collection, sorting, and delivery of mail. And at your bank, operations managers direct activities ranging from sorting checks and printing statements, to interacting with customers at teller windows, to tellerless dispensing of cash by machines in scattered public places. In each case customer-serving objectives, such as those pursued by AT&T-USC, are keys to operations success.

In other words, **operations** is where the organization's goods and services are produced and provided. Usually, operations is where most of the people work and where the company spends most of its budget. That does not mean operations is more important than other functions, such as sales and marketing or finance and

Back-office processing center at First National Bank of Chicago, which processes checks and deposits for other correspondent banks. Like AT&T-UCS, First Chicago bank has developed remarkably quick response, achieving turn-around times of just one hour when required by the customer (more on this in Chapter 13).

Dennis O'Clair/Tony Stone Images

accounting. Rather, we should see operations as one of the essential functions of any organization. Operations is always there, always has been, and needs careful management.

Operations Management

There is little consistency in how operations are managed, as anyone who has held a job can confirm. Part of the problem is the sheer complexity of operations, which involve people with all levels of skill and knowledge, equipment ranging from screwdrivers to magnetic resonance imaging machines, materials and tools of the trade, all kinds of buildings and work areas, and product and process knowledge in people's heads or filed away. Finally, operations managers must watch over all of these with customer satisfaction and cost in mind.

Nevertheless, over the ages, trial and error and innovative minds have brought **operations management,** or **OM,** to a high level of refinement. We can find pockets of consistency, which show up agreeably through the processes and to the final customer. You know what you are getting when you buy a Honda Accord or a Ford Taurus. Likewise with a McDonald's basic burger. Or a Federal Express delivery. Do the employees who provide these goods and services follow consistent, rational practices? Mostly, they do.

On the other hand, if you go to Notorious Motors to buy a pre-owned car or to The Bent Fork for a meal, you don't know what you are getting. Ask yourself why. You may see weaknesses in employee training, poor scheduling of staff, failure to anticipate and plan for customer requirements, poorly functioning facilities, lack of controls, and apparent unawareness of best practices of local or global counterparts.

When you are impressed with a delivered product, you should also be impressed with the assemblage of consistent, high-performance practices that were responsible. Putting them all together is an amazing feat. It requires teamwork and clockwork-like meshing of plans, actions, and follow-through.

In this chapter we will not say much about how such feats happen. That is the task of the remaining chapters. Here our first concern is with the meaning of operations and operations management. That takes us to matters such as commonalities and differences between OM for goods and for services and operations manager roles. In addition, we consider the recent bumpy trend in upgrading OM practices along with grand matters such as competitiveness, productivity, and customer service.

Transformation

Think of OM as a function that transforms inputs—including people, capital, energy, materials, and technology—into outputs, namely, goods and services. See Exhibit 1–1. These terms—*inputs, transformation,* and *outputs*—define operations management.

The main objective, of course, is the outputs—the goods and services—which form a continuum. Pure examples at either end of the continuum are rare; that is, most of the characteristics of goods and services overlap. The main differences are fairly obvious. We can store goods, whereas we consume services as they are provided. Services such as design, janitorial, and freight handling are closely tied to tangible goods: It is tangible items that are designed, maintained, and shipped. In human services, however, it is the client who is transformed. Despite the differences between these kinds of outputs, operations management is much the same for both. The following list highlights some of the main commonalities and differences for both goods and services.

The *Economist* defines services as "anything sold in trade that could not be dropped on your foot."

Commonalities

- Entail customer satisfaction as a key measure of effectiveness.
- Include common measures of satisfaction (e.g., quality and speed).

EXHIBIT 1-1

Operations: A Transformation Process

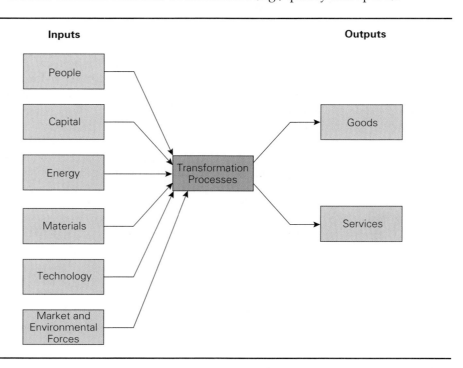

- Employ the same set of standard process improvement tools.
- Benefit from both individual initiative and teamwork.
- Can be either prescheduled or provided on demand.
- Require demand forecasting.
- Require design of both the product and the process.
- Can involve routing the product through more than one process.
- Depend on location and arrangement of resources for success.
- Can be provided in either high or low volume and be standard or customized.
- Involve purchase of materials, supplies, and services.
- Require maintenance of equipment, tools, and skills.
- Are subject to automation.
- Are affected by do-it-yourself trends.
- May be either commercial or nonprofit.
- Are shaped by an operations strategy, dovetailing with business strategy.

Differences

- Goods may be stored; services are consumed during delivery.
- Goods are transformed from other goods; in services, sometimes the clients themselves are transformed.

Each line in the list includes an object of operations management: satisfaction, forecasting, purchasing, automation, and so forth. They have to be planned for, executed, monitored, and improved. In view of the many commonalities—those listed and others—we treat OM for goods and services together rather than in separate chapters or sections. Where the differences have an impact, we discuss how and why.

Operations in the Organization

We've noted the presence of operations in all organizations. Equally basic are three other functions; one takes care of money, another design, and the third demand. Whether the organization is private or public, manufacturing or service, these four functions, portrayed in Exhibit 1–2, are present. In very small startup companies the functions are indistinct and overlapping. As the organization grows, these functions become the first departments. They often show up as separate boxes on an organization chart, such as the departments of finance, research and development, marketing, and operations. Alternately, they may be called accounting, design, sales, and production.

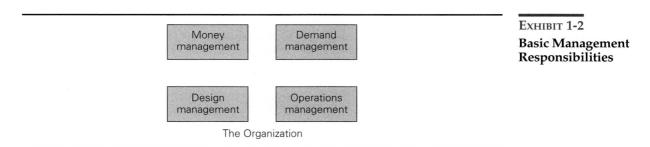

EXHIBIT 1-2

Basic Management Responsibilities

The terms *line* and *staff* have military roots but have become mainstream management terminology. We use them from time to time in later chapters.

Later, other departments form. They appear on organization charts as new boxes—human resources, purchasing, materials management, and maintenance, to name a few. These, called *staff* departments, provide support to the four basic departments, called *line* departments.

To take care of customers effectively, all the departments must function together, like the players on a well-trained sports team. It is not hard to achieve this when the business is small. Growth, however, brings problems. The boxes truly act like boxes, and coordination among the departments retrogrades. Therefore, the common box style of an organization chart is misleading. It does not show how a top-notch company finances, designs, markets, and provides goods and services. Teams, task forces, and committees—temporary or permanent—must cut across departmental boundaries.

We should understand, also, that every department has its own subfunctions. A human resource department, for example, must manage its own money, design, demand, and operations. The Into Practice box gives an example of how improvement in the operations within the accounting department at Johnson & Johnson led to higher quality results.

Thus, operations cannot stand alone, apart from finance and accounting, sales and marketing, and the rest. While college courses usually do separately treat these different functions, in application they overlap and link in complicated ways. When they do not, the organization falters and serves its customers poorly.

OM Elements

The subject matter of operations management is dynamic. It continues to evolve, expand, and intermesh with accounting, human resources, and other functions. In this and upcoming chapters, we discuss a few of the key situations in which success in operations depends on teaming up with accounting, human resources, and other functions.

Evolution of ideas—or the procedures and tools that accompany them—sometimes occurs rather suddenly and at other times gradually. A time-line look at this evolution, next, is a fitting lead-in to remaining chapter topics.

Quality Improvement in Accounting Operations at J&J

``Nowadays, the accounting departments with the highest quality have the lowest relative costs. Johnson & Johnson saved $84 million on accounting costs between 1990 and 1994. Among other things, the company trimmed the accounting staff . . . from 203 to 76 in accounts payable and from 106 to 28 in payroll. Meanwhile, the department's performance improved. For example, the staff now sprints to close the monthly financial report in seven days, compared to the old standard of 26 days.

``Conversely, the evidence suggests that, in accounting and other areas, companies with high costs have poor quality. Before streamlining, nearly two months had passed before Johnson & Johnson executives received financials on a new fiscal year. That's not quality.''

Source: Adapted from E. Bradley Wilson, ``Accounting: Your Next Competitive Edge,'' *Quality Digest*, July 1995, pp. 40–44.

Time Line

History is dotted with remarkable achievements in operations management. The building of the pyramids, the Arsenal of Venice, and certain of Napoleon's military campaigns come to mind. (Yes, military operations must be counted, too.) Whatever the methods used by operations managers in those cases, they were not passed on and perpetuated.

A brief history of OM, highlighted in Exhibit 1–3, notes concepts and methods that have been documented, taught, and carried forward. It begins in the first years of the twentieth century, the formative years of scientific management. The innovators were Frederick W. Taylor, Frank and Lillian Gilbreth, Henry Gantt, and several others; they brought science to the planning, scheduling, and control of factory work. A bit later, W. H. Leffingwell and C. C. Parsons carried scientific management into the office.[2] At the same time, the efforts of these pioneers broke ground for modern human resource management and advanced cost accounting. In fact, noted management authority Peter Drucker credits Taylor as the father of training. Taylor pioneered in documenting work elements so that people could be trained to do the work efficiently and consistently. Without well-documented work, skills training flounders. As an example, Drucker says that Adolf Hitler was confident the United States would be unable to play a serious role in World War II. Hitler knew that on sea, in the air, and on land, war-making depended heavily on optics for precision targeting. Germany had a large force of highly skilled optical technicians. America did not. But, Drucker says, U. S. industry had—as a legacy of Frederick Taylor—a compensating response. With amazing speed, massive training in optical technology provided industry with the necessary technical skills. High-precision war-making equipment soon poured forth.[3]

One way of looking at scientific management is as an extension of the industrial revolution, which began in England in about 1760. We think of that era, lasting some 100 years, as one of mechanization and standardization of parts. It yielded a flood of products, such as the cotton gin; and machines to make products, such as motor-driven lathes. Managing the human element was still nonstandard and uncontrolled. That is where Taylor and Gilbreth had their greatest

1760–1860	Industrial revolution: invention, mechanization, factory system.
1900–1920	Scientific management: standardized work tasks for better training, scheduling, and control of work and workforce.
1927	Hawthorne studies: Emotional and social factors shown to be as relevant to human motivation as logical factors; launched organizational behavior subfield of management.
1938	Operations research: quantitative—or management science—approach to management, which developed rapidly during World War II.
1960s	Just in time: lean, short-cycle production methods, pioneered by Toyota.
1960s	Total quality management: systematic management of quality in the process—becoming a competitive force among leading Japanese manufacturers.
1970s	Computer-driven production planning: material requirement planning systems, perfected in the United States.
1980s–?	Widespread service-sector applications of best OM practices.

EXHIBIT 1-3

Operations Management Time Line— Major Milestones

impact. They documented and timed human tasks, which created standards for training, planning, and controlling the workforce.

OM was affected in modest ways by the next milestone in management, occurring in the late 1920s and early 1930s. The Hawthorne studies at a Western Electric plant in Cicero, Illinois (near Chicago) revealed that human motivation is complex. People respond to attention as well as pay. The "Hawthorne effect"—that recognition temporarily raises motivation—still is a well-used term in business and social psychology. These findings triggered wholesale changes in management studies, launching the subfield of organizational behavior (OB).[4] Today, OB and OM are cross-fertilizing each other—as will be explained later in this time-line discussion.

Quantitative modeling run on computers was the next major influence on OM studies. Mathematical models proved useful in radar siting and planning complex ship convoy maneuvers in World War II. Since operations within the firm also are complex, modeling seemed to offer exciting possibilities in OM. Management scientists (also called operations researchers) went to work on applications such as making sense out of complex routing and scheduling problems in factories.[5] The models began to fill the pages of OM textbooks in the 1960s.

The same era spawned the first business computers, which quickly took over mass record keeping and data processing. Some companies made use of these computers to model complex problems, mostly in operations. As it turned out, however, the major use of computers in OM lay elsewhere. Computer-driven material requirements planning (MRP), developed in the 1970s, coped with complex material and job planning in factories. Another sea change in the content of OM studies had been launched. By the early 1980s some OM textbooks were devoting nearly a third of their pages to MRP and related factory and logistics planning and control. At the same time, business and engineering students were studying modeling in separate quantitative and statistics courses.

The changes in OM came fast and furious in the 1980s and 1990s. Service-sector content had to grow because the majority of the workforce is employed in service operations: financial, hospitality, medical, governmental, and back-office support areas of manufacturing companies. Would service applications drive factory talk into the background of OM textbooks? Not at all. Along came three unifying forces: quality, the customer, and teamwork, which are centerpieces of the **total quality management (TQM)** movement. An overarching theme, dominant in the third, fourth, fifth, and now this sixth edition of this textbook, is the voice of the customer—who demands ever higher levels of quality, which requires teamwork in the delivery system.

Customers and Requirements

Customers (all of us) energize the operations function like electricity does a light bulb. A customer arrives—at a bank, hardware store, or optometrist's office—hears a greeting ("May I help you?"), conveys a want or need, and has it fulfilled. That, at least, is how it should be. Too often, however, the current (customer needs and wants) never gets to the light bulb or does so too slowly. The light does not go on or goes on when it isn't needed. For want of a close customer-provider linkage, operations flounders and customer service falters.

Casually informed people sometimes view JIT as an inventory reduction technique. Most authoritative sources, including companies with mature JIT applications, view it more broadly. JIT aims most directly at reducing cycle times, secondarily at improving quality, flexibility, and various costs. In these pursuits, the JIT concept employs cross-trained employees, organization of resources into self-contained "work cells," reduced inventories precisely positioned and labeled, quick changeover of equipment, high levels of maintenance and housekeeping, close partnerships with suppliers and customers, schedules closely synchronized to demand, simplified product designs, and high levels of quality. (Quality and flexibility facilitate JIT as well as derive from it.)

In view of its breadth, we treat JIT's components in several chapters. Chief among these are Chapters 10, which treats two bedrock JIT topics, kanban and the pull system; 11 on quick equipment changeover; 12 on work cells; and 13 on synchronized scheduling.

EXHIBIT 1-4
Just-in-Time: Broad Concept

The old view of customer, as someone outside the organization, is not unifying. The newer view, however, is that everyone has a **customer:** the next process. That is, whomever receives the work that I do is my customer. This view allows people deep inside the organization, far removed from the final user, to develop customer sensitivities proximate to those of a waiter, dentist, or sales clerk. Moreover, both external and internal customers have many of the same general demands, which include quality, speed, and flexible response. The quest for speed and flexibility is central to **just-in-time (JIT)** processing, or time-based competition, which became a movement of its own, roughly in parallel with total quality management. A major empirical research project found strong support for the hypothesis that JIT and TQM are mutually reinforcing.[6] Actually, both JIT and TQM are broad-reach concepts that help unify diverse organizational processes; see Exhibit 1–4 on JIT's breadth.

The next-process-as-customer idea is owed to the late Kaoru Ishikawa, one of the giants of the quality movement. More on this in Chapter 3.

Companies that strive for a customer focus soon find that it requires broad changes in management of their human resources. People must unite for quality across departmental lines. In this cause, OM and organization behavior have converged on a common purpose. OB is weak without customer and quality objectives. OM is weak without cooperative processes. The integrating effects of the customer and quality movements extend to most of the other business and engineering functions as well. It may seem natural for companies to have a customer focus. Actually, it takes hard work and systematic procedures.

The Customer Interface—and Backup Support.   Consider the sequence of designing a custom good, producing it, and getting it to the user. Not only is the customer not around during design, it takes place weeks or months before pilot testing or prototyping. Then, after some redesign and further testing, production may take place across a continent or an ocean. Shipping and handling time intervenes more than once, and finally the goods are ready. By then, the customer's need for the goods may have disappeared or already have been fulfilled.

Though the example is for a custom-manufactured good, two of the three steps—designing and transporting—are services. Pure on-demand services are simpler—on the surface. The visible surface is what Jan Carlzon, CEO of SAS Airlines, calls "the moment of truth," a metaphor drawn from bullfighting. Consider a grocery store, where the clerk is almost eyeball-to-eyeball with customers:

Question: "What's your job?"
Answer: "I run the cash register and sack groceries."
Question: "But isn't your job to serve the customer?"
Answer: "I suppose so, but my job description doesn't say that."

Thus, even on the front lines, face-to-face with a customer, the moment of truth may be a moment to forget.

In the background, well away from the visible customer interface, service organizations entail a full range of planning, scheduling, and control processes. All contribute to results at the later moments of truth, just as many supporting steps contribute to final delivery of manufactured goods. How can the remote planning people feel any kinship with ultimate consumers?

The best answer is the Ishikawa idea: for all employees to think of the next process as their customer. The next, and the next, and the next, . . . lead finally to the consumer. The viewpoint has emerged as a core concept in the worldwide quality movement. Companies with strong quality programs train everyone, including front-line associates, in this concept. (See Contrast box, "Classifying People," on the shift toward unifying words like *associate*—and away from divisive terms.) They tell buyers that their customer is the associate in the department to whom the purchased item goes; a cost accountant's customer is the manager who uses the accounting information to make a decision. A test technician's customer is the packer who packs what was just tested, and a foundry associate's is the milling machine operator who mills the casting from the foundry. The next-process concept makes it clear that every employee, not just the caseworker or salesperson, has a customer. Just as clearly, everybody not only *has* a customer, he or she *is* a customer; with his or her own wants and needs.

In this book names for employed people include *associate, employee,* and *manager*—plus specialized names such as *sales clerk, assembler,* and *front-line* employee (*front-liner,* for short). *Worker* was abolished from the second edition and hasn't been used since, except in quotations.

Customer Wants and Needs: A Short List.   The provider has one notion about what the customer wants; the customer may have quite another. The real requirements, which tend to be poorly or incompletely stated, may have these three components:

1. A statement of recognized need.
2. The expected manner in which that need should be met.
3. Some idea of the benefits of having the need met.[7]

This is the customer's view. The provider's or supplier's view of the requirement is called a specification. The "spec" is the provider's target, which should match,

Classifying People

Them versus Us	**We**
Common people terminology: Managers and professionals versus workers. Salaried versus wage earners. Skilled versus unskilled. Exempts (from U.S. Wage and Hour Law) versus nonexempts.	Uncommon alternative: Some firms call all employees associates; they banish words implying that a manager class has charge of improvements and a worker class carries them out.

as closely as possible, the customer's actual needs. Close partnerships with customers help create good specs, increasing the supplier's ability to satisfy users.

What else do customers want? As consumers, our personal requirements constantly change. The same is true for consumers of business products. Though customers' requirements can be stated in great detail, the number of persistent general wants appears to be small (see Exhibit 1–5), and they seem to apply universally. Regardless of type of business, internal and external customers generally have these six basic requirements:

1. *High levels of quality.* From the customers' standpoint, quality has multiple dimensions, which will be presented in Chapter 3.
2. *A high degree of flexibility.* Customers' admire a provider's ability to react easily to shifting requirements and irregular arrival patterns.
3. *High levels of service.* Subjective measures of customer service include humanity in service delivery; objective measures can include having a required item in stock.
4. *Low costs.* External customers are price conscious; internal customers are concerned when they see costly wastes.
5. *Quick response (speed).* Customers want delay-free service and quick response to changing requirements. The provider aims to satisfy by shortening cycle times and quickly introducing attractive new goods and services.
6. *Little or no variability.* Customers expect consistency; the ideal is zero deviation from targeted or expected results.

These six requirements are part of the foundation of a well-conceived operations management system. Inasmuch as they apply to internal as well as external customers, the requirements have a unifying effect, that is, they permit each employee along the chains of customers to have a common, small set of goals. Being linked to the final customer also gives these goals the stature of being important, not artificial, which can make the work more personally meaningful. Scott Adams, creator of the Dilbert cartoon series, which pokes irreverent fun at popular management concepts, cautions employed people about going overboard on the customer. He tells them,

> You, personally, are No. 1—you!—and then your family and then your co-workers. And somewhere after that is the customer and the stockholder. Of course, it's often in your, your family's, and the stockholders' best interest to treat customers as No. 1.[8]

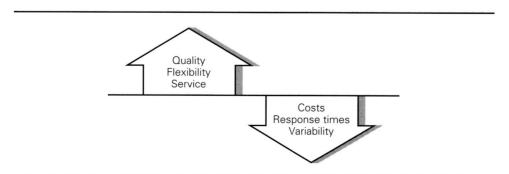

EXHIBIT 1-5

General customer requirements

In the last chapter we re-address the concept of employee needs, which we think needs to be better woven into the fabric of modern management thinking.

Be careful not to view the requirements listed in Exhibit 1–5 as potential trade-offs. Customers don't. As customers, we do not want to settle for just high quality or just low costs, or for just increased flexibility or just quicker response. We require that all these needs be met.

From the provider's standpoint, excelling in all six basic needs is a considerable challenge. Though not trade-off candidates, they do need to be priority ordered. If competitors are beating the company on speed, then quick response becomes a high-priority objective. Later on, the main issue may shift toward flexibility, but not at the expense of speed. Customers want and expect ever better performance in the direction of the arrows in Exhibit 1–5. Recognizing this, superior organizations commit themselves to continuous improvement, which is one more theme of the book.

Competitiveness

At the most basic level, operations management's aim is to please customers. Doing that gains their allegiance and brings in revenue. Doing it better than the competition gains market share. It could even drive a competitor out of your markets or product lines. These scenarios presume, of course, that sales and marketing and other functions are doing their part. We see that the six factors (Exhibit 1–5) important for customer satisfaction also build competitiveness.

These remarks apply to nonbusiness entities as well as commercial firms. Public agencies, churches, charities, and other nonprofits have their own kinds of customers and competitors. They compete with one another, and sometimes with profit-making businesses, for funding, clients, volunteers, and so forth.

competitor
Another organization vying with yours for sales and customers as well as for employees, permits, funding, supplier loyalty, and so on.

A top-down, look-back way of assessing competitiveness is to examine aggregated results. In highly competitive sectors, staying power is the first test. Internationally, the Red Cross, Coca Cola, and Canon endure among tough competitors for donations, soft drinks, and cameras; thus, they are competitively strong. Market share, revenue growth, return on equity, and so forth are other aggregated measures of company competitiveness. We judge national competitiveness by rates of productivity improvement.

Productivity

Do any aggregated statistics relate to down-to-earth operations management activities? Perhaps so. The years from 1980 to 1995 saw an outpouring of new, improved OM concepts and methods. Applied initially in the manufacturing sector, most of them fall under the general categories of total quality management or just-in-time operations. These developments coincide rather well with a spurt in manufacturing productivity in the United States. In the 1960 to 1977 period, the sector's productivity grew at an anemic annual rate of 2.8 percent. From 1980 to 1995, the rate grew to 3.2 percent.[9] (Here, productivity equals value of goods produced divided by number of hours worked; productivity is more extensively treated in Chapter 16.)

While OM people will want to pat themselves on the back, they would have to arm-wrestle other interest groups who have their own plausible claims. Some economists will say that monetary policy explains the increased productivity. Political scientists might cite the ending of the Cold War. Computer mavens might say that, finally, information systems are reaping a bonanza of productivity improvement. Job-conscious college business students will say business downsizing explains it. The truth may lie in a combination of these and other factors.

OM-Related Measures

We need better measures of how OM activities affect competitiveness. While there are many candidates, we shall offer three that seem to have breadth. One is a rather new index of customer satisfaction; the second, for inventory-intensive operations, is an old measure, inventory turnover; and the third distinguishes between value-adding and non-value-adding activities along the supply chain. The index of customer satisfaction relates to the total quality management thrust in OM. Inventory serves as a rough surrogate of just-in-time achievement. And elimination of non-value-adding wastes is a dominant goal of continuous improvement, which is central to both total quality and just-in-time operations.

Customer Satisfaction.   The National Quality Research Center at the University of Michigan's School of Business Administration administers a national customer satisfaction index. Claes Fornell of the center first created the index for Sweden in 1989. Germany set up its own similar index in 1992, and several other countries are at work on theirs.

The U.S. version, called the American Customer Satisfaction Index (ACSI), had its start in 1994. The data come from telephone interviews from a sample of the nation's households. Respondents report on their usage of a company's product, and satisfaction registers on a scale of 0 (lowest) to 100 (highest). The initial ACSI measured seven sectors and 40 industries, included over 200 organizations, and sampled about 50,000 households. Service organizations make up five of the sectors: transportation, communications, and utilities; finance and insurance; retail; services; and public administration and government. The sector called services includes three industries: hotels and motels; hospitals; and motion pictures. In the motion pictures category, six companies were measured: Times Warner, Walt Disney/Touchstone, Paramount, Tri-Star/Columbia, Universal Studios/MCA, and Fox. The two manufacturing sectors, nondurables and durables, included 18 industries. For example, Procter & Gamble, Unilever, Colgate Palmolive, Dial, and Clorox make up the personal-care products industry under manufacturing—nondurables.[10]

The ASCI provides a way for a company to compare itself over time and benchmark against industry averages. It may also help predict future performance and show customer acceptance of a new company initiative. Fornell and his colleagues believe the index also can gauge a sector's and a country's performance better than, say, the consumer price index.[11] Exchange rates, trade, and other factors can push and pull on consumer prices. Marketers may sometimes be able to manipulate customer satisfaction, but not much and not for long.

No long ago, indexes of customer satisfaction would have been less meaningful. Many of the world's consumers had no basis for crabbing about their own countries' poor workmanship, high defect rates, long delays, and inflexible labor and equipment. Political and trade barriers have that effect. Now, with the globalization of trade, Internet services, Hertz car rentals, American Express cards, Benetton sweaters, and Compac PCs are everywhere. Global communications bring visual portrayal of how others live and work to TV sets in parlors all over the world. Consumers are no longer in the dark but can judge their local services and goods against high world standards. Thus, the introduction of customer satisfaction indexes is timely.

Inventory Turnover.   Manufacturing, wholesaling, and retailing are inventory intensive. Thus, for those sectors, inventory management expertise is a common measure of performance. Weak companies generally have excessive inventories; strong ones, such as Wal-Mart and Toyota, generally are very lean on inventories. A standard measure is **inventory turnover,** which is easily computed from data obtained from a firm's annual report. It is simply cost of goods sold divided by total inventory. Thus, less inventory equals higher inventory turnover.

While it may seem that inventory turnover is just one of many internal measures, it actually can serve as a composite indicator of operations management excellence, much as customer satisfaction indexes can. A single inventory turnover number says little. A several-year trend, on the other hand, can track the pace of a company's continuous improvement effort. If the trend is sharply upward, the reasons are likely to include

- *Improving quality.* With higher quality, the firm may reduce the inventories it has been holding to cover items that end up as scrap or go through rework or customer returns.
- *Improving responsiveness.* Inventory piles up around every delay. By freeing itself of delays (e.g., in booking orders, purchasing, planning the work, production, and invoicing), a company may reduce the inventories.
- *Improving flexibility.* As the firm becomes more able to easily increase or decrease output, it may carry less inventory to meet peak demands. Also, as the firm becomes more agile in shifting from one product to another, it may carry less of everything.
- *Reducing variability.* It is not enough to have quality, responsiveness, and flexibility, *most* of the time. Occasional lapses may not seem serious, but they require extra inventory to cover the problem periods. Less variability reduces the need for such just-in-case inventories.

We have just made the connection between inventory trend and four of the six customer needs (from Exhibit 1–5). An upward trend in inventory turnover signals that a company is getting better at delivering quality, flexibility, quick response, and invariability; a downward trend suggests the opposite. Cost, the fifth customer need, also enters in. Not having to carry extra inventory saves money. Companies with good and rising inventory turnovers usually even see improvements in service, the sixth customer need. In Chapter 8, we examine research data that shows a connection between global trends in inventory turnover and competitiveness of nations and companies.

The Value Chain.   Value is in the eye of the customer. It is a complex mixture of product quality and usefulness at a low cost. The organization often gets sidetracked, however. Many steps in the chain of activities—from the earliest inkling of a product through delivery and after-sale customer interactions—produce non-value-adding wastes. The **value chain** (accounting for addition of value as an item goes through multiple transformation steps) is cluttered.

Thus, another route to improved customer service is cleaning up the value chain. Companies endeavor to eliminate the non-value-adding wastes. Robert W. Hall labels as waste anything "that does not add value to the product or service, whether material, equipment, space, time, energy, systems, or human activity of any sort."[12] Waste-busters use many of the same tools of measurement and analysis as quality improvers and cycle-time reducers. The tools get a prominent place in this book.

Operations Managers

Attacking non-value-adding wastes, with a focus on the six basic customer wants, is too important to be left up to people with manager in their titles. It is a job for the entire workforce, who, taken collectively, are the actual operations managers. They include:

1. *The associates who provide the service or make the product.* Every employee is a manager of the immediate workplace,[13] which consists of materials, space, equipment, tools, and information. In the best companies, employees team up with others in a work-flow relationship and periodically join a special project team. They strive to meet current demand exactly and to devise ways to improve processes and products. This role involves data collection, problem solving, and process control—all in the name of ever better service to customers, both internal and external.

2. *First-line supervisors.* Their proper role involves little traditional supervision; rather, they are facilitators who coordinate mixtures of human and physical resources in the cause of customer satisfaction and continuing improvement. Some companies have replaced supervisors with working coordinators, often called leads or lead persons. The role is the same: facilitator and coordinator.

3. *Upper-level managers, such as department heads and general managers.* One of their more important tasks is managing the training, reward, and recognition system with an eye toward helping line associates to become active in improvement. Good managers are teachers and coaches. Another role is as focal point for coordinating the support staff of experts, whose skills back up the direct efforts of front-liners to solve problems.

4. *Staff experts.* These include designers, buyers, hirers, trainers, engineers, schedulers, maintenance technicians, management accountants, inspectors, programmers, and analysts. Most organizations over-rely on staff experts because of failure to solidly tap line associates' capacities. Still, staff expertise will always be needed. The role of staff is to plan for change, respond expertly to problems, and serve on improvement teams.

Critical Themes in Operations Management

We have introduced a few of the themes in operations management that appear to be critical for success:

Dedication to customers, internal as well as external.

Six general targets for serving the customer: high quality, flexibility, and service; low costs, quick response, and minimal variability.

Competitiveness measures that are relevant globally as well as at the level of operations: indexes of customer satisfaction, trends in inventory turnover, and value-chain analysis.

All employees as contributors to operations management.

The following two chapters add more key themes to this list, including teaming up cross-functionally, universal principles of OM, and quality as a superordinate objective.

Summary

The operations end of an organization is where resources are transformed into goods and services. Operations, along with product development, marketing, and finance, are line functions of an organization—more basic than the staff support functions. Operations management (OM) is more the same than different between services and goods organizations.

Major milestones in OM include, at the turn of the century, the scientific management movement, which provided ways to document work such that people could be trained. Three more milestones affected OM. One was the Hawthorne Studies at Western Electric in the late 1920s, which revealed the power of recognition to influence work behaviors. The second was quantitative modeling based on advanced military operations in World War II. The third was computers, which could be harnessed to plan complex material scheduling tasks in factories.

OM's modern era began around 1980, or a bit earlier in Japan. It was centered on quality improvement, which was the main weapon used by Japanese exporters to kill off established competitors in North America. Quality is a matter of serving the customer, which includes the next process as well as the final user. Every employee is a manager, whose job is to improve processes in the eyes of the next-process customer.

Primary customer wants are high quality, flexibility, and service, coupled with low cost, quick response, and little variability. To be competitive, companies must strive for excellence in all six; customers do not view them as trade-off objectives. The years since the beginning of the quality movement are also years of heightened productivity, which suggests cause and effect.

For customer-sensitized organizations, the new customer satisfaction index seems timely. Administered by an agency of the University of Michigan, the index has been adopted by a few nations as well as by business sectors and certain companies. For inventory-intensive businesses, an old measure, annual inventory turnover, emerges as a good, single indicator of numerous kinds of improvement and waste elimination in the value chain.

1. What are *operations*? Explain using examples other than those in the chapter.
2. How have trends in operations management affected *consistency* in the delivery of goods and services?
3. What does the word *transformation* mean in connection with operations management?
4. Arrange the following in order of their appearances as major influences on operations management studies: Computer-based material requirement planning. The customer. Scientific management. Quality. Service operations. The Hawthorne Studies.
5. Why must operations be carried out in harmony with the rest of the organization?
6. To what extent does operations management treat services and goods the same? Differently?
7. Explain the impact of training on developments in operations management.
8. What is profound about this sentence: "The customer is the next process"?
9. What is a requirement? A specification? What is the relationship between the two?
10. What are the six basic customer wants?
11. What is the world-class approach to trade-offs?
12. What is the importance of a national customer satisfaction index?
13. What is the relevance of inventory turnover in manufacturing operations?
14. How does operations management deal with the value chain?
15. Identify the four types of operations managers and explain the role(s) of each type.

Exercises

1. Services once were neglected in operations management studies. Manufacturing dominated. From what you've learned about operations management in this chapter, why did OM develop earlier and more extensively for manufacturing than for services? Explain using examples of two different services.
2. The chapter identified four line functions of any organization. Sometimes, however, operations seems to encompass one of the other functions. For an architectural firm, operations focuses on designing buildings; thus, operations (one of the four basic functions) encompasses design (another of the four). Give an example of this same phenomenon (operations encompassing another function) for the two other line functions and for one staff function.
3. The following functions or departments are found in most businesses: human resources, sales, design, and management (cost) accounting.
   a. Why should professionals in each of those departments have a thorough understanding of the operating end of the business?
   b. Describe a company program that will achieve the right amount of exposure of people in those four departments to operations.

4. Think of three diverse examples of nonprofit organizations. For each, describe what its four line management functions (money, design, demand, and operations management) would consist of.

5. For each of the employee positions below, give an example of a next-process customer. Also give an example in which the listed employee would be the next-process customer.

   a. Assembler on a production line making kitchen cutlery.

   b. Product design engineer in a toy-manufacturing plant.

   c. Data processing manager in a bank.

   d. Employee benefits counselor in a large law firm.

   e. Cost accountant for a department store chain.

   f. Economist employed by the United States Federal Reserve Board.

6. As the chapter notes, customers do not view the six basic customer wants as trade-offs. They do, however, prioritize. Two customers waiting for the same service or product might have opposite priorities for the same basic want (e.g., one might consider speedy service first in importance; the next might give speed last priority). Give examples of this—for your choice of three different services or kinds of products.

7. Explain how the six basic customer wants apply in each of the following kinds of organizations:

Cattle ranch	Cruise line
Construction company	Manufacturer of fashion clothing

8. Obtain data for the American Customer Satisfaction Index (ACSI) for the most recent year and all preceding years. What trends are most significant (select at least three)? Discuss.

9. To what extent can a national customer satisfaction index explain or predict the economic well-being of a country? Outside study will provide you with authoritative viewpoints on this question.

10. Business news magazines some years ago were declaring a "productivity crisis" and speaking of the "hollowing of industry." What did they mean, and when did these stories appear? Try to relate your answer to the trends in inventory turnover discussed in the chapter.

11. Suzaki offers a special manufacturing listing of "the seven wastes." Find his discussion in Kiyoshi Suzaki, *The New Manufacturing Challenge: Techniques for Continuous Improvement* (New York: Free Press, 1987) (HD9720.5.S98). Describe each of the wastes in your own words.

12. From your library, obtain annual reports covering any 10-year consecutive period for a manufacturer, wholesaler, or retailer of your choice. Calculate inventory turnover for each year, and look for a trend. Compare your results with points about inventory turnover trends as presented in the chapter. Try to explain any differences.

13. Describe a value chain that you have participated in. Point out some of the obvious non-value-adding wastes and comment on how they affect final customer satisfaction.

For Further Reference

This section at the end of each chapter provides limited help for further research. (It does not necessarily list books cited within the chapter.) The book lists are intended to lead you to the parts of the library that hold material on a given topic. Thus, a list might include one book with a management (HD) United States Library of Congress call number, one with an industrial engineering (T or TA) number, one with a management accounting (HF) number, and so forth. That will guide you to the right shelf, where there are likely to be other books on the same topic. (Library of Congress numbers are given only for more recent books, many of which have the number printed on the copyright page.) Magazines, journals, and professional societies useful for people interested in operations management are also included.

An extensive Endnotes section at the back of this book contains all the footnote references listed in the chapters. This also can lead you to interesting and informative books, newspapers, and periodicals for your reference.

Internet

We have incorporated the Internet into our presentation of *Operations Managment* in the following ways:

1. We maintain a World Wide Web page through which we present periodic updates on selected OM topics and related materials. Please visit us at

   URL: http://www.irwin.com/management/pom

2. On the back endpapers, exercises for each chapter ask for general searches on key topics, or direct your attention to selected Internet sources (e.g., posted government data). Popular Internet search tools will suffice in these instances. We've listed these exercises by chapter in a special location at the end of the book on the inside back cover.

3. In the *For Further Reference* sections that close the chapters, we will list selected hard-copy and/or Internet references of a general nature that are either germane to chapter topics or are themselves pathways to useful Internet sites.

Books

Drucker, Peter F. *Post-Capitalist Society.* New York: Harper Collins, 1993. (HC59.15.D78).

George, Claude S. Jr., *The History of Management Thought.* Englewood Cliffs, N.J.: Prentice-Hall, 1968.

Myers, M. Scott, *Every Employee a Manager,* 3rd ed. San Diego: University Associates, 1991. (HF5549.M93).

Periodicals/Societies

Business Periodicals Index, an index of articles published in a limited number of business magazines and journals.

Engineering Index, an index of articles published on engineering in a large number of periodicals.

Interfaces (Institute for Management Science), a journal aimed at the interface between the management scientist and the practitioner.

Journal of Operations Management. (American Production and Inventory Control Society).

National Productivity Review.

Operations Management Review (Operations Management Society).

Target (Association for Manufacturing Excellence).

2   COMPETITIVE STRATEGIES AND PRINCIPLES

Chapter Outline

Operations Strategy
Getting Its Due
Strategic Evolution
Elements of Operations Strategy
Distinctive and Core Competency
Regional and Global Influences

Continuous Improvement as Strategy

Universal Strategies

Principles of OM—As Strategy

Case Study: Titeflex Corporation

> "On [General Motors'] 14-man strategy board (women and other minorities remain extremely rare at GM's uppermost levels) sit the top executives from manufacturing, engineering, sales and marketing, finance, personnel, logistics, purchasing, and communications. No matter what the issue, it tends to spill over into several functional areas, and the strategy board aims to get everyone involved in the resolution."[1]
>
> 3M Corporation "shakes the trees of its labs and customers," relying on them to "set the agenda. It is of course a strength to get ever more intimate with customers, and a strength to let creative flowers bloom . . . . Those virtues, however, beget a startling vice: 3M has no strategy." How then does 3M decide on such strategic questions as what is or isn't the right product line? According to vice chairman Ronald A. Mitsch, "That's a good question. None of us is foresightful enough to decide that, because our people might find some way to make whatever they're doing work."[2]

The very different strategic approaches of GM and 3M are not surprising, nor is the apparent lack of strategy at 3M. Strategic management in business, and the operations component of business strategy, are relatively young and still evolving.

A look back through dictionaries for the word *strategy* or *strategic* is revealing. If we go back to, say, before 1955, we will find the word, but the definitions refer to warfare, not business. For example, one of these early dictionaries calls *strategy* "planning and directing of military movements and operations."[3]

Applying this military concept to business, however, was a natural. Both have complex assemblages of resources to plan for and move out against the "enemy," which in business is more politely called the competition. General Electric is said to have been the first company to fashion a strategic business plan, in the 1950s. After that, management consultants, business schools, and large organizations of all kinds became advocates or adopters of strategic planning.

Whereas military strategies deal mainly with operations, business strategies often do not. Instead, their main focus may be financial, such as plans for acquiring or merging with other companies. New products and new markets are other common targets of business strategies, all of which affect and are affected by operations, sometimes a great deal. The elements of operations strategy, and their linkages with business strategy, are the subjects of this chapter.

Operations Strategy

A business strategy is a high-level plan for business effectiveness or competitiveness. To be complete, a business strategy must include four major components: finance, product development, marketing, and operations. Further, it must consider customers, competitors, and the company's own resources: the strategic triad.[4] The company's resources, one-third of the triad, are the purview of operations management. The other two-thirds—customers and competitors—affect operations strategy in many ways, such as the following:

- Locating a plant or store in order to go after a competitor's customers. (Location: Chapter 17.)
- Using better quality as a strategy for gaining market share at competitors' expense. (Quality: several chapters.)
- Cutting costly wastes in operations, which allows lowered prices to customers, putting pressure on competitors. (Waste and cost reduction: most chapters.)
- Gaining customer allegiance by including customers on product development teams. (Product development: Chapter 4.)

These examples help show the potential breadth of operations strategy, a potential that has not always been recognized. In recent years, however, operations strategy has evolved rapidly. In the next sections, we consider the past and recent evolution of operations strategy. In addition, we examine the concept of distinctive competency and how regional and global factors affect operations strategy.

Getting Its Due

At times it has seemed that the operations component of business strategy receives less than its share of attention. Too often, executives have concentrated on finance and marketing strategies. They've treated operations and product development as an afterthought, or, worse, as a given. Harvard Professor Wickham Skinner perceived this and became a strong voice for giving operations strategy its due. His oft-cited 1969 article, "Manufacturing—Missing Link in Corporate Strategy,"[5] expresses that point of view. A firm lacking proper OM strategy is like an anchored ship. Finance, design, and marketing may set the rudder and expect the ship to steam off, but with anchor set, the ship won't move, or moves reluctantly, dragging its burden.

Skinner's article appeared during a period of high merger and acquisition activity, which involved both goods and services companies. This activity was, in part, a legacy of World War II. The post-war boom years had created concentrated wealth among the more successful businesses—from big steel to automotive to financial services and retailers. Cash-loaded companies saw opportunities to grow and enhance their common stock prices by buying up, at cheap rates, the capacity, product lines, and customers of failing companies. Sometimes companies could make more money that way than by producing products and serving customers. It did not seem to matter much if there was a good fit. Manufacturers bought hotel chains, financial service companies, and rental-car agencies. Some service firms bought manufacturing companies. If the strategy had been aimed at acquiring a direct competitor, a key supplier, or a critical technology, it would have been a meaningful operations strategy, but it was usually not. This was the era of the conglomerates.

Conditions change; the cycle comes around and reveals repercussions of neglect of a basic function. By the early 1980s, business magazines in the United States were declaring a productivity crisis,[6] and the hollowing of industry.[7] Most of these writings cited Japan's emergence as an industrial powerhouse. They fretted about the possibility of Japan's complete takeover of a few industries that American firms had been preeminent in.

Why? What propelled Japan's ascendancy? Opinions shifted but finally zeroed in on a single, dominant competitive advantage: quality. For large numbers of firms, quality became the critical new business strategy. CEOs and presidents of such companies as Texas Instruments, Ford Motor Company, and IBM invited the giants of the quality movement to their companies. They listened and learned. Some executives led their company's intensive quality improvement campaigns, which were centered primarily in the operations function. So, at about the same time as Professor Skinner was raising business managers' consciousness about operations strategy, Japan was making quality its first clear target.

This does not mean that operations strategy could be summed up in the single word *quality*. While certain strategic constants—quality among them—are emerging, strategies differ from firm to firm, industry to industry, and over time. Quality may have only minor bearing on certain other critical strategic questions in operations, such as when and where to expand. Still, for many organizations, quality has become a superordinate strategy, a vital success factor. By the 1990s, total quality management campaigns had been mounted in hospitals, financial institutions, transportation firms, government agencies, and educational institutions, sometimes all the way down to elementary schools. Moreover, quality has durability: It may hold up as a key business and operations strategy forever.

Strategic Evolution

It did not take long for quality to be joined by other highly visible targets of operations strategy (listed in Exhibit 2–1). In short order, time followed quality. Just-in-time production and supply systems, also developed in Japan, became common operations strategy in big industry. Chronic delays would no longer be tolerated. Delays kill market response, obscure causes of defects, and generate administrative complexity and costly controls.

Later, George Stalk, Jr., vice president of the Boston Consulting Group, helped make speed more than just an operations strategy. His article, "Time—The Next Source of Competitive Advantage," got the attention of CEOs, presidents, and directors. Stalk said, " As a strategic weapon, time is the equivalent of money, productivity, quality, even innovation."[8] The management of time, like quality, became a serious strategy for business as a whole as well as for the operations function.

Globalization (or multinational expansion), third in Exhibit 2–1, emerged as another broadly attractive company and operations strategy. Political and economic realities had severely restricted international trade. To Japanese exporters,

Operations Strategy	Rationale
Quality	Quality-driven success proves itself in competitive industries.
Time (speed)	Delay-free response draws customers, exposes causes of bad quality, and avoids complex, costly controls.
Globalization	As political and trade barriers fall, massive new markets open up (e.g., the European Community, the former Soviet Bloc, China, India).
Teaming and partnering	Teaming up internally and externally facilitates fast-paced improvement in quality and customer response; global business expansion often builds on external partnerships.
Flexibility and agility	Quick, flexible response from an agile organization is part of quality and time-based competition.

Exhibit 2–1
Wide-Reach Operations Strategies, Circa 1980–Present

carved-up Europe—each nation with its own rules, regulations, tariffs, and cultures—had less appeal than the huge U.S. market. Formation of the European Common Market, however, created a second wealthy mass market. Then, the Iron Curtain fell, China and India saw fit to become full members of the global trading community, and nations signed various trade pacts (e.g., GATT and NAFTA).

Globalization can transform an industry. Take, for example, major home appliances. The two biggest U.S. makers, General Electric and Whirlpool, have rapidly expanded beyond their home bases in the last 10 years, as has their European counterpart, Electrolux. All three have become multinational giants, which for them raises new strategic issues. One is whether to customize—design and produce to national tastes—or standardize. The industry knows, for example, that the French prefer top-loading washing machines, while the Germans buy front-loaders. In the past that meant entirely different washers, right down to the screws. The new global alliances, however, permit enormous economies.[9] While the outsides and certain features, such as top loading versus frontloading, may make the appliances look entirely different, the global manufacturer standardizes—and mass produces—hundreds of internal parts, from wiring harnesses to hose clamps to screws. The external appearance and functions can be extremely different and still retain the economies of standardization inside. For example, washers made by Whirlpool affiliates in Brazil and Mexico range from high-tech and high-style (a

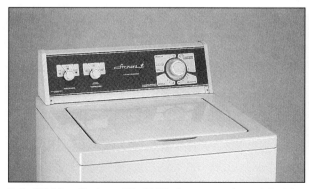

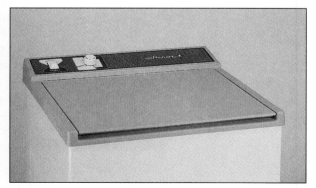

Left: Whirlpool's Aeros World Washer—upscale model with full control panel.

Right: Aeros World Washer with on-off switch and simple dial.

sharp European look with rounded tops) to ultra-simple (controlled by just an on-off switch and filled with a garden hose); see the accompanying photos. Yet these models are essentially the same inside.

Teaming and partnering, fourth in Exhibit 2–1, are in part elements of total quality management. In quality organizations people must partner up backward with supply-chain organizations and forward into the customer chain. Partnership strategies get a shot in the arm when competition is global. Companies may quickly expand their reach by linking with foreign partners, branches, suppliers, distributors, government agencies, cross-national business groups, and so forth. In its efforts to expand its European operations through wholly owned service units, Federal Express ran into a competitive buzz saw. Forced to waive the white flag in some markets, FedEx retreated to a partnership strategy with established European private mail and package services.

The complement of outside partnering is inside teaming. To ensure that the functions do not strategize and operate at cross purposes, representatives must team up across the functions. At the strategic level, the organization needs multifunctional product strategy teams. Besides developing joint strategies, their role includes sponsoring improvement projects for each product line. For example, they might agree to expand operating capacity, invest in an electronic data interchange system, or initiate a training program for the entire workforce.

Fifth on the list in Exhibit 2–1 are flexibility and agility, which relate well to the other four wide-reach strategies: A quality organization provides quick, flexible response to its external partners. To do so, it upgrades its people and processes to a high state of agility.

> The Iacocca Institute at Lehigh University, sponsored by major companies, targets agility as a major competitive concern for the future. The institute distinguishes between two similar terms thus: *flexibility,* an ability to react to expected change; *agility,* an ability to react to unexpected change.

Elements of Operations Strategy

Any business strategy needs to be translated downward into **operations strategy.** The latter has a narrower focus and covers the breadth of the operations function: inputs, transformation, outputs. (See Into Practice, "Technology Unseen, Unheard . . . ," for a unique application of some of the elements of operations strategy.)

Inputs. The inputs are the organization's capacity, or operating resources. Strategies deal with such matters as when and where to add or remove a unit of capacity, skills and flexibility of the workforce, level of commitment to safety and the environment, and whether or not to outsource. (Outsourcing is contracting for the service or materials instead of doing it "in house.")

Transformation. The transformation of inputs into outputs employs processes, methods, and systems in the production of goods and services. Strategies might include level of investment in product and process development, commitment to standardization, type of control system, and automation of information processes.

Outputs. Determining the outputs—the line of goods and services—is usually a high-level business strategy. Operations strategies for outputs should be customer focused, and they must consider (from Exhibit 1–5) product quality, flexibility, service, cost, customer responsiveness, and variability.

When the three strategic elements—inputs, transformation, and ouputs—come together effectively, the company develops distinctive competency, which helps fend off competition.

$\mathscr{I}$nto $\mathscr{P}$ractice

Technology, Unseen, Unheard—at Fidelity Investments

Selling securities to the public requires fine offices in financial districts in every major town, cold calls, and face-to-face customer interactions. At least that's the formula for the Merrill Lynches and Dean Witters of the investment community. But not at Fidelity Investments.

Edward C. Johnson III, the reticent innovator who took over Fidelity Investments when it was a modest family business, had another idea. In turning Fidelity into the largest U.S. mutual funds company, Johnson's

passion was computers. His strategy was to employ giant mainframes to transform operations. He spent countless hours in the computer room, observing, questioning, and tinkering. Naturally, his staff thought he was sinking far too much into computer operations, and saw his obsession as folly. Naturally, they were proved wrong.

Fidelity was able to bring Wall Street to millions of new investors without talking to them face to face. Customers placed their orders through massive phone centers and sent their checks to a post office drop box. This new way of doing business was well suited to capturing a dominant share of middle-class investors—without the expense of setting up brokerage offices from coast to coast.

In addition to operations technology, Johnson's strategy featured high quality service: Answer phone calls promptly, deliver statements accurately, and conduct business efficiently. Under the Fidelity system, people could judge the firm and its service based on technology they couldn't see and were only vaguely aware of.

Source: Adapted from Stephen D. Solomon, "Finances in Cyberspace," *Technology Review,* July 1995, pp. 67–68; book review of Joseph Nocera, *A Piece of the Action: How the Middle Class Joined the Money Class* (New York: Simon & Schuster, 1995).

Distinctive and Core Competency

After a series of biological experiments in 1934, Professor G. F. Gause of Moscow University postulated his principles of competitive exclusion: No two species that make their living the same way can coexist.[10] In strategic terms, the Gause principle says that a firm must strive to distinguish itself from its competitors. The business strategy is to strive for distinctive competency. When purpose gets muddled, indicating a need to restructure or downsize, a cogent strategy is to preserve core competencies.

Consider a town with three hospitals. The average citizen may see little difference among them. But ask an administrator or board member of one of the hospitals. "We are the only hospital in the city with a fully certified burn center" might be the reply. Or, perhaps, "We have the only neonatal care unit in the entire region." These are distinctive competencies.

Sometimes an organization is able to concentrate its entire being around a standout competency. Shouldice Hospital near Toronto, which treats only hernia patients, is an example. Facility layout, medical staff, cafeteria, surgery and recovery rooms,

distinctive competency
A strength that sets the organization apart from its competitors.

Courtesy of Shouldice Hospital Limited

and lounges all cater to that type of patient. By doing numerous hernia repairs each year, and no other surgeries, Shouldice doctors have become proficient. The narrow focus allows nurses to give better care to a greater number of patients, avoids the need for expensive general-purpose equipment that diversified hospitals must have, and, most important, results in higher-quality results. As measured by number of patients needing repeat hernia treatment, Shouldice is 10 times more effective than other hospitals.[11]

This strategy, focusing on a certain type of customer or product, earned prominence in another milestone article by Wickham Skinner called, "The Focused Factory."[12] This broad strategy can be applied to the whole company (e.g., Shouldice) or to subdivisions of it. For example, where the facility is large and unfocused, Skinner suggested the "plants-in-a-plant" concept: two or more focused "plants" within a larger plant. The idea is to break up a large, complex, difficult-to-manage unit into small units in which everyone knows everyone and each operates like an independent business. The concept has wide application: schools-within-a-school, prisons-within-a-prison, and so on. (We look more closely at the concept in Chapter 12.)

An organization's distinctive competency might, like Shouldice Hospital, be a whole focused business unit, complete with financial management, sales and marketing, operations, and other functions. Just as often or more often, it is excellence in some aspect of operations. Fast service, very clean premises, and superior quality are examples. While these competencies might be obvious to customers, less apparent factors also qualify. Examples are expert maintenance, low operating costs, and cross-trained labor. These abilities allow the firm, as Professor Gause put it, to make its living a little differently from its competitors in order to survive and succeed.

When a company is unable to sustain any special competencies, it goes under. But when a company can be distinctively competent in several ways, it wows the world. Walt Disney Co., Hewlett-Packard, McDonald's, United Parcel Service, and Toyota are examples. All five have dependably high quality. UPS and Toyota have very low costs of operations. Hewlett Packard has highly dedicated employees. Disney offers customer service unparalleled in its industry. Toyota, McDonald's, and UPS have highly efficient process controls, which lead to product and service uniformity. McDonald's provides very fast response to customer orders. Toyota is extremely flexible, admired for its ability to rapidly change stamping presses and production lines from one car model to another. These examples again highlight the six basic wants of customers: quality, cost, service, flexibility, speed, and predictability.

The competencies just mentioned have to do with how the goods or services are delivered. The earlier examples of whole focused units, such as the Shouldice hernia hospital, deal with the goods or services themselves. When Michael D. Eisner became CEO at Walt Disney, one of his first actions was to rebuild the company's animation infrastructure, and successive hits such as *Beauty and the Beast, Aladdin,* and *The Lion King* poured forth. The distinctive competency was resource based, which David J. Collins and Cynthia A. Montgomery call "competing on resources."[13]

Can a distinctive competency go unappreciated? Sometimes, yes. Those who guide the firm strategically need to sort out the special competencies from the broad array of activities the firm engages in. Professors C. K. Prahalad and Gary Hamel, among the more prominent strategic thinkers, advise company CEOs to wrap their company strategies around those **core competencies.**[14]

Regional and Global Influences

Until fairly recently, most of the world's businesses and nonprofit organizations operated in relatively small, dissimilar, protected markets and communities. Notable exceptions include the Roman Catholic Church, the Red Cross, and the Benetton retail clothier. For such organizations to set up and sustain operations in multiple countries required hard work and patient money.

Today, deregulation and privatization (e.g., of airlines and telephone companies) have gained a foothold throughout the former Soviet bloc, India, Argentina, and assorted other countries. These measures remove competitive restraints. Trade pacts and adoption of more uniform economic laws and policies further expand opportunities to do business globally.

In sum, the world is becoming more uniform economically and more wide open to business expansion, relocation, alliances, and partnerships. Most of the world's organizations are still small and local, but many others are exposed and vulnerable. Those that learn how to deliver quality efficiently and to achieve continuous improvement should find rich rewards. But no-change businesses may get trampled by new competitors expanding across old barriers.

We are not talking about nations competing economically against other nations; rather, many of the toughest competitors are multinational firms whose national headquarters are relatively unimportant. As Michael Porter states:

> There has been no shortage of explanations for why some nations are competitive and others are not. Yet these explanations are often conflicting, and there is no generally accepted theory. It is far from clear what the term "competitive" means when referring to a nation.[15]

The more important issue, Porter contends, "is to explain why firms based in a nation are able to compete successfully against foreign rivals in particular segments and industries."[16] In keeping with this view, we will not try to unravel the factors that make nations competitive. Rather, we will refer occasionally throughout the book to the success factors of leading companies in, say, Germany, Japan, or Mexico.

For any company, such factors as quality and continuous improvement are strategic elements of competitive success, and they go to the heart of operations

*C*ontrast

Takeover versus Investment

We Win, You Lose

Strategy: Take over a weak business with other people's money and make it strong and us rich by mass shutdowns and layoffs of its weakest elements. It's legal, yes, but is it ethical?

Win–Win

Strategy: For a weak business, invest not just, or mainly, money but also training and help in implementing customer-centered quality, efficiency, and continuous improvement.

management. We should see that some paths to wealth, such as buying companies and milking them dry, that were exploited in recent decades and that raise ethical questions, are riskier today. Moreover, a tired, run-down hotel chain in Romania or Estonia needs more than private ownership and Western money. It needs customer- and quality-centered operations management. This kind of help cures basic weaknesses, thereby protecting the investor, and it helps preserve and strengthen the business and the jobs and skills of its associates. When a management action yields a good result for each party, managers call it a win–win situation (see the Contrast box). Of the various win–win strategies, continuous improvement ranks highly.

Continuous Improvement as Strategy

Much that is in this book was absent from the OM field just a few years ago. Vigorous international competition has generated a lot of the newer concepts and methods. These changes are best captured in the term *continuous improvement.*

To be strategically effective, continuous improvement must account for the needs of customers and competencies of competitors, and it must build on the organization's internal capacities and capabilities.

However, if continuous improvement is confined to the ranks of management and technical experts, it is a weak strategy. It must be woven into the fabric of everyday work of all employees. Sometimes the strategy is easier for front-line employees to accept than labor union leaders. However, even union leaders have frequently come around. Jack Sheinkman, president of the Amalgamated Clothing and Textile Workers Union offers an insightful distinction between the "high road" and the "low road":

> High-road strategies entail continuous improvement in the quality of products, the organization, and the workers' contribution to the production process. Low-road strategies find competitive advantage in low wages and benefits and the elimination of jobs.[17]

Continuous improvement got its start in operations, first in leading Japanese export companies, then in competing companies elsewhere in the world. The idea is to continually, and incrementally, change and improve *everything:* equipment, procedures, employee skills, throughout time, quality, supplier relations, product and service designs, and so on.

Since this idea, and many supporting techniques, were perfected first at Toyota, they have been called the **Toyota production system.** In an MIT study of

The Japanese term for continuous improvement, *kaizen,* is in use in a few Western firms.

worldwide automobile assembly, the system was labeled **lean production.** According to the study's authors,

> [It] is lean because it uses less of everything . . . half the human effort in the factory, half the manufacturing space, half the investment in tools, half the engineering hours to develop a new product in half the time. Also, it requires keeping far less than half the needed inventory on site, results in many fewer defects, and produces a greater and ever growing variety of products.[18]

The lean production approach is so persuasive that it seems to have become the strategic leading edge in some companies. This occurred first within Japan's manufacturing sector, where furious competition reduced the number of motorcycle makers from over 1,000 to a handful. Similar outcomes occurred in many other industries, which resulted in a few very strong companies that turned their sights first to the United States, the world's largest market.

The pattern has repeated itself in other countries in response to competition. The enabler is widespread transfer of knowledge on how to generate continuous improvement. A survey of superior manufacturers in the United States, Japan, and Western Europe indicates that the strategic focus among these nations has evolved and become much alike. The 1992 survey, summarized in Exhibit 2–2, shows conformance quality, on-time delivery, and product reliability on all three lists. Performance quality, on the U.S. and Europe lists, is not on Japan's perhaps because an issue is not an issue when it has been resolved. Price is on the minds of executives in the highly price-competitive United States, while delivery speed concerns Europe, which was late in getting just-in-time efforts under way. If the survey were taken today, fast design change might appear on everyone's list. As will be discussed in Chapter 4, some recent trends have cast a small shadow on product customization, on Japan's top-five list.

While the survey included only U.S., European, and Japanese plants, there is some evidence that plants elsewhere are focusing on similar pathways to competitiveness. For example, MIT's international automotive study cited Ford's assembly plant in Hermosillo, Mexico, as the world's most efficient.[19]

Eicher Tractors Ltd., operating nine factories in India, is another example. Eicher intensively trains its workforce for continuous improvement. In Eicher's Faridabad tractor assembly plant, evidence of improvements, as well as process controls, is everywhere (see photos). Output incentive payments have been abolished in favor of producing just in time for use at the next process. Improvement projects are under way in support departments as well as in the factory. In

	U.S.	Europe	Japan
Conformance quality	1	1	4
On-time delivery	2	2	2
Product reliability	3	3	1
Performance quality	4	4	
Price	5		
Delivery speed		5	
Fast design change			3
Product customization			5

EXHIBIT 2–2

Top Five Competitive Capabilities for 1990–1995, Rank Ordered (1 = highest rank)

Source: Jay S. Kim and Jeffrey G. Miller, "Challenges for Building the Value Factory: Key Findings from the 1992 U.S. Manufacturing Futures Survey," *OM Review*, 9, no. 3 (1992) pp. 1–21.

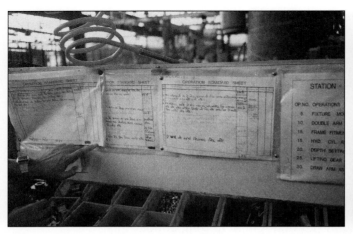

Process specification sheets are posted in each work area at the assembly plant of Eicher Tractor Ltd. These sheets include operating procedures and aid process control, process improvement, and cross-training   Left: Close-up of specs sheets. Right: Assembly team in white gloves; specs sheets are above parts trays at either side.

company transportation, drivers are assuming ownership of vehicle maintenance and have teamed up on a parking lot improvement project. In the finance department, an improvement team has cut the time to issue stock certificates (to investors) from three months to one week.

Eicher Tractor's application of continuous improvement in the back office is a natural extension of doing it in the plant. The same thing has been taking place in the offices of leading manufacturers globally.

At the same time, continuous improvement is becoming a competitive force among leading organizations in services. Although manufacturers have several names for this strategy (e.g., lean, world-class, or Toyota system), the service industries tend to favor a single term, **total quality management (TQM).** While TQM can take on a narrow definition, it is also used broadly, encompassing organization-wide continuous improvement in meeting customers' requirements. At any rate, continuous improvement has gained prominence as an OM strategy (as well as a business strategy) in services as well as in manufacturing.

Universal Strategies

We have seen that a certain degree of uniformity has evolved in operations strategy. Continuous improvement, customer or product-focused organization, speed, flexibility—many companies have gravitated toward these kinds of strategies. This is especially true of those on the leading edge of excellence. Is it too much to ask? Can operations deliver on so many strategies?

For some time, business schools taught strategy as a matter of trade-offs. Harvard professor Michael Porter's best-selling 1980 book, *Competitive Strategy,* typified the viewpoint. Porter suggested that a company could effectively pursue only one of the following three strategies: cost leadership, product differentiation, or customer/product focus.[20] That viewpoint began to melt at about the same time as the book was published. We came to realize that companies like Toyota and

Canon were beating their Western competitors every which way: on quality, cost, flexibility, and more. The competitiveness of the more successful Japanese companies was rooted mainly in these kinds of customer-sensitive operations strategies, which might be thought of as universal strategies. The proof strengthened when their subsidiaries in North America, and then Western companies such as Hewlett-Packard, Deere, and Intel, successfully put the same system into practice. Aleda V. Roth recently reported on a research study in which she found a number of health care organizations that "have begun to pioneer new operational models that emphasize quality, service, flexibility, innovation, and cost—simultaneously."[21]

The trade-off view continues to surface now and then. Current prevalent opinion, however, seems to be that companies can "do it all"—or most of it anyway.

Good operations build on good operations strategy. Therefore, to set the tone for the remainder of this book, we further develop the universals of operations strategy. These universals, stated in the next section as principles of operations management, cover a good deal of territory. They are a lot to introduce this early in the book. Thus, we present them as briefly as possible while still expressing their essence. Throughout the book, we re-state a given principle as a margin note near to a concept or procedure to which it applies.

Principles of OM—As Strategy

The elements of operations strategy that seem to apply universally may be thought of as principles of OM. Exhibit 2–3 is a 15-point set of the principles. They hang together in that they are customer focused, employee driven, and data based. They serve as a strategic foundation for operations in goods or services, just as running and blocking are fundamentals for any team in a variety of sports. The principles are like a sport team's game plan. Execution—playing the game well—depends on strength in the fundamentals.

A **principle** is "a fundamental, primary, or general law or truth, from which others are derived".[22] It applies in nearly all, but not every case.

The 15 principles are in two broad groups and seven categories. The first group, formulation of operations strategy, must account for customers, the company, and competitors if the OM strategy is to be complete. The second group, implementation, includes the other four categories, which are the building blocks of strategic support for the first group.

$\mathscr{C}$ontrast

Strategy

Conventional Wisdom

Strategy is something done by senior executives, often with advice from highly paid consultants.

Strategy permeates the organization through level-by-level, top-down planning.

New Thinking

Much of strategic management can be reduced to basic principles.

Widely shared information and involvement in strategic planning fosters unified purpose and eases implementation of strategies.

EXHIBIT 2–3
Principles of Operations Management

Operations Strategy—Formulation

Customers:
1. Know and team up with the next and final customer.
2. Become dedicated to continual, rapid improvement in quality, cost, response time, flexibility, variability, and service.

Company:
3. Achieve unified purpose via shared information and team involvement in planning and implementation of change.

Competitors:
4. Know the competition and the world-class leaders.

Operations Strategy—Implementation

Design and Organization:
5. Cut the number of product or service components or operations and the number of suppliers to a few good ones.
6. Organize resources into multiple "chains of customers," each focused on a product, service, or customer family; create work-flow teams, cells, and "plants-in-a-plant."

Capacity:
7. Continually invest in human resources through cross-training (for mastery of multiple skills); education; job and career-path rotation; and improved health, safety, and security.
8. Maintain and improve present equipment and human work before thinking about new equipment; automate incrementally when process variability cannot otherwise be reduced.
9. Look for simple, flexible, movable, low-cost equipment that can be acquired in multiple copies—each assignable to work-flow teams, focused cells, and plants-in-a-plant.

Processing:
10. Make it easier to make/provide goods or services without error or process variation.
11. Cut flow time (wait time), distance, and inventory all along the chains of customers.
12. Cut setup, changeover, get-ready, and startup times.
13. Operate at the customer's rate of use (or a smoothed representation of it); decrease cycle interval and lot size.

Problem solving and control:
14. Record and *own* quality, process, and problem data at the workplace. Ensure that front-line improvement teams get first chance at problem solving—before staff experts.
15. Cut transactions and reporting; control causes, not symptoms.

The principles have a common sense ring. Nevertheless, numerous companies take a different path—sometimes an opposite one—as we discuss below.

1. Know and Team Up with the Next and Final Customer.   The customer, whether final consumer or next process, is the object of the first and most important principle. The remaining principles, which follow from this one, concern *how* to serve the customer better.

Getting to know and teaming up with the customer often requires breaking barriers, especially departmental walls. Teaming up can mean moving associates out of functional departments and into teams and cells—that is, organizing associates by how the work flows. If that isn't practical, then organize cross-functional improvement teams. Although these teams do not "live" together, they meet periodically to solve problems.

Geography is often a barrier (e.g., a customer is located miles away). But responses to such barriers can get creative. For example, Globe Metallurgical, supplier of additives to steel mills and foundries, buses its factory associates to customer plants where they get to know their counterparts. This facilitates quick, easy communication, associate to associate, when the customer has a problem, or when Globe people have questions about customer needs. Globe's strong customer focus contributed to its being named the first (1988) recipient of the Malcolm Baldrige quality prize in the small business category.

A metal foundry makes castings by pouring hot metal into a mold, letting it set, and breaking the mold.

2. Become Dedicated to Continual, Rapid Improvement in Quality, Cost, Response Time, Flexibility, Variability, and Service.   Continual improvement means little without an object. The natural objects are the six general customer wants. This principle makes the connection and applies to any organization. Still, each organization is unique. The next two principles aim at tailoring OM strategy to the particular firm and its competitive environment.

3. Achieve Unified Purpose via Shared Information and Team Involvement in Planning and Implementation of Change.   Information must be shared throughout the organization if employee-driven continuous improvement is to occur. Few companies apply this principle as effectively as Zytec, a producer of power supplies for computing equipment and a 1991 Baldrige quality prize winner. In developing its five-year strategic plan, Zytec involves 20 percent of its workforce, from all corners of the firm; it even has a few key suppliers and customers comment on the plan. Then, every employee and team has a role in translating the plan into action elements with measurable yearly goals.[23]

4. Know the Competition and the World-Class Leaders.   In many firms, getting to know the competition has been viewed as a sales and marketing function, useful for competitive pricing, product positioning, and promotion. But for superior companies, that approach is insufficient. Operations management associates cannot be effective without competitive information. They need to learn about competitors' designs, capacities, skill base, and supplier/customer linkages—as well as costs, quality, flexibility, and response times.

Old-style competitive analysis is limited to sampling competitors' services and acquiring and "reverse-engineering" their products; continuous improvement requires that and much more. Blue-chip companies conduct benchmarking

Benchmarking was developed by Xerox Corporation, whose first benchmarking study took place in 1979. Benchmarking was quickly adopted by many other companies.

studies, in which they gather data and exchange visits with other companies, often in totally different industries. They seek to discover the best practices, not just the best services and products. A number of manufacturers have benchmarked Federal Express in order to learn better ways of handling deliveries.

Failure to learn about the strengths of the competition or about the best performance in any industry (e.g., the ability to deliver better quality or offer quicker response) leads to complacency and decline. But obtaining and using such information helps motivate a company's people to make necessary improvements, which are stated as principles 5 through 15.

5. Cut the Number of Product or Service Components or Operations and Number of Suppliers to a Few Good Ones.   Having too many components of a product or service or too many suppliers makes it difficult to do justice to any of them. Reducing the number of product components has become a centerpiece of continuous improvement in many top-flight manufacturing companies. Cutting down on the number of suppliers (of component parts or services) is closely related, and it is becoming common practice in both manufacturing and service organizations.

This principle, the first of two in the design and organization category, pertains to *things;* the next deals with *people.*

6. Organize Resources into Multiple Chains of Customers, Each Focused on a Product, Service, or Customer Family; Create Work-Flow Teams, Focused Cells, and Plants-in-a-Plant.   This principle addresses problems implicit in familiar bureaucratic statements like, "This office is responsible for issuing the permit," or "Our department processes those forms." Department-to-department work flows can be impersonal and invite finger pointing—at the other department—when things go wrong.

To ensure good coordination, error prevention, and continuous improvement, a customer—ideally a single person—at the next process should be known and familiar, a real partner or team member. Also needed is a dependable work-flow path. These are among the reasons why many organizations have re-engineered themselves: Hospitals have broken up specialty departments and reorganized into patient-focused care units. Insurance companies have broken up underwriting and claims-processing departments and regrouped into multifunctional teams. And factories and their support offices have re-engineered to create focused work cells by families of products.

7. Continually Invest in Human Resources through Cross-Training (for Mastery of Multiple Skills); Education; Job and Career-Path Rotation; and Improved Health, Safety, and Security.   Capacity is high in cost and has long-term impact. That goes not only for physical capacity, treated in principles 8 and 9, but also for human resource capacity.

Human resources are involved in formulating OM strategy and are the driving force for carrying it out. Like all the elements of capacity, the human resource is an object of continuous improvement. Old static approaches won't do.

Old practices: Divide work into jobs so small and simple that any unskilled person, paid minimum wage, could master it the first day. Assign managers, experts, and professionals to a single career track and keep them there for life so they can really learn the function.

Continuous improvement: Each associate continually masters more job and job support skills, problem-solving techniques, and self-(team) management. Through job switching, associates learn the impact of job A on job B; they discover their collective impact on the whole service or product, as well as their effect on customer satisfacton; and they understand their contribution to employee health, safety, and security. Managers and professionals require occasional career-path switching to gain a broader outlook, to increase their value to the company, and to achieve greater personal career security.

8. Maintain and Improve Present Equipment and Human Work before Thinking about New Equipment; Automate Incrementally When Process Variability Cannot Otherwise Be Reduced.   People are variable, and variability stands in the way of serving the customer. Progress will therefore require new equipment and automation. The easy, cheap way to achieve progress is for associates to tighten up their slack habits and bad practices. This defers the cost and complexity of automation. It also avoids succumbing to the glamour of automation and the tendency to automate for the wrong reasons, such as the following:

- "Replace run-down, poorly maintained present equipment, and cope with quality variation." Automation actually requires a higher degree of attention to equipment care and maintenance and better process controls on quality.
- "Become more flexible." But the most flexible resource is people, not flexible automation.
- "Invest retained earnings." Investing retained earnings in automation sometimes makes sense, but investing in the company's existing human and physical infrastructure is always a good choice.
- "Eliminate the 'labor problem'." Automation causes major workforce changes and potentially even greater labor problems. Such matters (which often are management problems) are best resolved before piling on other major changes.

9. Look for Simple, Flexible, Movable, Low-Cost Equipment that Can Be Acquired in Multiple Copies—Each Assignable to Work-Flow Teams, Focused Cells, and Plants-in-a-Plant.   How is growing demand to be served? The common tendency is to speed up the existing process: to add more people or to replace a small machine with a bigger, faster, costlier one.

Companies that have followed such practices for several generations of growth may find themselves with serious capacity obstacles. Their single, fast process is not divisible into focused units; it can process only one model at a time in huge amounts, which usually will be out of phase with actual customer demand patterns; it may be in the wrong location and too costly to move. Main-frame computers come to mind.

This plurality principle is the antidote. Planning in multiple-capacity units allows growth to occur at the same time as the firm is becoming product/customer focused. Moreover, focusing equipment and operating teams on narrow families of products/customers helps large and growing companies act like small, customer-service-minded ones. PCs and laptops come to mind.

10. Make it Easier to Make/Provide Goods or Services without Error or Process Variation.   This and the next three principles involve the processing itself—the transformation of resources into goods and services. The broad principle might be abbreviated as *Do it right the first time*. It enlists concepts and practices stretching from designing for quality, to partnering up with suppliers and customers for quality, to controlling processes for quality, to collecting and analyzing data for removal of the sources of poor quality.

This approach replaces poor but conventional practices in which causes of good and bad quality were not treated. Instead, manufacturing companies had sizable inspection staffs for sorting bad output from good, typically in late processing stages. Service organizations relied on complaint departments. Usually, plenty of bad results still slipped through.

11. Cut Flow Time (Wait Time), Distance, and Inventory All along the Chain of Customers.   This and the next two principles are closely associated with just-in-time operations, which shorten **cycle time** and improve responsiveness to customers. By cycle time, we mean elapsed time to complete one unit of output in a process that recycles. The output may be one manufactured item, one processed document, or one served client.

In human services, customers' main gripe is usually long waiting lines. One way to cut the waiting time is for the service organization simply to set queue limits in combination with flexible labor. Some banks and retailers are doing this (see further discussion in Chapter 10). Queue limitation works just as well in processing documents or materials.

Processing inventories can involve multistage waiting lines. The stages from factories to distribution centers to retail storerooms and display counters are typically choked with work-in-process and pipeline inventories. It's a long, loose chain full of waste and delay. Reaction to changes in demand patterns are cumbersome and slow, and the customer may not wait. Mistakes can pile up before they are noted. By then, their causes may be unclear because the trail is cold. Removing excess inventory at each stage might permit delivery while the customer is still interested, and that can preserve or increase sales and market share. Other benefits include reducing delay-related operating costs, such as extra handling, more transactions and documentation, and excess scrap and rework. Often it is possible to achieve quick response by moving process stages closer together—that is, shortening the flow path.

12. Cut Setup, Changeover, Get-Ready, and Startup Times.   This principle deals with preparation-to-serve delays of all kinds. For example, if you want to run a program on your personal computer, you must first get set up. You have to boot the disk, which, on your older model, takes 29 seconds. Then you make a menu selection (19 seconds), instruct the computer to read disk drive A (10 seconds), and call the desired program into memory (12 seconds). After a total of 1 minute and 10 seconds of setup, you are ready to perform useful work. Not so long, perhaps, but what if you need to switch from a word-processing program to a spreadsheet? Would you have to go through another partial setup? And then perhaps another, to use a database program?

Setup, changeover, get-ready, or startup time: The time to switch from useful output in one mode to useful output in the second.

Excess setup time on a computer can be a mild annoyance, or it can seriously detract from someone's productivity. Or, if a client is waiting for the computer to process something, it's a real problem of poor service.

In manufacturing, machine setup and production-line changeovers can eat up enormous amounts of costly capacity and render the company unable to change quickly from one product model to another as customer demand patterns change.

As just-in-time methods have come into use, many manufacturers have become aggressive about cutting equipment setup times. For example, at Pepsi's bottling plants, bottle size changeovers have been reduced from 90 minutes to 20 minutes.

However, the problem of long preparation time does not have to involve a machine. A customer may fume while a clerk hunts for an order book or a nurse opens cabinets looking for a roll of tape. Such examples of unpreparedness are commonplace and usually easy to fix. Systematic procedures for attacking these problems have migrated from the manufacturing sector to a growing number of service organizations.

13. Operate at the Customer's Rate of Use (or a Smoothed Representation of It); Decrease Cycle Interval and Lot Size.   That is: Don't go as fast as you can go, only to see the work pile up in front of your customer at the next process. Don't invest in equipment that runs many times faster than the work can be processed downstream. And don't save up large piles of work before sending it on to the next process. Although those practices are common in typically disconnected companies, they are wasteful and stretch out the response time. Customers may not be willing to wait.

14. Record and Own Quality, Process, and Problem Data at the Workplace. Ensure That Front-Line Improvement Teams Get First Chance at Problem Solving—Before Staff Experts.   Problem-solving and control, the topic of the last two principles, are ineffective if problem-solving *data* ends up in the wrong place. A common mistake is sending quality, process, and problem data from the front lines to experts in back offices. That leaves front-line associates (the majority of company employees) out of the problem-solving, control, and process ownership loop. Data is what gets them back in. Then they can do plenty, especially in teams in which knowledge, skills, and ideas are readily shared. Staff experts may have more problem-solving skills, but they have less understanding of the processes where problems occur. Also, staff people are not only expensive and relatively scarce, they are often tied up in other projects. This leaves little time for solving ongoing process problems and on-the-spot emergencies, which are the natural responsibility of front-line associates.

15. Cut Transactions and Reporting: Control Causes, Not Symptoms. Transactions and reports often deal with symptoms (e.g., our warranty costs are too high, too much overtime last month, etc.). Effective quality control and production control replace transactions and reports (as much as possible) with process data—categorized and detailed as to causes. Those data fuel the continuous improvement effort and need not end up in a report. In fact, in the continuous process-improvement mode, by the time a report of a problem comes out, a team of associates would probably already be working on it—or may already have solved it.

The 15 principles may serve *as* strategy, but they do not cover the whole strategic waterfront. For example, they cannot directly guide a decision on where to locate a warehouse or set up a branch office, or if or when to do this. Complex issues like these simply involve too many variables, and executive-level strategic planning will still be required. But that planning should follow principle number 3, enlisting the broadest possible involvement in the effort.

Summary

Operations has had a history of being strategically neglected, as compared with finance, marketing, and product development. Quality-based competitive pressures from Japanese exporters helped raise company consciousness about the need for a quality focus—which is mainly an operations strategy. Other wide-reach business and operations strategies of the past 15 or so years include time (speed), globalization, teaming and partnering, and flexibility/agility.

An effective OM strategy ties in with other company strategies and has the firm's customers, competitors, and the firm itself as its components. While every organization needs to carve out its own distinctive competency, worldwide competitive pressures tend to push every firm toward a roughly similar OM strategy. It is one in which all associates team up for continuous improvement. Although strategic commonality in OM affected manufacturing first (emerging from the just-in-time/total quality crusade), the service sector has also taken up the cause, generally calling it total quality management.

The goods and services sectors are now on the same course, with an underlying strategic foundation consisting of 15 basic principles of operations management: know the customer; be dedicated to continual, rapid improvement in the six basic customer wants; achieve unified purpose; know the competition and the world's best performers; cut the number of components and suppliers; organize multiple focused chains of customers; develop and broaden human skills; maintain and improve present resources and employ them to reduce variability before investing in new or automated equipment; seek plural, low-cost units of equipment that are movable into focused capacity units; make it easy to reduce error and variation; cut flow time, distance, and inventory; cut setup or other readiness times; operate at the customer's use rate and decrease cycle interval and lot size; record and own operating data at the workplace and give line associates the first chance at problem solving; and cut the need for transactions and reports by controlling causes.

Review Questions

1. How are operations strategy and business strategy related?
2. OM strategy must account for customers, competitors, and the company itself in profit-making firms. What about nonprofit organizations?
3. What events triggered resurging interest in operations strategy?
4. How is a globalization strategy related to an external partnership strategy?
5. How is a teaming strategy related to a quality strategy?
6. In what sense is quick response (speed) a broad-reach strategy?
7. Name five business elements that are associated with operations strategy and five that are not.
8. What is the likely fate of an organization that has no distinctive competencies? Explain.
9. When does an organization most need to be aware of its core competencies?

10. What is the world-class approach to trade-offs?
11. What is meant by *universal strategies?*
12. How do the principles of operations management relate to company strategy?
13. Which principles of operations management most directly pertain to operations costs? Explain.
14. Which principles of operations management most directly pertain to flexibility? Explain

Exercises

1. Give two examples of service-sector organizations that seem to be strong in all five of the wide-reach operations strategies of Exhibit 2–1.
2. Find two articles on operations strategy by Professor Wickham Skinner *not* mentioned in the chapter. What are his key points?
3. When Whirlpool elected to develop a line of washing machines for Europe with standard components, was this a business strategy or a strategy of one or more of the business functions? Explain.
4. The chapter discusses the unique strategy that led Fidelity Investments to become the largest mutual fund company. Another maverick is the Charles Schwab stock brokerage firm. Find out enough about Schwab to compare and contrast the operations strategies of these two firms.
5. What are the distinctive competencies of the following organizations? Discuss.
   a. Holiday Inn.
   b. U.S. Marines.
   c. Boeing.
   d. Procter & Gamble.
6. How does competition affect operations management? Consider, for example, some of the most successful firms in the highly competitive fast-food, lodging, and grocery industries. What do the successful firms do in operations management that their less successful competitors (maybe some that went under!) do not?
7. What are two examples of North American companies that generally have been successful in achieving both cost leadership and quality leadership? Discuss.
8. Most of the equipment (automatic screw machines, grinding machines, boring machines, etc.) is old and badly run down at North American Bearing Company. That leads to problems in holding tolerances and meeting specifications.
   a. What strategy do you recommend for correcting the situation? Refer to the relevant principles of operations management in your answer.
   b. Suggest a long-term strategy for continuous improvement so that North American Bearing does not experience such problems in the future.
9. One element of First City Bank's operations strategy is the opening of 15 new cash machines in locations around the area.
   a. What business strategy does this operations strategy most likely support? Express that business strategy in one sentence.
   b. With which principle of operations management does this strategy seem most consistent? Explain.
10. Classical Wooden Toy Company's business strategy includes "responding more quickly to changes in sales patterns for our different toy models." Develop an operations strategy to support that business strategy, taking care not to violate the principles of operations management. Explain your answer.

11. The food and restaurant division of a city health department is under pressure from the department director to improve its performance. The local newspaper has been running a series of exposés on filth in some popular restaurants. The stories have criticized the health department for (*a*) infrequent inspections and (*b*) long delays in responding to written and telephone complaints about certain restaurants. The division, consisting of 5 inspectors, 20 clerical employees, and 5 managerial and supervisory employees, claims that it does not have enough staff and budget to be thorough and quick to respond, as well as make frequent visits. Select four principles of operations management that might help the division. Explain your choices.

12. In the 1960s, companywide job announcements at Deere & Company's headquarters were regularly posted on bulletin boards in the information systems department. The department's policy was to encourage computer programmers and analysts to apply for jobs in marketing, production, and so forth. Is that policy outdated or up-to-date? Does it support or inhibit service to the customer? Does it relate to any of the 15 principles of OM? Discuss.

13. Arbor Nurseries, Inc., does a large business in planting trees for real estate developers, who invariably want service "right now." Which four principles of operations management must Arbor heed in order to be responsive to this customer want? Discuss.

14. At one Seagate plant, which manufactures disk drive products, automatic process-monitoring devices capture data from the assembly processes and put them into a computer system. Operators in the work centers plot summarized data (taken from computer terminals) by hand onto visual display charts, even though the computer system has full capability to print out impressive charts with color graphics. Why not use the color graphics? What principle of operations management seems to be the basis for this Seagate practice?

15. What organization that you have dealt with as a customer or client seems best at following principle number 11—cutting flow time and travel distance for you (as client) or for your order? How is this done? (You may need to conduct a small investigation to answer this.)

16. What organization that you have dealt with as a customer or client seems best at following principle number 12—being able to switch quickly from one kind of work (or customer) to another without long changeover delays? How is this done? (You may need to conduct a small investigation to answer this.)

17. In your experience as an employee or volunteer, you undoubtedly have encountered annoyance over delays and high error and rework rates. To what extent do these problems seem to be related to separation into departmental specialities (needed expertise in other departments)? Suggest a solution, specific to your experience, using concepts from the chapter.

CASE STUDY

TITEFLEX CORPORATION*

On December 1, 1988, Jon H. Simpson, 41, became president of Titeflex Corporation, located in Springfield, Massachusetts. In that year Titeflex produced and sold $45 million worth of high-performance hoses to the aerospace, industrial, and automotive sectors. Earlier that

* Adapted from Ravi Ramamurti, "Titeflex Corporation: The Turnaround Challenge," North American Case Research Association. Used with permission.

year, Titeflex's parent, the Bundy Group, had been acquired by the British engineering conglomerate, Tube Investments (TI). Simpson had been vice president of operations in CHR Industries, another Bundy company, when TI's management made him president of Titeflex.

Strategy

TI's initial strategy was to divest Bundy's Performance Plastics Group, which included CHR Industries and Titeflex. After further study, however, TI pulled Titeflex out of the divestment package, because its technology had value for Bundy's automotive business as well as for TI's flourishing aerospace business. All was not well with Titeflex, however. While the company was profitable and its sales were growing, competitors were nibbling away at Titeflex's market share, production was slow, deliveries were more often late than on time, and relations between management and Titeflex's union were abysmal.

TI's CEO, Sir Christopher Lewinton, would not be satisfied with Titeflex's performance. He wanted each of TI's 70 companies to be worldwide leaders in technology and market share. He expected sales and profits to grow at 15 percent per annum while yielding at least a 15 percent return on sales and a 30 percent return on net assets before interest and taxes.

Prior to the acquisition by TI, Simpson had been taking time away from CHR to help the Boston Consulting Group (BCG), which Bundy had brought in to study Titeflex's operations. As internal consultant, Simpson worked with BCG on flowcharting processes in every area to identify how efficiency and speed of response could be improved.

The promotion to the Titeflex presidency transformed Simpson's life. Suddenly, he found himself in Springfield, Massachusetts, managing a new division under a new set of (British) bosses. Simpson felt sandwiched between irate customers, warring employees, and demanding superiors. How should he deal with his customers? What could he do to improve Titeflex's operations and relations with the union? Simpson wondered what his priorities ought to be, where to begin, and how to proceed.

Products

According to customers that Simpson met in his first few days in the company, Titeflex had a reputation for producing "pricey" products of excellent quality. The product line consisted of some 100,000 different hoses varying in size, shape, fittings, and type of protective sleeving. Customers were clustered in three market segments: aerospace (50 percent of sales), industrial (30 percent), and automotive (20 percent).

Titeflex and two other firms had a 90 percent share of the aerospace market. Few competitors existed because of the long time it took for products to prove themselves through usage by the customer and for a supplier to become certified as "qualified." While the number of pieces sold was only 10 units per day, products were highly customized and had high profit margins. Some complex hoses went through all 44 manufacturing processes, traveling 2 1/2 miles. Titeflex's market share had declined to about 25 percent, and two of the company's largest customers had told Simpson they were considering dropping Titeflex as a supplier.

Hoses for the industrial sector were used in applications ranging from oil field apparatus to refrigeration equipment. Titeflex was a minor player in the price-sensitive part of this market. However, it competed well in the high-pressure and high-temperature segment where quality and reliability were more important than price. Meeting delivery schedules was crucial for new hoses, whereas quick response to customer requests was critical for hose replacements.

Product variety was small and price competition intense in the automotive sector. Late deliveries could shut down an auto assembly plant, and early deliveries were not accepted. High-performance auto engines had increased the technology involved in these hoses. This gave Titeflex, with its aerospace expertise, somewhat of an advantage. Of the three markets, automotive was expected to grow the fastest.

Operations

Titeflex's employment totaled about 750 people. Nearly 600 worked in its largest facility, in Springfield, with the rest in plants and offices in Canada and France. About half of the Springfield contingent were shop-floor people, while the rest worked in front-office support functions. Bundy had invested significant sums to expand and modernize the Springfield plant and strengthen the MIS system but had not tampered with its organization or processes.

For a standard product, total throughput time, from order receipt to shipment, totaled 10 to 15 weeks, provided that all went according to plan. Of that time, sales took 3 to 5 weeks for order entry and processing, while operations took 7 to 10 weeks for manufacturing. In operations, there were six organizational levels from the shop-floor employee to the head of the department. A purchase order for a bearing to fix a machine might require seven or eight signatures. Departmental loyalties were strong, and interdepartmental coordination required numerous formal meetings. Said one busy manager, "We have morning meetings, afternoon meetings, quality review meetings, engineering review meetings, purchasing meetings, make-buy meetings, and meetings to schedule meetings!"

The production process for an average hose began in the plant engineering department, which developed the manufacturing drawings—except when supplied by the customer. The hose fabrication shop manufactured the basic hose, while the machining department produced the fittings. All parts passed through a handful of very expensive machines in the two departments. The hoses and fittings, along with purchased parts, wound up in the assembly department, which assembled them into finished products.

All production employees and equipment were organized by type of activity rather than type of hose or type of customer. For instance, the same machine or operator might be used in the fabrication of a $10,000 hose for a jet engine and a $50 exhaust-recovery hose for a car. Most machine operators were paid on a piecework basis. Material handlers, accounting for nearly 20 percent of the shop-floor workforce, moved material from machine to machine and shop to shop in carts specially designed to minimize damage.

Shipments were frequently held up for want of outside parts or because of internal production bottlenecks. In some cases delays extended for several weeks, infuriating customers. To cope, Titeflex built up inventories of parts and work-in-process at all stages. By 1988, inventories had risen to four months of sales. A computerized material requirements planning (MRP) system introduced in the mid-1980s at a cost of nearly $1 million generated detailed reports on schedules, inventories, and manufacturing costs (by order, by department, etc.). In addition, production planning and control (PPC) held periodic meetings to review the status of various jobs. When all else failed, the "sales action" group in the PPC department shepherded high-priority orders through the production maze to placate angry customers. Despite this, in 1988 only a fourth of all industrial orders and a tenth of all aerospace orders were delivered on time.

To maintain a reputation for high-quality products, a large quality department inspected parts and subassemblies at every stage of the production process. Inspectors sent to rework anything that fell short of meeting specifications. Rework typically accounted for 25 percent of the output. A competent 15-person (recently downsized) new-products engineering department focused heavily on product development for the automotive industry.

Questions

1. Develop an operations strategy for Jon Simpson and his colleagues at Titeflex. To what extent is your operations strategy also a business strategy?

2. Which of the 15 principles of operations management applies most directly to your strategy? Explain.

For Further Reference

Books

Ettlie, John E; Michael C. Burstein; and Avi Fiegenbaum. *Manufacturing Strategy: The Research Agenda for the Next Decade,* Proceedings of the Joint Industry University Conference on Manufacturing Strategy Held in Ann Arbor, Michigan, on January 8–9, 1990. Boston: Kluwer Academic Publishers, 1990 (HD9720.5.J65).

Garvin, David A. *Operations Strategy: Text and Cases.* Englewood Cliffs, N.J.: Prentice-Hall, 1992 (TS155.G348).

Hill, Terry. *Manufacturing Strategy: Text and Cases.* 2d ed. Burr Ridge, Ill: Richard D. Irwin, 1994 (TS155.H46).

Moody, Patricia E. *Strategic Manufacturing: Dynamic New Directions for the 1990s.* Burr Ridge, Ill.: Dow Jones-Irwin, 1990 (HD9725.S73).

Ohmae, Kenichi, *The Borderless World: Power and Strategy in the Interlinked Economy.* New York: Harper Business, 1990 (HF3838.D44043).

Ohno, Taiichi. *Toyota Production System: Beyond Large-Scale Production.* Portland, Ore.: Productivity Press, 1988.

Porter, Michael. *The Competitive Advantage of Nations.* New York: The Free Press, 1990 (HD3611.P654).

Schonberger, Richard J. *Building a Chain of Customers: Linking Business Functions to Create the World Class Company.* New York: Free Press, 1990; Chapter 2, "Universal Strategy" (HD58.9.S36).

Skinner, C. Wickham. *Manufacturing: The Formidable Competitive Weapon.* New York: Wiley, 1985.

Periodicals/Societies

Academy of Management Executives (Academy of Management)
Harvard Business Review
Strategic Management Journal
Strategic Management Review

3 THE QUALITY IMPERATIVE

Chapter Outline

- At first Hawaiian Bank, tellers tend the drive-up windows and lobby counters in much the same way as their counterparts the world over. Between customers and during other free periods, however, First Hawaiian tellers telephone long-time depositors to thank them for their business and inquire if service might be improved.

- Members of the 217-person student body of Mt. Edgecumbe High School in Sitka, Alaska, spend 90 minutes weekly in training—learning to apply the tools of continuous process improvement and problem solving. They team up with faculty on improvement projects and have traveled the continent telling their story to managers in blue-chip companies.

- At Mitsubishi Motor Company's plant in Normal, Illinois, a multifunctional team is systematically working its way through automobile warranty claims. In one recent project, the team applied its problem-solving skills to power-window regulators with a goal of complete elimination of faulty window operation and the underlying causes—that is, zero defects. Within a few months, the goal was met and the team moved on to another problem.

- Calgary-based Canadian Airlines International introduced its Service Quality program in 1990, and it's paying off. Mishandled or delayed baggage has been reduced by 75 percent, for example, and speed of telephone response has increased by 79 percent. Kevin J. Jenkins, president and CEO, sums it up this way, "Organizing a basic flight schedule and loosely adhering to that schedule will not make an airline stand out. Having exceptional service quality will."[1]

> • Nestle, headquartered in Vevey, Switzerland, follows a simple strategy: back up top-quality products with top-quality service. Its service operations follow two cherished customer rights: the right to security and the right to information. Accordingly, customer service lines are answered by culinary and nutrition experts, not by public relations specialists. Further, it is company policy that every customer complaint be investigated at the factory level—by the plant manager working with production line associates.

These brief vignettes are a snapshot of the pervasive, global quality imperative.[2] This final chapter in Part 1 elaborates on an already-mentioned theme of the book: Quality is a driving force in contemporary operations management and a potent strategic weapon. The chapter focuses on the meanings of quality and total quality management, briefly traces the evolution of quality ideals, examines how quality affects competitiveness, considers ways in which quality performance is recognized, and explores employee-driven quality.

Quality: A Broad View

Shakespeare's eternal question, "What's in a name?" can be asked of quality. Does the word *quality* denote a desirable characteristic in output goods and services? Or, does it describe processes that make and deliver those outputs in ways that please customers? Or, especially when appended with the word *management* and preceded by the word *total*, does it refer to an even bigger picture—an overall approach to running organizations? The answers are *yes, yes,* and *yes.* The quality concept is both comprehensive and complex.

Quality Terminology

Today, it's hard to find a business that doesn't have some manner of formal program for ensuring quality in the goods or services that it provides. Hospitals, schools and universities, and government agencies have also joined the movement. Unique names, acronyms, logos, and company- or customer-specific jargon abound. Thousands of publications (books, articles, films, etc.) on some facet of quality have appeared since the early 1980s.

Although consumers welcome the widespread attention to quality, some observers lament the lack of clear definitions. For example, Philip Crosby and the late W. Edwards Deming, both respected pioneers in the quality movement during the twentieth century, avoid the term total quality management (TQM), arguing, respectively, that it lacks clear definition or even meaning. Joseph M. Juran, another respected voice in the quality field, says that part of the problem stems from a failure to distinguish quality goals from the steps taken to reach those goals; that is, quality and quality management need to be defined separately.[3] First, we consider quality.

Quality.   As the quality movement has evolved, so has the definition of quality. The layperson might still have a foggy I-know-it-when-I-see-it definition. Brief, general definitions of quality (e.g., fitness for use and conformance to requirements) have remained popular for others. But to keep demanding customers happy, businesses have expanded the concept of quality and at the same time have improved their ability to deliver on a wider array of quality dimensions. Exhibit 3–1 contains two itemized lists that exemplify this broadened view. The first was proposed for services; the second is more goods oriented. Despite differences in wording, the lists share two characteristics:

- Both reflect how *customers* think about quality.
- Both suggest action—things managers at all levels need to address if quality is to happen.

Thus, they point the way for quality management.

The term *total quality*, or *TQ* is becoming a popular shortcut to refer both to the characteristic of quality and to quality management.

Total quality management (TQM).   Juran provides a straightforward yet very inclusive definition of TQM: those actions needed to get to world-class quality.[4] The word total is a contribution of Armand Feigenbaum and the late Kaoru Ishikawa—two additional respected quality pioneers: In top organizations, quality management is no longer treated as a staff responsibility or functional speciality tucked away somewhere behind a door labeled "Inspection Department." Instead, it is everybody's business, a total commitment—organizationally as a competitive requirement; collectively as people pool their skills and special talents

---

Exhibit 3–1

Dimensions of Quality

10 Dimensions of Service Quality[*]
Reliability—consistency of performance and dependability.
Responsiveness—willingness or readiness to provide service; timeliness.
Competence—possession of the skills and knowledge required to perform the service.
Access—approachability and ease of contact.
Courtesy—politeness, respect, consideration for property, clean and neat appearance.
Communication—educating and informing customers in language they can understand; listening to customers.
Credibility—trustworthiness, believability; having customer's best interest at heart.
Security—freedom from danger, risk, or doubt.
Understanding—making an effort to understand the customer's needs; learning the specific requirements; providing individualized attention; recognizing the regular customer.
Tangibles—the physical evidence of service (facilities, tools, equipment).

8 Dimensions of Quality[†]
Performance—primary operating characteristics.
Features—little extras.
Reliability—probability of successful operation (nonfailure) within a given time span.
Conformance—meeting preestablished standards.
Durability—length of usefulness, economically and technically.
Serviceability—speed, courtesy, competence, and ease of repair.
Aesthetics—pleasing to the senses.
Perceived quality—indirect evaluations of quality (e.g., reputation).

[*] Adapted from Leonard L. Berry, Valerie A. Zeithaml, and A. Parasuraman, "Quality Counts in Services, Too," *Business Horizons*, May–June 1985, pp. 44–52.

[†] Adapted from David A. Garvin, *Managing Quality: The Strategic and Competitive Edge* (New York: The Free Press, 1988), p. 49ff.

as members of improvement teams; and singly as each individual performs job tasks.

TQM in Practice

A broad view further manifests itself in the multitude of programs, techniques, and tools being implemented under the banner of TQM and its close cousins. At about the same time some leading Western companies were fashioning their TQM agendas in the early 1980s, others were placing equal or greater emphasis on just-in-time (JIT) operations. From its inception in Japan, JIT had a strong quality improvement component in addition to its main emphasis on cycle-time reduction. The early view by companies like Toyota was that TQM and JIT are mutually reinforcing. Today, most competitive organizations embrace and extend that notion; they include benchmarking, re-engineering, supplier development, total preventive maintenance, quick-response programs, and a host of team-related tools, along with the more "hard-science" quality management techniques such as statistical process control, design of experiments, and scientific problem solving.

Research evidence also supports a broad description of TQM. In one recent study, for example, researchers grouped quality management into four broad dimensions—relationships with suppliers, relationships with customers, product design, and transformation processes. They found that all four dimensions were important contributors to high quality performance.[5]

As they will with any management initiative, however, some people prefer to focus their attention on flaws or failures in TQM implementations. And indeed, here have been many instances when tools that might be considered part of a TQM program haven't worked out. So, how can we know if application of a new (or old) tool or procedure, training program, or process change is sound TQM? GEC Plessey Semiconductors (GPS), headquartered in Wiltshire, England, answers that question with a simple test based on three fundamentals: customers, teamwork, and improvement.[6] GPS personnel evaluate all company programs on the seven dimensions shown in Exhibit 3–2. Using a scale to measure success on each item, GPS employees keep vital opportunities for improvement in focus.

GPS is among the organizations that have grown with TQM. They see it as having evolved into a broad set of teachable practices, a centerpiece of good management, and an imperative for successful global operations. While much of that evolution has taken place within the last two decades, the roots of TQM are deeper, as we shall see next.

Is it TQM?
• Is there a clear link to customers?
• Is there a clear link to company objectives?
• Have improvement measures been defined?
• Are managers and employees involved as a team?
• Is the team using a TQM (scientific problem-solving) process and tools?
• Is the team accomplishing and documenting its work?
• Are team decisions derived from data?

EXHIBIT 3–2

GEC Plessey Semiconductors' TQM Test

Source: Adapted from Samuel Feinberg, "Overcoming the Real Issues of Implementation," *Quality Progress*, July 1995, pp. 79–81.

TQM: History and Heritage

In tracing TQM's development, a few milestones stand out. We begin with artisan-based quality assurance, then move forward to note influences of the industrial revolution and consumerism, move to an overview of the major contributions of twentieth-century quality pioneers, and conclude with a brief contemporary perspective on the OM–TQM interface.

Quality Assurance

Interest in quality is centuries old. The code of Hammurabi, which dates from 2150 BC, mandated death for any builder whose work resulted in the death of a customer. Other quality-related codes, often equally harsh, are found in the writings of the ancient Phoenicians, Egyptians, and Aztecs.[7] Despite the harsh codes, however, it was the artisan's pride, not fear, that contributed most significantly to supporting quality assurance for centuries to come.

Quality assurance, in the view of George Edwards of Bell Labs, who coined the term in the 1920s, requires deliberate managerial planning and action, interlocked quality activities throughout the firm, and a senior officer in charge companywide.

The Artisanship Connection.   One of Robin Hood's merry men needed a new long bow. He got in touch with the best bow maker in all of Sherwood Forest. Together, they selected the proper limb, and throughout the fabrication process, the bow maker asked the archer to grasp the bow, try the draw, fire an arrow, and so forth. She took pride in her work and wanted the archer to be happy with his bow. A little carving here and shaping there, more testing, and finally the bow maker had a satisfied customer—one who would return when another new bow was needed and one who would recommend her to his friends. The provider–customer relationship was brief but close.

Today, their descendants *might* interact like their ancestors, but a more likely scenario would have the modern archer visiting a sporting goods store, where many bows would be available for trial. Today's retail transaction itself retains the provider–customer closeness of Sherwood Forest, but much is missing: Who designed the bow? Built it? Tested it? Who decided what brand of bow to stock? The missing elements constitute part of a much longer provider–customer chain. If the customer becomes unhappy, there is no single bow maker to blame. Many individuals in perhaps several companies were involved before the modern transaction occurred.

The Industrial Revolution.   Long supplier–customer chains are a product of the industrial revolution. In order for the masses to enjoy a wider array of goods, production costs had to decrease. New machines allowed production operations to be broken down into minute steps that unskilled labor could utilize. Demand and output increased as production costs decreased. Labor became specialized and disconnected from the big picture. Production people focused on quantity rather than quality; the reward system supported such behavior. In an attempt to stem the tide of deteriorating quality, managers assigned inspectors to check the work of line employees. Inspection, however, merely became another job specialty. Inspectors were unable to improve production quality; they could only find and remove some of the bad output after it had been produced. In many companies, quality fell apart and customers were angry.

Consumerism and Liability Laws.   Product quality and safety began to capture public attention in the mid–1960s. Activist Ralph Nader, consumer federations, action-line columns in newspapers, and investigative TV and newspaper journalists all contributed to increasing the public's interest. In 1965, the American Law Institute issued its "Restatement of the Law of Torts," which defined strict liability: making manufacturers liable for product defects even without proof of negligence.

Since the 1980s, physicians, accountants, attorneys, corporate directors, and volunteer members of civic organization boards increasingly became defendants in civil litigation. Liability insurance rates skyrocketed.

Concern for safe consumption of goods and services also led to regulatory action. In 1972, the U.S. Congress passed the Consumer Product Safety Act, which aims at preventing hazardous or defective products from reaching the consumer. Most other Western countries have followed the same pattern. Some companies extended their product warranties in the 1980s and early 1990s, but well-publicized product recalls seemed to say that quality on the warranty paper was not quality in fact. At the same time, in affluent nations large numbers of a new and demanding type of consumer emerged: the consumer of average means, who prefers to do without rather than pay for second best. There was a revival of neglected crafts such as handweaving, stone grinding of flour, and creation of stained-glass windows. Consumers once again sought the quality of the earlier age of the artisan.

We aren't suggesting that the bows of Robin Hood's era were superior to modern ones. As customers, we want the convenience, safety, technology, and low cost of modern goods. But we also want to know (or at least feel) that the provider of the goods or services is listening to us, cares about our needs, and will "make it right the first time." The influences of an artisan-based quality taproot linger.

The quality imperative is also rooted in the experiences, research and writings, and teachings of modern era quality pioneers, some of whom we've mentioned in the previous section.

The European Community's Product Liability Directive of 1985 called for the passage of strict liability laws in each EC country.

Quality Pioneers of the Twentieth Century

As the concepts and practice of total quality continue to evolve, the contributions of other leaders of the quality movement will emerge, but for now the work of six individuals stands out: W. Edwards Deming, Joseph M. Juran, Armand V. Feigenbaum, Kaoru Ishikawa, Philip B. Crosby, and Genichi Taguchi. Exhibit 3–3 contains a summary of their more noteworthy contributions to the field of quality. [A chapter supplement provides detailed explanations and suggests reference materials by and about these individuals.]

Though known, respectfully, as quality gurus, their thinking and influence extend well beyond the management of quality alone. They all speak of

- Companywide integration of purpose—a shared culture manifested by a top-down commitment to quality that is embraced at all levels.
- High regard for humans, as individuals and as vital components of teams.
- Continuous improvement in all facets of operations—a never-ending program of looking for problems (defects, delays, waste, etc.); finding and eliminating root causes of those problems.

Exhibit 3–3
**Quality
Pioneers—Major
Contributions**

W. Edwards Deming (1900–1993)
- 14 Points (for obtaining quality)
- Plan-Do-Check-Act cycle for continuing improvement
- Ardent support for training and data-based problem solving

Joseph M. Juran (1904–   )
- Editor-in-Chief, *The Quality Handbook*
- Management breakthrough (precursor to process re-engineering)
- The quality trilogy—planning, control, and improvement

Armand V. Feigenbaum (1920–   )
- Concept of total quality control
- Clarification of quality costs—those associated with poor quality
- Concept of "hidden plant"—plant capacity required for rework

Kaoru Ishikawa (1915–1989)
- Registered the first quality control circle (in 1962)
- Cause–effect diagrams (fishbone charts)
- Elemental statistical method—simple but effective tools for data-based decision making

Philip B. Crosby (1926–   )
- Concept of zero defects as the only acceptable quality goal
- Published *Quality Is Free;* argued that lack of quality is what costs
- Defined quality as meeting customer requirements

Genichi Taguchi (1924–   )
- Simplified pathway for greater efficiency in experimental design
- Robust designs to withstand rigors of production and customer use
- Quality loss function; idea that any deviation from target value of a quality characteristic costs society in some way.

- Widespread service to all segments of society through sharing of total quality management ideas, programs, data, and results.

OM and TQM: Contemporary Interfaces

Reflection on the concepts and heritage of TQM along with the principles of OM might prompt the question, "Isn't there a great deal of common ground?" Indeed there is; and the flow of influence goes both ways. Operations in any organization contain primary transformation processes—key targets for obtaining built-in quality improvement. These same processes, however, are also targets for other changes such as increased productivity, greater flexibility, or faster throughput. A change in methods, for example, though initially intended to improve output timing, may surprise implementors by also yielding better output. Rather than quietly accepting the "good luck," today's enlightened firm will eagerly seek to understand the cause of the unforeseen improvement. A second round of changes, perhaps with a quality improvement aim this time, may also result in greater speed or in some other desired outcome. In some cases, long-held beliefs about relationships among variables go by the wayside, as the Contrast box "Quality and Speed" illustrates.

ontrast

Quality and Speed

Old View

Good quality takes time. Speed (e.g., shorter cycle times) makes poor quality.

New View*

"It may sound absurd, but perhaps the surest way to improve quality is speed—by cutting the cycle time from inception to delivery, be the product a car, a piece of research, or an insurance claim."
James F. Swallow, vice president
A. T. Kearney (consultants)

*Source: Otis Port and John Carey, "Questing for the Best," *Business Week,* October 25, 1991, p. 8–16.

The continuing rounds of change and improvement have competitiveness, our next topic, as a dominant target.

TQM and Competitiveness

Dictionaries tell us that competition is effort expended by two or more parties to win the favor of a target individual or group. In this section, we look more closely at how TQM efforts can make an organization more competitive.

In the late 1980s, Gabriel Pall, director of the IBM Quality Institute and former line manager, described two primary pathways through which improved quality enhances a company's profitability; Exhibit 3–4 illustrates. Market-route benefits begin when improved quality increases the product's value in the eyes of customers. The provider may raise prices or—by holding prices steady—realize a gain in market share; revenue increases in either case. Cost-route benefits accrue because increased defect-free output cuts operating costs per unit, and lower costs also enhance profits.

Profitability is one time-honored indicator that customers are as a whole satisfied with a company's output. Demonstrating linkages from better quality to profits might seem a waste of time to the TQM "believer," but it is often a necessary step in convincing budget-minded managers (who face demanding stockholders) to cough up funds for process improvements. When managers evaluate a pending TQM program, Pall's two pathways define issues of concern: "How will it help us in the marketplace?" and "What will it cost?" Let's look first at costs.

Market and cost-route benefits also apply to government agencies, charities, and other not-for-profit groups. Those served by a quality-improving agency are more satisfied and more inclined to make donations or improve tax referendums, thus providing more revenue and resources to the organization.

Cost of Quality

Perhaps the earliest method of trying to incorporate costs of quality into modern managerial decision making was known simply as the **cost-of-quality** approach. Four categories of quality-related costs were identified:

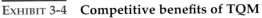

Exhibit 3-4   **Competitive benefits of TQM**

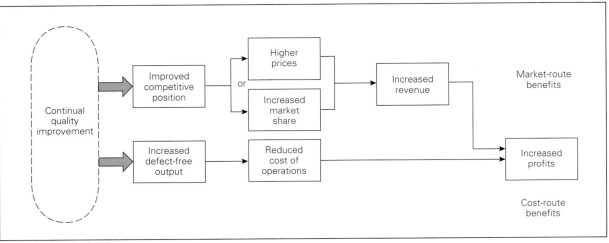

Source: Adapted from Gabriel Pall, *Quality Process Management* (Englewood Cliffs, N.J.: Prentice-Hall, Inc., 1987), chap. 1.

Internal failure costs. Costs the provider incurs directly—prior to delivery or shipment to customers—as a result of defective output. Examples are scrap, rework, retest, downtime, and searching for something misplaced.

External failure costs. Costs to the provider when defects are discovered after delivery or shipment to customers. Included are returns, warranty expenses, allowances, returned material handling, complaint processing, and service recovery. In extreme cases, liability settlements and legal fees would be included.

Appraisal costs. Costs of determining the degree of quality. They include monitoring, materials inspection and testing, maintenance of test equipment, and materials and other resources consumed during inspection and testing (e.g., destructive testing of flash bulbs or food items).

Prevention costs. Costs of efforts to minimize appraisal and failure costs. They include quality planning, training, new-products review, reporting, and improvement projects.

Though few firms' cost accounting systems bore expense accounts with these names, the cost-of-quality expenses did receive considerable attention in more theoretical cost-versus-quality debates. And in some instances, these concepts guided quality planning and budgeting efforts. Astute quality pioneers noted, however, that "these costs are associated solely with defective product—the costs of making, finding, repairing, or avoiding defects. The costs of making good products are not a part of quality costs."[8]

Thus, the term *cost-of-quality* itself is misleading. Taguchi (with his quality loss function) and others have correctly pointed out that the worrisome costs are those associated with *not having quality.* (See the Into Practice box titled "Escalating Cost of Defects" for an example.)

Quality advocates in a number of well-known firms, such as Motorola, Texas Instruments, and Xerox, used the cost-of-quality argument for shock value in the formative stages of their TQM efforts. Cost-minded senior managers were often

Escalating Cost of Defects

The following rule of thumb has become an article of faith in the electronics industry:

- If a defective part is caught by the supplier (before leaving supplier's plant), then there is no cost to the customer (the manufacturer).

- If that part is caught as it enters the manufacturer's plant, the cost is $0.30.

- If that part is caught at the first stage of assembly (after paperwork, handling, scheduling, and other activities that assume the part is good), the cost is $3.00.

- If that part is caught at the final test (common in electronics manufacture), the cost is $30.00.

- If that part is not discovered until after it leaves the manufacturer's plant, the cost is $300.00. It must be returned, replaced, and so on. (This figure, $300.00, *does not* include certain additional costs such as insurance, warranty, lost business, or loss of customer goodwill.)

Note: Raymond A. Cawsey, vice president of quality, Dickey-john Corp., confirms that these figures are "very close" to the true mark for his employer, an electronics firm.

startled to learn that "costs of *un*-quality" in their companies were 10 percent to 20 percent of annual revenue. When other arguments for managerial commitment to quality improvement programs failed, the cost-of-quality speech often got results.

Should firms that already have thriving TQM programs continue doing annual cost-of-quality audits? Maybe not. Consider, for example, a process improvement that prevents defective output. In a TQM company, it's a better-than-even bet that the change has other benefits; perhaps it results in faster or better engineering, reduces cycle times, or improves safety. Is the expense of the change a cost of quality? Or of engineering, production, or employee safety? Under TQM, quality is everybody's business; it's woven into the fabric of every job. So, the amount spent to achieve quality is difficult to state precisely. But even if we could find it, it isn't a cost we want to eliminate.

Leading Japanese companies, having launched TQM by other means, had little use for cost-of-quality accounts or logic and have avoided this usage.

In retrospect, it seems the main value of the cost-of-quality concept was in raising consciousness about quality's competitive importance. Recent studies on quality's impact have been broader. They consider quality-induced performance gains in addition to reductions in costs. As such, they look more at the *value* of TQM.

Value of Quality

As TQM gained momentum, companies poured large sums into its implementation. Not surprisingly, critics raised two good questions: "Is quality being improved?" and "If so, are the improvements showing up on the bottom line?" In short, is Pall's model valid? Numerous studies have addressed these questions; we shall mention but a few.

The General Accounting Office (GAO), the investigative arm of Congress, studied data from 20 finalists in the 1988 and 1989 Malcolm Baldrige National Quality Award competition to ascertain whether TQM improved performance.[9]

The researchers found that the quality-minded companies experienced general improvements after beginning TQM programs (see Exhibit 3–5).

Those results complement other survey data, especially the widely quoted PIMS (Profit Impact of Market Strategy) studies, which draw data from over 2,000 businesses.[10] Exhibit 3–6 summarizes the PIMS analysis of the impact of quality on return on investment (ROI) and return on sales (ROS). Across the entire range of relative quality, we see a strong, positive relationship between quality and business success. ROI increases 2.7 times, from a low of 12 percent for firms in the bottom quintile of quality to a high of 32 percent for those in the top quintile, and ROS

EXHIBIT 3–5
TQM—Impact of Quality on Performance

Market Share and Profitability
Fifteen companies supplied a total of 40 observations in this area: 34 improved; 6 got worse.
Market share—increased in 9 of 11 respondents, by an average of 13.7 percent annually.
Sales per employee—increased in all 12 respondents, by 8.6 percent.
Return on assets—increased in 7 of 9 respondents, by 1.3 percent.
Return on sales—increased in 6 of 8 respondents, by 0.4 percent.

Customer Satisfaction
Thirty observations came from 17 companies: 21 improved, 3 got worse, and 6 showed no change.
Overall customer satisfaction—increased in 12 of 14 respondents, by 2.5 percent.
Number of customer complaints—declined in 5 of 6 reporting companies, by 11.6 percent.
Customer retention—4 of 10 improved, 4 no change; slight increase averaging 1 percent.

Quality and Cost
Sixty observations came from 20 companies: 54 improved, 2 got worse, and 4 showed no change.
Reliability—improvement reported by 12 of 12 respondents, by 11.3 percent.
Delivery timeliness—improvement reported by 8 of 9 respondents, by 4.7 percent.
Order-processing time—reductions reported by 6 of 6, by 12 percent.
Errors or defects—decreases reported by 7 of 8, by 10.3 percent.
Product lead time—decreases reported by 6 of 7, by 5.8 percent.
Inventory turnover—turnover rate increases reported by 6 of 9, by 7.2 percent.
Cost savings from employee suggestions—all 9 respondents reported savings increases, ranging from $1.3 million to $116 million per year.

Employee Relations
Eighteen companies supplied 52 observations: 39 improved, 9 worsened, and 4 showed no change.
Number of employee suggestions—up 16.6 percent, increased in 5 of 7 respondents.
Employee satisfaction—up 1.4 percent, increased in 8 of 9 respondents.
Attendance—above industry averages in 9 of 11 respondents, increased further in 8 of those 9.
Employee turnover—below industry averages in 10 of 11 respondents, declined further in 7.
Safety and health rates—exceed industry averages in 12 of 14 respondents, improved further in 11.

Note: All percentages are average annual changes measured from when the responding companies began TQM programs.

Source: U.S. General Accounting Office, *Management Practices: U.S. Companies Improve Performance through Quality Efforts* (Gaithersburg, Md.: U.S. General Accounting Office, Report GAO/NSIAD–91–190, 1991).

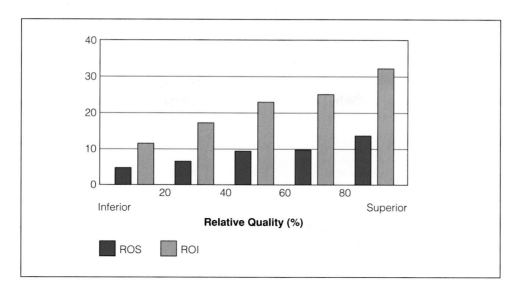

Exhibit 3-6

Relative Quality and Rates of Return

increases from a low of 5 percent for the inferior-quality group to 13 percent for the superior quintile.

Shortly after the PIMS studies, inception of the Malcolm Baldrige National Quality Award in the United States provided an opportunity to continue to track the value of quality to investors. To test the wisdom of investing in top-quality companies, one financial advisor created a mythical "Baldrige mutual fund." On the day Baldrige Award winners are announced, he invests a fictitious $1,000 in each publicly owned company or its parent. From 1988 (when the first awards were bestowed) through September 1, 1994, the fund value has increased by 99 percent. This compares with a 41.9 percent gain on principal if the same dollars were invested in the Dow Jones Industrials or a 34.1 percent gain if invested in the Standard & Poor's 500—again, investments assumed to have occurred on award dates. [This does not include gains from dividends.][11]

The GAO findings, PIMS study, and Baldrige-winner stock-fund analysis clearly support a positive conclusion about TQM's returns. Collectively, the results point to market share improvement, financial benefits, customer satisfaction, and better employee relations—in addition to better quality and lower costs.

In-depth analysis of relationships among these dimensions continues. For example, Professor James L. Heskett and a team of colleagues, all members of Harvard Business School's service management interest group, studied successful service companies, including Banc One, Intuit, Southwest Airlines, ServiceMaster, USAA, Taco Bell, and MCI. The researchers place special emphasis on the roles played by the human elements—customers and service providers' employees. Working backwards along what they refer to as the **service-profit chain,** they suggest that

> Profit and growth are stimulated primarily by customer loyalty. Loyalty is a direct result of customer satisfaction. Satisfaction is largely influenced by the value of services provided to customers. Value is created by satisfied, loyal, and productive employees. Employee satisfaction, in turn, results primarily from high-quality support services and policies that enable employees to deliver results to customers.[12]

Though they prefer to call these linkages propositions until further study bears them out, the Harvard team appears to support the general idea of Pall's model—quality promotes value. Moreover, their extension and refinements suggest that the reverse might also be true.

In sum, there appears to be ample evidence of a quality–competitiveness linkage. Customers acknowledge quality with their loyalty, but, as the next section shows, quality can also lead to more formal recognition.

Recognizing Quality

Twenty years ago, most of the topics in this section didn't appear in OM books or elsewhere. As the quality imperative caught on, however, the scramble to discover and recognize excellence in quality was on. Benchmarking, supplier certification programs, ISO 9000 registration, and competition for quality awards have all contributed to global definitions of quality and quality management. They serve to *recognize* quality.

Benchmarking

Benchmarking, developed at Xerox Corporation in the late 1970s, is the systematic search for best practices, from whatever source, to be used in improving a company's own processes.

Competitive benchmarking of **processes** is a relative of a much older technique: competitive analysis of **products**, which is a topic of Chapter 4.

At first, Xerox people called it competitive benchmarking. As the words suggest, they limited its application to finding their direct competitor's best practices. Xerox benchmarking teams boldly contacted competing manufacturers of copiers, computers, and other Xerox products. They asked, "How about we visit you and you visit us? We'll exchange information."

Why would rivals go for such a brazen proposal? Because the two companies would each benefit relative to other competitors not involved. (See the Contrast box, "Benchmarking." But, why restrict benchmarking to competitors? Why not *non*competitive benchmarking—searching for best practices anywhere?

*P*RINCIPLE 4:

Know the competition and world leaders.

Xerox manager, Robert Camp describes a benchmarking visit to L.L. Bean, the mail-order retailer, to learn what's behind Bean's legendary excellence in customer service.[13] Other companies have followed Xerox to L.L. Bean. Another frequently benchmarked company is Federal Express, for its overnight delivery ability.

*C*ontrast

Toward Benchmarking

Keep It a Secret

Our results, practices, and process knowedge are for our eyes only. Lock the doors, frown on outside visitors.

Trade It

Our results, practices, and knowledge are valuable assets; so are those of other good companies. Let's trade.

Now, benchmarking is in wide use by major hotels, accounting firms, transportation companies, banks, manufacturing companies, and others. Marriott Hotels have benchmarked the hiring, training, and pay practices of fast-food companies because hotels hire out of the same labor pool. Corporate attorneys at Motorola have even employed benchmarking. Richard Weise, general counsel at Motorola, says "We began to compile information on how many lawyers and paralegals it takes for each $1 billion in sales. We looked at how other law departments use tools such as computers [and] learned from them. Finally, we determined relative costs of delivering legal services domestically versus internationally."[14]

With so many firms involved in benchmarking—and trying to visit some of the same high-performance firms—the idea of putting benchmarking data into data banks arose. Thus, under the sponsorship of subscribing companies, the American Productivity and Quality Center in Houston has established an International Benchmarking Clearinghouse.

Xerox divided its initial benchmarking procedure into 10 steps, but Camp and other experts have noted successful programs based on as few as four defined stages. What matters is that all necessary actions are accomplished. Exhibit 3–7 shows one common format.

First comes planning and organization. The next step is all-important; selecting the process to be benchmarked and the team members. However, the team should not immediately set off to benchmark another company. First they need to benchmark their *own* process, in the following terms:

> *Metrics* (measurements in numbers). For example, a team from accounts payable may find it takes 18 hours average elapsed time but only 23 minutes of paid labor to process an invoice.
>
> *Practices.* The team documents every step in the process, noting delays, sources of errors, departments and skills involved, and so forth.

The third step is collecting information on whom to benchmark and what questions to ask. The fourth is to gain approval and establish plans for exchange visits.

Fifth is the benchmarking itself, including a visit to the benchmarked firms' sites. Information sought must parallel that already gathered by the team for its

Houston's Second Baptist Church, serving 12,000 parishioners weekly, uses benchmarking (e.g., Disney World's parking and people skills) in its own customer quality program.

Exhibit 3-7   **The Benchmarking Process: Common Steps**

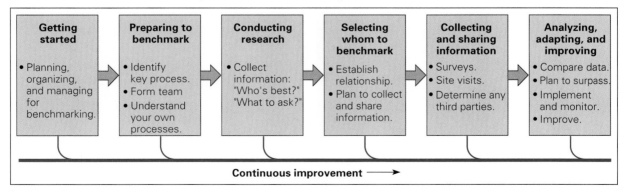

Source: Reprinted with permission from QUALITY (March 1992), a Capital Cities/ABC, Inc., Company.

own firm—namely, metrics and practices. Last, the benchmarking team analyzes the data, develops plans for change, and follows through.

Benchmarking has spread from its North American origin to many corners of the globe, and like other tools, it has been improved. Benchmarking teams may now tap computer networks and the clearinghouse database for much information, but the site visit remains popular. Camp, assessing benchmarking practice in an update of his earlier (1989) volume, notes other changes, including the following:[15]

- The overall benchmarking task really has two major components: a user process and a management process. The former consists of the steps that actually make up the benchmarking study (e.g., Exhibit 3–7). The latter is much broader, containing all those actions that support the user process before, during, and after the actual investigation.
- To the original (Xerox) benchmarking procedure, Camp adds what he calls a "step zero," to ensure consensus on key facets of benchmarking before it is begun. Camp says that step zero is best described as the quality process. Benchmarking has a greater chance of success when launched in an environment already steeped in TQM philosophy and procedures.
- *Problem-based benchmarking*—reaction to a specific trouble spot—was the right approach for early benchmarking efforts. Now, leading-edge firms realize that *process-based-benchmarking*, which targets those key business-wide processes contributing most to company goals, offers greater payback.

Most likely, benchmarking will continue to evolve as additional successes emerge. Its place in the TQM toolkit seems secure, however, inasmuch as it is one of the criteria used in the Malcolm Baldrige National Quality Award.

Camp (1995, p. 4) notes that benchmarking is mentioned over 200 times in the 1994 Baldrige Award criteria, and directly or indirectly affects up to 50 percent of the award's scoring.

EXHIBIT 3-8

Supplier Certification at Upright-Ireland

Left: Wall chart listing Upright's certified (just-in-time, with no inspection) suppliers, in four categories.
Right: Color-coded bins, which some of Upright's certified suppliers refill daily. Clipboards, one for each supplier, give daily feedback information to suppliers.

Supplier Certification

We've seen that in the third step, the benchmarking team asks, Who's the best? The team's purchasing associate might suggest taking a look at the company's own certified, high-quality suppliers.

Traditional assessments of supplier performance and capability were not stringent enough for TQM-driven companies. A quality-centered approach, called supplier certification, fills the need. Certification can have several levels. For example, Upright-Ireland, a maker of custom scaffolding, uses four levels (see Exhibit 3–8). As at other companies that certify suppliers, Upright's highest level of certification (registered firm suppliers) means there's no need to inspect the supplier's goods or services; an Upright certification team is satisfied that the supplier has processes capable and under control. Upright has only about 180 employees. But it is one of many small- and medium-sized firms that have extensively implemented total quality management concepts.

Receiving an important customer's highest certification is grounds for celebration at any supplier company. But someone should note that awards can also be lost if improvement does not continue. Other customers' certifications are the next challenges.

Marketers—always on the lookout for a competitive edge—quickly insert certification information into promotional materials. For example, if a company called Acme Office Supplies Co. were to receive, say, Kodak's "Quality First" certification, that might be the clincher for an Acme sales team to sign up an insurance company as a new client.

The growth of certification programs parallels another, related trend. Beginning in the late 1970s, a few pioneering large original-equipment manufacturers (OEMs) began to reduce the number of their suppliers. That movement has picked up steam as more companies, service as well as industrial, see the competitive advantages of dealing with but a few good suppliers. What suppliers do they keep? Those that can meet their quality certification requirements.

Suppliers may grumble about coercion, but those that are certified by big customers may find that effort an extra payoff when the time comes for them to seek registration to the ISO 9000 standard.

ISO 9000 Series Standards

The **ISO 9000 Standard** is actually an umbrella name for five separate but related quality standards originally published in 1987 (and revised in 1994) by the

*𝒫*RINCIPLE 5:

Reduce to a few good suppliers.

"ISO" is not an acronym for the International Organization of Standardization; it is Greek for "uniform" and is used as a prefix in words like isobar and isotherm. The intent is that ISO standards are uniform the world over.

Standard	Title
ISO 9000	Quality Management and Quality Assurance Standards—Guidelines for Selection and Use
ISO 9001	Quality Systems—Model for Quality Assurance in Design, Development, Production, Installation, and Servicing
ISO 9002	Quality Systems—Model for Quality Assurance in Production, Installation, and Servicing
ISO 9003	Quality Systems—Model for Quality Assurance in Final Inspection and Test
ISO 9004	Quality Management and Quality System Elements—Guidelines

EXHIBIT 3–9

ISO 9000 Series Standards

International Organization for Standardization, based in Geneva, Switzerland. Though support has been particularly strong within the European community, its use is global. Exhibit 3–9 shows the ISO 9000 standards in their 1994 format. Significant changes from the 1987 version include

- Making a company quality manual a requirement rather than an option.
- Stronger and more frequent references to the need to "establish and document procedures."
- Greater emphasis that the standards are meant to be generic—independent of any specific industry or sector.
- General reorganization of material to make section numbering more consistent among the various standards.[16]

The first financial management firm to receive ISO 9002 registration is Lawton/Russell, Inc., a Chicago-based investment advisor firm.[17]

Many companies require their suppliers to register to ISO 9000, and expect those suppliers to, in turn, require their own suppliers to register as well. As customers, their rationale is understandable: The quality imperative demands reliable suppliers. Under the ISO 9000 scheme, a company (or a division or plant within a company) arranges to have its *quality systems documentation and implementation* audited by an independent accredited registrar. The phrase "third-party registration" is used to refer to this objective assessment. As Exhibit 3–9 reveals, the particular role(s) to be played by a supplier (design, production, etc.) determine which of the three contractual standards—ISO 9001, 9002, or 9003—must be met.

If the quality systems—specifically, the plan, the implementation, and the documentation—are in order, the company is registered, and is permitted to advertise that fact in its promotional materials and other documents. The registrar continues to survey the supplier and makes full reassessments every three or four years.

Registration isn't cheap. For a prospective supplier to register a small plant (200–300 employees) with a single product line, to ISO 9002 level, registrars place the cost at between $10,000 and $15,000 if the registration is obtained on the first try and no corrective action or reassessment is necessary. This does not include expenses for assessment team travel, application preparation, and subsequent reassessment. Typically, that minimum cost ideal isn't the reality. One large international corporation registered 20 of its plants at a per-plant cost of $200,000 to $300,000. When asked how his company could justify such expenditures, one manager replied, "We can't afford not to.[18]

Is registration to ISO 9000 standards the ultimate quality performance achievement? No. As mentioned earlier, the standard does not certify quality of goods and services, but rather registers the existence of proper quality plans, programs, documentation, data, and procedures. Some customers may wish to probe deeper and require additional assurances of quality, but they might opt to not bother if a supplier balks at going for ISO registration. Another supplier will want the business.

In the final analysis, registration *is* a form of service to customers. And, managers who have taken companies through ISO 9000 registration offer another perspective; "The only approach to ISO 9000 registration that works is to improve the company's quality system for the benefit of those who function within it; ISO 9000 registration is a by-product of quality system improvement."[19]

Deming Prize and Malcolm Baldrige National Quality Award

Until the late 1980s, the **Deming Prize,** named after W. Edwards Deming and administered by the Union of Japanese Scientists and Engineers (JUSE), was the only quality award of note. First presented in 1951, the Deming Prize was largely un-appreciated outside Japan for over 30 years. As the quality of Japanese goods caught the world's attention in the 1970s and 1980s, however, the Deming Prize—along with a wealth of Japanese insight into quality philosophy and technique—gained international acclaim. It is the esteemed grandfather of other quality awards, including the Malcolm Baldrige Award in the United States.

On August 20, 1987, President Ronald Reagan signed Public Law 100–107, the Malcolm Baldrige National Quality Improvement Act. Named after the late secre-tary of commerce, the legislation reflected growing belief that the U.S. government should take a more active role in promoting quality and established the **Malcolm Baldrige National Quality Award (MBNQA)** that would recognize total quality management in American industry.

Responsibility for managing the award rests with the National Institute of Standards and Technology (NIST), a branch of the Department of Commerce. In 1991, NIST awarded the American Society for Quality Control (ASQC) a contract naming the society as administrator. The criteria are applied on an absolute (not relative) scale, and judges have the discretion not to give the award if applicants fail to measure up. The award is presented annually, usually in October (National Quality Month), to no more than two winners in each of three categories: manufacturing, small business, and service. Exhibit 3–10 shows the award history during its first eight years.

Hundreds of thousands of Baldrige award application forms are mailed out each year, but very few companies are good enough to apply. In 1991, for example, 235,000 applications were requested, but only 106 companies applied. Typically, only about 10 percent of those that apply merit a site visit by examiners, who are selected annually by NIST. If it's so hard merely to get a visit—much less win—why do companies bother with the application?

EXHIBIT 3–10   **Malcolm Baldrige National Quality Award Winners (1988–1995)**

Year	Manufacturing	Small Business	Service
1988	Motorola, Inc. Westinghouse Commercial Nuclear Fuel Division	Globe Metallurgical, Inc.	(None)
1989	Milliken & Company Xerox Business Products	(None)	(None)
1990	IBM Rochester Cadillac	Wallace Co.	Federal Express
1991	Solectron Zytec Corporation	Marlow Industries	(None)
1992	AT&T Network Systems Group TI Defense Systems & Electronics Group	Granite Rock Co.	AT&T Universal Card Services The Ritz-CarltonHotel Co.
1993	Eastman Chemical Company	Ames Rubber Corp.	(None)
1994	(None)	Wainwright Industries, Inc.	AT&T Consumer Communications Services GTE Directories Corp.
1995	Armstrong World Industries Corning Telecommunications Products Division	(None)	(None)

Some applicants act under duress. In 1988, just after it won a Baldrige Award, Motorola announced that it expected all of its suppliers to apply. Motorola knew that few if any would get far, but it wanted to make sure that all of its suppliers were exposed to the introspection that the application process demands. Other firms are more proactive; they apply on their own. They know that while winning would be a major accomplishment, the self-assessment has rewards of its own.

Although the basic structure, intent, and mechanics of the Baldrige award remain largely as originally designed, the award continues to evolve; slight changes in criteria and their weights reflect evolving ideas about TQ.[20] At the heart of the examination criteria, however, are the *core values and concepts*, which, for the 1996 award, were

1. Customer-driven quality.
2. Leadership
3. Continuous improvement and learning.
4. Employee participation and development.
5. Fast response.
6. Design quality and prevention.
7. Long-range view of the future.
8. Management by fact.
9. Partnership development.
10. Corporate responsibility and citizenship.
11. Results orientation.

Earlier, we noted Juran's definition of TQM as those actions needed to get to total quality. He goes on to state that, "Right now, the most comprehensive list of those actions is contained in the Baldrige Award criteria."[21]

The core values and concepts are embodied in seven broad *categories* containing 24 *examination items*. Exhibit 3–11 shows the 1996 categories and items along with possible point values, reflecting the relative weight given to each item in scoring.

Originally, not-for-profit organizations were ineligible for the Baldrige, although Public Law 100–107 anticipates that eligibility might be extended. In 1995, pilot program criteria were distributed for health care organizations and for educational institutions. For-profit, nonprofit, public, and governmental health care provider organizations were eligible to participate, as were public and private, for-profit, or nonprofit educational institutions.

Criteria for the two new pilot programs are similar to that of the established Baldrige Award, but differ somewhat in assignment of points and in titles. For example, whereas category 7.0 in the established criteria is called "customer focus and satisfaction," for health care it is "focus on and satisfaction of patients and other stakeholders," and for education, "student focus and student stakeholder satisfaction." It is too early to judge the success of the new programs. However, it seems likely that one effect will be to raise quality consciousness to even higher levels in health care and education.

As with the Deming Prize, the Baldrige has its critics. For example, some people lament the marketability of success that comes from winning the award, or feel that the Baldrige award mandate for winners to share the secret of success with other companies (even competitors) is unrealistic. Despite the criticisms, however, Baldrige winners continue to attract attention. Perhaps the greatest contribution of

Examination Categories/Items	Point Values	
1.0 Leadership		90
1.1 Senior Executive Leadership	45	
1.2 Leadership System and Organization	25	
1.3 Public Responsibility and Corporate Citizenship	20	
2.0 Information and Analysis		75
2.1 Management of Information and Data	20	
2.2 Competitive Comparisons and Benchmarking	15	
2.3 Analysis and Use of Company-Level Data	40	
3.0 Strategic Planning		55
3.1 Strategy Development	35	
3.2 Strategy Deployment	20	
4.0 Human Resource Development and Management		140
4.1 Human Resource Planning and Evaluation	20	
4.2 High Performance Work Systems	45	
4.3 Employee Education, Training, and Development	50	
4.4 Employee Well-Being and Satisfaction	25	
5.0 Process Management		140
5.1 Design and Introduction of Products and Services	40	
5.2 Process Management: Product and Service Production and Delivery	40	
5.3 Process Management: Support Services	30	
5.4 Management of Supplier Performance	30	
6.0 Business Results		250
6.1 Product and Service Quality Results	75	
6.2 Company Operational and Financial Results	110	
6.3 Human Resource Results	35	
6.4 Supplier Performance Results	30	
7.0 Customer Focus and Satisfaction		250
7.1 Customer and Market Knowledge	30	
7.2 Customer Relationship Management	30	
7.3 Customer Satisfaction Determination	30	
7.4 Customer Satisfaction Results	160	
Total Points		**1,000**

EXHIBIT 3–11

Malcolm Baldrige National Quality Award Examination Criteria—1996

the Baldrige award to date, however, is the fallout in the form of other awards that closely follow its format and the widespread acceptance of its criteria by companies as guidelines for internal improvement efforts, often independent of any award application process.

Winning a quality award is not the signal to relax. In 1990, consultant Richard Dobbins participated in a study of several Deming Prize-winning companies in Japan. The study team members were especially impressed by auto parts supplier Nippondenso. Its proud, highly involved workforce had thoroughly mastered tools of process improvement, and the company made a lot of money and rarely produced a defective part. Dobbins said to a Nippondenso plant manager, "It's easy to see how you won a Deming Prize with a management system like this." The manager replied, "Oh no, we won our Deming Prize in the 1960s; all of this we have learned since then."[22] The learning goes on among Nippondenso's employees. The next section further examines workforce involvement.

Employee-Driven Quality

We have considered the roots and development of the quality imperative. We now turn to implementation—specifically, the need for broad-based human involvement and commitment. Gaining that commitment requires action on three fronts:

1. *Training.* Everyone needs training in the tools of continuous improvement, problem solving, and statistical process control. In addition, people require training in job skills, plus cross-training for an understanding of the bigger picture.
2. *Organization.* People need to be put into close contact with customers (next process) and suppliers (previous process). This calls for organization of multifunctional customer-, product-, or service-focused cells, teams, and projects.
3. *Local ownership.* The management, control, and reward systems need to be realigned with the goals of employee- and team-driven, customer-centered quality and continuous improvement.

Time Out for Training

Quality is free, Philip Crosby says. It pays its own way—but not without an up-front investment. The investment is for training, the essential catalyst for action.

Amid all the evidence that businesses have taken the quality imperative to heart, the elevated commitment of certain firms to quality-oriented training and cross-training stands out. For example:

- Univar, the largest U.S. chemical distributor, committed $2 million to TQM training and implementation.
- At Xerox, within 90 days of being hired, salespeople receive TQM training.
- At Quad/Graphics, associates spend one day per week in the classroom—a "day a week, forever," as a leader in the firm's educational program puts it.

*C*ontrast

Management Theories

Theory X	Theory Y	Theory T (for Training)
Experts plan: operators do as they are told.	Listen to your people: they are intelligent and earnest.	Training provides the tools for continuous employee-driven improvement: no training, little improvement.

- Banc One Mortgage in Indianapolis has reorganized into teams averaging 17 cross-trained people who work on all aspects of a loan application at once.
- Carolina Power & Light trains all service specialists in two job areas foreign to them.
- A Miller brewery reserves an hour every day for employee training and an array of team-based management activities, even though the plant bottles and cans beer 24 hours a day; see the details in the Into Practice box below.

*P*RINCIPLE 7:

Cross-training, mastery, education.

There are thousands more examples like these. Most come from companies—including large, well-known ones—that had been spending virtually nothing on training front-line employees. In the past, only managers and professionals had received company-sponsored training. The old view was that training is an expense, takes away time from real work, and is down the drain when an employee leaves the company. The new view is that it is a necessary investment.

To avoid spending on training, businesses exploited the division-of-labor concept: Break the work down into its simplest elements, bundle a few elements into a job classification, and hire an unskilled person at minimum wage to do it with no training. Many companies, of course, still follow those practices, leaving them with fewer resources (minds) for making improvements or even for seeing what needs to be improved.

Lack of training also deters teamwork because, at least in Western cultures, people do not seem to be naturally team oriented. Athletic coaches and managers, for example, have to spend years molding lone wolves into wolf packs. In response to the demands of TQM, consultants are out in force providing team-building assistance.

*I*nto *P*ractice

Star-Point System at Miller Brewing Company, Trenton, Ohio

The million-square-foot Trenton brewery produces about the same amount of bottled and canned beer with some 400 production associates as other similarly sized breweries do with 800 employees. A key to the Trenton plant's success is its unique staffing plan: In this three shift, 24-hour-a-day operation, all production associates work nine-hour shifts instead of the usual eight. This adds up to five hours more than the 40-hours-per-week maximum stipulated as regular pay in U.S. wage laws, which means the workforce must receive five hours of "time-and-a-half" overtime pay every week all year long. The extra hour per day per shift, however, offers time for extensive training and for use of that training in the cause of continuous improvement. Within 18 months of being hired, an employee will have advanced through 25 training topics in five modules, called star points: quality, safety, productivity/maintenance, personnel, and administrative. Under quality, for example, the training topics are process improvement, product specifications, housekeeping/good manufacturing practices, raw materials, and records. All employees are on various kinds of teams, and each team designates a member to serve on other teams who deal with matters related to each of the five star points. In sum, the star-point system provides a pathway toward a self-managed team mode of operation.

Getting Organized—Team Formats

Team *organization* comes before team building. If a group of angry prisoners received team-building training, they might unite to burn down the jail. The same holds for businesses and agencies. The first priority is getting the right people on the team.

Quality Circles   One useful kind of team is the quality circle (which was popularized by Kaoru Ishikawa in Japan, where it is called a quality control [QC] circle). In the late 1970s, Western visitors to Japan were mesmerized by their apparent potency. Japan's QC circles contributed as many as 100 times more suggestions per employee than Western companies could elicit. In short order, quality circles were organized from Melbourne to Calcutta, Cape Town to Oslo, and Montevideo to Anchorage. The results were favorable, but not much more so than certain other programs, such as suggestion plans. It now seems clear that most quality circles were organized in a way that *avoided* a customer focus—that is, they excluded next processes.

  Part A of Exhibit 3-12 shows two examples of a quality circle composed of five people in a single department. The first consists of four welders and a supervisor, while the second has four order-entry clerks and a supervisor. Those circles could meet every day and never hear a complaint about the quality of welds or errors in recording customer requirements. Also, the circles would not be inclined to discuss causes of their own delays. Since their customers are not in the circles, the circles will discuss shared annoyances: room temperature, lighting, company recreation and benefits, work hours, and so forth. While all deserve attention, they are only indirectly related to serving a customer. In fact, circles like these may spend much of their time complaining about the demands of customers, instead of teaming up to serve them.

EXHIBIT 3–12   **Quality Circles: Gangs versus Teams**

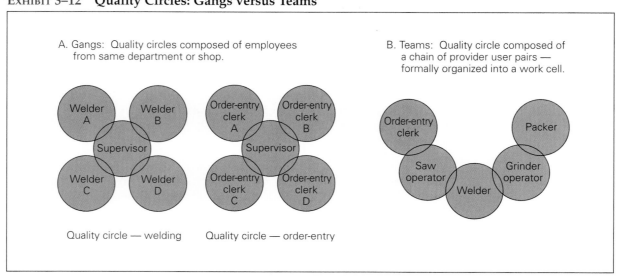

Into Practice

Four Team Formats at Globe Metallurgical

At Globe Metallurgical (producer of additives for steel making and foundries), winner of a 1988 Baldrige Quality Prize in the small-business category, there are four kinds of teams. Within Globe, all four are frequently referred to as quality circles; the first three meet weekly, sometimes with pay and sometimes off-shift without pay:

1. Departmental teams—hourly associates from one department. The volunteer rate is about 60 percent.

2. Cross-departmental teams—appointed groups, including representation from all departments within a single plant.

3. Project teams—multidisciplinary teams assigned to specific quality improvement projects.

4. Interplant teams—hourly and salaried associates from Globe's two plant sites exchange visits quarterly.

Source: Adapted from "Quality through Consistency: Globe Metallurgical Makes Improvements Quickly," *Target*, Fall 1989, pp. 4–12.

Cells.   Part B of Exhibit 3–12 shows how to organize quality circles for effective process improvement. This type of circle is hard to organize because it requires moving people and equipment out of functional departments. Here an order-entry clerk is teamed up with the customer who processes the order at the first production operation: a saw operator. The order-entry terminal and the saw are moved close together. Then add more maker–customer pairs from other departments: a welder and welding equipment, a grinder and grinding equipment, and a packer and packing tools and supplies. The five operations become one, a **work cell,** or simply a **cell.** A few companies call it a natural team.

Document processing cells and manufacturing cells are rarely organized for the purpose of creating quality circles. Rather, they are formed to quicken response time, cut out many clerical activities and transactions, eliminate bulk handling across long distances, and slash inventories along with potential rework or scrap.

One result, however, is a group of associates who can scarcely avoid some quality circle behaviors. The welder who closes a seam incompletely will hear about it very soon from the grinding machine operator at the adjacent work station. The two are a team whether or not they care to be. A "bad pass" from one cell member to the next gets prompt attention.

Teams.   Ten years after the first wave of Western interest in quality circles, a new wave surged, this time generally called *teams.* As 1980s circles did, 1990s teams often employ a facilitator, whose job may include keeping team meetings on track and providing training. One set of team training topics includes team dynamics, communications, and other behavioral matters, including how to interview and choose new employees and how to evaluate one another's performance. Another set aims at general problem-solving tools, such as brainstorming, nominal group techniques, role playing, and multivoting. Still another set focuses on the "hard sciences" of quality: process flowcharts, Pareto analysis, fishbone and run diagrams, and other process control tools (all discussed in Chapter 5).

To be effective, teams need all three kinds of training. Research by Andersen Consulting and two English universities, however, suggests that Western teams too often emphasize the human issues and neglect process control. In contrast, in Japan, which has more years of experience with teams than the West, the main role of teams is to "support process control and improvement."[23]

To some extent the manufacturing sector already has passed through the phase of teams focused primarily on human issues, as was generally the case during Western industry's first attempts in the early 1980s to implement quality circles. By now, many manufacturers have learned to use the full potential of teams—for both human and quality improvement issues.

Service organizations seem to be going through a similar learning process: Early efforts favored human issues and the less effective team membership pattern of Exhibit 3–12A (gangs). Numerous service companies, however, have evolved to more effective forms. An example is Fidelity Investment's "Monetary Gate" team, which, in its own corner of a single building in Texas, is able to process monetary corrections in 24 hours; formerly, corrections went back and forth among offices in dispersed cities and sometimes took months to complete.

Project Teams.   What happens when associates in the work flow are separated. They may be out of view, in different departments, or in different cities. That situation calls for still another kind of team: the multifunctional problem-solving or project team. Since most people in a work flow sequence do tend (rightly or wrongly) to be separated, this team form has an important place in total quality management.

*𝒫*RINCIPLE 1:

Team up with customers.

In some situations, such as in the transportation industry, it is impossible for people to co-locate and form a cell. Chemical Lehman Tank Lines, a Pennsylvania-based petroleum hauler, creates projects across distance by sending action teams of its employees to customer sites. In an unusual twist to cross-training, Lehman has even initiated exchanges of employees with its customers. Those employees are likely to gain insights that will improve their ideas in any team format.

In Chapter 4, we consider a concept related to teaming up for quality: the extended product or service design team, which can involve assigning component design people from a supplier company to serve on an end-product design team at a customer company. This subject arises again in the chapters on flow control (Chapter 8) and purchasing (Chapter 9).

Local Ownership of TQM

Unfortunately, smoothly functioning teams don't spring forth directly out of TQM training sessions. Individual behaviors change slowly, and frustration breeds in the void.

It need not be so. An excellent quick outlet for initial TQM enthusiasm is your own *personal quality checksheet*, which is a list of a few standout personal defects that you can record by a simple tally stroke on a checksheet in your pocket or on your desk. In their book *Quality Is Personal*, Harry Roberts and Bernard Sergesketter explain using their own experiences, plus those of colleagues.[24] Sergesketter, a manager for AT&T's Central Region of Business Network Sales, developed the method, and many of his associates quickly picked it up. His initial checksheet is as follows.

On time for meetings.

Answer phone in two rings or less.

Return phone calls same or next day.

Respond to letters in five business days.

Clean desk.

Credenza: only same-day paper.

Sergesketter counted his total number of defects monthly. The total quickly fell from about 100 in spring 1990 to 10, then 5. Also, he has implemented changes, such as date-stamping mail, that help with measuring defects and attaining improved performance.

Roberts, a University of Chicago professor, has found that just making the list has resulted in virtual elimination of some defects. Many of his executive MBA students have taken up the personal quality checksheet habit in their studies and back on their jobs as well. Experience so far suggests the following:

1. Define the defect unambiguously so it can be recognized easily and tallied.
2. No New Year's resolutions. Focus on attainable defects, especially waste reducers and time-savers. Later refine the list, perhaps including activity expanders to make productive use of the time saved.

As personal quality checksheets lead the way and teams follow, everyone needs to feel a sense of ownership of control, of improvements, and of results. It also means less control from on high and fewer levels of management to review improvement proposals. Further, the company must shift toward rewarding specific results at local levels rather than general ones at high levels.

To support local ownership, managers need to be out of their offices and visible locally, where they admire control charts and process experiments, help remove obstacles, and pass out awards. When local ownership has truly taken root, the evidence is likely to include charts of all kinds—on walls, doors, and partitions—*in the workplace* rather than in managers, offices. Exhibit 3–13 shows two examples from Florida Power & Light, 1989 winner of Japan's Deming Prize (the first non-Japanese winner of the prize).

*P*RINCIPLE 14:

Retain local ownership of quality, data, results.

Exhibit 3-13   **Drawings Based On Two of the Many Quality Improvement Charts at Florida Power & Light**

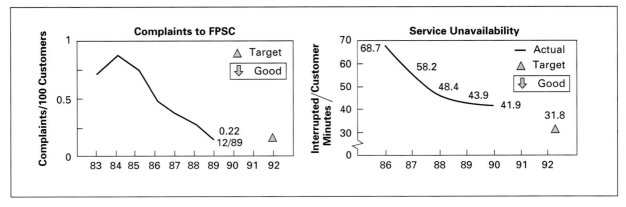

There is much more to be said about local ownership and total quality control. We will continue to explore these topics in detail in the remaining chapters.

Summary

The definition of quality has evolved into multidimensional descriptions of customers' wants and perceptions. Total quality management—actions that managers at all levels take to ensure that quality happens—promotes organization-wide continuous improvement in meeting those customer needs.

In enlarged form, the modern TQM toolkit may include JIT, benchmarking, re-engineering, supplier development, total preventive maintenance, quick-response programs, and team-related skills in addition to the hard-science tools of quality control and improvement. TQM may be thought of as good management in general and an imperative for global competitiveness.

Artisanship—pride in one's work—acted to promote quality from the time of ancient cultures until the industrial revolution weakened provider–customer connections. Ensuing quality degradation ushered in consumerism movements, stricter liability laws, and a desire for a stronger customer orientation. Contributions from pioneers like Deming, Juran, Feigenbaum, Ishikawa, Crosby, and Taguchi set the stage for the modern view of total quality, which closely interfaces with modern operations-management principles.

Recent studies suggest a strong relationship between TQM and competitiveness. Market-route benefits include increased market share, profitability, and customer satisfaction. Cost-route benefits include better quality, lower costs, and improved employee relations. As for costs, the main concern is with those costs associated with *not* having quality. Emphasis appears to be shifting to a value-based perspective, as studies of quality award winners have tended to support the value of quality.

Benchmarking is the systematic search for best practices that can help improvement efforts. The procedure includes startup organization, key process identification and analysis, research on "who's best," selection of benchmark targets, information collection and sharing, and adapting for continuing improvement.

Quality certifications, registrations, and awards have become influential. As companies pare down their lists of suppliers, surviving suppliers are usually those that achieve customer-certified status. Companies and their suppliers increasingly seek to become registered to the ISO 9000 standards, which are internationally recognized. Most prestigious are the public quality awards, among which the Deming Prize and the Malcolm Baldrige National Quality Award stand out.

Implementation of TQM occurs through broad-based human involvement and commitment. Success demands action on three fronts: training, organization into customer-oriented teams, and realignment for local ownership of control, improvement, and results.

Review Questions

1. Which principles of OM apply to "the quality imperative"?
2. What is the difference between quality and quality management?

3. What is the broad definition of quality? Of TQM?

4. Explain why quality ought to be everybody's business, not delegated to a few specialists.

5. What is artisanship? What has been its role in quality evolution and in development of the modern customer-oriented view of quality?

6. How was quality affected by the industrial revolution? The consumerism movement?

7. List one major contribution to the evolution of the concept of total quality from each of the following: Deming, Juran, Feigenbaum, Ishikawa, Crosby, and Taguchi.

8. Identify common themes in the contributions of the quality pioneers.

9. Give an example of how modern OM practices support TQM. Give an example of how TQM supports OM.

10. List ways in which TQM has been shown to improve performance and competitive position.

11. Explain what is meant by the "cost of un-quality."

12. Why are costs of improving quality hard to isolate?

13. What is meant by the value of quality?

14. What is benchmarking? What are the common steps in the benchmarking procedure?

15. How does supplier certification serve as an incentive to improve quality?

16. What are the ISO 9000 series standards? Comment on the importance of ISO 9000 registration.

17. How does competition for a major quality award (e.g., The Deming Prize or the Malcolm Baldrige Award) affect applicant companies?

18. What do we mean by employee-driven quality? Explain in terms of training, organization, and ownership.

19. Name and define three types of teams one might find in world-class organizations.

20. What does local ownership mean?

21. How does the personal quality checksheet contribute to TQM goals?

Exercises

1. Interview two managers, one in the private sector and the other from the public sector. Ask the following questions:

   a. Is quality increasing or decreasing in importance in your field?

   b. Does improved quality pay? Why or why not?

   Discuss your findings.

2. "The only acceptable performance is zero defects." Discuss the application of that phrase to each of the following situations:

   a. Surgeons performing elective surgery.

   b. Machinists fabricating automobile engines.

   c. Lawyers defending accused child molesters.

   d. Grocers stocking the supermarket deli display.

   e. Investment counselors giving financial advice.

   f. Police officers apprehending a suspect.

   g. County clerks recording tax payments.

   h. Merchants selling exercise equipment.

   i. College students typing term papers.

3. How do you determine quality in products? For example, how do you distinguish a good automobile (or bar stool, topcoat, aspirin, or golf ball) from a bad one? Does the item's price influence your thinking? What are society's beliefs regarding a relationship between price and quality? Are these beliefs realistic?

4. How do you determine quality in services? For example, how do you distinguish a good lawyer (or accountant, professor, athlete, or barber) from a bad one? Does the service's price—fee charged or salary received—have any influence on your thinking? Does society pay the same attention to price when judging the quality of services as it does in the case of goods? Why or why not?

5. Refer to Exhibit 3–1, "Dimensions of Quality":

   a. Explain each of the 10 dimensions of service quality as it applies to one service of your choice.

   b. Explain each of Garvin's eight dimensions of quality as it applies to a product of your choice.

6. Apply the Plan-Do-Check-Act cycle [Details contained in Chapter Supplement]—suggest specific actions for each of the four steps—to one of the following problems:

   a. Fellow employees (or students) are habitually late or absent from team meetings.

   b. Cashier lines at the cafeteria take too much time.

   c. Utility bills at home (house, apartment, dorm, or fraternity or sorority house) are too high.

   d. The bookstore always runs out of blank computer diskettes.

   e. Printer ribbons in the computer lab run out of ink (creating light print) too soon.

7. *John:* Hi Jane! How's it going?

   Jane: Lousy! My grandmom sent me a sweater for my birthday, but there's a flaw in the weaving. I have to mail it back to her, she has to return it to the store and hope they have another of the same style and color in my size, and then send it back to me. What a pain! She shouldn't have to go through that hassle.

   John: Yeah, I've been through that no-questions-asked returns policy too many times myself.

   a. List the members of the provider–customer chain in the above story.

   b. Where did quality break down?

   c. What social costs occurred in the above story?

   d. How might situations like the above be prevented?

   e. Is a free-returns policy high-quality service? Why or why not?

8. Acme Inc. has just installed a high efficiency motor-generator set to clean up the electrical power supply (remove unwanted fluctuations) to its precision equipment lab. Results include more accurate readings for tests, longer equipment life with less downtime, lower maintenance costs, shorter turnaround times for lab services for Acme's customers, and more accurate job scheduling due to increased equipment reliability. Is the expenditure for the motor-generator set a cost of quality? Discuss.

9. *Suzy:* Sam, they've reduced our training budget again! How can my people provide

the TQM training our company needs in order to achieve preferred supplier certification from Caterpillar? And we're also trying to get ISO 9002 registration!

Sam: I know. I talked to Betty in budgeting this morning. The feeling among the powers that be is that during the current business slump cuts have to come from soft areas—places that aren't value-adding. I guess their feeling about training is, "Adds costs but no proven value." Do you think we might present a convincing argument to change their minds?

Write a brief essay containing arguments that Suzy and Sam could use in trying to get the training budget restored.

10. At Ace Repair, at the completion of each job, the mechanic uses a prepared checklist to inspect his own work. For large jobs, this can consume up to half an hour. A wall sign informs customers that labor is billed at $45 an hour.

    a. Should the mechanics inspect their own work? Why or why not?

    b. Is the inspection time a cost of quality? Discuss.

    c. Does the value-of-quality notion apply? Why or why not.

    d. If "do it right the first time" is a company policy, is the inspection really necessary? Why or why not?

    e. Suppose we were talking about maintenance or repairs to commercial jet aircraft; how would your responses to parts a, b, and c change?

11. A young athlete aspires to win an Olympic medal in speedskating. She is well aware of the accomplishments of Bonnie Blair, the United States' gold medalist, and decides that benchmarking can help. She records Ms. Blair's winning times for each skating event and proclaims, "Those are my benchmarks." Discuss this approach to benchmarking.

12. At Sandwiches-Are-We, the manager of the second shift, which covers the dinner-hour rush, declares: "We have too many customer gripes about cold sandwiches. Any ideas?" One young part-time employee (who happens to be taking an OM course at City University) replies, "Not now, but we can use benchmarking to solve the problem." Discuss the pros and cons of this approach to benchmarking.

13. Abdul and Alice are co-chairs of the University Student Service Club's fundraising committee. For the past few years, fundraising has been on the decline, but Abdul and Alice are determined to reverse that trend. They plan to benchmark other campus organizations, and copy the successful ones. What are the pros and cons of their plan?

14. Review the list of Malcolm Baldrige National Quality Award winners in Exhibit 3–10. Then refer to Exhibit 3–5, "TQM—Impact on Performance," for examples of performance criteria, and pick two of the winners and investigate their performance since winning the award. Discuss your findings.

15. Would quality circles work well in improving the performance of a hockey team? Of a group of students banding together to study? Discuss.

16. After 12 to 19 percent increases in tuition and other fees across the state university system, a group of concerned students, parents, and other friends of higher education formed an ad hoc group to investigate the problem of runaway college costs.

    a. Is this group a team as defined in the text? Discuss.

    b. Who (what agencies, groups, etc.) ought to be represented in the group to prevent the *gang* syndrome from taking over.

17. At Rocky Mountain Academy, the basketball and skiing coaches have decided to employ the quality circle concept. Each circle will consist of the top five athletes on the team. The coaches' purpose is to try to tap their athletes' intelligence and thereby generate ideas that will improve the teams' effectiveness. Considering what

makes quality circles work well or poorly, assess the likely results of the quality circle experiment for each coach.

18. Seven bank tellers volunteered to form the bank's first quality circle. The human resources department conducted an attitude survey just before the quality circle was formed and again after it had been meeting for six months. The survey showed a dramatic improvement in morale and attitude. Further, the circle produced 38 suggestions in the six-month period. Is this quality circle well conceived? Are its results excellent, or not?

For Further Reference

Books

Camp, Robert C. *Business Process Benchmarking.* Milwaukee: ASQC Quality Press, 1995 (HD62.15.C345).

Crosby, Philip B. *Quality Is Free: The Art of Making Quality Certain.* New York: McGraw-Hill. 1979 (TS 156.6.C76).

Deming, W. Edwards. *Out of the Crisis.* Cambridge, Mass: MIT Center for Advanced Engineering Study. 1986.

Dobyns, Lloyd, and Clare Crawford-Mason. *Quality or Else: The Revolution in World Business.* Boston: Houghton Mifflin, 1991 (HD62.15.D63).

Feigenbaum, Armand V. *Total Quality Control,* 3rd ed. rev. New York: McGraw-Hill, 1991.

Garvin, David A. *Managing Quality: The Strategic and Competitive Edge.* New York: The Free Press, 1988 (HF5415.157.G37).

Huyink, David S., and Craig Westover. *ISO 9000: Motivating the People, Mastering the Process, Achieving the Results!* Burr Ridge, IL: Irwin Professional Publishing, 1994 (TS156.H895).

Ishikawa, Kaoru. *What Is Total Quality Control? The Japanese Way.* Translated by David J. Lu. Englewood Cliffs. N. J.: Prentice-Hall, 1985 (TS156.18313).

Juran, Joseph M. *A History of Managing for Quality: The Evolution, Trends, and Future Directions of Managing for Quality.* Milwaukee: ASQC Quality Press, 1995.

Juran, Joseph M. *Managerial Breakthrough,* Rev. ed. New York: McGraw-Hill, 1995 (HD31. J815).

Lamprecht, James L. *ISO 9000 and the Service Sector.* Milwaukee: ASQC Quality Press, 1994 (HD9980.5.L3).

Roy, Ranjit. *A Primer on the Taguchi Method.* New York: Van Nostrand Reinhold, 1990 (TS156.R69).

Sewell, Carl, and Paul B. Brown. *Customers for Life: How to Turn That One-Time Buyer into a Lifetime Customer.* New York: Doubleday Currency, 1990 (HF541.5.S49).

U.S. General Accounting Office. *Management Practices: U.S. Companies Improve Performance through Quality Efforts.* Gaithersburg, Md.: U.S. General Accounting Office, Report GAO/NSIAD–91–190, 1991.

Walton, Mary. *The Deming Management Method.* New York: Dodd, Mead, 1986 (HD38.W36).

Periodicals/Societies

Benchmarking for Quality and Technology Management
Quality, a Hitchcock publication.
Quality Digest
Quality Progress (ASQC).
Quality Management Journal (ASQC).

QUALITY PIONEERS OF THE TWENTIETH CENTURY

Discounting the ancient artisan's pride in doing the job right, we may place the roots of TQM in the twentieth century. Britain's R.A. Fisher's classic agricultural experiments during the first two decades set the stage for the experimental design and statistical process control tools we have today. Walter Shewhart, a physicist at Bell Labs, applied Fisher's concepts directly to manufacturing, and the modern era of quality was off and running[25].

Shewhart, in turn, exerted strong influence over the late W. Edwards Deming and Joseph M. Juran, perhaps the two dominant figures in the quality movement. In this supplement, we present some of the major contributions of Deming and Juran, along with those of Armand V. Feigenbaum, Kaoru Ishikawa, Philip B. Crosby, and Genichi Taguchi.

W. Edwards Deming

Although relatively unknown in his native country, the late W. Edwards Deming has been a Japanese hero for some 40 years. He began to gain recognition in the United States for his contributions to quality management on June 24, 1980, when NBC broadcast "If Japan Can . . . Why Can't We?" That documentary highlights Deming's role in Japan's industrial ascendancy.

Japan named its top national prize for contributions to quality after Deming and first awarded the Deming Prize in 1951. Deming continued to travel to Japan over the next three decades, sharing his concepts on data-based quality, developing a competitive edge, and management's role in these areas in general.[26]

In recent years, Deming traveled extensively, advocating his 14 points for management (see Exhibit S3–1). He believed that while quality is everyone's job, management must lead the effort. Further, he stated that his 14 points apply to both small and large organizations and in the service sector as well as in manufacturing.

Deming was an ardent proponent of training. He argued that doing your best simply isn't good enough until you know what you're doing. According to Deming, there is no substitute for knowledge. Classic Deming may be seen in the following excerpt from one of his (self-reported) communications to one organization's management:

> This report is written at your request after study of some of the problems that you have been having with production, high costs, and variable quality, which altogether, as I understand you, have been the cause of considerable worry to you about your competitive position. . . . My opening point is that no permanent impact has ever been accomplished in improvement of quality unless the top management carries out their responsibilities. These responsibilities never cease: they continue forever. No short-cut has ever been discovered. Failure of your own management to accept and act on their responsibilities for quality is, in my opinion, the prime cause of your trouble.[27]

As a statistician, Deming was an ardent proponent of the use of process data to make decisions and solve problems: use analysis if the data exist; if not, use experimentation and data collection. He followed an orderly approach to continuous improvement known as the **Plan-Do-Check-Act (PDCA) cycle,** which is among the best-known tools in the TQM arsenal. One form is shown in Exhibit S3–2.

Deming was known for his "rough" style in his seminars. He would not let managers off the hook if he sensed that they lacked sufficient commitment to quality.

The PDCA cycle is referred to as the Deming cycle by many, perhaps because he is largely responsible for its popularity. Deming, however, gave credit for its creation to his mentor, Walter Shewhart, who also developed the control chart.

Exhibit S3–1

Deming's 14 Points

1. Create constancy of purpose for the improvement of product and service with a plan to become competitive, stay in business, and provide jobs. Decide whom top management is responsible to.
2. Adopt the new philosophy. We are in a new economic age. We can no longer live with commonly accepted levels of delays, mistakes, defective materials, and defective workmanship.
3. Cease dependence on mass inspection. Require, instead, statistical evidence that quality is built in. (Prevent defects rather than detect defects.)
4. End the practice of awarding business on the basis of price tag alone. Instead, depend on meaningful measures of quality, along with price. Eliminate suppliers that cannot qualify with statistical evidence of quality.
5. Find problems. It is management's job to work continually on the system (design, incoming materials, composition of material, maintenance, improvement of machine, training, supervision, retraining).
6. Institute modern methods of training on the job.
7. The responsibility of foremen must be changed from sheer numbers to quality. . . [which] will automatically improve productivity. Management must prepare to take immediate action on reports from foremen concerning barriers such as inherited defects, machines not maintained, poor tools, fuzzy operational definitions.
8. Drive out fear, so that everyone may work effectively for the company.
9. Break down barriers between departments. People in research, design, sales, and production must work as a team to foresee problems of production that may be encountered with various materials and specifications.
10. Eliminate numerical goals, posters, and slogans for the workforce asking for new levels of productivity without providing methods.
11. Eliminate work standards that prescribe numerical quotas.
12. Remove barriers that stand between the hourly worker and his or her right to pride of workmanship.
13. Institute a vigorous program of education and retraining.
14. Create a structure in top management that will push every day on the above 13 points.

Source: Adapted from W. Edwards Deming, *Quality Productivity and Competitive Position* (Cambridge, Mass: MIT, Center for Advanced Engineering Study, 1982), pp. 16–17.

Exhibit S3-2

The Plan-Do-Check-Act Cycle for Continuing Improvement.

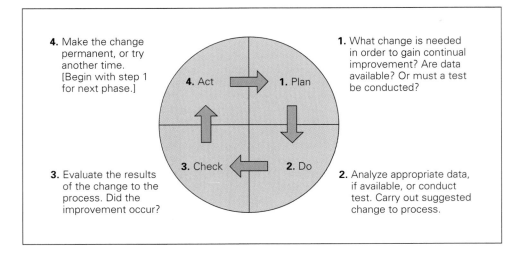

4. Make the change permanent, or try another time. [Begin with step 1 for next phase.]

1. What change is needed in order to gain continual improvement? Are data available? Or must a test be conducted?

3. Evaluate the results of the change to the process. Did the improvement occur?

2. Analyze appropriate data, if available, or conduct test. Carry out suggested change to process.

4. Act   1. Plan

3. Check   2. Do

Joseph M. Juran

Like Deming, Joseph M. Juran was a pioneer of quality education in Japan. He has also been known in the Western world for his textbooks and as editor-in-chief of *The Quality Control Handbook.* Unlike Deming, however, Juran was largely ignored by American management until the 1980s.

Juran's research has shown that over 80 percent of quality defects are *management controllable,* and it is therefore management that most needs change. He published *Managerial Breakthrough* in 1964 as a guide for the solution of chronic quality problems.[28] The breakthrough procedure is designed to gain and maintain improvements in quality. The sequence is as follows.[29]

1. Convince others that a breakthrough is needed.
2. Identify the *vital few* projects (involves Pareto analyses, discussed in Chapter 5).
3. Organize for a breakthrough in knowledge.
4. Conduct an analysis to discover the cause(s) of the problem.
5. Determine the effect of the proposed changes on the people involved, and find ways to overcome resistance to these changes.
6. Take action to institute the changes, including training of all personnel involved.
7. Institute appropriate controls that will hold the new, improved quality level but not restrict continued improvement—perhaps through another breakthrough sequence.

Juran's now-classic definition of quality is *fitness for use.* He intends those words to apply broadly, to include such properties as reliability, maintainability, and producibility; also, in certain situations, service response time, service availability, and price.

Juran defines quality management in terms of the *quality trilogy,*[30] which consists of:

Quality planning.

Quality control.

Quality improvement

Proper quality planning results in processes capable of meeting quality goals under certain operating conditions. Quality control consists of measuring actual quality performance, comparing it with a standard, and acting on any difference. Juran believes that inherent planning deficiencies might result in chronic waste, and it is up to the control process (initially) to keep the waste from getting any worse. Finally, quality improvement is superimposed on quality control. Quality improvement means finding ways to do better than standard and breaking through to unprecedented levels of performance. The desired end results are quality levels that are even higher than planned performance levels.

Armand V. Feigenbaum

Armand V. Feigenbaum is best known for originating the concept of **total quality control (TQC).** In his book *Total Quality Control* (first published in 1951 under another title), Feigenbaum explains that quality must be attended to through all stages of the industrial cycle and that

> control must start with identification of customer quality requirements and end only when the product has been placed in the hands of a customer who remains satisfied. Total quality control guides the coordinated actions of people, machines, and information to achieve this goal.[31]

To Feigenbaum, responsibility for TQC must be shared and should not rest with the quality assurance (QA) or quality control (QC) function alone. Feigenbaum also clarified the idea of *quality costs*—costs associated with poor quality. He was among the first to argue that better quality is, in the long run, cheaper. He defines "hidden plant" as the proportion of plant capacity that exists in order to rework unsatisfactory parts. This proportion generally ranges from 15 to 40 percent of the plant's capacity.

Kaoru Ishikawa

Kaoru Ishikawa, the late Japanese quality authority, acknowledged Deming's and Juran's influence on his thinking. However, Ishikawa must be recognized for his own contributions. He was responsible for the initial deployment of **quality control circles**—small groups of employees that meet regularly to plan and (often) carry out process changes to improve quality, productivity, or the work environment.

He also developed Ishikawa cause–effect charts, or "fishbone diagrams," so named because of their structural resemblance to the skeleton of a fish (discussed in Chapter 5). Like Deming, Juran, and Feigenbaum, Ishikawa also emphasizes quality as a way of management.

Ishikawa felt that there is not enough reliance on inputs to quality from nonspecialists. In 1968, he began using the term *companywide quality control (CWQC)* to differentiate the broadened approach to TQC from the more specialized view. Today, the terms TQC and CWQC are used almost interchangeably.

Another significant contribution of Ishikawa is his work on taking much of the mystery out of the statistical aspects of quality assurance. Conforming to the belief that without statistical analysis there can be no quality control, Ishikawa divided statistical methods into three categories according to level of difficulty, as shown in Exhibit S3–3.

The intermediate and advanced methods are for engineers and quality specialists and are beyond the scope of our discussion. The elemental statistical method, or the *seven indispensable tools* for process control, however, are for everyone's use and should be mastered by all organization members. Ishikawa intends that to include company presidents, directors, middle managers, supervisors, and front-line employees. His experience suggests that about 95 percent of *all* problems within a company can be solved with these tools. (We examine them in Chapter 5.)

EXHIBIT S3–3

Ishikawa's Statistical Methods

I. Elemental statistical method.
    A. Pareto analysis (vital few versus trivial many).
    B. Cause-and-effect diagram, also known as the *fishbone chart* (this, Ishikawa points out, is not a true statistical technique).
    C. Stratification.
    D. Checksheet.
    E. Histogram.
    F. Scatter diagram.
    G. Graph and Shewhart process control chart.
II. Intermediate statistical method.
    A. Theory of sampling surveys.
    B. Statistical sampling inspection.
    C. Various methods of statistical estimation and hypothesis testing.
    D. Methods of utilizing sensory tests.
    E. Methods of experiment design.
III. Advanced statistical method (using computers).
    A. Advanced experimental design.
    B. Multivariate analysis.
    C. Operations research methods.

Source: Adapted from Kaoru Ishikawa, *What Is Total Quality Control? The Japanese Way*, trans. David J. Lu (Englewood Cliffs, N.J.: Prentice-Hall, 1985), chap. 12 (TSI56.I8313).

Philip B. Crosby

Philip B. Crosby, former corporate vice president and director of quality control at ITT Corp., is the author of the popular book *Quality Is Free: The Art of Making Quality Certain*. In his book, Crosby explains that quality is not a gift but is free. What costs money is all the things that prevent jobs from being done right the first time. When quality is made certain, an organization avoids these expenses.

Crosby proposes **zero defects** as the goal for quality. To any who find that goal too ambitious, he simply asks, "If not zero defects, then what goal would you propose?" One often-used figure is the acceptable quality level (AQL), which is used in acceptance inspection. Briefly, AQL allows a certain proportion of defective items. Crosby explains that an AQL is a commitment to a certain amount of defects—before we start! The AQL idea is certainly out of step with a commitment to continuous improvement. Taking the consumer's view, Crosby makes his point bluntly:

> Consider the AQL you would establish on the product you buy. Would you accept an automobile that you knew in advance was 15 percent defective? 5 percent? 1 percent? One half of 1 percent? How about the nurses that care for newborn babies? Would an AQL of 3 percent on mishandling be too rigid?[32]

Crosby says that mistakes are caused by two things: lack of knowledge and lack of attention. Lack of knowledge, he argues, is measurable and can be attacked with well-known means. Lack of attention, however, is an attitude problem and must be changed by the individual. The individual, in turn, has a better chance of making the change if there exists a company commitment to zero defects. Crosby also states that while the tools of quality control are useful and available, they must be put into perspective. The important factor, he insists, is understanding and meeting a customer's requirements.[33]

Genichi Taguchi

Is it sufficient to control processes, inspect output, identify and remove defects, and rely on customer feedback? Genichi Taguchi says no. To improve quality, he argues, one must look upstream at the design stage because that is where quality begins. Quality must be designed in; it cannot be inspected in later. One fact of obtaining better design is experimentation on variables that contribute to a product's performance. Taguchi's strong belief in this approach has brought **design of experiments (DOE)** into wider use by quality experts, designers, and other members of design-build teams. Taguchi also believes that teams should aim for **robust designs**—designs that can withstand the hard-to-eliminate variabilities that occur in transformation processes or later in customer use.

Little was known of Taguchi's ideas in North America until the American supplier Institute (formerly a Ford Motor Company training unit) began to offer courses on Taguchi methods to the general public in 1984. Taguchi's short-cut variations on conventional DOE tools are efficient, working only with those variables that are most likely to contribute to large improvements quickly. For example, suppose that a compound is being created from 15 chemicals; each chemical can be purchased from two suppliers, and there is a slight variation in chemical concentrations between the two sources. Classical experimental design, calling for a *full factorial experiment*, would need 2^{15} (or 32,768) test runs to determine the mix of suppliers that yields optimal compound performance, with all chemical interactions considered. Taguchi would use a form of *fractional factorial experiment*, referred to as an *orthogonal array*, to perform the experiment in only 16 test runs.[34] The orthogonal array is a balanced plan for experimentation. Only those design variables deemed (by experts) most likely to affect output or performance are included.

While purists have faulted Taguchi's methods on various technical grounds, advocates argue that optimal design is not the important aim. Rather, a design that is nearly optimal *and* very quickly obtained is preferable.[35] Taguchi's approach tends to appeal to engineers—his customers—who find the presentation understandable and usable.

Exhibit S3-4

Taguchi's Quality Loss function

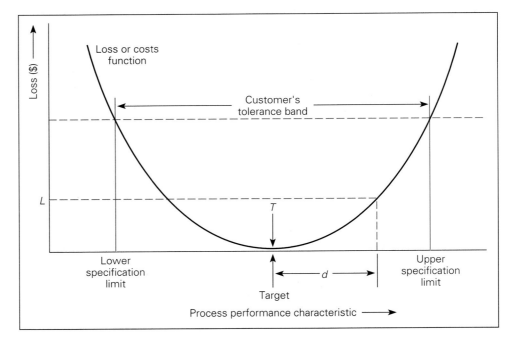

In addition to his work in design, Taguchi is known for development of the **quality loss function** (see Exhibit S3–4), a statement that any deviation from the target value of a quality characteristic results in extra costs to some segment of society. In fact, Taguchi defines quality in terms of the social loss, to producers or consumers, from the time a product is conceived.[36] The smaller the value of this social loss, the more desirable the product.

Briefly, Taguchi holds that unwelcome costs are associated with *any* deviation of process performance from the quality characteristic's target value. Thus, he favors going beyond zero deviation from specs to continual reduction in variability. The loss from performance variation (L) is directly related to the square of the deviation (d) of the performance characteristic from its target value (T).

Taguchi intends that the loss function remain valid at all times during a product's life. In theory, when process output performance reaches the specification limit, the customer's *economic* interest in the item is neutral; that is, the losses will exactly offset any gain from having the item.

For Taguchi, social loss must affect quality cost management decisions; that is, investments in quality improvement should be compared with savings to society rather than to the firm alone. Ultimately society will reward (or penalize) the firm for its record of societal savings; thus, Taguchi's view is meant to be sound for business.

Source: Smithsonian Museum, Washington, DC. Used with permission.

DESIGN AND CONTROL FOR CUSTOMER SATISFACTION

II

Machine designers and builders in the nineteenth century, especially those in the New World, had grand ideas. Their creations were often extravagantly ornate and colorful, with flourishes resembling those found on Roman temples or Gothic cathedrals. The photo on the preceding page is a good example.

Today, we're more down to earth. Factory machines look like, well, machines (sometimes pretty ugly and greasy, too). So do vending machines, cash registers, and personal computers. Most everything these days is utilitarian—to the point where a manufactured voice handles our phone inquiries and a cash machine dispenses folding money. What's important to us is that things work, do their jobs well, and hold down the costs.

The two chapters in Part II have the same aims. Chapter 4 gets at how, in the design phase, to make things work with high quality and low costs. Chapter 5 does the same thing, but for the execution phase of the product life cycle. Actually, these chapters do not advocate pure efficiency without any trace of pizzazz. In Chapter 4, we hear a bit about industrial design awards, which favor aesthetic appeal along with utility. And in Chapter 5, the quality emphasis is not on function alone, but on the overall goal of meeting—even exceeding—customer requirements.

For example, all the 100-plus branches of Seafirst Bank (in Washington State) promise customers $5 if they have to wait for a teller more than 5 minutes (see photo). The designers of that service feature aimed at *delighting* the customer, and they did! What's more, the $5 in payments get recorded to the branch and to the minute. The recorded data become one measure of quality of service for the given branch—since to customers, waiting in lines is poor service. (The five minutes/five dollars story continues as a case study in Chapter 14.)

Oh. *Why* did our forebears toss aside their innate practicality and embellish their machines? Partly to counter public worries about safety of anything mechanical. Riverboat boiler explosions, flywheel disintegrations, and runaway trains had made people wary. Then, too, ornamentation might counter impressions of vulgarity and ill-breeding among the nouveaux riches who were harnessing the machines and building industries. Cloaked in aristocratic dress, the machines "acquired cachet, appearing genteel and stately."[1]

4 DESIGNED-IN QUALITY: PRODUCTS, SERVICES, PROCESSES

Chapter Outline

Design: The First Step to Quality

Research, Design, and Development
Strategy

Research and Development Spending
Weaknesses of Conventional Design
Comprehensive Design Program

Teaming Up for Effective Design
Concept Development

Concurrent Design
Environmental Awareness

Quality Function Deployment

Design Objectives
Design for Operations: Guidelines
Design for Reliability and Serviceability
Design for Automation

Design Review and Appraisal

Black & Decker, based in Towson, Maryland, is the world's leading producer of power tools, specialty fastening systems, security hardware (lock sets, deadbolts, etc.), and glass container-making equipment. It is also the largest full-line supplier of small household appliances in North America and competes in lawn and garden products, plumbing supplies, and other commercial and industrial product lines.[1] Goods from Black & Decker's 50 manufacturing facilities in the United States and 15 other nations produced revenues of $5.3 billion in 1994. Profits were up by 93 percent from the previous year.[2] Though hard to tell from this description, the mid–1990s found Black & Decker just beginning to emerge from a decade of trouble.

Despite a reputation as the company that defined the power tool industry, Black & Decker's market share began to erode in the mid–1980s. Production costs crept up, product quality slipped, and customer service deteriorated. By 1991, B&D was battling with foreign producers in both professional power-tool and consumer-appliance markets. Professional builders and tradesmen were bypassing B&D in favor of innovative tools from companies like Makita, and they had all but abandoned B&D's DeWalt line—heavy duty power tools for commercial applications. Likewise, retail consumers rejected B&D's home appliance lines in favor of high-quality, state-of-the-art appliances from Matsushita and Braun.[3]

Black & Decker fought back. Part of its strategy called for a strong design effort, and in 1991 teams from several of B&D's global units banded together to invigorate tired product lines. New designs typically had to meet multiple goals. For example, the DeWalt cordless, pistol-grip drill/screwdriver (shown in Exhibit 4–1A) had to:

• Be compact, easy to carry around, and comfortable for the carpenter who might use it all day.

continued

Exhibit 4–1

Black & Decker's Award-Winning Products

A. DeWalt cordless drill/screwdriver   *B. Black & Decker Snakelight*

Courtesy Black & Decker.

concluded

- Have a cushioned grip, thin enough to grasp yet wide enough to accommodate the battery pack that makes the tool cordless.
- House a motor powerful enough for commercial use. (Designers also opted for a better motor than those available off the shelf.)
- Have a list price in the $170–$200 range.
- Be marketable on a global basis.[4]

The design hallmark of Black & Decker's highly successful SnakeLight (Exhibit 4–1B) is flexibility—in more ways than one. Its tubular, flexible body can be coiled or twisted around objects to provide hands-free illumination in almost any setting. Operational flexibility is further promoted through enhancements to the standard (home model) design: A shop model comes with a mounting bracket, and an automobile model is powered from the vehicle's battery via the cigarette lighter outlet.

Apparently, customers appreciate Black & Decker's design effort; by 1995, the company had reestablished a solid lead in the professional cordless drill market. The design community is also impressed, for both the DeWalt drill and the SnakeLight won gold awards in the 1995 Industrial Design Excellence Award Competition (no company won more than two gold awards).

Other consistent winners of this design award include AT&T, GM, Steelcase, Apple, IBM, Herman Miller, and Fisher-Price.

A chronic weakness among many companies is undermanagement of design and development. Even though design is one of the basic management functions, we probably know more about poor design practices than we do about good ones. Problems in design, in turn, ripple into operations. Quality suffers, processing delays and costs mount. Customers may look elsewhere for better service, perhaps provided by a competitor that is mastering the art of designing to meet multiple customer needs.

Design has two main targets: the outputs (goods and services that customers want) and the processes that provide them. In this chapter, much of our focus will be on the former. Process design doesn't get its own chapter in the book—the topic is much too broad. Transformation processes—whether for delivering a service or producing a good—are at the core of practically every chapter. This chapter is no exception; the coverage of reliability later in this chapter, for example, certainly applies to processes. And, when we address product design, we're talking about the items that become process equipment, so environmentally friendly design topics (addressed in this chapter) have strong influence on process design.

Furthermore, both quality analysis (Chapter 5) and methods analysis (Chapter 16) discuss process flowcharts. Benchmarking and re-engineering, also addressed in Chapter 3, are almost exclusively process oriented. Positioning of plant and equipment (Chapter 17) and layout (Chapter 12) also constitute significant process design components. More topics in still more chapters take in other elements in a complete process design.

Moreover, design of outputs greatly defines choices of process and method. In fact, as we shall see, one criterion of good product and service design is that it bring about ease of processing. Thus, we shall pay particular attention to how design-related activities affect operations and to the contributions operations managers make to design programs. We begin by recognizing design as the first step in quality.

Design: The First Step to Quality

The problem that plagued Black & Decker—tired product lines—is common to many well-regarded companies. Their goods fare well in the marketplace, which breeds the attitude, "Don't tamper with a winner!" But improved design concepts are taking root. Innovative competitors lurk, ready to beat existing industry standards and crow about it through performance-comparison advertising.

For example, computer system hardware and software providers almost always introduce new products by comparing performance of those products with the industry leaders.

Since new features stem from market feedback or reflect advances in technology, designs that incorporate those features are likely to advance quality in the eyes of customers. Thus, a strong design program, including one that wins prestigious design awards, is itself one mark of organizational quality.

Design is the first step to quality in another, more specific manner: The quality of output goods and services—and the processes that provide them—begins during the initial design activities. Exhibit 4–2—applicable to products, services, and

Exhibit 4–2

Quality Action Cycle

processes—shows how an iterative action cycle of design, discovery, and improvement provides quality.

In practice, the five phases of the quality action cycle overlap, and sometimes, we're even able to eliminate parts of the third (discovery) phase. Picture it this way: The *ideal* way to attain quality is to have perfectly designed outputs that are created without defect or variation by perfectly functioning processes. When perfection fails to materialize, the next best thing is to discover problems as soon as possible and work quickly to develop remedies for the underlying causes of those problems, before any "bad output" finds its way downstream to customers. Continuous improvement toward the ideal is the hallmark of total quality management.

Reserving analysis of the latter stages of the quality action cycle for Chapter 5, we continue our focus on design by examining some of the strategic issues.

Research, Design, and Development Strategy

Often, design is financed through a company's research and development (R&D) budget. Thus, as a starting point, we may view R&D spending as a broad indicator of strategic commitment to design. Regardless of spending levels, however, an effective design strategy for *any* firm is one that overcomes weaknesses inherent in conventional design efforts. But even that is not enough, for in the 1990s and beyond, design programs must also directly support immediate business needs—that is, customer wants. Successful contemporary design programs are comprehensive, containing a relatively defined set of characteristics aimed at increasing the overall productivity of design. In this section, we explore each of these issues further.

Research pushes the boundaries of science, aiming for new products, services, and processes. **Development** translates those innovations into useful tools for employees *(implementation)* and/or into practical outputs for customers *(commercialization).*

Research and Development Spending

Exhibit 4–3 lists R&D allocations, as percentages of sales, for selected industries and countries. The top spenders (computer and health care companies) invest over 15 times as much as those industries at the bottom of the list. Providers of food and fuel require less R&D, probably because their products are sold almost as they are obtained from nature. At about 1 percent, services providers also utilize relatively little R&D; services are sold almost as they arise from human nature.

R&D spending also varies a good deal from nation to nation. With the possibility of an era of relative peace, growing opportunities for trade may nudge low-spending nations (e.g., Britain and the United States) to invest more, especially in nondefense R&D, in order to be competitive. For the same reason, perhaps top spenders will shift spending somewhat from R&D to marketing. In other words, R&D (and marketing) spending patterns may become more alike among nations.

Knowing the average R&D commitments shown in Exhibit 4–3 might help a firm develop its own design strategy. For almost any firm, this strategy should focus on correcting chronic weaknesses of conventional design.

Weaknesses of Conventional Design

Sometimes customers sound off when they encounter poorly designed goods and services. They express themselves on consumer information cards that accompany new products or on feedback forms found on restaurant tables or in bank lobbies; maybe they even write letters. The providers in these cases are fortunate, for they

EXHIBIT 4–3
R & D
Expenditures

Industry (indented entries are selected U.S. industries)	Percentage of Annual Sales Spent on Company-Financed R&D (1993)
Computer software and services	13.5
Health care: drugs and research	13.0
Computer systems design	11.6
Health care: medical products and services	6.8
Switzerland: all-industry composite	6.5
Data processing services	6.2
Germany: all-industry composite	5.9
Leisure-time equipment (toys, sporting goods, etc.)	5.4
Canada: all-industry composite	5.4
Japan: all-industry composite	5.3
Non-United States: all-industry (200-company) composite	4.7
Aerospace	4.2
Automotive	4.0
United States: all-industry (900 company) composite	3.8
United States: manufacturing composite	3.0
Britain: all-industry composite	2.9
Housing	1.8
Consumer products	1.5
United States: service industries composite	1.0
Containers and packaging	0.9
Food	0.8
Fuel	0.8

Source: "R&D Scoreboard," *Business Week*, June 27, 1994, pp. 78–103. Obtained by *Business Week* from Standard & Poor's Compustat Services, Inc.

get the feedback necessary to make changes. But more often, customers just take their business elsewhere. Providers don't get the specific details, but—as was the case with Black & Decker—falling revenues signal possible design problems.

Though we applaud attempts to gather customer feedback, some improvements in design programs needn't wait. Many of the problems deserving immediate attention can be traced to one or more of the historical weaknesses of conventional design:

- *Design is slow.* Consequently, a product or service is late to market, arriving after competitors are entrenched. Or, ineffective transformation processes continue to operate because redesigns are delayed. Negative effects ripple through the three other primary line areas: (1) marketing must play catch-up in sales, and advertising can't tout the firm as the innovator; (2) operations loses the learning-curve advantage and also plays catch-up to competitors' post-introduction improvements; and (3) delayed financial returns prolong (or worse, preclude) investment recovery. Exhibit 4–4 shows the financial consequences of being late to market. For example, a company that is late to market by four months can expect an average reduction in gross profits of 18 percent.

- *Design is myopic.* This has been a common blind spot even for Western companies known for commitment to research. Though the problem takes many forms, perhaps the classic example occurs when people take the word *design* to mean *product design,* and pay little or no attention to design

	Number of Months					
If a company is late to market by:	6	5	4	3	2	1
Then average gross profit potential is reduced by:	33%	25%	18%	13%	7%	3%

EXHIBIT 4–4

Cost of Arriving Late to Market

Source: McKinsey & Company data, cited in Joseph T. Vesey, "The New Competitors: Thinking in Terms of 'Speed to Market,'" *Manufacturing Engineering*, June 1991, pp. 16–24.

of the processes—often made up largely of support services—needed to develop and commercialize discoveries. For service providers, design myopia acts in the same fashion; firms concentrate on the front-line service—the point of customer contact—and give scant attention to design of back-office support services. Resulting problems in purchasing, maintenance, training, delivery, installation, and after-sale service detract from any high regard customers might have for the front-line service.

- *Design is staffed-off.* In traditional design settings, designers are a breed apart—literally. They perform their work in isolation from their various customers, including those who transform designs into outputs, sell or distribute those outputs, and buy or consume the outputs. They often work with a paucity of information about requirements. Guesses substitute for facts because too many constituencies are not represented at the design table. When designs don't pan out, counterproductive finger pointing ensues.

- *Design is unfocused.* This problem may also appear in several forms, but all suggest the lack of clear guidelines for channeling the design program to remain true to function or purpose. Massachusetts Institute of Technology professors Karl Ulrich and Steven Eppinger note that early European industrial design theory emphasized the importance of precision, simplicity, and economy; it was believed that design should flow from the inside out as form follows function.[5] That is, designers should devote primary attention to the core components that make the "thing" being designed perform its intended function. However, according to Ulrich and Eppinger, dedication to function has not been as strong in the history of North American design strategy. In their haste to embellish external appearance, designers here placed more emphasis on nonfunctional features (e.g., tailfins and chrome-teeth grillwork on automobiles) than on inner workings so critical to functional performance.

Individually, each design weakness is bad enough. When acting in concert, they give customers—internal as well as external—cause to scream. Frequently, the effects of weak design show up as shoddy performance in operations. For example, when a new product or service is a hit and demand exceeds expectations, operations scurries to increase production or service capacity. Undesirable results include poor recruiting, inadequate training, reliance on untested equipment and sources of supply, and postponement of essential maintenance. In these cases, *all* of the right people weren't included during design discussions. The public sector is guilty, too. A commission or legislative subcommittee may spend a year creating a new program for, say, protecting the forests or housing the poor, and a law will be passed. But because the agencies (and citizens) that must implement the law are not involved in drafting legislation, development of implementation processes may further drag on for months or years.

Broadly speaking, whenever a good or service can't be easily built or installed, operated, delivered, or maintained, operations personnel are likely to take the heat for what is actually a manifestation of one or more of the traditional weaknesses of design. When it won't sell, marketing gets the blame. If it costs too much to provide, accountants feel the pressure to sharpen their pencils.

In general, as industry has begun to recognize the effects of poor design programs, and as employees in all areas of organizations have begun to understand how design has been affecting their work, the reaction has been positive. Comprehensive design programs that attack traditional weaknesses—and do much more—have emerged.

Comprehensive Design Program

Design program specifics differ, of course, but superior companies seem to agree on several common characteristics that describe effective product, service, and process design. Exhibit 4–5 presents a model for a comprehensive design program; it contains six integrated and overlapping parts.

The first two parts are strategic. First, senior managers decide which businesses to pursue and then select products and services to offer within the chosen industries; this determines the overall competitive environment in which the firm will operate. Next, the firm's design strategy must be positioned and implemented within that environment. This requires continuous environmental scanning and analysis—with

EXHIBIT 4–5

Comprehensive Design Program

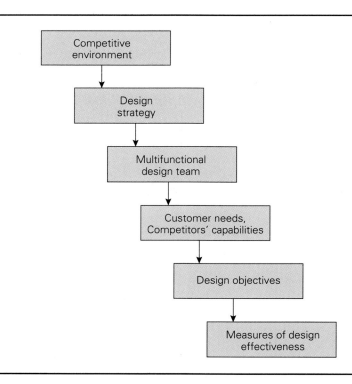

One-Coffeepot Teams

"For your average General Electric Co. researcher accustomed to the quiet, contemplative life in Schenectady, New York, being a member of a 'one-coffeepot' product-development team is no tea party. The teams unite GE researchers, manufacturers, and marketers in a single location, where they can sweep away obstacles to a new lightbulb or locomotive as they swill hot java.

"Lonie Edelheit, GE's senior vice president for research and development says most of the company's researchers have embraced the one-coffeepot concept. In any case, he says, there's no alternative: 'Speed means change. Everybody's got to understand that.' "

Source: Peter Coy, "Blue-Sky Research Comes Down to Earth," *Business Week,* July 3, 1995, pp. 78–80.

specific attention to customers' changing wants and competitors' shifting abilities and weaknesses. Since environmental change often evokes modifications in business strategy, some reformulation of design strategy might be needed. (Of course, operations, marketing, and financial strategies might need to be altered as well.)

*P*RINCIPLES 1 & 4

Get to know the customers and the competitors.

With strategies set, the multifunctional design team goes to work putting strategy into action. Among companies with leading R&D programs, the multi- or cross-functional team concept is the vehicle of choice for addressing all of the historical design weaknesses. (See the Into Practice box, "One-Coffeepot Teams.") When teams also include customers and suppliers, design efforts become fully sensitized.

The bottom three boxes in Exhibit 4–5 represent broad categories of design team responsibilities. We've mentioned the collection of customer and competitor data as it affects design strategy, but such information also plays a tactical role during design efforts. Later in the chapter, for example, we see how information about customers and competitors is incorporated into quality function deployment—one of the design team's tools.

To overcome the traditional weakness of lack of focus, effective design programs need guidelines and targets, as the next-to-last box in Exhibit 4–5 shows. Objectives will vary from setting to setting, but since our main interest is the design/ operations interface, we shall concentrate mostly on operations examples. Finally, represented by the last box, teams must have relevant measures of design program effectiveness. Feedback sparks improvement.

Thus far in this chapter, we've talked a bit about design strategy. We use the rest of this chapter to examine the remaining elements of the comprehensive design program. Teams are the first topic.

Teaming Up for Effective Design

A dominant theme of this book is the power of teams throughout organizations' activities, but what specifically do multifunctional teams do to improve design? Quite a bit. Furthermore, benefits accrue to both providers and customers: Providers overcome weaknesses in traditional design with powerful design techniques and tools that teams make possible. Customers enjoy improvements evident in final designs, often having made direct contributions to those designs. We will discuss but two of the more significant items in each category. First, teams facilitate concept development and make concurrent design possible. Second, when design is team based, products, services, and processes are more likely to have strong ergonomic and aesthetic appeal, and they are more apt to be environmentally friendly.

Concept Development

At the heart of any design program lies the notion of *concept development*. Crawford defines a **design concept** as "a combination of verbal and/or prototype form that tells what is going to be changed and how the customer stands to gain (and lose)."[6] Three essential parts must exist for an idea or plan to be elevated to the status of concept:

- *Form.* This is the physical thing itself—its shape, materials content, and so on. In the case of a service, form is often described by the steps needed to provide the service.
- *Technology.* The principles, techniques, equipment, mechanics, policies, and so forth to be employed in creating or attaining the good or service collectively constitute the technology. Examples include a particular assembly sequence or delivery plan. [Perhaps we're not stretching to suggest that Crawford's *technology* is essentially the *process*.]
- *Benefit.* Benefit is the value the customer plans to derive from the good or service.

According to Ulrich and Eppinger, design concept development begins with *concept generation*, itself a procedure. It transforms a set of customer needs and target specifications into a set of possible design concepts from which the team will select the most promising alternative.[7] One part of concept generation is **competitive analysis**—investigation of competitors' offerings.

Unfortunately, many companies have too few probes into the outside world. Competitive feedback is sparse, late, and narrow-gauged—for example, limited to sales totals and warranty claims. For services, competitive analysis requires going to the competitor, being served, and taking extensive notes for later use by your own service design teams. In manufacturing, the usual procedure is to buy a competitor's product and bring it in for thorough study, perhaps including complete disassembly, which is called *reverse engineering*. When many competitors are involved, or when a great number of performance characteristics must be studied, multidisciplinary teams are essential for even basic levels of competitive analysis.

After selection of the most promising design concept, development continues with refinements of specifications, economic analyses, and other fine-tuning activities. As the design nears final form, interest naturally shifts to production and delivery systems. Again, with effective use of team-based design, the transition will be smooth, for those charged with process design and operation will have already been active contributors to the design effort. That is, concurrent design will be ongoing.

Benchmarking (discussed in Chapter 3), a newer "sibling" of competitive analysis, seeks out best practices and products anywhere, not just from competitors.

Concurrent Design

Concurrent design, also known as **simultaneous engineering,** occurs when contributors to an overall design effort provide their expertise at the same time (concurrently) while working as a team instead of as isolated functional specialists working in serial fashion. Concurrent design is the norm in many leading companies; the examples from Hallmark, Boeing, and Rubbermaid in the accompanying Into Practice box illustrate.

From an operations perspective, significant benefits stem from getting those who design, operate, and maintain transformation processes included early and on the same team as those who design products. James Lardner, vice president at Deere and Company, maintains that "we can cut capital investment for automation by 50%–60% just by getting the design and manufacturing people together from the beginning."[8] Though our focus is operations, we should note that a full concurrent-design team also includes people from marketing, finance, purchasing,

Hallmark's Holiday Design Teams

Hallmark "lives or dies on new stuff—some 40,000 cards and other items a year, the work of 700 writers, artists, and designers. . . . Developing a new card had become grotesque; it took two years—longer than the road from Gettysburg to the Appomattox Court House. The company was choking on sketches, approvals, cost estimates, and proofs." But now, about half the staff will "work on cards for particular holidays. . . . A team of artists, writers, lithographers, merchandisers, bean counters, and so on,

will be assigned to each holiday. Team members are moving from all over a two-million-square-foot office building in Kansas City so they can sit together. Like a canoe on a lake, a card will flow directly from one part of the process to the next within, say, the Mother's Day team; before, it had to be portaged from one vast department to the next."

Source: Thomas A. Stewart "The Search for the Organization of Tomorrow," *Fortune*, May 18, 1992, pp. 92–98.

235 Design/Build Teams, One Boeing Airplane

Boeing's new "fly-by-wire" commercial airplane, the 777, involved 235 design/build teams—each with members from Boeing's vaunted design group, the airlines (the customers), the mechanics who will maintain the planes, the suppliers, "and the many others who will help build it, price it, and market it."

Shin-ichi Nakagawa, leader of a group of 250 engineers from Japanese supplier companies, says

Japanese companies "are familiar with teams of design and production engineers, but they haven't experienced Boeing's all-embracing teams that include customers, suppliers, and support teams."

Source: Jeremy Main, "Betting on the 21st Century Jet," *Fortune*, April 20, 1992, pp. 102–17.

Continuous Innovation at Rubbermaid

"Unlike many consumer-product companies, [Rubbermaid] does no test marketing. Instead, [it] has created entrepreneurial teams of five to seven members in each of its four dozen product categories. Each team includes a product manager, research and manufacturing engineers, and financial,

sales, and marketing executives. The teams conceive their own products, shepherding them from the design stage to the marketplace."

Source: Valerie Reitman, "Rubbermaid Turns Up Plenty of Profit in the Mundane," *The Wall Street Journal*, March 27, 1992.

human resources, and other inside departments; customers, suppliers, and freight carriers; and perhaps community and regulatory officials.

When a business is young or small, teaming up for effective design is easy and natural. But as the firm grows, people split off into functional specialties. How specialized? One reported example is of an automotive engineer who had spent his entire career designing door locks:

> He was not an expert in how to make locks, however; that was the job of the door-lock manufacturing engineer. The door-lock design engineer simply knew how they should look and work if made correctly.[9]

In that overspecialized system, product designers are accused of "throwing the design over the wall" to manufacturing or service process designers and saying in effect, "Let's see you figure out how to build that!" When process planners need to make changes, the design goes back "over the wall" to product designers, with the implication that, "If you had been smart enough to create a producible design in the first place . . ." Round after round of changes and attempts at production follow, usually creating disruptions and increased costs throughout the organization.

In some business sectors, shrinking product lives push designers into short design cycles; improvements must be rapid. Yearly (or even more frequent) announcements of everything from new computer hardware and software to new financial services to new types of disposable diapers favor concurrent design. But even when product life cycles are long, concurrent design has merit. For one thing, it avoids time-consuming misunderstandings and costly "do-overs" during the design phase. For another, it reduces costly bugs, errors, rework, and warranty claims during production, delivery, and customer use phases. "If a bonus system or orientation program needs to be redesigned because employees could not understand it, this is clearly 'rework.'"[10]

In the left margin, beside the paragraph beginning "In that overspecialized system":

In manufacturing, redesign results in **engineering change orders (ECOs),** each of which can go through many time-consuming and costly approval steps.

Contrast

Design

Over-the-Wall Design

- Becomes common practice as organization grows and splits into functional departments.
- Common, especially, in businesses, with long product lives (little urgency to develop new products).
- Tends to be slow.
- Tends to require several costly rounds of debugging.

Concurrent (Team) Design

- Tends to be common practice in very small organizations and where product redesigns occur often.
- Elevated competition has made it common in consumer electronics, cars, consumer credit, mortgage loans, and so on.
- Is fast and avoids problems (design rework) stemming from poor coordination and lack of shared information.

Environmental Awareness

Some businesses retain the notion that environmentally-friendly product designs—or, "green" designs—are too costly to be in their own or their customers' direct interests. Process design is another matter. Images of factories spewing smoke into the air or dumping toxic wastes into streams keep environmental groups and government officials vigilant—that is, in most of the world's industrial regions. Unfortunately, much remains to be done, especially in emerging economies.

In North America, the 1980s and early 1990s were a time of generally increasing public concern for the environment; tough pollution laws were passed and recycling became the norm in many homes, schools, and workplaces. Reluctance sometimes changed to willing compliance, which translated into planning for recycling and recovery in early design phases. The change in attitude occurred when, for example, paper once dumped into landfills and now recycled became a cash generator. Spent lubricants and chemical wash fluids turned out to be reprocessible and reusable, for less than the cost of new fluids. Recoverable metals in electronic trash and in plating acids were "gold in the trash barrel"—literally, in the case of gold-plated semiconductor leads.

Competitive one-upsmanship can be the attraction that gets environmental and social concerns on the design team's agenda. For example, a supermarket chain makes its competitor look bad by being the first to start a network of can, bag, and bottle recycling.

Sometimes reaction to a social or environmental concern opens up a set of promising new design options. For example, in attempting to design products easily operable by disabled consumers, designers have unearthed an attractive new approach called **universal design.**[11] It often turns out that, say, easy-to-open doors or easy-to-access information services are popular with young and old, able and disabled. That's good news for the maker because it allows the design team to focus intensively on just a few universal designs. With fewer, more universal product and service variations, designers can focus on better quality and other customer wants.

In this section, we've looked at selected strengths of team-based design. Next, we see how those benefits and others can be integrated within the context of a powerful yet relatively new tool—quality function deployment.

A Dow Chemical ethylene plant was designed to cut wastewater releases into the North Saskatchewan River from 360 gallons per minute to just 10, while also cutting energy usage 40 percent. Though construction cost 8 percent more, Dow projected full recovery in lower maintenance costs. "Growth versus the Environment," cover story, *Business Week*, May 11, 1992, pp. 66–75.

Quality Function Deployment

Quality function deployment (QFD) provides a structured way of viewing the big picture and of organizing the details of both product and process design.[12] The structure comes from a series of matrices. The first and most important matrix spells out customer needs—the "voice of the customer"—and compares the company's and key competitors' abilities to satisfy those needs. When the matrix is filled in and "roofed over," it takes the shape of a house—the **house of quality.**

Exhibit 4–6 is a house of quality developed with the aid of the owners of a chain of dry cleaning stores. The owners might use the matrix for improving one or more of their existing stores or for planning a new one. We interpret the QFD matrix as follows:

- The central portion shows what the customer wants and how to provide it.
- Symbols in the central portion show strong, medium, small, or no relationship between whats and hows. A double circle, strong, worth nine

QFD: Procedure for transforming customer requirements and competitor capabilities into provider targets, extending from design research to operations, marketing, and distribution.

Like many quality techniques, QFD got its start in manufacturing; that may change as its uses in services (e.g., Exhibit 4–6) become better known.

Exhibit 4-6
"House of Quality" for a Dry Cleaner

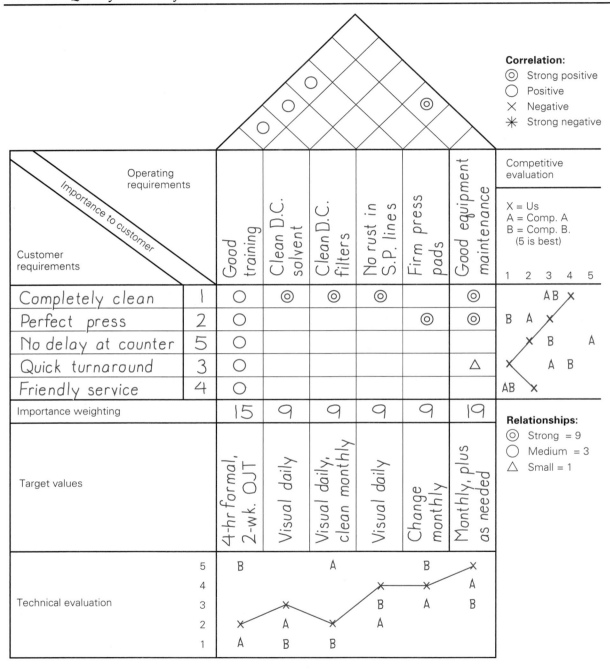

relationship points, appears six times. For example, a "perfect press" strongly depends on "firm press pads" and "good equipment maintenance," which account for two of the double circles.

- The five customer requirements are ranked 1 to 5 in importance. "Completely clean" is the customers' number-one concern; "no delay at counter" gets a 5.
- The ratings in each *how* column add up to an importance weighting. Good training, of medium importance for satisfying all five customer requirements, adds up to 15 points, which is second in importance to equipment maintenance, with 19 points.
- The house's roof correlates each *how* with each other factor. Only four of the combinations show a correlation. The double circle indicates a strong correlation between "good equipment maintenance" and "no rust in steam-press lines," meaning that steam-press components are subject to rust and thus must be cleaned out or replaced regularly.
- Target values, in the "basement" of the house, give a numeric target for each *how*: Change press pads monthly to keep them firm.
- The house's "sub-basement" and right wing show comparisons of the company and key competitors. We see at the bottom that the company is slightly better than competitors A and B in keeping solvent clean, in avoiding rust, and in maintenance. Ratings in the right wing show that both competitors are better in counter delays and quick turnaround.

The tough part for the design team is getting good data to enter into the matrix. Data sources may include focus groups, surveys, studies, comparison shopping, competitive analysis, public information, calculations, and reckoning. The emphasis is on relevant data, which may require tapping the minds of leading-edge customers (see Into Practice box, "Listening to Leading-Edge Customers"). QFD is (with good data) a structured, inclusive approach that helps keep the design team from overlooking something important.

The design team uses the basic house of quality in the product-planning stage. More detailed matrices may be developed for three remaining stages of design—that is, product design, process planning, and process control planning (see Exhibit 4–7).[13] According to one report, though, only about 5 percent of QFD users go beyond the basic house.[14]

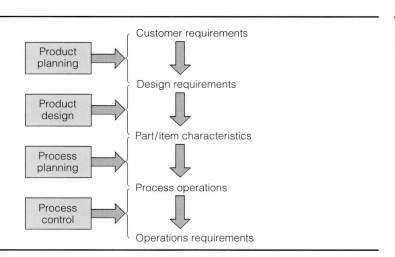

EXHIBIT 4–7
QFD Overview

Listening to Leading-Edge Customers

"MIT professor Eric von Hippel makes his living studying the sources of innovation. He says that sophisticated early adopters of new products, whom Hippel labels 'lead users,' can be worth their weight in gold."

While the search is for sophisticated users, the product can be as mundane as pipe hangers. Von Hippel, along with Cornelius Herstatt of the Swiss Federal Institute of Technology, helped Hilti AG, a leading European manufacturer of fastening-related products, to find lead users of pipe hangers. After surveying eight industry experts on likely developments in the next generation of pipe hangers, von Hippel and Herstatt turned their sights toward lead users.

"A random sample of 120 Hilti customers were asked, 'Do you/did you ever build and install pipe-hanging hardware of your own design?' 'Do you/did you ever modify commercially available pipe-hanging hardware to better suit your needs?'"

Von Hippel and Herstatt found 74 tradesmen who installed pipe hangers. Based on in-depth interviews, that number was reduced to 22 "true pace-setters," who were culled further to 12, who seemed

to have personal interests in new-product development. Finally, three design engineers from Hilti organized a three-day product-concept generation workshop with the 12 tradesmen, two of the eight industry specialists, a marketing manager, and a product manger.

"The first day, participants reviewed the specialists' findings, then broke into five subgroups to consider issues. They spent half the second day in their groups, then did generic creativity exercises. The third day, groups presented their solutions, which the entire workshop evaluated on originality, feasibility, and comprehensiveness. Then they formed a new group to explore the most promising concepts. In the end, all hands converged on a single product concept.

"But were these pace setters too far ahead of the industry? To find out, Hilti tested the workshop's idea on a dozen regular customers, not at the leading edge. Ten preferred the new product and said they'd pay up to 20 percent more for it."

Source: Tom Peters, "Just Listening to Customers Isn't Enough," syndicated column appearing in *Seattle Post-Intelligencer*, May 25, 1992.

Design Objectives

Quality function deployment is at its best when the aim is to satisfy a prescribed set of customer needs in the face of rather well-defined competitors' capabilities. Design objectives flow somewhat naturally from specific performance targets. On a broader level, however, general guidelines have emerged and are gaining widespread acceptance by design teams across a variety of industries. Though the guidelines do pose targets for product designs, operations managers can appreciate their substantial emphasis on design of transformation processes.

In this section, we examine design-for-operations guidelines and then turn to applications. First, we see how design teams improve product and process reliability, and then we look at how designers plan for robotics and other forms of process automation.

Design for Operations: Guidelines

Design lore is replete with examples of what have come to be known as DFX criteria: Design for X, which can mean design for quality, reliability, or other desired ends. AT&T Bell Laboratories incorporates design for the environment (DFE) into its computer-aided design software.[15] Here, the purpose is to steer the product development engineers toward product designs that are environmentally friendly; for example, easily disassembled for sorting into different recycling bins.

Another slant on DFE is designing plants and industrial processes for minimal damage to the environment. Managing products and processes for the environment is the subject of a new set of standards developed by the International Organization for Standards: the ISO 14000 series of standards. Since ISO 14000 is oriented more toward plant emission issues than product recycling, further discussion of this standard is reserved for the plant maintenance discussion in Chapter 17.

Product designers can too easily overlook the realities of front-line operations: the moment of truth with an unpredictable customer or the many sources of surprise, variation, agony, and error in operations. The design team may be able to avoid some of these pitfalls by following design-for-operations guidelines, which have evolved from the works of professors Geoffrey Boothroyd and Peter Dewhurst.[16]

In the early 1980s, Boothroyd and Dewhurst (originally from England, now professors in engineering at the University of Rhode Island) began to publish on design for operations for manufactured products. By the 1990s, tens of thousands of design engineers had studied **design for manufacture and assembly (DFMA).** (For a comprehensive Boothroyd-Dewhurst example, see Solved Problem 2 on pages 114–16).

Although the DFMA guidelines were aimed at manufacturing, they have proven to be general enough to apply well to services; thus, we use the more general term, **design for operations (DFO).** Exhibit 4–8 lists one version of DFO guidelines.

Exhibit 4–8   Design for Operations Guidelines

General Guidelines:

1. Design to target markets and target costs.
2. Minimize number of parts and number of operations.

Quality Guidelines:

3. Ensure that customer requirements are known and design to those requirements.
4. Ensure that process capabilities are known (those in your firm and of your suppliers) and design to those capabilities.
5. Use standard procedures, materials, and processes with already known and proven quality.

Operability Guidelines:

6. Design multifunctional/multiuse components and service elements and modules.
7. Design for ease of joining, separating, rejoining (goods) and ease of coupling/uncoupling (services).
8. Design for one-way assembly, one-way travel (avoid backtracking and return visits).
9. Avoid special fasteners and connectors (goods) and off-line or misfit service elements.
10. Avoid fragile designs requiring extraordinary effort or attentiveness—or that otherwise tempt substandard or unsafe performance.

The first two guidelines are general in that they have wide-ranging benefits.

1. Target Markets and Target Costs.   This guideline reinforces the need for a multifunctional design team; it is approached from two points of view. First, customer and marketing representatives bring sales targets, profit data, and competitors' pricing policies to the team. If it looks like, for example, the new product's production costs or the proposed process's operating costs will exceed competitive levels by a great deal, the project gets dropped quickly.[17] If the gap is closer, the team may opt to benchmark, brainstorm, and experiment on ways to reduce build or operating costs and thus salvage the project.

A newer tool allows design teams to approach costs from a different yet complementary view. By applying the concepts and mathematics associated with the Taguchi loss function (shown in Chapter 3, Exhibit S3–4), the team's engineering and operating experts are able to project savings resulting from designs that reduce product or process variation.[18] Taguchi's broad concept includes losses (e.g., stemming from design deficiencies) to society, not just to the provider or the customer.[19]

PRINCIPLE 5:

A few good product/service components.

2. Minimize Parts and Operations.   The Boothroyd-Dewhurst methodology focuses especially on this guideline, minimizing the number of parts or, outside of manufacturing, the number of operations. For example, a data-entry terminal may be used to input client data in one operation, instead of several times in several different offices of, say, a college or a clinic.

Exhibit 4–9 illustrates a manufacturing example. The design team is minimizing number of parts as it designs "a better mouse." The next step, in the Boothroyd-Dewhurst method, is separately analyzing each part to ascertain the best type of material and the best manufacturing method.

The next three guidelines pertain to quality: quality requirements of the customer (guideline 3), quality capabilities of internal and external processes (guideline 4), and use of standardization to make quality easier to deliver (guideline 5).

PRINCIPLE 10:

Eliminate error and process variation.

3. Customer Requirements.   Guideline 3 calls for the design team to find out customers' precise requirements, or their best estimates of them, and to keep finding out because requirements can change during the design project. Requirements may take the form of brightness, smoothness, size, speed of service, minimal waiting time, ease of maintainability, and so on. The design team must be clear on the matter because one of its jobs is to transform requirements into specifications and tolerances.

Since the total design—of product and process—may be split up among more than one organizational unit, it is important that designers from each unit get together on requirements. If they are kept apart, quality problems are likely. Suppliers will cite "ambiguous requirements." They will say, "We followed your requirements [or specifications] and now find out you really want something else."

Such failures to communicate are not just the fault of the customer. Good suppliers, inside or outside the firm, do whatever they can to find out their customers' real requirements, avoid misunderstanding, and make their customers look good. When communications are good, design tips flow both ways, and sometimes it's the customer who makes the supplier look good.

EXHIBIT 4–9 **Designing a Better Mouse**

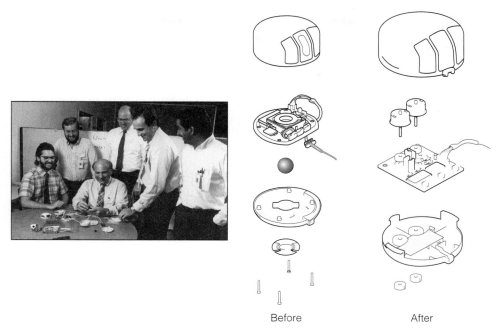

Before   After

Digital Equipment Corp. policy used to forbid design engineers from talking to suppliers (they had to go through purchasing); now they're required to talk to suppliers.

DFMA team at Digital Equipment Corp. designs a better mouse (computer accessory). New design cuts screws from seven to zero, assembly adjustments from eight to zero, assembly time from 592 to 277 seconds; also cuts material costs 47 percent, package costs 59 percent.

4. Process Capability.   Guideline 4, designing to process capability, affects the design team in two ways. First, the team is held responsible if the design cannot easily be delivered or produced using available processes (including those of the supplier), people, equipment, facilities, and other resources. Second, in being held responsible, the design team must become familiar with process capabilities, which usually are measurable to some degree.

Capability measures might include years of experience, amount of cross-training, and educational attainment of associates; documentation of procedures; safety devices in place; low equipment failure rates; and ability to achieve and hold tolerances. The latter may be measured using the process capability index, C_{pk}, which has become important in manufacturing in recent years (see Chapter 5).

5. Standard Procedures, Materials, and Processes.   The fifth guideline advises designers to favor standard procedures, materials, and processes. Related to standardization are questions about creativity, satisfying customer needs for variety, and new opportunities for global marketing. Each of these issues warrants brief discussion.

Standardization. Nonstandard designs are risky because of lack of knowledge about their performance. Xerox found this out the hard way. One consultant observed that, for lack of competition, the company's large staff of bright engineers developed machines with "incredibly complex technology. . . . Everything inside a Xerox machine was special. You could not go out and use a normal nut. It had to be a specially designed nut. The concept of using as many standard parts as possible was not even thought of."[20] Design complexities led to costly field service to make copiers work properly. High costs opened the door to competition, which actually was good for Xerox.

Standardization and creativity. Now Xerox—a 1990 Malcolm Baldrige prize winner—along with many other companies, has firm policies on use of standard parts. Some apply the guideline quantitatively. For example, a plastics recycling team at Xerox worked to reduce the 500-odd plastic formulations that its designers had been using. The team initially recommended fewer than 50 formulations—now they are down to about 10.[21] Similarly, an opinion survey firm might settle on just two or three standard formats for its survey forms, or a fast-food company may limit the number of sizes of cups or food containers. While it may seem that such restrictions could stifle creativity or effectiveness, they actually may have the opposite effect. By not spending time evaluating so many plastic varieties or survey forms or fast-food containers, designers have more time to be creative and thorough on what counts and to explore new materials, technologies, and competitors' procedures.

Standardization and personalized design. Is standardization in conflict with trends toward personalized design? Not necessarily. In fact, standardization may be the only way to make personalized design profitable: Carefully design a small number of standard elements that can be delivered in volume at low cost, and have the flexibility to quickly customize them right in front of the customer.

This formula—personalization but with standard components—is the basis for Panasonic's personalized bicycle, which starts out with customer fitting in a retail store.[22] The clerk enters customer measurements, color choice, and other specs (see Exhibit 4–10A) into a computer, and a computer-aided design routine at the factory produces a customized blueprint in three minutes.

While final assembly is still mostly manual, frame welding employs flexible automation. Racks of a limited number of frame models surround the automation equipment and are selected following the customer's specs. The frame models are somewhat standardized, which holds down production costs, perhaps by using dedicated equipment to make each model; the same applies to many smaller standardized bicycle parts.

Customer-run greeting card machines follow much the same formula (see Exhibit 4–10B). A large variety of customer choices are possible from a few standardized components, such as plain card, envelope, and inks. According to American Greetings Corp. president Edward Fruchtenbaum, the CreataCard machine is the "ultimate combination of just-in-time manufacturing and micromarketing."[23]

Standardization and globalization. Taken in conjunction with guideline 2 (minimize parts and operations), this guideline has strategic implications. As goods and services are designed with fewer, more standardized components and operations, costs go down and quality becomes more dependable. In turn, this increases their appeal, sometimes to the point where people around the globe know about and want the item—be it a Big Mac, a pair of Nikes, or an American Express card.

More broadly, three trends seem to be interrelated: (1) better designed goods and services (based on these design guidelines) and (2) widespread lowering of political and trade barriers create (3) markets of awesome size. One result is that

EXHIBIT 4–10   Personalized Design from Standard Components

A. 11,231,862 variations of Panasonic bicycle. Customer fitting in retail store.

Used by permission of Matrix, Inc.

B. Personalized greeting card machines.

Used by permission of American Greetings Corp.

Copyright © by Hallmark Cards. Used with permission.

companies with hot products and services may be able to prosper through rapid global expansion coupled with massive-volume production and service delivery.

Guidelines 6 through 10 generally offer further guidance on attaining high quality. More specifically, their focus is on operability—avoiding difficulties in front-line operations.

6. Multifunctional/Multiuse Elements and Modules.   The do-it-yourself industry is alive and thriving. Buy some plumbing modules, shelving components, or mix-and-match clothing, and combine to taste. Good design in accordance with this guideline makes it possible.

Insurance companies, investment funds, health care, and other service companies do much the same thing: design a self-contained service module (e.g., payroll processing) and offer it to companies that seek ways of cutting their own overhead and getting out of service areas beyond their expertise. For an example of manufacturing modules, see the Into Practice box, "Modular Design . . . at Scania Truck."

7. Ease of Joining/Separating, Coupling/Uncoupling.   Push, click, snap, whirr. That's the sound of the modern keyboard, clock, or auto dashboard being assembled. It's easy, quick, and if the design team has heeded guideline 7, mostly error-free.

Are snap-together connections hard to notice? That's good—until someone needs to take off a cover for repair, or until the junked unit gets to the recycler to be separated into reusable materials. Today's designer needs extra ingenuity to make disassembly and separation as easy as push-and-snap assembly. (Yet another DFX term: *design for disassembly,* or *DFDA.*)

Into Practice

Modular Design with Standardized Parts—Competitive Advantage at Scania Truck

"Scania, the Swedish maker of heavy-duty trucks, buses, and diesel engines, has parlayed a modular design strategy into a robust formula for low costs and sustained profitability." A comparison of Scania and Volvo truck performance in the 1980s is telling. The two companies sold about the same number of trucks in those years. Volvo's trucks, however, required about twice as many part numbers. (Each different part gets a different number, so "part numbers" is widely used in industry to indicate variety of parts.) By designing from half as many part numbers, Scania's product development costs averaged about half of Volvo's costs. Moreover, Scania enjoys a higher customer retention rate than either of its two main European rivals. Scania retains about 80 percent, Volvo about 60 percent, and Mercedes-Benz trucks about 60 percent.

It took Scania's design engineers about 15 years to achieve, by 1980, what they consider to be full-scale modularization and component standardization. Scania's product design route to success is notably different from that of many other manufacturers. The Toyota production system, for example, is based primarily on process simplification and flexibility rather than component design. Leif Östling, Scania's general manager, explains the cost advantages of Scania's design concept: Reducing part numbers results in higher production volumes of each retained part. He maintains that production costs per unit fall about 10 percent when standardization permits the production quantity of the part to double. Furthermore, distribution costs (from ordering and storing) fall about 30 percent when part numbers are cut in half.

Source: H. Thomas Johnson and Anders Bröms, "'The Spirit in the Walls:' A Pattern for High Performance at Scania," *Target,* May/June 1995, pp. 9–17.

A salesperson with cellular phone and data diskette can go to work on the road, at home, or in the sales office. This design of the sales process permits easy service coupling/uncoupling as the need arises. Increasingly, facilities (in hotels, airlines, restaurants, etc.) are designed so that service people can easily plug in and plug out.

8. One-Way Assembly and Travel.   Who hasn't had to stand in one line for a certain service element, wait in another line for the next element, and then later go back to the first line? Guideline 8 aims at avoiding that kind of backtracking and in manufacturing is helping to revitalize some assembly plants. For example, IBM was an early convert to designing products for layered assembly. The bottom layer may be the box itself. Then comes a bottom plastic cover for, say, a personal computer. Next are the inside components, then the top cover and loose accessories, and finally the top of the box. Since all assembly motions are up and down, IBM can equip the assembly lines with its own simple pick-and-place robots; no need for elaborate, costly robots with multiple axes of motion.

9. Avoid Special Fastening and Fitting.   This guideline avoids special steps. In manufacturing, the guideline applies especially to connectors and fasteners (*fasteners* is industry's term for bolts, washers, nuts, screws, etc.). For example, the number of screws in IBM's redesigned LaserPrinter was cut from dozens to a handful. "IBM had expected to assemble [them] by robot. Instead, engineers found that simplicity yielded yet another dividend: It turned out to be cheaper and easier to make them by hand."[24] A misfit service would include one that requires a server to leave a client to fetch a file folder or get an approval.

10. Avoid Fragile Designs.   Tendencies or temptations to take unsafe shortcuts, to be careless with sensitive equipment, to be brusque with customers, to steal, or otherwise misperform are partly avoidable by using designs that make such tendencies difficult.

One approach is to design controls into the process. Examples: design the process to maintain strict segregation of personal and business possessions, clearly labeled locations for all files and materials, easy access to backup help, and safety-guard gates to keep associates from blundering into an unsafe area.

Another approach is the use of **robust design** concepts. Examples: shatter-resistant glass, a waterproof watch, carpeting that comes clean even if smeared with black grease, and keyboards you can spill Coke on. See the Into Practice box, Looking for Trouble, for an example of redesign for robustness. In this case, in which a team of operators led the redesign, both a customer company and its supplier were the beneficiaries.

Design for Reliability and Serviceability

The DFO quality guidelines, especially guideline 3, are deliberately quite broad—they must encompass diverse customer needs and they must apply to both product and process quality. We can illustrate how the guidelines are put into practice, however, by looking at reliability and serviceability.

Reliability is the probability that an item will function as planned over a given time period. It may be calculated as follows:

$$R = e^{-\lambda t} \qquad\qquad (4\text{--}1)$$

where

R = Reliability, a value from 0 to 1.0

e = the base of natural logarithms (approximately 2.718)

λ = a constant failure rate

t = specified point in time

Serviceability is a bit harder to define; it means different things to various constituencies. One common thread, however, is the degree to which an item may be maintained: either kept in service through preventive maintenance (discussed in Chapter 17) or restored to service after a breakdown. Popular measures that relate to serviceability include:

- **Failure rate,** denoted by the Greek letter *lambda* (λ), is the average number of times an item is expected to fail within a given time period. As we saw in Equation 4–1, lambda is the critical determinant of reliability.
- **Mean time between failures (MTBF)** is the average time between failures of a repairable item, or the average time to first failure of a nonrepairable item. MTBF is usually denoted by the Greek letter *mu* (μ.) MTBF is the inverse of failure rate; that is, $\mu = 1/\lambda$.
- **Mean time to repair (MTTR)** is the average time required to repair (or replace) assuming that appropriate parts and sufficient expertise are available. In some circles, MTTR is used almost synonymously with serviceability.

At process-industry plants (e.g., refineries), where failures can be catastrophic, emphasis is on prevention of failure through planned, regularly scheduled maintenance. Many such facilities place primary interest in *mean time between planned maintenance* (MTBPM) rather than MTBF.

Into Practice

Looking for Trouble

At Eaton Corporation's Cutler-Hammer plant in Lincoln, Illinois, a team of assembly operators had completed one project and went looking for another trouble spot to attack. High scrap rates and ensuing rework on the company's ground fault interrupter (GFI) line caught their attention. (A GFI is a circuit breaker used where electrical current might come in contact with water, in bathrooms and around sinks, for example.) Not only were scrap and rework costs excessive, but production was being slowed.

Analysis—with Pareto charts and cause–effect diagrams—traced the likely cause of the bulk of the trouble to broken coils on the GFI printed circuit boards. Since the purchased coils were received in good condition, the coil breakage had to be occurring during GFI assembly at the Lincoln plant. After a series of experiments and other tests, the team was able to attribute the breakage to the close proximity of components—including the coil—inside the GFI housing. The design, though it met other objectives such as performance, compactness, and durability

during use, left the coil unprotected and subject to contact during assembly.

Complete redesign was one option—a time-consuming and costly one. The team tried another: they added a small insulator to protect the coil during assembly. The team assembled 50 test breakers a day for a week, all using the new insulators. The result was no broken coils in the test batches. They verified the solution by building controlled lots of GFI breakers—with the new insulators—for a month. Results? No broken coils.

When the coil supplier was notified of the assembly team's findings, the added insulator became a permanent design feature on the coil and was supplied to Cutler-Hammer at no additional charge. The supplier, who had been suffering the same problems with the delicate coils, found that the added insulator resulted in substantial reductions in its own scrap rates.

Source: Information courtesy of and used with permission of Eaton Corporation, Cutler-Hammer Division, Lincoln, IL.

- **Availability** is the proportion of time that a resource is ready for use. One version of availability (A) considers only designated operating time (thus excluding planned downtime for preventive maintenance, overhauls, etc.) and combines MTBF and MTTR:

$$A = \frac{\text{MTBF}}{\text{MTBF} + \text{MTTR}} \tag{4-2}$$

Examples 4–1 and 4–2 illustrate how design teams incorporate these measures into their work.

EXAMPLE 4–1:   BATTERY RELIABILITY

Westport Communications Systems builds heavy duty, portable radios for use by emergency service personnel such as firefighters and rescue personnel. The standard rechargeable batteries Westport has been buying to package with its radios have a rated MTBF of 10 hours under conditions of normal use; failure is said to occur when battery charge fails to register at a prescribed point on a test meter. A representative from the battery supplier announced that a design team was working on a new deluxe battery that would have an MTBF rating of 20 hours. What effect would the new battery have on the performance reliability of the radios? What other options might Westport suggest to its customers?

Solution

Westport employees can observe the effects on reliability by constructing reliability curves—which demonstrate reliability decline over time—for both the standard and deluxe batteries. They must first invert each MTBF value to obtain the failure rate, λ, for each battery:

$$\text{Standard battery: } \lambda = 1/\mu = 1/10 = 0.10 \text{ failure per hour}$$

$$\text{Deluxe battery: } \lambda = 1/\mu = 1/20 = 0.05 \text{ failure per hour}$$

Then, from Equation 4–1, reliability values for selected time values are determined. For example, reliability of the standard battery after three hours of service is

$$R = e^{-(\lambda)(t)} = e^{-(0.1 \text{ failure/hr.})(3 \text{ hrs.})} = e^{-0.3} = 0.74$$

Thus, there is a 74 percent chance that a battery will continue to retain the prescribed charge after three hours of operation. A note of caution: This is an average; some batteries will last longer, others not as long. By repeating the calculation for various time points and then doing the same for the deluxe battery, a table of reliability values may be constructed:

	Reliability Values					
Time (hours)	1	2	3	4	5	6
Standard battery (MTBF = 10 hours)	0.90	0.82	0.74	0.67	0.61	0.55
Deluxe battery (MTBF = 20 hours)	0.95	0.90	0.86	0.82	0.78	0.74

Exhibit 4–11A shows the reliability graphs for the two batteries, plotted from data in the table. The time could be extended, of course, but the general downward trend would continue. If a customer stated that even greater reliability was needed, Westport might suggest that they keep sets of spare batteries and change them at regular intervals, say, every hour. In such a case, reliability would be approximately as shown in Exhibit 4–11B, assuming the customer had elected to use standard batteries.

EXHIBIT 4–11

**Battery
Reliability Curves**

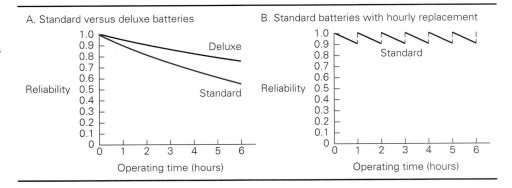

A. Standard versus deluxe batteries

B. Standard batteries with hourly replacement

EXAMPLE 4–2:   ENSURING RESOURCE AVAILABILITY

A redesign team is planning modifications to a line of its high-speed office photocopiers. A major customer's representative is on the team and has requested that every effort be made to provide an availability rating of at least 0.96. The historical MTBF for that line of photocopiers is 50 hours and the MTTR is 3 hours. What options might the team consider?

Solution

Initial availability calculations reveal the magnitude of the problem. From equation 4–2:

$$A = \frac{50}{50 + 3} = 0.94$$

The customer has requested a higher availability than currently exists, so that problem must be addressed. Team members suggest two approaches: First, the team might try to achieve a higher MTBF rating by designing out failure-prone components. Suppose one design alternative could result in an MTBF of 60 hours. Application of Equation 4–2 reveals:

$$A = \frac{60}{60 + 3} = 0.95$$

Improvement is evident, but more is needed. An alternative approach, suggested by team members who have operated and maintained the photocopiers, focuses on increased parts standardization and easier compartment access; their aim is a shorter repair time. Their estimates show a realistic value of two hours for MTTR. That, in turn, results in an availability rating of 50/52, or 0.96, the figure specified by the customer. Of course, the team ought to implement both changes, improving availability even more.

Example 4–1 showed that designers might be able to increase reliability by choosing a more robust component—in the example, a battery with a larger MTBF. Or, they might suggest that operators replace the component at regular intervals (e.g., change batteries hourly). But what if the best, perhaps state-of-the-art, component is already in place, and changeover is impractical or impossible? Often, the answer lies in improving reliability through redundancy—the backup parachute idea. The technique is popular with process designers stymied by a weak-link (unreliable), but necessary, system component. A simple example borrowed from basic electrical circuit design illustrates.

In circuits, parallel connections allow each circuit branch to operate independently (or very nearly so); loss of one branch doesn't interfere with operation of other branches. Failure of one light bulb, for instance, won't knock out bulbs on other branches, and the overall job (i.e., lighting a space) still gets done. Suppose item *A* in Exhibit 4–12A (maybe just a light bulb, but it could be any component, or an entire service process) has a reliability, which can be determined by using equation 4–1, of 0.9 at time equal to one week. The process reliability between points *X* and *Y*, then, is simply 0.9 at the end of any one-week operating period.

Now, suppose another *A* is added, operating independently of (or parallel to) the first. Exhibit 4–12B illustrates. System or process reliability between points *X* and *Y* at the end of one week may be determined as follows:

$$R_{XY} = 1 - (1 - R_A)^n \qquad (4\text{--}3)$$

where

R_{XY} = process reliability

R_A = item or component reliability of an *A* after a certain time period

n = number of identical redundant items in the process system

Substituting appropriate values for R_A and n yields:

$$R_{XY} = 1 - (1 - R_A)^n$$

$$= 1 - (1 - 0.9)^2 = 1 - (0.1)^2$$

$$= 0.99$$

Addition of yet a third item *A* branch is shown in Exhibit 4–12C. The reliability, again of the process contained between points *X* and *Y* at the end of a one-week period, may be determined with the same equation:

$$R_{XY} = 1 - (1 - R_A)^n$$

$$= 1 - (1 - 0.9)^3 = 1 - (0.1)^3$$

$$= 0.999$$

The marginal increase in reliability decreases (by tenfold in this example) for each iteration—clearly an economic consideration that would come into play. Practical physical constraints—such as the weight limits imposed on spacecraft—also restrict the luxury of increased reliability through unbounded redundancy. But even short downtime for repairs can prove catastrophic—say, in nuclear

We've used identical components in this discussion, and assumed that reliability decay functions are the same whether the component is experiencing operating life or merely shelf life. Variation of components types or variation of reliability function within type of component doesn't alter the gist of the message; the math just gets more cumbersome.

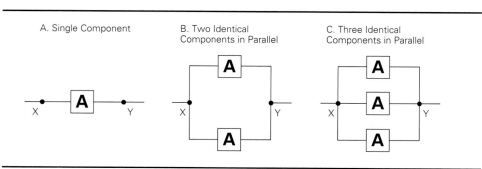

A. Single Component

B. Two Identical Components in Parallel

C. Three Identical Components in Parallel

EXHIBIT 4–12

Improving Process Reliability through Redundancy

power plant coolant systems, refinery flow control systems, and hospital power supply systems. In such cases, increased reliability through redundancy is often the design team's best bet.

Design for Automation

Boothroyd and Dewhurst's operability guidelines—6 through 10—are particularly useful as design teams cope with automation, a topic of continuing concern for operations managers. Three broad issues, affecting output and process design efforts, come into play:

- Wasteful or unnecessary processes should not be automated. Clean up the former and eliminate the latter *before* considering automation.
- The theme of the five guidelines is simplification for good reason: The simpler the task, the easier it will be to design equipment to do it. Development will also be faster and cheaper.
- When design teams strive for an easy-to-automate design, they sometimes get an unexpected dividend: Following the operability guidelines might simplify the process to such an extent that the firm can avoid the time and expense needed to acquire and install the automation.

Solved Problem 2 at the end of this chapter provides an application of the operability guidelines.

Design Review and Appraisal

Design and development is a loop. Preliminary designs are critiqued, improved, critiqued again, improved again, and so on. This commonly continues after the product designs are in production or services are being delivered, and customers are sampling the results. The inescapable questions remain: "Has quality been designed in?" and "How do we know?"

We don't know. To find out, the extended design team must listen to customers, keep track of competitors, and when necessary, modify the design. External feedback begins to reach the design team as soon as the first customers begin to work with the designs. Quite often, these first customers are operations personnel. Later, marketing and advertising associates get their turn; they must present the new designs to external customers—the final arbiters. Systematic, measurement-based design checking all along the chain (called design review) provides a near-constant flow of design appraisal data.

The tools and guidelines we've covered in this chapter suggest several specific measures of design-team performance. Percentage of standard parts or new parts, attainment of target costs, availability, reliability, design cycle time, frequency and magnitude of design changes, rework, and warranty costs are a few examples. Other more general measures address ergonomics, environmental concerns, and aesthetic factors.

But the list of those who evaluate designs, the criteria they use, and their sophistication all seem to be expanding. Several trends bear watching: First, businesses are increasingly aware of the financial impact of design—in short- and long-term operations and marketing. As such, many are turning to outside expertise—outsourcing their design work. Providing design services is a booming business. Second, customers all along the chain have elevated their willingness to sound off about design. They know more about design, are more demanding of design excellence, and appear to be less intimidated by so-called experts who fail to listen. Perhaps it's fair to say that design appraisal has gone public. Finally, customers want design teams to do more—to cover more territory, so to speak. *Business Week* editors summed it up this way:

> In the '70s, companies wanted designers to provide styling for their products. In the '80s, they began to ask for mechanical engineering as well. In the '90s, corporations are demanding that design firms deliver the whole shebang in product development— user research, industrial design, mechanical engineering, rapid prototyping, ergonomics, software interface design, graphics, packaging. And some even demand global capability—products that sell in Asia and Europe as well as the U.S.[25]

Summary

Elevated competition has led many companies to reassess their research and development (R&D) strategies. As Black & Decker discovered, tired product lines make even industry leaders fall prey to aggressive competitors. Also, the quality movement has reinforced advantages of the design-quality-in approach.

Though R&D spending varies by industry and by country, advanced design programs aim at overcoming traditional weaknesses—slow, myopic, unfocused design left solely in the hands of isolated staff personnel. Comprehensive design takes advantage of competitive environments, employs multifunctional design teams, pays close attention to the voice of the customer, establishes and meets design objectives, and acknowledges the presence of more sophisticated and changing sources of design appraisal.

Increasingly, design success demands a team approach—where design engineers are joined by associates from marketing, finance, operations, purchasing, human resources, and other functions. Customer and supplier representatives frequently join the teams as well. Teams facilitate concept development, make concurrent design possible, and ensure that products and processes are more likely to have ergonomic and aesthetic appeal and be environmentally friendly.

Quality function deployment (QFD)—a powerful design tool—helps teams translate customer desires into design requirements, then into production and service specifications, and on into detailed product characteristics and process operations. As design teams pay increasing attention to customers, they become aware of an expanding array of requirements. "Design for X" criteria—where the specific need, X, might be maintainability, reliability, and so on—are being refined and documented in many industries.

Design-for-operations (DFO) guidelines link product and process designs to operational success factors. The first two general guidelines include designing to a target cost, based on the market, and minimizing parts and operations, which reduces sources of error and overhead cost.

Quality-oriented guidelines 3, 4, and 5 are designing for customer requirements (3), which requires close customer contact; measurable process capability factors

(4); and standardization of procedures, materials, and processes, with quality already known and proven (5). Standardization of components can hold down costs and make personalized design affordable at the end-product level, where the components may be finished in numerous ways.

Guidelines 6 through 10, aiming at operability, also improve quality in that they avoid difficulties in making the product or providing the service. These guidelines call for designing for multiple functions and uses (6); ease of joining, separating, rejoining, coupling, and uncoupling (7); one-way assembly and one-way travel (8); avoidance of fasteners and connectors and misfit service elements (9); and avoidance of fragile designs that tempt incorrect performance (10).

DFO guidelines are deliberately broad. In application, however, teams have many specific measures at their disposal—each contributing to the aim of meeting customer needs. Quality guidelines might focus on reliability and serviceability, for example, and operability guidelines might be employed as a firm prepares for automation.

Design review and appraisal procedures are changing. "Has quality been designed in?" is an overall concern as various customers appraise the work of design teams. Greater recognition of the short- and long-term financial impact of design causes many companies to outsource design work. More sophisticated design review by a knowledgeable public and pressure on design teams to deliver a broader spectrum of services combine to keep design teams on their toes.

Solved Problems

Problem 1

Betty's daughter will soon open her new advertising agency, and Betty is shopping for a small office gift to present when she visits the agency next week. At an office supply store, Betty finds an electric pencil sharpener she likes. A label on the box informs her that the sharpener has a mean time between failure (MTBF) of two years. A clerk who arrives to assist informs Betty that the MTBF figure means that after two years, there is a 50–50 chance that the sharpener will still be working. Is the clerk correct?

Solution 1

The value of the sharpener's reliability at a time period of two years is the issue. First compute the failure rate (we must assume that it is constant): $\lambda = 1/\mu$, or ½ per year. Then, apply equation 4–1.

$$R = e^{-\lambda t} = e^{-(1/2)(2)} = e^{-(1)}$$

$$= 1/e = 1/2.718 = 0.368$$

So the clerk is incorrect. A common mistake is to assume that reliability at MTBF is one-half, or 50 percent. The correct value, however, is about 0.37, slightly more than a one-third chance of successful operation.

Problem 2

Exhibit 4–13 shows an assembly diagram for a simple product. Redesign the product for ease of assembly and robotics.

Solution 2

First, the design team evaluates the present method in terms of the strict and well-defined requirements for assembly by a robot. Then it simplifies the design.

Step 1: Robotic assembly. The design team specifies the following robotic assembly method. The robot starts by putting four bolts upright into four pods in a special fixture,

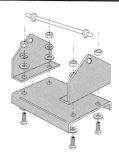

Source: Adapted from G. Boothroyd and P. Dewhurst, "Product Design . . . Key to Successful Robotic Assembly," *Assembly Engineering,* September 1986, pp. 90–93. Used with permission.

Exhibit 4–13
Assembly Using Common Fasteners

one at a time. Then it puts a washer on each bolt. Next, the robot must position the base so the holes line up with the four bolts—a difficult alignment unless the holes are large. The robot's next tasks are to grab a bracket, position it, and secure it at each end with a washer, a lock washer, and a nut. Tightening the nuts requires that the robot return its ordinary gripper to the tool rack, fasten its "wrist" to a special nut-turning device, and then, after the nuts are tight, switch back to the ordinary gripper.

Exhibit 4–14 gives the design team's estimated times for the seven tasks described (some done more than once), plus five more. Their estimate of 12 seconds for assembling the two nuts may be optimistic. They assume that bolts or nuts have special self-alignment features so threads will engage correctly and not bind or get cross-threaded.

The robot continues by inserting the spindle into one bracket hole and then moving the second bracket to receive the spindle. Since the robot has only one hand, it cannot hold the spindle and move the second bracket into place at the same time. It must move a fixture into place to hold up the spindle momentarily. Finally, the bracket is fastened down with washers and nuts.

The complete set of tasks includes insertions in several directions, which the team agrees would require an elaborate, costly robot. The total assembly time is 84 seconds, of which 86 percent is fastening. Of the 24 parts in the assembly, 20 are just for fastening. Are all those bolts, nuts, and washers really necessary? Perhaps not. But they are common and cheap, and assembly designers routinely choose such means of fastening.

Step 2: Simplified design. One way to simplify the design is to look for simpler ways to fasten the brackets. But why fasten them? Isn't it possible to make the brackets and base as one piece? The team believes it is. Their new design is shown in Exhibit 4–15. In that design, plastic inserts secure the spindle; both spindle and inserts may be assembled from above, which allows use of a simpler, cheaper type of robot with no special grippers or holding fixtures. There are only four parts, and a robot could assemble them in, say, 12 seconds. That improves output and productivity by 600 percent (from 43 to 300 assemblies per hour).

There may be better solutions. If specifications permit, the team realizes, the spindle could be made from material that will bend or flex. Then a two-piece design, as in Exhibit 4–16, will be possible. Now assembly consists of just one step and one motion: Snap spindle downward into place. The simplest of robots may be used.

Now, however, the design team has made assembly so simple that using a robot begins to seem excessive. If a robot were used, the parts would have to be presented to the robot on some sort of carrier—probably loaded by hand. Clearly it is just as easy—or even easier—to do the whole assembly by hand. Save the robot budget for tasks difficult for people.

*𝒫*RINCIPLE 8:

Automate incrementally when process variability cannot otherwise be reduced.

EXHIBIT 4–14   **Approximate Robotic Assembly Time—Bracket-and-Spindle Assembly**

Part	Repeats	Time(seconds)	Operation
Screw	4	12	Place in fixture
Washer	4	12	Place on screw
Base	1	3	Place on screws
Bracket	1	3	Position on base
Washer	2	6	Place on screw
Lock washer	2	6	Place on screw
Nut	2	12	Secure bracket (requires tool change)
Spindle	1	3	Insert one end in bracket (needs holding)
Bracket	1	3	Position on base and locate spindle
Washer	2	6	Place on screw
Lock washer	2	6	Place on screw
Nut	2	12	Secure bracket (requires tool change)
Totals	**24**	**84**	

EXHIBIT 4–15

One-Piece Base and Elimination of Fasteners

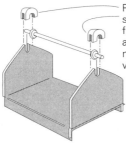

Plastic inserts allow spindle to be assembled from above. Integral base and brackets eliminate need for screws, washers, and nuts

EXHIBIT 4–16

Design for Push-and-Snap Assembly

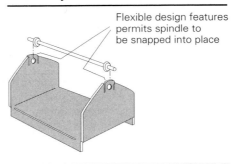

Flexible design features permits spindle to be snapped into place

Problem 3

Grittelbane Optics grinds special lenses for eyewear and for optical equipment used in medical and scientific laboratories. Almost without exception, the main grinder, an SL–54, gets out of alignment once during each standard five-day (40-hour) workweek. Grittelbane technicians call in a service representative from the manufacturer, SightLines, to realign the grinder, a tedious job that takes an average of four hours. Karl Grittelbane, company president, forecasts business growth and plans to purchase an additional grinder. His call to the sales V.P. (Vice President) at SightLines goes like this, "Except for the alignment problem, your grinder suits me just fine. I'd like to buy another SL–54; it would make my training and maintenance easier, but the downtime is killing me. I've got to look elsewhere if your designers can't come up with a fix . . . and soon." As SightLine's sales V.P., how should you respond?

Solution 3

First, whether or not Grittelbane is correct in blaming poor design, SightLine's design team ought to investigate. With access to Grittelbane's failure and repair records, the team can assess the magnitude of the downtime problem by computing availability. From these data, SightLines personnel find that MTBF = 5 days, and MTTR = 0.5, on average. Then from equation 4–2:

$$A = \frac{\text{MTBF}}{\text{MTBF} - \text{MTTR}} = \frac{5}{5.5} = 0.91$$

With just over 90-percent availability, Grittelbane will feel the loss of capacity—especially if the business is growing. The team *might* set an availability target (e.g., 98 percent or higher) for future redesign work on the SL–54, but there are other issues to address here.

First, Grittelbane needs some quick help. As a temporary fix until further investigation transpires, a preventive-maintenance program might be suggested, with weekly—or more frequently if needed—alignment performed during non–business hours. Meanwhile, the team should study the repair (realignment) process; maybe it can be streamlined, cutting the MTTR value. A permanent solution, however, requires that the cause of the out-of-alignment condition be identified and eliminated. That might involve grinder design changes, operator training (new procedures or manuals might be needed), and site visits to study the operating environment at Grittelbane. If poor design is the culprit, competitive analysis or benchmarking could be warranted. Clearly, this is a team task for SightLine and Grittelbane personnel.

Oh yes, the question about what the *sales V.P.* should do? . . . Write some soothing letters while the design team carries out the work? Not in today's competitive company! With sleeves rolled up, he or she will likely be an active member of the investigation team!

Problem 4

A value control assembly is part of a chemical company's process design for an upcoming plant addition; its rated MTBF is two years. Due to the inherently unstable nature of some of the chemicals the plant will process, equipment failure could be catastrophic. Typical of process industry operations, long periods of sustained flow—several months to a year, perhaps—will be the norm. As one of the design team's representatives from plant operations, you and fellow team members will evaluate the reliability of the value control assembly and report back to the team.

Solution 4

You know that the control assembly reliability at two years, the MTBF, is about 0.368; an unacceptably low figure in your judgment. Perhaps you perform a quick reliability calculation for the one-year point, given the duration of some of the plant's processing runs. First, the failure rate (assumed constant) using *year* as the unit of time:

$$\lambda = \frac{1}{\mu} = \frac{1}{2} = 0.5 \text{ failures/yr.}$$

Then, from equation 4–1, the reliability at the one-year point is:

$$R = e^{-(\lambda)(t)} = e^{-(0.5 \text{ failures/yr.})(1 \text{ yr.})} = e^{-0.5} = 0.607$$

The low reliability figure suggests that a more robust process design is needed. One option is to select control assemblies that have higher reliability (i.e., longer MTBF ratings), *if they are available*. Another possibility is to increase overall reliability through redundancy. For example, if two parallel control assemblies were employed, equation 4–3 is used to find reliability at the one-year point:

$$R = 1 - (1 - R_c)^2 = 1 - (1 - 0.607)^2 \approx 0.85$$

where R_c is the reliability of one control assembly after one year. For three control assemblies in parallel, the reliability—again at the one-year point—is:

$$R = 1 - (1 - R_c)^3 = 1 - (0.393)^3 \approx 0.94$$

You and your colleagues might present to the team a full set of reliability decay curves (similar to those found in Exhibit 4–11) for these and other options, but perhaps it's time to look at cost figures, or maybe brainstorm or benchmark for other ways to control chemical flow.

Review Questions

1. How might design of a company's products and transformation processes affect its competitiveness?
2. Explain why design is the first step in quality.
3. How might financial commitment to R&D be measured?
4. Contrast traditional company commitments to product design versus process design.
5. What are the effects of being late to market? What can design teams do about it? Explain.
6. What principles of operations management help prevent the "over the wall" problem in design?
7. Should design teams interact with suppliers? Why or why not?
8. Design teams should begin with function and follow with form. What is meant by that statement?
9. Draw and explain a process map—"boxes" connected with arrows—of the steps for creating a comprehensive design program.
10. What is a design concept? How does a concept differ from an idea or plan?
11. What role does competitive analysis play in comprehensive design programs?
12. What is concurrent design? What are its advantages?
13. What is industrial design? In what areas might industrial designers be expected to contribute to the design team?
14. What can design teams do to protect the environment?
15. What is universal design? How can it affect marketing? Operations? Costs?
16. Where does the information come from for use in a quality function deployment matrix? Why is the matrix called a house of quality?
17. What effect has the quality movement had on the number and variety of "DFX" guidelines? Explain.
18. Explain the meaning of *design to target costs*.
19. What is the effect of ambiguous specifications on quality?
20. When designers create multiuse or multifunctional components or procedures, how are they helping their associates in operations? In marketing?
21. Why should design teams avoid special fasteners? Fragile designs?
22. Designing for layered assembly in manufacturing is like what in services? Explain with an example.
23. Define *reliability, serviceability,* and *availability.* What measurable design characteristics might teams use to improve these properties? Explain.
24. Identify two ways design teams might improve the reliability of a product. A service process?
25. When processes are being redesigned for automation, they are typically streamlined. What ancillary benefit often flows from this streamlining? Explain.
26. Cite ways in which design review and appraisal procedures are changing. Explain.
27. Which principles of OM are especially relevant to design? Why?

1. Shrinking product life cycles are sometimes leading to premature conclusions about shifting customer demand patterns, thus breeding "design nervousness." Is there a practical limit on how short product life cycles should go? Support your answer with examples.

2. Download the most recent copy of *Business Week's* annual R&D scorecard from the Internet; it is published in June or July for the preceding year. For one of the industry classifications, prepare a table similar to Exhibit 4–3. Decide which companies are best at R&D and tell why you think so.

3. For two of the following McDonald's end products and components, find out who the principle designers/developers were and how the developments took place: sauces for Chicken McNuggets, special chicken for McNuggets, fish sandwich, Egg McMuffin. How does McDonald's deal with the quality of ingredients?

4. A chess clock shown in the accompanying illustration is housed in a molded plastic case that is closed up in the rear with two flat plastic square plates. (Chess clocks contain two identical clocks, one for each player in a timed chess game.) The three pieces are represented below, along with a sample of the special screw that goes into the eight drilled holes that fasten the clocks to the square plates. (Two other holes in the case and four holes and two half-moons in the squares are for clock adjustment. For purposes of this question, ignore them.)

   Suggest two practical design improvements based on the guidelines in Exhibit 4–8. (Mention the specific guidelines you are using as the basis for your suggestions.)

   Chess clock

   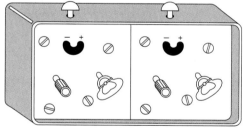

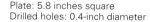
Plate: 5.8 inches square
Drilled holes: 0.4-inch diameter

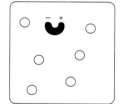

0.3 Inch

Screw specifications:
- Brass
- Flat head with slot
- Threaded on inside

5. Following are passages from an article on IBM's typewriter and keyboard factory:

   In the IBM Selectric System/2000 Typewriter, the new products are made with a layered design. The parts go together sequentially in one direction—from the bottom up—so that robots can do the job easily. There are many common fasteners [a limited number of different kinds], and nearly all screws were eliminated. Plastic molding offered many possibilities for more manufacturable designs.

   Detailed parts were combined wherever possible. Self-alignment reference points were designed for locating such things as posts and countersinks. Since robots are not efficient at finding a plug at the end of a wire, integrated packaging and solid connectors had to be used.

The changes resulted in fewer parts and fewer adjustments. There are about 900 parts in the new typewriters, compared with 2,700 in the Selectric typewriter. The number of adjustments needed is down to 6 from 121 originally.[26]

The above description indicates use of some of the 10 guidelines for effective design listed in Exhibit 4–8. Which of these guidelines can you identify in the passage? Give brief explanations where required.

6. Faceplates that cover electrical wall outlets and wall switches fasten with one or two screws. Suggest a modification that would eliminate the need for screws. Would the benefits be significant? Explain. Can you offer any arguments against redesign to eliminate screws?

7. Play the role of dietitian, fashion designer, architect, or financial portfolio designer. Describe the problems you can avoid with the proper degree of interaction with your suppliers.

8. At Monitor Manufacturing Company, product development engineers operate under a strict policy of frequent interaction with customers to ensure that designs match customer requirements. Still, customers view Monitor's designs as only average. What can the problem be?

9. When Mazda first came out with a rotary (Wankel) engine, there were serious performance problems. The public virtually quit buying the car, and Mazda's existence was threatened. Survival measures included sending design engineers all over Japan to sell cars. Besides cutting costs, what design engineering problem would this practice have helped deal with?

10. (Group exercise) UPS, based in Greenwich, Connecticut, announced in late 1994 that it was converting 500 of the 888 delivery trucks operating in Connecticut to operate on compressed natural gas (CNG). The reason? The state had recently decided to allow 50 percent of the investment in alternative fueled vehicles to be written off of corporate taxes and to exempt clean-running vehicles from the 31-cent/gallon state gasoline tax.

   As a group, brainstorm to identify a list of design factors that UPS, its suppliers, customers, and other stakeholders might need to consider in such a conversion program. [Hint: Don't limit your thinking to changes on the vehicles.]

11. (Group Exercises) Sony Corporation's 1.5-million-square-foot TV assembly plant in San Diego used to receive cathode ray tubes (CRTs) in cardboard boxes; after the tubes were removed, the boxes were destined for the trash bin. In the mid–1990s, a design team developed alternative packaging for tube transport—a collapsible wire basket that could be stacked and returned to the CRT supplier. John Pion, Sony's director of purchasing, says, "The [design] program was driven not only by environmental consideration, but there was approximately a 2 percent cost reduction in the piece price when all costs are included. We've been able to eliminate 1,700,000 pounds of materials from the waste stream according to this year's [1994] figures." Also, the plant's annual savings in disposal costs is around $300,000.[27]

   Your group has three tasks:

   a. Decide whether the basket design represents a product or process design change. Be prepared to present your reasoning.

   b. Prepare a list of the functional activities (at Sony and other organizations) that would most likely have input on, or be affected by, the packaging design change. Should all of these parties be on the design team? Explain your logic.

  c. Could reusable packaging (e.g., wire or plastic baskets or crates) be used on most or all large home appliances throughout the production, distribution, and retailing cycle—with the end consumer returning the packaging? Prepare a list of the product and process design considerations that would need to be faced.

12. Tokyo Seating Company operates TRI-CON, a subsidiary manufacturing division in the United States. Some years ago, TRI-CON asked an American metal products company to bid on a contract to provide TRI-CON with metal seat pans for motorcycle seats. TRI-CON's request for proposal specified a steel gauge and little else. The American firm was uncomfortable with TRI-CON's minimal specifications and refused to bid. Why would TRI-CON say so little about the kind of seat pan it wanted?

13. Team or individual assignment: A partial QFD matrix is given below for a fast-food hamburger container. Your assignment is (*a*) to add the house of quality's roof, (*b*) collect real data from two fast-food hamburger restaurants and use it to complete the QFD matrix, and (*c*) draw conclusions about the excellence of the two containers.

	How			
	Design of container	Ergonomics	Insulation	Biodegradability
Hold the heat				
Container appeal				
Ease of opening/use				
Environmentally sound				

(What is labeled to the left of the rows.)

14. According to one report, Japanese automakers are talking about building networks of small market-driven factories that will allow fabrication of a car from just 37 snap-together parts. Each such factory would economically produce about 10,000 autos a year, versus a typical break-even volume of over 200,000 in today's auto plants.

    To make this prediction a reality, name and discuss the five most important design principles and guidelines that would need to be employed.

15. From your own experiences, give, and explain, an example of (*a*) robust design of a service (to reduce chances of misperformance), (*b*) design of a service to reduce or eliminate backtracking and return visits, and (*c*) easily plugged-in service modules.

16. From your own experience, give three examples of reducing the number of operations (service steps). Explain.

17. Which of the following is best suited for robotic assembly: (*a*) assembling a clock consisting of a frame, faceplate, mechanism, backplate, and three screws; or (*b*) assembling a clock into a plastic box, which requires inserting a bottom liner

into the bottom box piece, placing an instruction card, clock, and top liner on top, and snapping the top box piece downward to engage with the bottom piece? Explain.

18. A security system timer controls lights, and other electrical components. The MTBF for the timer is advertised to be 2,000 hours. When should the operator or maintenance associate consider replacing the timer? Discuss your recommendations.

19. Equation 4–2 defined availability in terms of mean time between failure (MTBF) and mean time to repair (MTTR). To what extent are design teams responsible for these two parameters? To what extent are front-liners and maintenance associates responsible?

20. A control valve for a fuel supply system has an average failure rate of one failure per two years. Suppose the fuel supply system is to be used on an upcoming space mission that will last two weeks.

    a. Is this part of the vehicle safe enough? (Calculate value of reliability at mission end.)

    b. What might be done to improve reliability of this, or any other, component?

21. A design team at a test equipment provider has the following problem: A (potential) new customer wants the availability of any new computer testing units to be at least 0.99; that is a target for the team. Team members (maintenance personnel and the customer's operators) argue that, because of the need to recalibrate, a realistic figure for average repair time (should a breakdown occur in a test unit) is one hour. What options are open to the team?

22. A furnace thermostat has a constant failure rate of one failure per 36 months, and a mean time to repair of two hours.

    a. What is the thermostat reliability after 12 months? After 24 months? After 36 months?

    b. What is the availability?

    c. Should a design team try to streamline the repair process to reduce the MTTR? Explain.

23. A rechargeable electric razor battery provides an average of 45 minutes *of operating time* before the razor's recharge warning light flashes. It takes an average of three hours for the battery to fully recharge. Is it appropriate to compute the razor's availability with Equation 4–2? Why or why not?

24. A coolant line sensor has a reliability of 0.92 after one year of operation. What would the reliability be at the one-year point if

    a. Two of the sensors were used in a parallel configuration?

    b. Three of the sensors were used in a parallel configuration?

25. The photocopying machine in the management department at Acme University is in nearly constant use. But, breakdowns are frequent, and repairs typically consume a half-day or more. Professors, teaching assistants, secretaries, and student office assistants are starting to grumble, so the department chair promises to find the funds for a new machine. Professor Brown says the new copier ought to have a very high mean time between failures. Professor Green—who disagrees with Professor Brown on just about every topic—argues that a low mean time to repair is more essential. The department chair invites you for coffee and poses the question, "Who is correct, Brown or Green? And, oh yes, please tell me why."

For Further Reference

Barker, Thomas B. *Engineering Quality by Design.* Marcel Dekker, Inc., 1990 [TS156.B3748].

Boothroyd, Geoffrey, and Peter Dewhurst. *Product Design for Assembly.* Wakefield, R. I.: Boothroyd Dewhurst, Inc., 1987.

Burgelman, Robert A.; Modesto A. Maidique; and Steven C. Wheelwright. *Strategic Management of Technology and Innovation.* 2nd ed. Burr Ridge, Ill.: Richard D. Irwin, Inc., 1996 [HD45.B799].

Clark, Kim B., and Steven C. Wheelwright. *Managing New Product and Process Development.* New York: The Free Press, 1993 [HG5415.153.C58].

Crawford, C. Merle. *New Products Management.* 4th ed. Burr Ridge, Ill.: Richard D. Irwin, Inc., 1994 [HF5415.153.C72].

Graedel, T. E. and B. R. Allenby. *Industrial Ecology.* Englewood Cliffs, N.J.: Prentice-Hall, 1995 [TS149.G625].

King, Bob. *Better Designs in Half the Time: Implementing QFD Quality Function Deployment in America.* Methuen, Mass.: Goal/QPC, 1987.

Roy, Ranjit. *A Primer on the Taguchi Method.* New York: Van Nostrand Reinhold, 1990 [TS156.R69].

Schonberger, Richard J. *Building a Chain of Customers: Linking Business Functions to Create the World-Class Company.* New York: The Free Press, 1990 [HD58.9.S36]. See especially Chapter 10, "World-Class Product Development."

Ulrich, Karl T., and Steven D. Eppinger. *Product Design and Development.* New York: McGraw-Hill, Inc., 1995 [HD31.U47].

Wheelwright, Steven C. and Kim B. Clark. *Revolutionizing Product Development: Quantum Leaps in Speed, Efficiency, and Quality.* New York: The Free Press, 1992 [HF5415.153.W44].

Zangwill, Willard I. *Lightning Strategies for Innovation: How the World's Best Firms Create New Products.* New York: Lexington Books, 1993 [HF5415.153.Z36].

C　　H　　A　　P　　T　　E　　R

5　Quality Control and Process Improvement

Chapter Outline

Quality Improvement—At the Source
Quality Improvement in Action
Quality as a Specialty
Inspection
Time–Quality Connection

The Process Focus
Process Description and Performance
Process Output and Quality Characteristics

Process Improvement Overview

Coarse-Grained Analysis and Improvement
Process Flowchart
Check Sheet and Histogram
Pareto Analysis
Fishbone Chart

Fine-Grained Analysis and Improvement
Fail-Safing
Design of Experiments (DOE)
Scatter Diagram and Correlation
Run Diagram
Process Control Charts

Process Capability Analysis
Process Capability Graph
C_{pk} Computation
Variation Stackup

Process Improvement in Perspective

Case Study: Quadruples Restaurant

Quality Digest (to Richard L. Chitty, vice president of parts, service, and customer satisfaction for Lexus, the luxury car division of Toyota Motor Sales, U.S.A.): How do you identify and deal with process problems in a service environment?
Chitty: We developed Lexus service by flowcharting everything. . . This forms the basis for our service training. If some problem occurs, you go back and look at the flowchart and say, OK, here's our problem. [For example,] normally, if a customer has a tire problem, they go to the Goodyear or the Firestone store. But Lexus doesn't want that. We want customers to come back to us. That was the problem we identified. The next step was to map out the process. We flowcharted it. We examined the process, took the emotions out of it, determined the right thing to do, and then got the vendor in and figured out a system to deal with the issue.[1]

Quality doesn't happen by itself. It takes know-how, plus a few tools—such as flowcharting, as the Lexus service example points out. Flowcharts and the other tools of quality control and process improvement are simple, yet powerful. They are easily taught and ready-made for infusing a quality imperative into the work lives of every employee. The basic approach is to eliminate root causes of poor quality by focusing on the processes in addition to the products themselves. We begin with a few broad issues: the cycle of improvement, quality as a profession, the role of inspection, and how time and quality interrelate.

Quality Improvement—At the Source

A. V. Feigenbaum wrote, in his milestone book, *Total Quality Control,* that the burden of proof rests with the maker of the part, not with inspectors.[2] Businesses have extended the idea and made it action oriented. The *primary responsibility* for quality rests with the front-line producers or servers. Their responsibility extends from participating in teams for product and service design all the way through the transformation processes.

Quality Improvement in Action

The cycle of improvement, shown in Exhibit 5–1, is a repeating design-discover-improve sequence. Front-line associates become involved in the design and the improvement phases. In between are the failures: defects discovered by colleagues in a later process in the same organization, by next-company users, or by the final customer. A full description of the cycle follows:

Design.   The first two steps build quality into the process or stop a wayward process in its tracks.

1. Design a capable, fail-safe process. The best approach is prevention. In the first place, design a capable process. **Process capability** means capable of meeting customer requirements or specifications. Since no design is perfect, add back-up protection: fail-safe devices or procedures. The aim of **fail-safing** is to equip a process with features that prevent a mishap from going forward or even happening at all. For example, an invoice-payment computer routine won't write a check for an out-of-bounds amount.

    Some companies refer to fail-safing by its Japanese name, pokayoke.

2. If the process is not fail-safe, the next best response is self-inspection and correction. This requires shifts in responsibility: Each associate receives authority to correct a problem, such as placating an angry customer, on the spot, or to stop operations, even a whole production line, to avoid making bad products. And every work group takes responsibility for correcting its own mishaps; no passing problems on to a separate complaint or rework department.

Detection.

3. When the process cannot be fully controlled, we are pushed into the poor practice of inspection and discovery at a later stage (dark, shaded zone in Exhibit 5–1). Delayed detection is costly and damaging to reputations. Quick-as-possible feedback provides some damage control. The early-warning system should provide specific feedback from all subsequent

EXHIBIT 5–1

Quality Action Cycle

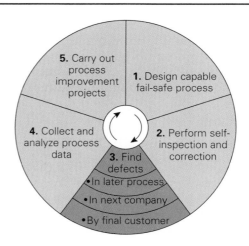

error discovery points: in a later process in the same organization, within the next company, and by the final customer.

$\mathscr{P}$RINCIPLES 2
AND 14:

Dedicate to continuous improvement. Involve front-line associates in problem solving.

Improvement.   Process improvement requires collection and use of data about process problems:

4. Collecting process data cannot be a random effort. Supervisors and operators need training in how to measure quality, collect quality data, and analyze quality statistics in order to isolate root causes.

5. The collected data become the raw material for problem solving. Process improvement teams analyze the data and attack the problems. Improvement projects aim at making deficient processes capable and fail-safe, and the quality action cycle begins again.

Quality as a Specialty

With a quality-at-the-source mindset and front-line associates assuming primary responsibility for quality, is there still a need for a quality assurance (QA) department? Usually there is, except in very small organizations. However, the quality movement changes the role of that department.

Exhibit 5–2 notes the changes, which are toward greater professionalism and heightened responsibilities for quality professionals. They plan, report, audit, coordinate, train, consult, and develop new methodologies for quality. In applying their unique expertise to a wider array of quality problems, their jobs are enriched. Instead of merely inspecting someone else's work, they audit entire quality-assurance systems. Last in the exhibit, they help with the transition of various quality-assurance activities to the source. Noted quality authority Frank Gryna explains: "By far the best way to implement quality methods is through line organizations rather than through a staff quality department. Isn't it a shame that it took us so long to understand this point?"[3]

Kelly Air Force Base, San Antonio, Texas, is making the transition. One hundred seventy-one teams were formed to focus on quality improvement. According

- Companywide quality planning.
- Generating executive reports on quality.
- Auditing outgoing quality.
- Auditing quality practices.
- Coordinating and assisting on improvement projects.
- Training for quality.
- Consulting for quality.
- Developing new quality methodologies.
- Transferring activities to line departments.

Source: Adapted from Frank M. Gryna, "The Quality Director of the '90s." *Quality Progress,* April 1991, p. 37.

EXHIBIT 5–2
The Quality Department: Emerging Roles

to Rodney House, assistant to the base commander, "Inspection has always been a separate operation by certified personnel. We are now trending toward production workers doing their own inspection and we will certify a limited number of them for it."[4] Many businesses and the general public, however, are confused about inspectors and inspection—as we note next.

Inspection

Surely you have seen the TV ad of the inspector in the white smock at the end of the production line saying something like, "I do a complete inspection of every [pair of jeans, telephone set, etc.]. Nothing goes out of here without my stamp of approval on it. You can count on it!"

But we cannot count on it. Inspection is the least effective way to control quality. As Exhibit 5–1 shows, we try first to design quality into the process. We want to handle remaining defectives and process variation through process improvement. Still, what do you do when design and improvement are weak? You rely on inspection. The modified quality action cycle, with a much enlarged detection zone, is shown below.

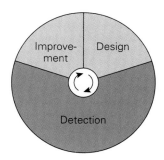

The following are some situations where inspection is likely or necessary:

- To enter an airport concourse, everyone and their hand-carried items goes through security X-ray screening.
- An important potentate is on somebody's death list. Someone inspects (taste-tests?) every item of food served to this VIP.

Contrast

Quality-Assurance Staff

Inspected-In Quality

Quality professionals and inspectors were responsible for quality.

There were never enough inspectors, so:

- Parts sat around for days waiting to be declared good or bad.
- Clients had to wait for an inspector to approve a service (e.g., authorize payment on a check) or review paperwork.

Built-In Quality

Front-line associates are responsible for their own process integrity and output quality.

Quality professionals serve as expert back-up to line people, giving advice on improvement projects, training, and other quality assurance support.

Inspectors are reassigned and carry their expertise into other line and staff work.

- A process for handling nuclear materials is fully capable and under strict process control. Still, to be doubly safe, regulations require inspection.
- The quality- and process-control situation for a brand new supplier are unknown. It's prudent to inspect the incoming products.
- One of your own processes varies wildly. It's prudent to inspect the output.

Thus, even though quality by design and by improvement is much preferred, inspection cannot be eliminated. The following are five approaches to inspection, all of which aim at catching mishaps efficiently.

Opinion surveys. Service clients fill out a form or answer questions about quality of a service. Open-ended questions require judgmental review; answers on, say, a seven-point numeric scale may be reduced to service-quality statistics. Willingness of clients to participate affects survey reliability.

100-percent inspection. An associate checks every unit, typically for highly critical quality characteristics, for new suppliers, and for new designs. This approach is subject to inspection errors and fatigue unless automated.

First-article inspection. In low-volume operations, after the process is set up, the operator checks the first unit; if the unit is good, the process is thought to be set up right so that it will produce good units. A better approach is for the operator to do a first- and last-article inspection; if the first and last units are good, probably the process did not change and the intervening units are good.

Destructive testing. The associate tests an item by destroying it (e.g., running a car into a wall to see how the bumper holds up); destructive testing necessarily is done on a sampling basis.

Acceptance sampling. Based on statistical sampling tables, the associate checks a random or stratified sample from a larger lot. If the sample is within the acceptable quality level (AQL), the lot passes inspection. A bad lot receives a 100-percent rectifying inspection, and bad units are replaced with good ones.

Acceptance sampling should not be confused with **statistical process control (SPC).** Both are statistical and both date back to work at Western Electric in the

1920s and 1930s. Drs. W. Edwards Deming and Joseph M. Juran were among the experts in the employ of that company who were in on development of both acceptance sampling and SPC. The big difference is that SPC occurs during the process—in time to prevent defects—whereas acceptance sampling merely detects some problem output—after it has been created. As in most things, we prefer prevention to detection.

While many organizations have not made the transition from detection to prevention, many others have. Usually the prevention of quality deficiencies is part of a large package of improvements and waste elimination. Two examples follow:

- *Jostens Diplomas, Red Wing, Minnesota, a printer of graduation diplomas.* This business unit of Jostens (which also is the leading cap-and-gown and class-ring maker) transferred 45 inspectors from an end-of-line inspection department into positions side by side with printing associates. At the same time, four of six personal computers were moved to the production floor for immediate processing of corrections, cross-training and skills certification programs were established, and cycle times fell from nearly four or five weeks to 24 hours.
- *AMPEX, Colorado Springs, Colorado, a producer of high-end recording products.* This AMPEX facility reduced its number of inspectors from 100 to zero. This improvement was part of a broad package of improvements: Cycle time for one recorder was reduced from 120 days to 18 days, flow distance from a mile to 150 feet, annual scrap and rework from $9.7 million to $1.1 million, and setup time on a key machine from eight hours to 30 minutes. At the same time, yearly training per person was raised from about 6 hours to 20 hours, and operators began ordering material directly from suppliers without the need to go through the purchasing department.[5]

PRINCIPLE 11

Cut flow time and distance.

Time–Quality Connection

As the Jostens and AMPEX examples suggest, improvements in quality, time (speed), plus other factors often go together. Sometimes, in fact, our definition of quality *is* time: That is the case when we stand, fidgeting impatiently, in long lines waiting for service. Usually, however, the time–quality connection is more subtle than that. As Robert Galvin, former CEO of Motorola, put it, "One can focus on time and improve quality" and "one can focus on quality and accomplish time."[6] The following points explain this apparent contradiction:

- *Quick response.* Improving quality eliminates delays for rework, process adjustments, and placating customers, thus providing quick response for a greater percentage of customers.
- *On-time.* Quality the first time—every time—removes a major cause of delays, late completions, and unpredictability, thereby improving on-time performance.
- *Quick feedback.* All efforts to cut out delays (the whole just-in-time, or quick-response, agenda) provide quicker feedback on causes of bad quality, allowing earlier process improvement efforts. To quote from Western Electric's classic handbook on quality control, "It is an axiom in quality control that the time to identify assignable causes is while those causes are active," and further, "delay may mean that the cause of trouble

$\mathscr{P}$RINCIPLE 10:

Make quality easy to achieve.
Get to know the competition.

is harder to identify, and in many cases cannot be identified at all."[7] In other words, anything that reduces delays is a powerful technique for process quality improvement.

- *Enough time for quality.* The time saved by removing delays and making quality right must not be squandered. It needs to be reinvested in training, design collaboration, inspection and on-the-spot correction, feedback and consultation with people in earlier and later processes, data collection, and improvement projects. If those activities are neglected, for example, under pressure for more output, quality suffers, and a chain reaction of delays and variations results in *less* output and *slower* response.

These interlinkages—time, quality, and problems in general—suggest that improvement should be looked at broadly. Discussion through the rest of the chapter follows through with that idea in mind.

The Process Focus

Dr. Lucian L. Leape of the Harvard School of Public Health says, "If an airplane goes down, we don't sue the pilot, we sue the airline. When a patient is injured, we sue the doctor."

But it's not the doctor's fault. It's the whole process in the hospital. That is the conclusion of a research team headed by Leape. They studied causes of mistakes that put patients at risk in two Boston hospitals. The team's data convinced Leape: "Most preventable injuries are not due to just one system failure but result from breakdown at several points in the system."[8]

And so it is in any other line of work. Recognition of the multiplicity of causes has led to today's strong belief in a process focus as the underpinning of total quality management. It's not the person, not the job, not the machine. It's the whole process.

Process Description and Performance

A process is what takes place during the transformation (which was part of our definition of the operations function in Chapter 1). It's time to look more closely at the transformation process and its multiple components. See Exhibit 5–3.

A **process** is the unique set of conditions (seven M's) that creates certain outcomes. Change a process (deliberately or accidentally) and different results (better or worse) are likely to occur. In many processes, not all of the M's are apparent. Some human services, for example, involve virtually no materials. In some cases, maintenance might be considered a part of methods. In other instances, people prefer to use category names that better fit their company or industry; *tooling* might be a category for a manufacturer, *packaging* for a warehouse, and *reservations system* for a resort. Whatever the category names, however, the aim is to understand processes in terms of all the variables that can affect process output.

Process components change over time: one data-entry person replaces another, materials come from a different supplier, a machine or its cutting tool is changed, a different maintenance schedule is started, and so on. This can result in constant process restabilization, with quality losses and costs each time.

TQM provides a better idea: Make process elements easily substitutable with no negative impact on process performance, thereby avoiding the burden of restabilization. Fail-safe designs, training for mastery of multiple jobs, supplier

Definition:	Process: A unique combination of elements, conditions, or causes that collectively produces a given outcome or set of results.
Composition:	Components of a process may be classified according to the "seven M's": Materials (raw materials, components, or documents awaiting processing). Manpower (the human factor; better yet, *people power*). Methods (product and process design and operating procedures). Machines (tools and equipment used in the process). Measurement (techniques and tools used to gather process performance data). Maintenance (the system for providing care for process components, including training of people). Management (policy, work rules, and environment).
Performance:	Process performance (output, intended or incidental) depends on how the process has been designed, built or installed, operated, and maintained.

EXHIBIT 5–3

A Transformation Process

certification, and standardization of equipment and tools are among the ways of pursuing that aim. While these improvements take time to implement and incur some cost, the results usually are long lasting. But how do we know whether a substitution has changed a process or not? We analyze the process output.

Process Output and Quality Characteristics

In the 1920s, Western Electric's Walter Shewhart and George Edwards pioneered the use of statistical analysis of process output data. They gave us the process control chart, discussed later in the chapter, and they showed what distributions of process output data reveal about how the process is working.

Though not all process output distributions are the same, we can gain insight from looking closer at a frequently occurring one. According to an American Society for Quality Control training manual:

> It has been well established that most machines and processes yield dimensions or other characteristics in the form of a normal curve [see Exhibit 5–4]. If a machine were set to turn a shaft with a target diameter of 6 cm, we know that all shafts would not be exactly the same. The precision of the machine would determine how close the variation could be held. From past experience we might know that the parts would fall in a distribution with *almost* 100 percent of the items being within ±0.12 cm of the mean value of the process output (here, equal to the target of 6.00 cm). Normal curve theory establishes that about 99.7 percent of the parts will fall within three standard deviations—3σ, or 3-sigma—of the mean. Here, three standard deviations equal 0.12 cm, thus one sigma equals 0.04 cm.[9]

Shaft diameter might be designated a **quality characteristic,** a performance output of a process that is of particular interest to a customer. If so, the maker would want to know more about the diameter's actual process output distribution. The distribution might be as shown in Exhibit 5–4. Note that the distribution is centered precisely at the target. While centering on target satisfies one aim, there still is output variation around the target to be concerned about.

Assignable and Common Causes.   Two kinds of variation affect every process output distribution. **Assignable-cause variation** is one kind. **Common-cause variation** is the other.

Imagine yourself driving down the highway trying to stay in your lane. The blowing wind, the crown of the road, and highway imperfections are some of the

−3σ	−2σ	−1σ	μ	+1σ	+2σ	+3σ
5.88 cm			6.00 cm			6.12 cm
			Target			

Source: Adapted from Ross Johnson and William O. Winchell, *Production and Quality* (Milwaukee: American Society for Quality Control Press, 1989), p.10.

Shewhart coined the term *assignable variation.* Deming, it is said, preferred to call it *special cause variation.* AT&T, where both men once worked, uses the term *unnatural variation.* All three terms refer to the same thing.

common causes of variation in your driving. Low tire pressure would be a special cause; fill the tire and the assignable variation goes away. Usually the operator can pinpoint such special causes; it doesn't require the skills of a quality scientist.

Common-cause variation is random and harder to trace. In driving, the multitude of small-chance fluctuations that occur are the source. The process as a whole is the likely culprit. Not being any individual's fault, common-cause reduction may require an administrative decision costing some money: Erect shelter belts of trees to dampen the wind; smooth the roadway.

Since less variability is a basic customer want, attacking the two types of variation is an excellent approach to process improvement. The general sequence is as follows:

1. Eliminate the special-cause variation by correcting the problems. When a process output distribution is free of all special-cause variation, that process is said to be in a state of **statistical control,** or simply in control. Removal of special causes results in a stable, predictable process output. A process that is in control still has common variation in its output, however.

2. Reduce that common variation. Required actions might include product or process redesign or some other substantial investment.

Any associate may employ this variation reduction sequence. The sequence gets best results, however, in the hands of a team of people representing elements of the whole process. The Into Practice box, Variation in the Campus Mails, illustrates.

Variables and Attributes.   Those studying variation need process output data, which come in two forms: variables data and attributes data. **Variables data** result from measuring or computing the amount of or value of a quality characteristic. The shaft diameter distribution of Exhibit 5–4, for example, would come from measuring shaft diameters. Variables data are continuous; any value within a given output range (5.88 cm to 6.12 cm for the shaft diameters) may occur. Other examples of outputs captured as variables data are packaged weights of foods, times required for county clerks to record documents, density of pollutants, brightness in an office, loudness at a rock concert, price-earnings ratios, and grade point averages.

Attributes data, the other type, are simpler than variables data. A measurement isn't required, just a classifying judgment: maybe yes-or-no for friendly service;

$\mathcal{I}$nto $\mathcal{P}$ractice

Variation in the Campus Mails

Statistician and quality expert George Box relates what a colleague told him. The secretary in the colleague's department said, "Don't ever circulate stuff through the campus mail. They take forever to get it delivered." But Box suggests that, if campus mail really is a problem, the best way to fix it is to make up a team of the department secretary, mail sorter, and mail deliverer. The team might find a special cause for the delay. On the other hand, it may want to design and recommend a new system that eliminates a number of common causes. For example, change the delivery routes, devise new mailing envelopes, or revise address designators.

Source: George Box, "When Murphy Speaks—Listen," *Quality Progress,* October 1989, pp. 79–84.

good-or-bad for a car wash; small, medium, and large for farm melons; or AAA, AA, or A for debt obligations in a portfolio. A battery tester with a red zone and a green zone provides an attributes check. Similarly, we test a night light by putting it into a socket and flipping the switch. It either lights or it doesn't. A table setting in a fancy restaurant may be checked by the head waiter. If one fork or glass is out of place, the headwaiter judges the table setting to be defective. Diameters of ball bearings could be checked by rolling them across a hole-filled surface. Those that fall through are too small; their diameters needn't be measured.

We see from these descriptions that variables data must be measured, whereas attributes data are usually counted. And while attributes data are easier to collect, variables data yield more information. Example 5–1, using variables data, presents some of the issues involved in studying a process.

EXAMPLE 5–1:   PROCESS FOCUS APPLIED

Consider a process for the production of bolts (see Exhibit 5–5). Components from each of the seven M's make up the process and create bolts with several quality characteristics. Customers would indicate the following:

1. *Quality characteristics important enough to receive close attention.* For a simple product like a machine bolt, customer-critical characteristics might be length, diameter, and thread depth; each would be represented by a frequency distribution. Here, we look at but one characteristic, bolt length.
2. *A desired value—and thus the maker's target—for each quality characteristic.* Here, assume customers have requested 3-inch-long bolts.

As Exhibit 5–5 shows, the output distribution of bolt lengths has a certain central tendency, or location, and an amount variation (dispersion). Studying the distribution is a simple, cheap, and effective method of understanding quite a bit about the process.

The distribution reveals two useful pieces of process output information: One is whether the process is centered on 3 inches, as the customer wants, or on the high or low side. The other is the amount of variation—the less of it the better. The bolt-making machinist knows that, as shown in Exhibit 5–5, the output of this process is the input to the next. Even if it is not a problem here, bolt-length variation may cause trouble at the next or any other downstream process.

Unfortunately, process output distributions are not always as stable as this bolt-length distribution appears to be; stability requires work. Suppose the machinist measures bolt

EXHIBIT 5–5

**The Process Focus:
Contributing
Variables and
Performance**

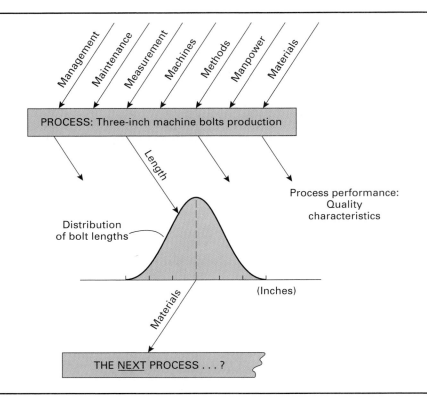

lengths every hour and finds them to be distributed as shown in the upper section of Exhibit 5–6, that is, centered around 2.9 inches for one hour, around 3.1 inches the next, back to 2.9, and so on. This odd pattern tells the machinist to look for a special cause for the hour-to-hour variation. It may be that the machinist had been switching methods of cutting the bolt bar-stock about every hour. Suspicion falls on cutting method as the special cause.

The machinist stops switching cutting methods and focuses on the method leading to bolts averaging about 2.9 inches. Exhibit 5–6B shows how this *new* process might appear. Continued measurement, say, for several hours, could convince the machinist that the special variation has been eliminated, resulting in a process that is in control. But process control is not enough. A larger issue remains: the bolts are still not meeting the target of 3 inches.

The machinist makes another process change: "I increased the feed of the bar-stock into the cutting tool by $\frac{1}{10}$ of an inch by moving a stop block. That got the process centered on target." The result, in Exhibit 5–6C, shows that the process is centered on target and stable across time. If there are no other special causes, the process is once again in control. Remember, the main benefit of statistical process control is predictability; as long as control is maintained, process output will be stable. Even better, however, the process now is in control and on target.

PRINCIPLE 10:

Eliminate process
variation.

The machinist in Example 5–1 dealt with two of the three main concerns in process analysis: achieving process control and getting the process on target. But, as is clear from Exhibit 5–6C, the process still exhibits variation in output. Process capability analysis attacks that common variation. We reserve that topic for later in the chapter.

EXHIBIT 5–6

Bolt Length Process Output

A. Two cutting methods

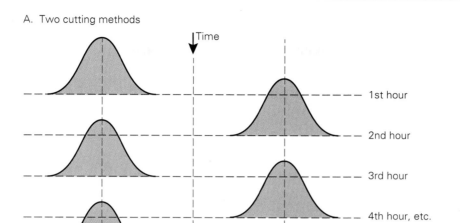

B. Single cutting method

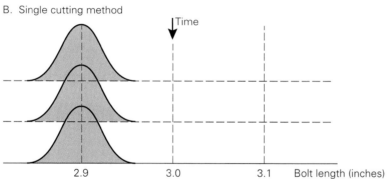

C. Single cutting method with bar-stock feed adjustment

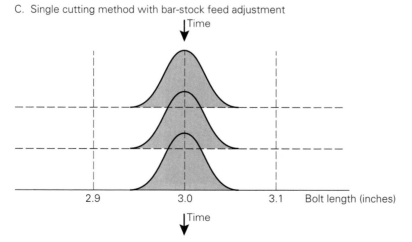

Also, the machinist followed a systematic approach: First, collect process output data and analyze it—what quality control people call listening to the process. Make a change if necessary, and then repeat. In the simple bolt-making example, one person achieved control and (some) improvement. Usually, problems are bigger, more ill-defined, and require the efforts of teams. We look now at a systematic approach to guide those efforts.

Process Improvement Overview

The systematic approach to process quality improvement follows the scientific method of investigation, familiar from physical or social science studies (see Exhibit 5–7). Briefly, the sequence is to find and study a problem, generate and evaluate possible solutions, implement and review the chosen solution, then repeat for a new problem.

The scientific method provides an overall plan of attack. But process improvement teams still need a set of tools to use at each step.

Exhibit 5–8 lists widely accepted tools for process improvement. The two in the general category require little explanation. Team building and group interaction tools, with deep roots in the social sciences, have a new home in team-based TQM. The specific process and technology tools relate or apply to a certain work specialty. They might include a computer spreadsheet, stethoscope, backhoe, accident claim form, customer satisfaction survey card, or coordinate measuring machine—anything that helps improve process output.

The four coarse-grained and five fine-grained tools are the basic techniques of quality science. A growing belief is that every employee should know and regularly use these tools—except for DOE, which requires special statistical analysis skills. Discussion of them makes up most of the remainder of the chapter.

EXHIBIT 5–7
Scientific Method for Process Improvement

1. Identify and define the problem.
2. Study the existing situation: collect necessary data.
3. Generate possible solution alternatives.
4. Evaluate alternatives and choose the preferred one.
5. Implement the improvement and measure results.
6. Evaluate and revise if required.
7. Otherwise, return to step 1 and start again with a new problem.

EXHIBIT 5–8
Tools for Process Improvement

General Tools	Coarse-Grained Tools	Fine-Grained Tools
1. Team-building and group-interaction tools.	3. Process flowchart.	7. Fail-safing.
2. Specific process/ technology tools.	4. Check sheets and histograms.	8. Design of experiments (DOE).
	5. Pareto analysis.	9. Scattergrams.
	6. Fishbone charts.	10. Run diagram.
		11. Process control chart

Coarse-Grained Analysis and Improvement

Tools 3 through 6 are a starting point for listening to the process: process flow-chart, check sheet and histogram, Pareto analysis, and fishbone chart. They help sift the data and point to the most promising targets for improvement. Sometimes these tools reveal the root causes clearly enough to make the solution apparent. Other times, they segregate the most promising target for further fine-grained analysis.

Process Flowchart

A flowchart gets the analysis started. It helps the team visualize the value chain. The **process flowchart** pictures the full process flow in all its complexity.

As they develop the flowchart, team members often are surprised by what they see. Someone might point out that certain sequences were put into effect years before under different conditions. The team may agree that whole sequences no longer are necessary or that certain steps should be eliminated, combined, or rearranged. While the process flowchart is nearly 100 years old, it has elevated stature today in helping identify process activities that add value and others that do not.

Exhibit 5–9 shows and describes widely used flowcharting symbols. Of the five, only the operation symbol denotes a **value-adding activity.** The other symbols reflect an addition of cost, not value. The symbols used in computer systems analysis, which are slightly different, can be used instead of or intermixed with these five. Any consistent set of symbols will work.

Exhibit 5–10 shows how an improvement team might document a company's travel authorization process. The before version, part A, has eight value-adding operations, five transportations, two inspections, and three delays. The stream-lined version in part B uses personal computer communication by E-mail. It cuts the operations to five, transports to two, inspections to one (combined with an operation), and delays to one. The reduction from eight to five operations does not mean less value, because value-adding operations also consume costly resources and time. The result is a simpler process that does the job.

Computer program flowcharts are another type. Their purpose is to provide documentation needed later on for program maintenance. Another term for process flowchart is *process map.*

○	**Operation**	Activity that adds value to a workpiece or provides a value-adding service to a customer; usually requires a setup.
⇨	**Transportation**	Movement of object from one work station to another; movement of customer from one operation to another.
□	**Inspection**	Work is checked for some characteristic of quality; may call for 100-percent inspection or inspection by sampling.
▽	**Storage**	Applies to materials or documents; may be temporary or permanent.
D	**Delay**	Time person, materials, or documents wait for next operation; in *lot* delay, wait is for other items in the lot to be processed; in *process* delay, entire lot waits for workstation or other bottleneck to clear.

EXHIBIT 5–9

Flow Chart Symbols

As with the other coarse-grained techniques, sometimes the flowchart alone tells the improvement team what it needs to know to complete the project. More often, the flowchart maps the process for further analysis.

Check Sheet and Histogram

A **check sheet** is the simplest of all the data collection tools. Just make a check mark each time the mishap occurs. One form of the check sheet has just a single category, such as "meeting started late today." Usually more useful is a multicategory version, which tracks occurrences of problems in more detail. The Into Practice box shows the advantage of more categories at Akron General Medical Center.

Exhibit 5–10 **Flowchart: Travel Authorization Process**

A. Original travel authorization process

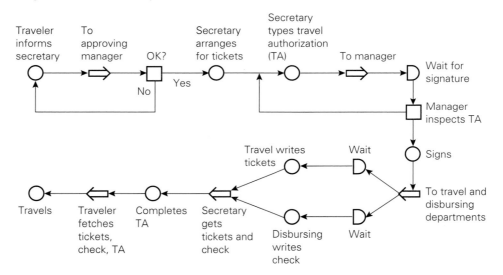

B. Improved travel authorization process — with e-mail

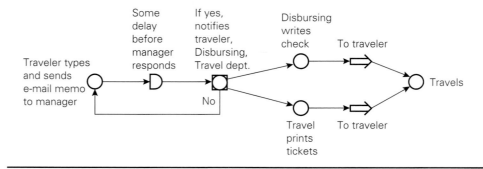

Source: Adapted from Dennis C. Kinlaw, *Continuous Improvement and Measurement for Total Quality* (Burr Ridge, Ill.: Business One Irwin, 1992), pp. 214–15.

Histograms offer another way to display frequency data. A histogram, which is more structured than a check sheet, has equal-interval numeric categories on the X-axis of an X-Y graph.

In the example of Exhibit 5–11, the X-axis is in 10-minute time intervals. The improvement team is tracking how long it takes for a hotel crew to do a typical ballroom conversion: Tear down a ballroom that has been set up for a conference, and reset it for a banquet. The histogram shows in some detail what the events department probably was concerned about: high variability, which makes it difficult for the sales people to schedule time for ballroom events. Since 9 of the 17 setups took 50 or more minutes, perhaps the improvement team will want to focus on those worst cases. One solution might be to increase the crew size for some of the more complex tear-down/setup cases.

Pareto Analysis

Pareto analysis helps separate the vital few from the trivial many. In process improvement, Pareto analysis proceeds as follows:

1. Identify the factors affecting process variability or product quality.

Into Practice

Check Sheet for Mishap Analysis at Akron General

Quality-data collection is an important first step to isolating root causes of medication errors, says Gayle Joiner. A quality management specialist at the 550-bed Akron General Medical Center, Joiner is also a member of Akron's improvement group and liaison team, comprising clinical nursing and pharmacy staff. The team first began looking at medication errors in 1992. They discovered a variety of systemic problems, including inadequate reporting on the type and severity of errors.

The team's original data collection method provided enough data to plot trends, says Joiner, but it was too vague to be useful for action planning and intervention. For instance, one of the check-boxes on the original form simply said, "Incorrect dose."

The team revised the check sheet to include four subcategories under that heading. They included the following: "Incorrect dose dispensed from pharmacy," "Verbal order taken incorrectly," "Incorrect dose ordered," and "Dosage calculation error." See sample below.

With the new form and more-specific data, the team reduced medication errors by 30 percent. In addition, the information provides useful material for training and orienting new staff.

Source: Adapted from "Hospital Improves Reports," *Quality Digest, April 1995, p. 9.*

	Frequency of Occurrence			
	Week 1	*Week 2*	*Week 3*	*Week 4*
Incorrect dose dispensed from pharmacy	✓✓✓	✓✓	✓	✓✓✓✓
Verbal order taken incorrectly	✓		✓✓	✓
Incorrect dose ordered	✓✓	✓✓✓✓	✓	✓
Dosage calculation error		✓	✓	

2. Keep track of how often a measurable defect or nonconformity is related to each factor.

3. Plot the results on a bar chart, where length of a bar stands for (or is proportional to) the number of times the causal factor occurs. Position more serious causes (longest bars) to the left of less serious ones.

Exhibit 5–12 is a Pareto chart derived from study of the drive-through-window (DTW) operation at a Kentucky Fried Chicken (KFC) restaurant in Oklahoma City. In that region, KFC had been losing market share to other fast-food companies that had quicker DTW service. Special timers had collected the data. The Pareto highlights the main cause, window hang time, accounting for 58 percent of the total service time. Hang time is KFC jargon for how long a customer waits—"hangs"—at the window to receive the order, pay, and leave.[10]

Checksheets and Pareto analysis often preceed—and feed problem data to—fishbone analysis (see photo, Exhibit 5–13).

Fishbone Chart

The process analysis continued at KFC Oklahoma City. The team displayed causes and sub causes of service delay at DTW on a **fishbone chart,** so named because it looks like the skeleton of a fish. See Exhibit 5–14.

In fishbone analysis, the team works backwards from the target for improvement on the spine bone, identifying causes down through the **"bone structure."** The lowest level of detail (finest bones) may reveal root causes, which are worthy targets for further problem solving.

The KFC team set up its fishbone in a typical way: with four general categories—people, equipment, materials, and methods—main causes. (Purists prefer not to use

Giving an item the degree of attention it deserves has been called the principle of parsimony (parsimony means frugality). The more general principle, widely applicable in society, is the Pareto principle, named after economist Vilfredo Pareto (1848–1923). His observation that most of the wealth is in the hands of a small percentage of the population makes it simple (frugal) to study wealth by studying just the wealthy.

EXHIBIT 5–11

Histogram: Ballroom Setup Time Requirements

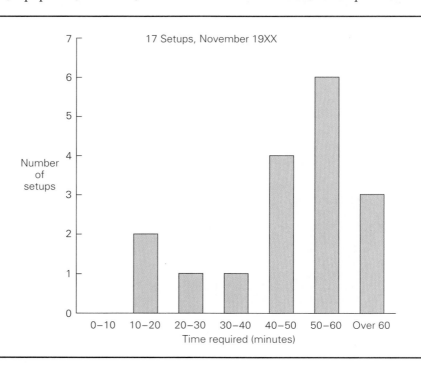

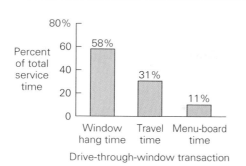

Source: Reprinted by permission, Uday M. Apte and Charles C. Reynolds, "Quality Management at Kentucky Fried Chicken," *Interfaces* 25, No. 3, May–June 1995, pp. 6–21, the Institute for Operations Research and the Management Sciences, 290 Westminster Street, Providence, RI 02903.

EXHIBIT 5–12

Pareto Chart: DTW Time

Improvement team member at Atlanta's West Paces Ferry Hospital leads team developing a fishbone chart, while another member updates a Pareto chart labeled "Causes of Delay."

EXHIBIT 5–13

Process Improvement Team in Action

these general categories. Instead they would look for case-specific main causes, such as "behind-counter confusion," "customer confusion," and "conflicts with KFC corporate standards.")

The team's next step was to return to check-sheet data. It found three of the root causes to be the most frequent and highest-impact problems. The three, designated with asterisks are "No headsets and headsets not working," "Poor equipment lay-out," and "Out of product." The following are among the team's improvements on these three problems:

- Instituted a procedure for regular testing of all headsets, and stockpiled supplies of headset batteries and replacement belts.

*P*RINCIPLE 2:

Dedicate to continual improvement.

EXHIBIT 5–14

Fishbone Chart: Service Delays at KFC

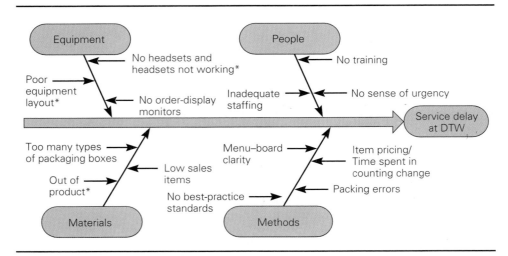

*Most frequent problems/highest impact.

Source: Reprinted by permission, Uday M. Apte and Charles C. Reynolds, "Quality Management at Kentucky Fried Chicken," *Interfaces* 25, No. 3, May–June 1995, pp. 6–21, The Institute for Operations Research and the Management Sciences, 290 Westminster Street, Providence, RI 02903.

- Rearranged the packing area, cutting the number of steps a packer had to move from six to two.
- Eliminated certain slow-selling products and replaced multiple desserts with a single dessert item.[11]

Fine-Grained Analysis and Improvement

We have just seen examples of how the coarse-grained tools can sometimes lead to solutions—without further, more-detailed study. It's like the apple that fell on Sir Isaac Newton's head. He deduced the gravity concept from the coarse-level "analysis."

The five more refined analysis tools from Exhibit 5–8 study one quality characteristic at a time. The purpose might be to further test a good idea, such as Newton's. More often, it is to impose a control on a varying quality characteristic or to find a solution that so far has been elusive. Fail-safing has the latter purpose.

Fail-Safing

The KFC example furnished us with one example of fail-safing: Eliminating multiple desserts makes it impossible for order takers or packers to make wrong-dessert mistakes. A common fail-safing example for suppliers of boxes of parts is egg-crate box dividers so that only the correct number of parts—no more, no less—can be packed and sent to a user.

Unlike other tools of improvement, fail-safing does not rely on any particular sources of process data. Rather, it is a mind-set that can help direct associates, positively, toward a permanent if unrealizable process fix: Expand the improvement zone of the quality action cycle, and shrink the detection zone to nothing.

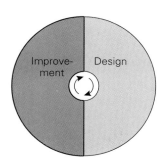

Quality action cycle. No detection zone since process is fail-safed.

Fail-safing is best applied at the root-cause level of analysis—for example, a third- or fourth-level sub-bone of a fishbone chart. It can prevent, for instance:

- Leaving out parts or steps.
- Fitting components or service elements together improperly.
- Failing to follow the right process sequence.
- Bad process result (e.g., the machine stops itself because of excess tool wear).
- Passing errors along to the next process (because the root cause has been found and eliminated).

Fail-safe devices may be as simple as templates, egg-crate dividers, velcro, glue, and paint, or as fancy as limit switches, electric eyes, scales, locks, probes, timers, and scopes. Exhibit 5–15 illustrates fail-safing achieved by painting a black surface white to prevent order fillers from leaving black disks in the previously all-black hoppers.

EXHIBIT 5–15

Fail-safing a Process at Microsoft-Ireland

Disk duplicating machines at Microsoft-Ireland. Production team painted black inside walls of take-up hoppers white, which fail-safed the process so that a black diskette would not be inadvertently left in the hopper and omitted from the order.

Fail-safing embraces a realistic view of people, processes, and errors. It recognizes that people need to be protected from their own naturally variable behaviors. To illustrate, imagine the thought process of packers at KFC-Oklahoma city—if they had been trained in the fail-safing concept:

First packer: Anybody is going to mess up and grab the wrong dessert once in a while—with all these dessert items to worry about.
Second packer. Yeah. Why don't we recommend cutting down to just the really popular desserts—or even just one of them. That'll fail-safe the task. No more blaming us—when the real root cause is too many desserts!

This is an excellent attitude—whether or not it is the right solution. If people are unaware that processes can and should be fail-safed, their tendency is to hide the mishap when it occurs to avoid the possibility of blame.

Design of Experiments (DOE)

Sometimes the improvement team is stumped: flowcharts, Pareto analyses, or fishbone charts have brought too many potential causes to the surface. The team asks, "Which are the *actual* causes?" It needs help from statisticians or engineers who are seasoned veterans in the art and science of experimentation.

As noted in Chapter 3, the early 1990s witnessed renewed interest in **design of experiments (DOE)** as the quality movement progressed. The intricacies of DOE, including the Taguchi short-cut methods, are beyond the scope of this discussion, but some comments about how to bring experimentation into the improvement process are in order. The best way is to have those with DOE expertise join process improvement teams as consultants. It is important that experts and front-line associates rub shoulders. Experts have much to learn about applications, and front-liners need to learn what they can about advanced methods. Cross-learning is the key to joint ownership of processes and results.

While not everyone should try to master DOE techniques, another experimental tool, the scatter diagram, is easy for everyone to learn and use.

The statistician may reply with a phrase popular in TQM: Torture the data and it will confess.

Scatter Diagram and Correlation

As used in TQM, a **scatter diagram** (scattergram for short) plots process output effects against experimental changes in process inputs. The correlation coefficient (discussed in Chapter 6) pins down the relationship in precise numeric terms. Usually, however, we can adequately estimate the strength of the association just by looking at the scattergram. Scatter diagrams are most useful for complex processes where cause–effect relationships are unclear.

Suppose that associates producing rubber inner tubes have noted wide variation in tube strength, as revealed by overfilling the tubes with air. They run an experiment seeking ways to reduce the variation. At the previous process in their work cell, in which formed tubes are cured in ovens, they vary the curing time. Next, they test the tubes, plot curing times against tube strength on a scatter diagram, and look for a correlation.

Exhibit 5–16 is the resulting scatter diagram. Each point represents one tube. Cure time is a point's horizontal location, and strength is its vertical location. The team's conclusions:

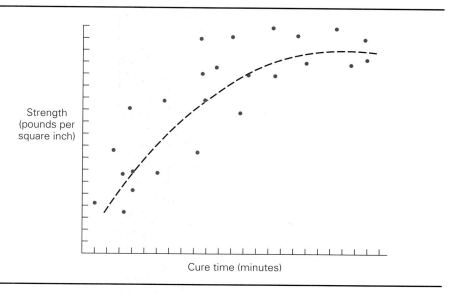

Exhibit 5–16

**Scatter Diagram—
Cure Time for
Inner Tubes**

1. Tube strength correlates well with cure time, as shown by a definite clustering of points about the curving line.
2. Tube strength increases with cure time up to a point, after which further cure time does no more good and may even be harmful.

Having found one source of variation, the team presses on, looking for other factors that might correlate with tube strength.

Run Diagram

When we aren't doing experiments or solving problems, what should we be doing—besides the task itself? Watching the process.

Here again we need tools. Relying on impressions won't do. The **run diagram** is the simplest of the process-monitoring tools.

A run diagram is simply a running plot of a certain measured quality characteristic. It could be number of minutes each successive airplane departs late. It might be number of customers visiting the complaint desk of a store each day. In these cases, the company might specify an upper limit, which would be plotted on the run diagram. Any point above the upper specification (spec) limit would be obvious—and perhaps grounds for taking some kind of action.

In other cases, there might be both an upper and a lower specification limit. Consider a plastic part made in an injection-molding process. It might be a component for a toy, a home appliance, or a consumer electronics product. The customer's specifications, probably stated in the purchase order or contract, are targets for the operation. Example 5–2 shows how the run diagram works.

In injection molding, hot, liquid plastic is injected into a mold containing one or more cavities in the desired shape of parts. The plastic cools and hardens forming the part.

Example 5–2:   Run Diagram—Injection-Molded Parts

Part: Round plastic part with a target (nominal) diameter of 5.00 cm
Specification (tolerance band): 5.00 ± 0.05 cm

EXHIBIT 5–17

**Run Diagram—
Outer Diameters
of 30 Pieces**

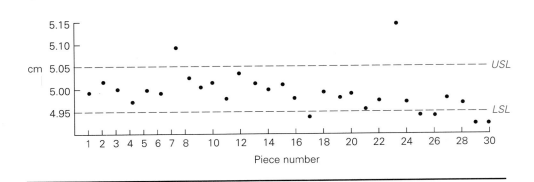

EXHIBIT 5–18

**Run Diagram—
Outer Diameters
of 30 More Pieces**

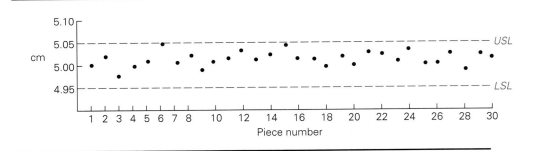

Quality objective: Continually improve quality and productivity by reducing the fraction of parts that do not meet the specifications, which call for diameters in the range of 4.95 cm to 5.05 cm.

Analysis phases: The improvement process follows distinct phases:

Phase 1: Operator measures every piece and plots outer diameter on the run diagram. Exhibit 5–17 shows diameters for 30 pieces. Pieces 7 and 23 are larger than the upper limit (5.05 cm), and pieces 17, 25, 26, 29, and 30 are smaller than the lower limit (4.95 cm). Also, there is a discernable drift downward over time. Action is needed.

Phase 2: The improvement team looks for causes. Some possibilities are

- The operator suspects machine heat buildup. In that case, a likely root cause is a faulty thermostat. A mechanic pulls out the old thermostat, finds it is indeed bad, and replaces it.
- The supervisor wonders about raw material impurities. A simple, no-cost solution is carried out: A sheet of clear plastic covers the containers of resin, so that passersby won't think the open box is a trash receptacle.

Phase 3: The operator again starts producing, measuring diameters, and plotting. Exhibit 5–18 shows that, for 30 more pieces, the diameters fall within specs and exhibit no drift.

Phase 4: Output has improved, so measurement frequency may be reduced. Process improvement, however, continues.

Process Control Charts

While the run diagram plots data on every unit, the **process control chart,** less precisely referred to as the quality control chart, relies on sampling. The method requires plotting statistical samples of measured process output for a quality characteristic. The sampling must be done initially to establish the control charts. Then, sampling continues with the results plotted on the control charts. By watching the plotted points, the observer can detect unusual process variation, which calls for some kind of corrective action.

Control charts come in several forms. We examine three of the more popular kinds: **mean and range charts,** which operate as a pair; **proportion-defective chart;** and **number-of-defects chart.** The mean and range charts rely on measurements of a continuous variable, such as weight, height, or specific gravity. Both the proportion-defective and the number-of-defects charts, on the other hand, count occurrences of a quality attribute within a sample. The underpinnings of the three charts are three different statistical probability distributions: normal distribution for the mean chart, binomial distribution for the proportion-defective chart, and Poisson distribution for the number-of-defects chart.

We consider the mean and range first. The example is a continuation of our injection-molding process, which operators first monitored using run diagrams (Example 5–2). They had concluded that "measurement frequency may be reduced," in this case to statistical samples from which we determine the mean and range. As with the run diagram, mean and range charting has distinct phases, which we follow in Example 5–3.

EXAMPLE 5–3:   MEAN AND RANGE CHARTS—INJECTION-MOLDED PARTS

Phase 1. Collect and record data. The left two-thirds of Exhibit 5–19 display the operators' (perhaps more than one since it could be a multishift operation) measures of diameters for 20 hourly samples of four parts each (that is, $k = 20$ and $n = 4$). Each sample mean, $\overline{X}$, shows process location, and the sample range R shows process dispersion or spread at the time the operator drew the sample. (Historically, in order to simplify the calculations, dispersion was measured by the range instead of by standard deviation. With computers, saving on calculations is no longer important.)

Phase 2. Calculate chart center lines and control limits. This phase has several steps. The first is to compute sample averages and ranges for each of the 20 samples. For the first sample,

$$\overline{X}_1 = \frac{\sum x}{n} = \frac{5.06 + 5.00 + 5.03 + 5.01}{4} = 5.025$$

$$R_1 = 5.06 - 5.00 = 0.06$$

These two calculations, repeated for the other 19 samples, fill out the two rightmost columns of Exhibit 5–19.

The center lines for the mean and range charts are the grand average of the sample averages, $\overline{\overline{X}}$ (referred to as "X-double-bar") and $\overline{R}$ (referred to as "R-bar"). In this case,

$$\overline{\overline{X}} = \frac{\sum \overline{X}}{k} = \frac{100.195}{20} = 5.010 \text{ cm} \tag{5–1}$$

$$\overline{R} = \frac{\sum R}{k} = \frac{1.50}{20} = 0.075 \text{ cm} \tag{5–2}$$

Next, calculate control limits. Typically, the limits are set at three standard errors above and below the center line; they are commonly referred to as three-sigma limits. The *central limit theorem* (a standard topic in statistics studies) applies. The theorem holds that (for our

EXHIBIT 5–19

Measurements for Designing Mean and Range Charts

Sample Number	Date	Measurements (cm)				Mean ($\overline{X}$)	Range (R)
		x_1	x_2	x_3	x_4		
1	10/10	5.01	5.00	5.03	5.06	5.025	0.06
2		4.99	5.03	5.03	5.05	5.025	0.06
3		5.03	5.04	4.99	4.94	5.000	0.10
4		5.05	5.03	5.00	5.01	5.022	0.05
5		4.97	5.04	4.96	5.00	4.992	0.08
6		4.97	5.00	4.99	5.02	4.995	0.05
7		5.06	5.00	5.02	4.96	5.010	0.10
8		5.03	4.98	5.01	4.95	4.992	0.08
9	10/11	5.05	5.03	5.05	4.98	5.028	0.07
10		4.99	5.03	5.01	4.96	4.998	0.07
11		4.98	5.05	5.05	4.94	5.005	0.11
12		4.95	5.04	4.99	4.99	4.992	0.09
13		5.00	5.05	5.01	4.97	5.008	0.08
14		4.96	5.03	5.05	5.00	5.010	0.09
15		5.08	5.01	5.02	4.96	5.018	0.12
16		5.02	4.98	5.04	4.95	4.998	0.09
17	10/12	5.02	4.99	4.99	5.04	5.010	0.05
18		4.99	5.00	5.05	5.05	5.022	0.06
19		5.03	5.02	5.01	4.96	5.005	0.07
20		5.02	5.04	5.04	5.04	5.040	0.02
Totals						100.195	1.50

purposes) the sample averages will form a normal (bell-shaped) distribution, regardless of the population from which the samples are taken. Then, approximately 99.72 percent of all sample averages should fall within three standard errors of the mean. That holds *if* the process is in a state of statistical control.

To simplify the calculations, we obtain the control limits by approximation (rather than by actually calculating the standard error). Exhibit 5–20 contains frequently used approximation factors for mean and range charts. The tables are derived from the mathematics of the normal distribution and the distribution of ranges. For the sample mean chart,

$$\text{Upper control limit } (UCL_{\bar{x}}) = \overline{\overline{X}} + (A_2)(\overline{R}) \tag{5–3}$$

$$\text{Lower control limit } (LCL_{\bar{x}}) = \overline{\overline{X}} - (A_2)(\overline{R}) \tag{5–4}$$

From 5–1 and 5–2, $\overline{\overline{X}} = 5.010$ and $\overline{R} = 0.075$. Then, the control limits are

$$UCL_{\bar{x}} = 5.010 + (0.729)(0.075) = 5.010 + 0.055 = 5.065$$

$$LCL_{\bar{x}} = 5.010 - (0.729)(0.075) = 5.010 - 0.055 = 4.955$$

Then, $\overline{R}$ becomes the center line of the range chart. The three-sigma limits for the range chart use the D_4 and D_3 factors from Exhibit 5–20, with sample size $n = 4$:

$$UCL_R = (D_4)(\overline{R}) = (2.282)(0.075) = 0.171 \tag{5–5}$$

$$LCL_R = (D_3)(\overline{R}) = (0)(0.075) = 0 \tag{5–6}$$

Phase 3. Draw the control charts. Most companies use preprinted forms or computerized templates for their control charts. The operator adds center lines and control limits, then plots the data, sample averages and ranges. Exhibit 5–21 shows the resulting mean and range charts.

Sample (or subgroup) Size (n)	Control Limit Factor for Averages (mean charts) (A_2)	UCL Factor for Ranges (range charts) (D_4)	LCL Factor for Ranges (range charts) (D_3)	Factor for Estimating Process Sigma $(\hat{\sigma} = \overline{R}/d_2)$ (d_2)
2	1.880	3.267	0	1.128
3	1.023	2.575	0	1.693
4	0.729	2.282	0	2.059
5	0.577	2.115	0	2.326
6	0.483	2.004	0	2.534
7	0.419	1.924	0.076	2.704
8	0.373	1.864	0.136	2.847
9	0.337	1.816	0.184	2.970
10	0.308	1.777	0.223	3.078

EXHIBIT 5–20

Process Control Chart Factors

EXHIBIT 5–21   **Initial Mean and Range Charts**

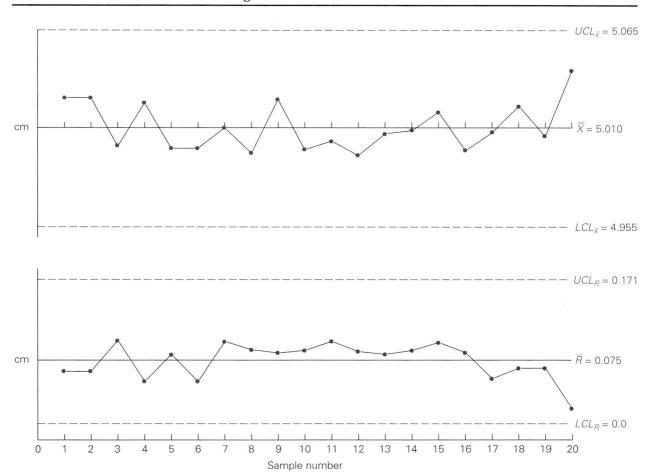

Phase 4. Analysis of control chart data. Is the process in control? The operator does a few tests to answer the question. The obvious test is simple. Are any points outside the control limits? Two other commonly used tests are as follows: Do seven consecutive points either rise or fall? Do eight or more consecutive points fall on the same side of the center line? Failure of any of the tests indicates presence of special variation, unstable output, and an out-of-control process.

The operator inspects the two charts (Exhibit 5–21) and sees that one of the tests fails: On the range chart, 10 successive points are above the center line. That suggests some shift in a process component—special variation.

Phase 5. Check for causes of special variation. It might be a new operator, new raw material lot, or a different measurement gauge. A process improvement team must investigate. After dealing with the special causes, they construct new control charts to confirm that the process is under control.

Process control has nothing whatsoever to do with meeting specifications. A process may be in control and still produce totally unworthy output. Control means consistency only.

What's next—after achieving process control? It is investigation of process capability. We shall return to capability analysis for our injection-molding process after examining two kinds of control charts for attributes.

EXAMPLE 5–4:   PROPORTION-DEFECTIVE CHART—BILLS OF LADING AT P*I*E NATIONWIDE[12]

The first use of process improvement tools at P*I*E Nationwide, fourth largest trucking company in the United States, was for billing errors. In eliminating special variation and bringing the billing process into statistical control, a P*I*E improvement team was able to eliminate all inspectors and cut the error rate from 10 percent to 0.8 percent in one year.

In the spirit of continuous improvement, the team's next step was to use process control charting to track the proportion, p, of defective bills per day. That attribute, a defective bill, was defined as one having any type of error.

Phase 1: The first step with a proportion-defective chart, as with any process control chart, is to make some decisions. The team decides on a sample size (n) of 50, to be taken every day for 20 days. Exhibit 5–22 summarizes the collected data.

Phase 2: Next, a team member calculates the chart center line ($\bar{p}$) and control limits $\pm 3\sigma$ from the center line. Since the chart plots proportion defective, there are only two values for the attribute: good or bad (defective or nondefective). Thus, the binomial (two numbers) distribution applies. Sigma (σ) in the binomial distribution is

Sample size for attributes is usually from 50 to a few hundred.

$$\sigma = \sqrt{\frac{\bar{p}(1 - \bar{p})}{n}}$$

EXHIBIT 5–22
Attribute Inspection Data— Defective Bills

Day	Defective Bills	Proportion Defective	Day	Defective Bills	Proportion Defective
1	25	0.50	11	30	0.60
2	22	0.44	12	32	0.64
3	33	0.66	13	35	0.70
4	25	0.50	14	33	0.66
5	37	0.74	15	30	0.60
6	25	0.50	16	30	0.60
7	35	0.70	17	35	0.70
8	33	0.66	18	40	0.80
9	35	0.70	19	35	0.70
10	35	0.70	20	25	0.50
				Total 630	

where

$\bar{p}$ = Average (mean) fraction defective

n = Number in each sample

Therefore, the control limits, at 3σ from the center line, $\bar{p}$, are

$$UCL = \bar{p} + 3\sqrt{\frac{\bar{p}(1 - \bar{p})}{n}} \qquad (5\text{--}7)$$

$$LCL = \bar{p} - 3\sqrt{\frac{\bar{p}(1 - \bar{p})}{n}} \qquad (5\text{--}8)$$

The average fraction defective, $\bar{p}$, is total defectives divided by total items inspected, where total items inspected equals number of samples, k, times sample size, n:

$$\bar{p} = \frac{\text{Total defectives found}}{kn} \qquad (5\text{--}9)$$

Since 630 defectives were found in 20 samples of 50 bills,

$$\bar{p} = \frac{630}{(20)(50)} = 0.63$$

The control limits are:

$$UCL = \bar{p} + 3\sqrt{\frac{\bar{p}(1 - \bar{p})}{n}}$$

$$= 0.63 + 3\sqrt{\frac{(0.63)(0.37)}{50}}$$

$$= 0.63 + 0.20 = 0.83$$

$$LCL = 0.63 - 0.20 = 0.43$$

Phase 3: The team member plots the points back on the chart. Exhibit 5–23 shows the result. All points are within the control limits, and there are no suspicious patterns of con-

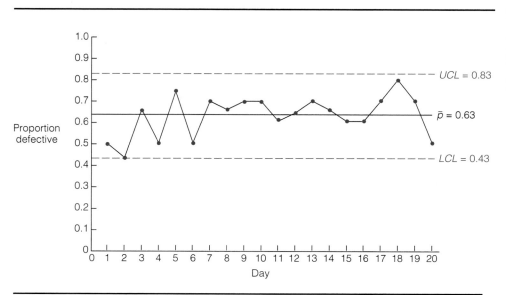

EXHIBIT 5–23

Chart of Proportion of Defective Bills per Day

secutive points. If the process were out of control, bill processing associates would undertake a search for a special cause. For example, they might find an incomplete address for a major customer in computer memory. An address correction could reduce errors on days when that customer places several orders, or an associate may trace a pricing error back to a previous process, such as in sales.

Phase 4: Associates use the charts daily, watching them for an out-of-control condition that requires investigation and action. Meanwhile, the team employs other tools of process improvement in keeping up the attack on causes of defective bills and process variation. (With the aid of fishbone charting and Pareto analysis, the actual P*I*E team found "that 77% of the errors could be corrected by drivers during pickup and that only 23% were actual billing errors. The original error rate of 63% fell in less than a month to [below] 20% and was approaching 8%.")[13]

EXAMPLE 5–5:   NUMBER-OF-DEFECTS CHART—HOTEL SUITE INSPECTION

A luxury hotel has five suites for visiting dignitaries and other VIPs—like operations management professors. The hotel's TQM effort has a strong advocate, the housekeeping supervisor, who has implemented a quality-check system for those five suites. Housekeeping associates, on a rotating basis, serve as inspectors, checking the suites immediately after completion of housekeeping. They record as defects any deviation from the hotel's standards of excellence (a ruffled towel, wilting flowers, unstocked bar and refrigerator, etc.). Every day the inspector records on a control chart the number of defects, c, found.

Phase 1: As always, decisions about data collection are mostly defined by the circumstances. In this case, suites may be cleaned only at the guests' convenience, and the inspector must follow shortly thereafter. Defect totals apply to the entire five-suite inspection; Exhibit 5–24 shows those totals for a 26-day period.

Phase 2: Calculate center line and control limits. The center line ($\bar{c}$) is the sum of the defects found divided by the number of inspections (k, which should be at least 25). Here,

$$\bar{c} = \frac{\sum c}{k} = \frac{39}{26} = 1.50 \tag{5-10}$$

To get control limits, the supervisor needs to know the standard deviation. Since the basis for the number-of-defects chart is the Poisson statistical distribution, rather than the binomial or normal, the formula for the standard derivation (σ) is very simple:

$$\sigma = \sqrt{\bar{c}}$$

Thus the 3σ control limits are:

$$UCL = \bar{c} + 3\sqrt{\bar{c}} \tag{5-11}$$

$$= 1.50 + 3(1.22)$$

$$= 5.16$$

$$LCL = \bar{c} - 3\sqrt{\bar{c}} \tag{5-12}$$

$$= -2.16, \text{ or } 0^*$$

---

*There cannot be a negative control limit on attribute control charts.

Exhibit 5–24
**Hotel Suite
Inspection—
Defects
Discovered**

Day	Defects	Day	Defects	Day	Defects
1	2	10	4	19	1
2	0	11	2	20	1
3	3	12	1	21	2
4	1	13	2	22	1
5	2	14	3	23	0
6	3	15	1	24	3
7	1	16	3	25	0
8	0	17	2	26	1
9	0	18	0	Total	39

Exhibit 5–25
**Number-of-
Defects Chart
for Hotel Suite
Inspection**

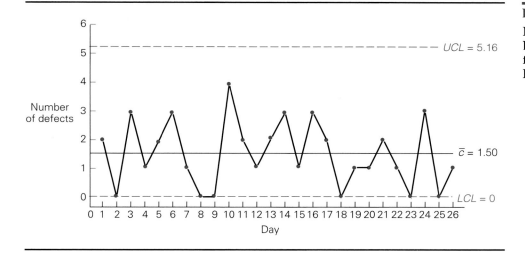

Next, the housekeeping staff construct the process control chart (in much the same fashion as for a proportion-defective chart). They draw the center line and control limits and plot the 26 data points. Exhibit 5–25 shows the completed chart. The process is within limits and does not violate the consecutive-points rule. The group concludes that the process is in control. The housekeeping supervisor and staff, however, aren't satisfied with control; they want perfection.

Phase 3: Process improvement efforts continue. The group's ideas might include checklists to avoid forgetting, a closer supplier of freshly cut flowers (maybe just outside the hotel's front door), and prestocked bar and refrigerator shelves that are inserted each day and refilled at night.

Process Capability Analysis

Process capability refers to the ability of the process to meet specifications. Usually, process capability is expressed using one or more **process capability indexes.** The best known index is C_{pk}. A process improvement team must know the specification for a quality characteristic and what the process output looks like before it can compute C_{pk}. The foundation for capability indexes, and perhaps a better understanding of their meaning, comes from a process capability graph.

Process Capability Graph

To see how an improvement team could develop a process capability graph, we return to the injection-molding process used in Example 5–2 (run diagram) and Example 5–3 ($\overline{X}$ and R control charts). Assuming that injection-molding associates have attained process control, the only variation in process output is the natural (common) variation. That variation, equal to six standard deviations (6σ), is referred to as the inherent process capability. The team first determines inherent capability.

The standard deviation of process output is unknown but is estimated as follows:

$$\hat{\sigma} = \overline{R}/d_2 \tag{5–13}$$

where

$\hat{\sigma}$ = Estimate for σ

d_2 = Conversion factor found in quality control tables (see Exhibit 5–20); it is a function of sample size

From Exhibit 5–20, for a sample size (n) of 4, d_2 is 2.059; and from Example 5–3, $\overline{R}$ is 0.075 cm. Then:

$$\sigma = \frac{\overline{R}}{d_2} = \frac{0.075 \text{ cm}}{2.059} = 0.036 \text{ cm}$$

The value for 6σ becomes:

$$6\sigma = 6(0.036 \text{ cm}) = 0.216 \text{ cm}$$

This inherent capability, 0.216 cm, is a statement of variation only; it makes no claim as to location. Process output location is already known, however. From Example 5–3 the injection-molding process is centered at 5.01 cm—the value of $\overline{\overline{X}}$. Thus the team can fully describe the expected process output distribution. It is centered at 5.01 cm and extends 3σ (0.108 cm) above (to 5.118 cm) and below (to 4.902 cm) that center.

To complete the process capability graph, the team adds the specification for the outer diameter of the part. In that specification, 5.00 ± 0.05 cm, the tolerance band extends from the center (target) of 5.00 cm down to 4.95 cm and up to 5.05 cm. The allowable tolerance band is just 0.10 cm wide, much less than the inherent capability (0.216 cm) of the process. Exhibit 5–26 shows the process capability graph.

The shaded areas at each end represent molded parts that do not meet specifications. With the normal curve areas table (Appendix A), the team could compute the proportion of output that fails to meet specification. (We leave that for an end-of-chapter solved problem.)

C_{pk} Computation

Improvement teams usually do not need to go to the extreme of constructing a figure such as Exhibit 5–26 in order to compare process output with specifications; they calculate C_{pk} instead. That index is a single number that conveys most of the information in Exhibit 5–26. The formula for C_{pk} is as follows:

$$C_{pk} = \min\left(\frac{USL - \overline{\overline{X}}}{3\sigma}, \frac{\overline{\overline{X}} - LSL}{3\sigma}\right) \tag{5–14}$$

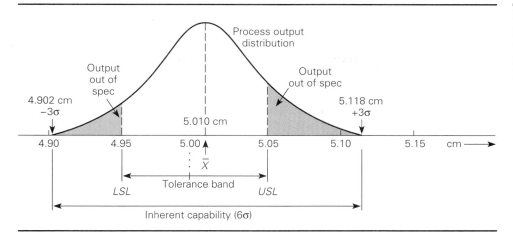

Exhibit 5–26

Process Capability Graph: Injection-Molding Process

where

USL = upper specification limit

LSL = lower specification limit

If process output is not centered on the spec target, danger of out-of-spec output is greater at the nearer spec limit; hence, the focus on the minimum numerator value. In the present case, since $\overline{\overline{X}}$ (5.01) is closer to the upper limit than to the lower one, the minimum numerator is $(USL - \overline{\overline{X}})$, and the team calculates the value of C_{pk} as follows:

$$C_{pk} = \frac{5.05 - 5.01}{3(0.036)} = \frac{0.04}{0.108} = 0.37$$

What does that value mean? Is it good or bad? The improvement team knows that—unfortunately for the customers or suppliers—it is a poor value for C_{pk}. It means that a large portion of the injection-molding process output is not meeting specs, which we already know from the process capability graph of Exhibit 5–26. In sum, C_{pk} reveals considerable process information. Exhibit 5–27 graphically shows the four relevant C_{pk} conditions along with a brief explanation of what each value says regarding process output.

Some companies require their suppliers to show C_{pk} values of at least 1.33, a somewhat arbitrary indicator of acceptable performance. Teams increase C_{pk} in two ways. First, they improve process output location by getting the process average ($\overline{\overline{X}}$) closer to specs target. Second, they take actions to decrease variability (σ). Wouldn't capability also improve if they just extended the spec limits (widened the goal posts)? Yes, but that option is ridiculous. Continious improvement—better customer service—requires narrowing of spec limits, not extending them.

Why the persistent attack on process variability? Isn't it overkill, especially if C_{pk} satisfies customers? There are two reasons why improvement teams must not let up. First, specification limits are always somewhat arbitrary (even with maximum customer input). A customer might define *fresh fish* as fish caught that day, but would prefer fish caught within the hour, or even within a few minutes. Until the universe is prefect, quality is a matter of degree, though tolerance bands tend to make it yes–no

C_{pk} shows not only whether process output is capable of meeting specs, but whether it does *meet specs.*

EXHIBIT 5–27   Capability Index C_{pk}: Four Examples

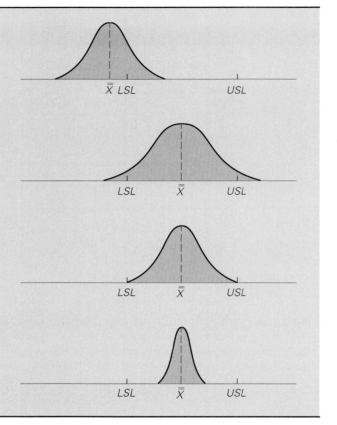

• If C_{pk} is negative, then $\overline{\overline{X}}$ is not within tolerance limits, indicating a very high defect rate; process improvement is urgently needed.

• If C_{pk} is positive but less than 1.0—the case for the injection-molding process—the process is centered somewhere within the tolerance band but its width exceeds the tolerance band; again, serious work is needed, for some output is out of spec.

• If C_{pk} equals 1.0, the process just (barely) meets specs; it is centered somewhere within the tolerance band.

• If C_{pk} is greater than 1.0, all process output is within tolerances; the higher the value of C_{pk}, the better.

(within specs, or not). No matter where one positions the spec limits, improvement can *always* be defined as getting more of the process outcomes closer to the target.

A second, and perhaps more practical, reason for continued improvement and narrower spec limits is a phenomenon called variation stackup, or tolerance stackup, explained next.

Variation Stackup

Output that meets specs may be unsatisfactory when the customer has to put it to use with other outputs. **Variation stackup** occurs when two or more outputs that must be used jointly each lie at the extreme of their spec limits. Consider this example:

Door specifications: 36.0 ± 0.25 inches.
Frame specifications: 36.5 − 0.25 inches.

Even if all doors and frames are within their respective specs, one of the smaller doors placed within one of the larger frames results in gaps through which unwelcome weather passes. The opposite possibility, a larger door in a smaller frame, requires planing and sanding to get the door even to close. Sorting and matching doors to frames is a weak solution, since it treats the symptoms but does not resolve the problem.

Variation stackup can apply in services as well. Consider a municipal bus system. For the customers, the bus riders, the bus system's specs might be the following: Be at the bus stop up to five minutes before scheduled departure. Specs for the bus drivers might be to arrive at each stop no more than five minutes behind schedule. If the customer is five minutes early and the bus is five minutes late, however, it is bad service. Just-in-time arrival of the customer coupled with an early departing bus is equally poor service.

The best cure for these and other variation stackup problems is reduction of process variability. Make all doors close to 36.0 inches and all frames close to 36.5 inches. Put enough slack in the bus schedule so that buses are rarely late and set a rule that a bus may never leave a stop early. Northwest Airlines did exactly that and went from being chronically late to having the best-on-time performance of the major airlines operating in the United States in the early 1980s.

The variation stackup problem is amplified in the mixing stages of continuous process production. Often several ingredients, not just two, are mixed together. Purities, specific gravities, and fineness of various liquid and solid ingredients may all be within specs, but on the high (or low) side. When mixed and processed, the result might be tacky rubber, cloudy glass, unstable chemicals, rough surfaces, crumbly pills, brittle plastics, or M&Ms that melt in your hands.

Process Improvement in Perspective

Does anybody besides industry leaders use these quality control and improvement techniques? Students and teachers at the Lower Nazareth Elementary School in Pennsylvania do. Together with business partners from the Martin Guitar Company, they went after behavior problems in the cafeteria. The project team collected baseline statistics, developed improvement options, and put several into effect. Bad behaviors, including shouting, running, and leaving the building, decreased by 56 percent.

Contrast

Approach to Quality

Old Approach

- Worry about output volume first, and then worry about quality—when it becomes a problem.
- Produce large lots and rely on sampling inspection to accept or reject; sort to find good ones; scrap or rework bad ones.
- Declare some proportion defective (1–2 percent, perhaps) as acceptable quality level (AQL) and strive to meet that goal.

Process Improvement (TQM) Approach

- Everyone serves a customer and all customers want quality.
- Aim for fail-safe processes.
- Control processes for consistent output.
- Use capability analysis to guide continued efforts to improve processes.
- The only acceptable goal is zero defects.

Second graders at Western Salisbury (Pennsylvania) School are in the learning mode. Their subject matter includes flowcharts, Paretos, and fishbone diagrams. Using these tools, they developed baseline data on time to make a peanut butter and jelly sandwich. After study and improvement, they cut the sandwich production time from an average of about 3 minutes to 1.4 minutes.[14]

Process improvement is for everybody—but not without tools. Education is the starting point. Making data-based continuous quality improvement a part of everyone's job—or even school life—sustains the improvement pattern, which avoids sinking into a work life of frustration over chronic problems that never get solved. The transition to the process improvement approach is summarized in the Contrast box, Approach to Quality.

Summary

The responsibility for quality rests with the makers of goods and providers of services. Team and individual actions that carry out that responsibility revolve around the quality action cycle: designing quality into the process, detecting the failures, and using data to drive continuous process improvement. Reducing dependence on detection (inspection) is a measure of overall success, although quality gains usually closely relate to other improvements such as time and flexibility. Quality as a specialty continues, but emphasis shifts toward the upgraded role of facilitator as companies shed many of their inspectors. Where inspection is still needed, the preference is for efficient methods such as sampling.

Modern quality management takes a process focus. Transformation processes are complex, consisting of materials, manpower, methods, machines, measurement, maintenance, and management. Process performance yields quality characteristics. Studying the distribution of those characteristics is at the heart of process improvement. Process output may exhibit common-cause and special-cause variation; when the latter is eliminated by removing assignable causes, the process is said to be in control or stable. Typically, those working closest to a process are better able to remove special-cause variation, but management action (e.g., expenditures for new equipment) is often needed to reduce common-cause variation. Process output may be collected as variables data, where the degree of presence of a quality characteristic is measured, or as attributes data, where output is merely classified and counted.

Process improvement is guided by the scientific method. A growing collection of general, coarse-grained, and fine-grained tools are of proven help at each stage. General tools include team-building, group-interaction skills, and specific process technology knowledge. Coarse-grained tools are the process flowchart, check sheets and histograms, Pareto analysis, and fishbone charts. Fine-grained tools include fail-safing, design of experiments, scattergrams, run diagrams, and process control charts. Many improvement efforts are accomplished with the general-level and coarse-gained tools alone, but more persistent problems may also require fine-grained tools.

In coarse-grained analysis and improvement, the focus is on the flow or relationships of materials, documents, or people. Data-sorting efforts to identify targets of opportunity also characterize this level of improvement. The process flowchart identifies each step in a process for analysis that detects the cause of error. Check sheets and histograms are simple, quick data-collection and presentation tools. Pareto analysis arranges problems or possible causes in decreasing order and thus focus attention on the most immediately promising targets of opportunity. Fishbone charts help teams break problems down into manageable segments of cause–effect linkages.

Fine-grained analysis aims at quality characteristics one at a time. Fail-safing entails a mind-set of prevention: devices and procedures that do not allow a mishap to pass onward or do not allow it at all. Design of experiments techniques test underlying relationships among causal variables. The scatter diagram correlates behavior of one variable (such as a quality characteristics) with that of another (perhaps a deliberate team action on process components).

The run diagram is a plot of sequential units of output. Comparison to spec limits is straightforward. Process control charts typically show plots of statistics taken from samples of process output and compared with computed control limits. Mean and range charts are the most widely used of the variables control charts. The mean chart shows between-sample variation, while the range chart shows within-sample variation. Popular attributes control charts include the proportion-defective chart and the number-of-defects chart (number of defects in a sample, typically of one unit). Process capability analysis compares process output with specifications. The natural process width (6σ) is referred to as the inherent capability. Capability indexes such as C_{pk} combine in a single number most of the information of a process capability graph. Companies often set minimum values of C_{pk} for their suppliers to maintain.

Process improvement at any level is a matter of attacking and reducing variation in output. It ought to occur in ever-widening teams of empowered employees dedicated to continuous improvement.

Solved Problems

Problem 1

Connector leads for electronic ignition components are produced to a specification of 8.000 ± 0.010 cm. The process has been studied, and the following values have been obtained:

$$\text{Process average} = \overline{\overline{X}} = 8.003 \text{ cm}$$

$$\text{Standard deviation (estimate)} = \hat{\sigma} = 0.002 \text{ cm}$$

Calculate:
   a. The inherent process capability
   b. The capability index C_{pk}

Solution 1

   a. Inherent process capability $= 6 \times \hat{\sigma}$
       $$= 6 \times 0.002 \text{ cm}$$
       $$= 0.012 \text{ cm}$$

   b. Since the process average (8.003 cm) is closer to the upper spec limit than to the lower, the appropriate form of Equation 5–14 (with values inserted) is:

$$C_{pk} = \frac{USL - \overline{\overline{X}}}{3\sigma} = \frac{8.010 - 8.003}{3(0.002)} = 1.167$$

The value of C_{pk} is greater than 1.0, so all process output meets spec. Some buyers in today's marketplace, however, would not be satisfied with so low a value. A process improvement team needs to take a look.

Problem 2

Samples of 180 units are drawn from production in order to construct a proportion-defective chart. Develop the chart for the following 16 samples of percentages defective. Is the chart satisfactory for use on the production line? Explain.

Sample	Percent Defective	Sample	Percent Defective	Sample	Percent Defective	Sample	Percent Defective
1	2	5	1	9	6	13	4
2	5	6	0	10	2	14	3
3	5	7	2	11	7	15	2
4	3	8	2	12	1	16	3

Solution 2

First, calculate $\bar{p}$, UCL, and LCL, using Equations 5–7 through 5–9.

$$\bar{p} = \frac{\text{Total percent defective}}{k}$$

$$= \frac{2 + 5 + 5 + 3 + 1 + 0 + 2 + 2 + 6 + 2 + 7 + 1 + 4 + 3 + 2 + 3}{16}$$

$$= \frac{48}{16} = 3 \text{ percent, or } 0.03$$

$$UCL = \bar{p} + 3\sqrt{\frac{\bar{p}(1 - \bar{p})}{n}} = 0.03 + 3\sqrt{\frac{0.03(0.97)}{180}} = 0.068$$

$$LCL = \bar{p} - 3\sqrt{\frac{\bar{p}(1 - \bar{p})}{n}} = 0.03 - 0.038 = -0.08, \text{ or } 0$$

Next, develop a chart and plot the 16 data points on it:

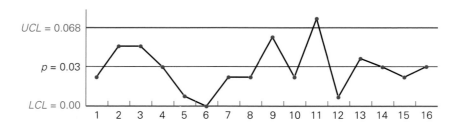

The chart is not satisfactory. Sample 11 is above the *UCL*, which indicates that the process is unstable, out of statistical control. Look for a special cause, eliminate it, and try again.

Problem 3

I. B. Poorly is director of Employee Wellness Programs for Alpine Escapes, a chain of winter sports resorts. He knows that Alpine's employee health care costs have risen 78 percent in the last three years. Absenteeism, low productivity, and poor attitudes (especially in the presence of customers) are other symptoms of poor health among employees. I. B. organized a largely volunteer process improvement team to turn things around. The team interviewed and tested a sample of 60 Alpine employees and recorded health problems on a check sheet. Join I. B.'s team and show how process improvement tools might be used to systematically tackle the health improvement task at Alpine.

First, analyze the following check sheet:

Health Problem	Occurrences	Total	Health Problem	Occurrences	Total
Poor sleep habits	ꟷꟷꟷꟷ IIII	9	Smoking	ꟷꟷꟷ ꟷꟷꟷ ꟷꟷꟷ III	18
High cholesterol	ꟷꟷꟷ ꟷꟷꟷ IIII	14	Overweight	ꟷꟷꟷ ꟷꟷꟷ ꟷꟷꟷ ꟷꟷꟷ ꟷꟷꟷ I	
High blood pressure	ꟷꟷꟷ ꟷꟷꟷ ꟷꟷꟷ II	17		ꟷꟷꟷ ꟷꟷꟷ	36
Poor circulation	IIII	4	Alcohol abuse	ꟷꟷꟷ III	8
			Other problems	ꟷꟷꟷ I	6

Clearly, some of the 60 members of the sample had more than one health problem, and perhaps there are interrelationships among the listed ills. A Pareto analysis, however, would call for more-detailed study of the most frequently occurring problem. Thus, the team ought to focus on weight by making it the spine of a fishbone chart. Such a chart, including some of the team's brainstorming (possible causes and effects), is sketched here.

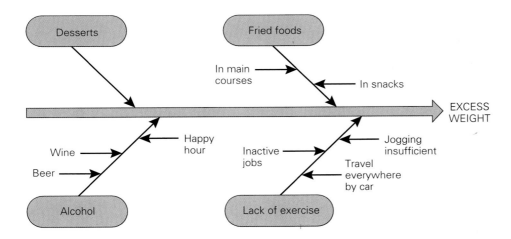

Each end point on the fishbone chart suggests action. The team might use process control charts to track percentage of employees who succumb to various poor health habits (snacks, no exercise, smoking, etc.). Effects of process interventions such as healthy cafeteria food, flexible work hours, exercise periods, and so forth, ought to show up on the charts.

Pareto analysis may again be used for the "jogging insufficient" end point. The accompanying Pareto chart provides concrete data on specific reasons for insufficient jogging. In this case, the dominant cause, "skipped entirely," might be used as the spine for another, finer fishbone analysis indicating reasons for skipping (e.g., bad weather or working late).

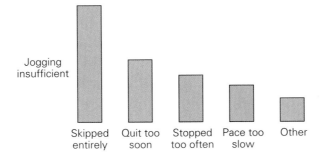

Problem 4

The fill process for 9-ounce bottles of Island Sunscreen Lotion is under scrutiny by a process improvement team. Sample average and ranges from 20 samples of four bottles each are shown in the table below. Construct mean and range charts and analyze the information given by the charts.

Sample Number	Average (oz.)	Range (oz.)	Sample Number	Average (oz.)	Range (oz.)
1	9.025	0.2	11	9.025	0.3
2	9.050	0.1	12	9.100	0.2
3	9.100	0.3	13	9.125	0.3
4	9.100	0.3	14	9.150	0.5
5	9.000	0.5	15	8.950	0.2
6	9.025	0.3	16	9.000	0.5
7	9.050	0.4	17	9.025	0.2
8	9.075	0.1	18	9.100	0.2
9	9.000	0.2	19	9.050	0.1
10	8.975	0.3	20	9.075	0.4

Solution 4

Following the procedure used in Example 5–3, calculate center lines and control limits for both mean and range charts. First, the center line for the mean chart:

$$\overline{\overline{X}} = \frac{\Sigma \overline{X}}{k} = \frac{181}{20} = 9.05 \text{ oz.}$$

For the range chart:

$$\overline{R} = \frac{\Sigma R}{k} = \frac{5.6}{20} = 0.28 \text{ oz.}$$

Next, (using factors from Exhibit 5–20) control limits for the mean chart:

$$UCL_{\overline{x}} = \overline{\overline{X}} + A_2\overline{R} = 9.05 + (0.729)(0.28) = 9.25 \text{ oz.}$$

$$LCL_{\overline{x}} = \overline{\overline{X}} - A_2\overline{R} = 9.05 - (0.729)(0.28) = 8.85 \text{ oz.}$$

MEAN CHART

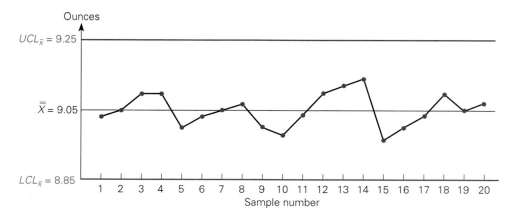

RANGE CHART

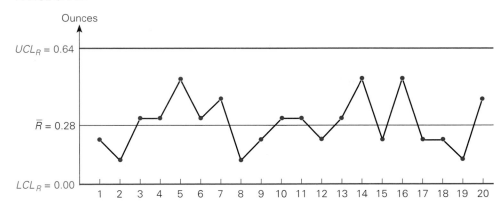

Limits for the range chart:

$$UCL_R = D_4(\overline{R}) = 2.282(0.28) = 0.64 \text{ oz.}$$

$$LCL_R = D_3(\overline{R}) = 0(0.28) = 0$$

Place the center line and control limits on the respective mean and range charts and then plot the sample averages and ranges. The accompanying charts illustrate.

Comparison of chart patterns with tests for process control reveals that all tests pass. Close inspection does show what seems to be a cyclic pattern—high to low about every four or five samples—on the mean chart. The team must investigate. Perhaps they will find that the on-off cycling of large motors such as air conditioners is affecting the lotion-filling machines. If a special cause for the apparent pattern is found, it must be eliminated.

The cycling might disappear on its own after a few more samples, and if stability continues, the team will begin capability analysis by comparing process output with specifications.

Exhibit 5–26 is the process capability graph for the injection-molding process discussed in Example 5–3. The improvement team has asked you to compute the percentage of molding process output that fails to meet specifications and to comment on the implications.

Problem 5

Use the normal curve areas (see Table A–1 in Appendix A) to find the proportion of output that lies beyond each spec limit; that is, the areas that are shaded in Exhibit 5–26.

Recall from Example 5–3 that the process center is: $\overline{\overline{X}} = 5.01$ cm

Also, from Equation 5–13, $\sigma = 0.036$ cm

To use Table A–1, find the number of standard deviations (called z values) that each spec limit lies from $\overline{\overline{X}}$, the process average. The formula is:

Solution 5

$$z = \frac{\text{Spec limit} - \overline{\overline{X}}}{\sigma}$$

Two z values are needed, one for each spec limit:

$$z_{LSL} = \frac{4.95 - 5.01}{0.036} = -1.67$$

$$z_{USL} = \frac{5.05 - 5.01}{0.036} = 1.11$$

From Table A–1, read directly the area between the distribution average and the z values. Then subtract each of those areas from 0.5, the area in half the distribution. The remainder is the area or proportion (or, for present purposes, percentage of output) that lies outside the respective spec limit. For the lower spec limit:

$$\text{Table area} = 0.4525, \text{ so } (0.5 - 0.4525) = 0.0475, \text{ or } 4.75 \text{ percent}$$

For the upper spec limit:

$$\text{Table area} = 0.3665, \text{ so } (0.5 - 0.3665) = 0.1335, \text{ or } 13.35 \text{ percent}$$

Add the two out-of-spec percentages, to get the total for the molding process:

$$(4.75) + (13.35) = 18.1 \text{ percent of output fails to meet specs}$$

In your report to the improvement team, you might mention something about getting that errant output within specs—a free 18-percent boost in capacity. Tell the team about the key goal in all process improvement: Hit the target, the first time and every time!

Review Questions

1. As TQM takes hold in a firm, how should emphasis shift among process design, detection, and process improvement (the quality action cycle in Exhibit 5–1)?
2. What are the likely roles of quality departments in the future?
3. What is the changing nature of inspection?
4. Explain the time–quality connection.
5. What is a transformation process? How might process performance be described in terms of quality characteristics?
6. How do special-cause variation and common-cause variation relate to process control and process capability?
7. How do variables data differ from attributes data? Give examples of both.
8. What is the purpose of the scientific method in process improvement efforts?
9. What is the importance of data in process improvement?
10. How do flowcharts help identify value-adding transformations?
11. How is fail-safing used in improvement efforts?
12. How might check sheets and histograms complement one another in process improvement?
13. How might Pareto analysis and fishbone diagrams complement one another in process improvement?
14. How is a scatter diagram used in process control and improvement?
15. What are the roles of run diagrams and process control charts in improvement programs? What are the similarities and differences?
16. How do specifications and tolerances figure into process control? process capability?
17. In control charting for variables why use two charts (e.g., mean and range)?

18. Compare and contrast four types of process control charts and their uses.

19. What are some tests for process control? How are they applied?

20. What does a process capability graph show? Is the same information given by the inherent capability? Explain.

21. Discuss the meaning of different values for C_{pk}.

22. What is variation stackup? How does it affect good output? How might the effects of variation stackup be diminished?

Exercises

1. Fix-M-Up, Inc., is a small chain of stores that clean and repair typewriters, photocopiers, and other office equipment. Define a process for the company along the lines of that discussed in the chapter for the manufacture of three-inch bolts. Prepare a list of quality characteristics you might wish to use if you were considering using Fix-M-Up as the maintenance contractor for your company's office equipment.

2. Using either the Jostens Diplomas or the Ampex examples in the chapter (see page 129) fully explain why so many improvements occurred at the same time.

3. A listing of products/services follows. Select two from each column and do the following:

   a. For each of your four selections, decide on two attributes and/or variables that you think are most suitable for inspection. Explain your reasoning.

   b. Discuss whether a formal statistical sampling method or an informal inspection method is more sensible for each selection.

Column 1	*Column 2*
Telephone	Auto tire mounting
Ball-point pen	Bookbinding
Pocket calculator	Data entry
Dice	Proofreading
Space heater	Wallpaper hanging
Electric switch	Library reference services
Glue	Nursing care
Bottle of cola	Food catering
Watch	Cleanliness of dishes
Handgun	Bank teller service
Light bulb	Roadside rest stop

4. An office furniture manufacturer (which employees 1,000 people) is planning to adopt a total quality program. Following are some characteristics of its present production system:

   a. There is a quality assurance department of 50 people, including 30 inspectors.

   b. Rejected products discovered at the end of final assembly are sent by conveyor to a rework area staffed by 120 people.

   c. All purchased raw materials and parts are inspected on the receiving docks using acceptance sampling.

   d. All direct laborers are paid by how much they produce, which is measured daily.

   What changes would you suggest? Discuss.

5. Exhibit 5–10 shows flowcharts of a travel authorization process, one before improvements and the other after. What principles of operations management were used to improve the process? State specifically how each principle you list was beneficial.

6. The improved travel authorization flowchart in Exhibit 5–10 relies heavily on E-mail (computer-to-computer communications). Assume that the company does not have that technology. Develop an improved process, displayed on a process flowchart, under that assumption. Compare these results with the E-mail results.

7. An Into Practice box in the chapter presents check-sheet data for Akron General Medical Center. Those data are reproduced below.

	Frequency of Occurrence			
	Week 1	*Week 2*	*Week 3*	*Week 4*
Incorrect dose dispensed from pharmacy	✓✓✓	✓✓	✓	✓✓✓✓
Verbal order taken incorrectly	✓		✓✓	✓
Incorrect dose ordered	✓✓	✓✓✓✓	✓	✓
Dosage calculation error		✓	✓	

   a. Rearrange the data as a Pareto chart.

   b. The data do not easily rearrange into the form of a histogram. Why not? What raw data would be needed to develop one or more histograms?

   c. Compare the usefulness of a Pareto analysis with histograms for Akron General's project.

8. American Pen and Pencil (AmPen) has had most of the market for ball-point pens, but now it is under great pressure from a competitor whose product is clearly superior. AmPen operators have identified several quality problems, including viscosity of ink, which is affected by the temperature of the mixing solution; purity of powdered ink and amount of water; the ball-point assembly, which is affected by ball diameter, ball roundness, and trueness of the tube opening into which the ball goes; and strength of the clip, which is affected by the thickness of the metal and the correctness of the shape after stamping.

   a. Draw a fishbone chart for these ball-point pen factors. How should the chart be used?

   b. An inspection procedure at the ink-mixing stage reveals that 80 percent of bad samples are caused by impurities, 15 percent by wrong temperature, and 5 percent by wrong amount of water. Draw a Pareto chart. How should it be used?

9. A waiter is trying to determine the factors that increase tips. Some of his ideas are how long it takes to serve, how many words he speaks to a table of patrons, how long it takes the kitchen to fill the order, time between taking away dishes and bringing the check, and how far the table is from the kitchen.

   a. Arrange these few factors into a logical fishbone chart. Explain your chart.

   b. Which of the factors is likely to plot on a scatter diagram as an upside-down U? Explain.

10. Some mathematics instructors and students are developing a fishbone chart on how to improve the average math score on the Scholastic Aptitude Test (SAT). So far, the chart is as shown below; only one primary bone, "materials and machines," is filled out.

   a. Fill out the rest of the primary bones with reasonable cause and subcause arrows.

   b. Suggest three actions to be taken next.

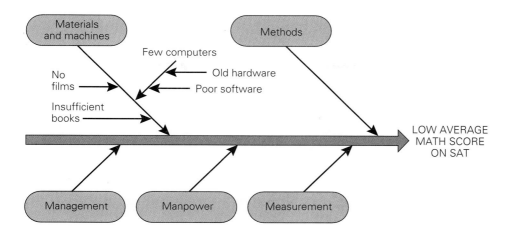

11. Suggest a fail-safe device that could be used at a popcorn stand to prevent too many unpopped kernels from ending up in customers' bags.

12. Suggest a fail-safing approach for each of the following problems:

    a. Forgetting to set the alarm clock.

    b. Missing appointments.

    c. Running out of gas.

    d. Not having correct change for unattended tollway exit booths.

    e. Losing one sock, earring, or glove from a (matching) pair.

13. Following is a scatter diagram showing inches of deviation from the correct length of wooden blinds and humidity in the shop.

    a. What does the shape of the scattered points indicate?

    b. Sharpness of the saw blade is also known to affect the correctness of blind length. Make a drawing of how the scatter for those two factors (sharpness and deviation of length) would probably look.

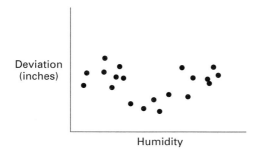

14. You are manager of one of the Oil Can (speedy auto oil change and lubrication) stores. You've been collecting data on time, in minutes, to service cars. Your purpose is to reduce variability in the completion times, and you believe that job specifications will help. Completion times for one day's business, 25 cars, follow:

    6, 10, 14, 14, 9, 11, 13, 8, 16, 15, 19, 15, 9, 18, 15, 16, 15, 17, 12, 17, 17, 15, 18, 14, 9

    a. Plot the points on a run diagram. What does the diagram reveal about the process?

    b. Create spec limits and insert them on your run diagram. What investigations are suggested?

c. Plot the data as a histogram. What questions does that histogram raise?

d. Explain how these data and tools might be used advantageously in your store.

15. An associate measures current loss in a circuit and plots the means of sample measurements on an existing process control chart. Most of the means fall below the lower control limit—less current loss than before. What is the implication of this on such factors as pricing, marketing, purchasing, production, training, design, and control charts?

16. Redraw the following chart. Fill in your chart to show which of the four types of tool could be suitable for each of the products on the left. Briefly explain each of your answers.

	Run Diagram	Mean and Range Chart	Proportion-Defective Chart	Number of Defects Chart
Alcoholic content in beer batches				
Billiard balls—ability to withstand force in a destructive test				
Vibration of electric motor right after a process improvement				
New electronic component				
Number of fans that do not turn when plugged in				
Percentage of lenses having a scratch				
Number of scratches per table surface				

17. An improvement team for a medical supply manufacturer subjects hypodermic needles to a bend test, and the results, in grams, are plotted on mean and range charts. A suitable number of samples have been inspected. The resulting $\overline{\overline{X}}$ is 26.1, and the resulting $\overline{R}$ is 5.0.

a. For $n = 8$, calculate the control limits for the control charts.

b. What should be done with the data calculated in question a?

c. Assume that process control charts have been developed for the above data and that the operator has been using the charts regularly. For one sample of hypodermics, $\overline{X}$ = 26.08 and R = 0.03. Should there be an investigation for a special cause? Explain.

18. Spark-O-Plenty, Inc., periodically takes random samples, each with a sample size of six, from a production line that manufactures $\frac{1}{2}$ volt batteries. The sampled batteries are tested on a voltmeter. The production line has just been modified, and a new quality control plan must be designed. For that purpose, 10 random samples (of six each) have been taken over a suitable period of time; the test results are as follows:

	Test Voltages					
Sample Number	V_1	V_2	V_3	V_4	V_5	V_6
1	0.498	0.492	0.510	0.505	0.504	0.487
2	0.482	0.491	0.502	0.481	0.496	0.492
3	0.501	0.512	0.503	0.499	0.498	0.511
4	0.498	0.486	0.502	0.503	0.510	0.501
5	0.500	0.507	0.509	0.498	0.512	0.518
6	0.476	0.492	0.496	0.521	0.505	0.490
7	0.511	0.522	0.513	0.518	0.520	0.516
8	0.488	0.512	0.501	0.498	0.492	0.498
9	0.482	0.490	0.510	0.500	0.495	0.482
10	0.505	0.496	0.498	0.490	0.485	0.499

a. Compute and draw the appropriate process control chart(s) for the data.

b. What should be done next? Discuss.

19. A process improvement team at Hang-M-High, a manufacturer of coat hangers, decided what constitutes a defective hanger. Samples of 200 hangers were inspected on each of the last 20 days. The numbers of defectives found are given below. Construct a proportion-defective chart for the data. What should the team do next? Explain.

Day	Number Defective	Day	Number Defective	Day	Number Defective	Day	Number Defective
1	22	6	16	11	21	16	24
2	17	7	12	12	21	17	14
3	14	8	11	13	20	18	8
4	18	9	6	14	13	19	15
5	25	10	16	15	19	20	12

20. OK-Mart, a chain retailer, contracts with Electro Corporation to manufacture an OK brand of photo flashbulb. OK-Mart states that it wants an average quality of 99 percent good flashbulbs—that is, 99 percent that actually flash. Electro's marketing manager states that their goal should be for 99.9 percent to flash (better than OK-Mart's stated goal). After production begins at Electro, sampling on the production line over a representative time period shows 0.2 percent defective.

a. Where should the center line be drawn on a process control chart? Why?

b. What, if anything, needs to be done about the difference between goals and actual quality?

21. A pottery manufacturing firm constructs process control charts. Thirty pottery samples are taken, and the mean proportion of pottery samples that fail a strength test is 0.02, which becomes the center line on a proportion-defective chart. Control limits are put in place, and the 30 defect rates are plotted on the chart. Two of the 30 fall above the upper control limit, but all 30 meet the requirements of the major customer, a department store. Explain the situation. What should be done?

22. Rescue Services Training (RST) trains emergency rescue squads for state, county, and municipal police and fire departments. The training program development and improvement group at RST evaluates company training effectiveness, in part, by performance of trainee teams on the Simulated Emergency Rescue Exercise (SERE). During the SERE, trainee teams may err by omitting required steps as well as by committing acts that they shouldn't. The training group records total errors for each team. The table shows error data for the last 25 trainee teams:

SERE Team	Errors	SERE Team	Errors	SERE Team	Errors	SERE Team	Errors	SERE Team	Errors
1	4	6	1	11	3	16	3	21	3
2	3	7	4	12	7	17	6	22	2
3	11	8	3	13	4	18	4	23	4
4	2	9	2	14	1	19	4	24	1
5	6	10	4	15	8	20	12	25	3

a. Plot the error data on a number-of-defects chart.

b. Analyze the chart and comment on process stability.

c. Prepare a list of recommendations to the training program development and improvement group.

23. The training program development and improvement group at RST (see problem 22) suspects that the SERE error rate may depend on experience level—that is, trainee team members' years on-the-job in police or fire departments before coming to RST's program. How might that suspicion be investigated? Be specific in the tools and procedures that you recommend.

24. A food processing company has large tanks that are cleaned daily. Cleaning includes the use of packaged detergents, which dissolve in a solution inside the tanks. The company purchases detergent packages with a fill-weight specification of 12.00 ± 0.08 oz.

    A supplier representative claims that his company uses statistical process control and will promise an inherent process capability of 0.20 oz. for the fill-weight specification. The brochure says nothing else about the process except that the advertised weight of the detergent packages is 12 oz.

    a. Should the food processor buy detergent from this supplier? Why or why not?

    b. If the supplier had control chart evidence that its fill-weight process was in fact centered at 12.00 oz. and was in a state of statistical control, how would your answer to question *a* change? Does all output meet specs?

    c. Suppose the supplier is a reliable provider of other products and can reasonably be expected to improve the detergent-packaging process. What advice would you offer to the food processor on seeking alternate suppliers? What advice would you offer the supplier regarding the relationship with the food processor?

25. Plug-N-Go, Ltd., makes valve covers to a diameter specification of 0.500 ± 0.020 cm. The normally distributed process is in control, centered at 0.505 cm, and has an inherent process capability of 0.024 cm. The next sketch shows the process distribution.

    a. Calculate the process capability index C_{pk}.

    b. Should Plug-N-Go be concerned about reducing the variation in the diameter process output? Why or why not?

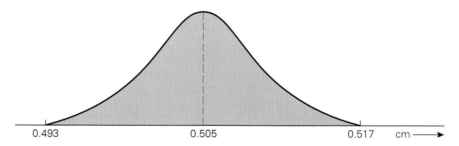

26. Suppose the valve cover process in Exercise 25 is in control but centered at 0.510 cm. The inherent process capability and the diameter specification are as given in Exercise 3. The process would appear as follows:

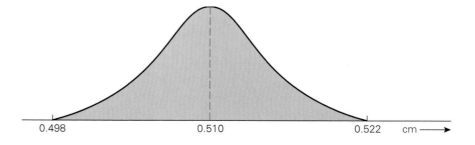

    a. Calculate C_{pk}.

    b. Use Appendix A (areas under the normal curve) to determine what proportion, if any, of the valve covers would fall outside the specifications.

    c. What action, if any, should Plug-N-Go take regarding the valve cover process?

27. Give two examples of tolerance stackup for a goods producer.

28. Give two examples of variation stackup for a service provider.

QUADRUPLES RESTAURANT

Restaurants Limited, a Seattle-based restaurant group, has recently hired an aggressive person to manage Quadruples, which caters to business travelers. The new manager, a total quality management (TQM) enthusiast, is concerned over complaints about Quadruples' self-service breakfast buffet. In the interest of improving customer service, the manager develops a survey form, obtains responses from customers over a three-month period, and summarizes the results on a Pareto chart (see Exhibit 5S–1). The chart shows that customers' biggest gripe is having to wait too long to be seated.

Next, the manager collects base-line data on percentage of customers waiting over one minute. The data are as follows:

M	T	W	T	F	S	S	M	T	W	T	F	S	S	M	T	W	T	F	S	S
7.3	8.2	6.3	6.3	5.3	3.5	3.0	8.1	7.0	6.4	7.3	5.4	4.7	4.0	8.4	9.3	7.3	7.2	6.7	4.9	4.0

Officers at Restaurants Limited have observed these preliminary initiatives—in the interest of possibly applying TQM to other restaurant management issues. Several questions need to be answered, and a step-by-step project improvement methodology would need to be established.

Before addressing the following questions, organize the data into a run diagram.

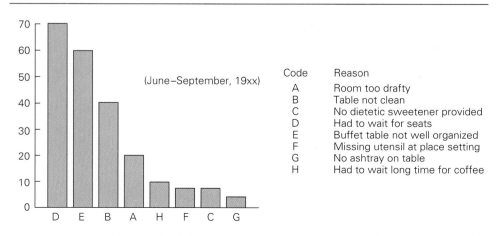

EXHIBIT 5S-1

Pareto Chart of Complaints

(June–September, 19xx)

Code	Reason
A	Room too drafty
B	Table not clean
C	No dietetic sweetener provided
D	Had to wait for seats
E	Buffet table not well organized
F	Missing utensil at place setting
G	No ashtray on table
H	Had to wait long time for coffee

Source: Adapted from Marie Gaudard, Roland Coates, and Liz Freeman, "Accelerating Improvement," *Quality Progress,* October 1991, pp. 81–88.

Discussion Questions

1. Can these kinds of customer response data be obtained reliably, systematically, and cheaply enough for a restaurant? If so, how?

2. Which of the Exhibit 5S–1 complaints are natural targets for continuous improvement in the restaurant (or any enlightened firm), thus, perhaps, not requiring solicitation of customer inputs to reveal the target for problem solving?

3. All of the complaints in Exhibit 5S–1 clearly are things customers would notice. If restaurant staff, instead of customers, were asked to express their complaints, suggest at least five complaints that would probably come forth. To what extent could the staff's mind-set be altered so that they would worry about the same things as customers? How could this change occur?

Project Assignment

Devise a project for dealing with the complaint data from Exhibit 5S–1 and the run diagram. Consider the relative merits and uses (for this case) of each of the tools for process improvement listed in the chapter plus brainstorming, competitive analysis, benchmarking, and quality function deployment (QFD) (covered in Chapters 3 and 4).

For Further Reference

Books

Brassard, Michael. *The Memory Jogger Plus +*™. Methuen, Mass.: GOAL/QPC, 1989.

Continuing Process Control and Process Capability Improvement. Dearborn, Mich.: Ford Motor Company, 1983.

DeVor, Richard E.; Tsong-how Chang; and John W. Sutherland. *Statistical Quality Design and Control.* New York: Macmillan, 1992 (TS156.D53).

Duncan, Acheson J. *Quality Control and Industrial Statistics.* 5th ed. Burr Ridge, Ill.: Richard D. Irwin, Inc., 1986.

Juran, J. M., and Frank M. Gryna, eds. *Juran's Quality Control Handbook.* New York: McGraw-Hill, 1988.

Montgomery, Douglas C. *Introduction to Statistical Quality Control.* 2nd ed. New York: John Wiley & Sons, 1991 (TS156.M64).

Statistical Quality Control Handbook. 2nd ed. Indianapolis: AT&T Technologies, 1956.

Periodicals/Societies

Journal of Quality Technology, American Society for Quality Control (ASQC).

Quality, a Hitchcock publication.

Quality Management Journal (ASQC).

Quality Progress (ASQC)

A Federal Express delivery: intermittent process, and somewhat customized service for each client (Courtesy Federal Express)

A Federal Express sorting operation: rather repetitive process of commodity-like products (parcels) (Courtesy Federal Express)

Manufacturing Portland cement, a commodity product, in the continuous processing mode (mixture of limestone and clay, kiln-heated at 2700°F, ground with gypsum, in 24-hour-a-day, seven-day-a-week operation unchanging for sometimes months) (Courtesy Portland Cement Association)

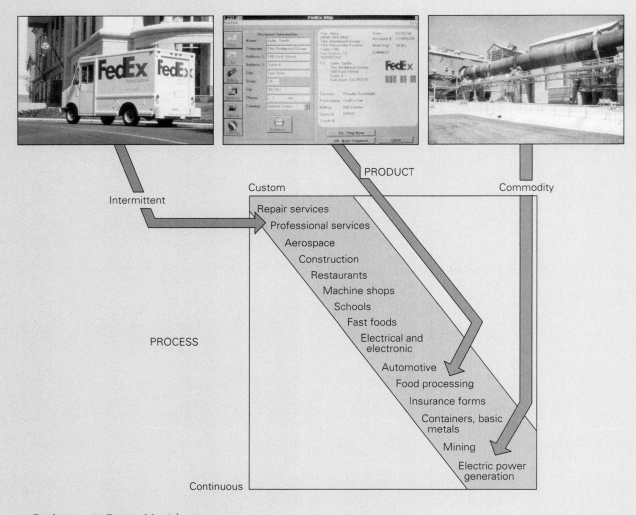

PRODUCT

Custom   Commodity

Intermittent

PROCESS

Repair services
Professional services
Aerospace
Construction
Restaurants
Machine shops
Schools
Fast foods
Electrical and electronic
Automotive
Food processing
Insurance forms
Containers, basic metals
Mining
Electric power generation

Continuous

Product versus Process Matrix[1]

TRANSLATING DEMAND INTO ORDERS

III

Customers are relentless. They expect everything. One customer demand might be for a customized window display—requiring flair, artistic talent, and construction abilities. The next demand could be for 2,000 sets of Barbie doll swimwear. Part III is all about planning for every kind of demand. To properly study the six chapters, it's prudent first to get one's arms around the diverse kinds of demands. The exhibit on the facing page provides a way to do that. Its horizontal axis sweeps across a full range of products (goods and services), and its vertical axis does the same for processes. In the middle is a broad band of examples of how products usually pair off with processes.

High and left in the exhibit is one extreme mode of operations. It is the irregular, intermittent (on-and-off) kind of processing that repair services must deal with. The product is **custom** (customized), which means unique. Planning is difficult to say the least. At the other extreme, lower right, is the opposite case. Processing is ultracontinuous, as it must be for a generator of electric power. (But just in case, the hospital or on-line computer service has its own backup generator.) The product is a **commodity,** very common or undifferentiated. Set it up right—in the design phase—and planning is easy from day to day. All kinds of processes and products are in between the two extremes, as is suggested by the three photo examples in the exhibit.

As we shall find in the upcoming chapters, companies sometimes find ways of shifting from their usual places on the product–process matrix. Intermittent processors strive to become more continuous, while repetitive and continuous processors seek even greater degrees of continuity. They aim for more predictability and easier planning—more like electric power generation. Doing this without losing flexibility to meet fickle customers' ever-changing demand patterns is a tall order. A trend in the other direction, for any kind of organization, is striving to become more flexible without losses of predictability and simplicity in planning. Superior companies are getting ever more clever at accomplishing these ambitious goals. As is the case throughout the book, the clever new ideas are intermixed with the more commonplace approaches.

DEMAND MANAGEMENT AND FORECASTING

6

Chapter Outline

McDonald's ARCH system, "in theory, will enable a store manager to have a customer's food ready when he or she walks through the door. . . . [It] tells the manager how many fries, hamburgers, or cheeseburgers he or she can expect to sell over the next 10 minutes. It indicates how many packages of tartar sauce or Big Mac sauce the manager should have on hand for the day. It recalls the store's history for, say, the four most recent Friday afternoons with regard to Filet-O-Fish sandwiches. Or, if a particular store normally gets a bus load of customers every Friday afternoon at 3 P.M., ARCH . . . 'knows' that, too."[1]

Customer demand is the lifeblood of any enterprise. Sometimes, however, customers appear unexpectedly—no advance warning. When that happens, the organization scrambles. Quality, responsiveness, and customer service suffer. That should rarely happen. The well-managed enterprise (e.g., McDonald's) forecasts demand, which allows being reasonably prepared when the demand actually occurs. More broadly, the business strives to manage demand, a task which includes

Customers line up at a McDonald's, their arrival anticipated via the ARCH demand forecasting system.

Wide World Photos

1. Planning for demand—developing readiness and flexibility.
2. Recognizing and accounting for all sources of demand—demand forecasting.
3. Pre-processing of demand—the order-processing activity.

Planning for demand, first on the list, is multifaceted. Human resources, equipment, materials, and other elements of operations management are involved. We will find discussion of readiness and flexibility in most chapters of the book. Preprocessing, the third demand management element, is narrower in scope. Order processing ties closely to the purchasing and order-fulfillment function, which is the subject of Chapter 9. We reserve the bulk of this chapter for the second item on the list, demand forecasting. First, however, a brief overview of demand management is warranted—to show how forecasting fits into the larger picture. Following that overview, we examine key issues in demand forecasting, how to measure forecast error, and forecasting techniques themselves.

Demand Management Overview

*𝒫*RINCIPLE 3:

Achieve unified purpose through team involvement in planning.

Demand management is a shared responsibility. A master planning team, with ties to marketing, finance, and operations, needs to take charge of and coordinate demand management activities. One of the team's roles is to account for all sources of demand: historical demand patterns, sales force estimates, actual orders and direct selling, within-company (division-to-division) demands, and economic influences. Another is to try to influence demand—for example, through special

Demand Management in . . .

Transportation

The governing council for Sea-Tac Airport (Seattle-Tacoma area) has approved a plan to evaluate demand management strategies. The plan includes assessment of "increasing landing fees during peak travel times, . . . use of more efficient aircraft sizes and types for the number of existing passengers, [and] increased use of Stage 3 [quieter] aircraft. . . . 'Until a decision is made on adding physical capacity, demand management has to be a part of what happens,' said Port Commissioner Paige Miller."

_____

Source: *Sea-Tac Forum*, July 1993, p. 1

Manufacturing

At Digital Semiconductor, demand forecasting was divided among three functions: marketing, materials, and finance. And it wasn't working. The leaders of the three departments formed a core team, which proceeded to map the current process. The process map (flow chart) revealed the following problems:

1. Use of different definitions for key terms and data elements.

2. Marketing and materials were duplicating each other's data collection and analysis.

3. Painful reconciliation of materials' short-term (zero-to-two-year) forecast with marketing's long-term (two-plus-year) forecast at the year–2 overlap.

4. Separate and different information systems, data, and analysis tools.

5. Outdated demand data by the time it took to review and reconcile the differences.

The core team identified six potential solutions, then brought in a much larger group of people as a project group. The extended team brainstormed 34 potential solutions to the top six issues, culled them down to a smaller number, and chartered three subteams to carry the solutions through to successful implementation.

_____

Source: Jill Phelps Kern, "The Chicken Is Involved, But the Pig Is Committed," *Quality Progress*, October 1995, pp. 37–42.

promotions; see the Into Practice box. Still another is to evaluate the impact of any demand management plan on capacity and cash flow. These matters must consider the full planning horizon—the breadth of the time interval for demand management.

Demand management has short-, medium-, and long-term purposes. The short-term question concerns item demand. That is, the organization needs to plan for demands in the near future for each item in its mix of goods and services.

The medium term covers 6 to 18 months in manufacturing, but usually much less in the service sector. The purpose is to project aggregate demand so that productive capacity can be planned. In the medium term the plans particularly apply to labor, machine usage, and aggregate inventory, which we address further in Chapter 7.

Long-term demand management affects planning for buildings, utilities, and equipment, which we focus on in Chapter 17. Long-term demand management also affects the introduction of new products and services and the phasing out of older ones—already treated in Chapter 4.

Medium- and long-term demand management decisions are made infrequently. The short-term product mix (item demand) activities, in contrast, keep a

Whether in short-, medium-, or long-term mode, demand management effort can be simplified if lead time, the time required to get things done, is shortened.

good many employees busy much of the time. Some are handling current business. Others watch current sales, adjust forecasts, and modify plans for capacity and output. The issues in making and adjusting forecasts are our next topic.

Issues in Demand Forecasting

Red sky at night, sailors delight. This and other homespun weather forecasting saws are part of our culture. Weather forecasts, however, are beyond our scope. So are harvest forecasts and economic forecasts, though all of these can and do have effects on operations. Our interest is in sales forecasting, or, preferably, demand forecasting, a term that accounts for the nonprofit sector as well as sales-oriented businesses. Key issues, taken up below, include the purposes of demand forecasting, lead-time requirements, data sources, forecasting for support services, time-series behavior, and forecast accuracy or error.

Purposes

Demand forecasting, like demand management, has uses across the planning horizon: short, medium, and long term. The forecasts help plan both quantities and timing of

1. Items/services provided or goods produced—in the short term.
2. Labor and inventories—in the medium term.
3. Facilities—in the long term.

Item forecasts are short term and must express demand in natural units. Examples are tons of steel and gallons of diesel fuel in the process industries, and clients or client hours, light bulbs, paper tablets, trucks, and so forth, in discrete output businesses. Those units apply to both the forecast and the schedule for creation and delivery.

The medium term could cover just a few days for a firm that uses untrained labor and hires and lays off based on a few days' notice as demand rises and falls. Most firms adjust the labor force less often because of the cost of training labor. In that case, the medium-term forecast would extend several months or quarters into the future. Medium-term forecasts are often expressed in labor-hours' or machine-hours' worth of demand. Planners can work with other units of measure, including dollars, since they may be converted to labor, machine usage, and aggregate inventory.

Long-term forecasts for facilities (plant and equipment) may go 10 to 20 years into the future for plants that require extensive hearings, licenses, debate, and approvals. Nuclear power plants are one example. At the other extreme, the long-term forecast for a restaurant may need to extend only a few months out. Monetary volume is the preferred measure of long-term demand. Usually, however, planners must restate total monetary demand as units of each major category of the product line, which indicates how to equip the facility: types of space, equipment, utilities, and so forth for each product line. (See Into Practice box, Fashion Forecasting.)

While organizations need to forecast for all three components of the time horizon, all do not do it the same way. Conditions always allow varying amounts of lead time for forecasting, as we see next.

Fashion Forecasting

Insiders at Limited, Inc. (retail fashion apparel), speak reverently of the "Weiss calendar." Michael Weiss, vice chairman, developed the calendar during his 12-year presidency of Express, Limited's most profitable retail chain. The calendar—really a forecasting aid—pinpoints what stores and what days of the year to run test marketing of a new garment. The method is highly accurate in predicting success for the garment across the entire chain. The calendar also "marks optimum dates for ordering fabric, beginning production, and starting markdowns."

Source: Teri Agins, "Limited Puts 'Weiss Methodology' to Test," *The Wall Street Journal,* August 9, 1993.

Lead-Time Requirements

Companies may need to forecast demand for only one stage of their transformation process, or for several stages. It depends on the product line and the competitive lead times—that is, the time interval from when the customer orders until the provider is able to deliver. Exhibit 6–1 shows five transformation stages, along with the forecasting requirements. At the bottom of the chart are industries with competitive pressures to meet customer demand immediately on receipt of an order. Most services and deliveries from stock, such as clothing, auto replacement parts, and cafeteria foods, require that everything except the delivery time be forecast and made ready in advance for phantom customers. Those future customers will expect to have to wait only as long as it takes for shipment, delivery, or on-site purchase—and no longer. Delivery is the allowable lead time.

Next up the ladder are industries in which customers expect to wait for assembly and delivery; everything else—capacity, raw materials, components, and so forth—must be forecast. These are make-parts-to-stock and assemble-to-order firms. Consider a Subway sandwich shop: customers wait and watch while their sandwich is assembled and delivered; components, however, have been forecast and prepared in advance. Other examples include machine tools, electronics, and custom assemblies.

Job-oriented firms form the next class. After placing orders, customers wait for manufacture or creation of components in addition to assembly and delivery. Organizations in this class, such as foundries, hospitals, and landscape/nursery firms, forecast for capacity and raw materials; they make or provide to order, but from raw materials already on hand.

At the top of Exhibit 6–1 are industries with very long manufacturing lead times, such as ships, locomotives, and heavy construction. Customers know that these heavy-capital-goods firms are project oriented and make only to order. Thus, allowable lead time includes procurement of raw materials in addition to the other transformation stages already discussed. Companies in this class need only long- and medium-term forecasting for planning capacity; everything else happens after orders are received.

Two additional points about Exhibit 6–1: First, it suggests that up to four types of forecasts might be required for a firm. Implementation of just-in-time processing,

EXHIBIT 6-1
Demand Lead Times and Forecasts Required

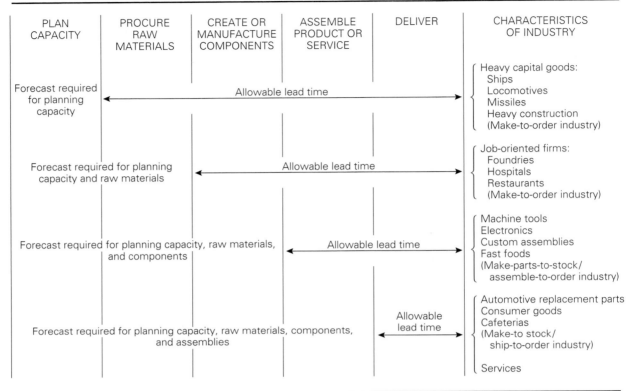

PLAN CAPACITY	PROCURE RAW MATERIALS	CREATE OR MANUFACTURE COMPONENTS	ASSEMBLE PRODUCT OR SERVICE	DELIVER	CHARACTERISTICS OF INDUSTRY
Forecast required for planning capacity	Allowable lead time				Heavy capital goods: Ships Locomotives Missiles Heavy construction (Make-to-order industry)
Forecast required for planning capacity and raw materials		Allowable lead time			Job-oriented firms: Foundries Hospitals Restaurants (Make-to-order industry)
Forecast required for planning capacity, raw materials, and components			Allowable lead time		Machine tools Electronics Custom assemblies Fast foods (Make-parts-to-stock/ assemble-to-order industry)
Forecast required for planning capacity, raw materials, components, and assemblies				Allowable lead time	Automotive replacement parts Consumer goods Cafeterias (Make-to stock/ ship-to-order industry) Services

Source: Adapted from Figure 2–2 of G. W. Plossl and O. W. Wight, *Production and Inventory Control: Principles and Techniques* (Englewood Cliffs, N.J.: Prentice-Hall, Inc., 1967), p. 16. Copyright 1967 by Prentice-Hall, Inc. Reprinted by permission.

*P*RINCIPLES 6 & 11:

Organize chains of customers. Cut inventory all along the chain.

Delayed differentiation
Keeping items in a lower-cost state as long as possible by delaying transformation of generic items into differentiated items.

with its tight stage-to-stage linkages, however, might cut this to as few as two forecasts: (1) a medium- to long-term forecast for facilities and labor, and (2) a shorter-term forecast of final product demand linking fabricated and purchased items.

Second, customers judge competing firms' timeliness only on allowable lead time—the time from order placement until receipt of goods or services. The customer is blind to the preceding forecasting and demand management effort. Consider, for example, two competing companies in bicycle repair services. The one with the longer allowable lead time in this business is at a competitive disadvantage. Perhaps the opportunity for shortening lead time can be found in better forecasting and demand management activities. To reinforce a point made earlier: When lead times exceed those of competitors, it's time for smarter demand management.

Wouldn't it be more competitive just to stock large inventories of finished goods and wait for the orders to roll in? Not really; there are risks of being stuck with costly inventories when forecasts have been too high just as there are risks of lost sales when forecasts have been too low. Demand management teams walk a thin line between those two risks, but sometimes they can help themselves by applying delayed differentiation.

Basically, the principle of delayed differentiation (postponement) works like this: At each stage of operations and for each class of inventory, strive to keep items in a lower-cost or lower-value-added state as long as possible. For example, paint stores show a rainbow of available colors on small paper cards, but they certainly don't stock all those colors; rather, they make them up by mixing pigment (dye) in white paint after the customer has ordered a particular color. Grilled-to-order steak is another example: Keep the steak in its raw, lower-cost state until the customer specifies how it is to be done. Delayed differentiation works best when choice of type, style, or model is large but demand for each is low, as is true of nonstandard paint colors; or the value of the item changes a good deal from one state to the next, as with grilled steaks.

> Standardization— expressed as a design guideline in Chapter 4 and as a goal for effective purchasing in Chapter 9—facilitates delayed differentiation.

Data Sources

Your $1,000 certificate of deposit is maturing and you are thinking about a higher-yielding investment. A friend suggests stock, currently about $9 a share, in a company that has just diversified into the knee pad business (for skateboarders, volleyball players, tile layers, and spelunkers). Friendship is nice, but a little more checking is in order. You want to know about the company's past financial performance (time series of past stock prices, earnings, etc.), and operating performance (innovations, capacity, technology, management, etc.). In addition, you want more general information about what lies ahead. What are market projections? How is the general economy going to do? And what about demand for knee pads, as well as other goods and services provided by the prospective company?

Large corporations are no different. They want to chart a course with inputs from a variety of sources. Consequently, demand forecasting is often three-pronged, perhaps coordinated by a corporate planning department. Exhibit 6–2 shows the three major groups of projections that help create a demand forecast.

- *Marketing projections.* Planners base marketing projections, typically measured in monetary units, on sales projections, sales force estimates, test market results, other kinds of consumer surveys, and special promotions.
- *Economic projections.* Economists look at how the economy is likely to affect the organization's demand. Economic forecasting based on sets of computer-processed mathematical equations is known as econometrics.

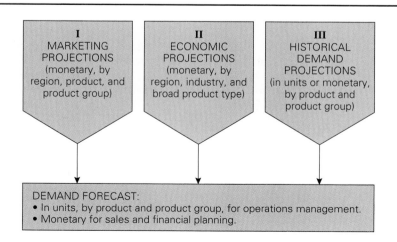

EXHIBIT 6-2

Three Determinants of Demand Forecast

• *Historical demand projections.* Computerized statistical packages help teams project past demand patterns into the future.

$\mathcal{P}$RINCIPLE 10:

Improve accuracy;
reduce variation.

While further exploration of marketing and economic projections is beyond our scope, we do recognize their importance. They show the big picture so that planners can sharpen their judgment about future demand and reduce variation between what customers want and what the firm provides. Historical demand projections (taken up later), on the other hand, are at the core of demand management. Regardless of the sources of data for forecasting, every manager should be involved. The reasoning behind this statement is the next topic.

Forecasting for Support Services

It is obvious that demand forecasting should be done by those with responsibilities for final products. In other words, forecast demand for items earning revenue, or major mission items—for example, in social work, number of eligible clients. That view of forecasting is necessary but not sufficient. All managers should forecast. Put another way, all staff services and nonrevenue items should be forecast in addition to forecasting for revenue and major mission items. Example 6–1 shows why forecasting is necessary in support departments.

EXAMPLE 6–1:   APEX BUS AND LIMO CHARTERS

O. R. Guy is the new president of Apex. One of his first acts is to create the department of management science and assign corporate forecasting to it. Corporate forecasting applies to the firm's revenue-earning services: its charter bus rentals.

Management science department analysts arrive at a forecast of a 10 percent increase in total bus charter sales for next year. Mr. Guy informs key department heads that they may consider 10 percent increases their targets for planning departmental budgets. Mr. Guy hears the following protests at the next department head meeting:

Engineering chief: O. R., I hate to protest any budget increase. But I'd rather wait until I need it. The engineering workload often goes down when bus charters go up. That's because marketing pressures us less for new bus cabin customization designs when sales are good. But then, in some years of good sales, we have a lot of new design and design modification work. This happens when several bus interiors are in the decline phase of their life cycles. So you can see that our budget should not depend strictly on corporate sales.

Director of human resources: We are the same way, O. R. The personnel workload depends more on things like whether the labor contract is up for renewal. Sure, we need to do more interviewing and training when corporate sales go up. But we have bigger problems when they go down. Layoffs and reassignments are tougher. Also, when sales go down, we may get more grievances.

Marketing chief: Well, I hate to be the crybaby. But it's marketing that bears most of the load in meeting that 10 percent forecast sales increase. I was going to ask for a 20 percent budget increase—mainly for a stepped-up advertising campaign. I don't dispute the management science projection of a 10 percent sales increase. The market is there; we just need to spend more to tap it.

Based on those three comments. Mr. Guy rescinds his note about a 10 percent targeted budget increase. He then informs managers at all levels that they are expected to formally forecast their key workloads. That becomes the basis for their plans and budgets. A management science associate advises those managers requesting help.

To explain what is meant by key workloads, Mr. Guy provides each manager with a simple forecasting plan developed by the director of human resources:

Workloads	Forecast Basis
1. Hiring/interviewing.	Number of job openings is based on data from other departments. Number of job applicants is based on trend projection and judgment.
2. Layoffs and reassignments	Number of employees is based on data from other departments.
3. Grievances.	The number of stage 1, 2, and 3 grievances, estimated separately, is based on trend projection and judgment.
4. Training.	The number of classroom hours and the number of on-the-job training hours; both are based on data from other departments.
5. Payroll actions.	Number of payroll actions is based on number of employees and judgment on impact of major changes.
6. Union contract negotiations.	Number of key issues is based on judgment.
7. Miscellaneous—all other workloads.	Not forecast in units; instead, resource needs are estimated directly based on trends and judgment.

Our discussion thus far suggests that managers have to exercise common sense and judgment in forecasting. One of their aims is high forecast accuracy, usually measured by forecast error.

Forecast Error

The popular ways of measuring **forecast error** have this in common: All are after the fact. That is, a manager must wait one period (sometimes longer) to unearth the error in the forecast.

Forecast error for a specific item in a given time period is:

$$E_t = D_t - F_t \tag{6-1}$$

where

E_t = Error for period t

D_t = Actual demand that occurred in period t

F_t = Forecast for period t

The period t depends on the purpose of the forecast. It might be a year for forecasting demand for a new facility (e.g., new motel units), or it might be 15 minutes for a hot prepared fast food (e.g., a hamburger). Usually, there is little value in knowing the error for just one period. Forecast error over several periods, however, indicates the validity of the forecasting method.

Mean Absolute Deviation.   Among the ways of calculating average error, one of the simplest and widest used is the **mean absolute deviation (MAD).** The MAD is the sum of the absolute values of the errors divided by the number of forecast periods; that is,

$$MAD = \frac{\Sigma |E_t|}{n} \tag{6-2}$$

where n is number of periods.

Example 6–2 shows the calculation of the MAD for eight business days in a small service firm.

EXAMPLE 6–2:   FORECAST ERROR—RÉSUMÉS-A-GLOW, LTD.

Kathy and Kyle have just opened their new business, a résumé preparation service. As part of their business plan, needed to secure startup financing, they forecast a level daily demand of 10 customers. After the first eight days of business, they evaluated the wisdom of the level forecast. Exhibit 6–3 shows the demand pattern and the error. The table below shows the day, actual demand (number of customers), and forecast in the first three columns. In column 1, −8 is the first business day, −7 is the next, and so on through the eighth business day.

(1) Period (day) (t)	(2) Demand (customers) (D_t)	(3) Forecast (customers) (F_t)	(4) Error (E_t)	(5) Absolute Error $|E_t|$
−8	10	10	0	0
−7	8	10	−2	2
−6	13	10	3	3
−5	5	10	−5	5
−4	9	10	−1	1
−3	8	10	−2	2
−2	11	10	1	1
−1	12	10	2	2
		Sum:	−4	16

Error, in column 4, is column 2 minus column 3, and column 5 is the absolute value (ignore the minus signs) of column 4. The sum of column 5 provides the working figure needed in the formula:

$$MAD = \frac{\Sigma |E_t|}{n} = \frac{16}{8} = 2.0$$

Is a mean absolute error of 2.0 too high? If so, does it suggest changing the forecast or the forecasting method? Kathy and Kyle decide to watch closely for another week or two, then decide.

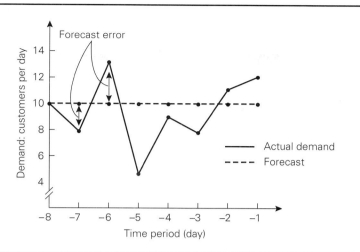

Exhibit 6-3

Demand and Forecast Plot—Résumés-a-Glow, Ltd.

Forecasting Specific versus Aggregate Demand.   Forecast error is likely to be high for a specific product such as number of vanity vehicle license plates. Error is less, however, when forecasting the aggregate demand for a group of several related products, such as vanity, common, commercial, and government vehicle plates. The reason is that the high and low forecasts for each product tend to cancel out in the aggregate.

This can affect capacity planning. Example: The human resource department of vehicle licensing is planning labor requirements for the next four quarters. First they project historical demand for all types of licenses. Next, they translate the aggregate projection into labor hours and then number of people.

Using aggregate forecasting in this way works fine if employees are flexible. If not, the method is a sham. Say that the licensing agency has four service counters, one for each type of vehicle license. If vanity plates surge in popularity, that service counter and its support people will need help. If employees at the next counter—say, common plates—are cross-trained, no problem. The common-plates service counter puts up a sign saying "Common or Vanity Plates," and one or more common-plate associates help process the vanity-plate paperwork. Service does not degrade, and the aggregate forecast has done its work well.

Forecast Error: Near versus Distant Future.   Make an honest effort at answering these three questions: How many hours will you spend reading this week? How about the third week in April? The week of your 85th birthday? Obviously, forecasts are more accurate for near-future periods than for more distant ones. This somewhat intuitive point is illustrated in Exhibit 6–4 with data from a picture frame assembly shop.

Initially, the supervisor set a level forecast of 500 frames per week (column 2) for the next two quarters, far enough out for capacity-planning purposes. The cumulative forecast for selected weeks (2, 5, 10, 15, 20, and 26) appears in column 3; column 3 equals column 1 times column 2. Column 4 shows cumulative actual demand—for the same selected weekly periods. Cumulative absolute error (column 5) is actual (column 4) minus forecast (column 3). Error rises as the forecast takes in a longer time period.

EXHIBIT 6–4

Cumulative Forecast Error: Picture Frames

(1) Week Number	(2) Weekly Demand Forecast	(3) Cumulative Demand Forecast $[(1) \times (2)]$	(4) Cumulative Actual Demand	(5) Cumulative Absolute Error $[\,|(4) - (3)|\,]$
2	500	1,000	1,162	162
5	500	2,500	2,716	216
10	500	5,000	5,488	488
15	500	7,500	8,110	610
20	500	10,000	11,250	1,250
26	500	12,500	14,010	1,510

The picture frame example raises several issues concerning length of forecast period and other more general points:

𝒫RINCIPLE 2:

Cut response times.

1. Long-term forecasting, even with the threat of increasing error, is often necessary in order to plan medium-, and long-term capacity. Forecasts must project as far into the future as the firm's lead times.

2. Level or smooth demand is easier to serve. The demand pattern in the picture frame example is actually rather steady, about 540 frames per week, so a level forecast was the correct move on the supervisor's part. It was a good pattern guess, but a bit low on magnitude or amount.

3. As time passes, forecasts should be refined by interjecting newer data (e.g., recent demands) and rolling the forecast over. Had the frame-shop supervisor examined cumulative error after week 5 and perhaps switched to a weekly forecast of 600 frames at that point, the cumulative absolute error at the end of the 26-week period would have been slightly over 1,000, but in the other direction; that is, an over-forecast. Of course, making adjustments approximately every month could serve to reduce the cumulative error.

4. Forecast error analysis is hindsight. We can speak about what the frame shop supervisor should have done because we can see the entire two quarters—the historical demand time series. At the five-week point, however, the supervisor didn't have that knowledge; a guess had to be made.

If the frame shop supervisor asked you now what to forecast for the next two quarters, your response might be, "About 540 frames per week—that is, if the past demand pattern holds true for the future."

You've just used one of several popular projection techniques. We examine others in the remainder of the chapter.

Historical Demand Projections

Getting a good forecast may require trying out several techniques and selecting the best one—the one with lowest forecast error. The matrix in Exhibit 6–5 relates

Forecasting Technique	Forecast Horizon		
	Short Term	Medium Term	Long Term
Multiperiod pattern projection (mean, trend, seasonal)	Yes	Yes	Yes
Patternless projection (moving average, exponential smoothing, and simulation)	Yes	No	No
Associative projection (leading indicator and correlation)	Yes ↑	Yes ↑	Yes ↑
	Product scheduling	Labor and inventory planning	Facilities planning
	Forecast Purposes		

EXHIBIT 6–5

Historical Demand Projection Forecasting Techniques

techniques to purposes. We are familiar with the short-, medium-, and long-term purposes (from earlier discussion). The techniques group into three categories, all relying on historical demand data. The first two, multiperiod pattern and pattern-less projections, employ time-series data. The two "No's" in the patternless row indicate that those techniques have limited applicability; their only effective use is for short-term product scheduling. Associative projections, the third group in the matrix, do not involve time series; rather, they track demand against some variable other than time.

By time series, we mean a series of demands over time. The main recognizable time-series components are

1. **Trend,** or slope, defined as the positive or negative shift in series value over a certain time period.
2. **Seasonal variation (seasonality),** usually occurring within one year and recurring annually.
3. **Cyclical pattern,** also recurring, but usually spanning several years.
4. **Random events** of two types:
   a. Explained, such as effects of natural disasters or accidents.
   b. Unexplained, for which no *known* cause exists (UFDs: unidentified flying demands).

Each of the first three variations appears in pure form as a separate three-year time series in Exhibit 6–6A. The trend line is positive. In the undulating seasonality series, the seasonal high occurs in the first quarter of each year and the seasonal low is in the third quarter. The cyclical series peaks in about the middle of year 2. Exhibit 6–6B shows how a time series might appear with all three of the pure components along with some random events, shown as spikes.

Forecasting models exist for use with time series containing any or all of these components. Many demand forecasts are rather simple extensions of past series behavior into the future. For example, suppose the demand for tow-truck and jump-start services has peaked in the winter season in the 10 years for which

Time series
A sequential set of observations of a variable, such as demand, taken at regular intervals; useful in both historical analyses and future projections.

EXHIBIT 6-6

**Components of a
Time Series**

Seasonal effects
surround us (the flu
season, the tourist
season in a given locale,
the harvest season),
and all usher in
demand peaks and
valleys for goods and
services. The
magnitude may vary,
but the pattern goes on
and on.

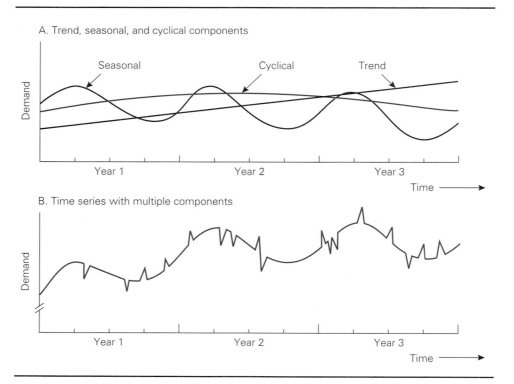

A. Trend, seasonal, and cyclical components

B. Time series with multiple components

records exist. We would expect this seasonal component to continue, and that would affect the tow-truck firm's planning of service to troubled motorists in the future.

Demand Forecasting in Practice

A survey by Professors Nada Sanders and Karl Manrodt sheds light on current forecasting practices in U.S. corporations.[2] The survey included a slightly greater number of service companies than manufacturers and tended more toward large than small companies. It reveals that the most popular methods of demand forecasting include none of the quantitative techniques listed in Exhibit 6–5. Rather, the most popular method is simply to use the most recent period's actual sales as the forecast for next period. For obvious reasons, that approach has usually been called the **naive method.**

Next most popular are judgmental methods. For medium- and long-term forecasting, which are infrequent and high in impact, the companies tend to rely on the opinions of a number of executives; this method is often called the "jury of executive opinion." For short-term forecasting, which occurs far more often, a single high-level executive may do the judging.

Why are these nonquantitative methods so widely used? The survey respondents tended to name lack of good demand data as the number-one reason. It suggests that practicing managers often fail on the basics—in this case setting up an infrastructure for data collection.

The high rate of business failure, especially among startups and small firms, surely is partly owed to such record-keeping failures, and consequent misjudging (really, mismanaging) demand. Thus, it is important for managers to set up a record-keeping procedure. At a minimum the records must note each sale, by date. A more complete procedure also keeps tabs on demands that the company is unable to meet, perhaps because of lack of capacity or materials.

Until records are available, managers will have to rely on judgment or the naive methods, which can be fraught with error. The consequences are idle resources some of the time and failure to meet demand at other times.

Among the quantitative demand forecasting models listed in Exhibit 6–5, the Sanders-Manrodt survey revealed moving average to be the most widely used. (For economic forecasting, regression is the favorite.) As we shall see later in the chapter, moving average is comparatively easy to understand, which, the researchers speculate, explains the preference for its use. Comparing their results with previous similar ones, the researchers had cause for cheer: The level of awareness and positive views of advanced forecasting methods is higher than in the past.

Though on average, firms seem not to use advanced techniques, some companies live and die by their sophisticated demand forecasting models. The rental car industry, which has suffered low profitability or losses in recent years, is an example. Demand management in this business is complicated by several factors; notable among them are allowing customers to pick up and return at different locations, and serving business customers who prefer larger cars and airport pickups on weekdays versus leisure customers who prefer small ones and downtown hotel pickups on weekends. Industry-leader Hertz has developed elaborate demand management and forecasting models to cope.[3] Its models try to project needs for number of cars in the fleet, best locations to which to deploy the cars, diversity of types of vehicles, and pricing combinations (one-day rentals, weekend rentals, and so forth).

A major element of the Hertz procedure, called a yield management system (YMS), is actually two separate forecasts combined. The more accurate of the two, which is based on extensive history, estimates demand for any date including holidays. The second forecast reflects the pace of bookings and cancelations over just the previous one to two months. The YMS merges the history-based and bookings-based estimates to produce a forecast whose standard deviation of error is lower than that of either separate forecast. Periodically, Hertz checks its forecasts against actual demand and uses the results to change the weights for combining the two forecasts. The Hertz system forecasts at a detailed level: expected net bookings for a given city, day of the week, time of day, length of rental, and time prior to pickup.

One YMS module is designed for ease of use by Hertz's local city managers. They tap into the system on their personal computers, and a graphical user interface employs color and shadings to highlight days requiring management attention. Days of excess demand show up in red, which alerts managers to take action to restrict demand; days of excess fleet availability show up in green, which requires action to stimulate demand. Managers can use their PCs to access detailed data, by date, enter updated data that will affect forecasts, make recommendations as to car availability, create graphs, or keep a diary of special occurrences such as holiday car-rental patterns.

Bar-code scanning at point-of-sale terminals is retailing's answer to the data-collection problem.

The details on the models that make up the YMS are specific to Hertz. In this chapter, we examine general concepts and models, which can be elaborated upon by any organization.

Multiperiod Pattern Projection

Consideration of the historical forecasting models listed in Exhibit 6–5 constitutes most of the remainder of the chapter. First are the three models used in multi-period pattern projection.

Mean and Trend

The simplest projection of a time series uses the arithmetic mean. When historical demand lacks trend and is not inherently seasonal, the simple mean may serve well. More often there is at least some upward or downward trend, which could even be projected as a curve. Exhibit 6–7 illustrates the mean and trend for Data Services, Inc., which offers commercial computer programming.

Three years of past quarterly demand in hours of programmer time are plotted. A first impression might be that there is no strong trend, and a bit of study shows no seasonal pattern either. If a certain quarter's demand is high one year, it looks as likely to be low the next. The up-and-down movement seems random. Also, one would not consider programming to have a seasonal demand pattern. What should the forecast be for upcoming quarters in the year 2000? Perhaps the mean (which works out to be 437) is the best way to minimize forecast error for such a nondescript demand; see the level dashed line.

Alternatively, we might look at only the most recent data, say, the last seven quarters. The trend is downward; see the "eyeball" projection (done by eye with a straightedge) slanting downward in the exhibit. Data Services's analysts may consider the projection to be valid for one or two quarters into the year 2000. They do not accept it for the longer term, since it is trending toward out-of-business

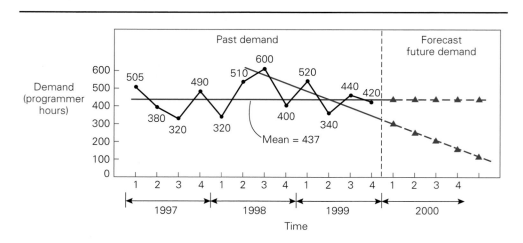

status! If they know the business is strong enough to carry on and prosper, the analysts would look for a more realistic way to project the future.

For a better forecast, better demand data might help. Let us assume that 20, not 12, quarters of past demand data are available; see Exhibit 6–8. Quite a different pattern emerges. The long-run trend, projected with a straight edge two years (eight quarters) into the future, is definitely upward. The year 2000 quarterly forecasts are now in the range of 500 programmer-hours instead of the 300 to 200 range resulting from the 7-quarter downward trend projection in Exhibit 6–7.

Another interpretation is that the 20-quarter demand data describe a slow curve. The exhibit shows such a curve projected by the eyeball method through 2001. The 2000–2001 forecast is now between the two previous straight-line forecasts. This projection is for a leveling off at about 450.

The curving projection looks valid. In other cases, of course, a straight-line projection may look valid. In any event, forecasting teams may use the graphic projection only to sharpen their own judgment. For example, Data Services's people may know something about their customers that leads them to a more optimistic forecast than the projected 450 programmer hours. As Al Ries and Jack Trout point out, "Trends change very slowly. It's only a fad that is fast-moving."[4] Even where outside information, perhaps about a fad, seems to overrule historical projections, the projections are worth doing. The procedure is quick and simple.

Another method of trend projection is mathematical projection using regression analysis. The least-squares technique of regression analysis, discussed in the chapter supplement, results in an equation of a straight line that best fits the historical demand data. To get a trend projection, teams extend the line into the future. The least-squares method may be modified to yield nonlinear projections as well.

The accuracy of least squares is not its main value. Eyes and straightedge are generally accurate enough for something as speculative as forecasting. But drawing graphs for eyeball projections is time-consuming, prohibitively so if a large number of products must be forecast. Least squares takes time to set up,

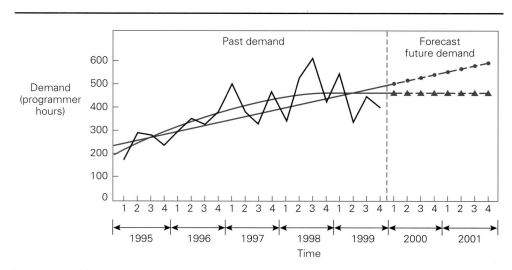

EXHIBIT 6-8

Twenty-Quarter Eyeball Curve— Data Services, Inc.

but after that it goes quickly, using a programmable calculator or computer. Computer-based forecasting routines have an extra benefit: They are usually able to print out mathematical formulas as approximations of the demand pattern, graphic projections, and tabular listings. Thus, least-squares regression is valued not for its forecasting accuracy but because it aids in routinizing some of the forecasting steps.

Seasonal

Often an item showing a trend also has a history of demand seasonality. In fact, perhaps most goods and services exhibit at least some seasonality, which calls for the **seasonal index** method of building seasonality into a demand forecast.

Seasonal Index: An Example.   The moving business is seasonal, so let's consider how a mover might make use of seasonal indexes. Exhibit 6–9 shows four years of demand data, in van loads, for Metro Movers, Inc. Since moving companies experience heavy demand surges during summer school vacations, Metro groups its demand history into three-month seasons—summer, fall, winter, and spring.

From the demand graph, summer demand is clearly the highest and fall demand is generally the lowest. (Note: Besides seasonality, there appears to be a slight upward trend over the 16 periods, but we'll ignore that for now.)

Using fall 1994 as an example, we calculate the seasonal index as follows:

1. Find the seasonal average. Fall 1994 is in the middle of a year that includes half of spring 1994, all of summer, fall, and winter 1994, and half of spring 1995. Thus, the seasonal average demand for the year that surrounds fall 1994 is

$$\frac{(90/2) + 160 + 70 + 120 + (130/2)}{4} = 115 \text{ van loads}$$

2. Find the seasonal index by dividing actual demand by the seasonal average. Since actual demand for fall 1994 is 70, the seasonal index is

$$\frac{70}{115} = 0.61$$

EXHIBIT 6-9

Seasonal Demand History—Metro Movers

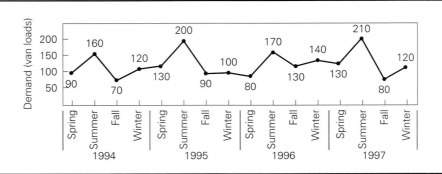

In other words, the fall 1994 demand was only 61 percent of an average season's demand for the surrounding year.

By the same two-step procedure, the four years of demand history yield the following seasonal indexes:

Fall 1994	0.61	Spring 1996	0.70
Winter 1994	0.96	Summer 1996	1.36
Spring 1995	0.98	Fall 1996	0.95
Summer 1995	1.51	Winter 1996	0.95
Fall 1995	0.73	Spring 1997	0.89
Winter 1995	0.88	Summer 1997	1.53

The final step is to reduce the three indexes for each season to a single average value. For the three summer indexes the average is

$$\frac{1.51 + 1.36 + 1.53}{3} = 1.47$$

The other three average seasonal indexes are: 0.85 for spring, 0.76 for fall, and 0.93 for winter. These numbers are rounded so that the four indexes sum to 4.0—exactly four seasons.

Now, Metro's forecasters have what they need to do a seasonally adjusted forecast. Suppose Metro expects to move 480 van loads of goods in 1998, which is simply an arithmetic mean projection of recent past years' demand. It would be foolish to just divide 480 by 4 and project 120 vans per season. Instead, multiply the average-season value, 120 loads, by the seasonal index for each season, yielding seasonally adjustable forecasts. The procedure is as follows:

$$120 \times 0.86 = 102 \text{ vans forecast for spring 1998}$$

$$120 \times 1.47 = 175 \text{ vans forecast for summer 1998}$$

$$120 \times 0.76 = 91 \text{ vans forecast for fall 1998}$$

$$120 \times 0.93 = \underline{112} \text{ vans forecast for winter 1998}$$

$$\text{Yearly total} = 482 \text{ (not exactly 480 because of upward rounding)}$$

Seasonally Adjusted Trends.   The seasonal index method may also be applied to projections when a trend component is present. Suppose forecasters at Metro Movers believed that the 1999 moving demand would reflect a 5 percent upward trend over the 1998 demand. On an annual basis, that increase would be calculated as

$$480 \times 1.05 = 504 \text{ vans for 1999}$$

And the average-season demand for 1999 would be:

$$504 \div 4 = 126 \text{ vans}$$

Next, the seasonal indexes may be applied to the value of the average season. The procedure is as follows

$$126 \times 0.86 = 107 \text{ vans for spring 1999}$$

$$126 \times 1.47 = 185 \text{ vans for summer 1999}$$

$$126 \times 0.76 = \ \ 96 \text{ vans for fall 1999}$$

$$126 \times 0.93 = \underline{117} \text{ vans for winter 1999}$$

$$\text{Total} = 506 \text{ vans}$$

Exhibit 6–10 shows the 1998 and 1999 forecasts. The figure shows what might be expected: trend effects, which are so important over the long run, tend to be overshadowed by seasonality when the short run, say, one year or less, is the focus. For forecasting and capacity management teams, the dominant message of Exhibit 6–10 is the seasonal pattern; the upward trend is secondary.

Cyclical Patterns—Natural and Induced.   Our previous discussion has described seasonal demand patterns and cyclical demand patterns as different time-series components. However, the patterns are alike except for the wavelength—the time it takes to make a complete cycle. Thus, forecasters can treat seasonality, whether with a standard one-year wavelength or one that recurs, say, every 5, 10, or 15 months in much the same way. Other tricks of seasonal or cyclic demand management depend somewhat on whether the cause of the pattern is natural or artificial.

Naturally occurring seasons are sometimes accompanied by extraordinary events that affect the magnitude of seasonal peaks. For example, a summer heat wave might raise temperatures from the seasonally normal high 80s to record 100-degree heat and create unusual demand for electricity. Also, accountants know that every spring is income tax season; newly revised tax laws, however, can further increase the peak demand for their services. In both cases, extra capacity will be needed beyond that associated with the usual seasonal surge. A public accounting firm that saw a 17-percent increase in its tax-related business following the 1986 U.S. tax law change, for instance, might plan on an additional 15 to 20 percent demand surge when new changes occur. Retailers have long known that holiday season sales create demand for more capacity (more clerks, longer store

> Steady growth, reflected by an upward trend, is great for business. Seasonal demand ups and downs, however, can give managers fits when they try to plan capacity to meet that demand.

Exhibit 6-10

Seasonal Adjustment of Trend Projection— Metro Movers

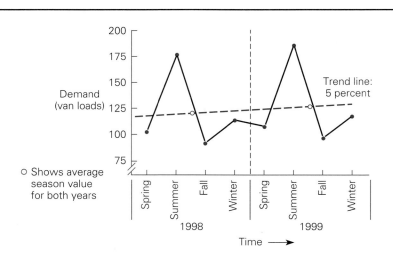

hours, etc.). They also know that extraordinary events, such as a mild winter, new toy or fashion craze, or negative report from a consumer advocacy group, further affect capacity needs in various departments or specialty shops.

Other seasonal patterns are artificial. For example, some firms often fall into a pattern of inflating current sales totals—by various means—to meet some sort of goal. One version, well known in manufacturing circles, is called the end-of-month push (also end-of-week, end-of-quarter, and end-of-year push). People relax in the early part of the period and then go into a frenzy at the end to meet the target.

One company, Physio Control, a producer of a medical electronic product line, tried mightily to escape from its end-of-year demand-surge pattern. So far, it has been unable to do so because most of its customers, emergency and medical institutions, have money to spend at the end of the year and spend a lump of it on Physio's products.

Another version, *channel stuffing*, arises from pressures to meet sales quotas in selling to wholesalers and retailers. In a few cases, pressures to meet goals have driven people to desperate, sometimes illegal, acts (see the Into Practice box entitled "Stuffing the Channel").

In such cases, where artificial demand patterns are a fact of life, seasonal analysis can and should account for them. That should not stop people from attacking the problem directly in an effort to eliminate the causes of spikey demand patterns.

To summarize the multiperiod pattern projections, keep in mind that their source is historical demand data described as time-series patterns. Finding the patterns can require some computations, but projecting them into the future is direct and simple. If there is evidence suggesting that future conditions will differ markedly from past ones, the forecasting team should avoid the pattern projection techniques or use them with extreme caution.

We now turn to patternless projection.

Into Practice

Stuffing the Channel

"Hitting the number became a company-wide obsession. Although many high-tech manufacturers accelerate shipments at the end of the quarter to boost sales—a practice known as *stuffing the channel*—MiniScribe went several steps beyond that. On one occasion, an analyst relates, it shipped more than twice as many disk drives to a computer manufacturer as had been ordered; a former MiniScribe sales manager says the excess shipment was worth about $9 million. . . .

"Other accounting maneuvers, starting as far back as 1986, involved shipments of disk drives from MiniScribe's factory in Singapore. Most shipments went by air freight, but a squeeze on air-cargo space toward the end of each quarter would force some shipments onto cargo ships—which required up to two weeks for transit. On several occasions, says a

former division manager, MiniScribe executives looking to raise sales changed purchase orders to show that a customer took title to shipment in Singapore, when, in fact, title wouldn't change until the drives were delivered in the United States. . . .

"To avoid booking losses on returns. . . defective drives would be tossed onto a 'dog pile' and booked as inventory, according to [a technician]. Eventually, the dog-pile drives would be shipped out again to new customers, continuing the cycle. Returns of defective merchandise ran as high as 15 percent in some divisions [according to the same technician]."

———
Source: Andy Zipser, "How Pressure to Raise Sales Led MiniScribe to Falsify Numbers." *The Wall Street Journal,* Monday, September 11, 1989.

Patternless Projection

The patternless projection techniques make no inferences about past demand data but merely react to the most recent demands. These techniques—the moving average, exponential smoothing, and simulation—typically produce a single value, which is the forecast for a single period into the future.

rolling forecast
Forecasts redone or rolled over at intervals—for example, every week, month, quarter, or year.

In practice, forecasters extend the projection several additional periods into the future. In the absence of trend and seasonality, extending the single value is appropriate and results in a rolling forecast. In each new period, the previous projection is dropped and the newly computed forecast becomes the new projection for periods in the new forecast horizon. It is like driving at night with headlights aimed 300 feet out, always reaching out another 300 feet as the car moves over the next stretch of pavement. These techniques are best suited to short-term forecasting for scheduling product mix. The forecast period typically is a week, a month, or a quarter.

Moving Average

The **moving average** is simply the mean or average of a given number of the most recent actual demands. Formulas and explanations for the moving-average technique are presented in Exhibit 6–11.

EXHIBIT 6–11

Moving Averages: Formulas and Explanation

A general expression for the moving average forecasting model is

$$F_t = \frac{\displaystyle\sum_{i=t-n}^{t-1}(D_i \times W_i)}{\displaystyle\sum_{i=t-n}^{t-1}W_i} \qquad (6\text{--}3)$$

where

F_t = Moving average forecast for period t

n = Time span, the number of demand periods included in the computed average

D_i = Actual demand for period i

W_i = Weight value given to data in period i

When different weights are used for the various data values, the computed forecast is referred to as the *weighted moving average*. Typically, higher weights are assigned to more recent periods. When the demand for each time period is weighted equally, usually with a weight of 1, we compute a *simple moving average* forecast. The sum of the weights (the denominator in equation 6–3 will then equal the number of periods in the time span (n). The numerator is also simplified for simple moving averages, resulting in

$$F_t = \frac{\displaystyle\sum_{i=t-n}^{i-1}D_i}{n} \quad \text{or, simply, } F_t = \frac{\sum D}{n} \qquad (6\text{--}4)$$

The weighted moving average recognizes more important demands by assigning them higher weights. The advantages of weighting are somewhat offset, however, by the added burden of selecting weights: Just how much more important is last month's demand than that from two months ago? From three months ago? Fortunately, exponential smoothing (discussed in the next section) provides an easier way to achieve about the same results as weighted moving averaging. Therefore, we shall limit our discussion of moving-average forecasting to the simple moving-average model, which is derived from the more general model as shown in Exhibit 6–11.

The examples in the remainder of the chapter include much tabled data and calculation. We have, in most cases, rounded to the tenths place to facilitate presentation.

Like other time-series methods, the moving average smooths the actual historical demand fluctuations, as illustrated in Exhibit 6–12. The data are for our moving company, Metro, except this time the demand history is in weekly instead of quarterly increments.

Demands for the last 16 weeks are shown on the left in Exhibit 6–12, where -1 means one week ago, -2 means two weeks ago, and so forth. On the right in Exhibit 6–12 is a column of three-week moving averages.

In Exhibit 6–13, the three-week moving average for weeks -16, -15, and -14 is projected as the forecast for week -13. The result, 9.0, which smooths the peaks in demand that actually occurred in the first three periods (6, 8, and 13), can be obtained from equation 6–4.

$$F_t = \frac{\sum D}{n}$$

$$F_{-13} = \frac{\sum D}{3} = \frac{6 + 8 + 13}{3} = 9.0$$

Since actual demand in week -13 was 11, the forecast error is $11 - 9 = 2$. That is a shortage or underestimate of two vans for that week. The moving average for weeks -15, -14, and -13 then becomes the forecast for week -12. The forecast error is $11 - 10.7 = 0.3$. The process continues, the average moving (or rolling

Week		Demand (van loads)	Three-Week Moving Average
−16	6		
−15	8		9.0
−14	13		10.7
−13	11		11.7
−12	11		12.7
−11	16		12.7
−10	11		11.7
−9	8		8.7
−8	7		10.0
−7	15		10.7
−6	10		12.0
−5	11		8.7
−4	5		8.3
−3	9		8.7
−2	12		11.0
−1	12		

EXHIBIT 6–12

Demand Data and Moving Average—Metro Movers

EXHIBIT 6–13

Three-Week Moving Average and MAD—Metro Movers

(1) Week	(2) Actual Demand	(3) Forecast Demand (three-week moving average)	(4) Forecast Error [(2) − (3)]	(5) Sum of Absolute Values of Forecast Errors
−16	6			
−15	8			
−14	13			
−13	11	9.0	2.0	2.0
−12	11	10.7	0.3	2.3
−11	16	11.7	4.3	6.6
−10	11	12.7	−1.7	8.3
−9	8	12.7	−4.7	13.0
−8	7	11.7	−4.7	17.7
−7	15	8.7	6.3	24.0
−6	10	10.0	0.0	24.0
−5	11	10.7	0.3	24.3
−4	5	12.0	−7.0	31.3
−3	9	8.7	0.3	31.6
−2	12	8.3	3.7	35.3
−1	12	8.7	3.3	38.6

$$\text{MAD} = \frac{38.6}{13} = 3.0 \text{ vans per week}$$

over) each week, dropping off the oldest week and adding the newest; hence, a moving average.

The three-period moving-average forecast results in a forecast error (MAD) of 3.0 vans per week (see calculation at the bottom of Exhibit 6–13). But the choice of three weeks was arbitrary. Also, use of the MAD in this and other examples is arbitrary. Another measure of forecast error would work just as well.

Suppose forecasters decide to try a different time span, say, six weeks. The six-week moving average, forecast errors, and MAD calculations are shown in Exhibit 6–14. The mean error of 2.4 is better than the previous 3.0 value. They could try other moving average time spans and perhaps further reduce the error. In a larger firm with many products, searching for the best time span is a job for the computer.

Moving average time spans generally should be long where demand is rather stable (e.g., groceries) and short for highly changeable demand (e.g., white-water rafting). Most users of moving average are producers or sellers of durable goods, which tend to have stable demand patterns in the short run. Therefore, longer time spans, say, 6 to 12 periods, are common.

The time span resulting in the lowest MAD is the best choice for actual use in forecasting future demand. But keep in mind that the forecasters relied on past data. As long as they think the future will be similar to the past, that is fine. If the future will be different, however, there is little point in expending much time analyzing past demand.

History-based forecasting methods such as moving average attempt to wash out some of the forecast error from historical demand data. The effect is a series of fore-

(1)	(2)	(3)	(4)	(5)	
Week	Actual Demand (vans)	Forecast Demand (six-week moving average) (vans)	Forecast Error [(2) − (3)]	Sum of Absolute Values of Forecast Errors	**EXHIBIT 6–14** **Six-Week Moving Average and MAD—Metro Movers**
−16	6				
−15	8				
−14	13				
−13	11				
−12	11				
−11	16				
−10	11	10.8	0.2	0.2	
−9	8	11.7	−3.7	3.9	
−8	7	11.7	−4.7	8.6	
−7	15	10.7	4.3	12.9	
−6	10	11.3	−1.3	14.2	
−5	11	11.2	−0.2	14.4	
−4	5	10.3	−5.3	19.7	
−3	9	9.3	−0.3	20.0	
−2	12	9.5	2.5	22.5	
−1	12	10.3	1.7	24.2	

$$\text{MAD} = \frac{24.2}{10} = 2.4 \text{ vans per week}$$

cast values that are smoother—less variable—than the time series itself. These smoothing effects are illustrated in Exhibit 6–15 for the three-week and six-week data in the moving-average example. The actual demand pattern, taken from Exhibit 6–12, exhibits some extreme high and low spikes. The three-week moving-average data pattern, from Exhibit 6–13, has spikes that are much less pronounced. The six-week moving-average data pattern, taken from Exhibit 6–14, is smoothed to look like gently rolling hills. Taken to the extreme, the 12 weeks of actual data would be smoothed to a single flat prediction line, no peaks or valleys, which is the mean (discussed earlier). The correct amount of smoothing—the correct moving average time span—is the one resulting in the least amount of error (smallest MAD).

Exponential Smoothing

Many firms that adopted the moving average technique in the 1950s saw fit to change to **exponential smoothing** in the 1960s and 1970s. Today it is among the most widely used quantitative forecasting techniques.

Simple exponential smoothing smoothes the historical demand time series. However, it assigns a different weight to each period's data and thus is really a weighted moving average. Weight values are obtained by selecting a single smoothing coefficient, α, such that $0 \leq \alpha \leq 1.0$. The exponential smoothing formula is:

$$F_{t+1} = F_t + \alpha(D_t - F_t) \tag{6–5}$$

EXHIBIT 6-15

Smoothing Effects of the Moving Average

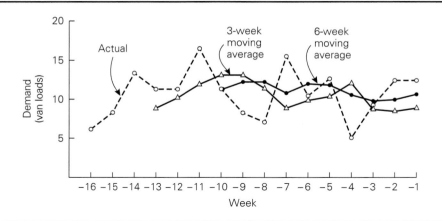

where

F_{t+1} = Forecast for period $t + 1$

α = Smoothing constant

D_t = Actual demand for period t

F_t = Forecast for period t

Equation 6–5 shows that each smoothed average has two elements: the most recent demand, D_t (new information), and the historical smoothed average, F_t (old information). The term in parenthesis, $D_t - F_t$, is the forecast error for period t. Thus, the exponential smoothing forecast for a period may be thought of as the forecast for the preceding period adjusted by some fraction (α) of the forecast error. That is:

Next forecast = Last forecast + α(Last demand − Last forecast)

For example, assume that the last forecast was for 100 units but demand was only 90. If α is set at 0.2, the exponential smoothing forecast is

$$\text{Next forecast} = 100 + 0.2(90 - 100)$$

$$= 100 + 0.2(-10)$$

$$= 100 - 2 = 98$$

This forecast of two fewer units than the forecast for last period makes sense because the last period was overestimated. Thus, exponential smoothing results in lower forecasts where teams have recently overestimated and in higher forecasts where they have underestimated.

Exhibit 6–16 illustrates this, again using Metro Movers as the example (the data come from Exhibit 6–12). In the exhibit, α is set equal to 0.2. In exponential smoothing, there must be a startup forecast; in this case, it is 10.6 for week −5. Following the suggestions of Brown,[5] the startup value here is the simple mean of past demand data.

The underestimate for startup week −5 was slight: only 0.4 units. Multiplying that 0.4 by the 0.2 smoothing constant yields an adjustment of 0.1, rounded off.

EXHIBIT 6–16   **Exponentially Smoothed Demand Forecasts—Metro Movers**

(1)	(2)	(3)	(4)	(5)	(6)	(7)	
Week	Actual Demand	Forecast	Forecast Error [(2) − (3)]	Smoothing Adjustment [(0.2) × (col. 4)]	Exponentially Smoothed Forecast [(3) + (5)]	Sum of Absolute Values of Forecast Errors	
−5	11	10.6	0.4	0.1	10.7		Startup phase
−4	5	10.7	−5.7	−1.1	9.6	5.7	
−3	9	9.6	−0.6	−0.1	9.5	6.3	Forecasting
−2	12	9.5	2.5	0.5	10.0	8.8	phase
−1	12	10.0	2.0			10.8	

$$\text{MAD} = \frac{10.8}{4} = 2.7 \text{ vans per week}$$

Adding that 0.1 to the old forecast of 10.6 yields 10.7 as the forecast for the next week, week −4.

In week −4, the 10.7 forecast exceeds actual demand of 5; the error is −5.7. That times 0.2 gives an adjustment of −1.1. Thus, the next forecast, for week −3, is cut back by −1.1 to 9.6. And so on.

Exhibit 6–16 results may be compared with the three-week moving-average results in Exhibit 6–13. Moving-average absolute forecast errors for the last four weeks from Exhibit 6–13 sum to 14.3 (7.0 + 0.3 + 3.7 + 3.3). Exponential smoothing forecast errors in Exhibit 6–16 are better at 10.8 (week −5 is not counted). However, this is by no means a fair comparison, since the number of demand weeks is so small and exponential smoothing has not run long enough for the artificial startup forecast to be washed out. Yet it indicates the tendency for exponential smoothing to be more accurate than moving-average forecasts.

In testing for the proper value of α, the mean absolute deviation is again helpful. Using past demand data, forecasting teams could calculate the MAD for various values of α, then adopt the α yielding the lowest MAD. It is common to use an α in the range of 0.1 to 0.3. The reason is the same as that mentioned earlier for using longer moving-average time spans: Most larger firms using exponential smoothing are makers or sellers of durable goods having rather stable short-run demand patterns. A small α, such as 0.2, fits this situation well. A small α means a small adjustment for forecast error, and this keeps each successive forecast close to its predecessor. A large α, say, 0.7, would result in new forecasts that followed even large up-and-down swings of actual demand. That would be suitable for the less-stable demand pattern of a luxury good or service.

It may appear that the next exponential smoothing forecast is always based solely on what happened last period, with no regard for all preceding demand periods. Not so. Metaphorically, if the forecast for next period, F_t, is the child, the parent is F_{t-1}, the grandparent is F_{t-2}, the great-grandparent is F_{t-3}, and so forth. The current offspring, F_t, has inherited a portion, α, of the error attributable to the parent, F_{t-1}, a smaller portion of the error attributable to the grandparent, and so forth.

Consider the manner in which weights are assigned in an exponential smoothing series. In a case where $\alpha = 0.2$, we would get the following results:

0.2 is the weight assigned to the F_{t-1} error.

$(0.2)(0.8)$ is the weight assigned to the F_{t-2} error.

$(0.2)(0.8)^2$ is the weight assigned to the F_{t-3} error.

$(0.2)(0.8)^3$ is the weight assigned to the F_{t-4} error.

In general, $(\alpha)(1-\alpha)^{i-1}$ is the weight assigned to the F_{t-i} error.

The pattern of decreasing weights for $\alpha = 0.2$ is plotted in Exhibit 6–17. Also plotted are the calculated weights for $\alpha = 0.5$. The exponential smoothing weights extend back into the past indefinitely.

It is possible to construct a weighted moving average that closely approximates exponential smoothing. But why bother? Exponential smoothing is actually simpler and less expensive to perform than moving average; it requires but one small formula. Furthermore, exponential smoothing can be extended to handle forecasting chores for data with trends and seasonality. Such models are beyond our scope, but may be found in forecasting texts.

Is forecasting-model simplicity a true advantage? Research evidence suggests that it is. Simple models are not only easier to implement, but they frequently outperform more complicated ones. When two or three simple models are used together (e.g., with results averaged) performance improves even more.[6]

The main weakness of exponential smoothing and moving average is one of those pesky what-ifs. The underlying assumption of both models is that past demand data is the best indicator of the future. But what if it isn't? Sometimes the very fact that a good or service has been in very high demand causes demand to drop in the near future. Customers become sated and demand drops. As was observed earlier, wise managers use multiple forecasting sources.

Adaptive Smoothing

Adaptive smoothing is usually used as an extension of exponential smoothing, and thus is often called adaptive exponential smoothing. Forecasters may adjust

EXHIBIT 6-17

Example Weight Patterns for Exponential Smoothing

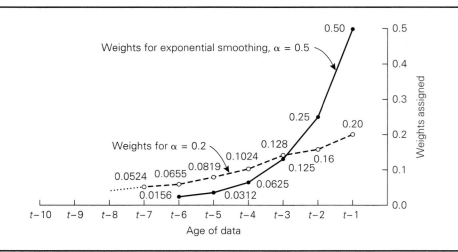

the value of the smoothing coefficient (α) if cumulative forecast error gets too large, thus adapting the forecasting model to changing conditions.

Cumulative forecast error is called the running sum of forecast error (RSFE). To signal the need for a change in α, the magnitude of RSFE is divided by the MAD to compute what is known as a **tracking signal:**

$$\text{Tracking signal} = \frac{RSFE}{MAD} \qquad (6\text{-}6)$$

Sustained increase in tracking-signal magnitude reflects bias in the forecasting model, which the forecasting team would want to eliminate. Two bias conditions may arise; fortunately, both are corrected in the same manner:

1. *Tracking signal magnitude increases, positive direction:* The RSFE is getting larger in the positive direction due to underforecasting. The cure is to increase forecast values by increasing α, since the forecast errors are positive. A larger α then increases the forecast.
2. *Tracking signal magnitude increases, negative direction:* The RSFE is getting increasingly negative due to overforecasting. The cure is to decrease forecast values by increasing α, since forecast errors are negative. A larger α then decreases the forecast.

It is known that when forecast errors are normally distributed, one standard deviation equals approximately 1.25 times the MAD. From the table of areas under the normal curve in Appendix A, we may obtain probabilities associated with various portions of a hypothetical tracking-signal distribution assuming that no forecast model bias exists. The approximate probabilities are:

Area	Probability
0 ± 1 SD (or ± 1.25 MAD)	0.6826
0 ± 2 SD (or ± 2.50 MAD)	0.9545
0 ± 3 SD (or ± 3.75 MAD)	0.9972

Thus, the likelihood of the tracking signal exceeding a value of ±3.75 is very remote if the model is not biased. Continued tracking-signal values with magnitudes less than 3.0, with some alternation in sign, usually denotes an unbiased forecasting model. A helpful rule of thumb is to consider changing the smoothing constant when the tracking signal exceeds 4 for high-value items or 6 for low-value items. For example, if the cumulative deviation is 650 and the MAD is 100, the signal is 650/100 = 6.5, which is above the maximum. Forecast error is overly positive, that is, forecasts are too low. Larger α values should be tested on recent data to reduce the error.

Forecasting by Simulation

Trend and seasonal analysis, moving average, and exponential smoothing are standard forecasting tools, especially for durable-goods manufacturers. The techniques do not require a computer, but most firms have computerized them for efficiency reasons. The computer, however, provides the firm with computational power to run forecasting simulations involving several techniques. Forecasting simulation has the potential to surpass in accuracy any of the individual forecasting techniques.

In each simulated trial, the forecast values are subtracted from a set of actual demands from the recent past, giving simulated forecast error. The forecast method yielding the least error is selected by the computer, which uses it to make just the next period's forecast. Each successive forecast requires a new simulation, possibly based on a new technique. (In contrast, the search for a time span or a smoothing constant—for a moving average or exponential smoothing—is performed as an occasional review rather than every forecasting period.)

Perhaps the best known forecasting simulation routine is **focus forecasting,** which was devised for use by buyers for hardware stores.[7] In this system, each product is simulated every month for the next three months and seven forecast techniques are tested. Each is simple for buyers and other inventory people in the company to understand. For example, one of the seven forecasting techniques is a simple three-month sum (which is not quite the same as a three-month moving average). The simulation for that method uses historical demand data for only the past six months, which are grouped into two three-month demand periods.

To illustrate the simulation, let us assume that demand for giant-size trash bags was 500 in the last three-month period and 400 in the period before that. In a three-month-sum forecasting method, the latest three-month sum is the forecast for the next period. Therefore, the computer simulation treats 400 as the forecast for the three-month period in which actual demand was 500. The simulated forecast error is $500 - 400 = 100$ trash bags. That forecast error is converted to a percent error so that it can be compared with six other computer-simulated methods for forecasting trash bags. The percent error is $1 - (400/500) = 0.20$, or 20 percent.

The simulation continues through six other simple, easy-to-understand methods (including simple trend and simple seasonal) to see what percent error results. If the three-month-sum method turns out to have a lower percent error than the other six simulated methods, the computer uses that method to make the next forecast. The forecast would be 500 for the next three months, and for each of those months the forecast is simply $500/3 = 167$ trash bags. The forecast rolls over (is recomputed) each month. The computer prints out the forecast for each of the 100,000 items, but buyers may overrule the printed forecast if they disbelieve it.

Focus forecasting was developed by Bernard T. Smith, as inventory manager at American Hardware Supply, for use in buying 100,000 hardware products.

Associative Projection

In all of the preceding techniques, forecasters track demand over time. Associative projection tracks demand, not against time, but against some other known variable, perhaps student enrollment or inches of precipitation. The associative techniques are the leading indicator and correlation.

Leading Indicator

If another variable precedes changes in demand, the other variable is a **leading indicator.** The leading indicator is helpful if the patterns of change in the two variables are similar (i.e., they correlate) and if the lead time is long enough for action to be taken before the demand change occurs.

Few firms are able to discover a variable that changes with demand but leads it significantly. The reason probably is that demand for a given good or service usually depends on (is led by) a number of variables rather than a single dominant one. The search for such a variable can be costly and futile. Therefore, most of the work with leading indicators has centered on national economic forecasting instead of local demand forecasting. Nevertheless, the leading indicator is a valued predictor in those cases where it can be isolated.

One story about leading indicators has been widely circulated. It is said that the Rothschild family reaped a fortune by getting advance news of Napoleon's defeat at Waterloo. Nathan, the Rothschild brother who lived in England, received the news via carrier pigeon. On that basis he bought depressed war effort securities and sold them at a huge profit after the news reached England.[8] (One historian disputes the story, asserting that the Rothschilds made more money during the war than at its end and that the news was forwarded by a courier in a Rothschild ship, not a carrier pigeon.)

The leading indicator in this case was news of the war, and it led prices of securities. The Rothschilds' astuteness was not in realizing this, for it was common knowledge; rather, it was in their development of an information network with which to capitalize on that knowledge. A costly information system like that set up by the Rothschilds can provide highly accurate information rapidly. In contrast, personal judgment as a basis for action is cheap but tends to be less accurate, and hindsight rather than foresight; that is, personal judgment often does not lead events.

In sum, leading indicators should have long lead times as well as accuracy. That requires good information systems. Example 6–3 illustrates.

EXAMPLE 6–3:   STATE JOBS SERVICE AND LEADING INDICATORS

Mr. H. Hand, manager of the Metro City office of the State Jobs Service, sees the need for better demand forecasting. The problem has been that surges in clients tend to catch the office off guard. Advance warning of demand is needed in order to plan for staff, desks, phones, forms, and even space.

One element of demand is well known: many of the job seekers are there as a result of being laid off by Acme Industries, which is by far the largest employer in Metro City. Hand is able to obtain Acme records on layoffs over the past year. He plots the layoff data on a time chart, along with the Jobs Service office's data on job applicants, in Exhibit 6–18. The chart shows the number of job applicants ranging from a high of 145 (period 8) to a low of 45 (period 20). Layoffs at Acme range from a high 60 (periods 6 and 7) to a low of zero (several periods).

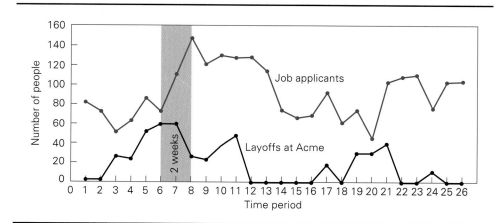

EXHIBIT 6-18

Layoffs at Acme and Job Applications at Jobs Service, with Time Scale

Exhibit 6-19

Exhibit 6-19

Correlation of Layoffs at Acme ($T - 2$) with Demand at Jobs Service (T)

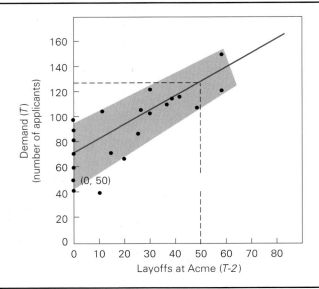

Plotting the points seems well worth the effort because Hand notes a striking similarity in the shapes of the two plots. Further, the layoffs plot seems to lead the applicants plot. For example, the high of 145 applicants occurred two weeks after the high of 60 layoffs and the low of 45 applicants occurred two weeks after layoffs spiked downward to zero. Weeks 1, 3, 17, 21, and 22 are other places on the layoff plot in which a two-week lead appears; the lead is close to two weeks in weeks 11 through 15.

Does a two-week lead make sense, or could it be coincidence? Hand feels that it makes sense. He bases this on the impression that laid-off Acme people tend to live off their severance pay for a time—two weeks seems reasonable—before actively seeking other jobs. Hand therefore takes the final steps. First, he establishes an information system. This is simply an agreement that every two weeks Acme will release the number of its laid-off employees to the Jobs Service office. Second, he establishes a forecasting procedure based on that layoff information and the two-week lead pattern in Exhibit 6–18.

In setting up a forecasting procedure, Hand regraphs the data from Exhibit 6–18. The new graph, shown in Exhibit 6–19, is a scatter diagram. It plots layoffs at Acme for period $T - 2$ and applicants at the Jobs Service for period T as the two axes of the graph. For example, the first point plotted is (0,50), which is taken from Exhibit 6–18, where for period 1 layoffs are 0 and two weeks later applicants are 50. Every other point is plotted in the same way. The points tend to go upward left to right, clustering around the solid line (an eyeball regression line).

Hand uses the solid line for forecasting. Suppose, for example, that he learns today that Acme is laying off 50 people this week. In Exhibit 6–19 a dashed vertical line extending from 50 to the solid line and leftward yields a forecast demand of about 125. This tells Hand to plan for 125 applicants in two weeks.

Correlation

Correlation means degree of association.

How good is Mr. Hand's leading indicator? By one measure—the supporting information system—it is very good! The layoff data from Acme are cheap to obtain and highly accurate. But in terms of lead time, it is not so good. Two weeks' notice seems insufficient for the purpose of adjusting resources on hand. In terms of validity, the leading indicator seems good, but how may we measure good? One answer is to measure it by the correlation coefficient.

The correlation coefficient, r, is a measure of degree of association. The value of *r* ranges from 1.0 for perfect positive correlation to 0.0 for no correlation at all to −1.0 for perfect negative correlation. In positive correlation, a rise in one attribute occurs along with a rise in the other; in negative correlation, a rise in one occurs along with a fall in the other. To calculate *r*, forecasters need a number of pairs of values. The chapter supplement provides a formula and sample calculations.

For the Jobs Service example, the correlation coefficient is quite good (about +0.78, calculations not given), which one can see by looking at Exhibit 6–19. The points tend to cluster along the broad, shaded band running upward at about a 30-degree angle. This is the pattern of a positive correlation. (Negative correlations go downward left to right.)

In the Jobs Service example, the amount of lead was determined visually. The two variables were plotted on the time scale in Exhibit 6–18, and brief inspection showed that the two curves were generally two weeks apart. Sometimes the amount of lead is hard to see, and where there are many potential leading indicators to check out, manual plotting and visual inspection become tedious. In such cases, computers may take over. It is simple for the computer to calculate *r* for a number of different lead periods. Planners may then select the one with the best *r*.

What about a lead period of zero? That would exist where a pair of events occur at the same time. Even if the correlation is perfect ($r = 1.0$), it appears that it is useless in forecasting. No lead time means no forewarning and, it might seem, no forecasting. This impression is incorrect. Correlation with no lead can be valuable if the indicator (independent variable) is more predictable than is demand.

Zero-lead-time correlation is usually covered in the introductory statistics course.

As an example, phone company planners in a large city may know that new residential phone orders correlate nearly perfectly with new arrivals in the city—with no lead time. There is probably value in knowing this because in most large cities careful studies are done to project population increases. Fairly reliable projections of new residences may be available. The phone company need not spend a lot of money projecting residential telephone installations; instead, forecasters may use the city's data on new residences. For these reasons, most large firms are indeed interested in establishing good correlations, even without lead time.

Summary

Demand forecasting, or estimating future demand, is a major activity of demand management. Because planning usually must begin long before actual customer orders are received, forecasting is essential. The demand that is to be forecast consists of long-, medium-, and short-term components in addition to noise. Analyses of historical time-series data often justify using simple projections of past patterns as forecasts of future demand performance. Demand is more certain in the immediate future, for which there usually exist customer orders specifying needed goods and services.

Forecasting results may be evaluated by studying forecast error. For a given time period, error is equal to demand minus forecast. Typically, however, a measurement of error over multiple time periods is more useful than that for single periods. One popular measure of forecast error is mean absolute deviation.

Aggregate demand forecasts are used for planning product or capacity groups. Error for group forecasts is usually lower than an average of comparable errors for individual items.

Forecast accuracy deteriorates as projections extend into the more distant future. Thus, as time passes, older forecasts should be refined in light of more recent developments. Also, planning and control systems dependent on forecasts should be segmented according to the importance of forecast accuracy.

Like demand management, demand forecasting has short-, medium-, and long-term components. Three primary sources of demand forecasts are marketing, economic, and historical demand projections. Accurate records greatly aid historical demand projection. Forecasting procedures are affected by industry and organizational variables such as required customer lead time, but all managers should forecast.

Demand forecasting often is based on a projection of a historical demand time series. Historical demand analysis addresses the simple mean, trend, and seasonality in time-series data.

Multiperiod pattern projection techniques are often used in a rolling-forecast mode. These techniques project the mean, trend, and seasonal components and are useful in short-, medium-, and long-term forecasting. The least-squares procedure (see chapter supplement) for trend projection may be used when precision is desired or where many products or services must be forecast. Seasonal indexes are combined with trend to produce projections that are more sensitive to seasonal influences on demand. The multiperiod projection techniques are useful only when past demand patterns are expected to remain valid in the future. In the short run, forecast inaccuracies can stem from artificial conditions, such as stuffing distribution channels to make sales figures look good.

Patternless projection tools include moving average, exponential smoothing, and simulation. Although they are most useful for short-term forecasts, they may be extended further into the future if certain conditions are met. A moving average is a mean of recent past demands, rolling over as time progresses. The number of periods used to compute the mean is the time span of the moving-average forecast.

Exponential smoothing, perhaps the most popular of the single-period techniques, is really a form of weighted moving averaging. It is simple and inexpensive and has been shown to be accurate. The single or simple exponential smoothing forecast is the forecast for the last period plus some fraction (α) of the last period's forecast error. Adaptive smoothing uses a tracking signal—a ratio of the running sum of forecast error to the MAD—to permit adjustment of α should forecast error become too large.

The widespread availability of microcomputer-based forecasting software has resulted in computerization of much business forecasting. The computer is essential in forecasting by simulation, in which several forecasting models are studied simultaneously in the search for the best forecast.

In associative projection, demand is tracked against some variable other than time. Techniques include leading indicator and correlation. Attempts to isolate an association (correlation) between one known variable and demand are most productive if the predictor variable can be shown to lead demand. The greater the correlation and the longer the lead time, the better the leading indicator as a forecasting aid. Correlation without lead may itself be useful, however, if the correlated variable is more predictable than demand. Multiple regression/correlation permits use of more than one independent or predictor variable.

While all of the historical techniques are potentially useful, demand forecasting is inherently imprecise. No amount of mathematical analysis can change that. Recently, the preference seems to be for the simple models, such as those discussed in this chapter.

Solved Problems

Problem 1

Historical demand data and forecasts exist for the eight-period time interval shown below:

Period	−8	−7	−6	−5	−4	−3	−2	−1
Demand	100	110	104	98	106	102	100	98
Forecast	104	102	104	100	100	104	103	102

Arrange the information in a table similar to the one in Example 6–2. Compute the forecast error (MAD). Plot the demand and forecasts as time series as in Exhibit 6–3.

The period, demand, and forecasts are shown in the first three columns of Exhibit 6–20. The rest of the table is constructed as in Example 6–2; it contains the computations necessary for determining the required error measures. The actual historical demand and forecasts for the eight time periods are plotted in Exhibit 6–21.

Solution 1

Period (t)	Demand (D_t)	Forecast (F_t)	Error (E_t)	Absolute Error $|E_t|$
−8	100	104	−4	4
−7	110	102	8	8
−6	104	104	0	0
−5	98	100	−2	2
−4	106	100	6	6
−3	102	104	−2	2
−2	100	103	−3	3
−1	98	102	−4	4
		Sum:	−1	29

$$\text{MAD (from Equation 6–2)} = \frac{29}{8} = 3.625$$

EXHIBIT 6–20

Forecast Error Measures: Solved Problem 1

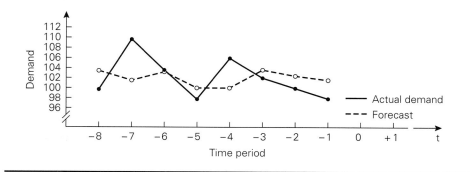

EXHIBIT 6-21

Demand and Forecast Plots: Solved Problem 1

Problem 2

Consider again the historical demand and forecast data in Solved Problem 1. Determine the running sum of the forecast error (RSFE) at the end of each period, and calculate the tracking signal after period -1.

Solution 2

Exhibit 6–22 contains the given data, forecasts, and error calculations in the first five columns. The sixth column contains the RSFE values at the end of each period. The tracking signal at the end of period -1 is calculated below the table.

EXHIBIT 6–22

Date and Solution Table: Solved Problem 2

Period (t)	Demand (D_t)	Forecast (F_t)	Error (E_t)	Absolute Error $|E_t|$	RSFE
-8	100	104	-4	4	-4
-7	110	102	8	8	4
-6	104	104	0	0	4
-5	98	100	-2	2	2
-4	106	100	6	6	8
-3	102	104	-2	2	6
-2	100	103	-3	3	3
-1	98	102	-4	4	-1
				Sum = 29	

$$\text{MAD} = \frac{29}{8} = 3.625$$

$$\text{Tracking signal} = \frac{\text{RSFE}}{\text{MAD}} = \frac{-1}{3.625} = -0.276$$

Problem 3

Following are historical demand data for 12 periods:

Period	-12	-11	-10	-9	-8	-7	-6	-5	-4	-3	-2	-1
Demand	40	42	41	44	40	39	39	41	45	41	38	40

a. Calculate simple-moving-average forecasts and mean absolute deviation for the data, using a time span of 4.
b. Plot the demand data and the forecasts on a time axis.

Solution 3

The time periods and historical demand data are shown in the first two columns of Exhibit 6–23. Moving average forecasts are in column 3, and error terms are in columns 4 and 5. Sample calculations and MAD values appear below the table.
Sample calculations: simple moving average (from equation 6–4):

$$F_t = \frac{\Sigma D}{n} = \frac{40 + 42 + 41 + 44}{4} = \frac{167}{4} = 41.75$$

$$MAD = \frac{17.0}{8} = 2.125$$

The plots of the 12 periods of historical demand data and the moving-average forecasts are shown in Exhibit 6–24. We see how the moving average technique smooths the peaks in the data.

(1) Period (t)	(2) Demand (D_t)	(3) Simple-Moving- Average Forecast (F_t)	(4) Error (E_t)	(5) Absolute Error $|E_t|$
−12	40			
−11	42			
−10	41			
−9	44			
−8	40	41.75	−1.75	1.75
−7	39	41.75	−2.75	2.75
−6	39	41.00	−2.00	2.00
−5	41	40.50	0.50	0.50
−4	45	39.75	5.25	5.25
−3	41	41.00	0.00	0.00
−2	38	41.50	−3.50	3.50
−1	40	41.25	−1.25	1.25
				Sum = 17.00

EXHIBIT 6–23

Date, Forecasts, and Errors: Solved Problem 3

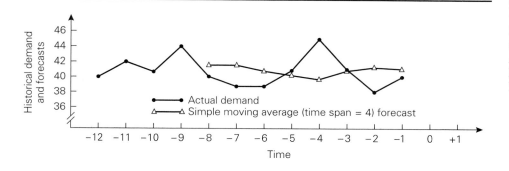

EXHIBIT 6-24

Demand Data and Moving-Average Forecasts: Solved Problem 3

The first five periods of demand data from Solved Problem 3 are shown in the following table. Using a smoothing coefficient, $\alpha = 0.3$, compute simple exponentially smoothed forecasts for periods −4 through −1. Initialize the procedure with a forecast value for period −5 of 41.

Problem 4

Period	−5	−4	−3	−2	−1
Demand	40	42	41	44	40

The data, forecasts, and absolute errors for the five-period interval are given in Exhibit 6–25. Sample calculations and the MAD follow.

Solution 4

Sample calculations (from Equation 6–5):

$$F_{t+1} = F_t + \alpha(D_t - F_t)$$

$$F_{-4} = F_{-5} + \alpha(D_{-5} - F_{-5})$$

$$= 41 + 0.3\,(40 - 41) = 40.700$$

$$F_{-3} = F_{-4} + 0.3\,(D_{-4} - F_{-4})$$

$$= 40.7 + 0.3\,(42 - 40.7) = 41.090$$

$$\text{MAD} = \frac{7.271}{5} = 1.454$$

EXHIBIT 6–25

Data, Forecasts, and Errors: Solved Problem 4

Period (t)	Smoothed Demand (D_t)	Exponentially Smoothed Forecast ($\alpha = 0.3$) (F_t)	Error (E_t)	Absolute Error ($\mid E_t \mid$)
−5	40	41.000	−1.000	1.000
−4	42	40.700	1.300	1.300
−3	41	41.090	−0.090	0.090
−2	44	41.063	2.937	2.937
−1	40	41.944	−1.944	1.944
				Sum = 7.271

Review Questions

1. What are the purposes of demand management?
2. Who is responsible for demand management?
3. What is the relationship between lead time for providing a product and requirements for demand forecasts?
4. Marketing projections and economic projections are both done in monetary units. How, then, do they differ?
5. If a manager told you, "I don't need to do demand forecasting," what arguments would you use to counter that statement?
6. What are the consequences for organizations that keep no demand records?
7. How is forecast error measured? What are the limitations of this measure?
8. Compare the accuracy of item and group forecasts. Explain.
9. Since forecast error is worse for distant future periods than for the near future, is it prudent to forecast only for the near term? Explain.
10. What does the term *historical demand pattern projection* mean?
11. What are the short-, medium-, and long-term purposes of demand forecasting?
12. What is a time series? What are its principal components?
13. When is a simple mean a suitable forecast? When would a trend forecast be preferable over the mean?
14. Is it permissible to make eyeball projections? Discuss. Under what conditions should the least-squares technique (see supplement) be used for trend projection?
15. Why is it sometimes difficult to decide whether to use the mean, straight-line trend, or curve trending as a forecast basis?
16. What is the purpose of calculating seasonal indexes? What is done with them?
17. Compare pattern with patternless projection.
18. Compare the time span of a moving average with a smoothing constant of exponential smoothing.
19. How is the effectiveness of a leading indicator determined?
20. How is one forecasting model compared with another in selecting a model for future use?

1. Demand management can include demand forecasting (estimating existing or natural demand) and also manipulating demand. Give three examples of the latter (demand manipulation).

2. Following is a list of organization types. Exhibit 6–1 shows that forecasts may be required for planning (*a*) facilities and adjustable capacity, (*b*) raw materials, (*c*) components, and (*d*) assemblies. Refer to the concepts presented in the figure to match up the listed organizations with the four purposes. Briefly explain your matchups.

Furniture manufacturing	Roller-skating rink
Clothing manufacturing	Natural gas distributor
Highway construction	Orthodontist
Air conditioning/heating contractor	Church parish
Airframe manufacturing	Sound-system manufacturing
Commercial printing	Small-appliance manufacturing
Tractor manufacturing	Toy manufacturing

3. At Apex Bus and Limo Charters, the human resources director was the first manager to separately forecast key workloads (see Example 6–1). Mr. Guy, the president, wants key workload forecasting extended to other departments. Your assignment is to prepare logical workload lists and forecast bases, similar to the table in Example 6–1, for the following departments or sections: public relations, advertising, and information systems.

4. Planners at county hospital are preparing a staffing plan and budget for next quarter. The following listing is computer data on labor-hours in various departments for last quarter. The trouble is, the average forecast error looks very high. Is the forecast error too high, or could next quarter's computer forecast be useful as the basis for a quarterly staffing plan? Perform any necessary calculations and discuss. (Hint: See discussion on page 184 of "Forecasting For Support Services.)

Department	Last-Quarter Labor-Hour, Actual	Last-Quarter Labor-Hour Forecast
Anesthesia	208	130
Cardiopulmonary	175	210
Emergency	589	650
Obstetrics	391	380
Pathology	68	90
Physical therapy	71	110
Radiology	277	200
Surgery	950	810

5. At Henry, Henry, and Henry, Public Accountants, the administrative vice president is responsible for forecasting demand for professional accounting services. The forecast for the preceding six-month period (made six months prior to that) was 120 client-days of work per month. Actual demand turned out to be 130, 100, 150, 150, 90, and 80. Calculate the MAD for the six-month time interval. From your calculations, what would you say about the pattern of error? Is it about what you expect? Why or why not?

6. Metro Auto Sales forecasts new-car demand 12 months into the future. The forecast is updated every month. Metro's supplier, a large U.S. auto maker, requires a 12-month forecast of total number of cars of all types so that it may plan equipment, space, labor, and so on in its manufacturing plants. It also requires a two-month forecast of numbers of each model. Internally, Metro finds the forecast useful for staffing (new-car salespeople) and for ensuring the correct amount of lot space on lease. Metro and its new-car supplier clearly are practicing a number of the concepts and principles of demand forecasting discussed in the chapter. Your assignment is to discuss the principles and concepts that apply to this situation (as many as you can think of).

7. Following are the recent actual demands and forecasts for a *service part* (industry's term for a spare or replacement part).

Time (t)	−5	−4	−3	−2	−1
Actual demand	9	10	17	25	27
Forecast	10	12	15	19	25

   a. Calculate the MAD.
   b. Plot the demand and forecasts on a graph similar to Exhibit 6–3. If you had to forecast the next two or three periods, what would your concerns be? Why?

8. Should the manager of a television or radio station forecast demand? Why or why not? What sort of demand are we talking about? (A brief interview with such a manager would be informative.)

9. In a certain time-sharing computer system, the quarterly number of "connects" or "logons" is one useful indicator of demand. Recent data are as follows:

	Quarter							
	−8	−7	−6	−5	−4	−3	−2	−1
Number of connects (in thousands)	8	9	11	10	11	13	16	12

   What is your forecast for next quarter? Look for seasonality and trend. Explain.

10. Service-part demands for lawn mower blades at Lawngirl Manufacturing Company, along with three-week and nine-week moving-average data, are as follows:

	Week							
	−16	−15	−14	−13	−12	−11	−10	−9
Demand	800	460	630	880	510	910	420	740
Three-week moving average		630	657	673	767	613	690	650
Nine-week moving average					682	671	713	710

	Week							
	−8	−7	−6	−5	−4	−3	−2	−1
Demand	790	700	840	600	930	680	900	800
Three-week moving average	743	777	713	790	737	837	793	
Nine-week moving average	716	734	733	776				

a. For weeks − 12 through − 5, plot the raw demand data, the three-week moving-average data, and the nine-week moving-average data on one graph. Comment on the smoothing effects of the different time spans (note that the raw data constitute a one-week moving average).

b. Assuming a nonseasonal demand, what is the forecast for next week if a one-week moving average is used? If a three-week moving average is used? If a nine-week moving average is used?

c. Consider your answers from question *b* and the nature of the product: lawn mower blades. Which moving average time span seems best?

11. Recent monthly caseload in a public defender's office was as follows:

January	*February*	*March*	*April*	*May*	*June*
180	100	90	110	110	120
July	*August*	*September*	*October*	*November*	*December*
140	170	150	160	160	170

a. Graph the demands as (1) a two-month moving average and (2) a six-month moving average. What do the graphs show about the smoothing effects of different moving-average time spans?

b. Calculate a five-month moving average centered on June. Then use that value to calculate a seasonal index for June.

c. What factors would determine the usefulness of the seasonal index in question *b*?

12. Demand data and seven-month moving-average data are as follows:

		Month										
	−12	−11	−10	−9	−8	−7	−6	−5	−4	−3	−2	−1
Actual demand	130	160	80	130	100	40	150	160	210	200	150	170
Seven-month moving average	133	121	107	113	117	124	141	144	154			

a. Compute a seasonal index applicable to next month.

b. If the trend projection, not adjusted for seasonality, is 168, what is the seasonally adjusted forecast for next month? Use the seasonal index from question *a* in your calculation.

c. If the product is not seasonal but the seven-month moving-average time span is optimal, what should be the forecast for next month?

13. Examine issues from the last two months of *Business Week.* In the "Business Week Index" section, find the production index and the leading index.

a. How are they determined? Verify this with calculations of your own.

b. Why would indexes such as these be smoothed? Discuss.

14. The stockroom manager at Citrus Life and Casualty Company forecasts use of office supplies by exponential smoothing using $\alpha = 0.3$. Three weeks ago, demand for letterhead envelopes and the forecast were both 12. Actual demands since then were 18 and 5 boxes, respectively. What is the forecast for next week?

15. The captain of the *Pescado Grande,* a sport-fishing boat that docks at Ensenada, Mexico, is trying to develop a plan for crew needs by day of the week. The basis is the number of paying customers per day. Following are data for the last three weeks:

	Monday	Tuesday	Wednesday	Thursday	Friday	Saturday	Sunday
Week −3	12	6	10	12	18	30	26
Week −2	9	4	5	8	22	32	34
Week −1	3	10	8	7	14	27	31

a. Calculate "seasonal" (daily) indexes for Sunday and Monday. Base the calculations on the appropriate seven-day average demand. What index should be used for planning the crew on Sunday and Monday of this week? Explain.

b. If the average number of paying customers per day next week is expected to be 16, how many should be forecast for Monday?

16. Huckleberry Farms, Inc., has three years of monthly demand data for its biggest seller, Huckleberry Jam. The planning director aims to use the following data for demand forecasting:

	Cases of Huckleberry Jam		
	Three Years Ago	Two Years Ago	Last Year
January	530	535	578
February	436	477	507
March	522	530	562
April	448	482	533
May	422	498	516
June	499	563	580
July	478	488	537
August	400	428	440
September	444	430	511
October	486	486	480
November	437	502	499
December	501	547	542

a. Calculate a six-month moving-average forecast. To which future time period is this forecast applicable?

b. Which of the following moving-average time spans is best: three months, six months, or nine months? Prove your answer by calculating mean absolute deviations (MADs) using data for the last 12 months only. (If suitable compter facilities and software are available to you, use the full 36 months' data.)

c. If the most recent forecast—for December of last year—was 495, what is the next exponential smoothing forecast? Use $\alpha = 0.3$. To which future time period is this forecast applicable?

d. Which of the following alphas is best for exponential smoothing forecasting: 0.1, 0.3, or 0.5? Prove your answer by calculating MADs using monthly data for the last three months only. In each case, assume that 570 was the exponentially smoothed forecast for September of last year.

e. Although the given data are monthly, Huckleberry also needs a forecast for next quarter and next year. Manipulate the monthly data (i.e., create new tables of data) to make them useful for a quarterly and annual forecast. Now compute a quarterly and annual moving-average forecast using a three-period (not three months, in this case!) time span. Then compute a quarterly and annual exponential smoothing forecast using $\alpha = 0.3$ and assuming that the last-period forecast was (1) 1,596 for quarterly and (2) 5,990 for annual.

f. Plot the data on a scatter diagram with time as the horizontal axis (use graph paper or carefully create a substitute on ordinary lined paper). Use the eyeball trend projection method to produce a forecast (not adjusted for seasonality) for Huckleberry Jam for the next 12 months. You may use either a straight or curving line—whichever fits better. Write down each of the 12 forecast values. (If suitable computer facilities and software are available to you, verify your plotted trend line by processing the data on a computer.)

g. Most consumer products show some degree of demand seasonality. What kind of seasonality pattern would you expect for Huckleberry Jam? Why? After responding to that question, examine the three-year history to see if the data tend to follow your reasoning. You may find it helpful to plot the three sets of 12-month data on top of one another on a graph to see if there is a seasonality pattern. Now comment further on Huckleberry's demand patterns.

h. Select any 3 of the 12 months and calculate seasonal indexes for those months for each year. Use a 12-month moving average on the basis. Now develop projected (next-year) seasonal indexes for each of the three months. (If suitable computer facilities and software are available to you, develop seasonal indexes for the full 12 months.)

i. Combine your results from (g) and (h), that is, your trend projection with your seasonal indexes. What are your seasonally adjusted trend forecasts for next year?

17. Following are the last four months' demand data and exponential smoothing forecasts for the custom drapery department at a local department store. The data are in number of customer orders:

Month	Actual Demand	Forecast
−4	18	20
−3	6	18
−2	12	16
−1	9	15

a. Determine the mean absolute deviation of forecast error.

b. Calculate the tracking signal as of today. What does it suggest?

18. Q. R. Smith, owner-manager of Smith's Kitchens, Inc., sees some evidence that demand for kitchen cabinets is related to local tax mill rates, which are adjusted twice yearly. Following are recent data that Smith has collected:

	Half-Year Period									
	−10	−9	−8	−7	−6	−5	−4	−3	−2	−1
Cabinet demand	55	70	75	70	80	85	90	80	70	75
Mill rate	110	125	135	145	140	140	160	150	150	140

a. Develop a graph (scatter diagram) with cabinet demands (Y_t) on the vertical axis and mill rates three periods earlier (X_{t-3}) on the horizontal axis. Plot each combination of demand and mill rate three periods earlier (i.e., Y_t and X_{t-3}) on the graph. For example, the first point would be the demand, 70, for period −7 and the rate, 110, for period −10. Examine your graph, Is there enough association between demand and mill rates three periods (one-and-a-half years) earlier to be useful for forecasting? Explain.

b. Calculate the formula for the straight line of best fit for the data in (a). Using your formula along with the appropriate mill rate, what is the forecast cabinet demand for the next six-month period?

Exhibit 6-26

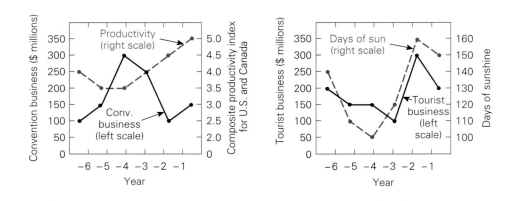

c. Calculate the coefficient of correlation. Is your impression from (a) confirmed?

19. The chief of planning at North American Hotels, Inc., suspects that convention business may be associated with productivity indexes and tourist business with weather. The graphs in Exhibit 6–26 show two of his attempts to make these associations:

a. Based on your inspection of the productivity–convention business graph, what should the chief of planning conclude? Comment on the usefulness of the analysis for the hotel.

b. Based on your inspection of the sunshine–tourist business graph, what should the chief of planning conclude? Comment on the usefulness of the analysis for the hotel.

20. The safety division at Acme Manufacturing Company has written the following numbers of safety citations in the past seven months:

	Month						
	−7	−6	−5	−4	−3	−2	−1
Citations	71	63	60	58	61	40	42

a. Using the eyeball method, plot the data and project the number of citations that might be expected next month.

b. The chief safety inspector suspects that safety citations are related to number of new hires. She has collected the following data on new hires for the same seven months.

	Month						
	−7	−6	−5	−4	−3	−2	−1
New hires	40	31	27	33	10	25	25

Analyze the association between new hires and citations. Look for a leading indicator.

c. Calculate the formula for the straight line of best fit (line of regression) for the last seven months of citations. Use the formula to calculate the projected demand for the next two months.

    d. Calculate the coefficient of correlation between new hires and citations. Make the same calculation but with new hires leading citations by one month. (Base the calculations on citations for months −6 and −1 and new hires for months −7 to −2.) Comment on the difference and on which type of associative forecast is more appropriate.

21. Anderson Theaters owns a chain of movie theaters. In one college town, there are several Anderson Theaters. Anderson wants to find out exactly what influence the college student population has on movie attendance. Student population figures have been obtained from local colleges. These, along with movie attendance figures for the past 12 months, are as shown in the table that follows:

    a. What is the correlation coefficient?

    b. Is this correlation analysis useful for Anderson Theaters? Discuss fully.

	Month											
	1	*2*	*3*	*4*	*5*	*6*	*7*	*8*	*9*	*10*	*11*	*12*
Students*	8	18	18	18	15	9	11	6	17	19	19	13
Attendance*	14	15	16	12	10	8	9	7	11	13	14	17

*In thousands. The student figures are monthly averages.

22. Large utilities typically forecast energy demands far into the future to ensure that adequate production facilities and distribution networks are available to meet customer needs. In 1992, Illinois Power Company prepared a 20-year forecast of the electrical power demand for its service territory; that forecast (not including reserve margin requirements) is shown in Exhibit 6–29.

    a. From the forecast, what would you conclude about the company's needs for financing, personnel, and facilities in the years to come? Why?

    b. Why are there three forecasts—high, medium, and low? Does the presentation of three sets of numbers detract from the credibility of the forecast? Discuss.

    c. Exhibit 6–29 is a demand forecast that does not include electrical power margin requirements. How might a company such as Illinois Power incorporate margin requirements into its forecasts? (You might want to interview a manager at a utility company.)

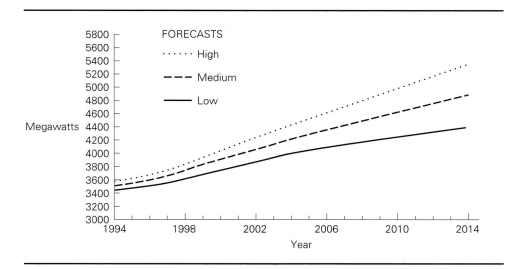

Source: Data courtesy of Illinois Power Company. Used with permission.

EXHIBIT 6–29

Forecasting in Utilities Services— Elecrical Power Demand

For Further Reference

Books

Abraham, B., and J. Ledolter, *Statistical Methods for Forecasting.* New York: John Wiley & Sons, 1983 (QA279.2.A21).

Bails, Dale G., and Larry C. Peppers. *Business Fluctuations: Forecasting Techniques and Applications.* 2nd ed. Englewood Cliffs, N.J.: Prentice-Hall, 1992 (HB3730.B25).

Box, G. E. P., and G. M. Jenkins, *Time Series Analysis, Forecasting, and Control.* Rev. ed. San Francisco: Holden-Day, 1976 (QA280.B67).

Chatfield, Christopher. *The Analysis of Time Series: An Introduction.* 4th ed. London: Chapman and Hall, 1989 (QA280.C4).

Makridakis, Spyros G., and Steven C. Wheelwright. *Forecasting Methods for Management.* 5th ed. New York: John Wiley & Sons, 1989 (HD30.27.W46).

Smith, Bernard T., and Oliver W. Wight. *Focus Forecasting: Computer Techniques for Inventory Control.* Boston: Monochrome Press, reprint ed. 1994.

Willis, Raymond E. *A Guide to Forecasting for Planners and Managers.* Englewood Cliffs, N.J.: Prentice-Hall, 1987 (HD30.27.W55).

Periodicals

Interfaces
Journal of Forecasting
Journal of the Operations Research Society
Management Science

Supplement

LEAST SQUARES AND CORRELATION COEFFICIENTS

In this supplement we examine two related techniques. Both concern the straight line that most closely fits a set of plotted data points:

1. The least-squares technique, which yields an equation for the straight line of best fit (line of regression).

2. The correlation coefficient, which measures how well a given straight line or line of regression fits a set of plotted data points.

Least Squares

The general formula for a straight line is:

$$Y = a + bX$$

For any set of plotted data points, the least-squares method may be used to determine values for a and b in the formula that best fits the data points: a is the Y intercept, and b is the slope. Least-squares formulas for a and b follow, first in the general form and then in a simpler form for a special case.

General form:

$$a = \frac{\Sigma Y}{N} - b\left(\frac{\Sigma X}{N}\right)$$

$$b = \frac{N\Sigma XY - \Sigma X \Sigma Y}{N\Sigma X^2 - (\Sigma X)^2}$$

Special form (when $\Sigma X = 0$, i.e., an odd number of periods):

$$a = \frac{\Sigma Y}{N} \text{ and } b = \frac{\Sigma XY}{\Sigma X^2}$$

where

ΣY = Sum of Y-values for all plotted points

N = Total number of plotted points

ΣXY = Sum of product of X value and Y value for all plotted points

ΣX^2 = Sum of squares of X values for all plotted points

ΣX = Sum of X values for all plotted points

The least-squares technique is shown in Example S6–1 using the special form of the equation.

EXAMPLE S6–1:   LEAST SQUARES TREND LINE—DATA SERVICES, INC.

At Data Services, Inc., demand in the last seven quarters in programmer-hours was as follows: 510, 600, 400, 520, 340, 440, and 420. What is the trend line?

Solution

The following table simplifies computation of a and b values. The fourth quarter, in which demand was 520, is treated as the base period; it is numbered as period 0. The three previous periods are numbered -1, -2, and -3; the three succeeding periods are numbered $+1$, $+2$, and $+3$. The low numbers simplify calculation and, since their sum is zero—that is, $\Sigma X = 0$—the simpler least-squares equation apply. The Y values are the seven demand figures.

Y	X	X^2	XY
510	-3	9	$-1,530$
600	-2	4	$-1,200$
400	-1	1	-400
520	0	0	0 ← Base period
340	$+1$	1	$+340$
440	$+2$	4	$+880$
420	$+3$	9	$+1,260$
Sums = 3,230	0	28	-650

Since

$$a = \Sigma Y/N \text{ and } b = \Sigma XY/\Sigma X^2,$$

$$a = \frac{3,230}{7} = 461$$

$$b = \frac{-650}{28} = -23.2$$

The formula for the line of best fit is:

$$Y = 461 - 23.2X$$

The formula may be used to forecast, say, the next quarter. With the base or centermost period numbered 0, the next quarter is numbered $+4$. Then,

Exhibit S6–1

Seven-Quarter Least-Squares Trend—Data Services, Inc.

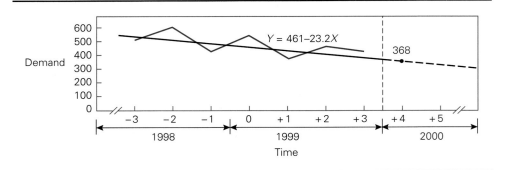

$$Y = 461 - 23.2\,(+4)$$

$$= 368 \text{ programmer-hours}$$

Exhibit S6–1 summarizes the results of the least-squares computations and the forecast for next quarter; note the very close pattern of the demand data here with that in Exhibit 6–7. Dates are added to the figure to make it agree with the dates for 6–7 in the chapter. Clearly the least-squares trend is very nearly the same as the eyeball trend in Exhibit 6–7, as we would expect it to be.

Correlation Coefficients

The coefficient of correlation (r) ranges from ± 1.0 for perfect correlation to 0.0 for no correlation at all. An r of ± 1.0 applies to the case where all plotted points are on the straight line of best fit.

A widely used formula for r is

$$r = \frac{\Sigma XY - \Sigma X \Sigma Y/N}{\sqrt{[\Sigma X^2 - (\Sigma X)^2/N][\Sigma Y^2 - (\Sigma Y)^2/N]}}$$

Example S6–2 demonstrates the formula for the State Jobs Service.

EXAMPLE S6–2:   CORRELATION COEFFICIENT—STATE JOBS SERVICE

Layoffs at Acme two weeks earlier are plotted against job applicants at the Jobs Service office. Exhibit 6–18 in the chapter shows the correlation visually. What is the calculated coefficient of correlation (r)?

Solution

Exhibit S6–2 provides the necessary totals to solve for r. All X and Y values are taken from Example 6–3 in this chapter. Since there are 24 data items, $N = 24$. Calculation of r is as follows:

$$r = \frac{\Sigma XY - \Sigma X \Sigma Y/N}{\sqrt{[\Sigma X^2 - (\Sigma X)^2/N][\Sigma Y^2 - (\Sigma Y)^2/N]}}$$

$$= \frac{51,825 - (2,130)(470)/24}{\sqrt{18,900 - (470)^2/24)(206,350 - (2,130)^2/24)]}}$$

$$= 0.78$$

An r of 0.78 is rather high. Layoffs at Acme may be considered a good leading indicator.

Number of Applicants (Y)	Layoffs at Acme (T−2) (X)	Y^2	X^2	XY
50	0	2,500	0	0
60	0	3,600	0	0
80	25	6,400	625	2,000
65	20	4,225	400	1,300
110	50	12,100	2,500	5,500
145	60	21,025	3,600	8,700
115	60	13,225	3,600	6,900
125	25	15,625	625	3,125
120	20	14,400	400	2,400
120	35	14,400	1,225	4,200
110	45	12,100	2,025	4,950
70	0	4,900	0	0
60	0	3,600	0	0
65	0	4,225	0	0
90	0	8,100	0	0
55	0	3,025	0	0
70	20	4,900	400	1,400
45	0	2,025	0	0
100	30	10,000	900	3,000
105	30	11,025	900	3,150
105	40	11,025	1,600	4,200
70	0	4,900	0	0
95	0	9,025	0	0
100	10	10,00	100	1,000
Sums = 2,130	470	206,350	18,900	51,825

EXHIBIT S6–2

Working Figures for Computing r —State Jobs Service

7 MASTER PLANNING—FOR CAPACITY AND OUTPUT

Chapter Outline

"Suffice it to say that, in the past, Caterpillar always waited until it was sure that the economy was turning down before it reduced production schedules. That is because with its previous inflexible production, it always took several months to raise or lower production rates by significant amounts. When Caterpillar finally did reduce production, it tended to be a sign that the peak in demand was already past, as Caterpillar tended to be unwilling to risk production cuts that might have to be quickly reversed.

"Today, with its flexible production, Caterpillar can respond to interim changes in dealer order rates during an economic upswing very quickly, and, even while the primary trend of the economy is upward, can fine tune its production schedules to interim demand changes without worrying that it might get caught short when a short-term slowdown suddenly reverses to the upside. For that reason, we believe a knee-jerk reaction—that when Caterpillar cuts production, it's a sign that the peak has been passed—would be wrong."[1]

Bulldozer assembly line at Caterpillar plant.

Source: Courtesy Caterpillar

Master planning works like a pair of scissors. Demand management, our focus in the last chapter, is one blade. Capacity planning and master scheduling—the topics of this chapter—form the other. Unless both blades exist, sharpened and well maintained, nothing gets done; there's no meeting of supply and demand. Unfortunately, however, the following exchange is all too common:

"How's business?"
"Great! Demand's up 15 percent! Only problem is that we're unable to meet it. I've got quite a few angry customers."

The reply reflects one problem that can face a master planning team— considerable demand but insufficient capacity to serve it. Customers can't or won't wait, and go elsewhere. On the surface, the solution seems simple—make sure you always have enough capacity to meet any level of demand that might arise. But that approach opens the door for master planning's other problem— substantial excesses in capacity and output. Costs go up, and eventually prices must rise. Though the effect is more subtle, and perhaps delayed, this problem also sends customers to the competition. Plus, the frequent remedy—downsizing—has other costs; plant closings and layoffs create short-term financial burdens and exact substantial human costs.

In a nutshell, master planning teams have the job of preventing either of these problems. In the remainder of the chapter, we see how they accomplish that task.

Master Planning Basics

The importance of master planning—demand management, capacity planning, and master scheduling—equals that of financial planning and market analysis; all three flow from the business plan and are mutually supportive. Human resources management, materials management, purchasing, and supplier management all make key contributions to the master planning process. Major customers and key suppliers are also frequently included in master planning deliberations. And increasingly, the strategic emphasis is on flexibility—due in no small part to the challenges of time-based competition.[2]

In all but very small business, master planning is a job for multifunctional teams—diverse expertise is required. Later in this section, we look specifically at what those teams do and examine the master planning sequence. But first, let's define some terms and look at master planning in a proprietorship.

Terminology

aggregate demand: Total demand, not broken down into different products; measured in broad units (e.g., customers, cartons, truckloads, or tons per day).

Capacity is the ability to accommodate. In operations management, it refers to a provider's capability of performing the transformations necessary to provide those goods and services that customers demand. **Capacity planning,** therefore, describes a broad range of activities—all focused on creating and maintaining customer-serving resources and adjusting the levels of those resources as required. As we saw in Chapter 6, the use of aggregate demand data simplifies the initial stages of capacity planning—if human and other resources are flexible enough to handle multiple tasks.

For every firm, capacity planning at some point has to include facilities planning; decisions regarding location and layout clearly affect capacity to serve customers. We address location in Chapter 17 and layout in Chapter 12. Also, process design, discussed in Chapter 4, plays a key role in determining production or service capacity.

When capacity is allocated—that is, when resources are assigned to specific tasks, projects, or customers—the focus shifts to outputs. The allocations constitute a schedule—a commitment to produce or serve. The **master schedule** is the general plan for providing those outputs according to specific configurations, quantities, and dates. In manufacturing, the master schedule is referred to as the **master production schedule (MPS);** in services, it usually has a more generic label such as the appointment book or facility schedule.

The Anita's Studio example relates to two other chapter examples: Koji Film Co., a manufacturer whose product Anita might use, and FastFotos, Inc., a service business that Anita might turn to for film processing.

We will expand and refine some of these concepts later, but with the basic definitions in place, we are ready to look more closely at the master planning challenges faced by businesses.

Introductory Example

Although the more complex master planning tools and most of the terminology evolved in North American manufacturing, all organizations perform master planning. Anita's Studio, a small service-oriented business, must consider the same issues—though on a smaller scale—as large multinational manufacturers. Example 7–1 illustrates. The margin notes, positioned beside appropriate text passages, highlight these issues.

Example 7–1:   Master Planning—Photography Services, Part I

Demand for
  outputs. . . . .

Demand for
  capacity. . . . .

Anita's Studio is a professional photography business. Anita specializes in individual and family portraits. She shoots in her own studio and does her own developing and printing. Demand may be expressed as the number of customers or, more precisely, the number of photos. But to Anita, demand has another, equally important meaning: demand for capacity. What capacity does she need in order to satisfy the demand for her services?

The first capacity item is Anita's time, which includes hours in the studio, developing, packaging, record keeping, management, and so forth. Second is the demand for paper,

Elements of capacity. . . . . developing chemicals, film, and other supplies. Next, she needs certain tools and equipment, such as cameras, lights, backdrops, enlargers, drying racks, and light meters. Finally, she needs the facility (studio) itself.

Capacity limits. . . . . . . Further, each item is limited. Anita's time is restricted to something less than 24 hours a day, the enlarger can handle only so many prints per hour, the studio accommodates only certain group sizes, backdrops, and so forth. If Anita knows that demand for her work is relatively stable, she may develop a relatively stable capacity plan.

Complexity created by diversification. . . . . . But what if she wants to change her business plan, say, by expanding into event photography—weddings and other social or sporting events? For one thing, demand for photographs and capacity to process them will grow, which requires further capacity planning. Also, while some capacity items are common to both portrait and event photography, others must be separately planned. Event work will require new kinds of capacity: It generates travel and on-site shooting time. Moreover, Anita may have to purchase faster lenses, battery packs, film winders, and other special equipment. Both event and portrait work, however, require capacity for developing and printing.

Capacity strategy and possible capacity plans. . . . . Another issue is seasonality. Weddings, anniversaries, graduations, and proms pile up in May and June. Thus, more capacity will be needed in those months. Anita may consider buying more equipment, hiring assistants, and contracting out some developing and printing. On the other hand, she may choose simply to limit the business she accepts, reasoning that any added springtime capacity will be unused during the rest of the year. She might wish to avoid the unpleasant task of dismissing assistants when there is not enough work. The point is that she has options in planning capacity.

Business plan influence. . . . . Anita's business plan, including goals, strategies, and policies, will affect her thinking about capacity options. What she wants to do influences what she plans to do.

Master scheduling. . . . . In developing an appointment book (master schedule), Anita must consider demand for her services as well as her capacity to provide them. Total (aggregate) demand for all photography services will determine the load on her developing and printing capacity and on her capacity to cover demand for billing and other clerical operations. The mix of portrait and event photography (major subgroups of aggregate demand) will determine the capacity requirements for studio shooting and travel/site-shooting times, respectively.

Schedule (meeting demand) allocates capacity. . . . . Finally, planning for each capacity item, such as each type of film and each size of printing paper, will require forecasts of each type of photography assignment, including number of shots, size and number of prints desired, and so forth. Actual customer bookings and ensuing print orders will most accurately help predict capacity needed, by type.

Capacity plan affects the master schedule. . . . . On the other side of the coin, the capacity plan Anita selects will determine how much and what type of demand she can satisfy. She might have to revise her appointment book, perhaps more than once, as she juggles demand and capacity, seeking a fit.

Master schedule revisions. . . . . It is easy to see that inattention to demand for photography services might lead to investment in too much or too little capacity. Likewise, failure to consider capacity could lead to overbooking and promising more than can be delivered. Adverse effects may include delays, customer dissatisfaction, lost business, and overall careless and hurried business practices.

Effects on service to customers. . . . .

Several points emerge from the Anita's Studio example:

1. Capacity is needed in order to meet demand—without panic or shortcuts.
2. The business plan (including plans for expansion or contraction) influences capacity choices (equipment quantity, staff size, etc.).
3. Greater variety of products or services offered (portrait photography, event photography, etc.) complicates capacity planning.
4. Demand planning and capacity planning set limits on what the appointment book (master schedule) can accommodate.
5. In a given period, one or more revisions of the master schedule/appointment book might be required.

We reemphasize that these points also apply to master planning in large firms, where the extra difficulty of reaching consensus among the many manager-planners adds further complexity. Two additional issues that affect master planning in large organizations were not evident in Anita's Studio; we add them to our list:

6. Flexibility makes master planning easier. Cross-trained personnel may be more readily moved to where demand is greatest, and flexible equipment may be assigned to a variety of jobs. (Proprietors like Anita should keep this point in mind as their businesses grow.)

7. Standard designs—in parts, components, and processes—make it easier to smooth out demands on capacity and also reduce the chance of stock outages or excessive inventory buildups. (Small businesses can benefit here, too. Sticking with the same types of equipment, for example, makes it easier to move jobs and employees around to balance demand and capacity.)

Let's expand our perspective now by looking at master planning in larger organizations. Teams come into play.

Master Planning Teams

In many larger companies, master planning is a two-team effort. One team—the **capacity planning team**—operates at the broader level.

The capacity planning team must strive to balance aggregate customer demand with the company's established capacity policies (upper right in Exhibit 7–1), which have evolved from the business plan. The result of this balancing act is a capacity plan that shows the big picture of overall resource requirements. This broad-level capacity planning is sometimes called **resource requirements planning.** In complex production settings, the capacity planning team might perform another capacity check after an actual production plan has been set. This activity—**rough-cut capacity planning**—ensures that the specific plan won't overload a scarce resource.

In Exhibit 7–1 we see possible membership on the capacity planning team. This list isn't fixed but is typical. As with formation of any team, what is important is to get all of the right people as members.

In practice, resource requirements planning and rough-cut capacity planning activities often overlap. Many companies use but one term to describe an ongoing broad-level capacity planning effort.

EXHIBIT 7–1

Capacity Planning Team and Its Responsibilities

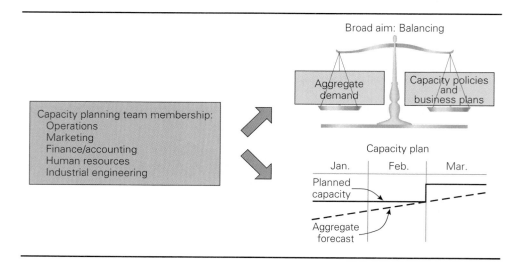

The lower right-hand portion of Exhibit 7–1 is a sample capacity plan for a three-month period. The vertical axis, representing planned capacity and aggregate forecast demand, may be in capacity units (e.g., labor or machine hours) or output units (gallons, pieces, etc.). Inspection shows that this plan calls for capacity to meet or exceed demand throughout the three-month planning period. The step-up in capacity in March ensures this.

There is nothing that says capacity plans must be in monthly increments. Time-based competitive pressures are driving some firms into weekly capacity planning, which requires commensurate capacity flexibility (such as on-call temporary labor). Whether in monthly or weekly increments, the capacity plan is subject to change before it runs its course. For example, if actual demands turns out to be less than the forecast, the planning team may want to delay the planned capacity increase until April 1.

The second master planning team is more narrowly focused. As Exhibit 7–2A shows, this team—the **master scheduling team**—steers the firm's capacity toward

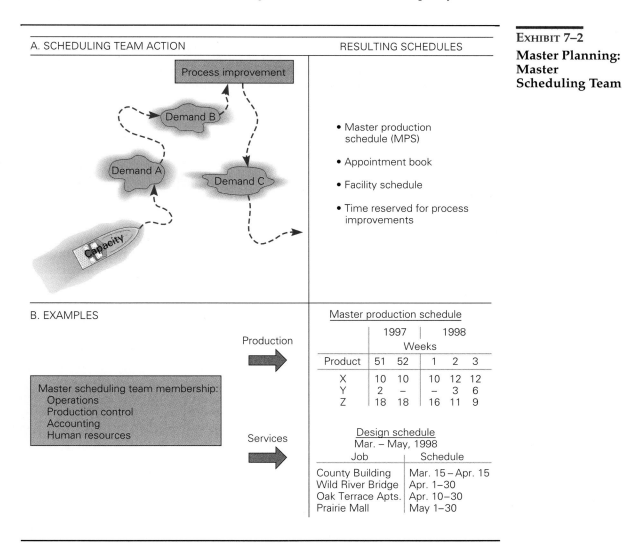

EXHIBIT 7–2

Master Planning: Master Scheduling Team

A. SCHEDULING TEAM ACTION

RESULTING SCHEDULES

Process improvement

Demand B

Demand A

Demand C

Capacity

- Master production schedule (MPS)

- Appointment book

- Facility schedule

- Time reserved for process improvements

B. EXAMPLES

Production →

Services →

Master scheduling team membership:
  Operations
  Production control
  Accounting
  Human resources

Master production schedule

Product	1997		1998		
	Weeks				
	51	52	1	2	3
X	10	10	10	12	12
Y	2	–	–	3	6
Z	18	18	16	11	9

Design schedule
Mar. – May, 1998

Job	Schedule
County Building	Mar. 15 – Apr. 15
Wild River Bridge	Apr. 1–30
Oak Terrace Apts.	Apr. 10–30
Prairie Mall	May 1–30

actual demand items and toward specific, budgeted, process improvement activities. Results take the form of a master schedule—the MPS, appointment book, or facility schedule—along with scheduled improvement activities such as maintenance, benchmarking, re-engineering, employee training, and so forth. Unlike the broad view taken by the capacity planning team, the master scheduling approach must account for individual customers, orders, facilities (buildings, rooms, airplane seats, etc.) and/or units of output.

Exhibit 7–2B provides a typical master scheduling team composition at the left, and examples of master schedules at the right. In the production example, the MPS shows a five-week schedule for three products. The services example might apply to a design firm; four projects are scheduled to be accomplished within the dates shown.

Questions about the plan may arise: What if product X needs components that get delayed? Or, what if the design firm doesn't have enough structural engineers to cover the scheduled work? Won't the team have to change the master schedule? Indeed, as we noted in the Anita's Studio example, that might happen. Detailed capacity planning and scheduling, topics we have yet to cover, often result in master schedule changes. Also, demand may change. Customers might increase orders for Product Y, or the owners of Oak Terrace Apartments might decide to add to the design effort, perhaps with a deck or patio.

Master schedule changes become more likely as product and service offerings and the transformation processes required to provide them become more complex. Regardless of organization size or complexity, however, the master planning process follows a common sequence.

Basic Master Planning Sequence

Exhibit 7–3 illustrates a basic master planning sequence. It shows one series of steps for prescheduled goods and services (e.g., dental appointments, contract home buildings, mail orders, or molding of plastic cases for camera assembly). A shorter sequence is shown for on-demand goods and services (e.g., freshly popped popcorn, electrical power outage repair, while-you-wait welding). For on-demand sales and services the capacity plan aims at providing the right amount of space, equipment, labor, and inventory (if any) to do business.

Prescheduling of demands, on the other hand, is in two steps. First, the planning team ensures that the master schedule states what and when, but not in detail. Second, the team completes detailed planning and scheduling: step-by-step tasks and work flow (covered in Part IV of the book).

At this point—their first brush with capacity planning—many students ask, why not just forecast demand or book customer orders, then plan whatever capacity is required to meet that demand?

The answer: As stated in the opening paragraphs of the chapter, competition requires that plans for capacity and output levels must be sufficient but not excessive (incurring costly waste). Capacity strategies and policies (the filter between customer demand and the capacity and output plans in Exhibit 7–3) help ensure that both requirements are met.

The arrows leaving the bottom of Exhibit 7–3 reflect continuation into subsequent, more detailed planning and scheduling activities. We pursue those matters in later chapters where they fit well with other topics. At this point, we turn our attention to the upper portion of Exhibit 7–3 and examine how capacity strategies and policies affect the creation of capacity plans.

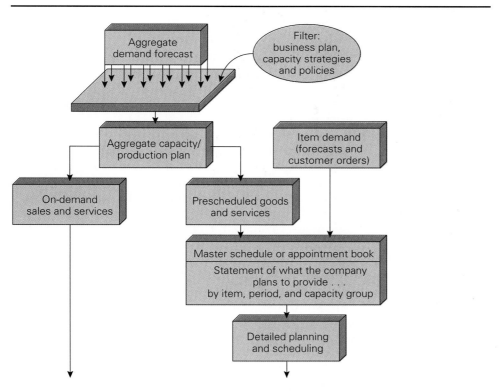

Exhibit 7–3
**Master Planning:
Sequence
Overview**

Capacity Strategies and Policies

As a rule, capacity level adjustments are costly. But broader, more general economic factors—as well as costs—influence decisions to increase or decrease capacity as demand swings occur. At the top level, the business plan evolves into strategies which are, in turn, implemented through capacity policies. Capacity to serve customers is also governed by desired resource utilization, which is affected by resource flexibility. This section explores these and related issues, beginning with a look at capacity strategies.

Chase-Demand versus Level-Capacity Strategies

Look again at the example capacity plan in Exhibit 7–1; the capacity level was increased in order to meet increasing demand. When demand falls, capacity follows. Such a strategy—**chase demand**—might be found in various settings. In labor-intensive businesses, especially services, where required skills (and therefore training needs) are minimal, for example, the strategy could be simply: Hire when demand is up; lay off when demand is poor. Or, in any setting—production or service—where the level of outsourcing is high (i. e., raw materials, components, and support services are purchased), chase-demand is accomplished by increasing or decreasing the volume of orders.

Capital-intensive businesses favor an alternate strategy—**level capacity.** Their challenge is to achieve consistently high capacity utilization in order to recover equipment costs. In labor-intensive settings, the preference is for level capacity if employees' skill qualifications are high or if skills are scarce. The aim is to retain good people through thick and thin.

The level-capacity strategy sometimes raises inventory levels and order backlogs. In a make-to-stock company, for instance, demand reductions might cause planners to allow inventory levels to increase just to keep capacity level. Or, planners at a make-to-order firm may let order backlogs build rather than change (increase, in this case) the capacity level.

backlog
Accumulation of unfinished work or unfilled orders.

Competitive conditions in the industry often dictate capacity strategy. Exhibit 7–4 presents a general comparison of conditions one might find in chase-demand and level-capacity settings. Businesses that employ low-wage, low-skill people in possibly unpleasant working conditions tend to use the chase strategy. With low skill levels, training costs are low per employee but could be high per year, since turnover tends to be high. Turnover also means high hire–fire costs and, along with low skills, contributes to high error rates. Forecasting and budgeting may be short term since lead times for adding to or cutting the workforce are short.

Level capacity has opposite features. To attract more skillful people, pay and working conditions must be better. Training costs per employee are high. The attractions of the job are meant to keep turnover and hire–fire costs low, and high labor skills hold down error rates. Forecasting and budgeting must be longer term, since hiring and training skilled people takes time.

In some companies, a single capacity strategy won't do. Consider, for example, ABC, Inc., a Wall Street brokerage firm.[3] ABC handles transactions coming in from branch offices around the country. Securities and Exchange Commission regulations require all transactions to be settled within three days; that gives ABC managers time to smooth out the daily volume fluctuations so that transaction-handling capacity will not be strained one day and underused the next. But stock market volume can swing dramatically overnight. For example, a rumor about a peace agreement somewhere in the world might cause volume to soar. This could tax ABC's capacity to process stock transactions. How would ABC cope? Here are what two ABC managers might propose:

Manager A: Our capacity should be set at 12,000 transactions per day. This will allow us to meet demand most days. Last year we had a few hot periods when demand ran at 14,000–15,000 per day, and we probably will this year, too. We can handle those problems by overtime for a few days—until new clerks can be hired. Our labor turnover rate is high, so when transaction volume drops we can ease capacity down by not filling vacancies.

Exhibit 7–4

Comparison of Chase-Demand and Level-Capacity Strategies

	Chase Demand	Level Capacity
Labor skill level	Low	High
Wage rate	Low	High
Working conditions	Erratic	Pleasant
Training required per employee	Low	High
Labor turnover	High	Low
Hire–fire costs	High	Low
Error rate	High	Low
Type of budgeting and forecasting required	Short term	Long term

Manager B: I think we should keep capacity right at 17,000 transactions per day. That will be enough to handle the spurts in volume, which are very hard to predict.

Who is right? In this case both are—and here's the rest of the story. Each is managing a different end of the business of handling the stock transactions. Manager A is in charge of cashiering: processing certificates, cash, and checks. Clerks and messengers with uncomplicated tasks are the workforce. Manager B, on the other hand, runs order processing. The workforce has higher skills: data entry, data processing, programming, and information analysis. Equipment is expensive, and lead times to change information processing procedures are long.

Manager A is advocating chase demand, which seems rational for his department. Manager B prefers a level-capacity strategy, which is logical for her department. Since A's lower-skill people cannot handle the work in B's department, A and B should have different capacity plans based on separate aggregate demand forecasts.

Still other companies strive to attain the best parts of both chase-demand and level-capacity strategies: the Into Practice box, "Hewlett-Packard's Flex Force," illustrates. Although the strategy options considered thus far stress the human component of capacity, facilities, equipment, information channels, and all other resources enter the capacity plan as well.

To sum up, the chosen strategy is a general statement of the degree of change in capacity level that a manager will—or can—tolerate. Once selected, however, strategy governs policies.

Capacity Policies

Suppose Anita chooses to follow a chase-demand strategy. She might adopt a customer-oriented policy of promising portrait proofs within 72 hours after the sitting. To meet that commitment, her capacity policy might be to make extensive use of subcontracting (to a friend's studio) for developing and printing. Other examples of specific policies follow:

policy
Guidance or technique used to carry out strategy.

- A municipal power company has a strategy of providing high employee security in order to gain a stable workforce (low employee turnover). Its enabling policies include (1) maintaining excess linespeople and installers in order to meet surges in demand and (2) subcontracting (to local electric contractors) extraordinary maintenance, especially repair of downed lines.
- A bowling lane proprietor's strategy is one of high utilization of bowling lanes. To act on that strategy, the proprietor offers lower prices for daytime bowling.
- At a food wholesaler, planners have adopted a competitive strategy of very fast service to retail grocers. Its supportive policies include shift work, weekend hours, overtime, cross-trained office associates who can help out in the warehouse or drive delivery vehicles, and large inventories.

Exhibit 7–5 shows examples of these and several other common capacity policies. As illustrated, some apply only labor, others to nonlabor resources, and still others to both.

Top company officers are responsible for setting capacity policies. But, as the ABC, Inc., example showed for strategy considerations, a team approach is most likely to result in all points of view making it to the table. Some capacity policies

Hewlett-Packard's Flex Force: Level Capacity Plus Chase Demand

At Hewlett-Packard's Lake Stevens Instruments division, demand spikes made capacity planning difficult. Their solution: flex force, a permanent pool of on-call temporary employees. At its inception, flex force was designed to meet these six requirements:

1. Provide 20-percent flexibility in the total capacity projections.
2. Assure short-term response (within 48 hours) to changes in capacity requirements.
3. Provide training necessary to maintain quality levels, regardless of changing workloads.
4. Be cost neutral. There should be no perceived cost advantage or disadvantage from using the flex force program.
5. Flex force employees should feel like HP employees and not be treated as second-class

citizens. They should be included in departmental meetings, enjoy equal access to the facility, and not be visibly identifiable as flex force employees.

6. Flex force employees should want part-time employment and not accept part-time employment as a means to attaining full-time employment.

Flex force grew from an initial pilot-test group to 80 employees. The six requirements were generally met, and "on-time delivery rates, frequently among the best in the company, have been largely attributed to the ability of the flex force to quickly respond to changing order rates on any product."*

*John Schneider, "Putting the Flex in a Flexible Work Force," *Target*, Special edition (1991), pp. 5–13.

EXHIBIT 7–5

Capacity Management Policies

Capacity Policy	Applicable Resource	
	Labor	Other
1. Hiring and layoffs.	X	
2. Job sharing (two or more people share the same job).	X	
3. Part-time help.	X	
4. Cross-training and transfers (of people or work) among departments.	X	
5. Mandatory (involuntary) leave, vacation, and so on.	X	
6. Overtime or extra shifts.	X	X
7. Outsourcing.	X	X
8. Refusing, backordering, or delaying work.	X	X
9. Service pools (e.g., resource sharing as with a typing pool).	X	X
10. Peak/off-peak price differentials (e.g., cheaper matinee movies).	X	X
11. Build inventories or backlogs.	X	X
12. Undercapacity scheduling.	X	X
13. Quick changeover techniques to increase capacity flexibility.		X
14. Rent (space, equipment, tools, etc.).		X
15. Use of secondary or marginal facilities.		X

are general, "Avoid overtime, and keep inventories low." Others are specific, expressed numerically as minimums, maximums, or ranges, and may also be priority ordered. For example, a set of priority-ordered policies aimed at maintaining a level permanent workforce might be

1. For insufficient demand:
    a. Keep employees busy by building backlogs—maximum of 10 percent buildup above predicted demand.
    b. Lay off employees only after a 10 percent backlog is on hand.
2. For excess demand:
    a. Use temporary labor for the first 5 percent of excess demand.
    b. Use overtime for the next 5 percent.
    c. Reduce customer service (serve best customers fully, but for lesser customers, postpone or even refuse the work, offer partial shipments, etc.).

The Into Practice box, "Working Hard at Avoiding Layoffs," illustrates how one company implemented policies in an ordered fashion.

With such specific policies, master planning is straightforward; managers just follow the policies. Usually, however, a company will not hem itself in so explicitly. For example, the lifetime employment policy of some Japanese firms is really only a goal. The employee tends to have a lifetime (or career-time) commitment to a single company, but the company may or may not be able to retain the employee that long. Although Japan has a highly competitive economy, each year many companies fail, laying off employees. Some successful companies throughout the world, of course, can claim with pride that they have never had layoffs. Have they just been lucky? Perhaps fortune has played a role, but then again maybe foresight

> Kawasaki's actions may actually have been more a series of reactions to a series of situations. (Such may be the case with much of so-called policy.)

Into Practice

Working Hard at Avoiding Layoffs

Kawasaki Motors Manufacturing in Lincoln, Nebraska, was faced with a double dilemma: Just-in-time and quality improvements had raised productivity, resulting in a labor surplus. Then a recession hit, severely cutting motorcycle demand and killing off Kawasaki's entire line of snowmobiles. To correct the capacity–demand mismatch, the management team took the following actions, in chronological order.

1. Assigned excess direct labor to essential support tasks, including modifying, moving, and installing equipment.
2. Assigned excess labor to maintenance work, such as painting, caulking, and minor remodeling.
3. In fall 1981, Kawasaki lent 11 of its excess employees to the city of Lincoln, where they worked for several months with Kawasaki paying wages and benefits.
4. The first layoffs (24 white-collar people) occurred in October.
5. In November, 16 blue-collar employees voluntarily took a six-month furlough with call-back rights.
6. In February 1982, 98 production employees were terminated.
7. In October 1982, the plant went to a four-day workweek to preserve jobs for the remaining workforce.

The only policy governing those actions was that of seeking to avoid layoffs in the face of insufficient demand.

and attention to detail—a proactive approach to master planning—helped create some of the good fortune.

Capacity policies work best when they're in place before they are needed. But how might a prudent manager anticipate such a need?

Policy Options: An Example

Let's return to Anita's Studio, a few years after we parted company in Example 7–1. Example 7–2, illustrating much of what we've learned thus far about master planning, finds Anita's business booming.

EXAMPLE 7–2:   MASTER PLANNING—PHOTOGRAPHY SERVICES, PART II

A few years ago, Anita expanded her photography business to include weddings and proms, in addition to her portrait and group photo work. She has found that the expansion has increased her portrait work as well, since many of her former wedding clients want her to take their anniversary portraits, children's pictures, and so on.

Wedding pictures, like portrait photographs, require manual developing in two stages—the proofs and the final prints of the customer's selected poses. Anita prefers to develop these herself, although for the past two springs she has had to hire an assistant to help with developing. Prom photographs, however, are like group photographs; machine developing is sufficient. She contracts all machine development work to FastFotos, Inc., a commercial photofinisher.

Word of Anita's expertise has spread; she enjoys a top reputation, and clients have learned to book her early. Each December, before leaving on her January ski vacation, Anita likes to plan her capacity requirements—especially the requirements for her own time—for the spring, her busy season. As she examines demand for her services, shown in Exhibit 7–6, she realizes just how much business is growing. Group photo, wedding, and prom demands are all in the form of orders; portrait work is a mixture of orders and Anita's forecast based on recent demands for this six-month period, but adjusted upward to reflect this year's projected increase.

Job Details

- Portrait photo: Requires 1 hour photograph time; manually developed—2 hours proof development time and 5 hours of final print development time.
- Group photo: Requires 2 hours photograph time; machine developed.
- Wedding: Requires 3 hours of photograph time; manually developed—6 hours proof development time, and 10 hours of final print development time.
- Prom: Requires 4 hours of photograph time; machine developed.

Business Plan

Anita prefers to limit her photography time to about 25 hours per week even during the spring season. If she goes much above that, time requirements for (manual) photo developing

EXHIBIT 7–6

Monthly Job Demand—Anita's Studio

Job Type	Feb.	March	April	May	June	July
Portrait photo	18	12	15	40	50	35
Group photo	6	4	8	5	7	5
Wedding	1	2	4	5	10	8
Prom	0	0	5	7	1	0

become excessive—especially since she prides herself on rapid turnaround time for her customers. She has found that bookkeeping consumes about five hours of her time each week; maintenance and housekeeping another three hours; and inventory management about one hour. She likes to include personal improvement time—for professional reading, seminars, and so forth—in her schedule as well; two hours each week is her aim.

If Anita uses the demand data in Exhibit 7–6 as a trial master schedule for the six-month period, what capacity planning issues will she face? What options might she pursue?

Solution

Since Anita is concerned primarily with capacity requirements for her time, the initial step is to convert the trial master schedule demand data into capacity units—that is, hours of Anita's time. Next, the other capacity demands, things she either has to do to run the business or wants to do for personal improvement, must be factored in. The result will be a rough statement of the demand for her labor (capacity) in hours per month; Exhibit 7–7 illustrates.

Example calculations, May:

$$Photographic\ hours = (40\ portraits \times 1\ hr./sitting) +$$

$$(5\ groups \times 2\ hrs./sitting) +$$

$$(5\ weddings \times 3\ hrs./wedding) +$$

$$(7\ proms \times 4\ hrs./prom)$$

$$= 93\ hrs$$

$$Developing\ hours = (40\ portraits \times 7\ hrs./sitting) +$$

$$(5\ weddings \times 16\ hrs./wedding)$$

$$= 360\ hrs.$$

The resulting labor-hour workload is about what Anita expected. She can handle February, March, and—with some long workdays—April loads, *as they are now.* But beginning in May, she will need some help. In addition to her own overtime, Anita has other capacity planning options available. She's interested in four:

1. Hire assistants, for one or more of the following:

- Most or all of the manual photograph developing work.

Job Type	Feb.	March	April	May	June	July
Portrait photo	18	12	15	40	50	35
Group photo	12	8	16	10	14	10
Wedding	3	6	12	15	30	24
Prom	0	0	20	28	4	0
Total photo hours	**33**	**26**	**63**	**93**	**98**	**69**
Developing hours	142	116	169	360	510	373
Bookkeeping	20	20	20	20	20	20
Maintenance/housekeeping	12	12	12	12	12	12
Inventory management	4	4	4	4	4	4
Personal improvement	8	8	8	8	8	8
Total hours	219	186	276	497	652	486

EXHIBIT 7–7

Rough Capacity Demand for Owner's Time— Anita's Studio

- Some of the photography work and some of the developing.
- Bookkeeping, maintenance, housekeeping, and inventory management.

2. Outsource more of the developing work; perhaps let FastFotos, Inc., do some of the portrait and wedding proofs and finish print developing. Maybe outsource bookkeeping and maintenance, too.
3. Attempt to alter the master schedule by shifting workload forward or backward in the schedule.
4. Limit future bookings to priority customers—existing clients, for example.

Example 7–2 ends without Anita having selected a particular capacity plan. She will incorporate information about costs, previous experience with these and other capacity options, and perhaps think again about what she *wants to do* before settling on a plan. Regardless of the chosen policies, capacity planners must deal with issues of capacity utilization.

Capacity Utilization

Utilization refers to intensity of use of capacity. A general expression for it is:

$$\text{Utilization rate} = \frac{\text{Time in use}}{\text{Time available}} \qquad (7\text{–}1)$$

where availability (as defined in Chapter 4) is the time that a resource is considered ready for use. Utilization planning involves two questions: (1) How shall we define full utilization? (2) What is planned utilization for the upcoming capacity planning period?

Typically, companies define full utilization at some high but attainable level. Usually it is less than 24 hours a day, seven days a week. For example, Anita would probably consider being up and running 24 hours a day to be unreasonable—in terms of both customer and staff expectations. For her business, a reasonable definition of full utilization might be 44 hours per week (five 8-hour days plus Saturday mornings). In some capacity planning periods, she may elect to remain open during those hours, which means 44 hours per week is also her planned utilization. During August, however, suppose she plans to close on Mondays and Saturdays, reducing her planned capacity utilization to 32 hours per week. Then, by equation 7–1, Anita's Studio would operate at a capacity utilization rate of 72.7 percent (32 divided by 44).

At some assembly plants, full capacity is defined as 3 shifts per day, five days a week, or 15 shifts per week. If the planning team sets next quarter's capacity plan (based on the latest demand forecast) at 2 shifts of scheduled assembly per day, or 10 shifts per week, then planned capacity utilization would be 67 percent (10 divided by 15).

For paper and metal processors, because their equipment is so expensive (see Exhibit 7–8), full capacity may mean 21 shifts per week (including scheduled maintenance time). If a paper plant's demand is slack and its master planning committee elects to run only 18 shifts a week, planned capacity utilization is 86 percent (18 divided by 21).

EXHIBIT 7–8
Paper Plant Operations

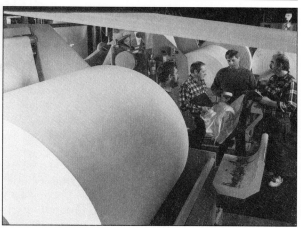

Top left—Parent roll of tissue.
Top right—Team (amid rolls of tissue) examines partially converted segment.
Left—Product segment, plus packaged final product (conversion machines in background).

Source: Courtesy of Pope & Talbot, Inc., Comsumer Products Division.

Over- and Undercapacity Planning

Whatever the definition of full capacity, should the goal be to utilize it fully? It depends. In times of superheated demand, companies will sometimes plan to overuse capacity: Anita, for example, might advertise special Sunday hours during the busiest season. Normally, however, high levels of performance in the eyes of customers require some slack: Plan for underuse of capacity by some percentage. In application, this means paying the price of extra capacity so that it is possible to respond to customers quickly and with high quality even when demand surges. (See Contrast box "Capacity Management.") For example, Solectron (a Baldrige prize winner in 1991) plans its operations "at about 75 percent to 80 percent capacity to accommodate customer order fluctuations due to market volatility." Solectron (producer of printed circuit boards and other sub-assemblies for high-tech manufacturers such as Intel and IBM) calls this practice "flexible capacity."[4]

*P*RINCIPLE 1:

Get to know the competition.

ontrast

Capacity Management

"By the Numbers" Capacity	Well-Managed Capacity
Plan for full utilization of capacity—for hours of demand to equal available hours of labor and facilities or even to overutilize capacity (e.g., work overtime on a regular basis).	Plan for enough capacity to ensure high quality, on-time performance every time, and reasonable time for improvement activities.

A deliberate policy of undercapacity planning may be set forth numerically (as at Solectron). A dental clinic, for example, might plan at 15 percent under capacity. If clinic capacity (measured in dentists' time, dental technician time, etc.) is 100 patients per day, the clinic will plan and schedule for 85 patients per day. The extra 15 percent is not to be squandered. Rather, the policy calls for using the time for data analysis; project work; preventive maintenance on equipment; training; and other activities aimed at reducing errors, rework, equipment trouble, and variation of all kinds. The benefits include fewer unplanned stoppages, greater staff efficiency, lower operating costs, time to fit in emergency patients, time for unexpected patient problems, less rework, and happier customers. Well-served customers, in turn, lead to higher customer retention, thus avoiding the costs of patient turnover or, worse, too few patients to keep the staff busy.

Example 7–3 illustrates some of the simple calculations that might be involved in applying undercapacity planning in a manufacturing setting, the planning takes place at the level of a master production schedule.

EXAMPLE 7–3:   UNDERCAPACITY SCHEDULING—KOJI FILM CO.

The star of the product line at Koji Co., a photographic film manufacturer, is 135 24-exposure, 100-speed color film. The yield per eight-hour shift has averaged 6,600 rolls, or 825 rolls per hour. Koji's master scheduling team has adopted a rate-based schedule of 6,000 rolls per shift—no more, no less—which is the current sales rate.
Is the schedule attainable? What is the underscheduling policy in percentage terms?

Solution

The target of 6,000 should be attainable in one eight-hour shift most of the time. In a shift with average problems, the 6,000 rolls would be produced in about $7\frac{1}{4}$ hours (6,000/825 rolls per hour = 7.27 hours). On a bad day with two or three line stoppages, the 6,000 may still get produced—by working right up to the bell. On a very bad day, the 6,000 might be made by working some overtime.

The underscheduling policy is 6,000/6,600 = 90.9 percent.

Though undercapacity planning is designed to work within a given work area, its power is amplified when resources are flexible enough to move among several areas. Resource flexibility also helps when natural work areas—groups or families—are the basis for capacity planning.

Group (Family) Capacity Planning

Group-based capacity planning is a commonsense partner of aggregate forecasting (discussed in Chapter 6). To some degree, it applies in most types of organizations.

Capacity Groups in a Small Business

Look again at Exhibit 7–7, capacity demand for labor hours at Anita's Studio. Anita might reasonably expect that if she hires an office manager, that person could do the bookkeeping, inventory management, and perhaps some or all of the maintenance and housekeeping chores, but should not be expected to have photography skills. A photography assistant, on the other hand, might be expected to take and develop photographs, but won't necessarily have office management skills.

Thus, Anita could manage the labor component of her capacity as two groups. Indeed, the capacity demand pattern shown in Exhibit 7–7 suggests some wisdom for this grouping: The office management duties (as we shall call them) impose a steady demand on capacity—about 36 hours per month. Perhaps Anita will seek a regular, part-time employee for this job, following a level-capacity strategy. The photography and developing work, however, varies with the season. Maybe outsourcing or temporary employees (with appropriate skills)—implemented on a chase-demand basis—are appropriate options for this group. Her most flexible resource—her own time—is her ace in the hole, available to meet any extra demand surges that come along. Example 7–4 illustrates how Anita might create a capacity plan using these policies.

EXAMPLE 7–4:   GROUP CAPACITY PLANNING—SMALL BUSINESS

Anita, a professional photographer and small business owner, has separated demand for labor capacity at her studio into two groups. The first, for office management activities (bookkeeping, inventory management, and maintenance and general housekeeping), is steady, and averages about 36 hours per month. The second is for photography services (taking and developing photographs) and is highly seasonal. Demand for each type of capacity (in hours) for an upcoming six-month period is shown below. (These data were obtained from Exhibit 7–7.)

	Month					
Demand for Labor Capacity—By Groups (hrs.)	*Feb.*	*March*	*April*	*May*	*June*	*July*
Office management activities	36	36	36	36	36	36
Photography services	175	142	232	453	608	442

Anita has decided to employ a part-time office manager on a regular basis; she will ask this new employee to work 10 hours each week, or 40 hours per month. Her plan now—in late December—is to get the new office manager on board within the next month. To meet the demand for photography services, she has elected to

- Hire two temporary assistants during April; she wants them both on board by May. They will each work 40 hours per week (160 hours per month).

- Limit her *planned* personal labor commitment to 40 hours per week (160 hours per month). [She knows that she will probably work more, but wishes to hold her own "overtime" in reserve to meet last-minute needs of her regular customers.]

EXHIBIT 7–9

Capacity Plan— Anita's Studio

Capacity Plan—By Group (hrs)	Feb.	March	April	May	June	July
Office management activities						
Demand	36	36	36	36	36	36
Capacity: New office manager (part-time)	40	40	40	40	40	40
Photography service						
Demand	175	142	232	453	608	442
Capacity: Photo assistant #1	—	—	80	160	160	160
Capacity: Photo assistant #2	—	—	—	160	160	160
Capacity: Outsourcing (FastFotos, Inc.)	15	—	—	—	130	—
Capacity: Owner (Anita)	160	142	152	133	158	122

- Outsource photo developing work to FastFotos, Inc., (a commercial photofinisher) whenever demand exceeds capacity available from the two assistants and her own time.

Develop a capacity plan that will meet Anita's capacity planning objectives.

Solution

Exhibit 7–9 shows one possible capacity plan that will meet Anita's goals. The plan is based on having one photography assistant working for half of April—an assumption, of course.

Outsourcing (15 hours) is planned for February simply to meet Anita's goal of holding her own planned time to no more than 160 hours per month. Of course, if no last-minute orders arise, she may elect to forgo the outsourcing and do the 15 hours of developing work herself. It's not important for her to make that decision now. What is important, however, is that she has a plan in place and is ready to deal with contingencies that might arise.

Group capacity planning in larger organizations follows the same three steps. To recap, they are:

1. Group products into natural families and select units for aggregate capacity planning. A family consists of goods/services that employ units of capacity going through roughly the same processes. It is a natural family only if capacity (skills and equipment) is flexible enough to process all the goods/services within the family.

2. Project aggregate customer demand for each capacity group. This forecast is in the units of measure chosen in step 1.

3. Develop a production plan (output units), and convert to capacity units if necessary. This step aims at having the right amount of aggregate resources on hand.

The 1–2–3 capacity planning procedure applies to both on-demand (make-to-order) businesses and make-to-stock production. Our next example is for on-demand commercial photo processing services.

On-Demand and Make-to-Order Operations

Example 7–5 illustrates the 1–2–3 procedure. The idea for the example (but not the data) comes from Ashton Photo, Salem, Oregon. Ashton's professional photo-processing business has been organized into 16 U-shaped photo finishing cells. Each cell has about nine cross-trained members, focuses on one type of photo (e.g., sports teams or school photos), and processes the entire job from incoming film to outgoing finished work and invoice.

EXAMPLE 7–5:   CAPACITY PLANNING—FASTFOTOS, INC.

FastFotos is a large photofinisher, handling both consumer and commercial film processing (including some contract work for Anita's Studios, especially in the school graduation season). It is an on-demand, make-to-order business.

The capacity-planning team (the personnel director and the operations manager) plans capacity a number of weeks in advance. Since there is plenty of equipment capacity, the plan includes labor only: the right skills, hiring, and training. Their day-to-day fine-tuning includes reasonable overtime and labor borrowing.

The capacity team uses the three-step method:

Step 1. They conclude that consumer and commercial photo processing make up separate capacity groups: Consumer processing is routine; commercial customers usually require special processing. Routine processing and special processing take place in different areas of the building. (Exhibit 7–10 shows an actual photo processing cell.) They agree that number of orders is an appropriate capacity measure for both groups. The team plans capacity for its all-important commercial accounts first.

Step 2. The capacity team uses recent past demand (number of orders) as a simple, reasonable projection of demand for the next eight-week capacity planning period.

Step 3. Exhibit 7–11 is the capacity-planning work sheet for commercial business. It includes recent demand data (second column) and two capacity options, both tight on capacity (team members are very cost conscious). Option 1 provides enough capacity to process 1,800 orders per week (100 fewer than the mean recent demand of 1,900 per week). Projected deviations range from +700 (excess capacity) to −1,000 orders per week. Since negative deviations signify backlogged orders, consecutive negative values carry over to the next week. The projected backlog grows to −2,100 orders in week 7, then falls to −1,500 in week 8. The capacity shortage in week 7 is more than one week's backlog (2,100 orders/1,800 orders per week = 1.17 weeks), which won't do in FastFoto's competitive business.

Here *orders* is the unit of measure in a production plan and is also a suitable (surrogate) measure of capacity. (Cars per year serves a similar dual role in the auto industry—as noted earlier.)

One of 16 U-shaped photofinishing cells at Ashton Photo, Salem, Oregon. (Ashton's customers are professional photorraphers.)

EXHIBIT 7–10

Photofinishing Cell

EXHIBIT 7–11

Capacity/Backlog Options at FastFotos, Inc.

Week	Recent Demand Orders	Option 1 Capacity: 1,800 Orders per Week				Option 2 Capacity: 2,100 Orders per Week			
		Orders	*Deviation*	*Backlog*	*Excess Capacity*	*Orders*	*Deviation*	*Backlog*	*Excess Capacity*
1	1,800	1,800	0			2,100	+300		300
2	1,100	1,800	+700		700	2,100	+1,000		1,000
3	1,800	1,800	0			2,100	+300		300
4	1,950	1,800	−150	−150		2,100	+150		150
5	2,300	1,800	−150	−650		2,100	−200	−200	
6	2,800	1,800	−1,000	−1,650		2,100	−700	−900	
7	2,250	1,800	−450	−2,100		2,100	−150	−1,050	
8	1,200	1,800	+600	−1,500		2,100	+900	−150	

Total 15,200

$$\text{Mean demand} = \frac{15,200}{8} = 1,900 \text{ orders per week}$$

Option 2 provides for 300 more orders per week than option 1. This results in projected excess capacity in the first four weeks, but insufficient capacity in the second four weeks; the backlog grows to a high of −1,050 orders in week 7. Since 1,050 orders is less than one week's backlog, the capacity planning team considers the plan workable (with the potential of marshaling additional labor hours during peak weeks).

Does this method of capacity planning assume that future demand will be like past demand? No. While total demand may be fairly close, the week-to-week demand pattern is sure to be different. Thus, maximum backlogs can be much more or less than projected. Still, the simple method illustrated in Example 7–5 employs existing demand data. It can work quite well because overtime, job transfers, and other flexible responses are available in weeks when the plan goes wrong.

Put another way, capacity planners generally should reserve their flexible options for when the plan does not work out. (Recall from Example 7–4 that Anita desired to reserve her own overtime—*her* most flexible resource—for times when her capacity plan might not fit the situation.) If they build overtime, subcontracting, and so forth into the capacity plan, there is no room for correction when actual demand patterns don't follow the plan.

In some businesses, such as transportation, restaurants, and lodging, an unmet order is lost; backlogs are not carryable. The method used in Example 7–5 needs to be modified in those cases. The altered method treats demand as noncumulative so that negative deviations are lost sales, not backlogs.

Make-to-Stock Operations

In the make-to-stock case, capacity planning follows the three-step process and often adds a fourth step: Refine the plan to provide for desired inventory levels. There may also be a fifth step: Further test the feasibility of the plan by examining how it affects critical resources (e.g., a heavily used machine or a specially skilled associate). The first four steps are presented in Example 7–6.

EXAMPLE 7–6:   CAPACITY (PRODUCTION) PLANNING—QUARK ELECTRONICS

Capacity planning at Quark Electronics was once reactive. If work was piling up in Shop A (long customer-order backlogs), a planner in that shop would request more labor, extra shifts, or other reactive capacity changes. Planning capacity based on demand forecasts seemed hopeless because there were too many different products and forecasts were too inaccurate.

However, a capacity-planning team was formed, and they have learned to apply group-based forecasting and capacity planning in four steps.

Step 1: The team divided its production processes into three product families, groups 1, 2, and 3. Each group covers a large number of electronic items, including end products, subassemblies, and component parts.

The team studied product routings (flow paths) and found three dominant paths through the four shops (see Exhibit 7–12). A few products do not fit any of these routings, but enough do to provide a solid basis for capacity (production) planning, with groups large enough for decent forecast accuracy.

Step 2: The capacity team obtains aggregate demand forecasts for each of the three product groupings; the forecast for group 1 is in pieces per week (see Exhibit 7–13).

Step 3: The team develops a capacity plan stated in pieces per week. The plan is based on careful evaluation to ensure that the plan is consistent with capacity policies and is realistic. The team's calculations (not shown) ensure that projected aggregate labor-hours in product group 1 are sufficient to meet projected demand each week, with time to spare for improvement work.

Step 4: Several years ago Quark's senior management decided to follow its competitors and focus, not on direct labor costs (which had fallen to less than 3 percent of production costs), but on intensive management of inventories (over 65 percent of costs). Thus, capacity planners are building inventory reductions into the capacity plans. The current four-week

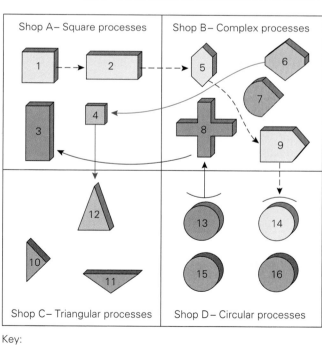

EXHIBIT 7–12

Common Routings—Quark Electronics

Note: Machines 13, 14, 15, and 16 are identical; thus 15 and 16 could be substituted for 13 and 14, if needed.

EXHIBIT 7–13
**Capacity Plan—
Product Group 1**

| | Pieces through Product Group 1 | | | | |
| | Forecast | | Capacity (Production) Plan | | |
Week	*Pieces per Week (000)*	*Cumulative*	*Pieces per Week (000)*	*Cumulative*	*Inventory*
0	—	—	—	—	14.0
1	10.0	10.0	10.1	10.1	14.1
2	10.0	20.0	10.1	20.2	14.2
3	10.4	30.4	10.1	30.3	13.9
4	10.4	40.8	10.1	40.4	13.6

capacity plan shows a decline from 14,000 to 13,600 pieces (see last column in Exhibit 7–13). But each year, just prior to Quark's busy season, the capacity planners allow a buildup of anticipation inventories. That is, they increase the production rate above the forecast sales rate in anticipation of a seasonal surge in demand.

Quark's capacity-planning team must repeat all of these steps for product groups 2 and 3. But is that the end of it?

To be on the safe side, the planners want to know that their capacity plan does not overload certain critical resources. For example, Machine 5, a complex machine in Shop B, is nearly always the first to be overloaded, thereby becoming a bottleneck. Since the capacity plan is stated in pieces per week, which represents a nonspecific mixture of products, the team cannot precisely project the workload of Machine 5. Instead, they use historical average machine-hours per piece as the basis for the rough-cut stage of capacity planning. For Machine 5, the data show 0.0075 hours per piece. Thus, for group 1 and week 1:

$$\text{Projected workload} = 10,100 \text{ pieces} \times 0.0075 \text{ hours per piece}$$

$$= 75.75 \text{ hours}$$

Marketing director's actions show capacity planning is more than translating demand into capacity numbers. If it were only number crunching, it could all be done by a computer—no need for a team.

This is within Quark's upper limit of 80 planned hours of workload per week. (Company policy is to operate two 8-hour shifts a day, five days a week, or 80 hours.) The capacity team finds this too close for comfort. It leaves little margin for error, and forecasts are notoriously erroneous.

What to do? The marketing director (a member of the team) says, "No problem." Promotion costs are too high, and sales people have been booking orders from customers whose credit is shaky. His actions to deal with these two problems will, he estimates, cut projected demand by 5 percent. Quick recalculation of all capacity figures yield a plan the whole team likes.

Capacity Planning in the Focused Business

*P*RINCIPLE 6:

Form multiple focused chains of customers.

The method just reviewed represents good capacity planning for the firm that is organized by function. The modern movement to get focused (which requires breaking up functional departments, offices, and shops) yields a bonus: simplified capacity planning.

Exhibit 7–14 shows how Quark Electronics might get focused. The four shops (see Exhibit 7–12) are gone. The people, their equipment, and accessories have been moved into product-focused clusters, called cells or plants-in-a-plant. This way of grouping capacity makes it natural and easy for associates to become cross-trained, to switch jobs, and constantly to interact and solve problems with suppliers at the previous process and customers at the next one. When the demand fore-

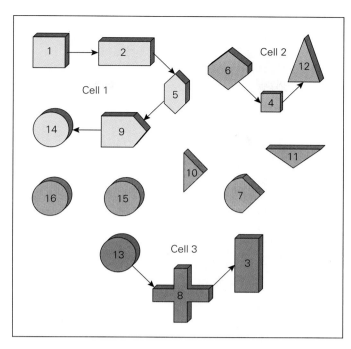

EXHIBIT 7–14
**Cells—Quark
Electronics**

Note: Work centers not organized into cells are shaded gray. Centers 15 and 16 are mobile, capable of quick replacement for center 13 or 14.

cast for their product family is wrong, the people in the focused unit may be able to quickly take corrective action on their own.

Master Scheduling

A capacity plan puts aggregate customer demand into time slots, but the master schedule puts actual orders into time slots. Exhibit 7–7, for example, shows that Anita's Studio has aggregate demand for 98 hours of photography services in June. But we would have to look at the master schedule (appointment book, in this case) to see an actual order: Mr. and Mrs. O'Grady will have their portrait taken on June 20 at 2:00 pm. in the portrait sitting room.

*C*ontrast

Capacity Planning

Reactive	**Product-Group Based**	**Product-Group Based, Capacity Focused**
Poor; hampered by functional organization and lack of product focus.	Good, but dispersed capacity for each product group hampers communication, cross-training, labor borrowing, and so on.	Very good; co-locating capacity and product groups simplifies planning, problem solving, and adjusting to wrong forecasts.

The scheduled order matches the O'Grady's demand with capacity—in this instance, one hour of photographer's time and a one-hour use (reservation) of the portrait room. If we look deeper and incorporate other capacity elements along with Anita's customer-service policies, we conclude that the master schedule entry actually commits even larger chunks of capacity, including

- Two hours of proof developing time within 72 hours of the O'Grady's June 20 sitting. (See "Job Details" in Example 7–2.)
- Five more hours of developing time for final prints. This requirement could occur immediately after proof delivery if the O'Grady's quickly return the proofs with their selected poses and print order.
- Office time for processing the O'Grady's order, billing, and so forth; plus the nonlabor capacity elements (film, paper, etc.) if developing is done in-house.

In principle, it works much the same way in large manufacturing plants. The capacity plan might show, for instance, that a package wrapper will be required for 100 hours during June, but we must turn to the master schedule—and perhaps to more detailed schedules, as well—to discover when that machine will be preparing a specific completed order for shipment. The detailed schedules also reveal commitment of other capacity elements as the order moves through the plant. In practice, due precisely to the large number of diverse capacity elements required to convert planned orders into actual outputs, master scheduling in manufacturing can become complicated. It may even be "more art than science."[5] Thus, we will save coverage of some of these complexities until we examine specific manufacturing environments in later chapters.

This section focuses on general master scheduling concepts and on how the master schedule relates to capacity planning and demand management. Let's ask the most basic question first: Do all organizations even need master scheduling?

Applicability and Scope

As we've noted, all organizations ought to perform demand management, and all must have some sort of capacity plan. But those organizations that provide on-demand services have no time to plan at the detailed level of a master schedule. That includes organizations catering to walk-in or call-in customers: retailers, fast-food restaurants, emergency rooms, police and fire departments, automobile registration facilities, buses, and so forth.

By contrast, reserved-seat businesses, professional services, and manufacturers draft a detailed master schedule. At Anita's Studios, the appointment book schedules customers into Anita's available time slots. A bigger service business such as a medical clinic would have a separate appointment book for each physician, and might also have appointment books for scarce, high-cost facilities like surgery suites.

Manufacturing is a bit more complicated. A master scheduling team (from operations, production control, sales, accounting, and human resources) weighs the master scheduling alternatives and sets priorities. Good customers, for example, get preferential slots in the master schedule; hence, the need for sales to be represented on the team. High-profit items ought to be preferred over marginal ones; hence, accounting needs a representative.

	Weekly Production Schedule				
Modules	Jan. 13–17	Jan. 20–24	Jan. 27–31	Feb. 3–7	Feb. 10–14
Mother Board:					
X–121	53	61	57	62	58
X–221	45	42	50	44	40
(Etc.)	—	—	—	—	—
Power Supply:					
Y–123	100	120	110	95	105
Y–223	220	210	240	220	235
(Etc.)	—	—	—	—	—
Hard Disk:					

Exhibit 7–15
Partial Master Production Schedule— Computer Assembly

The master scheduling team may construct the master production schedule (MPS) around major capacity-consuming modules (end items) of the final product. Major modules (e.g., a personal computer's mother board, power supply, hard drive, etc.) are costly and warrant careful advance scheduling. In contrast, putting the modules together into final products may be push-and-snap assembly, random testing, and a bit of packaging; it may take just a few hours and not cost much. Since each module consumes different resources (capacity) with different timing, each gets its own segment of the MPS. Exhibit 7–15 illustrates with a simple partial MPS covering a five-week period.

With these few examples of a master schedule's scope in mind, let's turn our attention to the process through which master scheduling is accomplished. We begin with a basic example from the services sector.

Master Scheduling: Services Example

Preparation of the master schedule is a key duty of department heads and other administrators in educational institutions. Example 7–7 illustrates.

EXAMPLE 7–7: MASTER SCHEDULING IN DEPARTMENT OF MANAGEMENT—FUNK UNIVERSITY

Each department chairperson in the College of Business at Funk University must prepare a master schedule of course offerings. They prepare the schedule twice each term, once based on preregistration, and again after general or final registration has occurred.

The procedure is illustrated in Exhibit 7–16. The Management Department faculty clusters its courses (perhaps 30 to 40 offerings) into three capacity groups (block 2):

1. Quantitative/management information systems (MIS)/operations management (OM)

2. Behavioral/human resources management (HRM)

3. General management/business policy

Although other departments would use the same master scheduling procedure, their aggregate forecast groups would differ. The groupings are not intended to correspond to

EXHIBIT 7–16
Master Scheduling—Department of Management

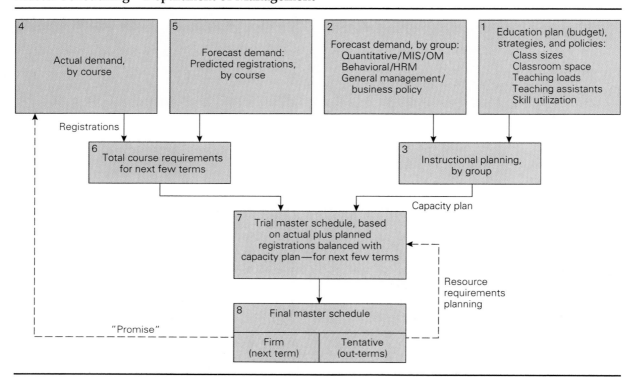

clusters of demand; rather, the intent is to form natural groups of capacity. At Funk University, the faculty consider courses within each capacity group similar enough so that faculty within that group have necessary expertise to teach most of the courses. While the groupings aren't perfect, they should be all right for the purpose: Arrive at a capacity plan (out of block 3) that matches up reasonably well with total course requirements (block 6), leading to a trial master schedule of course offerings (block 7).

The budget (education plan) and strategies and policies (block 1) are controls on the capacity plan. Policies are for class sizes (faculty–student ratios), classroom space, teaching loads (per faculty member), use of teaching assistants, and utilization of faculty skills (the extent to which faculty teach in stronger or weaker areas of expertise).

While blocks 1 through 3 concern aggregate demand and capacity, blocks 4 through 6 deal with unit demand course by course. Block 4 is actual demand, consisting of registrations by course. Block 5 is forecast demand: predicted registrations, by course, based on historical patterns plus other knowledge.

Next, in block 6, the chairperson assembles course requirements for the next few terms into a list. Then she matches this shopping list against what is available in the capacity plan. The result is the trial master schedule of course offerings for the next few terms. The feedback arrow from block 8 to block 7, resource requirements planning, indicates closed-loop control. It makes the master schedule an accurate reflection of capacity to meet demands by adjusting the master schedule until scarce resource overloads are eliminated.

A final master schedule emerges at block 8. It is firm for the upcoming term and tentative for future terms. At this point, Funk University's registrar sends out an order promise to students who have registered. He either confirms or denies their registration for a given course. If denied, he may offer a substitute.

Master Scheduling: Manufacturing Example

Exhibit 7–16 contains the basics of master planning. Exhibit 7–17, expanding those basics, yields a master planning model for the complex case of a manufacturer that fabricates and assembles in the job or batch mode.

Blocks 1 through 6 are the same for a manufacturer as for a service: A capacity planning team guided by business plans and capacity strategies (box 1) uses aggregate demand forecasts (box 2) to plan overall production activity (box 3), thereby yielding a capacity plan. The sales force goes to work booking orders (box 4), which combine with forecasts of future orders (box 5), adding up to total requirements (box 6).

jobs and batches
Irregular work, varying in time and quantity; covered in Chapters 12 and 14.

Scheduling End Products and Components.   After block 6, there may be a split into two different types of schedules, one for end products and another for component parts. The one for end products is the master production schedule (MPS), block 7 (trial) and block 8 (final). The master scheduling team, in generating the MPS, tries to smooth out lumpy demand streams and may also collect demands for the same products into production lots.

The schedule for component parts includes demands for parts needed to meet the master production schedule, and may also include independently demanded

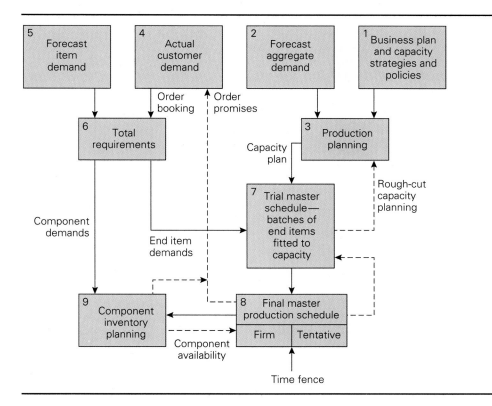

EXHIBIT 7–17

Capacity-Demand Matching Process

service parts
In manufacturing
lingo, spare parts and
repair parts for after-
sale service.

cumulative lead time
Total time from first
activity (e.g., drawing
materials from stock) to
completion of the item.
time fence   Point in
the future beyond the
longest total lead time;
separates firm
scheduling zone from
tentative zone.

component parts, such as service parts (see arrows from blocks 6 and 8 to block 9 in Exhibit 7–17).

Time Fence Policies (Avoiding Nervous Schedules).   After suitable trials, the master scheduling team produces a final MPS. The firm portion typically covers the products's cumulative lead time, which ends at a time fence. A different master scheduling policy is needed for the two sides of the time fence. On one side (in the firm zone where work has already begun) schedule changes are generally avoided, because they generate system nervousness—disruptions that ripple through many stages of planning and execution. On the other side of the time fence (in the tentative zone), schedule changes are just on paper. Thus, the firm portion of the schedule is changed only as a last resort, but the tentative portion may be changed frequently.

However, frequent schedule changes, even in the tentative zone, can upset schedules for suppliers. In some companies, therefore, the master planning team sets up a second time fence to cover maximum lead time for key supplier-partners. Capacity policy then calls for checking with those suppliers before making schedule changes in the zone between the first and second time fences.

Order Promise.   A primary concern of the customer is an order promise date, which comes from a salesperson. Salespeople must have reliable information from master scheduling so that they can make reliable promises. The importance of having a sales representative on the master scheduling team has already been mentioned.

In an attempt to improve delivery promises some companies install a complete information system that accurately calculates order completions. However, problems can persist under such a system. Better if the firm simplifies and integrates ordering, planning, scheduling, purchasing, and production, and thereby eliminates causes of the usual delays so all jobs get done quickly and predictably. Thus, salespeople can make promises based on firm order-promise policies (called "rules of the game" at Ahlström Pump, Mänttä, Finland, and Easley, South Carolina). Most importantly, good order-promise practices allow the master schedule to serve the needs of final

𝒫ᴿɪɴᴄɪᴘʟᴇ 10:

Make it easy to
avoid error or
variation.

*𝒞*ontrast

Master Scheduling

Conventional Narrow Outlook

Master scheduling czar.

   Focus on internal lead times, time fence, lot sizes, and avoidance of schedule nervousness that would disrupt internal work in progress.

   Final assembly scheduled to actual customer orders and with short lead times.

   Major modules master-scheduled mostly to a forecast and long lead times.

   Component schedule tied to major module schedule, with long lead times.

Broad Competitive Outlook

Master scheduling team.

   Focus on customers, and avoidance of schedule nervousness disruptive to customers, salespeople, and both internal and supplier work in progress.

   Final assembly, major modules, and component processes scheduled as a unit in one stage, with short total lead times.

customers as well as improve utilization of capacity. The contrast box master scheduling summarizes this point, along with other points from earlier discussions.

Master Scheduling in Make-to-Order Plants

A special case of master planning in manufacturing is make-to-order production. An
example is a producer of ultrasound machines for hospitals and medical clinics
—no production without a firm order. The bane of the make-to-order producer is
lack of planning lead time. Clinics order ultrasounds and want them right away.
With no lead time, can a master production schedule extend far enough into the
future to match demand with capacity reasonably well? The answer is yes. One
approach is to use a flexible, customer-oriented procedure that involves what is
called consuming the master schedule (or consuming the forecast).

    The method employs an MPS with three subdivisions: master schedule, actual de-
mand, and available to promise (see Exhibit 7–18). The procedure begins with the master schedule, based on forecasting. As salespeople book orders, the master scheduler
enters the quantities in the actual demand row. The term *available to promise* means the
computed difference between master schedule and actual demand quantities.

    We see in Exhibit 7–18 that in week 4, one unit of ultrasound A has been sold—to
be completed or delivered in that week—and five are available to promise. In the same
week, both master-scheduled units of ultrasound B have been sold, leaving none
available to promise. The master schedule is said to be consumed by actual orders
being booked by salespeople. The master schedule keeps sales informed about quantities available to promise so that the sales force will not overconsume the schedule.

    The master scheduler revises the MPS periodically. For example, Exhibit 7–18
shows two of the four ultrasound A's as available to promise in week 1. If the firm
never produces for inventory, the MPS would be revised at the last minute in order
to produce just two, not four, units of ultrasound A.

Rough-Cut Capacity Planning

The feedback loop from block 7 to block 3 in Exhibit 7–17 refers to rough-cut capacity planning. The aim is to assure the capacity-planning team that the production plan will not overload a scarce resource. Typically, a scarce resource is an expensive machine or a hard-to-get skill, such as a graphics designer or a
programmer for a numerically controlled cutting machine.

    In one sense, every organization does rough-cut capacity planning:

	Week				
	1	2	3	4	5
Ultrasound A:					
Master schedule	4	2	0	6	3
Actual demand	2	0	0	1	0
Available to promise	2	2	0	5	3
Ultrasound B:					
Master schedule	0	7	8	2	0
Actual demand	0	1	4	2	0
Available to promise	0	6	4	0	0

EXHIBIT 7–18

Consuming the Master Production Schedule

It might be as simple as saying, "I have a plan that calls for shipping $3 million worth of products this month, and I've always been able to ship $4 million per month. So we have the proven capacity to meet the plan." Alternately, you might say, "Management wants us to ship $7 million a month during the summer season. We have no precedent for being able to do that—management's new plan appears to be unrealistic at this time."[6]

bill of labor
States amount (hours) of each skill needed to produce/provide one unit. (Similarly, bill of materials states amount of each material needed to produce one unit.)

Running a rough-cut check requires data that show how much of the scarce resource is required per unit of product to be made or provided. Assume, for example, that a plastics manufacturer has a bill of labor stating that a newly designed plastic case for a computer keyboard requires, on average, 46 hours of mold-making labor. (The firm's senior mold-maker's skills are exceptional—nobody else has those skills.) To improve confidence that aggregate forecast demand will not overload the mold-maker, the capacity-planning team runs a rough-cut check on the amount of mold-making labor required.

Assume that the forecast is for eight new case designs in an upcoming quarter. Then

$$8 \text{ cases} \times 46 \text{ hours per case} = 368 \text{ hours}$$

Since a standard quarter equals 520 hours (13 weeks $\times$ 40 hours per week), the production plan looks doable. Capacity for the scarce resource is adequate.

But providing only 368 hours of molding for the mold-maker in a 520-hour quarter may seem inadequate to keep the expert busy.

Not so. In fact, being well below the 520-hour maximum is comforting at this stage of planning—no work has been scheduled and no orders have been received. When orders do arrive, they are unlikely to spread out evenly over the quarter. When orders pile up, the mold-maker will be quite busy. But when no orders require new mold design, the mold-maker will be occupied with repair and maintenance of existing molds and improvement projects. Vacations and possible illness may also intervene.

Load Profile

Load, as in load profile, is short for *workload.*

In addition to capacity planning, scarce resources are also an issue at the master scheduling stage (see dashed arrow from block 8 to block 7 in Exhibit 7–17). The master scheduling team may employ **load profiles** as a rather precise method. A load profile shows both how much of a given resource is required and when. However, like the rough-cut method, the profile does not deduct inventories already on hand or on order. Therefore, requirements might be overstated.

For example, in assembly of mass spectrometers, a final-test machine might be the scarce, or bottleneck, resource. A load profile may show that a model X spectrometer requires four hours of system test time on the second day prior to shipment. Exhibit 7–19 is a complete load profile, showing time requirements for nonscarce as well as scarce resources (only the processes, not the resources themselves, are shown). Other spectrometer models would have different load profiles.

The profiles may exist as computer records or written data in a file cabinet. If the master production schedule calls for production of five model X spectrometers, two of model Y, and three of model Z, the master scheduler may pull out the profiles and multiply the processing times by 5, 2, and 3, respectively.

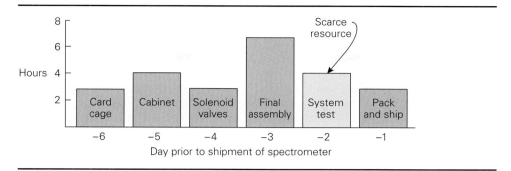

EXHIBIT 7–19

Load Profile for a Mass Spectrometer, Model X

The result is a composite workload profile showing whether the MPS will overload the scarce resource (the test machine). If so, the MPS quantities or timing may be changed.

Summary

Master planning works like a pair of scissors—demand management is one blade, capacity planning and master scheduling is the other. Customers' demand for outputs merged with demands on the provider's resource capacity yields the master schedule. The master schedule is referred to as the master production schedule (MPS) in manufacturing, but it might be an appointment book or a facility schedule for service companies. Capacity planning is integral to all businesses, and master scheduling is appropriate to all but sales or service-on-demand firms.

Meeting customer demand and utilizing capacity (not too much utilization or too little) are the aims of master planning, which is best accomplished by cross-functional teams that meet regularly.

Capacity planning is balanced against aggregate demand far enough out to permit changes in workforce, inventories, and other medium-range capacity elements. The capacity plan is based on aggregate forecasts for groupings of capacity or product families, and is easily translated into (or from) a production or delivery plan.

Capacity planning is governed by capacity strategies. A chase-demand strategy permits responsive customer service, but at a cost of fluctuating capacity. A level-capacity strategy has opposite characteristics. Policies translate the chosen capacity strategies into action and, along with strategies, are set by top management.

Often it is good practice to schedule under capacity by some percentage so that a fixed quantity of production is attainable in each run. When the quantity is produced early, employees engage in other useful activities, such as process improvement.

In companies with large backlogs, the capacity team may plan capacity in detail for months into the future. However, with or without backlogs, capacity planning may be improved by centering it around product families or capacity groups. By reorganizing resources into cells for each family or group, planning teams can avoid some of the hazards, inaccuracies, and complexities of capacity planning.

In a make-to-order business, options for capacity planning for a given capacity group may be tested on recent demand data, revealing effects on backlogs and order lead times. The capacity team may then select the plan that best fits company policies and customer needs.

In a make-to-stock business, capacity planning is also done by capacity groups. Based on demand forecasts, planners calculate the effect of a trial production rate on inventory levels and, in the complex case, on labor-hour and machine-hour requirements. They select the plan that yields the closest approximation to desired inventory levels while staying within available capacity.

Master planning for on-demand sales and services consists of capacity planning only. Prescheduled goods and services require an additional master scheduling step, which focuses on item demands for the next few periods. The capacity plan places upper limits on the master schedule or appointment book in an attempt to provide scheduled time slots for sales bookings plus item forecasts. An order promise conveys the firm's commitment to the customer.

In manufacturing, the master scheduling team creates the master production schedule, with separate sections for each major product. A subordinate schedule for component parts, plus parts sold outside, may also be developed.

Lack of planning lead time is the main problem in make-to-order plants, but an MPS based on forecasts can still work well. One approach—consuming the MPS—deducts actual customer orders as they arrive; MPS quantities not consumed are available to promise.

A rough-cut check shows capacity planners how the capacity plan affects scarce resources. Master schedulers also may use load profiles to do a more detailed check.

Solved Problems

Problem 1   Jack Sharp, a recent college graduate, seeks an entrepreneurial career. He started a consulting firm that helps small retail establishments and professional offices install microcomputer-based record keeping. Realizing that the only resources he has to sell are his expertise and workaholic tendencies, Jack plans on working about 280 hours per month. (Will all work and no play make Jack Sharp dull?) He has grouped his clients into three types: small retail outlets (such as shopping mall specialty stores), single-principal professional offices, and partnership professional offices. Jack estimates that time requirements for those clients will average 20, 40, and 50 hours, respectively.

Much telephone work and knocking on doors has resulted in a tentative client list for the next six months. Jack wants to match customer demand with available capacity (his time) and develop a trial schedule. The demand for each job type is as follows:

Client Type	Time Required (hours)	Demand—Customers/Month (month)					
		1	2	3	4	5	6
Retail store	20	4	—	6	3	4	2
Single professional	40	2	6	4	—	—	3
Multipartner professional	50	3	—	—	4	—	5

Solution 1   The following table shows Jack's capacity requirements by group (client type) for the six-month planning horizon as well as idle capacity or overload conditions:

Client Type	Demand—Resources/Month (Hours per client × Number of clients) (months)						Cumulative (for group)
	1	2	3	4	5	6	
Retail store	80	—	120	60	80	40	380
Single professional	80	240	160	—	—	120	600
Multipartner professional	150	—	—	200	—	250	600
Total capacity requirements (hours of time)	310	240	280	260	80	410	1,580
Capacity available	280	280	280	280	280	280	1,680
Extra capacity ("−" denotes overload)	−30	40	0	20	200	−130	100

For the total planning horizon, Jack has not overextended himself. He has 100 hours of excess capacity. He may have to work a few more hours during the first month, if demand estimates are accurate. His problem is months 5 and 6. He might try to entice some customers to use his services a month earlier than planned. But schedules very far out have a way of changing—often several times—prior to when the originally scheduled dates become current.

Problem 2

Exhibit 7–9, an example capacity plan for Anita's Studio, is based on a projected demand stream and some assumptions (e.g., one new assistant works half of April). As part of her master planning, Anita wonders if she might have to adjust her capacity plan if actual demand on her photography service is, say, 15 percent higher during the six-month planning period?

Solution 2

The lower part of Exhibit 7–9 is used as the format for the table shown below. Photography service demand (photo taking and developing work) has been increased by 15 percent in each month. Other assumptions, and Anita's desired policy of limiting her own work to 160 hours per month, remain in force.

Capacity Plan—By Group (hours)	Feb.	Mar.	Apr.	May	June	July
Photography service:						
Demand	202	164	267	521	700	509
Capacity: Photo assistant #1	—	—	80	160	160	160
Capacity: Photo assistant #2	—	—	—	160	160	160
Capacity: Outsourcing (FastFotos, Inc.)	42	4	27	41	220	29
Capacity: Owner (Anita)	160	160	160	160	160	160

If Anita sticks with her desire to limit her own planned time to no more than 160 hours per month, outsourcing will be used to absorb the extra capacity requirements. As she examines this plan, she sees no urgent need to alter her original strategy. A third photography assistant could be used full time during June if Anita desires to cut down on the amount of outsourcing, but even with a 15-percent demand increase, that person wouldn't be needed during other months. She does note, however, that this plan consumes all 160 hours of her personal (planned) time allocation. Maybe she should begin thinking about a regular, but part-time, assistant to work about 40 to 60 hours per month. That would free up some of her time and might be more flexible than outsourcing. Back to the basic issue in capacity planning: What does she *want* to do?

Problem 3

An assembly line currently staffed with 10 assemblers produces an average of 190 units per day. The current sales rate for the product is 200 units per day. If the company follows a policy of scheduling at 85 percent of capacity, what should it do? (Options include setting a new production rate or changing capacity.)

Solution 3   The production rate must be 200 units per day, exactly the number being sold. Then 200 is set equal to 85 percent of capacity, and capacity is solved for algebraically:

$$0.85X = 200$$

Then,

$$X = 235.3 \text{ units per day}$$

Since 10 assemblers can produce 190 on the average, we need to know how many assemblers are needed to produce 235.3. Therefore:

$$\frac{10}{190} = \frac{X}{235.3}$$

$$190X = 2,353$$

$$X = 12.38, \text{ or } 13 \text{ assemblers}$$

Thus, the company must assign three more assemblers to the production line.

Review Questions

1. What is master planning? How does it relate to demand management?
2. What is capacity planning? How does it differ from master scheduling?
3. Is master planning essential for all businesses? Explain.
4. What areas of an organization ought to be represented on capacity planning teams? On master scheduling teams?
5. The master schedule goes by various names: What is it called in manufacturing? In service? Does it perform the same function in both settings? Explain.
6. Once a master schedule is determined, may it be changed? Explain.
7. Why does the master planning sequence for prescheduled demands include more steps than for on-demand goods and services?
8. How does chase-demand strategy differ from level-capacity strategy? Why might one department in a company follow chase demand while another opts for level capacity?
9. What are capacity policies? Give examples. Should these policies be general or specific? Discuss.
10. Explain the statement, "Capacity policies are options; choose the one(s) you want."
11. What are the advantages and disadvantages of hiring as a capacity management policy?
12. What difficulties might arise if one uses master schedule revision as a capacity management policy?
13. How might we compute a resource utilization rate?
14. Capacity utilization rates may be misused. Give an example of your own creation. Explain fully.
15. When is an undercapacity scheduling policy effective?

16. Given the uncertainty of customer demand in on-demand and make-to-order businesses, how can capacity be planned in such firms?

17. In a make-to-stock business, how could a capacity plan provide for rising inventory levels in anticipation of seasonal peak sales?

18. How can principle 6 affect capacity planning?

19. What is a time fence in master scheduling?

20. Why might a manufacturer have both a master production schedule and a component parts schedule?

21. Explain how a master schedule may be consumed.

22. How does rough-cut capacity planning improve the validity of the master schedule?

23. How is a load profile used in master scheduling?

Exercises

1. Assume that you are president of a large company and have a strong aversion to laying off employees. Devise a multistep policy governing what your company would do if demand in certain product lines dropped, creating excess labor. Your last step should be employee terminations.

2. How has Hewlett-Packard been able to downsize and still avoid laying off employees, given the competition and short life cycle of many products in the fast-changing computer and electronics industry? You may need to research the subject or interview H-P people to answer this question satisfactorily.

3. Investigate one company in three of the following types to find out (*a*) what full capacity is in terms of hours or shifts per week, and why, and (*b*) what current capacity utilization is, and why:

Supermarket	Overnight mail service
Discount store	Manufacturing plant
Bank	Certified public accounting firm
Art gallery	Charitable institution

4. Investigate a retailer, a wholesaler, or a manufacturer to learn whether its current capacity plan includes both numeric labor and inventory levels. What are the plan's aims? Why? (If your company does not have a numeric capacity plan, find out why.)

5. City Sod is a small business that sells and lays sod (rolled strips of grass). The owner has devised a forecasting procedure based on demand history from previous years plus projection of demand in recent weeks. The forecast for the next six weeks, in labor hours of sod laying, is

860	880	900	920	930	940

   Currently City Sod has a staff of sod layers consisting of four crew chiefs and 15 laborers. A crew chief lays sod along with the laborers but also directs the crew. The owner has decided on the following staffing policies:

   a. A two-week backlog will be accumulated before adding staff.

   b. Plans are based on a 40-hour work week; overtime is used only to absorb weather or other delays and employee absence or resignations.

c. The ideal crew size is one crew chief and four laborers.

Devise a hiring plan for the six-week period covered by the forecast. In your answer, assume a current backlog of 1,200 labor hours of sod-laying orders. Does City Sod follow more of a chase-demand or level-capacity strategy of production planning? Explain.

6. Bright Way Janitorial Service has long followed a level-capacity strategy of capacity planning. Now, however, the company is considering a shift from level-capacity to chase-demand. Bright Way managers know that chase demand would greatly simplify production/capacity planning. Explain why this is so. What new management problems would chase demand tend to create?

7. Coast Limited Railways operates a car repair yard in Kansas City to repair its cars. In the six most recent months, Kansas City's car repair workload has been:

Month	1	2	3	4	5	6
Cars	83	72	71	90	49	56

a. Coast Limited headquarters has directed Kansas City managers to plan for a capacity level that will exceed demand by no more than half a month's average demand during the six-month planning period. Prepare the capacity plan following the backlogging method of Example 7–5 in the chapter. Explain the positive and negative deviations.

b. What important factors in (*a*) could be analyzed in terms of dollars?

8. The purchasing director and two senior buyers at Windward Sportswear, an apparel manufacturer, jointly prepare the purchasing department's staffing (capacity) plan. They test alternative staffing plans using recent demand data. Demand is measured as the number of purchase orders (POs) per week, based on purchase requests from other Windward departments. Data for the past five weeks follow:

	Week				
	1	*2*	*3*	*4*	*5*
POs	128	98	155	150	83

a. If the team elects to staff the department for 130 POs per week, will purchasing be able to serve its customers adequately? (Hint: Refer to the method of Example 7–5. Explain.)

b. What capacity plan would you recommend? Why?

c. If customers require very fast processing of purchase requests, what could the purchasing department do to efficiently accommodate the requirement?

9. Old English Tea Company blends and packages an average of 8,000 boxes of tea per shift. Eighteen people tend the production line, and the company follows a policy of undercapacity scheduling, scheduling labor at 90 percent of capacity. Demand is down, and the production rate must be reduced to meet the demand of 6,800 boxes per shift. How many people should be added or how many assigned to other work? Assume that labor and output rate are linearly related.

10. A computer software company has one production line that copies programs onto floppy disks and packages the disks. The line has been scheduled at full capacity and has been consuming 30 hours of direct labor per day. Demand recently has fallen from 1,400 to 1,200 packages per day; therefore, now is a good time to convert to undercapacity labor scheduling. (Problems in meeting schedules and resulting

lost sales have brought about the policy change.) Determine the new labor-hour requirements for a policy of 10-percent undercapacity scheduling.

11. Dominion Envelope Co. produces a variety of paper and light-cardboard envelopes, often with customer-specified printing on them. Dominion formed an order-processing cell for its biggest customer, Bank of North America (BNA). The cell consists of one person each from sales, accounting, materials, and operations. Orders from other customers go from department to department, but BNA orders are processed in the cell, then sent to operations for production, packaging, and shipping.

    a. How would capacity planning differ for BNA orders versus other orders?

    b. How could capacity planning be improved for other customers?

12. Concrete Products, Inc., makes reinforced concrete structural members (trusses, etc.) for large buildings and bridges. Each order is a special design, so no finished-goods inventories are possible. Concrete members are made by using molds that are bolted onto huge shake tables. A vibrating action causes the wet concrete to pack, without air pockets, around reinforcing steel in the molds. Concrete Products uses a chase-demand strategy of hiring labor to assemble, fill, and disassemble the molds. If it takes a week to hire and train a laborer, how can Concrete Products make the chase-demand strategy work well? What types of labor (capacity) policies would work? Recent work loads, in labor hours, on the shake tables are as follows:

Week	1	2	3	4	5	6	7	8	9
Labor hours	212	200	170	204	241	194	168	215	225

13. At a fiberglass products company, the dominant product line is fiberglass bathtub and shower units, which sell to the high-quality segment of the market. The company's best employees work in tubs and showers, which are treated as a separate capacity group. Forecast demands for this capacity group are in labor hours. For the next three months, demand is forecast at 300, 370, and 380 labor hours. The present inventory is 620 labor-hours' worth of tub and shower units, in all sizes and colors. The plan is to reduce the inventory to 300 after three months because the slow season is approaching.

    a. Prepare a production plan for the next three months that minimizes labor fluctuation.

    b. How would the master production schedule differ from the production plan?

14. Gulf Tube and Pipe Company prepares monthly production/capacity plans for three capacity areas, one of which is the pipe-forming, -cutting, and -welding (FCW) processes. The forecast FCW demand for next month is as follows:

Week	Forecast Lineal Feet (000)
1	6,000
2	5,800
3	5,400
4	4,600

The present inventory is 16 million lineal feet.

    a. Devise a production plan following a chase-demand strategy that results in an ending inventory of 14 million lineal feet.

    b. Devise a production plan following a level-capacity strategy that results in an ending inventory of 14 million lineal feet.

c. The following rule of thumb is used for purposes of capacity planning: two operators are required for every 1 million lineal feet produced. Develop two capacity (i.e., workforce) plans, one using data from (*a*) and the other using data from (*b*).

d. Cite data from (*a*) through (*c*) to explain the contrasting effects on inventories and labor of chase-demand and level-capacity strategies.

15. Devise a master scheduling procedure diagram similar to Exhibit 7–16 but for draftspeople in an engineering firm. Explain your diagram.

16. Devise a master scheduling procedure diagram similar to Exhibit 7–16, but for a maintenance department. Assume that maintenance includes janitorial crews, plumbers, and electricians, but does not include construction or remodeling personnel. Explain your diagram.

17. Capacity planning is never easy, and seems especially difficult in retail, where demand varies greatly throughout the day. Four retail situations are listed below. Pick any two and write a brief analysis of how each deals with the unpredictability factor in planning capacity (labor). You may need to interview one or more people in a real firm.

Post office   Fast-food restaurant

Motel   Bank

18. In general registration at your college, registering for classes might require you to pass through several work centers. Which work center is a bottleneck? Would the registrar's office find the rough-cut capacity planning idea useful in planning for that bottleneck work center? Explain. You will probably need to consider what the MPS would consist of in this case. (If you prefer, you can answer this question using drop-and-add or another administrative procedure instead of general registration.)

19. At Piney Woods Furniture Company, the scarce resource that most concerns master scheduling is the wood-drying kiln. One product, a cabinet, uses three types of wood, which go through the kiln at different times in the manufacture of the cabinet. The accompanying bar graph shows the kiln load profile resulting from a minimum cabinet order (50 cabinets). The unit of measure is cubic yard-hours, which accounts for size of the drying load and time in the kiln for one cabinet.

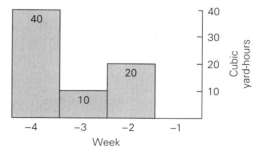

The current MPS includes an order for 1,000 cabinets in week 6 (six weeks from now). Projected kiln workload for all products other than the cabinet is as follows for the next six weeks:

	Week					
	1	*2*	*3*	*4*	*5*	*6*
Cubic yard-hours	5,000	5,200	5,300	5,800	5,700	6,000

a. Calculate the week-by-week kiln loads (workloads) for the cabinet order. (Assume that week −1 on the load profile means one week prior to the week in which an order is due on the MPS.)

b. If the kiln has a maximum weekly capacity of 6,000 cubic yard-hours, will the MPS overload the kiln? Explain.

c. If the cabinet order is adjustable (the customer would accept a change in delivery date), what MPS changes would you recommend, if any?

For Further Reference

Books

Berry, William L.; Thomas E. Vollmann; and D. Clay Whybark, *Master Production Scheduling: Principles and Practice.* Falls Church, Va.: American Production and Inventory Control Society, 1979 (TS157.5.B46x).

Blackstone, John H., Jr. *Capacity Management,* Cincinnati: South-Western, 1989 (HD69.C3B63).

Plossl, G. W., and O. W. Wight. *Production and Inventory Control: Principles and Techniques.* Englewood Cliffs, N.J.: Prentice Hall, 1967 (HD55.P5).

Proud, John F. *Master Scheduling: A Practial Guide to Competitive Manufacturing.* Williston, Vt.: Oliver Wight Publications, Ltd., 1994.

Vollmann, Thomas E.; William Lee Berry; and D. Clay Whybark. *Manufacturing Planning and Control Systems:* 3d ed. Burr Ridge, Ill.: Dow Jones-Irwin, 1991 (TS176.V63).

Wight, Oliver W. *MRPII: Unlocking America's Productivity Potential.* Williston, Vt.: Oliver Wight Limited Publications, 1981 (TS161.W5x).

Periodicals/Societies

APICS—The Performance Advantage (American Production and Inventory Control Society).

Decision Sciences (Decision Sciences Institute).

Industrial Engineering Solutions (Institute of Industrial Engineers).

Journal of Operations Management (American Production and Inventory Control Society).

Production and Inventory Management (American Production and Inventory Control Society).

(All of these periodicals contain articles on various facets of master planning.)

8 FLOW-CONTROL SYSTEMS OVERVIEW

Chapter Outline

"The automaker regularly got information from dealers about what car models were selling, what colors were popular, and so on. The automaker could pass that information on to its seatmaker to help anticipate what styles and colors of seats would be needed in the near future. The seatmaker dealt with a fabricmaker who in turn dealt with a yarn dyer who got material from a yarnmaker.

"Like most other customers and suppliers in traditional competitive industries, they kept most business affairs secret from each other, fearful that shared information might cause a competitive disadvantage and lost profit. [A consultant] found [that] the time it took for the yarnmaker's product to find its way into a car seat installed by the automaker averaged about 71 days."

It took seven months "to persuade everyone in the chain that it would be mutually advantageous to share information. . . . Once everyone agreed, the information was regularly distributed by fax. They could have installed computer linkups and shared information electronically, but that would have taken another two years to implement and wouldn't be any more efficient," the consultant maintained.

Results: "On average, everyone in the chain was able to cut inventory by 75 percent, and the time from yarnmaker to installed car seat dropped to 28 days."[1]

*Reduction of the overall flow time for auto seats from 71 to 28 days touched on the outward elements of the total **flow control system:** final auto sales patterns and the interfaces between the major players. Further improvement—below 28 days—requires fine-tuning of the flow control systems of each contributing organization: producers, freight handlers, wholesalers, retailers.*

Courtesy Johnson Controls Company

Flow control ensures timely, accurate, value-adding movement of goods, services, or customers—through the processing stages. Poor flow control produces highly variable, unpredictable results, such as late, or early, completions and out-of-bounds quality. Good flow control requires correcting the many weak points in the process stages.

There is no single department that can control the flows. Some companies have, however, a department of production control, which has some flow-control responsibilities, though not the full set. Actually, flow control is more a matter of control of *delays* between value-adding "production" processes than control of the production itself.

This chapter sets the stage for the remaining chapters in Part III on "translating demand into orders," which focus on purchasing and inventory management (Chapters 9, 10, and 11). Flow control issues extend further into Chapters 12 through 15 in Part IV on "translating planned orders into outcomes." Thus, flow control systems cover a lot of ground.

System Variability

Were you out of coffee this morning? Was the milk spoiled? Car battery dead? Situations like these interrupt the flow of work (or play). These are failures of the **flow-control system.** They can include inventory problems, faulty equipment, and various people and system shortcomings.

A business flow-control system is like your own, except that many more things can vary from targeted performance and break down in the business's system. In any organization, multiple process elements can vary at the same time, and

A flow-control system in wholesaling is mostly an inventory system; in manufacturing, a production and inventory system; in human services, a customer processing system.

the combined variations can result in extreme mistakes, delays, failures, and total shutdowns. Two common examples for purchased materials are variations in delivery time and in quality (see Exhibit 8–1).

*𝒫*RINCIPLE 10:

Eliminate process variation.

In the exhibit, the T stands for the performance target: what should happen every time. The variabilities are not pluses (goods) and minuses (bads) that cancel out over the long run: One uncooked cake and one burned cake do not add up to great baking. All variabilities are bad, and combining them only makes matters worse: Bad-quality material is not forgiven if delivery is too early. Ted Waitt, chairman and CEO of Gateway 2000, the computer-by-mail company, has the customer in mind: "I convinced our manufacturing people that an early shipment was as bad as a late shipment, so the 'on-time' [goal of 90 percent on time in less than five days] means just that. No more waiting for a UPS man that doesn't show, or having something show up unexpectedly."[2]

Variability, variation, uncertainty, and *undependability,* are used more or less synonymously, as are *invariability, certainty,* and *dependability.*

Process variability annoys, both because it yields bad results and because it equals uncertainty. If a bus is late by 10 minutes dependably, we might be able to live with it. But if it's 10 minutes late on average—sometimes much later, on time, or early—we may give up on bus riding.

Keeping buses on time requires controlling just a few sources of variability. But flow control in a complex organization involves many interacting sources of variability, such as multiple internal processes using many different external materials and other resources. Reducing interacting variability requires a three-pronged attack:

1. System designers avoid complexity so that there are fewer sources of variability.
2. Every associate and team finds ways to control process variation.
3. Cross-functional teams develop ways to detect and plan around or adjust to sources of variability, thus producing a satisfactory result.

Developing the flow-control system is this chapter's focus, and it requires a basic understanding of inventories, carrying costs, demand dependency, logistics, system delays, combined effects of timing and quality, and measurements of success. The remainder of the chapter addresses these topics.

Exhibit 8–1

Variability: Deviation from Target

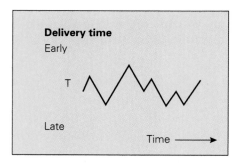

Late or early delivery of material

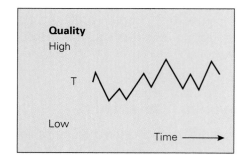

Material out of specification (bad quality) on the high or low side

Flow Control: Avoiding Slacks and Gluts

A tailor, a tax advisor, or a ticket-taker each seeks a steady flow of customers to and through the processes. This means avoiding both slack resources and "inventories" of customers waiting impatiently for services. To be successful, these businesses must keep their cloth, tax forms and ticket revenues (respectively) flowing.

In manufacturing, wholesaling, and retailing, inventories of materials must be kept flowing, while avoiding slacks that anger customers and gluts that raise the costs of carrying the inventories. Inventories are a major cost, typically over 50 percent of expenditures in manufacturing, 70 percent in retailing, and 90 percent in wholesaling. In these businesses, controlling inventories is a key to success. Highly efficient Wal-Mart spends less on inventory mistakes (too much or too little inventory), which enables it to spend more (85 percent) of its expenditures on the revenue-earning inventories themselves.

Control does not mean elimination. Inventories (materials, documents, or customers) must flow. But like life-giving rivers, they should neither dry up nor flood too often.

The world's best retailers team up with freight carriers and producers at several levels in the supply chain in order to keep goods flowing.

Whether linked to retailers or not, each manufacturing plant must keep the work flowing. Master planning teams see to capacity plans and master schedules. Then, buyers and schedulers perform their roles. They plan for materials to arrive just in time for processing or, for seasonal manufacturing, they plan for building stock to meet the seasonal peak.

In any business, planning and timing do not work out if equipment is out of commission. Thus, equipment maintenance is part of flow control. Also, long get-ready and changeover times often necessitate scheduling in large lots (batches), but each large-lot process is a lump in what otherwise could be a relatively smooth work flow. Therefore, efforts to cut change times and batch sizes are also important.

Quality is especially important. If quality is erratic, work may arrive on schedule but go directly to scrap, to rework, or to the complaint department.

*C*ontrast

Having the Right Inventory

No One Responsible	Everyone Responsible
Inventory managers *care for* inventory; processing and transporting in batches.	Everyone at every process keeps the work flowing.
Shortages of supply are blamed on purchasing, suppliers, operations, maintenance, and so on.	Avoid stops and starts, large process and transit batches, unnecessary storage, equipment stoppages, and so on.
Wrong items in inventory: Marketing and the demand forecast get the blame.	Everyone connects with and responds quickly and flexibly to customers and suppliers.

The point should be clear—poor flow control has diverse causes, including disconnection between supply chain levels, long get-ready times, batching, erratic processes, and poor quality.

Companies commonly address these causes defensively or reactively. Common defenses include flooding the distribution warehouses and internal processes with extra, just-in-case inventories. Common reactions are rerouting, rescheduling, or rearranging priorities of stalled orders. However, what's needed is to solve the problems in the first place. Otherwise, flow control activities—when carried out in a separate function and cost center (e.g., operations control or materials management)—become highly complex. Indeed, the costs of managing the delays and changes may rival the direct costs of the operations being controlled.[3]

Managing the Delays (the Carrying Costs)

To reiterate, the work must flow. That advice becomes doubly important when cost is considered, for cost is like dust—it tends to settle on anything that is sitting around. Rapid processing allows little time for costs to accumulate. Unfortunately, in almost any business the work is mostly in a state of delay or idleness. For example, for every minute that a piece of metal is under a cutting tool, it is likely to spend 5, 10, or even 100 minutes in front of the machine waiting. When material is idle, it incurs a cost above and beyond its unit price. That cost is called an **inventory carrying cost.**

Office work collects carrying costs, too. For example, office people sometimes spend more time searching (in-baskets, brief cases, computer files, trash barrels) for a document than working on it. Then, often enough, the work isn't done right and must be done over. In human services, customers waiting in line or holding the telephone "for the next available service representative" bear their own costs of idleness, which, they may estimate, sometimes exceed the value of the purchase or service sought.

Costs of Idleness

What do those delays cost? For a client the cost is hard to judge because most of it is poor-service cost, that is, the cost of the client's involuntary idleness. Likewise, for documents and files the cost of idleness is mostly the cost of slow service to the customer; costs of storing and carrying the documents and files are minor.

What about materials in a hospital, restaurant, or factory? First are the physical costs of holding inventory and the financial costs of having working capital tied up in idle inventory. But those are the obvious carrying costs, which accounting and inventory management writings have always recognized. More recently these writings have paid heed to less obvious and "hidden" costs. Obvious, semiobvious, and hidden inventory carrying costs are listed in Exhibit 8–2.

Obvious Costs

In order to be a true inventory carrying cost, a cost must rise with the growth, and fall with the reduction, of inventory. **Capital cost,** first on the list, clearly qualifies. Company financial managers frequently attempt to secure bank loans or lines of credit to pay for more inventory. Banks often use the inventory as collateral for loans.

Obvious carrying costs:
    Capital cost—interest or opportunity costs of working capital tied up in stock
    Holding cost—stockroom costs of:
        Space
        Storage implements (e.g., shelving and stock-picking vehicles)
        Insurance on space, equipment, and inventories
        Inventory taxes
        Stockkeepers' wages
        Damage and shrinkage while in storage
Semiobvious carrying costs:
    Obsolescence
    Inventory planning and management
    Stock record keeping
    Physical inventory taking
Hidden carrying costs:
    Cost of stock on production floor:
        Space
        Storage implements (e.g., racks, pallets, containers)
        Handling implements (e.g., conveyors, cranes, forklift trucks)
    Inventory transactions and data processing support
    Management and technical support for equipment used in storage, handling, and
        inventory data processing
    Scrap and rework
    Lot inspections
    Lost sales, lost customers because of slow processing

EXHIBIT 8-2

Carrying-Cost Elements

Only in abnormal situations can a company avoid capital costs. For example, Harley-Davidson people like to crow about the time when they got paid for production before they had to pay for the raw materials. On the books, the effect appears as negative inventory. (The product was not motorcycles but a subassembly they had contracted to make for another company.) The negative inventory situation arose because of Harley's successful just-in-time efforts: Work sped through the plant—raw materials to finished goods—in a day or two versus the weeks that it would have taken in Harley's pre-JIT days.

Next on the list is **holding cost,** which is mainly the cost of running stockrooms. While the accounting system may consider space and storage implements as fixed costs, they exist only to hold stock; therefore, they are true carrying costs. The other more or less obvious holding costs are insurance, taxes, material department wages, damages, and shrinkage costs.

Semiobvious Costs

Semiobvious carrying costs include inventory obsolescence and costs of inventory management and clerical activities (see Exhibit 8–2). People involved in inventory planning, stock record keeping, and physical inventory counting do not actually handle stock, and their offices often are far from stockrooms. Perhaps for these reasons, some companies include those costs as general or operating overhead. Clearly, however, they are inventory carrying costs.

Obsolescence cost is nearly zero when materials arrive just in time for use, but it can be high if companies buy in large batches and then find that the need for the items has dried up. High-fashion stores and high-tech electronics companies should be acutely aware of obsolescence as a cost of carrying inventory. Old-line manufacturers, however, might write off obsolete stock only once every 10 years; if so, they may fail to include obsolescence routinely in their calculated carrying-cost rate.

Hidden Costs

Carrying costs that commingle with other costs tend to be hidden. A prime example is stock released from a stockroom to operations (factory, sales floor, kitchen, etc.), where it sits idle between operations, tying up cash and occupying costly space. In manufacturing, idle in-process inventories commonly occupy half or more of factory floor space. Idle stock often sits on racks, conveyors, automatic storage systems, and other costly equipment, and it adds up to a major hidden carrying cost component.

Most companies once invalidly charged those costs as production costs. Today, accountants and operations managers and associates are increasingly asking: Does it add value? Does the activity produce something saleable or directly serve a paying customer? If not, treat it as an inventory carrying cost. Illustration: a conveyor literally carries inventory and adds no value to the product.

Another so-called **non-value-adding (NVA)** activity is processing inventory transactions, including the cost of associates' time for entering inventory usage and scrap data into terminals plus the cost of the terminals, usually treated incorrectly as operating costs. Much greater are the associated central processing costs (hardware, software, and computer operations) and the costs of corrections and report processing. In inventory-intensive firms, inventory management is the dominant computer application; its costs have been conveniently bundled into the information system department's total costs, but they are actually hidden inventory carrying costs. Costs of management and technical support for storage, handling, and data-processing equipment are also carrying costs, but they are rarely treated as such.

ℙRINCIPLE 11:

Cut inventory.

Scrap and rework costs also fall with decreases in inventories, including decreases in lot sizes. This is true in processing perishables (such as cutting off rot from food items), in wholesaling and retailing (e.g., an entire lot of garments missing a buttonhole), in information processing, and in manufacturing.

As an information processing example, suppose telephone sales associates send sales orders forward once a day in batches averaging 800 orders. Order entry clerks in the next department might find numerous defects, such as missing quantity, incomplete address, or lack of a promise date. Sometimes, especially for a new promotion, an entire lot of 800 orders will contain the same error. More commonly, errors will occur at some average percentage. Either way, order entry clerks end up sending the faulty forms back to the sales office for rework, probably the next day (see Exhibit 8–3A). Meanwhile, time has passed and sales people are busy with other orders. They are no longer clear about the details of yesterday's orders and the likely root causes of yesterday's order-processing errors.

Independent inspectors conducting sampling inspections may reject a whole lot based on a bad sample and send the lot back for rectification.

If salespeople processed and forwarded orders in lots of 20 instead of 800 (Exhibit 8–3B), maximum damage would be 20, which could be sent back while the trail of causes is still warm.

ℙRINCIPLE 13:

Decrease cycle interval and lot size.

Much better still would be for a sales associate to hand the order directly to an order entry clerk (Exhibit 8–3C). They become a team, intolerant of errors on order forms. Large defective lots are no longer possible. When an error occurs, the clerk usually discovers it right away while the cause is still obvious. The team finds ways to permanently eliminate the causes, steadily driving down the rate of defective order forms.

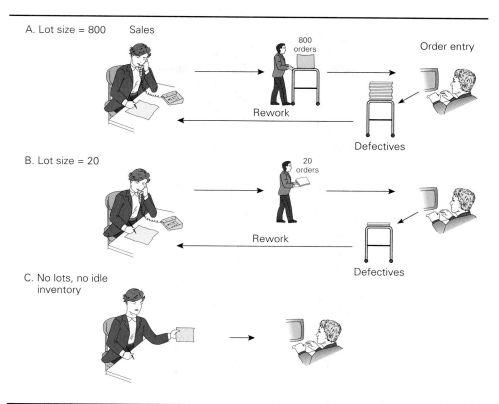

A. Lot size = 800   Sales

800 orders

Order entry

Rework

Defectives

B. Lot size = 20

20 orders

Rework

Defectives

C. No lots, no idle inventory

Exhibit 8–3

Effect of Lot Size on Rework/Scrap

Inspection costs merit similar scrutiny. Inspectors facing large lots have the big job of sorting out the bad ones. However, some companies avoid large lots by adopting just-in-time techniques. They avoid large *bad* lots by implementing strict process controls to prevent rather than merely detect defects. The tie-in between inspection costs and lot-size quantities is becoming clear, and the conclusion is that even inspectors may be treated as a carrying cost. (We leave it to the reader to speculate on machine repairpeople, parts expediters, and others who respond to work stoppages and stockouts: Are those too a type of carrying cost?)

Last and most important are the costs of lost sales and lost customer allegiance when the flow-control system is plagued by stalled orders. Thus, the negative impact of idle inventories on customer responsiveness is also a carrying cost. But by keeping lot sizes, queues, and transport distances short, the firm can ensure that the work flows through the system cleanly and quickly—perhaps surprising, delighting, and retaining the customer.

Uses of Carrying Costs

In some organizations inventories are such a dominant cost that virtually every investment proposal has an inventory effect. Therefore, it is important to use a realistic carrying cost when doing a financial analysis for a proposal.

Traditionally, carrying cost has been stated as an annual rate based on the item's value. Older books on inventory management suggested a rate of 25 percent as a good average. Many North American manufacturers still use 25 percent (or 24 percent—2 percent per month). But that rate is based on the obvious carrying costs (Exhibit 8–2) and possibly some of the semiobvious costs.

If all carrying costs are included, as they should be, what is the proper rate? No studies have answered that question definitively. However, the rate is surely at least 50 percent. Indeed, several manufacturers have upped their rates to 50 percent or higher.[4] When researchers have unearthed all carrying costs, more companies may use higher rates, perhaps as high as 100 percent. To see what 100 percent means, imagine a $50 chair sitting in a stockroom for a year. The owner would be paying another $50 for the chair in the form of the costs of carrying it.

Thinking about moving a machine and its operator across the building to team up with a machine and operator at the next process? How much inventory savings are there, and what carrying-cost rate is being used? Suppose that the cost of moving is $2,000 and that $3,000 of inventory would be eliminated. At a 25 percent rate, the savings are $750 per year ($0.25 \times \$3,000$); without doing a discounted cash flow analysis, payback on the investment will take $2\frac{2}{3}$ years ($\$2,000 \div \$750$ per year)—perhaps not very attractive. At 100 percent, carrying-cost savings are $3,000 per year and the investment pays for itself in less than a year:

$$\text{Simple payback period} = \frac{\text{Investment cost}}{\text{Annual savings}} \qquad (8\text{--}1)$$

The best-known financial analysis that uses carrying-cost rates is in calculating an economic order quantity (see Chapter 11). Another issue that bears on flow-control systems is whether demand for an item is dependent or independent of other items.

Dependent and Independent Demand

A taco that you buy and eat is an **independent-demand item;** it does not go into a **parent item.** The taco's ingredients, however, are **dependent-demand items,** which is the demand category for a **component item** that goes into a parent item. In delivery of services, client demands are independent, but supplies consumed and capacity engaged in service delivery may be dependent.

Sometimes an item appears to be dependent but its parent is unknown. An example is a new tire for sale in a service station. What kind of car or truck will it go on? The item must be treated as independent. However, that same tire, if destined for a car in an auto assembly plant, is a dependently demanded component.

The classification reasoning is as follows: The production or delivery schedule for a dependent item matches the demand for the parent; production of the component and parent can be tightly synchronized with little fuss or idle inventory. The schedule for the component is completely accurate relative to the schedule for the parent item or items.

Scheduling the independent-demand item is less simple. The service station keeps common tires on hand, a practice that generates a carrying cost. But which common tires and how many of each should be on hand? The station manager can only guess (forecast), and that introduces inaccuracy. To ensure an adequate level of customer service, the manager keeps **buffer stock** on hand in order to provide protection in the face of forecast inaccuracy.

Retail and wholesale inventories generally are independent-demand items, as are service parts (spare or replacement parts) in factories, since the parents into which they go are unknown to the provider.

Buffer stock
Stock inserted at any stage of production or order fulfillment to ensure continued supply when demand increases or production stalls; also called *safety stock.*

A few decades ago, flow-control systems were too primitive and data processing too costly to permit companies to sort out parent–component dependencies. Most parts were ordered based on guesses about how quickly they would be used up, and buffer stock provided protection from stockouts. Modern systems, especially **quick response (QR), just-in-time (JIT),** and **material requirements planning (MRP),** simplify the planning of dependent items. These systems handle independent-demand items, too, but with less precision and higher costs since independent demands must be forecast. JIT and MRP, briefly mentioned in this chapter, are more fully treated in Chapter 10. QR, a powerful multistage application of JIT, is our next topic.

Quick Response: Control of Intersector Flows

QR links different companies in several stages of production, supply, and freight hauling to final points of sale. The ultimate aim is tight synchronization: Pick the cotton that's spun into thread that's woven into cloth that's dyed and finished into fabric that's cut and sewed into a shirt that's delivered to the store just before you walk in to buy it—all of this, and transportation, too, in sync. Synchronization at each stage affects scheduling, purchasing, storage, logistics, capacity, marketing, and cash-flow planning. The accompanying Into Practice box gives examples of QR.

*P*RINCIPLE 13:

Operate at the customer's rate of use.

Basic and Enhanced QR

Quick response's unofficial kickoff was in June 1986 in Chicago. Roger Milliken, chairman of textile manufacturer Milliken & Co., was instrumental in getting together a few dozen retailers and textile and apparel suppliers to discuss foreign competition. The main issue was how North American fiber-textile-apparel industries could compete with low-wage companies offshore. Participants at this and following meetings wanted to use technology to exploit the proximity of U.S. companies to the American market, and the goal was to set standards so everyone from raw material supplier to the retail store could speak the same electronic language and share data.

Bennetton's and The Limited's home-grown versions of QR existed before 1986. But the Milliken-led group brought QR into general use.

The reasoning was that if U.S. companies could respond faster to market shifts, they could overcome the advantage of low wages paid by Third World competitors.[5]

QR has rapidly expanded. An annual Quick Response convention and exhibition has emerged to promote the concept and the technology. Quick Response '93, held in Atlanta, included special sessions devoted not only to textiles and apparel but also to housewares, health and beauty aids, footwear, menswear, consumer electronics, toys, tools, hardware, and jewelry; attendees came from dozens of other business sectors as well.[6] The photo, "Survival of the Quickest," comes from a promotional brochure for a trade group that has actively supported the annual QR conventions.

Technology is part of the QR equation: universal product codes, scanning equipment at the retailer, data communications hardware, and electronic data interchange (EDI) software. However, according to one executive "Technology is 10 percent of the issue." The other 90 percent, he says, involves tight "relationships with trading partners, reduction of inventories, and recrafting production processes."[7]

Basic QR requires point-of-sale (POS) data only from selected stores. This is like predicting election results. Pollsters use voter intentions from key precincts to predict election winners with high accuracy. Similarly, manufacturers—even if several echelons removed from final sales points—can schedule production based on recent POS samples. Conventional scheduling, on the other hand, is always weeks or months out of date.

$\mathscr{I}$nto $\mathscr{P}$ractice

QR at Luxottica Group SpA of Italy

"Luxottica [the world's largest eyeware manufacturer] reorganized its U.S. sales staff and started sharing with customers the advantages of computer power. It is equipping [independent] retailers with software that checks Luxottica's stock and orders goods for overnight delivery. In the past, delivery took days or weeks."

Source: Bill Saporito, "Cutting Out the Middleman," *Fortune*, April 6, 1992, p. 96.

QR in Apparel

"VF Corporation [maker of Wrangler, Lee, Jantzen, and Vanity Fair apparel] has devised and implemented a Market Response System (MRS), designed to reduce cycle time and inventory, lower costs, and offer retailers and consumers the products they want, when they want them. MRS is executed through a series of simultaneous rather than sequential marketing, production, and supply activities, linked by information technology."

According to Lawrence Pugh, CEO, "If we eliminate organizational barriers and encourage such a free flow of information, we can get a specific product replaced on the retail shelf in less than seven days—in an environment where 60 to 90 days has been considered good practice. . . . [By implementing MRS] we can make it so that the consumer can count on having the right product, size, and color in the store every day."

Source: Advertising supplement, *Fortune*, September 21, 1992.

"Today, when JC Penney sells a Mens Relaxed Fit in Pepper Wash in size 32 × 32, Avondale Mills knows they just moved 2.218 square yards of denim."

Source: Michael A. McEntire, "Consumer Responsive Product Development," Conference Proceedings, Quick Response '94, Automatic Identification Manufacturers, Inc. (AIM USA), 1994, p. 68.

SURVIVAL OF THE QUICKEST.

Source: This photo is reprinted with the expressed written consent of Automatic Identification Manufacturers, Inc. (AIM USA). For more information, contact AIM USA 412/693-8588.

Though a manufacturer started QR, retailers have largely taken it over and shaped it to meet their own special interests. Wal-Mart, a leading proponent, has publicly announced that it would cease doing business with distributors and would deal only with manufacturers—and their suppliers. For example, in dealing with an apparel manufacturer, Wal-Mart will also work with the fabric-maker and even the fiber producer. David Glass, Wal-Mart's president and CEO, says, "We just tie everyone into the loop. You won't call the apparel manufacturer and have them say, 'Gosh, we'd make that for you, but we don't have any fabric.'"[8]

In an advanced version of quick response, called **vendor-managed inventory (VMI),** retailers confer to producers the management of retail inventories. Retailers send point-of-sale data to producers daily via electronic data interchange, and producers have access to retailers' inventory files. Unlike basic QR, which requires scanning data only from a few stores, VMI can provide manufacturers with complete data—from every store.

Still another advanced form of QR is called **efficient customer response (ECR).** ECR provides additional supply-chain linkages, in four main ways.[9]

- *Efficient replenishment.* These are the practices already described for QR and VMI.
- *Efficient assortment.* Retailers use sophisticated "category management" software to stock store areas with what consumers want most. The twin aims are more sales per square foot and improved customer satisfaction.
- *Efficient promotion.* Order, produce, ship, and stock exactly what sells. Cease forward buying, trade loading, and BOGOs (buy one, get one free), which pay little heed to real customer needs or usage.
- *Efficient product introduction.* Product development is a joint effort. Producers, distributors, brokers, and retailers team up to get the right products to market quickly.

Regarding efficient promotion, Ronald Zarrella, GM's head of sales and marketing, introduced the following: Promote cars throughout their life cycle, instead of spending lavishly in the introductory year, then starving the model after that. Zarrella, formerly president of eyeglass maker Bausch & Lomb, had no previous experience in autos to becloud his views on good promotional practices.[10]

QR and JIT: Linking External and Internal Flow Control

QR is the offspring of just-in-time and it embodies JIT's core concept of final customers "pulling the strings" to cause production and delivery, back through the chain of supply. For QR to work, firms at each echelon in the supply chain must improve their internal processes—in office support, distribution, and freight areas, as well as in front-line operations (see Exhibit 8–4 on pages 278–79). These firms can use a broad array of proven JIT techniques for responding to customers' demands, plus TQM techniques for getting it right.

By involving retailers, QR uses sales scanning data that big retailers had collected for years but never used to good advantage. Before QR's introduction, firm-to-firm JIT arrangements were widespread but mostly limited to manufacturing: processed-material or component suppliers linked (by kanban, fax, EDI, etc.) to fabrication or assembly plants. QR establishes a common basis for sector-to-sector flow control, linking goods and service sectors seamlessly.

JIT was born in Japan and is now practiced worldwide, but QR is a uniquely North American contribution to good management. America's large open market

Kanban
A signal (e.g., an empty container or an order card affixable to the container) that more parts are needed.

*Top row: Consumers lose when manufacturers periodically stuff excess goods into distributors'
warehouses (sometimes called trade loading). Here a typical grocery item takes 84 days to go from
factory to store shelf*

The manufacturer stockpiles in-gredients and packaging supplies to meet peak production levels.

Plants prepare huge runs. Sche-duling is chaotic, with more over-time and temporary workers.

Freight companies charge premi-um rates for the manufacturer's periodic blow-out shipments.

No more panic purchases are nec-essary. The company cuts down on inventories, freeing up cash.

Factories run on normal shifts. The company cuts down on over-time pay and supplemental workers.

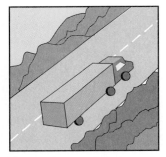

The manufacturer eliminates peak-and-valley distribution. That helps it save 5% in shipping costs.

and relatively efficient distribution system offered a favorable environment for QR's development. The necessary alliances have been difficult to attain in Japan with its many layers of middlemen between manufacturers and retailers. In Europe, despite geographical difficulties (national borders), QR is catching on.

Logistics: Moving the Goods

As we've seen, QR and JIT both rely on efficient freight and distribution manage-ment, which businesses refer to as **logistics.** In fact, logistics has become a high-visibility partner of marketing and operations management, after years of being left to disparate specialists. Producers and retailers increasingly see that they can-not be expert in managing the flow among parties in the supply chain. They must partner up with freight movers (air, rail, truck, barge) and distributors.

A growing trend is for a single logistics company to take over both freight and some of the management of distribution centers. Federal Express receives and stores personal computer components for IBM and Compac Computer.

Bottom row: Speeded-up cycle is more efficient, improves company's cash flow, and gives consumers a fresher product at a better price.

**EXHIBIT 8–4
(concluded)**

Distributors overstock as they binge on short-term discounts. Cartons sit for weeks inside warehouses.

At distribution centers, the goods get overhandled. Damaged items go back to the manufacturer.

Twelve weeks after the items leave the production line, they may not be fresh for the consumer.

Wholesalers' inventories get cut in half. That means storage and handling costs decline 17%.

Retailers receive undamaged products. Their perception of the manufacturer's quality improves.

The consumer gets the goods 25 days earlier, and—even better news—at a 6% lower price.

Source: Patricia Sellers, "The Dumbest Marketing Ploy," *Fortune,* October 5, 1992, pp. 88–94. Used with permission. Jim McManus, Illustrator.

Then, when a company (or a person) orders a customized PC system, Federal Express pulls the components, boxes them (with manuals thrown in), and makes the delivery. This role expansion has transformed Federal Express from an overnight mail delivery company into what is called a third-party distributor, which means it works under contract to handle logistics for major customer firms.

DSC Logistics, with a 1.2-million-square-foot warehouse in Melrose Park, Illinois, got itself into the business by a different route. It had been strictly a warehouser. Ann Drake, who runs the family-owned business, changed its name from Dry Storage Company in 1993.[11]

Trucking companies are metamorphosing into full-service logistics as well:

Just behind a vast field of corn on Packerland Drive in Green Bay, Wisconsin, stands the brain center of Schneider National. Once strictly a trucking company, Schneider now focuses on its highly profitable logistics business. It has about 140 logistics contracts, ranging from $2 million to $200 million, the last for a deal with GM.

Union Pacific's Bailey Yard.
Source: Union Pacific museum collection.

On one giant floor, hundreds of Schneider customer-service representatives in cubicles track freight using electronic data interchange technology. With a satellite system, a Schneider representative can tell customers exactly where its drivers are, and, more importantly, what time a given shipment will be delivered.[12]

Satellite-navigated trucks time their arrival at unloading docks to the hour— or even within a 15-minute window. Producers help by providing advance shipping notices to the freight haulers.

The retailer's distribution centers are shifting their roles as well, sometimes spurning their traditional storage role. Instead, they move incoming goods directly to other docks and outbound trucks. The following describes this no-stop procedure, called **cross-docking:**

> Every truck in industry-leading Schneider National's fleet has sprouted a jaunty little satellite antenna. . . . You look in the cab and see generally not a Teamsters truck driver but an 'associate' with a merit pay plan and an on-board computer that links him with headquarters. . . . When Schneider's tractor-trailer pulls up with a cargo of appliances, for example, Sear's home delivery trucks are lined up across the loading dock, scheduled to bring them to customers expecting delivery that day.[13]

Railroads, too, are involved. John Bromley, director of public affairs at Union Pacific, says, "No other country in the world has such a modern rail freight system [as does the United States]. And no other system operates at a profit without government subsidies. We may not have the high-speed passenger trains like Europe and Japan, but we've sure got them beat when it comes to hauling freight." Union Pacific's Bailey Yard in North Platte, Nebraska, is billed in the Guiness Book of World Records as the world's largest train yard. It is 10 miles end to end, has 150 branching, parallel tracks, and handles 120 trains and 9,000 freight cars daily.[14]

Ten other large (around $1 billion sales) rail freight companies operate in the United States, along with some 400 short lines that serve small communities "and feed to the giants boxcars filled with fruit, hoppers brimming with grain, and flatcars loaded with steel. Together they move 40 percent of the nation's freight, a figure that's climbing steadily. . . . Between 1983 and 1993, rail productivity shot up an incredible 157 percent. Revenues have increased 32 percent, while rates have dropped 40 percent."[15]

The fastest growing mode of transportation is international air freight. Until the 1980s,

> shipping air meant being assured that your goods would arrive at such-and-such an airport within 48 hours of a promised time. Today, for an average of one to four dollars per pound, a customer expects guaranteed, on-time delivery; and increasingly that service is door-to-door, not airport-to-airport. . . . Companies ship phone books from the United States to India to have the names inexpensively keyed in on mailing lists. Automobile insurance claims travel by the boxful from Miami to Manila to be processed by people who are not only cheaper to employ but who make fewer mistakes than the clerks for hire in Miami.[16]

Besides the external flow-control issues that involve logistics systems, companies must deal with internal flow-control problems. Avoiding getting stuck in a bottleneck is a persistent internal issue.

Bottleneck Management

If you're standing in line waiting to buy a ticket and the ticketing machine or computer breaks down, you get annoyed. You are idled at a **bottleneck,** which is any process (office, work cell, machine, manager, etc.) that impedes the flow of work. Generally, we say that demand exceeds capacity at a bottleneck. For the ticket-line example, repair of the ticketing computer removes the bottleneck.

When you finally buy your ticket and surrender it to a ticket taker, you may head for the restroom only to find a long queue there. In this case, the bottleneck stems from failing to plan enough restroom capacity.

Bottlenecks are serious and costly and they drive off customers. The cause of a bottleneck must be fixed, but that takes time; meanwhile, the flow-control system must go to work to minimize damages. We shall briefly consider four topics pertaining to flow control in the face of bottlenecks: finite and infinite capacity assumptions, capacity cushions, capacity enhancement, and the theory of constraints.

Capacity: Finite or Infinite?

Typically, computer-driven flow-control systems, such as material requirements planning (MRP), have operated in the **infinite-capacity planning** mode: The system's scheduling routine sets order start and finish dates assuming that equipment, labor, and other resources are available infinitely to produce the required parent-item components.

However, capacity is finite. In the case of a bottleneck, it is insufficient, and the schedule is said to be overstated. That need not be serious because

1. Various kinds of flexibility (not easily captured in a computer routine) have always existed. Such flexibility is used to its fullest in firms with a commitment to serving the customer and improving continuously, including improving things associated with bottlenecks, such as long changeover times or breakdown-prone equipment.

2. Priorities can be rearranged as the work proceeds from process to process. As we shall see in Chapters 10 and 14, advanced MRP systems can issue a new priority report every day. The report for in-progress jobs rearranges priorities, so the highest priorities go to the jobs farthest behind.

Composition of Demand.   Where departmental barriers have been removed, permitting the formation of a multifunctional master scheduling team, another approach to defeating bottlenecks is available. The team looks closely at the composition of orders flowing toward a bottleneck resource and separates good orders from not-so-good ones.

Exhibit 8–5A shows an apparent bottleneck situation. Demand has grown so that it consistently exceeds capacity. The master scheduling team breaks down current demand into three categories: orders for high-profit items, low-profit items, and loss items (see Exhibit 8–5B). The team immediately gives preference to high-profit items by removing some of the loss and lower-profit items from the current demand stream (delaying, canceling, or subcontracting those orders). Longer-term actions might include removing items from the product line; changing pricing, advertising, and promotion; and impressing salespeople with the need to discourage sales of loss items.

> Cost systems often don't yield true item cost; the master scheduling team may need to do its own activity-based costing audit to get good cost data for finding true item profitability.

Besides segmenting demand by profitability, the master scheduling team may also segment by type of customer: vital customers, average customers, and difficult customers. Good customers get priority service, but the annoying ones are turned away. Thus, the team rejects the view that "a sale is a sale." It segments demand on overloaded resources and takes commonsense actions to relieve the overloads.

A few companies are following this strategy. One is Queen City Treating Company, a small Cincinnati firm specializing in heat-treating metal parts. CEO Ed Stenger says that formerly the company policy was "Be everything to everyone. Compete on price. Quote all comers—regardless of part or process. Promise whatever it takes on delivery. And never tell a customer anything more than he absolutely needs to know." But Stenger had heard a different tune at a meeting on strategy spon-

Exhibit 8–5

Analysis of Demand at an Apparent Bottleneck

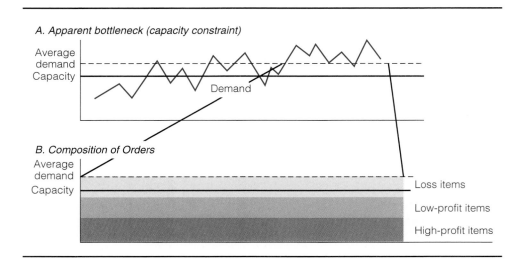

sored by the Cincinnati Chamber of Commerce. The message induced Stenger and some of his young managers to rethink their conventional strategy.[17] They studied their customer base and developed a strategy of targeted growth, as opposed to being all things to everyone. Stenger and his team arranged customers into three tiers. First-tier customers: high volume, common processes. Second tier: substantial volume, considerable process commonality. These two tiers are "key accounts." Third tier: low volume, irregular frequency, and little process commonality. A new price and delivery structure strongly favors key-account customers both in dollars and delivery times—at the expense of the third tier.

Stenger explains: "The simple fact is, and always has been, that the lowest tier customer interrupts our ability to service the upper tiers—those who pay the bills. . . . Which doesn't mean we won't service [the third tier]. It just means they'll pay more and wait longer if they want us to do the work."

Other companies going for targeted growth include

- Omni-Circuits, Inc., Glenview, Illinois. Omni has trimmed its customer list from 200 to 20.[18]
- Nypro, an injection molding (plastics) company headquartered in Clinton, Massachusetts. Nypro has cut its customer base from 600 small and large to 31 big ones.[19]
- Microelectronics Modules Corp., Milwaukee. Each Friday morning CEO Kenneth A. Hammer and key lieutenants sit down and decide which customers to accept or decline.[20]

Giving preference to best products and best customers is good business anywhere. Why wouldn't every company do it? we might ask. One reason is that companies have lacked team structures for joint planning across departmental lines. Another is that companies often expect too much from their computer scheduling routines. The computer system is unlikely to be able to sort out the best options as to which customer orders or which products to favor when demand is overheated. Prudence calls for involving experienced teams of human decision makers in such matters.

Finite-Capacity Planning.   Computer-based flow-control systems that operate under **finite-capacity planning** assumptions are also available. The methodology is as follows. The computer plans the workload for a certain work center or machine. If the workload exceeds capacity, creating a bottleneck, the computer moves some of the workload to the following period's schedule for that work center. The enormous complexities in such systems prevented widespread use of finite-capacity planning until recently. In the mid–1980s, a high-priced finite-based computer software package called optimized production technology (OPT) became available, and a number of finite-capacity planning systems are now on the market (some OPT software is still in use, mainly in Europe). Much improved finite-capacity system software has become available. Nevertheless, infinite-capacity planning approaches are in wide use and can be made to work well (see Contrast box).

Capacity Cushion

While computer-based flow-control systems offer ways for companies to plan around capacity obstacles, some companies are able to avoid the problem by planning for sufficient capacity in the first place. Not investing in enough capacity

Contrast

Finite or Infinite Capacity Planning?

Finite

If a computer-calculated schedule over loads a bottleneck resource, the system moves some jobs to later, or earlier, time slots.

While early finite schedulers made decisions, newer models conduct simulations and offer results to human decision makers.

Critique:[21] (1) Pushes customer orders around; rather than a "can-do" customer-focused approach. (2) Schedules are too often immediately dated, given the high rates of changing production variables.

Infinite

First generation: Human expediters use wits to overcome bottlenecks.

Second generation: Computer issues daily priority report, allowing delayed jobs to catch up.

Third generation: Low tolerance for bottlenecks or complex central planning. Emphasis on flexible, cross-trained people, under capacity scheduling, and restricting/diverting less-desirable orders that create bottlenecks

---

became common in North America and may have contributed to the productivity crisis that became apparent in the 1980s. Even some highly admired North American companies commonly suffered numerous permanent bottlenecks. This was caused largely by misguided strategies: Managers milked cash out of existing facilities and failed to invest to expand capacity or to improve the reliability and flexibility of existing capacity.

No approach works well in conditions of chronic capacity constraints. The most successful firms have understood that. Merck Company (pharmaceuticals) and Milliken & Company (textiles and chemicals), for example, as well as most supermarkets, hotels, hospitals, and transportation companies, plan for a healthy cushion of capacity. This enables them to respond to demand surges, rather than falling into periodic bottlenecks. The Mercks and Millikens of the world are setting an example for other companies, and perhaps prudently shifting to a policy of maintaining a reasonable capacity cushion will become a trend. Companies are also taking cues from JIT writings, which call for undercapacity scheduling so that firms can meet demand surges and serve customers dependably even with lean inventories.

Capacity Enhancement

Companies are also finding ways to make existing capacity more dependable and versatile. Exhibit 8–6 lists six approaches that teams of associates can take to reduce the firm's vulnerability to bottlenecks or constraints. The first two items (reducing service and capacity consumption for low-profit items and increasing flexibility to gain capacity) need not be discussed further. But the other four items need some explanation.

*P*RINCIPLE 9:

Multiple units of capacity.

Well-trained standby labor (number 3) protects against bottlenecks as long as there is enough available, not theoretical, physical capacity (equipment and space) for the standby labor to use. Having standby equipment capacity ties in with the ninth principle of operations management, calling for multiple smaller units of capacity. The rationale is simple. If one small unit breaks down, others of the same type keep humming, but if a single, large-capacity unit goes down, production comes to a halt.

Exhibit 8–6

Toward Capacity Enhancement

1. Less service (and therefore less demand on capacity) for less-profitable items or less-valued customers.
2. Cross-training and faster equipment changeovers to gain capacity, flexibility, and speed.
3. Maintaining capable standby capacity, including trained, on-call labor.
4. High involvement in improvement projects that cut capacity losses due to down equipment, lack of materials or information, rework, scrap, and low process yields.
5. Deliberately cutting stock to create temporary bottlenecks, thereby stimulating the need to solve basic problems.
6. Moving emergency buffer stock offline, thus cutting throughput time while retaining protection against random bottleneck conditions.

Number 4 aims at getting more output from existing capacity through improvement projects. Improvement teams especially focus on eliminating stoppages and preventing losses from bad quality.

In the lore of JIT, one purpose of cutting buffer stocks (number 5) is to stimulate problem solving. The procedure is to cut inventories between a pair of processes until the user process sometimes runs out of work (a stockout). The idea is to create a bottleneck, though not a severe or permanent one. This makes people in the process feel the actual pain of a shortage in order to create the incentive to expose and fix the underlying cause of variability. In other words, you create a small, temporary bottleneck in order to prevent a large, chronic one. This is an agressive, enforced-problem-solving approach that has sometimes been associated with JIT; it is not for the fainthearted.

Number 6 is a way of avoiding a trade-off dilemma. Prudent managers have followed the apparently commonsense practice of inserting buffer stocks wherever there is a capacity constraint. The trouble is that buffer stock adds lead time, which has multiple negative effects.

Let's turn this technique around: Where there is a serious but infrequent capacity constraint, move the protective buffer stock offline. For example, an Ontario, Canada, manufacturer keeps one day's supply of six sizes of steel blanks in a low-cost, offline location; historically the blanking equipment breaks down a few times a year. When it does, someone fetches the buffer stock, and operations carry on, avoiding late deliveries, while the equipment is fixed. If the buffer stock was on line, it would add one extra day of lead time all year long, even though it is needed only a few times a year. Furthermore, if on line, it would take up premium space and require constant handling and the usual administrative expenses of work-in-process inventory.

Offline buffer stock avoids these costs. In addition, offline stock can be purified, or subjected to 100-percent quality checking to ensure that, if needed, it will be good stock. If buffer stock is on line, constantly being used and resupplied (first-in, first-out), there is the chance of getting poor quality buffer stock just when it's needed.

Theory of Constraints

Another approach to bottleneck management is Eliyahu Goldratt's **theory of constraints** (an extension of OPT), which calls for altering the schedule and more frequent forwarding of completed work.[22] The goal is to maximize throughput: the rate of work flow and, therefore, cash flow. Managers may be especially at-

constraint
Inability to keep up with demand because of a capacity bottleneck or a demand surge.

tuned to throughput when their capacity is busy 24 hours a day, seven days a week, and still demand cannot be met. In a more normal situation, managers should place first emphasis on decreasing throughput *time,* which we emphasize throughout this text as a basic, customer-oriented, long-term objective. Throughput, on the other hand, is more of an internal, shorter-term financial objective (see the Contrast box, "Improving the Flow").

One feature of the theory of constraints is to treat a process batch and a transfer batch separately: If the process batch is large, break it down into smaller transfer batches. The next process, then, gets started on the job sooner, with a smaller amount, instead of waiting until the whole process batch arrives. Another feature is to increase the process batch size on a bottleneck machine, which cuts down on time lost stopping for machine changeovers to another product.

To these concepts (which were OPT elements) the theory of constraints adds policies on buffer stock. There are formalized rules for inserting buffer stocks either before or after certain bottlenecks. One example is stocking already machined parts just after (past) a breakdown-prone machine; another is placing finished stock as a buffer before an erratic-demand item.

There are two reasons for today's special emphasis on buffer stock policies:

1. In conventional manufacturing and distribution, lot sizes were very large. It was common to buy or produce weeks' or months' worth of most items at a time; that meant weeks or months before supplies dwindled to the point where stockout became a concern. In effect, the huge cycle stocks (lot-size stocks) did double duty, providing buffer stock protection as well.

   The convenience of using cycle stock as buffer stock disappears as lot sizes and cycle intervals shrink, as they do under QR or JIT. Suppose a dairy makes apple-lemon ice cream every day instead of once a month. Dairy managers had better think carefully about how much buffer stock to keep on hand. The buffer stock (raw materials, including apple and lemon flavorings, and semifinished product, such as apple-lemon mix) should be based on recent data on fluctuations of demand, yield, on-time deliveries, machine problems, and so forth. While all those variabilities were present when apple-lemon ice cream was made only monthly, the possibility of stockout occurred so seldom that the buffer stock decisions were not worth much thought.

ontrast

Improving the Flow

Theory of Constraints	**Capacity Enhancement**
Maximize throughput (e.g., cash per day generated by moving work quickly through the plant).	Minimize throughput time by solving a wide assortment of work-flow and quality problems.
Potential weakness: Old-line managers may use the theory as an excuse to continue watching short-term productivity reports and profit statements.	Has long-term customer-oriented emphasis

2. In pursuing just-in-time, some managers become sidetracked and begin to believe that the goal is to eliminate inventory. Most JIT authorities, however, stress that inventory reduction is a lesser benefit (by-product) and that the primary goals are quick, high-quality service to the customer. That often requires prudently placed buffer stock.

We've seen that flow control may involve two kinds of inventory: that arising from lot size and that serving a protective buffering purpose. Are these two kinds of stock related? A caterer's egg-buying behavior provides an answer.

Relating Inventory Timing to Quantity

Kevin and Karin systematically ensure that their catering business doesn't run out of key ingredients. For example, they always write *eggs* on their buy list when the stock in the refrigerator gets down to 10 eggs. At that point, they buy seven dozen eggs.

These two decisions—timing and order quantity—may seem independent but they are not, and here's why.

Kevin and Karin have two aims: (1) Don't tie up too much money and refrigerator space on eggs (seven dozen plus 10 eggs is enough), and (2) hold down the chance of running out (10 eggs as the trigger for restocking is the right amount of protection).

If Kevin and Karin maintained 10 eggs as their **reorder point** but changed their order quantity from seven dozen to one dozen, they would risk running out too often. That is, their egg supply would drop to the danger zone for running out (10 eggs) seven times more often than before. Their catering business won't stand for that much risk, so they would either need to go to a larger order quantity or raise their reorder point, say, from 10 eggs to two dozen. Either step reduces the long-term frequency (risk) of running out.

reorder point
Quantity of on-hand inventory that serves as a trigger for placement of an order for more.

Measuring Flow-Control System Performance

What is a gung-ho, high-performance flow-control (or production-control) group striving to achieve? Exhibit 8–7 summarizes traditional and newer answers to that question. Traditional (and still common) examples of flow-control measures include 95 percent on-time performance against internal schedules, 99 percent inventory accuracy, and five inventory turns per year.

Companies still care about each of these factors, but emphasis is shifting from internal due dates, stock records, and inventories to speedy response through the supply chain and customer chain.

Pipeline Efficiency

Quick response programs look beyond the department or company walls. QR-connected firms in the supply pipeline all work from the same scanning data: real customer demand. The supporting information system usually allows suppliers to send advance shipping notices to freight carriers via electronic data interchange (EDI) or fax transmission.

New pipeline-oriented measurements need to be devised to reflect flow control among suppliers, freight carriers, and retailers. Examples for suppliers include

EXHIBIT 8–7

Measurements of Flow-Control Performance

	Traditional	New
Pipeline control	None	Order-to-receipt time (supplier performance)
		Advance-shipping-notice-to-receipt time (freight carrier performance)
		Receipt-to-selling floor time (retailer performance)
Operation control	On-time order completion	Cycle time (thoughput time, response time)
		Response ratio
Inventory control	Stock-record accuracy	Invariable quantity of items/containers in fixed locations between each pair of processes
	Inventory turnover, company	Joint inventory turnover, company plus suppliers

time from ordering to receipt of material by the customer; for carriers, time from receipt of the advance shipping notice to customer receipt of the goods; and for the retailer, time from receipt of the goods to their availability on the sales floor.

Short Cycle Time

A prominent performance measure within company walls (complement to external pipeline measures) is cycle time, including time to process all information related to production or service. Aside from measuring quickness of response, cycle time serves as an overall indicator of flow control. Long cycle times (e.g., many weeks) are evidence that the work flow is out of control.

Better flow control means a smaller flow-control staff. That is, as cycle times fall and the work flow becomes more tightly controlled, the firm needs fewer expediters, schedulers, dispatchers, and clerical staff.

For example, JIT implementation teams at Physio Control (a manufacturer of defibrillators) were able to create 11 JIT cells (or *team-built* lines, as they are called at Physio). The focused cells used daily rate scheduling, revised monthly, thus eliminating thousands of work orders. Work-in-process (WIP) inventories plunged, emptied WIP stock rooms were torn out, and remaining small stocks became the property of each team-built line. Physio's 10-member production control department had no scheduling or inventory management to do and was abolished, and the 10 people were retrained for other duties, such as supplier certification and supplier development.

defibrillator
medical emergency device that electrically stimulates a failing heart.

Response Ratio

Cycle time is a fine measurement of overall flow through several processes, but what about measurements within each of those processes? The **response ratio** fills the need.

The three response ratios are cycle time to work content, process speed to use rate, and pieces to work stations or operators. The ideal ratio for each is 1 to 1, but in practice it is typically 5, 10, 100, or 1,000 to 1. What does a ratio of, say, 100 to 1 mean? Examples for each ratio serve to illustrate:

- In a drop-and-add line (at registration for college classes), there is an average of 99 minutes of delay for a 1-minute transaction to have a form signed. The 99 minutes of delay plus the 1 minute for signature yield a ratio of 100 minutes of total cycle time to 1 minute of value-adding work content.

- A wire-cutting machine currently is cutting 1,000 pieces of electrical power cord per hour for a certain model of lamp. Lamp assembly, the next process, installs that model of cut cord at only 10 per hour. The ratio or process speed to use rate, thus, is 1,000 to 10, or 100 to 1.

- A clerk in a purchasing department typically has a stack of 99 invoices in an in-basket and just 1 invoice being worked on. This constitutes a pieces-to-operator ratio of 100 to 1.

In each case, high ratios mean long queues of customers, documents, idle materials, or projects. Team members may calculate the ratio, post it in the workplace, and then work to lower it. But they cannot do so without making improvements: cut changeover times, limit the queues, have a system for borrowing labor when lines get too long, eliminate disruptive rework by doing it right the first time, keep all areas clean and well organized, run equipment at the use rate instead of at maximum speed, and so forth.

Following an improvement, the new ratio can be posted on the graph for all to see. The process continues, one improvement at a time, with 1 to 1 or 2 to 1 as the ultimate (though sometimes unattainable) goal. It is often a good idea to post before-and-after photos or schematic drawings showing waiting-line reductions as the ratios drop.[23] Use of the ratios helps instill the habit of improvement at the operator level (*kaizen* in Japanese) so that improvement becomes primarily a line, not staff, responsibility.

Some firms use response ratios for an entire sequence of operations (total cycle time to theoretical minimum time). This overall ratio can be a useful indicator for senior managers. But it is not very meaningful for front-liners, who should be concentrating on their own process responsiveness, measured by their own response ratios.

A main advantage of the response ratio is that it is unitless, devoid of numbers of minutes, clients, truckloads, and so forth. The goal of 1 to 1 or 2 to 1 is the same for any kind of work, and it enables comparison of improvement rates across the enterprise. In short, the ratio is promising as a universal measure of service speed, flow control, and, conversely, nonvalue-added wastes and delays.

Inventory Control

For material-intensive businesses, inventory control is a key aid to flow control of the work itself. This became clear to the early adopters of material requirements planning. They found that MRP success required high stock-record accuracy. Perfect accuracy is 100 percent agreement between counts of stock in the stockrooms and on-hand stock balances in the inventory master file.

Successful implementation of just-in-time doesn't require high stock-record accuracy so much as it yields record accuracy. One reason is that, to the extent that JIT cuts inventories, there are fewer chances for inventory-record inaccuracy. More important in advanced JIT, inventories are held in a set number of special fixed-quantity containers (see Exhibit 8–7). Thus, associates can count their own stock quickly and accurately.

Conventional large-batch production lacks that discipline. Items are likely to exhibit considerable stock variability, from zero (a back-order condition) to thousands of pieces on shelves or in nonstandard containers scattered throughout the facility. Since chances for error are high (sometimes baskets of parts are simply lost or misplaced), stock counting is a major undertaking and may be done only once a year.

To summarize, emerging external and internal flow-control focus is on fast processing—on time and in synch with real customer needs—and stable inventories.

Inventory Turnover

The last flow-control measure listed in Exhibit 8–7 is **inventory turnover.** For manufacturers, wholesalers, and retailers, inventory turnover remains a good overall measure accounting for many of the wastes tied up in inventory. Corporate management or improvement teams can use it to assess site performance, and site managers/teams can use inventory turnover, or turnover improvement, to measure their own performance. Low inventory turnover normally indicates poor performance, symptomatic of waste and inflexibility; high and increasing inventory turns indicate good performance and continuous improvement.

Moreover research evidence suggests that long-term trend in inventory turnover may be as good or better an indicator of company strength than the usual financial measures, such as profitability and sales revenue. This suggestion is based on a study of inventory turnover for well-known manufacturers in the United States and the United Kingdom over a 45-year period beginning in 1950; partial supporting evidence comes from France and Australia.[24] The research shows declining turnovers for about 25 years. Then, many manufacturers began to react. They learned about lean production concepts and put them to work. The assorted concepts include total quality, cross-training of employees, partnerships with suppliers and customers, design for manufacture and assembly, preventive maintenance, and just-in-time. One result of all of these improvement methodologies is less dependence on inventories as a cover for problems, so inventory turnovers improve.

Exhibit 8–8 shows the decline-incline pattern in inventory turns for Ford and General Motors. Ford's annual rate of improvement since 1994 was 3.6 percent; GM's was 3.3 percent. Other data from the study show roughly the same many-year pattern of decline-incline for Caterpillar, Emerson Electric, Eaton, Cummins Engine, Outboard Marine, and other U.S. companies, as well as similar firms in the other countries.

Beside measuring turnover within the firm, improvement teams should concern themselves with inventories held by suppliers. Exhibit 8–7 refers to joint inventory turnover, which includes the total of within-company inventory and supplier inventory. This measurement prevents companies from dumping inventories on suppliers to make internal inventory performance look good.

Annual inventory turnover is cost of goods sold divided by the value of average inventory:

$$T = \frac{CGS}{I} \qquad (8–2)$$

special case: Retail stores maintain what is known as *presentation stock,* which means excess inventory whose purpose is to convey an image of having plenty. Without such stocks customers may think the store is in trouble. Presentation stock puts a limit on how much the store can increase its inventory turnover.

An implementation team at one of IBM's first continuous flow manufacturing (JIT) facilities, in Raleigh, North Carolina, chose *joint* inventory as a performance measure.

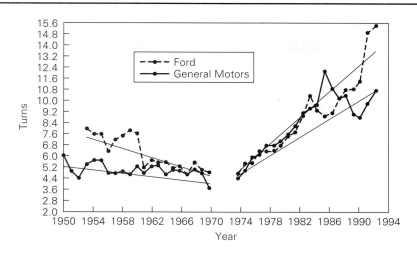

EXHIBIT 8–8

**Inventory
Turnover**

Source: Schonberger & Associates, Inc.

where

T = Turnover

CGS = Cost of goods sold (annual)

I = Average inventory value

To illustrate, assume that a modem costs $30 to produce, is selling at a rate of 1,000 per year, and average inventory is worth $6,000. What is the inventory turnover?

$$\text{Cost of goods sold (CGS)} = \text{Unit cost} \times \text{Annual sales}$$

$$= \$30 \times 1{,}000 = \$30{,}000$$

$$T = \frac{CGS}{I} = \frac{\$30{,}000}{\$6{,}000} = 5 \text{ turns per year}$$

The firm is selling its inventory, or turning it over, five times per year. Compared with an average of between three and four turns for North American industry, that's not bad. (The industry average is much higher in high-volume, continuous production and lower in one-of-a-kind production.) However, some North American plants that used to turn their inventories 3 or 4 times have, through lean practices, improved that to 10, 20, 30—even 100—turns.

A poor turnover (below three) could arise from flow times stretching out over many weeks or months. It could also result when demand response is fast but achieved with high inventories. Thus, turnover is a good measure of flow-control system performance.

It may be useful to calculate turnover by category: raw materials, work-in-process, finished goods, and total inventory. Extending the example of the modem manufacturer, assume that $1,500 of the $6,000 average inventory is finished goods, $1,500 is raw materials, and $3,000 is WIP. Assume further that the cost of labor and overhead to convert raw materials to finished goods is $12,000, which is used in calculating WIP turnover as follows:

$$T_{WIP} = \frac{\text{Manufacturing costs}}{WIP}$$

$$= \frac{\$12,000}{\$3,000} = 4 \text{ WIP turns per year} \tag{8–3}$$

To calculate raw material (RM) and finished goods inventory (FGI) turnover, we may assume the price of purchased materials plus purchasing overhead to be $14,000 and the overhead cost to carry finished goods to be $4,000. Then,

$$T_{RM} = \frac{\text{Purchasing costs}}{RM}$$

$$= \frac{\$14,000}{\$1,500} = 9.3 \text{ RM turns per year} \tag{8–4}$$

$$T_{FGI} = \frac{\text{Finished goods overhead costs}}{FGI}$$

$$= \frac{\$4,000}{\$1,500} = 2.7 \text{ FGI turns per year} \tag{8–5}$$

Some firms also compute an RIP turnover, which includes both raw materials and WIP. One company that uses the RIP measure is TRW's Mission Products Division in Texas. The division, one of the more successful JIT converts, improved its RIP turnover from 3 to about 35 per year.

Summary

The flow-control system in any business experiences variabilities: arrivals too early or too late; performance too high or too low, too fast or too slow; or machine breakdowns and yields varying randomly over time. The variabilities are undesirable and detract from serving the customer. When added to poor performance in meeting other customer wants, variability makes things worse. Flow-control systems try to plan around the variabilities; better flow control tries to eliminate them.

Managers/caretakers can only partially control the inventory element (documents and customers as well as materials) of the flow-control system. Inventory slacks and gluts are caused by process variabilities and thus must be dealt with by marketers, engineers, plant maintenance and quality specialists, and others who have the skills to dampen process variability. Their failures call the flow-control system into action, but the system costs themselves are high.

With inventory come inventory carrying costs: capital invested; stockrooms; obsolescence; inventory administration; space, storage, handling gear for front-line inventories, and support for them; data processing; scrap and rework; lot inspections; and lost business resulting from slow, inconsistent response. The last four items are hidden inventory costs, commonly commingled with other cost categories.

Annual carrying cost is commonly set at 25 percent of the inventory's cost. With hidden costs included, the rate goes as high as 50 percent or even 100 percent. The rate is important since in many businesses inventory is a dominant cost affected by almost any proposed major change.

Modern flow-control systems take advantage of the dependency of component parts on the parent item. The dependency can be reduced to computer calculation using material requirements planning (MRP) software, or to the simplicity of a visual just-in-time (JIT) signal from parent to component.

While MRP and JIT have operated mostly on dependencies within a firm (plus some first-echelon suppliers), quick response (QR) programs reach well back into the supply chain. QR requires extensive intercompany teamwork to install a system that feeds retail sales scanning data back through layers of suppliers, who may use it to synchronize schedules to recent actual sales.

One of the challenges to a flow-control system is coping with capacity bottlenecks and constraints. The MRP method is initially to presume infinite capacity and then adjust to bottlenecks by rescheduling affected jobs and by reprioritizing jobs already in process. A newer set of coping approaches is a theory of constraints, which aims at maximizing throughput and cash flow. It includes adjusting the sizes of transfer batches and production quantities, and prudently placing buffer stocks after an undependable process or before a spikey demand. Today's emphasis on buffer stocks stems from loss of buffering as JIT drives down lot-size (cycle-stock) inventories; too much inventory reduction causes too much exposure to risks and variabilities.

The multifunctional master scheduling team can often avoid bottleneck or constraint problems by examining the composition of the demand stream. Typically it contains some unprofitable orders or those from difficult customers; by canceling or delaying those orders, the team relieves the bottleneck.

Logistics entities (distribution centers and freight haulers), taken for granted in an earlier age, have been key cogs in flow control in the supply chain. Advanced distribution center management includes adding value (e.g., light assembly and packaging) and cross-docking (incoming stocks moved across the warehouse directly to outbound trucks). Similarly, trucking companies are taking on distribution center management and monitoring of the full shipping process. Trucking and rail companies are competing on speed and dependability, rail and air freight are in a growth spurt, and advances in air freight are permitting companies to have work done anywhere on the globe.

While flow-control systems help in dealing with capacity constraints, they do not deal with the root cause of many capacity problems: failure to invest in sufficient capacity. Spending enough on capacity avoids the chaos resulting when demand exceeds capacity. Permanent bottlenecks and the severity of temporary or floating bottlenecks are thus reduced.

Other ways of averting bottleneck problems include provision of capable, on-call backup labor, and improvement team projects that cut changeover times, keep equipment working, and so on, thereby continually freeing up wasted capacity. The JIT technique of putting buffer stock off line allows lead times to be compressed at the same time that risks of stoppages are reduced. Finally, the aggressive JIT approach of drawing down buffer stocks to the pinch point, thus making every process a temporary bottleneck, can drive the pace of improvements, many of which relieve capacity constraints.

Lot-size and buffer inventories are related; smaller lots mean more instances of low stock levels. Flow-control designs should allow for this and avoid increasing risks as stocks are drawn down.

Flow-control system performance had been measured by on-time work-order completions and stock-record accuracy. With JIT driving lead times down and inventories down and into exact positions in known quantities, the old perfection criteria are becoming givens. The new measures center around pipeline efficiency for QR-involved firms; short lead times and low response ratios convering every process; stable, invariable inventories between processes; and overall high inventory turnover jointly with suppliers.

Inventory turnover is the number of times average inventory is sold annually. Some JIT and QR facilities are driving up annual turnover from industry average values of 3 or 4 to 10 or 20 times that high.

Solved Problems

Problem 1

A print shop often has numerous jobs stacked up before the huge paper slicing machine. Even by running the slicer overtime and with extra shifts, some days the slicer cannot keep up with the workload. What is a JIT solution to the problem? What solutions would be consistent with the *theory-of-constraints* concept?

Solution 1

The JIT approach, based on continuous improvement, would be to seek permanent solutions to the capacity limitations. An improvement team might recommend acquiring one or two small, simple paper-cutting machines that could provide backup and ease the bottleneck. Other techniques favored under JIT are quick setup to reduce the machine time lost in changing from one paper size to another, high levels of preventive maintenance on the machine to keep it from breaking down in the middle of a busy day, high levels of quality control so that the machine's limited capacity will not be eaten up by rework, and moving materials from process to process in small quantities.

Usable theory-of-constraints concepts include (1) consolidating similar orders (e.g., same paper sizes) into a large production batch, thus minimizing setup frequency, and (2) moving small transfer batches forward from the slicer to the next processes rather than waiting for completion of an entire production run (same as one of the JIT solutions). Both concepts help get more work per day through the bottleneck machine during busy times.

Problem 2

At Computer Services, Inc., small software jobs start at the chief analyst's desk, where each job is assigned to one of the 10 systems analysts. On average, a job sits in the chief's in-basket for 7 ¾ hours before the chief starts processing it. Average processing time is 15 minutes. In systems analysis, there typically are 60 active jobs.

Use the appropriate response ratios to analyze the delay situation at the chief's desk and in systems analysis.

Solution 2

Chief: Lead time to work content is the proper ratio:

$$\text{Total cycle time} = 7\tfrac{3}{4} \text{ hours delay} + \tfrac{1}{4} \text{ hours work content}$$
$$= 8 \text{ hours}$$

Then:

$$\text{Ratio (cycle time to work content)} = 8 \text{ to } \tfrac{1}{4}, \text{ or } 32 \text{ to } 1$$

Analysts: Pieces to operators is the proper ratio:

$$\text{Number of pieces} = 60 \text{ jobs}$$
$$\text{Number of operators} = 10 \text{ analysts}$$

Then:

$$\text{Ratio (pieces to operators)} = 60 \text{ to } 10, 6 \text{ to } 1$$

Problem 3

One division of J. W., Inc., produces detergent. Its current RIP inventory turnover is 9. Another division, producing a line of electronic timing devices for home and industrial use, has an RIP turnover of 4. Both divisions have about the same annual costs of purchased materials plus cost to convert them to finished goods: $2 million.

   a. What is the average total of raw materials and WIP for each division?
   b. Should the turnovers be used for comparing the two divisions or for some other purpose?

a. The turnover formula must be inverted from

$$T_{RIP} = \frac{\text{Purchasing and manufacturing costs}}{RIP}$$

to

$$RIP = \frac{\text{Purchasing and manufacturing costs}}{T_{RIP}}$$

Then:

For detergent: $RIP = \$2,000,000/9 = \$222,222$
For timers: $RIP = \$2,000,000/4 = \$500,000$

b. It is unreasonable to compare turnovers. Detergent is made in a continuous process, which should not give rise to nearly as much idle inventory as do timers. It is reasonable to regularly assess the trends in RIP turnover separately for each product. Higher RIP turnover is an overall sign of improvement in division performance.

Review Questions

1. Describe three types of process variabilities. What are their effects on work flow? On customer service?
2. Can material managers control inventory excesses and shortages? Explain.
3. What are capital costs and holding costs?
4. Why have some costs of carrying inventory been semiobvious or even hidden?
5. What is the meaning of a 35 percent carrying cost? Is it realistic today? Discuss.
6. Give an example of a dependency chain four levels deep (component into parent, which goes into its parent, etc., through four levels).
7. Why are buffer stocks more necessary for independent-demand items than for dependent-demand items?
8. How are quick response (QR) systems different from JIT? Similar?
9. How do VMI and ECR differ from basic QR?
10. Can a flow-control system be effective under an infinite-capacity assumption? Explain.
11. When and why should a master scheduling team analyze the composition of demand?
12. What is the role of logistics in flow control?
13. What modern trends in distribution center management and freight handling have critical impacts on logistics?
14. What does the theory of constraints do about bottlenecks?
15. What is a good way of coping with permanent bottlenecks?
16. How is JIT supposed to handle bottlenecks?
17. How does lot size affect risk of stockout?
18. When should buffer stock be offline and why?
19. Why is 100 percent on-time completion of work orders inadequate as an indicator of perfection in operation control?
20. What is the usefulness of calculating inventory turnover?

Exercises

1. Process variabilities induce firms to carry protective excess inventories; the greater the excess, the greater the inventory carrying cost. Process variabilities also can result in inventory shortages. The greater the shortage, the greater which costs? Explain.

2. Iota Company produces bicycle reflectors. Currently Iota buys the main raw material, bags of plastic pellets, in large quantities about three times a year. Its policy is to order another lot when stock on hand falls to five days' worth (the reorder point). Now Iota is considering a just-in-time purchasing approach: small quantities ordered frequently, perhaps as often as every two weeks.

   There is a risk that the supplier will deliver late. Will JIT purchasing increase or decrease the risk? Should the reorder point be changed? Explain.

3. A plant specializing in precision machining is considering buying a numerical control (NC) machine with an installed cost of $200,000. The NC machine can perform multiple metal-cutting operations by successively rotating a mounted metal work piece and selecting cutting tools from a magazine. Thus, it would incorporate operations now done at scattered machine centers and would eliminate idle materials between machine and stockroom. Average inventory reduction from using the NC machine is estimated at $60,000. Also, the single machine will cost less to set up and operate than the present multiple machines, an additional savings of $50,000 per year.

   a. If 20 percent is used as the inventory carrying cost, how quickly can the investment pay for itself (what is the payback period)?

   b. Suggest four more important kinds of savings that are likely but less obvious than savings from materials and direct labor. Recalculate the payback period using a larger, more realistic carrying cost (your best estimate).

4. When Hewlett-Packard's Boise division converted to JIT, it eliminated all work orders. One result was 100,000 fewer computer transactions per month.

   a. In what sense may those eliminated transactions be considered as non-value-adding? An element of inventory carrying cost?

   b. This story is detailed in Rick Hunt, Linda Garrett, and C. Mike Merz, "Direct Labor Cost Not Always Relevant at H-P," *Management Accounting*, Feb. 1985, pp. 58–62. Find this article and explain how the transactions were eliminated.

5. Jack is an assembler at Penrod Pen Company. His job is to pack a gold-plated pen and pencil set, plus guarantee card, into a gift box. He puts the completed box on a chute, which feeds a machine that applies an outer wrap. (The chute holds a maximum of five boxes.) As an employee, Jack exhibits normal human failings, especially these:

   Occasionally he drops a pen, pencil, or card and while he searches for it on the floor, the outer-wrap machine runs out of boxes to wrap and stops. Several times the machine has lost 50 to 100 cycles while Jack was searching.

   Every few hours the assembly line is changed to produce a different model of pen and pencil set, which requires a different guarantee card. But Jack sometimes forgets to change to the correct card. (Inspectors discover the error through random sampling.) As many as 1,000 boxes may have to be torn open and reworked, and when that happens an order for an important customer is usually late.

   The supervisor has a solution to Jack's variable performance: extra inventory.

   a. Explain exactly how extra inventory could be worked into the process to serve as a solution.

   b. Jack has ideas for certain types of fixtures and automatic checkers that, he feels sure, would immediately catch either of his chronic errors. The devices, installed at his end of the feeder chute, would eliminate the need for the extra inventory that his supervisor has proposed. The supervisor weighs the cost of the devices against the savings on inventory carrying costs using Penrod's usual carrying cost rate of 25 percent. Jack feels the rate is too low. Is Jack right? Be specific in your answer.

6. The director of purchasing and materials management at Ivy Memorial Hospital wants her hospital to be the first in the area to implement a quick-response program with its suppliers of medical devices. How should she proceed?

7. Rate the following four types of businesses, one (poor) to four (good), as to the applicability of quick-response systems in the business. Explain your ratings.

   a. Welfare agency.   *c.* Producer of pigments.

   b. Fast-food restaurant   *d.* Trucking company.

8. Review the QR examples in the chapter, of Luxottica and VF Corp., both of which employ EDI. Also review the chapter-opening example from the automobile industry.

   a. Explain any significant differences between the first two examples and the example from the automobile industry, other than choice of communications media.

   b. Having adopted fax communications, should the fabric-to-auto chain upgrade to EDI? Why or why not?

   c. As other chains of customers, perhaps in other businesses, consider a quick-response alliance, would you recommend EDI or fax? Why?

9. Over-Nite Mail Corporation experienced two serious problems as business grew in the past 18 months: (1) Over 10 percent of its service orders take three days or more for successful delivery; (2) record accuracy (showing where orders are in its delivery system) is poor; random sampling shows that 30 percent of the records are inaccurate (e.g., a log book shows that a piece of mail is in the delivery truck while it is really still in the sorting room). A recent investment in a computerized order-tracking system has improved record accuracy to 99.5 percent. Should that give the company a significant competitive edge over competing overnight delivery companies? Explain. In your explanation, describe how the company should measure the effectiveness of its order control system.

10. A plant that produces industrial thermostats has successfully implemented MRP. One result is that mean production cycle time (from raw material to finished goods) has improved modestly, from 9.3 to 8.7 weeks. Two large improvements are (1) stock-record accuracy has risen from 68 to 99.2 percent, and (2) on-time completion of work orders is up from 60 to 97 percent. Plant management and the consulting company that assisted in the conversion to MRP are delighted; they claim that inventory control and production control are approaching perfection. They expect the results to stem some of their business losses to domestic and foreign competitors. Are their expectations realistic? Are the inventory and production control really so good? Discuss.

11. The following are examples of complex, delay-prone inter-sector material flows. For each one, recommend changes that employ advanced logistics concepts.

    a. A manufacturer of auto parts for the "after market" (i.e., replacement parts used in automotive repair) currently sends its production—over 2,000 different parts—to its own warehouse. The warehouse receives and fills orders from 25 distributors disbursed around Canada, the United States, and Mexico and forwards the ordered items to the distributors in its own trucks. The distributors receive and fill orders from several hundred auto parts stores and forward the items to the stores in their own trucks. Late deliveries, wrong shipments, and stockouts are common in the distribution centers and in the stores.

  b. A high-end furniture manufacturer in Michigan has learned, through market research, of large potential sales of its product in markets it has not tapped in the past: the U.S. and Canadian West Coast and most of Europe. The company has always shipped by independent truckers to its traditional markets in the Great Lakes area. The question is, can the new markets pay off, given the increased transportation challenges?

  c. Headquarters of a chain of dress shops contracts locally for design of private-label dresses and also contracts to local apparel makers to have the dresses made and delivered. However, sales have been falling and retail store managers in scattered markets are rebelling, saying the dresses cost too much and must be ordered too far in advance of each season. Company managers know that some competitors go "off shore" to have work done. They wonder if that option is practical, given the new logistics issues.

12. Currently the major bottlenecks at a plant that makes electrical fixtures are the paint line and the 600-ton press that stamps out sheet metal parts. Hundreds of different kinds of parts must pass through those two processes, and many jobs get stalled in queues before one or both.

  a. What kinds of solutions would be recommended if theory-of-constraints concepts were employed?

  b. What are likely to be the main kinds of solutions to these bottleneck problems under JIT?

13. The equipment used in a campus testing service includes order-entry terminals, optical scanning equipment, computers, and printers. At certain times, one or more of the machines has days' worth of jobs queued up. What do you recommend? Why?

14. Elmo's Burger Shoppe sells $50,000 worth of plain burgers per month. The profit margin is 10 percent. Total inventory on hand averages $12,000. What is the inventory turnover? Should Elmo separately calculate turnovers for purchased materials, WIP, and finished goods? Explain.

15. ABC Specialties, Inc., produces a wide variety of office and home products, one of which is a small mail scale. Annual cost of goods sold for the scale is $100,000, which includes $60,000 to purchase raw materials and $35,000 to convert them to finished goods. The average value of recently purchased plastic and metal parts and materials, plus fasteners, is $10,000; the value of partially completed production is $5,000; and the value of completed finished goods is $15,000. Compute separate and total inventory turnovers. Is ABC managing scale production well? Explain.

16. Exhibit 8–1 shows variability in relation to target performance. The point was made in the chapter that positive and negative variations do not cancel one another out. How does these ideas compare with Taguchi's social loss concept (discussed in Chapter 3)?

CASE STUDY

RIO BRAVO IV—A REPORT OF THE PLANT MANAGER

The Packard Electric division of General Motors is the leading producer of power and signal distribution products in the United States and wanted the same reputation internationally.

Case topics: Quality; housekeeping; continuous improvement (kaizen); quick die change; eliminating non-value-adding wastes; disciplined stock location practices; supplier partnerships; visual management; globalization and culture.

Source: Adapted from James P. Walker, "A Disciplined Approach to Continuous Improvement," Packard Electric Corp., 1988.

The company believed it was as capable as any producer anywhere, but that view was not shared in some foreign markets. There was one way to gain worldwide respect: take on an important international project and show everyone just how competent we were.

Little did I realize that I'd be in the middle of this project or that it would start as it did, when my boss drove me to an industrial section of Juarez, Mexico, and mysteriously stopped on a small street.

"You always wanted to do something in manufacturing," he began. "Here's your chance, Jim, it's all yours."

With knowing irony he motioned dramatically toward my new domain—a dilapidated warehouse building, previously used to store furniture, with weeds growing through the surrounding pavement. It was hardly what I envisioned when I imagined myself as manager of a manufacturing plant.

From this dirty, cobwebbed structure, our team would be expected to produce wiring harnesses for the most demanding company Packard had ever supplied: New United Motor Manufacturing Incorporated (NUMMI), a joint venture of General Motors and Toyota in Fremont, California. And initial units for the pilot vehicle were to be shipped in just four months.

Thus, I became manager of Plant IV of Rio Bravo Electricos, S. A. de C. V., a subsidiary of Packard Electric.

Packard decided to perform the manufacturing in northern Mexico, where other Packard facilities were in operation. The former furniture warehouse was leased and converted to an assembly plant, equipment was quickly installed in a layout similar to that of other Packard plants, and a management team was gathered.

It was an unlikely team. My background was primarily in quality control and sales; I had never supervised a manufacturing operation. Our manager of industrial engineering was a long-term tool-and-die guy who had no industrial engineering experience. The materials manager was an ex-U.S. Army captain whose involvement with automatic wiring had been nine months of scheduling production for a battery line in Ohio. We had three other Packard transferees. Only one of these five men spoke any Spanish. Completing the team were three Mexicans. One had worked two years at a wiring plant. The second had been in the clothing business with his father, and the third had been a mining engineer at an aluminium operation.

From our hastily equipped facility, this team had to supervise the prompt production of products that met NUMMI's lofty expectations. We thought we were a very high-quality producer, but we didn't realize that NUMMI was demanding something we had never had to accomplish: Not only did the parts have to be of the highest quality, but they had to be delivered

- In precise quantities.
- At the specified hour of the day.
- To the correct location.
- At an acceptable price.

It might be difficult, but how tough could it be? After all, we were good at making harnesses. What would be expected that we couldn't handle?

We quickly found out.

The Awakening

Despite Packard's long and successful history of producing wiring harnesses and electrical components, it did not take long for us to see that NUMMI's expectations were on a different plane from any we had previously encountered. Satisfying them was sometimes humiliating, often painful, and nearly always an ordeal.

When Packard was instructed to send 200 samples for a prototype vehicle, the Packard general manager decreed that the samples be flawless, regardless of the effort required. He wanted to impress NUMMI with Packard quality.

A special group was formed to assemble the samples. The division's best people were used. Every component was carefully checked. The samples, all in perfect order, were sent to NUMMI managers then located at Toyota in Japan.

We eagerly awaited the anticipated flattery. Instead, the Toyota people expressed grave disappointment. They disliked the tape used to wrap the assemblies! Our tape had small notches along one edge, cut intentionally to facilitate tearing. To the NUMMI people, the notches were unattractive, and the appearance of the wiring harnesses, not just their performance, was important.

We could not believe such nit-picking. We were certain they were creating objections in order to make us look bad. Nevertheless, we had to do something.

Question 1.   Are there any justifiable reasons for this response by NUMMI/Toyota people? Or was it just nit-picking?

So we entered into a joint technical agreement with Sumitomo Wiring, a company with a reputation for outstanding quality and a major supplier to the Japanese auto industry, including Toyota. Sumitomo sent a team of six engineers and a translator to Rio Bravo IV where they spent six months with us, living and working, teaching, and criticizing. Mostly teaching by criticizing. These advisors not only showed us how to read the NUMMI blueprints but also helped us institute the philosophies, techniques, and discipline necessary to produce harnesses acceptable to NUMMI.

The agonizing details of this six-month period of criticizing and learning are set down in the original, longer version of this report. I'll make that longer story short by skipping to our first shipment to NUMMI. It was rejected. The reason: There was too much variation in the colors of the cables.

Despite the negative evaluation and the initial rejection and the lack of appreciation for our efforts, Packard hung in there, and so did most of our workforce, though not without doubts and frustration. The pressure on everyone was disheartening.

One afternoon, two of my top Mexican managers said they wanted to quit. They complained that, no matter how hard they worked, I was never satisfied. After some conversation, the managers agreed to sleep on their decisions and talk about it the next day.

That day, by chance, Packard Electric staff members, including general manager Elmer Reese, visited the plant. In front of his staff and many of our beleaguered workers, our general manager optimistically announced, "Things look bad now, but I predict this plant will be a success." Buoyed by this show of faith from Mr. Reese himself, the Mexican managers decided to stay on, hoping eventually to share in the rewards.

During the same visit, Elmer said to me: "This is the cleanest plant I've ever seen at Packard Electric or General Motors. You can't serve a gourmet dinner from a dirty kitchen; I know this team will be successful."

Putting the Theories to Work

The many lessons we learned, with the guidance of the Sumitomo advisers, had to be put into effect in ways that fit the local nature. Still, we have instituted these techniques: customer is king, build it right the first time and every time, no repeat problems, eliminate waste, planned maintenance, minimal inventories, supplier involvement, kanban, visual controls, people power, and so on.

Kaizen.   Kaizen (continuous improvement) sheets are posted on boards around the plant. When a problem is identified, it is listed on the sheet. A sketch or Polaroid snapshot is placed on the board to illustrate the problem. There are columns for writing in the cause of the problem, the irreversible corrective action that will eliminate the cause, the person or persons responsible for the corrective action, the date when the action is completed, and a sketch or photo of the correction. Posting the problems not only establishes our desire to remove them but gives all members an opportunity to be involved in solutions.

We have also hastened problem solving by a very simple technique: reducing the size of our reject holders. A large rack encourages procrastination in taking corrective steps and makes it easier to discard the rejected item and think about it later. By cutting the size of our racks in half, the decision-making process was hurried. Since then, we have eliminated the reject racks altogether. Now, whenever there is a reject, the associate must immediately decide what action should be taken.

Question 2.   This practice (restricting the reject holders) is an application of what concept from this chapter?

Die Changes.   The delay caused by die changes has also been reduced. We have cut the time required of our cutting machine operator by 80 percent. All possible adjustments are made in a trial press before the die leaves the crib for the cutter. This minimizes the loss of the operator's production time and is an example of external adjustments, which, where possible, should be made offline before interrupting production.

Lead Time Reduction.   We use a simple diagramming method to look at ways to streamline our procedures (see Exhibit CS8–1).

Blocks representing each step in a procedure are drawn proportionally to the amount of time that step consumes. The blocks are laid out along a time line, with value-added steps on the left side of the line and non-value-added steps on the right. Our goals are to reduce the size of the boxes (i.e., the time required for each step) and eliminate steps on the non-value-added side of the line.

Question 3.   In what Rio Bravo IV operations would this diagramming method be effective? Discuss.

Inventory Control.   Inventory is like a drug: it makes you feel good, but it can be very expensive and even deadly (in a tough competitive environment). We order and maintain inventories of supplies that are as small as practicable. And we produce only what is needed for that day's shipments; when operators complete their scheduled work before the end of the shift, they spend the remaining time cleaning their work stations or checking their equipment or working on a plant problem or training.

To ensure that inventories are kept small, we build racks to accommodate only the size and number of boxes that we determine are necessary. This applies to our drinking water as well as our production materials.

One morning, while on a plant tour, I spotted two bottles of drinking water on the plant floor next to a completely filled bottle rack. I asked the water service man why they were there. He replied that two extra bottles were needed because of demand. I explained our everything-in-its-place philosophy and agreed to have another rack built to meet his needs.

A couple of days later I noticed that both racks were filled and two bottles were again on the plant floor. I waited for the water service man to arrive and, once he could see me, I broke one of the bottles with a hammer. The problem was eliminated.

Kanban.   We control inventory through the use of kanban. With kanban, material is pulled from the supplier to the customer. The cards make it easy to see how many pieces have been ordered, how many have been built, and how many remain to be built. The kanban card is the pull signal.

Kanban works; we have reduced inventories and related floor space by 80 percent (and we are not finished yet), discovered process and quality problems in their early stages, and cut the time necessary to make engineering changes. However, kanban works best only in combination with other measures. For optimum results, production schedules received from the customer must be level or with plus or minus 10 percent variation.

Three of our local suppliers (providers of pallets, boxes, and cable) have recognized the benefits of kanban and have adopted their own systems. Every day, at a specified time and

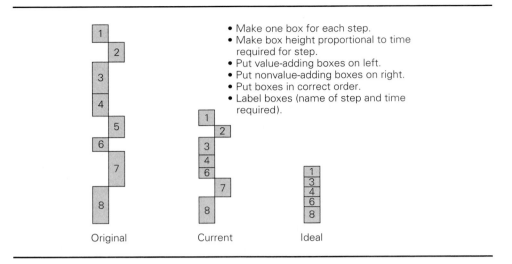

- Make one box for each step.
- Make box height proportional to time required for step.
- Put value-adding boxes on left.
- Put nonvalue-adding boxes on right.
- Put boxes in correct order.
- Label boxes (name of step and time required).

Original   Current   Ideal

loading dock, we receive from them exactly those materials we need for that day, and only that day.

Suppliers.   By involving a supplier or just by asking, "How about doing this for us?" it is surprising how often problems are eliminated. Occasionally, however, it is necessary to find another supplier.

For example, some of the shipping boxes we used were too easily crushed. The weak boxes were affecting the quality of our products—broken connectors were one of the biggest problems reported to us by NUMMI. Besides, boxes are not supposed to get damaged in normal handling.

We looked into the problem and found that (1) the boxes were too spacious for the amount of material being shipped within, (2) the box walls were probably too thin, and (3) internal liners would add support and protection, but also add cost. We discussed the needed changes with our box supplier. They were unable to make satisfactory modifications.

A supplier was found who designed and fabricated a stronger box, with internal dividers, that met our needs. In addition, the new box cost less than the box we had been using (see Exhibit CS8–2).

Question 4.   What benefits in addition to protection do the box dividers offer? Discuss.

Visual Management and Discipline.   As a visual control above critical equipment, we've installed a system of lights. When the machine is running, the green light is illuminated. The yellow light means the machine is momentarily idle, and red indicates assistance is needed.

Also above cutting machines are placards that show the date of the equipment's last maintenance work and when the next maintenance is scheduled. It is planned maintenance as opposed to crisis maintenance. In addition, daily adjustments are made by operators, who consider the machines their own.

Another simple visual control appears on the doors of our terminal die cabinets. On the metal doors, blocks are lined off that relate in size and position to the compartments inside. Each block is labeled with the compartment's part number and has small spaces corresponding to the dies within. When dies are in the compartment, magnets are put in the spaces. A green magnet indicates that a die is in use in a press, and a red magnet shows that a die is being serviced or replacement parts are on order.

With visual controls such as these, anyone passing can tell at a glance where things stand. There is no need to check computer screens, printouts, or reports.

We have a rule: when a light goes out in the plant, it is to be replaced within 10 minutes. (Fixtures are not supposed to hold burned-out lights and, more important, poor lighting

EXHIBIT CS8-2   Shipping Containers

A. Former method

B. New Method

obscures the operator's view of the work.) It is not left to a maintenance person to spot it; anyone can do it.

There is a place for litter, as there is for barrels of cable, terminal dies, and bottled water. Orderliness takes effort to establish but, once instituted, makes many tasks more efficiently done.

"Everything in its place" applies to the office area as well as to the production area. In our conference room is a small holder with slots for five felt tip markers. We placed bars of color on each slot to show what particular color of marker goes in that specific slot. All slots are to filled with the properly colored marker. I've threatened going even a step further and having a kanban card for each marker.

You may have thought that such details are ridiculous, but I hope by now you understand their significance. I have a quick way of judging how well things are going at Rio Bravo IV: If the markers are in their holder properly and if there are no burned out lights in the plant and if the terminal reels are stacked correctly, I can be fairly sure that everything is proceeding as it should and the harnesses are marching into their shipping containers.

The Beginning

The trials of Rio Bravo IV have been difficult, but the lessons learned have helped to establish Packard Electric as a worldwide leader in the manufacture of signal and power distribution systems. That was our objective when the NUMMI contract was bid, and it remains our objective today.

It would be comfortable to think that the goal has been reached and now we can relax. But the principle of continuous improvement does not allow for complacency. There is always opportunity for improving quality or productivity or costs; there is always a better way.

Though we have made giant strides in our first three-and-one-half years, the ongoing attention to continuous improvement will show that the steps taken so far are just the beginning.

Question 5.   What does this case suggest about management of the global company? What does it suggest about the influence of culture?

For Further Reference

Books

Goldratt, Eliyahu M., and Jeff Cox. *The Goal: Excellence in Manufacturing.* Croton-on-Hudson, N.Y.: North River Press, 1984.

Hall, Robert W. *Attaining Manufacturing Excellence.* Burr Ridge, Ill.: Dow Jones-Irwin, 1987.

Plossl, G. W., and O. W. Wight. *Production and Inventory Control.* Englewood Cliffs, N.J.: Prentice-Hall, 1967 (HD55.P5).

Schonberger, Richard, J. *Building a Chain of Customers: Linking Business Functions to Create the World Class Company.* New York: The Free Press, 1990 (HD58.9S36).

Vollmann, Thomas E., William L. Berry, and D. Clay Whybark. *Manufacturing Planning and Control Systems.* 3rd. ed. Burr Ridge, Ill.: Richard D. Irwin, 1992 (TS176.V63).

Periodicals/Societies

Journal of Operations Management (American Production and Inventory Control Society).

Production and Inventory Management Journal (American Production and Inventory Control Society).

Target (Association for Manufacturing Excellence).

ORDER FULFILLMENT AND PURCHASING

Chapter Outline

> The Vancouver division of Hewlett-Packard has realized the benefits of what H-P calls "design for supply-chain management." The division once had made all models of its printers in its factories, then shipped the printers to distribution centers around the world for order processing with customers. Variable demands from different countries, however, created stocking problems: excesses of some printers and shortages of others in the distribution centers. Instead of treating the issue as a forecasting or just an inventory problem, the new idea was to design the printers differently to partially eliminate the problem. Engineers redesigned the printers so that the power-supply module could be attached externally instead of being built in. That permits the factories to ship basic printer models to the distribution centers, who then customize the product for their local markets. This requires that the centers take on new functions: procuring power supply modules and manuals, performing a few final assembly and packing operations, and ensuring quality. While this plan would increase the cost of those operations, it would reduce overall costs and improve customer service.[1]

As the Hewlett-Packard example indicates, purchasing and order fulfillment do not stand apart from other functions of the organization. The design of the product, which was the subject of Chapter 4, can affect the entire supply chain.

That chain comprises several links, each centering around a purchasing function. The financial impacts can be considerable. Purchased inventories typically account for some 70 percent of expenses in retailing and 90 percent in wholesaling. In manufacturing, over 60 percent of the final cost of finished goods consists of purchased materials. In addition, organizations of all kinds contract for services ranging from janitorial to consulting to computer operations. While the purchasing function may be relatively small in numbers of people, its impact on effectiveness can be immense.

In this chapter, we focus first on purchasing as part of the full order-fulfillment sequence. With that as an overview, we proceed with examination of supplier partnerships and some of the better-known purchasing policies and procedures.

Order Fulfillment

When things go well, operations is able to keep up with customer demand. To keep things going well, company associates must play an active role in monitoring customer activities and being prepared. In most cases it is poor policy for a company to go for maximum customer traffic. If sales generates more demand than the firm can handle, the excess traffic just ends up in backlogs and waiting lines. To avert this kind of demand–capacity mismatch, the full planning team needs to devise a responsive order-fulfillment system that includes appropriate checks and balances. The following discussion focuses on this system.

Order fulfillment involves demands from both internal and external customers, features both appointments and immediate sales or service, and may or may not involve purchasing. Exhibit 9–1 details the common elements of order fulfillment. In compressed form, the demand or sale, order entry, and service occur all at once—1 to 2 to 7 in the exhibit. When the customer orders or makes an appointment in advance, the sequence is longer. In addition to 1, 2, and 7, it involves checking the appointment book (3), making the order promise (4), and finally service or delivery (7). A still

The Pentagon's ability to fill orders in a war zone has improved: For Desert Storm in fiscal year (FY) 1991, order-fulfillment time averaged 25.5 days; for Bosnia (FY 1995), it fell to 7.1 days.[2]

EXHIBIT 9–1

**Order-Fulfillment
Sequence**

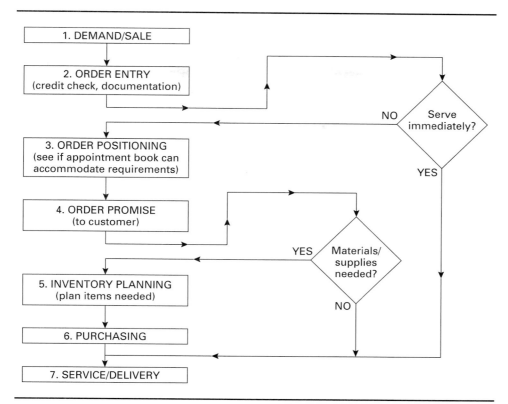

longer sequence requires purchasing. It includes all of the steps in the exhibit, including planning for (5) and buying (6) needed supplies (e.g., blood for a surgery) or materials for sale or conversion in manufacturing.

Sometimes order fulfillment has loops within loops. Consider, for example, a medical clinic. You, the patient, are an order. When you go to X-ray, the technician processes an X-ray order. When you go to the lab, lab people process several lab orders. After more stops, you are almost finished. What remains is a billing order—or invoice. Thus, the question, "Where's the customer?" or "Where's the order?" does not always have an easy response; the answer is in one of the order-fulfillment loops.

Some organizations make hard work of order fulfillment by stretching it out and failing to be ready for customers or orders. Departmental walls chop up the sequence and hinder unified preparation. Superior firms, however, rely on methods that combine or avoid certain steps. They may employ simple, visual "kanban" methods of triggering action. In addition, they may organize co-located teams, or work cells, to compress steps in the sequence (see Into Practice, "Speedy Order Processing . . . ").

Of the seven blocks (plus two decision diamonds) in the order fulfillment sequence of Exhibit 9–1, blocks 5 and 6 are major functions in their own right. Block 5, inventory planning, consumes two full chapters (10 and 11). Block 6, purchasing, is the subject of the remainder of this chapter.

𝒫RINCIPLE 2:

Dedicate to
continuous, rapid
improvement.

The case study at the
end of this chapter, the
Office Goes Kanban at
Boeing," illustrates
visual kanban in
practice.

Speedy Order Processing at Atlantic Envelope Company

Atlantic Envelope Company's seven sites had the same back-office problem: slow order entry. It was taking a week or so (nobody had actually measured it) from when salespeople booked a customer order (such as from a retail chain, an office-supplies wholesaler, or perhaps a high-volume mail handler like Federal Express) to the start of envelope production or shipment from stock.

Stage 1, 1990

Atlantic's effort to streamline order entry began at the company's home plant in Atlanta in the fall of 1990. Earlier, office partitions had been removed so that four order-processing associates (order editor, order typist 1, order typist 2, and order checker) could operate more as a work cell. By itself, working in a common area as an order-processing cell did not result in noticeable changes.

As a base line for improvement, it was necessary to measure the processing time. It averaged five days, but was highly unstable. Moreover, all orders, except those designated for special routing, were treated alike. No rational priority system existed. One quick result: Merely measuring processing time resulted in its being cut to an average of three days, without conscious efforts on the part of the cell associates.

Stage 2, 1992

Then the team went to work. By fall 1992, they had cut average processing time from five days to about eight hours (and reduced their processing team from four to three associates). They made the following primary improvements:

- An order-entry associate screens incoming orders and puts them into color-coded folders: one color for standard manufacturing orders, a second for rush orders, a third for "jet" orders (overprinting on existing envelope stock using a jet printer), and a fourth for orders filled through purchasing from another Atlantic plant or an outside printer. Color-coding sets the stage for separate, focused treatment of each type of order.

- Jet orders, for example, are processed by a jet coordinator (a new position), who is able to get a sample to the art and composition department in about an hour (formerly it took one day). She determines which jet press to use, assigns the completion date, and returns the jet order to the order-entry cell for final processing (price, commissions, etc.) and forwarding to the jet press department. Jet order processing time is now 5 days (15 days formerly).

- Large, split-lot orders and stock replenishment orders, both involving inventory actions, go directly to the inventory planner for more specialized handling.

- Order-entry associates now hold regular order review meetings with raw materials and scheduling people; these meetings resolve order-processing problems faster and reduce errors.

- Order entry now sends incorrect and incomplete orders to sales service associates, who are better able to take corrective action with salespeople and customers.

- Associates are becoming cross-trained, allowing people to help at another order-processing desk and across department lines as needed in order to handle surges in certain types of orders.

In the spirit of continuous improvement, further innovations are being considered. At the same time, Atlantic's other sites are involved in their own order-entry streamlining, mostly by adapting the Atlanta system.

Order processing cycle times charted by order-entry associates at Atlantic Envelope Company's Atlanta facility. Shows average time to process 47 orders on Thursday, March 5, to be 7.9 hours. Large chart in the center shows average for the first four days in March. To the left are charts for prior months.

Purchasing: Quest for High-Quality Supplier-Partners

When you go shopping, what do you look for? Quality? Brand name? Service with a smile? Probably, in most cases (unless you are wealthy) you go for price.

Purchasing departments are inclined that way too: The buyer gets quotes from potential suppliers and accepts the lowest price. It's the easiest way to look good as a buyer, since price is objective and attributes like quality are less so. Higher-up executives, or elected officials, also want to look good. So they may direct purchasing departments to use procedures that bring about price reductions.

Lowest price, however, can be like fool's gold, crumbling easily and not retaining a shine. Most executives and buyers know that price is only one element in life-cycle costs of purchased items and that costs of factors such as quality and maintenance add up quickly. Furthermore, administrative costs—costs of order fulfillment in both the buying and supplying organizations—sometimes dwarf the price. Dealing with these multiple issues, to get real value, requires a team effort — within the buying organization and in partnership with suppliers. Keki Bhote describes the transition toward partnership as a four-stage evolution:[3]

Stage 1: Confrontation with the supplier.

Stage 2: Arm's-length relationship, where adversarial attitudes gradually give way to a cautious, tentative assessment of a working relationship.

Stage 3: A congruence in mutual goals, a coming together.

Stage 4: A full-blown partnership between customer and supplier, a marriage "made in heaven."

We shall say no more about the confrontation stage, with its emphasis on price, its squabbling over contracts and compliance, and its occasional law suits. Rather, in the next three sections we examine the arm's-length, goal-congruence, and full-blown partnership stages.

Arm's-Length Purchasing

Most purchasing today is still probably done impersonally, the arm's-length approach. The purchasing department's organization is by commodity group. Each buyer has responsibility for one or a few commodities, such as sportswear, shoes, steel, electronics, paper and supplies, and contracted services. A typical week may bring hundreds of requisitions to be processed and forwarded to dozens of suppliers. In addition, the buying staff receives voluminous data from the receiving department. Some is for reconciliation—matching the original purchase order with what actually came in. Other data are for evaluating supplier performance, in order to help buyers make decisions on which suppliers to deal with in the future. Buyers keep busy as well in seeking new suppliers, then soliciting and processing bids. All the while, they are handling complaints from unhappy internal and external customers who have unmet materials needs.

> A requisition, prepared in another department, is a request for purchasing to place an order for a specific item.

Poor quality, wrong quantity, wrong items, and, especially, late deliveries keep requisitioners anxious and buyers busy. Changing delivery dates or quantities, arranging alternative transportation, and attending to the large flow of paperwork keeps buyers from getting to know suppliers.

Management may choose not to know what happens in the supplier's system, in effect, to treat it as a black box (see Exhibit 9–2). Order information (orders, requisitions, inquiries, change requests, etc.) goes into the box, and status information (acknowledgements, responses, etc.) and, eventually, goods and services themselves come out. But what's inside remains a mystery.

In a few companies, however, purchasing professionals have attempted to probe the black box (e.g., by phone or on-site visit to the supplier) to learn about suppliers. However, the result too often is like the following exchange:

Buyer: "What is the status of my order?"
Supplier's representative: "According to my current information, it is on time."
Buyer: "What do you mean by current information?"
Supplier's representative: "Well, I haven't received a delay notice."
Buyer: "Do you receive regular delay reports?"
Supplier's representative. "Yes."
Buyer: "How often?"
Supplier's representative: "Monthly."

EXHIBIT 9–2
Black Box View of the Supplier's System

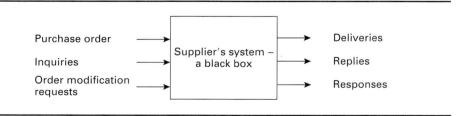

Buyer: (mentally noting that month-old delay reports are badly out of date): "Could you please check to see where the order is in your shops?"
Supplier's representative: "No, I've tried that before. Manufacturing tells me there are just too many orders on the floor to go searching for a particular one."
Buyer: "OK. Then could you just check with your master scheduler to see where my order is on your MPS?"
Supplier's representative: "MPS?"

Clearly, the supplier's representative is not in the habit of checking with production control or operations (nor does the rep know that MPS stands for master production shedule). The aggressive buyer will have scored a coup if the supplier's rep is induced to go to production control for order-status information and succeeds in getting it.

Too often, the arm's-length, black-box approach degenerates into an adversarial system: Buying companies distrust suppliers and change them often. In response, suppliers often do not do their best for customers, which makes their replacement by other suppliers likely. And the cycle repeats and degenerates.

Goal Congruence

Quality is a good starting point in moving away from an arm's length relationship: Both parties can only benefit from higher levels of quality. An important step is to shift the responsibility for quality from the buyer's inspectors or users to the supplier's processes. Just-in-time processing is another mutually beneficial target of goal congruence: Cut out all the delays—and costly wastes—that stand in both parties' way of delivering just in time for use.

Full Partnership

Ultimately, as a step in achieving full partnership, the buying company's purchasing department may need to be re-engineered. While a centralized purchasing core may be retained, portions of the department may split off to join product or customer-focused teams. The teams may count supplier representatives among their membership, which is another, strong step in the direction of supplier partnership. (See the Contrast box for a summary of the traditional and more-effective viewpoints.) A modern trend in manufacturing is to create a new job classification called **buyer-planner**: A buyer assumes the added role of job planner, or a job

Contrast
The Purchasing Associate

Traditional

- Commodity oriented.
- Burdened with paperwork.
- Out of touch with suppliers.

More Effective

- Captain of a purchasing team of colleagues and suppliers.
- Quality oriented and challenged by task variety.

Affiliation with the National Association of Purchasing Management (NAPM) provides a window to career opportunities in purchasing and related fields.

planner takes on buying responsibilities. The buyer then becomes a member of an extended production team.

A full partnership must involve internal functions as well as outside suppliers. Typically, the internal functions affected by purchasing activities include

Purchasing. Buyers and staff are the main action component of the purchasing effort.

Product design and development. This function may be called upon to develop specifications for the products or services to be bought.

Operations. Often operations teams or managers requisition, receive, and use the purchased item.

Material control. Plans inventory levels, releases material, and ensures record accuracy.

Information systems. The information system, usually computerized, handles order-processing transactions and related documentation.

Receiving. In the case of purchased goods, a separate receiving function may accept and process incoming items before the items make their way to the user.

Accounts payable. This section of the accounting department pays the supplier for accepted goods and services.

Legal. Purchase orders, even if conveyed orally, are legal contracts, which may need careful scrutiny.

In complex purchasing cases, all of these internal functions are active. The TQM concept of multi-functional teamwork is key to avoiding mistakes and maximizing chances for a successful acquisition.

The trend toward partnerships is strongest among big companies, such as Bank of Boston, Federal Express, and Chrysler. Some, such as Harley-Davidson, label their approach "partners in profit," which asserts the buying company's commitment not to skewer the suppliers but to help make them strong. A few companies have even dropped the "purchasing" department label; Frito-Lay, for example, has a vice president, and department, of supplier development. Advanced data communication systems and trade pacts have made partnering possible across borders and oceans. Between quality at the source and supplier teams are a number of other features of supplier partnership, discussed next.

Features of Supplier Partnership

Exhibit 9–3 contrasts the partnership and adversarial approaches. Most of the points under the partnership column in the exhibit could be called features of just-in-time purchasing, or of total-quality purchasing. As is noted often throughout this book, JIT, total quality, and external partnerships are closely related.

While few companies have been totally adversarial with suppliers, most have been that way to some degree. In contrast, certain leading-edge companies have embraced nearly all of the partnership items, and many others have adopted them in part. The extremes of adversary and partnership are anchors for discussion of the 12 dimensions in Exhibit 9–3.

Tenure

Under the adversarial approach, it's supplier musical chairs. A new supplier's price list might catch a buyer's eye and trigger a switch from the old to the new

Exhibit 9–3   Supplier Relationships

	Adversary	*Partnership*
1. Tenure	Brief	Long-term, stable
2. Type of agreement	Sporadic purchase orders	Exclusive or semi-exclusive contracts, usually at least one year
3. Number of sources	Several sources per item for protection against risk and for price competition	One or a few good suppliers for each item or commodity group
4. Prices/costs	High on average; low buy-in bids (below costs) can lead to unstable suppliers	Low; scale economies from volume contracts; suppliers can invest in improvements
5. Quality	Uncertain; reliance on receiving inspections	Quality at source; supplier uses statistical process control and total quality management
6. Design	Customer developed	Make use of suppliers' design expertise
7. Delivery frequency/order size	Infrequent, large lots	Frequent (sometimes more than one per day), small lots just in time.
8. Order conveyance	Mail	Long-term: contracts. Short-term: kanban, phone, fax, or electronic data interchange
9. Documentation	Packing lists, invoices, and count/inspection forms	Sometimes no count, inspection, or list—just monthly bill
10. Transportation	Late and undependable; stock missing or damaged	Dependably quick, on time, and intact
11. Delivery location	Receiving dock and stockroom	Direct to point of use
12. Openness	Very little; black box	On-site audits of supplier, concurrent design, visits by front-line associates

supplier. For large-volume (or big-ticket) services or items, buyers request bids from several suppliers at least yearly; the low bidder (often not the present supplier) usually gets the contract.

The partnership approach calls for staying with one supplier and letting the learning curve work for the benefit of both parties. Suppliers who get to know a customer's real requirements are valuable participants on improvement teams, quality function deployment, and other continuous-improvement efforts.

Type of Agreement

In the adversarial approach, sporadic purchase orders are the norm, and orders for a single item may rotate among 5 or 10 suppliers. Special, one-time buys will probably always require a purchase order. For regularly used items, however, the trend is toward one-year or longer contracts. Five-year contracts have become widespread in the North American auto industry; one-year contracts are more common in the volatile electronics industry. For example, the Lincoln, Illinois, plant of Eaton Corporation's Power Distribution Division treats selected vendors as internal departments and uses yearly master pricing agreements.

Some contracts specify the quantity for the next few months and provide a forecast for the rest of the year. Also, the contract may grant exclusivity to a supplier but not stipulate exact quantities.

Number of Sources

Having several sources for each purchased item is common practice among ad-versarially oriented buyers. Government regulations require it for certain classes of goods and services for reasons of price competition and a sense of fairness in public expenditures. In most cases, however, fear of supplier failure accounts for the many-supplier rule.

Over time, multiple sourcing has effects opposite to what is intended. It raises each supplier's costs and thus costs to the customer.[4] But sole- or preferred-supplier sourcing gives the supplier confidence that demand will continue. This encourages supplier investment in process and product improvements that offer economies of scale. Indeed, some believe that widespread multiple sourcing in North America and Europe in recent decades ruined part of the supplier base, which drove buying companies off shore, primarily to the Far East, in search of quality goods from reliable suppliers.

Multiple sourcing is also costly to buying organizations: Multiple sources mul-tiply costs of selection, evaluation, certification, data processing, communications, and administrative and clerical activities, for example. A less tangible cost is the loss of the opportunity to get to know and take advantage of suppliers' capabilities.

*P*RINCIPLE 5:

Cut the number of suppliers.

Competitive organizations strive to reduce these wastes, and a total quality or JIT program is often the impetus. A survey of North American companies revealed the average number of suppliers to be 1,096 prior to JIT. The number dropped to 759 after one year of JIT, to 656 after two years, and to 357 after five years. On average, the companies had cut their number of suppliers by over 67 percent in five years.[5] Other companies' programs aim at reducing the number of suppliers as a goal in it-self. For example, a 3M factory in New Ulm, Minnesota, trimmed its active vendor list from 2,800 to 600 in the first year, and to 300 in the second year.[6] Furthermore, the trend has spread from manufacturing to fast-food companies, hotels, retailers, and wholesalers. Wallace Company, a distributor of oil-drilling repair parts and a winner of the Malcolm Baldrige Quality Award, cut its number of valve suppliers from 2,500 to 325.[7] Reductions of suppliers usually are competitive rather than arbitrary, and buying companies are usually up-front about their intentions to cut suppliers.

McKesson Corp., a pharmaceutical distributor, reversed the process. In the early 1980s, it developed a total service plan that led to its becoming sole or pre-ferred distributor to many small drug retailers. The services employ electronic communication and include inventory and shelf management, pricing, credit, in-surance claims, and others. These services have created a strong dependency rela-tionship between the retailers and McKesson.[8]

Despite the obvious cost benefits of supplier reductions, some companies fear that the sole supplier might fail. Sole-sourcing is not always the answer; often firms maintain two suppliers for each commodity group but just one for each part within a group. For example, they buy business forms 1, 3, 5, 7, and so on from supplier A, and forms 2, 4, 6, 8, and so on from supplier B. If disaster strikes one supplier, the other is able to help without the expense of developing new supply channels. Added protection of buyer–supplier contingency plans (what to do in case of fire, flood, strikes, etc.) further reduces buyer's exposure.

Prices/Costs

In the adversarial approach, price tends to dominate the buy decision. This may make sense for commodities—items that scarcely differ from one source to the

Staying Lean with Low Risk

"Our inventory levels are at a fraction of where they were in the mid–1980s, but we feel there's no higher risk of shortages developing now than then," said Allen Hagstrand, in charge of purchasing for the Stamford, Connecticut, unit of Schweppes PLC, the London food and beverage producer.

Closer cooperation with a smaller but better-informed assortment of suppliers has helped, according to Mr. Hagstrand. "Today we get close to 80 percent of our glass containers from a single company, whereas seven years ago no one supplier provided more than 30 percent," he said. "We used to play one off against the other and keep them guessing, while now we all work very closely together, providing sales forecasts and other data we once kept to ourselves."

Source: Alfred L. Malabre, Jr., "Firm's Inventories Are Remarkably Lean," *The Wall Street Journal*, November 3, 1992.

next, such as a standard grade of coal or feed corn. For most items, however, design, quality, delivery, and service deserve their share of emphasis.

Overemphasis on price can backfire. For example, sometimes a supplier will outbid other suppliers with a discount or a bid price that is below its costs; then, however, it may overcharge on other contracts in order to stay in business. Also, when big customers with clout are able to force suppliers into making recklessly low bids, the suppliers become unstable and financially unable to invest in improvements. That instability, along with frequent changing of suppliers, introduces high change costs for both parties. Thus, while the adversarial approach focuses on getting good prices, it often causes the opposite.

By contrast, the partnership approach, offering stable high-volume contracts with opportunities for economies of scale, is attractive to suppliers. It persuades them to try to improve and do their best for customers.

Quality

When suppliers are distrusted, customers must protect themselves. The insurance may be a sizable staff of inspectors at the receiving dock or in a holding area. Sometimes it takes days to clear incoming inspection, while users watch their own schedules slip. For purchased services, the distrusted supplier's work must be checked, reports and claims must be filed and reconciled, and sometimes the service must be redone.

Instead of spending so much time discovering post-receipt errors, firms need to partner up and send customer teams to visit, develop, certify, and then nurture suppliers. Some companies furnish training and technical assistance to suppliers to prevent mistakes (fail-safing) or to help the supplier discover and correct them (process control). Sometimes supplier nurturing extends throughout an industry. For example, after decades of using unique SPC rules (thus forcing suppliers into the expense of multiple manuals, nomenclature, and reporting formats), General Motors, Ford, and Chrysler jointly developed the *Fundamental Statistical Process Control Reference Manual.*[9] That common set of procedures for inspection and reporting significantly reduces industry suppliers' costs of meeting carmakers' quality requirements.

*P*RINCIPLE 10:

Make it easy to provide goods and services without error.

Design

If the customer buys out of a catalog or off the shelf, the supplier clearly has control of the design specifications. However, the customer often wants special features or service. In the adversarial approach, the customer typically does the design work, passes the specs on to the supplier, and expects them to be followed. But that approach has come under attack from wise customers. Programs such as early supplier involvement, design-build teams, and quality function deployment tap suppliers' expertise and can reduce development time significantly.

Delivery Frequency/Order Size

Shipping costs depend partly on whether the volume is great enough to fill a truck (or barge or sea container). Since volume for a certain item traditionally has been split among several suppliers, each supplier must ship less often in order to get full-load freight rates. Thus, it has been normal for customers to have to receive large lots infrequently; many weeks' supply per shipment is common.

Under the partnership approach, in which a smaller number of suppliers each has a greater volume of business, shipping more often—weekly, daily, or even more frequently—becomes economical. If the bulk is insufficient to fill a semi-trailer, then a smaller truck or van may make the deliveries.

For remote suppliers, frequent, small-lot deliveries are made economical by what the auto industry calls milk runs. A single truck stops at several suppliers, collecting a small amount from each; when the truck is full, it delivers to one or more customers. Milk runs range from one a week to several loops per day.

Distance need not be a serious problem. One Chrysler milk run, extending from El Paso, Texas, to the Detroit area, takes 56 hours. Small-lot deliveries are even oc-curing across oceans; for example, a ship departing from a Far Eastern port may carry in a single sea container just a day's worth of several dozen different bulky auto parts; each day another similarly loaded ship departs, and each spends five weeks on the sea, but one arrives at a North American port to offload every day.

Conventionally, the truck or ship would carry one or more months' supply of a given item per delivery and would visit a given supplier just once every month or two for a pickup. That is a costly amount of inventory for the supplier to build up for each shipment and a costly amount to dump on the customer. While it may seem that loading and paperwork costs are much greater when pickups and deliveries are daily instead of monthly, that need not be the case. When partnered companies, including the freight hauler, get a regular milk run going, they usually are able to greatly simplify the data processing, including invoicing just once a month instead of per delivery and per part number.

◯RINCIPLE 13:

Operate at the customer's rate of use; decrease cycle interval and order size.

Order Conveyance

Exhibit 9–4 illustrates the order conveyance and documentation aspects of purchasing. We deal with order conveyance here and documentation in the next section. In traditional delivery systems, a mailed purchase order from the customer or an order booked by a salesperson starts the ball rolling in the supplier's plant (see the top portion of Exhibit 9–4A).

Under partnership with frequent deliveries, mail is too slow. New, faster methods of transmitting order information include phone, facsimile (fax) machine, and **electronic data interchange** (EDI) (see Exhibit 9–4B). EDI is a standardized

Exhibit 9–4

**Purchasing—
Order
Conveyance and
Documentation**

A. Traditional approach

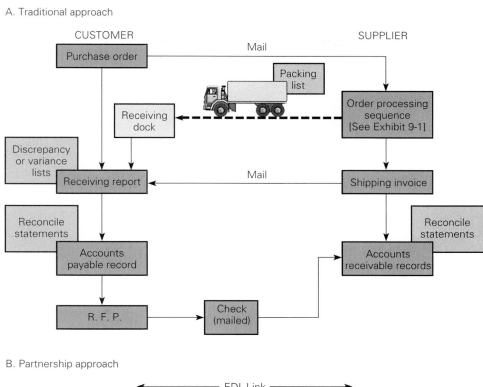

B. Partnership approach

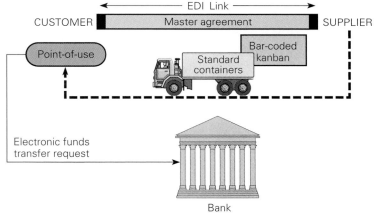

computer-to-computer messaging system open to any company and usable for billing and perhaps funds transfers as well as for ordering.

According to the National Association of Purchasing Management, EDI improves purchasing productivity by reducing paperwork, improving information management, and bettering supplier relationships.

Basic kanban is still another communications method. A kanban (identification card) is attached to the container, which is returnable; its return to the supplier is the authorization to forward one more containerful to the customer. Basic kanban is also usable in conjunction with electronic messaging. Standardized returnable containers provide physical discipline and control, while an electronic message or faxed kanban card provides early warning, before the empty container itself is delivered back to the supplier.

Documentation

Critical documentation associated with traditional purchasing occurs after the supplier receives the purchase order, completes required transformations, and ships goods to the customer (see Exhibit 9–4A). When the shipment arrives, receiving inspectors verify its correctness: right item, right quantity, and right quality. Receiving associates check the supplier's packing list against the receiving dock's copy of the purchase order and note discrepancies on forms that go to purchasing and accounts payable. After reconciliation, accounts payable issues a request-for-payment (RFP) to the controller's office, which cuts and mails a check.

*𝒫*RINCIPLE 16:

Cut transactions and reporting.

The partnership approach tries to eliminate or simplify paperwork. In an ideal system based on a master agreement (see Exhibit 9–4B), there is no purchase order, packing list, or receiving report. A bar-coded kanban card identifies standard containers as to contents, quantity, and so forth. Inspection isn't needed; supplier and item are certified. When an associate scans the kanban bar code upon receipt of the order, accounts payable receives payment authorization. Alternatively, front-line associates scan the bar codes, thus recording the receipt in appropriate inventory accounts and stock records. A monthly bill and electronic funds transfer may complete the process.

Transportation

Prior to the deregulation of trucking (which occurred in the United States in 1980 and in other countries in subsequent years), this dominant mode of transport was slow and unreliable. Along with the resulting keen competition, customers' demands for quality and speed have transformed the transportation industry. While in the old days freight haulers could not guarantee the *day* of delivery, today, sometimes, deliveries are to the *hour*. It is no wonder that, as noted in the Chapter 8 discussion of logistics, truckers increasingly rely on satellite navigation, cellular phones, and personal computers. The increasing demands for quick, on-time, zero-damage transport have thrust the various players in the total transport system into close partnerships and multi-modal freight agreements.

Delivery Location

More on kanban squares in Chapter 10.

Deliveries have historically gone to a single receiving dock (see the top portion of Exhibit 9–5; the vertical arrows depict internal flow of purchased items). The traditional relationship between the customer and Supplier A is costly, time-consuming, and wasteful. Materials may be handled four times: onto the dock for a quick check of contents and quantity, into quality hold in the receiving stockroom for counting and inspection, then to a free-to-use area of the stockroom, and finally to the point of use.

The partnership approach , on the other hand, would employ a quality-certified supplier (reflected as Supplier B in Exhibit 9–5) and would skip all or most of the non-value-adding steps. In industry parlance, they go dock-to-line (or dock-to-use), right to their destination in the plant, lab, kitchen, sales floor, or office. Some companies are remodeling their buildings to provide receiving docks and doors at

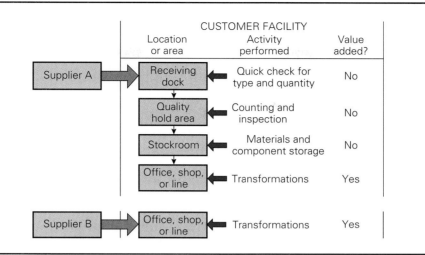

EXHIBIT 9–5

Delivery Location: Dock versus Point of Use

multiple locations around the building so that trucks can deliver close to use points.

In some cases, the driver is authorized to carry or push a trolley or parts through the dock to an interior user location. This is the case for paper and packaging materials delivered from Smurfit Company, a JIT supplier to Microsoft-Ireland, a Dublin-based plant producing software products for the European market (see Exhibit 9–6). The trolleys shown are specially designed, the paper quantities are counted out in 20s (Microsoft's lot quantity), and the driver pushes each to its proper location on a kanban square.

Relationship Openness

The adversarial approach is one of arm's-length relationship. The buyer, in the office or at trade shows, sifts through many suppliers' offerings and finally selects a few; from then on, communication is by mail and fax (except in times of materials scarcity, when the suppliers put their customers "on allocation"—1,000 Nintendo game sets to this store chain, 1,200 to that one, and so forth).

The partnership approach requires the buying organization to send teams to the supplier's site. That includes sending operations employees who use the purchased items. The visitors get to know people at the supplier's facility and acquire an understanding of the supplier's culture, skills, processes, nagging problems, and potential sources of misunderstanding. They invite the supplier's people to reciprocate the visit.

Some buying companies, in what is called supply-chain management, actively seek to extend the partnership to the supplier's suppliers and beyond. Sometimes the catalyst for such linkages is a supplier's trying to forge partnerships with customers and their customers. Such companies as Baxter Healthcare, Wal-Mart, and Levi Strauss & Co. have engaged in this form of customer development or customer-chain management.

The buyer's outreach effort usually also includes some kind of supplier evaluation or certification. (See the Ford Motor Company example in the supplement.) To some extent, evaluation teams supplement their own efforts with public, industry, or international quality recognition (e.g., ISO 9000 registration). Companies may formally evaluate and certify suppliers of both materials and services.

The buying company that is truly serious about a strong partnership must be a good customer. Motorola, for example,

> conducts quarterly confidential surveys of its main suppliers to evaluate its performance as a customer. Each Motorola plant is rated in nineteen areas that the company feels are important to the buyer–seller partnership. Motorola has established a fifteen-member council of suppliers to rate its practices and offer suggestions for improving, for example, the accuracy of production schedules or design layouts that Motorola gives them.[10]

Failure to visit and perform audits or obtain evaluations from external partners invites misunderstanding, bad feelings, and a return to adversarial relationships. It is perhaps like gardening: Till the soil, or weeds will grow.

Outsourcing and Related Strategic Issues

Despite the high levels of expenditures represented by purchased items in most companies, purchasing often hasn't been thought of as strategic. That is changing. As companies scour their environments looking for more places to cut costs, it doesn't take long to zero in on purchasing and order fulfillment. One of the popular targets for cost cutting is services provided and goods made inside that could better be purchased outside. Electing to shift to **outsourcing,** as it is called, has strategic significance in view of the large number of candidate activities, some of which appear in Exhibit 9–7. They extend across the gamut of the transformation processes, from design to service or delivery to the customer.

Issues relating to the outsourcing strategy include the converse—backward integration—along with the make-or-buy model, standardization, and modular buying. Each is discussed below.

Backward Integration versus Outsourcing ("Stick to Your Knitting")

When materials or services are scarce or supplier performance is inconsistent, panic sets in. Anxiety makes some companies opt for **backward integration.** That

EXHIBIT 9–7   **Candidates for Outsourcing**

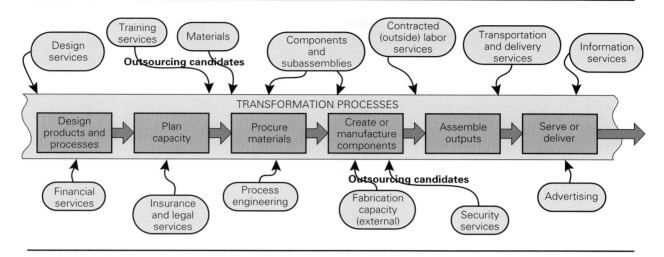

is, they set up to make goods or provide services formerly bought, or they simply acquire the supplier company and make it a part of the business.

Backward integration can consume considerable financial resources and managerial energy. And when the scarcity evaporates or the supplier upgrades its performance, the company that backward integrated may wish it hadn't.

The authors of "Managing Our Way to Economic Decline," an acclaimed 1980 article, commented on backward integration. Companies with stable, commodity-like products, such as metals and petroleum, often can gain economies and profit improvements through backward integration. The strategy may backfire, however, for companies in technologically active industries. Backward integration "may provide a quick, short-term boost to ROI figures in the next annual report, but it may also paralyze the long-term ability of a company to keep on top of technological change."[11]

In the adversarial era, backward integration often seemed to be the only way to get control of costs and quality. By now, many companies have had success with supplier partnerships. Some have experience partnering up with suppliers internationally. Thus, outsourcing—and global sourcing—appear less risky or difficult, and backward integration seems less attractive. Those are among the reasons why companies today are contracting for training, temporary labor, transportation, legal services, advertising, and the other items shown in Exhibit 9–7. Operation of the company information system, which touches on all the transformation processes, is perhaps the most common target for outsourcing. But as noted in Chapter 2, companies should not "give away the store." They should retain core competencies, otherwise known as "sticking to your knitting."

Sometimes, the mere threat of outsourcing can help shape up the inside organization. At Compaq Computer, cost concerns sent engineers around the globe searching for suppliers who could provide parts for less than Compaq's own costs. They settled on a Taiwanese producer that could deliver circuit boards for 30-percent less. At a briefing of plant associates, "one 'crusty old' employee stood up and [argued] that Compaq workers should be allowed to bid on the job." The

Bob May, director of quality at Physio Control Company, was put on special assignment to investigate outsourcing candidates. His team's conclusions: 80 percent of everything done at Physio should be outsourced. But that's impractical. They'll settle for 25 percent.

point hit home. Team engineers found a way to simplify board manufacturing, enabling in-house personnel to make a new computer model on one line, saving a lot of down time.[12]

In a variation on this idea, a number of companies have been bringing operations back to the United States or Canada to cut costs or improve quality—the same reasons for leaving some years earlier. An article on the subject notes further reasons for coming home:[13]

- Automation and "new product designs that shrink the number of parts and simplify assembly."
- Quick response. "What many companies compete on today is service—the ability to produce with lead times of a day or two."
- Fast product development. It is better for the "design and manufacturing folks to be physically close so that they can talk elbow to elbow, modifying continuously."

Any advantages of "stick to your knitting" or outsourcing depend on having reliable suppliers. The ideal is for the buyer company to exert control over a few vital factors of the supply channels, leaving the supplier free to innovate and keep up with technologies in its area of expertise. Reliable suppliers don't just happen; they must be nurtured.

Make or Buy

The question of whether to outsource or not is often a complex issue, not fully reducible to cost analysis. For an existing service or good, going outside means the firm no longer needs the employees currently doing the work; reducing the workforce is always unpleasant and costly. Moreover, some of the overhead costs connected to the outsourced item may not disconnect easily, thereby reducing the potential savings.

Another issue is possible loss of control in outsourcing. The loss-of-control argument, however, can be turned around: Highly vertically integrated companies such as General Motors do not seem to have better control of their internal suppliers than less-integrated companies like Chrysler or Toyota do with their external suppliers. One possible reason is that when a company owns its own suppliers, they become complacent. In a strong partner relationship, however, the external suppliers may fight hard to do the right thing for their customers, since there is always the threat of losing the contract to another supplier.

Some of the outsourcing decision, however, is a cost-volume issue. A simple form of break-even analysis captures the basic elements; see Exhibit 9–8.

As the exhibit shows, if the item is bought, there is no fixed cost. Instead, the total cost (TC) is simply the unit price (P) times demand (D):

$$TC_{buy} = P \times D \tag{9–1}$$

If the item is made, there is a fixed cost (FC) of setting up for production. The other element of total cost is the variable cost of production, which equals the assumed constant unit variable cost (V) times demand (D). Then

$$TC_{make} = (V \times D) + FC \tag{9–2}$$

We see in Exhibit 9–8 that the break-even demand (B) occurs where the total costs are equal. For demand less than B, the total cost to buy is lower; thus, *buy* is

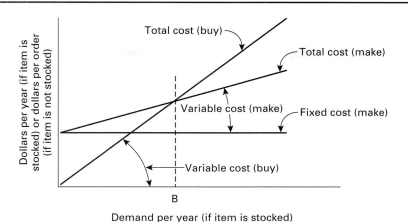

Exhibit 9–8

Make-or-Buy Break-Even Analysis

preferred. For demand greater than B, offsetting the fixed cost by the lower unit cost results in a lower cost to make; so *make* is preferred. The analysis should be based on annual demand and cost if the item is a stocked one that is bought year after year. The demand and cost of a single order should be used for a nonstocked item that may or may not be reordered in future years.

Since the total costs are equal at the break-even point, a break-even formula is easily developed. Using B (for break-even demand) instead of D, we have

$$TC_{buy} = TC_{make}$$

$$P \times B = (V \times B) + FC$$

Then, by algebraic transformation,

$$B = \frac{FC}{P - V} \tag{9–3}$$

For example, assume you can buy candles at the store for $1 each. Or you can pay $50 for candle-making apparatus and make your own candles for a unit variable cost (wax, wicks, etc.) of $0.75. What volume is necessary in order to recover your fixed cost—that is, break even?

Solution:

$$B = \frac{50}{1 - 0.75} = \frac{50}{0.25} = 200 \text{ candles.}$$

Classical make-or-buy is simple enough, but what about its overall usefulness? Like any model, the make-or-buy model entails certain assumptions. First, both options must be realistic. For the make option, this goes beyond the cost of the candle-making apparatus. To be realistic, there are questions of technical knowledge to be successful in such a new endeavor. And will management resources be spread too thin if candle-making is taken on? Another issue is technological obsolescence. What if a new, lower-cost method of candle-making appears? If you invested in the old method, you're stuck and could be underpriced by a competitor.

Concern over these kinds of questions and assumptions seem trivial in this candle-making example. But what if owners of a shopping mall are considering a

$10 million expenditure for installing their own power-generating facilities instead of buying power from the local utility? Now the issues (technical skills, managerial demands, obsolescence, etc.) loom large. The point is that the make-or-buy model does not make the decision but only helps sharpen decision makers' judgment.

The issue of obsolescence is related to the next two topics, standardization and modular buying.

Standardization

Standardization means settling on a few rather than many sizes, formats, and so forth. A standardization strategy is one way to ward off obsolescence, though that is by no means its only purpose. Standardization may apply to printed materials, software, hardware, methods and processes.

Lee and Dobler state that, in manufacturing, "standardization is the prerequisite to mass production." They credit Eli Whitney's development of standardization (initially of musket parts) as having led ultimately to the emergence of the United States as the world's dominant mass producer in the twentieth century.[14] This does not necessarily mean standardized end products. The more powerful strategy is being able to make a wide variety of end products from a small number of standardized parts and materials. The same goes for services. For example, serve a wide variety of training needs with a small number of standardized training methods.

The cost savings can be substantial. For one thing, standardization is key to delayed differentiation, discussed in Chapter 6. Furthermore, fewer items means less purchasing, receiving, inspection, storage, and billing. In manufacturing, standardization reduces the number of different kinds of production equipment and tooling, and production of some parts may be relatively continuous and just in time, instead of inefficient stop-and-go production with intermittent delays and changeover costs.

Some companies, and some industries, have standardization committees. National and world bodies also develop standards. The American National Standards Institute (ANSI) is a federation of over 100 organizations that develop industrial standards. After research and debate, ANSI may approve a recommended standard for adoption nationwide. Perhaps the most vexing standardization issue in America is metrics, since the United States is the only nonmetric country among major industrial countries. However, most American companies with good export markets have gone metric on their own.

Modular buying

How to tell if a plant has too many parts: Have a look. If most of what you see are vehicles, overhead conveyors, and storage systems, the plant is sinking in a sea of parts.

Related to standardization, make-or-buy, and backward integration is purchasing in already-put-together modules. This has special advantages for companies whose products are made from many hundreds or thousands of parts. Processing large numbers of parts in a single location tends to overload the system, causing quality problems, cascading shortages and work stoppages, and physical congestion.

If the firm is adversarial with suppliers, it tries to cope with these difficulties itself. But partnership companies look to their suppliers for a solution, such as having a supplier acquire and preassemble a collection of loose parts into a module, to be delivered with certified quality just in time for use. Though it takes years to implement, this solution has become attractive to manufacturers of such complex products as automobiles, aircraft, large appliances, and mass spectrometers. (A car has over 13,000 parts, and the newest Boeing airplane, the 777, has 132,000 engineered parts and over 3 million fasteners.)

Sometimes the initiative comes from supplier companies. The automotive group at Eagle-Picher Company has proposed to its automotive customers that it supply multipurpose rubber floor mats. The mats would include the underlayment, plus electrical wiring for tail lights and accessories. That gets wiring inside the car, for more reliable quality, instead of strung beneath the car where it is exposed to the elements. Eagle-Picher wants to become a stronger, more valuable supplier with business for *more* parts, while helping its customers to become stronger by needing to manage *fewer* parts.

In a still closer kind of partnership, the supplier moves onto the buying organization's premises in order to become almost like "family." The Into Practice box offers an example.

The outsourcing-related matters just discussed are, or can be, of strategic importance. The day-to-day business of carrying out sourcing strategies requires systematic policies and procedures, our next topic.

Purchasing Policies and Procedures

Commonsense policies relating to value and kind of items bought provide guidance for purchasing professionals. In considering those policies, we look first at ABC analysis and its influence on common buying procedures. Related to this are two final chapter topics: measurement and compliance issues and value analysis.

ABC Analysis

It makes sense to manage costly goods and services tightly and cheap ones loosely. That logic is the basis of **ABC analysis,** an old and still important tool of materials management. (ABC analysis is another example of Pareto's observation concerning maldistribution. Here, most of the value lies in but a few of the inventory items.)

Supplier in Residence

The purchasing department at Bose Corporation, producer of high-end speakers and sound systems, is a pioneer in an extension of the supplier-partnership concept. Their approach, registered under the trademark JIT II, features suppliers in residence at the Bose headquarters facility in Framingham, Massachusetts, as well as at Bose factories. Conceived in 1987, the Bose program has grown to include nine suppliers, of metal, plastics, packaging, printing, stationery, export/import, and transportation goods and services. The supplier representatives are "stationed at the Bose facility at the [supplier's] expense, on a full-time basis, [given] access to customer data, people, and processes, and granted the right to place purchase orders with their own organizations on behalf of Bose. . . . Simply put, JIT II eliminates buyer and salesman, and the [supplier] and customer work closely together."

Source: Adapted from "JIT II: An Inside Story," *APICS—The Performance Advantage,* October 1992, pp. 20–22.

ABC analysis begins by classifying all stocked items by annual dollar volume, that is, annual demand times cost per unit. Class A items, those needing close control, are the high-dollar-volume group. They may include 80 percent of total purchase cost but only 1 percent of total items bought. Class B is a medium-dollar-volume group, perhaps 15 percent of cost and 30 percent of items. Class C is the rest, say, 5 percent of cost and 69 percent of items. Some firms continue with D and perhaps E categories.

Computer processing makes ABC analysis easy to do. Item cost is available in the inventory master file. Any measure of annual usage may be used, such as actual usage last year, actual usage last month times 12, or a forecast. After the computer provides a list of items in descending dollar-volume order, associates divide the list into A, B, and C, based on the company's category break-point policies.

The resulting ABC listing may be used as follows (the details will vary from firm to firm):

1. *Purchasing.* Have each contract or purchase order for a class A item signed by the president or chief financial officer, for a class B item by a department head, and for a class C item by any buyer.

2. *Physical inventory counting.* Count A items weekly or daily, B items monthly, and C items annually.

3. *Forecasting.* Forecast A items by several methods on the computer with resolution by a forecasting committee, B items by simple trend projection, and C items by buyer's best guess.

4. *Safety stock.* No safety stock for A items, one week's supply for B items, and one month's supply for C items.

5. *Quick response.* Deliver A items frequently, perhaps daily, just in time. Deliver Bs weekly, and Cs monthly.

At a TQM team's suggestion, Microsoft USA provides each group assistant (serving a group of software engineers) with a credit card for buying low-value items, thus bypassing the purchasing department for nearly 40 percent of the firm's purchases.

ABC dipped a bit in popularity in the 1970s. Experts were saying that falling computing costs made it economical for a material requirements planning system to give B and C items as much attention as A items; one ordering system could be used for all items. The emergence of just-in-time brought us back to more conventional ABC thinking.

Class A items are often the best prospects for full JIT treatment because they have the volume to most easily justify frequent small-lot deliveries, perhaps daily. It is no small achievement to switch an item to daily deliveries; typical delivery intervals/lot sizes in the non-JIT mode are monthly or greater. JIT policies for B and C items are more modest: perhaps weekly deliveries for class B items and monthly for class Cs.

Actually, many companies have found ways to do much better than that for some Bs and Cs. For example, a sizable number of manufacturing plants now buy all their hundreds of hardware items (screws, bolts, grommets, etc.) from a single supplier. Commonly, that supplier visits the customer at least once a week, and sometimes even daily, goes right out to the factory floor to fill the bins and trays, and just invoices the customer monthly. While each hardware item is class C in annual value, the whole commodity group adds up to class A value, which makes it economical for the supplier to provide that kind of customer service.

A different twist on the same general idea was discussed earlier: buying completed modules instead of the individual parts. Past practice in automotive assembly, for example, was to buy and receive hundreds of class B parts for instrument panels, doors, and so forth for piece-by-piece installation on the assembly line. The sheer volume of parts made this system a receiving and material-handling nightmare.

The current trend is to have a subcontractor, a specialist in instrument panels or doors, for example, deliver completed modules to the assembly plant. While the individual parts are class B, the modules are class A in value, which makes daily deliveries (sometimes several times a day) economical.

ABC applies as well to inventory-intensive wholesaling and retailing as it does to manufacturing (see Example 9–1).

EXAMPLE 9–1:   ABC ANALYSIS—WHOLESALER

At Universal Motor Supply Company, the buyer has arranged 10 inventory items in order of annual dollar volume. Exhibit 9–9 shows the ordered list, with monetary volume expressed in percentages. The buyer examines the list to arrive at an ABC classification of the items.

Exhibit 9–10 shows the 10 items as the buyer grouped them into classes A, B, and C. The groupings seem natural: The three B items account for over seven (9.8 ÷ 1.3) times

Stock Number	Annual Demand	Unit Cost	Annual Dollar Volume	Percent
407	40,000	$ 35.50	$1,420,000	59.53%
210	1,000	700.00	700,000	29.35
021	2,000	55.00	110,000	4.61
388	20,000	4.00	80,000	3.35
413	4,400	10.00	44,000	1.84
195	500	36.00	18,000	0.75
330	40	214.00	8,560	0.36
114	100	43.00	4,300	0.18
274	280	1.00	280	0.01
359	600	0.25	150	0.01
		Totals	$2,385,290	~100.0%

EXHIBIT 9–9

Inventory Items in Annual-Dollar-Volume Order— Universal Motor Supply Company

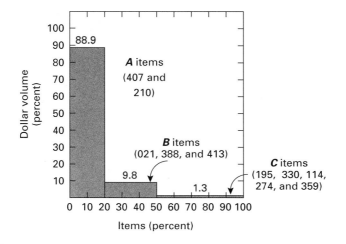

EXHIBIT 9–10

ABC Classification— Universal Motor Supply Company

as much annual volume as the five C items, and two A items account for about nine times as much as the three B items. It is clear that A items should receive major attention. Have them delivered often in small quantities, store them in flow racks at or near the receiving/shipping docks, and carefully monitor and control them. Class Bs should receive moderate attention, and class Cs little attention; for example, handle them manually and store them in conventional racks in a remote part of the warehouse.

Purchasing and Contracting Practices

Besides ABC analysis, there are other common purchasing practices and terms that managers should know. They have to do with arranging the supplier–buyer agreement and the terms of that agreement, and they group fairly well into the A, B, and C categories.

Class A Items.   A class A item may be a service contract, an expensive, seldom-ordered item, or a low-cost item that is ordered often or in large quantities. Common purchasing measures are:

>   **Soliciting competitive bids on specifications.** The buyer mails an invitation to bid or a request for quotation to prospective suppliers. The item to be bought is specified in detail; the description may consist of technical specifications (e.g., physical or chemical properties), performance specifications (mean time until failure, rated output, etc.), and procedural specifications (e.g., consultant will conduct an employee attitude survey). Specifications may be necessary because the item is nonstandard or because the buying firm wishes to exclude low-quality suppliers. Also, specifications can provide a sound basis for determining compliance with the buyer's requirements. Engineers often play a key role in developing specs, and blueprints may be attached. Attorneys may ensure that contractual obligations are legally correct.
>
>   Governments, especially the federal government, intermittently buy based on publicly available specs. Regulations require that for many types of purchases the invitation to bid be published in a widely circulated government document.
>
>   **Certification.** As Chapter 2 noted, quality-conscious companies conduct formal studies to quality-certify suppliers and items bought from them. Older approaches, which rank suppliers rather than certify them, are based on external price data, delivery timeliness, defect rates, and a few other factors. Quality certification sometimes includes such factors as quality of design, training, response time, and delivery performance (see chapter supplement).
>
>   **Negotiation.** Where sources of supply are stable, there may be no need to solicit formal bids. Instead, purchasing teams may just periodically negotiate with the regular source for better price or delivery terms. Typically, negotiation applies to nonstandard class A goods and services.
>
>   **Speculative buying.** In this type of purchasing, also called buying down, the buyer will purchase in excess of immediate needs when the price is down. The practice is risky in that price could fall further, and a need for the items bought may never materialize.
>
>   **Hedging.** Hedging applies especially to commodities, such as wheat, corn, silver, and lumber. Organized futures markets exist for some commodities. A

buyer can pay cash to buy a commodity now and at the same time sell a like amount of a future delivery of the commodity. Price changes will mean that losses on one order are offset by gains on the other.

Class B Items.   Class B goods and moderate-cost services usually warrant less purchasing effort. That applies to many kinds of standard off-the-shelf goods, such as maintenance, repair, and operating (MRO) supplies as well as standard services, such as those of a plumber or an auto body shop. For nonstandard items in the class B cost range, specifications might be necessary, but the expense of soliciting bids is harder to justify than for class A items. Buying procedures for the class B category include the following:

> **Approved supplier lists.** Companies like to buy from proven suppliers. Buyers rely on the approved supplier list, especially for class B items, though it also is used for class A and class C buying. The approved supplier list may be based on an old-style performance rating or on a full certification study.
>
> **Catalog buying.** Perhaps the most common purchasing procedure for off-the-shelf MRO goods is buying out of current catalogs, sometimes with the help of salespeople. Most buyers have shelves full of suppliers' catalogs for this purpose.
>
> **Blanket orders.** An ongoing but varying need for an item with class B annual volume may call for a blanket-order contract with a supplier. The blanket order covers a given time period, and deliveries are arranged by sending a simple release notice to the supplier. Price and other matters are covered in the contract.
>
> **Systems contract.** A systems contract is similar to a blanket order, but it is longer term and more stringently defined. The purchasing department negotiates the systems contract; purchasing then typically monitors, but does not particpate in, ordering. The contract may name certain responsible employees who may order, by mail, phone, or other means, directly from the supplier.

Class C Items.   Class C or low-cost items are worthy of little attention by purchasing specialists. Buying such items from a supplier on an approved supplier list provides a measure of control. For many items even that is too much control and red tape, and to avoid these, using departments buy out of petty cash funds. Until recently, petty cash buying has been restricted to office employees. Now a few progressive North American companies provide each improvement team with a petty cash fund for purchasing low-cost items that can improve performance.

Performance and Compliance: The Tangibility Factor

When teams buy intangibles (things that cannot be seen, touched, tasted, etc.), they must employ different purchasing practices than when buying tangibles. The distinction arises largely because the quality characteristics of tangibles can be measured (variables) or classified and counted (attributes). An intangible item, however, is sometimes difficult to identify, much less specify. Consequently, it may be hard to hold the provider accountable for the buyer's performance/compliance wishes.

Intangibility is relative (see Exhibit 9–11). At the highly tangible end of the scale, quality is generally determined by objective, measurable output standards. At the highly intangible end of the scale are few, if any, measurable output quality characteristics on which teams may judge compliance with requirements; thus, emphasis shifts to input or procedural factors as surrogate indicators of quality. Specific attention to these two extremes, as well as the intermediate levels of tangibility is warranted:

- Highly tangible items include simple parts like screws, diodes, and switches. Quality is easily measured.
- Commodities (corn, iron ore, bananas, etc.) are tangible but some of their properties are costly to measure. These may require a certain amount of subjective eyeball judgments to grade quality, thus moving from variables into attributes.
- Simple finished goods are less tangible than commodities. Books, furniture, and fabrics, for example, have several measurable physical properties, but visual inspection for scratches, flaws, and so on, may be more important. Again, buyers mix attributes assessment and variables assessment.
- Complex finished goods (autos, ships, mobile homes) have thousands of measurable physical properties of *form* (e.g., dimensions) and *function* (such as turning radius and speed). Nevertheless, partly subjective judgments of effectiveness (how well a destroyer protects the fleet, or a mobile home keeps the elements out) are also important. For complex goods aimed at consumer markets, even more subjective judgments—about style, comfort, and even status—come into play.
- Designs for tangible goods, such as those rendered by architects and engineers, are harder to judge until the end result (the tangible good itself) becomes reality. If a bridge caves in or a door handle keeps breaking off, we can (in hindsight) judge the design to be bad. The engineer might even be liable for damages. Perhaps the best *up-front* help for buyers of these items is design expertise on the buying team.

EXHIBIT 9–11

Tangibility of Purchased Goods

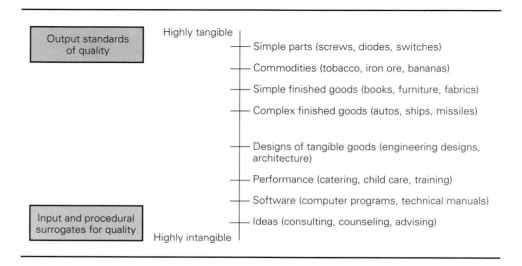

- Contracting for performance is on the upswing; catering, child care, and employee training are examples. Enterprising college students capitalize on the trend by starting part-time businesses to provide janitorial, yard care, computer dating, and a variety of other services. The end products or outputs are good food, well-adjusted children, requalified employees, clean floors, weed-free lawns, and well-matched dating couples. It is difficult to write standards for those outputs into a contract. Consequently, there is growing use of measures of compliance such as mean number of customer complaints and opinion polling involving customers, experts, or impartial panels using some form of Likert scale (a rating scale from 1 to 5, 1 to 7, etc.).

- Software (computer programs, technical or training manuals, operating instruction booklets, etc.) is slightly more intangible. Buyers of these items must distinguish between the quality of the item specified, a television set, for example, and the quality of the software (operating instructions manual) being purchased. A benchmark-class health care package may not impress employees because the benefits description booklet is poor. Buyers may set contract limits such as number of pages or lines of code, but these hardly measure quality, and the supplier is likely to receive full pay (even for a shoddy job) just by meeting those limits.

- Highly intangible items, at the bottom of Exhibit 9–11, have no physically measurable properties. Therefore, purchase contracts may be based on input and procedural factors. In a contract with a consultant, input factors may include specifying level of education and years of experience of the consultants sent out on the job; procedural factors may include number of people to be interviewed and number of pages on the final consultant's report. Those do not define the quality of the consultant's services, but they are often treated as surrogates for output quality.

We can conclude that the most serious measurement and compliance assessment problems occur when buying performance, software, and ideas—items at the intangible end of the scale. Buying from certified suppliers, or at least from those with good reputations, helps. But performance service providers tend to come and go rather than stay and build clientele and reputation. Software firms and consulting firms are somewhat more stable. Ironically, poor software or consulting is not notably destructive to firms' reputations. The reason is that dissatisfied customers may not admit their displeasure (1) because of the risk of defamation suits (bad quality is difficult to prove) and (2) because dissatisfaction would be an admission of having wasted time and money on poor software or consulting services.

On occasion, however, service providers' failure to perform is publicly recognized, especially when those providers charge stiff fees for their failure. An example is the attempted leveraged buyout of UAL Corp. (United Air Lines' parent) that fell through on October 13, 1989. Already reeling from plummeted stock values, UAL shareholders nevertheless received a bill for $58.7 million for professional services rendered by the lawyers and bankers hired to complete the deal. Irked by this high price for failure, shareholders and other observers criticized the banks and law firms involved and questioned the wisdom of the UAL Corp. board for its purchase of the services.[15] Even large corporations can have problems in buying service performance.

Public and corporate officials rely increasingly on consultants to help them with sticky decisions. But the inability to write tough contracts leaves the officials at the consultants' mercy. Fortunately, most consultants are professionally dedicated and motivated to maintain self-respect. Still, contracting for intangibles is a challenge for buyers, one that permeates all organizational transformations. Clearly, trust, openness, and a few good suppliers are key to meeting the purchasing challenge.

Value Analysis

value analysis (VA)
Team analysis of existing product design specifications with the aim of improving value; developed in the purchasing department of General Electric in 1947.

Purchasing means spending money. But purchasing professionals also may become involved in projects that offer long-term substantial savings (making money) for their company. Value analysis projects are of this type.

In large organizations, file cabinets in purchasing and design may be filled with specs developed years ago. New technology outdates some of the old specifications. Each time such items are reordered, the obsolescence becomes more apparent and purchasing takes the heat for not "buying modern." It is no surprise that VA was developed and promoted by purchasing people. As engineers got more involved, the concepts were extended to include new designs as well as old specs.

In some companies and in the federal government, engineers conduct the analysis, calling it **value engineering (VE).** While value analysis is sometimes applied to services, it is mostly associated with goods, especially where material costs and usage rates are high.

The VA step-by-step procedure has been adopted worldwide. The steps are a variation of the scientific method:

1. *Select product.* Select a product that is ripe for improvement.

2. *Gather information.* The team coordinator collects drawings, costs, scrap rates, forecasts, operations sheets, and so forth, before the team first meets. Team members provide whatever information they have.

3. *Define function.* The team, which sometimes includes the customer, meets and defines each function of the product. A function is defined in two words: a verb and a noun (e.g., "A barrel *contains fluid*."). Only essential functions are included. Next, the team estimates the present cost of each function. That reveals which functions are costing far too much. (Note: Defining functions in this way is unique and sets VA apart from other cost reduction techniques.)

4. *Generate alternatives.* Team members suggest ideas for new and different ways to accomplish the functions (known as brainstorming). Ideas are recorded and later culled to a list of manageable size.

5. *Evaluate alternatives.* The team evaluates alternatives based on feasibility, cost, and other factors, which cuts the list to one (or a few) good ideas.

6. *Present proposals.* Refine the final alternatives and present them to a management committee as change proposals.

7. *Implement plan.* Translate the approved change proposal into an engineering change order (ECO) and put it into effect.

In Example 9–2, the description of a real VA study helps show how the procedure works.[16]

EXAMPLE 9–2:   VALUE ANALYSIS OF PRE-PRINTED QUOTATION BINDERS

The marketing manager had a problem involving the binders used by her salespeople in making customer quotations: The commercial printer that had been producing the binders notified her that because of increased costs, they would have to charge her $1.75 each instead of $1.25. She mentioned the problem to the value analysis team member from her department.

That afternoon at the VA team meeting, the marketing representative commented on the increase. The team, seeing the effects that the 40-percent price increase would have on the cost of the multitude of quotations sent out by that company, decided to look into the matter.

First, they determined the functions of the binder: "provide advertising," "provide appearance," and "provide protection." Next, they asked some of the salespeople to participate in a VA study. Their task would be to generate creative ideas on different ways of accomplishing the three functions. One of the salespeople noted that the present binders were so thick that when received by customers, clerical assistants removed the quotation materials from the binders so they wouldn't take up so much space in their files; he had seen this done on several occasions. With this information, the team asked the question, Is the binder made by the right process, given the quantities used?

A team member from industrial engineering commented that his department had just purchased some simple binders to cover their master routing sheets. They were a clear plastic folder into which the sheets were inserted; then, a long, plastic clip the length of the folder "zipped" the folder closed on one side to hold the papers in place. The folders costs only $0.10 each.

Following up on this idea, the team obtained a copy of a customer quotation set and tried it out on one of the plastic folders. They found that the folder not only took care of the function, "provide protection", but it also accomplished the function "provide advertising" since the company letterhead showed through the clear plastic, and the function "provide appearance" since the folder looked better than the old binder. The team showed the folder to the marketing manager, who realized that the clear plastic jacket not only solved her cost problem but also was thin enough that it would not be removed by the customer, thus maintaining the appearance and protection of the quotation materials.

Source: Arthur E. Mudge, *Innovative Change: 101 Case Histories*, (Pittsburgh, Penn.: J. Pohl Associates, 1989), p. 68.

Impressed by the results of VA and VE in private industry, the Department of Defense issued VE regulations applicable to all DOD contracts costing more than $100,000. In 1964, the American Ordnance Association conducted a survey that randomly sampled 124 successful VE changes in the DOD.[17] The survey report showed not only impressive cost savings but also, in many cases, collateral gains in the areas of reliability, maintainablity, producibility, human factors, parts availability, production lead time, quality, weight, logistics, performance, and packaging. The DOD then implemented a formula for sharing VE savings (usually 20 percent) with contractors; that gave the contractors' VE teams added incentive to squeeze savings out of the design specifications.

An informal method of value analysis has recently come into use. In a JIT plant a problem might arise that threatens to stop production. That summons a buyer or engineer to the shop floor; a foreman and perhaps an operator will join in the problem analysis. Blueprints may be marked up and taken immediately to the inside or outside maker of the parts that are causing the problem.

Conducting value analysis in that way—on the fly—requires that blueprints and design specs not be too limiting. Design engineers traditionally have tried to specify

$\mathscr{P}$RINCIPLE 3:

Achieve team
involvement in
implementation of
change.

every dimension, type of material, finish, and so on, which greatly limits options for producing the item. The nonrestrictive specs concept aims at giving the maker latitude over nonessential design attributes so that easy, cheap ways of making the part may be searched for and easily changed when someone sees a better way.

The purist might say that making design decisions on the floor should not be called value analysis because the formal steps (defining functions, generating alternatives, etc.) are bypassed. While that is true, the less formal approach has the advantage of giving more attention to how product design affects producibility, a key element in overall product cost. Also, producibility is a vital concern in just-in-time production in which a production problem can starve later production stages of parts and bring operations to a halt.

Summary

Order fulfillment consists of up to seven steps, depending on whether the sale or order is on-demand or scheduled, service or goods. The seven steps are as follows: 1. the demand or sale; 2. order entry; 3. order positioning (scheduling); 4. order promise; 5. inventory planning; 6. purchasing; and 7. service or delivery. Every step has its own internal processing sequence. Teaming across the entire sequence can greatly reduce delays and costs.

Step 6, purchasing, is strategic in view of the trend toward supplier partnerships and the large potential for cost reduction: Purchased items typically make up over 80 percent of retailers' and wholesalers' expenses and about two-thirds of the final cost of manufactured goods.

Traditionally, purchasing has operated by commodity groups, with each purchasing agent responsible for one or a few commodities. Relationships between buyer and supplier have often been adversarial and standoffish. The supplier came to be viewed as a black box, whose internal workings could only be surmised. Some buyers attempted to probe the black boxes through plant visits and other modes of inquiry, but the majority accepted the adversarial relationship as the norm.

Disappointment with supplier performance, such as late deliveries, poor quality, and incorrect quantities, kept purchasing professionals busy searching for and switching to new suppliers. Suppliers had little commitment to do their best, sensing lack of support from customers. Each new prospective supplier created necessary but time-consuming supplier evaluation procedures, and new startup costs and problems.

Supplier partnership programs have come into existence to deal with these issues. Characteristics of the partnership relationship include longer contracts, more exclusivity in agreements, fewer (but better) suppliers, lower prices, quality at the (supplier) source, supplier-centered design, frequent delivery of small lots, less burdensome order conveyance and documentation, dependably quick transport, delivery to point of consumption (rather than to a receiving inspection), and mutual openness. Visits between buyer and supplier help maintain the open relationship, and supplier certification raises the confidence level.

In recent years, many companies have been making outsourcing a strategic initiative. The aims are to cut costs and to turn over provisioning of non-core items to outside experts. The contrary strategy, backward integration, still makes sense under certain restrictive conditions. The classical make-or-buy break-even model can provide assistance in this decision. Simplifying assumptions make this model less attractive for complex decisions but suitable for relatively low-impact items.

Risk of obsolescence is one concern in the make-or-buy decision. Standardization of product and service elements offer some protection agains sudden obsolesence. More important, standard items cut many costs. Several parts or features brought together in one unit constitute a module. Buying modules rather than loose parts can greatly reduce the purchasing workload and complex logistics, as well as strengthen the suppliers who assume modular responsibilities. Buying standard and modular items works best when a relatively small number of items can be combined into a wide variety of end products—at the last minute, just in time to fill a need.

Purchasing procedures depend on what is being bought. The ABC method of classifying materials uses annual dollar volume to assign items to one of three classes. High-valued (class A) items are purchased and controlled with more care than medium-valued (class B) items, which in turn are managed more closely than low-valued (class C) goods.

Purchasing intangibles, such as ideas and services, presents special problems for buyers because the quality of intangibles is difficult to measure. Often the buyer is at the mercy of the seller, and the seller's professionalism and self-respect are the only guarantees for quality.

Value analysis is a procedure that purchasers developed to meet materials needs (functions) with lower-cost materials and designs. Value engineering (VE) emerged as engineers began to influence value-analysis efforts. VE has received federal government support in the form of higher profits for contractors able to lower costs through VE studies of governemnt specifications.

Solved Problem

Consider the following list of parts, their unit costs, and annual requirements:

Part Number	Unit Cost	Annual Demand
M2	$ 20.00	120
A5	2.00	155,000
A7	8,000.00	13
L8	950.00	6
L4	0.30	7,000
A6	10.00	9,400
M9	6,000.00	70
Q2	400.00	240
Z1	0.50	200

Compute the annual value and percentage of total value for each part. Arrange the nine parts into ABC categories. Plot cumulative percentages in order from the greatest- to least-valued part.

First, we compute the annual value for each part, obtain the total annual value of materials, and derive the required percentages, which are shown in the next table (below Exhibit 9–12).

Solution

EXHIBIT 9-12

Cumulative Percentage of Total Annual Inventory Value

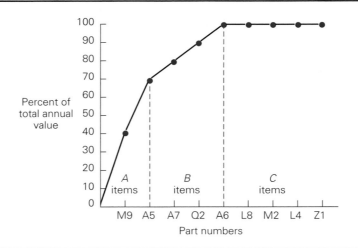

Part Number	Annual Value	Percentage of Total	Cumulative Percentage
M9	$ 420,000	40.61%	40.61%
A5	310,000	29.97	70.58
A7	104,000	10.06	80.64
Q2	96,000	9.28	89.92
A6	94,000	9.09	99.01
L8	5,700	0.55	99.56
M2	2,400	0.23	99.79
L4	2,100	0.20	99.99
Z1	100	0.01	100.00
Sum = $1,034,300			

We see that two parts, M9 and A5, account for over 70 percent of the total annual materials value and are likely candidates for treatment as A parts. We might select the next three parts, A7, Q2, and A6, as our class Bs. The remaining items, L8, M2, L4, and Z1, would be the C items. The plot is shown in Exhibit 9–12.

Review Questions

1. Under what conditions does the order-fulfillment sequence include purchasing, and when does it not include it?
2. Contrast the black-box and the probing-buyer approaches to purchasing.
3. How has team-based purchasing affected the role of the purchasing professional?
4. What is the adversarial approach to purchasing?
5. What principle of OM applies to supplier partnerships?
6. How does supplier partnership affect quality and cost?
7. How does the partnership approach affect freight and information handling?
8. How do supplier certification and approval programs fit into modern purchasing?

9. Why are many companies interested in outsourcing?

10. Under what conditions would classical make-or-buy analysis be appropriate?

11. How does standardization simplify purchasing?

12. How can an assembly plant choking on too many parts obtain help from its suppliers?

13. What information is needed to do ABC analysis?

14. What are MRO items, and how should they be purchased?

15. Identify ways that buying intangibles differs from buying tangibles.

16. Compare value analysis "on the fly" with formal VA.

Exercises

1. Give three real examples of your participation in the order-fulfillment sequence. Make one of the examples a spur-of-the moment service, one a scheduled service, and one an item you purchased.

2. The chapter discussion on partnership versus adversarial buyer–supplier relationships examines 12 dimensions on which the relationship might be rated. A number of organizational types are listed below. For each type, identify the relationship's most crucial dimensions. Explain your reasoning.
   a. Aerospace company that is highly project oriented.
   b. Chemical company.
   c. Foundry.
   d. Major accounting firm.
   e. U.S. Navy shipyard.
   f. Private shipyard faced with severe cost problems.
   g. Machine tool manufacturer.
   h. Retail hardware store.
   i. Integrated circuit manufacturer.
   j. Hairstyling salon.

3. You would like to negotiate a long-term (two-year), exclusive contract to sell your automobile-repair services to a city government. The city's purchasing agent believes that such a contract would not be in the city's best interests because "free competition wouldn't get a chance to work." Prepare a rebuttal, giving specific ways in which the city might benefit from a contract with you.

4. John Revere, operations director at CalComp, Inc., a producer of graphics peripheral products, "was given an ultimatum: Shape up the factory or it would be shipped to Singapore" (Bruce C. P. Rayner, "Made in America: CalComp plots a World-Class Future," *Electronic Business*, August 1, 1988, pp. 28–32). Among Revere's actions to preserve U.S. operations was his challenge to the team designing the new 1023 model pen plotter: Design it with no more than 20 fasteners (screws, bolts, etc.) bought from no more than 20 suppliers located no farther than 20 miles from the CalComp facility in Anaheim, California.

   How would achievement of these three objectives keep production in Anaheim? Cite concepts from the chapter in your answer.

5. David N. Burt reports ("Managing Suppliers up to Speed," *Harvard Business Review*, July–August 1989, pp. 127–35) that Xerox's copier division was in a cost squeeze and losing market share in the 1970s. Corrective actions included reducing its supplier base from 5,000 to 400 companies. Further, "it trained

suppliers in statistical quality control (SQC), just-in-time (JIT) manufacturing, and total quality commitment (TQC). Under a program of continuous improvement, it included suppliers in the design of new products, often substituting performance specifications for blueprints in the expectation that suppliers should design final parts themselves."

Which of the 12 characteristics of supplier partnership given in the chapter was Xerox following in these actions? Explain.

6. A home remodeling contractor presently subcontracts concete work, mainly pouring concrete patios. The patios cost an average of $400 each. If the remodeling company were to do the patios itself, there would be an initial outlay of $8,000 for a concrete mixer, wheelbarrows, and so forth, but the cost per patio for labor, materials, and extras would drop to $200.
   a. What is the break-even volume?
   b. Draw and fully label the break-even graph.

7. Othello Corporation has a company uniform that employees may wear if they choose. Othello spends $60 for each new uniform. If Othello made its own uniforms, the variable cost (labor, materials, etc.) would be only $50 each, but it would have to lease a sewing machine for $200 per year.
   a. What number of uniforms per year would be required to break even on the $200 lease cost for the machine?
   b. If 15 new uniforms per year is the projected need, is it better to make or buy uniforms? Explain.
   c. Draw and fully label the break-even graph.

8. A large corporation is considering establishing its own travel department, which would earn commissions on airline tickets. The current cost of airline tickets averages $122 per trip. With an internal travel department earning commissions, it is estimated that the ticket cost would drop to $105 per trip. The salaries and expenses of the travel department would come to $40,000 per year.

   What number of tickets per year would the corporation need to process in order to break even on writing its own tickets instead of buying tickets from an outside agency? If the corporation projects 2,000 trips per year, should it buy or make? Why?

9. Following are eight items in a firm's inventory. Devise an ABC classification scheme for the items. Show which class each item fits into.

Item	Unit Cost	Annual Demand
A	$ 1.35	6,200
B	53.00	900
C	5.20	50
D	92.00	120
E	800.00	2
F	0.25	5,000
G	9,000.00	5
H	15.00	18,000

10. Several examples of uses of ABC inventory classification were discussed in the chapter. Suggest four more uses and discuss their value.

11. Arrange the following six item numbers into logical A, B, and C classes (put at least one item into each class):

Item Number	Quantity Demanded Last Year	Unit Price
24	2	$ 800
8	10	15,000
37	1,000	0.05
92	3	12
14	80	50
35	20	1.25

12. Arrange the following five item numbers into logical A, B, and C classes (put at least one item into each class):

Item Number	Quantity Demanded Last Year	Unit Cost
109	6	$1,000
083	400	0.25
062	10	10
122	1	280
030	10,000	3

13. Danielle Weatherby is director of purchasing at Spark-o-Mation. Her company, a producer of sophisticated control and security systems, has had a successful supplier certification program in place for six years; Danielle herself laid much of the groundwork for the program. She attended several good seminars, benchmarked other supplier certification programs, and ensured that her own associates, as well as prospective suppliers, were well trained and informed as the program evolved.

    Spark-o-Mation's supplier base has been reduced to approximately 20 percent of its size since Danielle came on board, and the current suppliers are treated as partners. They've earned it; JIT delivery to the point-of-use is in place, receiving inspection at Spark-o-Mation is a thing of the past, EDI has reduced the paperwork, and suppliers have active roles in Spark-o-Mation's design efforts. Danielle feels that further reduction in the supplier base would be detrimental to Spark-o-Mation's performance.

    She reads a memo she just received:

    Memo to all Department Heads:

    As you know, earnings have been flat for three quarters, and last quarter's orders were disappointing. Several large customers cite problems with the quality and timely delivery of our product, and some are threatening to go elsewhere for their control systems. I want you all to conduct a thorough (internal) audit of your departmental operations with an eye for change. Let's get together next Tuesday at 8:00 A.M.

    Thanks,
    Mark Smith
    VP, Operations

Danielle has several thoughts:

- Clearly, Mark needs help from all of us; I must be a team player on this one.
- We've already done so much in purchasing. Can we be expected to improve on an already great system?
- I know we're getting good materials; the quality problems must be occurring elsewhere. How can I say that without pointing the finger?
- We get great delivery, but we can't give it. I wonder why?

How should Danielle respond?

14. Adam Pendleton is director of purchasing for THIS Company. THIS (The Healthcare Industry Supply) provides a broad line of MRO items to hospitals and clinics in several western, Rocky Mountain, and plains states and in the western provinces of Canada. One of the best performing of those items is uniforms. THIS offers surgical gowns and laboratory coats in many styles and colors as well as uniforms for nurses, technicians, orderlies, cafeteria employees, and so forth. THIS buys almost all of its uniforms directly from an apparel manufacturer with two plants located in two southeastern states. In both cases, the plant is the town's major employer.

THIS accounts for approximately 35 percent of the apparel manufacturer's sales. Over the years, THIS has lived with slow but steady price increases. Delivery from the supplier has been adequate, but there is room for improvement. Quality is average at best; often shipments have to be returned for some correction of sizing, color, special insignia, or other mistake.

Already today, Adam has had to make two calls to the supplier to straighten out details in orders. The uniform supplier stays in his mind as he reads a memo he just received:

> Adam,
>
> As you know, everyone is screaming about health care costs; our customers are getting hammered to keep their costs down, and the buck is being passed back to us. We've simply got to do two things: First, get our own costs down so we can be more price competitive; second, build up a better quality image. Maybe I've got those two reversed, but you get the idea. I've been wondering about getting rid of some of our poorer suppliers; I think there are better and cheaper sources out there. Any ideas? We can't sit on this; I'd like to get together with you early Tuesday morning if possible.
>
> Thanks,
> Nell Jones
> Executive VP

As Adam mulls over Jones's note, several thoughts come to mind:

- Clearly, Nell needs help and is counting on me to play a key role in this matter.
- The supplier certification program that I tried to implement three years ago—with little support from upper management—would have made things easier now.
- If changing suppliers is the answer, the uniform supplier ought to be among the first to go.

How should Adam respond?

15. The purchasing department at OK Industries uses different buying techniques for various items bought. What are two appropriate buying techniques for each of the following items?
    a. Bearings and seals for the factory machinery.
    b. Gear assemblies bought as direct materials in quantities of 8,000 per year.
    c. A special bottle of drafting ink for the company's one draftperson.
    d. Nails used in the maintenance department.

16. Several types of organizations are listed below, each with different kinds of purchases to make:

Fashions (apparel)	Car rental company
Liquor wholesaler	Glass manufacturer
City government	Plastics manufacturer
Major home appliance manufacturer	Computer manufacturer
Electric power company	Food wholesaler
Furniture manufacturer	Shipbuilder
Construction contractor	Aerospace company

    a. Discuss some key purchasing techniques that would be useful for four of the organization types.

    b. Which types of organizations on the list are most likely to be heavily involved in buying intangibles? Explain.

    c. Which types of organizations on the list are more likely to use an approved supplier list? Bid solicitation based on specifications? Blanket orders? Explain.

    d. Which types of organizations on the list are most likely to use value analysis? Explain.

17. Some years ago, the public school system in Gary, Indiana, contracted with a company to run the Gary schools. The contract featured incentive payments for raising scores on standardized math and verbal tests. What weaknesses do you suppose were present in this contract? Discuss.

18. Value analysis often begins by selecting VA projects from old specifications found in the design engineering files. How is value analysis modified in companies using the just-in-time production system? Why?

19. Following is a list of products to be analyzed by value analysis:

Classroom desk	Bookends	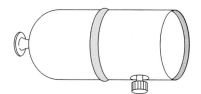
Mousetrap	Electric fan	
Backpack-style book toter	Bike handlebars	
Fireplace grate	Bike lock	
Coaster on which to set drinks	Lamp part shown at right	

    a. Select any four of the above and define their function or functions in two words as discussed in the chapter.

    b. Why is function definition an early and precisely done step in value analysis/value engineering? Explain what this step accomplishes, using some of your examples from (a).

20. Jane A. Doe has just moved to another city and taken a job with a company that manufactures lawn sprinklers, which was exactly the kind of company she had worked for in her prior city of residence. She finds that her new company has three or four times as many different part numbers going into essentially the same models of sprinkler. Is this good or bad? Discuss.

21. Contact the purchasing department of a service organization in your area. Conduct an interview to determine the level of interest and action on an outsourcing strategy. Evaluate the correctness of the organization's outsourcing activity.

THE OFFICE GOES KANBAN AT BOEING

The Boeing Commercial Airplane Company had reorganized. Far-flung functional departments were consolidated into "reponsibility centers"—units that could take full responsibility for a family of key airplane components or modules. One of the new units is the Door Responsibility Center, in Renton, Washington, which specializes in airplane doors and hatches.

In creating the Door Center, five support offices were consolidated. The office staffs brought all their supplies with them. Quantities of many items were clearly excessive. At the same time as the consolidation was taking place, trainer Bob Wiebe was conducting training sessions for the staff. For example, the materials group was learning about kanban. Annette Ludwig, a member of the group, saw an opportunity. She would develop a kanban system for the office supplies. Use of the system would provide hands-on lessons in how kanban works, as well as coping with the overstocks.

Ludwig's system features a wall-mounted location listing for all the supplies, minimum stock quantities, special containers, velcro-backed laminated kanban tags, a fabric MST (minimum stock tag) board, use of stick-on dots to indicate items on order, and an order desk with a designated order clerk, Lynn Thoma. Three types of supplies—small items, large paper items, and forms—are stored in separate cabinets. Three cabinets are for small items (down from nine cabinets required just after consolidation of the offices), one is for large paper-stock items, and one is for forms. Exhibit CS9–1 shows the layout of the office area where the kanban system operates.

Ludwig found electrical connector boxes from the shop that were just right to hold the many small items—pens, Post-Its, paper clips, highlighters, tape, and so on. Twelve of the boxes fit neatly into one shelf in a four-drawer cabinet. In Exhibit CS9–2, the photo on the left shows one of the drawers. The photo on the right shows a locator map affixed to one of the file drawers; it includes a listing of the rules, keys description of the 12 boxed items to their box locations, and states that a "green dot indicates item is currently on order."

The minimum quantity for an item is contained in a plastic bag, along with its blue kanban tag—called an MST tag. The bag goes at the bottom of the box, which is usually covered up by unbagged stock. For example, a bag might hold 12 of a certain pencil, and a few dozen of that pencil might cover it up. The rules are, whoever uses up the loose stock and breaks into the bag must place the blue MST tag on the MST board.

Exhibit CS9–3 shows two additional visual devices that help make the system work:

1. A one-page master location listing.
2. A replica of one of the MST tags, which measure 2 by 3 3/4 inches. The tag notes the item name (in this case, a 3×3 Post-It), ordering number, minimum ordering quantity (which once was 12 packages, then 5, and now 1), ordering unit (package of 12), cabinet location, page number (not used), and instructions for use.

In the cabinets holding stationery, tablets, forms, and similar bulky items, the small MST tags would be hard to spot. For this reason, Ludwig developed a larger velcro-backed tag, about 5 by 10 inches. In restocking an item, the responsible materials management associate

---

Case topics: Kanban for office supplies; order fulfillment; visual replenishment; containerization; training.

Note: Since the main kanban discussion is in Chapter 10, study of this case may be deferred until then. Alternatively, in using the case here, its purpose is to illustrate a simple, effective approach to order fulfillment as well as serving as an advance introduction to kanban.

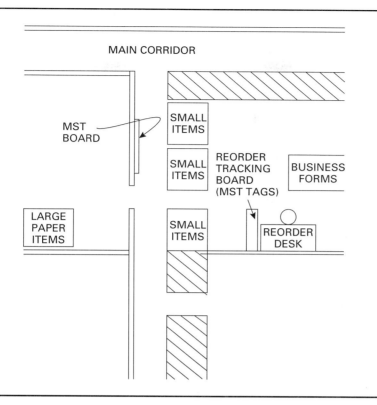

MAIN CORRIDOR

MST BOARD

SMALL ITEMS

SMALL ITEMS

REORDER TRACKING BOARD (MST TAGS)

BUSINESS FORMS

LARGE PAPER ITEMS

SMALL ITEMS

REORDER DESK

EXHIBIT CS9–1

Layout, Support-Staff Offices— Boeing Door Responsibility Center

---

EXHIBIT CS9–2   **Four-Drawer Kanban File Cabinet**

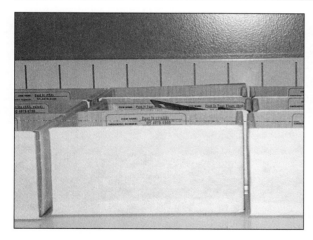

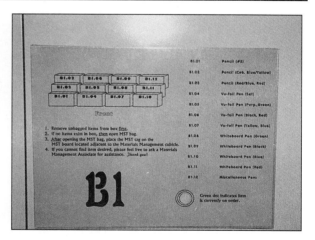

Twelve kanban boxes in one file cabinet
Source: Photos Courtesy of Boeing.

Locator map and rules of kanban sysem affixed to file drawer (usually Lynn Thoma) places the tag at the minimum quantity toward the bottom of the pile. When the user reaches the tag, the usual rule applies: Hang the tag on the MST board. The left photo in Exhibit CS9–4 shows two tags velcroed to the board. The right photo shows a stationery directory on a board next to the MST board.

At least daily, someone collects the tags that have found their way to the MST board. Thoma, at the ordering desk, uses the tags to reorder, which includes writing the order number and date on the tags. The lamination on the tags offers a surface on which to write, using an erasable marking pen.

Word about the Door Center's office kanban system has spread. Many other Boeing units have come to see it and to receive Ludwig's startup kit. As of this writing, about 15 other Boeing office support units have adopted the same system.

Questions

Case Questions

1. Construct a flow chart of the steps in the Door Center's replenishment system. Relate your flow chart to the order-fulfillment sequence shown in Exhibit 9–1.

2. What are the common and uncommon benefits/uses of this kanban system?

EXHIBIT CS9–3   Office Kanban Aids

Location	Container Content	Category
C2.06	ADDRESS LABEL (Inter-plant)	LABEL
C3.04	BINDER (Boeing blue)	BINDER
B2.09	BINDER CLIPS (Large)	CLIPS/CLAMPS
B2.08	BINDER CLIPS (Medium)	CLIPS/CLAMPS
A4.01	BINDERs (1″)	BINDER
B4.01	BINDERs (3″)	BINDER
B3.03	CLIPS	CLIPS
A2.11	CORRECTION DISPENSER (1/6″, 1/3″)	CORRECTION
A2.10	CORRECTION REFILLS (1/6″, 1/3″)	CORRECTION
A2.12	CORRECTION TAPE (1/6″, 1/3″)	CORRECTION
A2.08	DRYLINER DISPENSER (Permanent, Temporary)	ADHESIVE
A2.09	DRYLINER REFILLS (Permanent, Temporary)	ADHESIVE
C2.08	ENVELOPE (Airborne Express)	ENVELOPE
C2.07	ENVELOPE (Boeing)	ENVELOPE
C2.04	ENVELOPE (Business)	ENVELOPE
C2.03	ENVELOPE (Legal)	ENVELOPE
C3.13	ENVELOPE, 10×14	ENVELOPE
C3.11	ENVELOPE, 14×18 INTER OFFICE	ENVELOPE
C3.12	ENVELOPE, 7×10 BOEING	ENVELOPE
C3.10	ENVELOPE, 8×10	ENVELOPE
A2.01	ERASER, WHITEBOARD	ERASER
A3.05	ERASERS (Pink, Dispenser/Refill, Peel-off)	ERASERS
C3.01	FACSIMILE HEADER	FACSIMILE
B2.11	FASTENERS (Brass, 3/4″)	FASTENERS
B2.10	FASTENERS (Brass, 1¼″)	FASTENERS
C3.06	FOLDER, FILE ("Out")	FOLDER
C3.05	FOLDER, FILE (Manila)	FOLDER
C3.07	FOLDER, FILE (Pos.1)	FOLDER

Master location listing (reduced size)

ITEM NAME: Post-It (3X3)
ORDERING NUMBER: D2-4079-0600
MIN. ORDERING QTY: ~~12~~ ~~5~~ 1
ORDERING U/M: (12/pkg)
CABINET #: A1.01   **PAGE #:**   ?

Please place this tag on the MST board adjacent to the Mat'l Mgmt. group upon opening of the Minimum Stock Bag.

MST tag (reduced size)

Exhibit CS9–4   MST Board and Stationery Directory

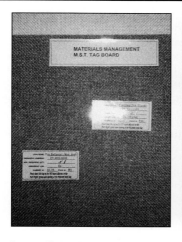

Source: Photos Courtesy of Boeing

For Further Reference

Books

Ansari, A., and B. Modarress. *Just in Time Purchasing.* New York: The Free Press, 1990 (TS156.A56).

Bhote, Kehi R. *Strategic Supply Management: a Blueprint for Revitalizing the Manufacturer–Supplier Partnership.* New York: AMACOM, 1989 (HD 39.5.B488).

Dobler, Donald W. *Purchasing and Materials Management: Text and Cases.* 5th ed. New York: McGraw-Hill, 1990 (HD39.5.D62).

Fearon, H. E.; K. H. Killen; and D. W. Dobler. *The Purchasing Handbook,* New York: McGraw-Hill, 1992.

Graw, LeRoy, and Deidre M. Maples. *Service Purchasing: What Every Buyer Should Know.* New York: Van Nostrand Reinhold, 1994.

Leenders, M. R.; H. E. Fearon; and W. B. England. *Purchasing and Materials Management.* 10th ed. Burr Ridge, Ill.: Richard D. Irwin, 1992.

Lewis, Jordon D. *The Connected Corporation: How Leading Companies Win through Customer–Supplier Alliances.* New York: The Free Press, 1995.

Mudge, Arthur E. *Value Engineering: a Systematic Approach.* Reprint ed. Pittsburgh, Penn.: J. Pohl Associates, 1989.

Zenz, Gary J. *Purchasing and Management of Materials.* 7th ed. New York: John Wiley & Sons, 1993 (HD39.5.W47).

Periodicals/Societies

Journal of Purchasing and Materials Management (National Association of Purchasing Management).

Production and Inventory Management (American Production and Inventory Control Society).

Purchasing.

Supplement

PURCHASING AT FORD MOTOR COMPANY: THE TOTAL QUALITY EXCELLENCE (TQE) PROGRAM

Ford Motor Company, like many other large companies, has an active program of supplier selection and evaluation. Ford people refer to their supply-base management program by the name of the award that top-level suppliers receive: Total Quality Excellence (TQE). The roots of TQE lie in Ford's quality-oriented Q1 supplier certification program.

The Q1 Supplier Certification Program

Ford started the Q1 program in 1981 to improve the quality of materials from outside suppliers. In the mid–1980s, Q1 was extended to internal (captive) suppliers and later to Ford's assembly plants. In 1989, Ford made Q1 certification a prerequisite for all suppliers. Under Q1, suppliers are required to have certain quality-related programs in place (e.g., incoming quality, SPC, and process capability) and to assist Ford with advanced quality planning and manufacturing feasibility studies. Though giving Q1 some credit for Ford's success during the 1980s, Ford planners realized the limitations of a program that focused solely on quality, and in 1987 the TQE program was launched. Exhibit S9–1 shows the evolution of both Q1 and TQE.

The Continuing Improvement Mandate

TQE requires suppliers to build on Q1 certification by demonstrating continuous improvement. Ford evaluation teams assess supplier improvements in four areas: (1) product quality; (2) engineering; (3) delivery; and (4) commercial performance. The evaluations place suppliers into one of three categories of excellence: short term, potential long term, and preferred long term.

Getting to Know Suppliers

TQE's basic documents are a *TQE Orientation Guide* and a *TQE Assessment Manual.* These documents mandate involvement by executives, managers, and employees in creating a culture of improvement across multiple dimensions, including leadership, information analysis, strategic quality planning, human-resources utilization, quality assurance of products and services, quality results, and customer satisfaction.

   Human-resources utilization, for example, covers all four areas of evaluation. Ford expects suppliers to

- Utilize cross-functional teams, employee involvement concepts, and improvement tools such as team-driven problem solving and the plan-do-check-act approach.

- Provide employees with opportunities for education and training in quality and other disciplines throughout their careers.

EXHIBIT S9–1

Ford's Supplier Certification Program Evolution

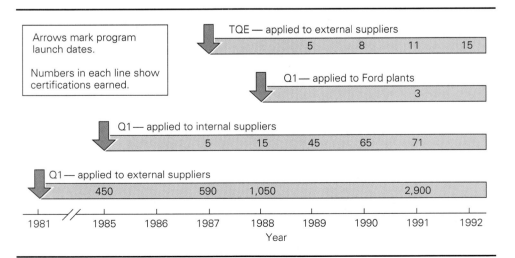

Source: Adapted from James Welch, Laddie Cook, and Joseph Blackburn, "The Bridge to Competitiveness: Building Supplier–Customer Linkages," *Target,* November–December 1992, pp. 17–29.

- Show commitment to health and safety, including ergonomically designed man/machine interfaces and work environments.

In commercial performance, Ford wants to know about a supplier's worldwide cost competitiveness, degree of support, and responsiveness to various business issues.

Throughout the TQE evaluation process, Ford's purchasing teams are to aggressively probe for partnership potential. The criteria are stiff: In the first five years of TQE, only 15 suppliers had made the grade.

Sources: *Total Quality Excellence Award Program Orientation Guide* (Plymouth, Mich.: Ford Quality Related Publications, 1990); *Total Quality Excellence Assessment Manual* (Plymouth, Mich.: Ford Quality Related Publications, 1990); James Welch, Laddie Cook, and Joseph Blackburn, "The Bridge to Competitiveness: Building Supplier–Customer Linkages," *Target*, November–December 1992, pp. 17–29.

The authors thank Ms. Susan E. Kobet, Manager of Supplier Relations and Quality, Ford Motor Company, for her cooperation and assistance in the preparation of this supplement.

10   TIMING: JIT/KANBAN, MRP, AND RELATED TOPICS

Chapter Outline

"Research has indicated that the most important factor to an air traveler is on-time performance. The industry measures on time [as] whether a flight leaves within 15 minutes of the scheduled departure time and, in fact, even later than that if the reason why it's late relates to bad weather, mechanical difficulties, or congested air traffic.

"But that's not how customers define 'on time.' They think on time means just that, not give or take 15 minutes . . . . So we decided that we were going to start measuring on-time performance by the customer's watch.

"Getting an airplane out on time is quite interesting because it requires a major cross-functional effort: . . . The coordination of the airport, which directs customers to the proper gate; the pilot who flies the plane; the flight attendant who makes sure that all safety requirements are met; the people who load the luggage and cargo; and the caterers who load the food. Both suppliers and employees have to be committed, so teamwork and partnering with suppliers are very important.

"We developed a process on how to count down to flight departures. By using this process, each person . . . involved . . . knows when he or she must complete the work in order for the flight to depart on time.

"Our on-time performance, as measured by the customer's watch, has gone from 57 percent to 74 percent. This includes all departures, whether the reason for the delay was controllable or not. This countdown process has resulted in a savings of about $35 million each year."

Source: Kevin J. Jenkins, president and CEO of Canadian Airlines International, in an interview by Karen Bemowski, "Quality Is Helping Canadian Airlines International Get off the Ground," *Quality Progress*, October 1995, pp. 33–35.

Not many organizations give timing the high priority that Mr. Jenkins and his staff at Canadian Airlines do. We hear too few stories of serious efforts to be quick, to be on time, and to do so invariably. But public transportation companies must publish schedules for their end-stage operations, a flight or cruise for example, thus providing highly visible checks on overall company performance. Even the casual observer can compare actual departure and arrival times with the schedule and determine how well the firm meets its commitments to customers. Such "quick-look" analysis, however, fails to reveal schedules for the hundreds or thousands of support operations—some mentioned in the opening vignette—that must be performed equally "on time" if the trip is to proceed on schedule.

We begin this chapter with a brief look at the broad impact of timing issues; move on to consider newer concepts and practices like kanban and pull-system operations that have widespread applicability for improving timing in both goods production and services delivery; and conclude with a discussion of older concepts more closely associated with inventory timing—material requirements planning, reorder point, and safety stock.

Timing: Another Imperative

All organizations face timing problems not too different from those encountered by Canadian Airlines. Whenever people or materials are late, carefully crafted schedules go awry and the negative effects—increased customer waiting, unplanned downtime, wasteful extra handling of materials and equipment, personnel shuffling, expensive rescheduling actions, and inventory excesses or outages to name a few—ripple up and down supply routes. One slip-up anywhere along the chain—a tardy supplier, perhaps, or a back-office paperwork mixup—and the end result is late delivery of a service or good. Not surprisingly, reports of company efforts to better manage time are appearing from a broad spectrum of industries. (See the Into Practice box, "Turnaround Time at Dun & Bradstreet.")

In Chapter 1, we saw that timing, like quality and cost, is a basic customer demand. On-time performance is one time-related requirement, but customers also want faster response times. Furthermore, they expect consistency—that is, decreased variation in providers' response times. Actually, timing affects most facets of operations management, and thus factors into nearly every chapter of this book. Exhibit 10–1 illustrates some of the more concentrated discussions of timing-related material. The listing in Exhibit 10–1 is not meant to be exhaustive; perhaps it is best viewed as a general statement of the many opportunities that operations managers have to positively affect timing.

In the remainder of this chapter, we focus on tools and techniques. We begin with kanban and pull systems, simple tools that have the power to synchronize multistage operations and eliminate much of the problem of unpredictable completion times.

Kanban and the Pull System

Kanban methodology and the pull-system concept have their roots in the just-in-time family of tools. As discussion and examples in this section illustrate, they are appropriate in both manufacturing and service settings.

Into Practice

Turnaround Time at Dun & Bradstreet

Millions of times a year, companies go to Dun & Bradstreet for information they need about other firms they might want to do business with. In 1991, it was taking Dun & Bradstreet an average of about five days to provide the information a client company requested. Since that beat its own turnaround standard of seven days, Dun & Bradstreet thought it was doing a good job. Customer surveys, however, revealed that though clients were satisfied with accuracy of the research reports and clarity of presentation, they were dissatisfied with turnaround time; often they wanted the reports in no more than three days.

The company launched Operation Clean Slate in a pilot project in its Greensboro, North Carolina, site, one of the largest and most productive of its 71 regional offices. Seven team members, who called

themselves the Greensboro Groundbreakers, went to work. Within two weeks the Groundbreakers had developed dozens of time-saving ideas, which cut turnaround time to three days. The improvements included such changes as eliminating duplicate steps and not allowing offices to build up backlogs of work. Within a year, the team had driven the time down to 1.85 days. After implementing the best ideas in all offices, average turnaround nationwide fell to 2.6 days, with improved quality level and no additional staff or other resources.

Source: Michael E. Berkin, "Dun & Bradstreet Conducts 'Operation Clean Slate,'" *Quality Progress*, November 1993, pp. 105—107.

General Area	Example Topics	Material
Operations strategy	Timing objectives	Ch.2
Meeting general customer requirements	Faster response time On-time delivery Reducing timing variation	Most chapters
Resource reliability	Available time Repair time (down time)	Ch. 4
Forecasting	Lead time Forecast time horizon	Ch. 6
Customer and materials flow	Quick response Materials order timing Queue time limits Customer throughput time	Ch. 8 and 10
Setups and changeovers	Quick-changeover/setup time	Ch. 11
Continuous operations	Cycle time Throughput time Work-content time Takt time	Ch. 13
Job and batch operations	Lead time Queue time Run time Setup/changeover time Inspection time Move/transport time	Ch. 14
Time standards	Elemental time Normal (rated) time Standard time	Ch. 16
Maintenance	PM time	Ch. 17

EXHIBIT 10–1

Timing Issues in Operations

Kanban (Queue Limitation)

Kanban, from the Japanese, literally means card or visible record. An ancient meaning of kanban is, however, shop sign, and Exhibit 10–2 is a kimono shop example. The colorful, artistic shop sign conveyed simple, accurate information about a shop's product or service to passing shoppers in Japanese villages hundreds of years ago. Less artistically, but just as simply and effectively, today's kanban tells a provider what and how much to forward to a customer. And—more important—it tells the provider *when* to act, using visual signals and simple rules.

How does kanban work? Many variations exist, but let's look at classic kanban— a card system. In such a system, kanbans recirculate; any container with parts in it must have a kanban attached. Kanban cards contain such information as item name, stock or part number, quantity in the container, user, provider, and card number.[1]

Exhibit 10–3 illustrates this version of kanban for an item, Part A, that might be a desk drawer going from a desk drawer manufacturing cell (maker) to desk assembly (user). In this example each of three carts holds five desk drawers, and has its own kanban card; the kanbans are numbered 1 of 3, 2 of 3, and 3 of 3. When an assembler takes the first desk drawer from the cart, the card is pulled, to be collected by (or sent to) the desk drawer production associates.

Exhibit 10–2

Japanese Shop Sign (Kanban) for Kimono Shop

Source: Dana Levy, Lea Sneider, and Frank B. Gibney, *Kanban: The Art of the Japanese Shop Sign* (San Francisco: Chronicle Books, 1983), p. 75.

Exhibit 10–3

Card (Kanban) System

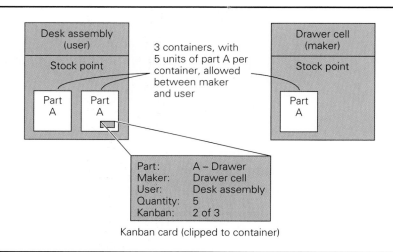

Kanban card (clipped to container)

At the drawer production cell, the card is the signal to act; specifically, it instructs the provider to make five more desk drawers of type A, and make them now. Thus, if the cell makes a family of parts, say, several types of drawers, shelves, and roll-tops, the kanban specifies which to produce. Two key points: (1) The user drives production. Had the desk assembler not needed the drawer, the card would not have been taken from the cart and returned to the drawer-making cell. And at the cell, the rule is (2) No card, no production. Thus, customer demand pulls work along the supply chain—the defining characteristics of the **pull system,** or **pull-mode operations.** We shall say more about pull systems later in this section.

As the desk drawer example illustrates, kanban keeps the provider attuned to customer usage. Thus, kanban is a queue limiter, a device that limits the length of the queue (waiting line) and thus the waiting time of items—or people—waiting

- Classical card kanban: Recirculating containers with detachable cards.
- Labeled containers: Recirculating containers and carts, permanent kanban identifying labels attached.
- Unlabeled containers or kanban squares: Contents of flow path obvious, so no identifying label (card) necessary.
- Timer or warning light or bell: Queue time limitation, instead of quantity limitation.
- Queue limit policy: Prominently displayed, hard-to-ignore queue limit.
- Colored golf balls, poker chips, abacus beads, discs, flags and so on: Queue depletion below queue limit signaled by a colored indicator.
- Electronic: Notification of queue depletion below queue limit via electronic communication.
- Automatic queue limiter: In automated system, notification of queue depletion, below queue limit, via automatic device.

EXHIBIT 10–4

Queue Limiter (Kanban) Variations

for service. Queue limitation replaces lax flow control with discipline. Throughput times, along with variation in throughput times, decrease, as customer satisfaction and competitive position increase. Exhibit 10–4 lists various queue limitation methods, but is not intended to be an exhaustive list. We've discussed classical card kanban; the remaining types listed in the exhibit are considered below.

Labeled Containers.   Here the card is permanently affixed to recirculating kanban containers, carts, dollies, trolleys—a limited number per item. At Harley-Davidson's engine and transmission plant in Milwaukee, nearly all component parts are controlled this way. Kanban for a certain gear, going from a machining cell to transmission assembly, might be set at four recirculating parts boxes (kanban = 4), each holding exactly 20 gears, and each having a plate riveted to it on which the usual kanban information is written. The rule: No box, no production (of that part) at the cell. (Harley had tried detachable kanbans, inserted into a box slot. But the cards got lost, torn, and grease-stained too often.)

Unlabeled Containers or Spaces (Kanban Squares).   Some firms use unlabeled recirculating kanban containers (carts, dollies, trolleys, etc.) or kanban squares (spaces on the floor or a table). An identifying label is unneeded under each of the following conditions:

- The container holds only one (homogeneous) item, such as a certain size gas tank. Exhibit 10–5 illustrates two special containers for defibrillators, made by Physio Control Company. The three-level container—queue limit (kanban) = 3—was devised for one of Physio's products in its first assembly-and-test cell. Associates assembling a similar product in Physio's second cell, seeking an improvement, adopted a one-unit version of the container (queue limit = 1).
- Various (nonhomogeneous) items are flowing through the same process sequence, such as different customer orders through order processing, or successive 10-person groups of tourists on a fixed-sequence guided tour.

Exhibit 10–5   Kanban Containers at Physio Control Company

- The empty square signals the need for production. For example, unlabeled kanban squares are common in electronic assembly plants. Typically, one square is taped off on each table on an assembly line (kanban = 1). Each assembler looks to the square at the next table for the customer's signal—an empty kanban square—that more work is needed. For big units, the kanban square is on the floor, and some kind of lifting/moving apparatus is usually needed for transport to the next process.

Timer or Warning Light or Bell.   Each Seafirst Bank has a clock and a sign, where customers queue up for a teller, that says the bank will pay $5 to anyone who waits more than five minutes for a teller (queue limit = 5 minutes). Since customer arrivals are extremely uneven, Seafirst uses part-time and flexible labor to keep queues below the limit. Some tellers work only the noon rush, some only on Mondays, Fridays, paydays for the area's biggest employer, and so forth. (See further discussion in the Chapter 14 case study, "5 Minutes, $5—Seafirst Bank.")

Queue-Limit Policy.   Ernst Home and Garden stores put up signs above cashier stations proclaiming the Three-Person Promise (queue limit = 3; see Exhibit 10–6). The sign explains that if a fourth person enters a line, an Ernst clerk comes immediately to open another cashier station.

Colored Golf Balls, Poker Chips, and Abacus Beads.   At a Kawasaki engine plant, when a certain part in subassembly is down to its queue limit, the assembler rolls a colored golf ball down a pipe to a machine center, which tells the operator what part to run next. Associates at a Seagate disk drive plant in Minneapolis came up with red and blue poker chips and abacus heads, one row for each product, where red means don't make it (we still have some), and blue means make it (we are down to the queue limit).

Electronic Signal.   Some users convey usage data, or notification of having reached the queue limit, electronically. Bar-code scanning of kanbans can capture the usage. From there, the data goes to a provider process internal to the organiza-

EXHIBIT 10–6

"Three-Person Promise" at Ernst Home and Garden Stores

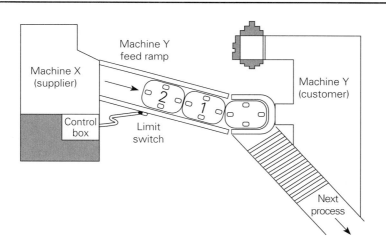

EXHIBIT 10–7

Automated Queue Limitation (Kanban) Example

tion or to an outside supplier. Internal transmission may employ radio frequency signaling or other wireless messaging.[2] External notification goes by fax or electronic data interchange, over phone lines, or by satellite. As noted in Chapter 8, these kinds of external communication are elemental in quick-response partnerships that link retailers, wholesalers, and manufacturers.

Automatic Queue Limiter.   When automated conveyor systems link processes, limit switches governing each feeder machine can keep the queues short before each user machine. Exhibit 10–7 is a schematic illustration. The limit switch, positioned in the conveyor or feed mechanism of Machine Y, limits the queue. When piece 2 slides into a position where it blocks the switch (queue limit = 2), a signal halts Machine X. When Machine Y pulls the next unit forward for processing, the switch is tripped and Machine X gets a signal to make and forward another piece.

At the other extreme from electronic and automated signaling, the notification could be just a shout to a provider at a nearby process. It doesn't matter how the message is conveyed. What is important is that the kanban system be disciplined: Send no more parts, or clients, until the current queue is below the limit.

Queue Limitation and Dependability

In each of the previous examples, queue limitation serves two basic customer needs: short lead time and invariability. It shortens the lead time by bringing average waiting delays below the queue (kanban) limit, and it prevents extreme wait-time variations.

Exhibit 10–8 shows eight customer experiences with a certain business, perhaps a bank. In part A, with no queue limits, the customer's total time commitment (wait time plus service time) is highly variable, ranging from a low of 3 minutes (fourth instance) to a high of 28 minutes (eighth instance). The average is 16 minutes. In part B, with a queue limit of 5 minutes, the variation is slight, ranging from 3 to 7 minutes, and the average is 5.25 minutes.

A high ratio of queue time to production or service time, as in Exhibit 10–8A, is the norm in manufacturing and office work as well as in human services. Therefore, queue limitation is the key to greatly improved response times.

In some companies, success with queue limitation in the direction of Exhibit 10–8B has led to the following results:

- The guesswork is removed. Rob Henderson, plant manager of Corning's ceramic filters business in Corning, New York, says: "We used to negotiate on the request date. We don't do that anymore." With a known, dependably fast throughput time, the Corning salesperson and customer needn't negotiate, which partly explains why this Corning plant was chosen "one of America's best plants" by *Industry Week*.[3]
- Reliable order promise dates are easy to set. At Ahlstrom Pump (Finland and U.S. facilities), the multifunctional product strategy team has worked out an order-promise policy they call "rules of the game," which is based on its dependably quick time to produce any pump, large or small. Nearly all parts, made or bought, are kanban controlled.
- On-time performance improves. In extensively employing kanban, Baldor Electric, a specialty (high-mix) electric-motor manufacturer, has cut its throughput time from an unstable average of four weeks to a fixed five days.[4] As a result, in March 1991, associates at Baldor's Westville, Oklahoma, plant celebrated a full year of on-time deliveries.

$\mathscr{P}$RINCIPLE 10:

Eliminate variation

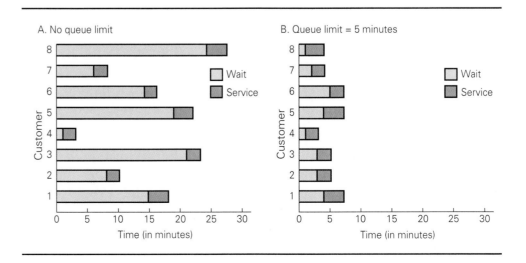

EXHIBIT 10–8

Effects of Queue Limit on Total Customer Time

Contrast

Materials Management

Conventional Stocking Systems

Kanban

Failure prone: Rely on fallible stock records, separated from actual stocks; stocks often poorly segregated, counted, containered, and susceptible to damage and unauthorized usage.

Few failures: Stock location and count well defined, easily verified; stocks well packaged or "containered"; simple, visual, disciplined.

In each of these examples, kanban system designers paid special attention to labeled stock locations, exact counts, and special containers. Then, with proper training, people can operate the kanban system effectively without cumbersome records; see Contrast box, "Materials Management."

Maintaining discipline with regard to physical stocks is one requirement of dependable kanban operations. Another is a high degree of human resource flexibility. Without it, a surge in business at Physio Control, Ernst Home and Garden, or Seafirst Bank will create long waiting lines of partially complete defibrillators (Physio) or customers (Ernst and Seafirst). These companies keep the queues short—within their kanban limits—by having backup labor options to meet the crunch. At Physio, the backup labor can include temporary transfers of people from other parts of the plant; working extra hours, extra shifts, and weekends; and bringing in temporary employees. Ernst and Seafirst rely on cross-trained employees who can restock shelves, unload incoming trucks in the back room, or work the cash registers; and on-call casual labor.

Continuous Improvement (Kanban Removal)

A special attraction of kanban, as described in early writings on it, is the kanban removal feature, a simple way of decrementally reducing the queue (See Example 10–1).

EXAMPLE 10–1:   KANBAN/EDI SERVICE AGREEMENT—MEDIVICE, INC., AND MUNY HOSPITAL

Last year, Muny Hospital contracted with Medivice, Inc., to provide medical devices under a kanban/electronic data interchange (EDI) contract. The initial, trial agreement included 30 high-use items—for example, bar-coded cartons of H1 disposable hypodermic needles.

For that item Muny Hospital's stores manager and a Medivice salesperson agreed to an initial kanban quantity of eight cartoons. Whenever Muny's demands for H1 needles requires a stores clerk to break open another carton, the clerk uses a wand to scan the carton's bar code. That sends an EDI message to Medivice, authorizing shipment of one carton next time the truck goes to the hospital. If the hospital has used, say, three cartons since the previous delivery, Medivice learns about it through EDI and ships three cartons instead of one.

But was eight the right kanban quantity? Experience soon provided the answer. In the midst of a serious flu epidemic, Muny Hospital quickly went through all eight cartons of H1s and experienced a stockout. The medical staff was in a panic until Medivice made a special midnight needle delivery. That seemed like an isolated exception, but several more

EXHIBIT 10–9
Kanban Status and Stockout Check Sheet— Hospital

Items on Kanban	Last Year	This Year								
		J	F	M	A	M	J	J	A	S ...
Hypodermic needle, H1										
Kanbans	8→ 10 → 8	8	8	7	6	6	6	6		
Stockouts	5				//					

Comments: April problem (damaged needle packages—two stockouts) quickly resolved by supplier; no need to increase kanban quantity.

.
.
.

IV bags. I1									
Kanbans	14 → 10	10	10	10	9	8	8	7	
Stockouts	0								

Comments: No stockouts last year or this year to date.

.
.
.

Nurserver carts									
Kanbans	30 → 25	25	25	25	22	22	22	22	
Stockouts						/			

Comments: June late delivery (8:30 AM instead of 5:30) due to large turnover of drivers (e.g., graduation of student drivers). Freight company has set up backup driver system, so no change in kanbans.

Note: Data shown for only 3 of 30 kanban items.

stockouts occurred in the next two months, caused by various system failures (miscount of cartons, a late truck, a stockout at Medivice's warehouse, and a defective lot of H1 disposable needles). As a result, the stores manager and the salesperson increased the kanban quantity of H1 needles to 10 cartons.

On I1 intravenous solution (IV) bags, the opposite happened. The initial kanban quantity, 14 containers, proved to be more than enough. Despite a few startup problems in getting I1 IV bags on kanban, they were always available at the hospital. The service rate on this item was 100 percent, which spelled too much inventory to the stores manager and called for kanban removal. The manager and the salesperson reduced the kanban quantity to 10 containers of IV bags. More reduction followed; primarily because hospital improvement teams, including representatives from the freight carrier and the supplier, implemented overall improvements in the kanban system.

Stores associates wanted a simple, easily noticed record of stockout incidence for H1 needles, I1 bags, and the 28 other kanban-controlled items. They developed a large visible wall-chart check sheet with preprinted categories of problem causes. A stores clerk makes a check mark beside the probable cause whenever a stockout occurs. Improvement teams later investigate the most frequently checked causes.

Stores associates treat reduction of kanban quantities as one measure of success; response ratios, in pieces rather than boxes, are another useful measure. Associates make check marks for stockouts, and they track kanban reductions on the same wall chart, shown in part in Exhibit 10–9. Out of Muny's several thousand stockkeeping units (SKUs), only 30 are currently under kanban, so it's feasible to chart them all.

The exhibit includes two individual SKUs (H1 hypodermic needles and I1-IV bags) and the Nurserver cart, a shelved cart filled with common supplies (tape, swabs, tongue depressors, etc.). Medivice takes Nurserver carts away each day for restocking and return.

service rate or fill rate Percentage of demands (items) filled out of existing stock (or immediate production).

*P*RINCIPLE 11:

Cut wait time and inventory.

stockkeeping unit (SKU) An item at a particular geographic location; a stocked item requiring separate management. SKU is used in retailing, manufacturing, and elsewhere.

Exhibit 10–9 shows a pattern of few stockouts (high fill rates), which is to be expected since kanban is a disciplined, highly reliable system. The exhibit shows that last year, the kanban quantity for H1 needles increased from 8 to 10 (as explained earlier) but then fell back to 8, with further reductions—from 8 to 6—occurring this year. The stockout problem that occurred twice in April this year was quickly resolved, but Muny's cautious associates agreed to keep kanban at six cartons for awhile. Good service experience has led to intermittent kanban removal for both I1 IVs (14 to 10 to 7 kanbans) and Nurserver carts (30 to 25 to 22 kanbans; a single late Nurserver delivery problem causing the June stockout was successfully resolved.)

Push versus Pull Systems

Just-in-time and kanban are often associated with the pull system. In following sections, we'll explore the difference between pull and push, why push is so commonplace, subtle pull–push distinctions, and when kanban is used in the push mode.

Vending Machine—Pure Pull System.   Imagine a coffee machine that keeps filling cups and setting them on a conveyor, regardless of the presence of coffee drinkers. That would be a **push system.** Driven by the maker (or provider), a push system pumps out product without queue limits or linkage to usage (user demand) and usage interruptions.

Of course, coffee machines are not push systems; they respond on demand, with a queue limit of zero. In other words, they respond to a pull signal, money dropped in the slot by the customer. Unless demand is present, the machine is inactive.

Dominance of Push Systems.   The push system has dominated nearly every type of operations. Factories typically contain conveyors, storage racks, and pallets on the floor, all loaded with stock, and more being pushed out with no queue limits. In services, long lines of customers form, and providers have no response that would shorten the queues.

Although apparently wasteful and insensitive to customer wants, the push mode has dominated for three main reasons:

1. *Inflexibility.* A surge in customers or order arrivals will cause the queue to lengthen unless the provider can quickly muster more resources. Sufficient physical capacity, plus cross-trained labor and a backup labor supply (as at Seafirst Bank), are some ways of providing necessary flexibility.
2. *Geographical distances.* In manufacturing and distribution, provider and users are often geographically distant, which tempts the maker/supplier to keep producing product and pushing it forward.
3. *Erroneous costing.* Costs of producing an item in advance and carrying it are often grossly underestimated (see discussion of carrying costs in Chapter 7).

Push–Pull Distinctions.   Fast-food restaurants often keep a small inventory of already-cooked and-wrapped sandwiches in a kanban-like slide, one for each product. When a slide is full, the cook stops preparing that item; when a server withdraws one or more, that is the pull signal authorizing the cook to make one or more.

In this system, slides are short, so the link between customers and cooking is short too. If the slide was long (holding dozens of sandwiches), the close linkage between customers and cooking would be lost. Quality deterioration (e.g., cold

For heavier stock, such a slide is called a flow rack and is often equipped with rollers.

burgers) signals that the cooks are operating in the push mode, keeping the slides overflowing rather than serving customers fast with high quality.

Sometimes the push system is built in. Conveyor-driven production lines (for bottling, canning, tableting, assembly, etc.) are examples. This kind of processing is relentless and associates describe it as "push, push, push." Increasingly, however, companies in these businesses are installing stop and slow-down switches accessible to any operator which in effect makes the line less "push" and more "pull." (See Exhibit 10–10.)

Numerous automotive and appliance assembly lines have been so equipped, and the main reason is to give associates ownership of quality: the means, the authority, and the duty to stop the line to get the quality right and eliminate the re-work lines. Associates are likely to carry out their duty if (*a*) the schedule includes time for stoppages (undercapacity scheduling, discussed in Chapter 7), and (*b*) expert help is nearby. Many companies have moved key technical-support people and engineers to the front lines so that they can respond just in time. When these changes are made, associates are less inclined to use the word *push* to describe their work environment. It begins to *feel* like a pull system to associates—and so it is. Thus, the pull system is, in some sense, a state of mind.

Kanban in the Push Mode?   Earlier we noted Ahlstrom Pump's "rules of the game" and Baldor Electric's success in driving throughput times down from four weeks to five days. Both companies produce a wide variety of models, some in one-piece lots (non-homogeneous production); both have achieved dependably short throughput times through extensive use of kanban; and both launch orders at the first stage in the processing sequence (e.g., blanking or rough-machining of

---

EXHIBIT 10–10

Operator Ownership of the Process-Line Start/Stop Switches

Operator hitting line-stop button at Ford assembly plant, Louisville, Kentucky.

Source: *Manufacturing Engineering Magazine,* Society of Manufacturing Engineers. Photo courtesy of Mid-West Conveyor Co., Kansas City, Kansas.

a cast metal part) rather than pulling orders through from the last stage in the process. Is this the push system? It is not.

Though orders are pushed (launched) at first process to identify which model of motor or pump to produce, all remaining processes are governed by queue limits, which disallow pushing. At Baldor, a coil-winding-machine operator may not produce unless an empty kanban container has come back from the stator assembly station (where the coil is assembled, with other components, into a stator). A few specially designed containers, holding a fixed kanban quantity of various coils, enforce the queue-limit rule, but they are not labeled with a particular coil's stock number. Usage at stator assembly empties a container, the pull signal to coil winding.

We've seen the advantages of good user-provider contact, enforced by queue limitation. But what if the provider is plagued by inflexible capacity, buried in other work, or far removed in time from the next process? Can there be reasonable coordination between provider and user? In manufacturing, yes, there can be, by using a timing system called material requirements planning, our next topic.

Material Requirements Planning (MRP)

Material requirements planning (MRP), perfected in North America in the 1970s, harnessed computer power to carry out complex manufacturing planning. Its first applications were in assisting order planners to determine parts needed to meet a known master schedule for end items.

Comparisons of JIT and MRP often omit this distinction: JIT does not require a software package, while MRP and its extensions do.

At its inception, MRP combined two old procedures, bill of materials (BOM) explosion and netting, with a new one, backscheduling. New in that the computerization made it feasible, backscheduling means subtracting required lead time from the due date to find when a required item should be started into production or ordered from a supplier.

Through the years, MRP has been updated to include planning for more than materials. Later in this section, we consider some of the extensions. First, however, we take a look at MRP in its basic form and progress through some of its primary features.

Basic MRP

MRP is said to be a push system, but that is an oversimplification. Though MRP usually does plan a push schedule for a week at a time, it may include a production activity control subroutine to adjust the work flow somewhat every day in response to the latest customer needs (pull signals). Also, MRP can be set to plan everything daily instead of weekly.

A process can switch from push to pull as the situation changes. Drink machines, labeled as natural pull systems earlier in this chapter, come to mind. A cola machine in the student lounge might better serve its clientele (and make more sales per day) with the following modification: Three minutes before change of classes, the machine converts itself from pull to push; it fills cups with cola and ice and pushes them onto a short conveyor inside the machine. Customers put in their money and get their cola right away; when customers don't come (rarely), the cups are dumped. In either case, the machine changes back to pull after the conveyor is emptied.

Though a fanciful example, it helps clarify push and pull and the value of each, or both in tandem. Example 10–2, also for a food product, illustrates basic

MRP graphically. Since MRP is easier to grasp graphically than in words, some MRP computer systems even show MRP results in graphical form. Two new terms are introduced: **planned order release,** which is found by backscheduling from the date of need, and **residual inventory,** which is inventory left over when an order is canceled or reduced in quantity.

EXAMPLE 10–2: MRP FOR A CATERER

Imagine you are a caterer and have a master schedule of parties to cater every night for the next two weeks. Your policy is zero stock (except for incidentals like seasonings). To plan for zero inventory, you consult menus for every food dish to be provided for each catering order in the next two weeks. Menu quantities times number of servings equals gross requirements. Let us say (without showing calculations) that gross requirements for salami are as shown in part A of Exhibit 10–11. Salami is required in the quantities shown on days 3, 6, 11, and 13.

You normally order salami from a deli two days ahead of time (purchase lead time for salami is two days). Therefore, you plan to release salami orders as shown in part B of Exhibit 10–11. Each planned order release is two days in advance of the gross requirement shown in part A. Backing up by the amount of required lead time is called **back-scheduling.**

The schedule of planned order releases is correctly timed and in the exact quantities needed. It is a material requirements plan for one of the components that go into the foods to be catered. It is a plan for zero inventory and is achieved if the deli delivers the salami orders in the planned two days. If deliveries come a day early, inventory builds. Also, if an order of salami arrives on time but a customer cancels the catering order, residual (leftover) inventory builds. Such supply and demand uncertainties create some inventory when MRP is used, but MRP cuts inventory considerably from what it is when the producer (caterer) *plans* to keep components in stock.

While this procedure seems sensible, most airline caterers today make grocery lists manually. (Exception: Sky Chef, when owned by American Airlines, used modified MRP.)

EXHIBIT 10–11

Planned Order Release Determination— Salami

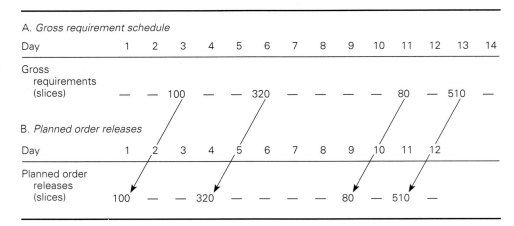

A. *Gross requirement schedule*

Day	1	2	3	4	5	6	7	8	9	10	11	12	13	14
Gross requirements (slices)	—	—	100	—	—	320	—	—	—	—	80	—	510	—

B. *Planned order releases*

Day	1	2	3	4	5	6	7	8	9	10	11	12
Planned order releases (slices)	100	—	—	320	—	—	—	—	80	—	510	—

MRP Computer Processing

Clearly MRP is a simple idea. The MRP calculations for salami (Exhibit 10–11) are easy because from salami slices to a master schedule of catered food dishes is only a single level of dependency. Now consider the partial product structure in Exhibit 10–12. (A product structure visually depicts a bill of materials and sometimes is used as a synonym for *bill of materials.*) It is a dependent-demand chain having five levels below the end item, an automobile. The end item typically is designated the zero level in a computer file storing a bill of materials. The figure shows raw metal (5) cut into a gear (4), fitted onto a shaft (3), placed in a gear box (2), installed in an engine (1), and assembled into an auto (0).

The timing and quantities of parts to be ordered at each level depend on needs for parts by the parent item directly above. Planned-order-release calculations must cascade, that is, proceed from the first level to the second, to the third, and so on. Cascading calculations are complex, however, and a good reason for planners to use computers, especially for products having thousands of parts.

But cascading or level-by-level netting is not the only complication. The same raw metal that is cut into a gear might also go into other parent items that ultimately become the vehicle. Moreover, the raw metal (and, perhaps, the gear, shaft, gear box, and engine) may go into other parent items that become other types of vehicles. Finally, dependent demands (i.e., demands that descend from parent items) for parts at any level must be combined with independent demands. Independent demands arise, for example, from orders for spare parts (service parts). Computers are needed to total and properly time-phase all those requirements.

Exhibit 10–13 shows the necessary inputs and outputs of an MRP computer run. The inputs are a master production schedule, an item master file, a bill-of-materials file, and an open-order file. The outputs include a planned-order-release listing, rescheduling notices, and management reports.

Master Production Schedule.   The master production schedule (MPS) is the action input. The end-item schedule (of the MPS) drives MRP. In most MRP-using firms, the master scheduling team plans in weekly time buckets (periods) extending a year into the future and updated monthly. As the month passes, the master production schedule gets increasingly out of date; that is, toward the end of the month some of the scheduled quantities are out of line with sales orders being booked. Often, the master scheduling team leaves the MPS as it is and deals with inaccuracies via weekly MRP runs, by component parts schedule changes, and by activity control measures on the shop floor.

Item Master File.   The **item master file** holds reference and control data, including on-hand stock balances and planning factors for every component item. The on-hand balance is simply the quantity that is supposed to be in stock.

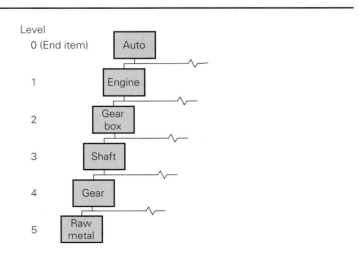

EXHIBIT 10–12
Partial Product Structure Showing Dependency Chain

EXHIBIT 10–13

MRP Computer Run

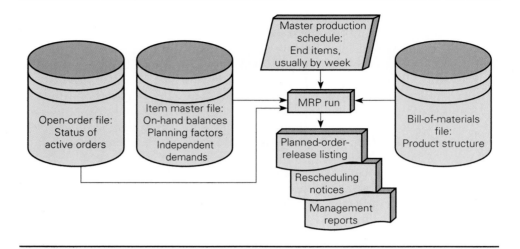

The on-hand balance is used by MRP to compute planned orders. First, the system computes gross requirements for a given part. Then it calculates projected stock balances to see if there is a net requirement, which would indicate a need for a planned order; that calculation is called **netting.** A net requirement is the same as a negative projected stock balance, where

$$\underset{\text{stock balance}}{\text{Projected}} = \underset{\text{stock balance}}{\text{Previous}} - \underset{\text{requirements}}{\text{Gross}} + \underset{\text{scheduled receipts}}{\text{Planned and}} \qquad (10\text{–}1)$$

Example 10–3 extends Example 10–2 to allow for an on-hand stock balance. Also, let's change salami into salamite, a hypothetical chemical compound. In keeping with the usual industry practice of scheduling in weeks, gross requirements for salamite are stated as a 14-week rather than 14-day schedule.

EXAMPLE 10–3:   MRP FOR A CHEMICAL PRODUCT

Let us say that 220 units of salamite is the on-hand balance at time zero (the start of week 1). Gross requirements are as shown in Exhibit 10–11 (for salami), but with days changed to weeks. For week 3,

$$\text{Projected stock balance} = 120 - 100 + 0 = 120$$

The positive projected stock balance of 120 shows that there is no need for an order. The projected balance stays at 120 in weeks 4 and 5. In week 6,

$$\text{Projected balance} = 120 - 320 + 0 = -200$$

Now the projected stock balance is a negative 200, which is a net requirement. In MRP, a net requirement is covered by a planned order. The planned order quantity is 200, and the planned order release, obtained by back scheduling, is two weeks earlier, since the planned lead time (*LT*) is two weeks.

Exhibit 10–14 shows MRP results as a four-row display. This type of display might be available for viewing on a video terminal or as printed output. (The scheduled-receipts row, which is empty in this example, is explained later.)

LT (lead time) = 2																
Week		1	2	3	4	5	6	7	8	9	10	11	12	13	14	
Gross requirements				100			320					80		510		
Scheduled receipts																
Projected stock balance	220	220	220	120	120	120	0 −200	0	0	0	0	0 −80	0	0 −510	0	
Planned order releases					200					80		510				
					↑LT = 2↓					↑LT = 2↓	↑LT = 2↓					

EXHIBIT 10–14

MRP Computations— Salamite

A planned order release of 200 in week 4 covers the net requirement of 200 in week 6. A negative stock balance is thus averted; therefore, the − 200 is crossed out and replaced by a zero balance. Recomputation of the stock balance in week 6 to account for the planned receipt of 200 is accomplished with equation 10–1:

$$\text{Projected stock balance} = 120 - 320 + 200 = 0$$

The projected balance goes negative twice more, in weeks 11 and 13. Planned orders cover the net requirements; thus, the negative quantities are crossed out and replaced by zeros.

Planning factors stored in the item master file include lead time, lot size, safety stock, and so forth. Those factors need less updating than stock balances. In Example 10–3, the lead time (LT) of two weeks would have been extracted from the item master file.

So far we have assumed that the planned-order-release quantity is the same as the net requirement. That policy is known as lot-for-lot (i.e., production lot size exactly equals lot quantity required). Sometimes the item master file specifies a preset order quantity or lot size, Q (for quantity). Example 10–4, adapted from Example 10–3, provides for a fixed Q.

EXAMPLE 10–4:   MRP FOR A CHEMICAL PRODUCT—FIXED ORDER QUANTITY

Assume that salamite is produced in a vat that holds 500 units. Even though 500 is unlikely to be the net requirement, it seems economical to make the salamite in full 500-unit batches. The excess is carried as a stock balance.

Exhibit 10–15 shows the MRP computations for the case of a fixed order quantity, Q, equal to 500 units. A net requirement of 200 arises when the computed stock balance goes negative by 200 in week 6. The computer covers the net requirement with a planned order two weeks earlier (since $LT = 2$). the order is for $Q = 500$, the fixed order quantity, which brings projected stock balance in week 6 to +300. The balance drops to 220 in week 11 and to − 290, indicating a net requirement, in week 13. To prevent the negative balance in week 13, the computer plans an order for 500. The planned order release is in week 11, which eliminates the negative balance in week 13 and leaves 210 units to spare.

Fixed order quantities compromise the MRP goal of low (or zero) inventories. Order-quantity policies are a topic in the next chapter.

EXHIBIT 10–15

MRP with Fixed Order Quantity—Salamite

LT = 2 Q = 500		1	2	3	4	5	6	7	8	9	10	11	12	13	14
Week		1	2	3	4	5	6	7	8	9	10	11	12	13	14
Gross requirements				100			320					80		510	
Scheduled receipts															
On hand	220	220	220	120	120	120	300 200	300	300	300	300	220	220	210 290	210
Planned order releases					500							500			

Bill-of-Materials File. A bill of materials (BOM) is not the kind of bill that demands payment; rather, it is industry's term for a list (often a structured list) of component parts that go into a product. The BOM names the parts detailed on the engineer's blueprints. Like the item master file, the computerized BOM file serves as a reference file for MRP processing.

The BOM file keeps track of which component parts, and how many of each, go into a unit of the parent item. In each MRP run, the computer (1) calculates planned order timing and quantity for the parent item, (2) consults the BOM file to see what goes into the parent, and (3) translates the parent's planned order requirement into gross requirements for each component. This sequence is known as

EXAMPLE 10–5:   MRP FOR A CHEMICAL PRODUCT WITH TWO LEVELS

Planned order releases for salamite have been calculated. The computer consults the BOM file to find what goes into salamite. The first ingredient is a chemical compound known as *sal*. There are two grams of sal per unit of salamite. Therefore, the planned order quantities for salamite are doubled to equal gross requirements for sal. The simple translation of salamite orders into sal needs is shown in Exhibit 10–16. (The salamite data are from Exhibit 10–15.)

EXHIBIT 10–16

BOM Reference Data and Scheduled Receipts in MRP

Week		1	2	3	4	5	6	7	8	9	10	11	12	13	14
Parent—Salamite															
Planned order releases					500							500			
Component—Sal LT = 5															
Gross requirements					1,000							1,000			
Scheduled receipts					1,000										
On hand	0	0	0	0	1,000 0	0	0	0	0	0	0	1,000 0	0	0	0
Planned order releases							1,000		LT = 5						

×2 (from Salamite 500 week 4 to Sal gross requirements 1,000 week 4); ×2 (from Salamite 500 week 11 to Sal gross requirements 1,000 week 11); LT = 5

Projected stock balances and planned order releases may now be calculated for sal as shown in the figure. Then the computer does the same for the next ingredient or component of salamite.

bill of materials explosion. For example, if there are three of a certain component per parent, the gross requirement for that component will be equal to triple the planned order quantity for the parent. The grand total of gross requirements for the component would also include requirements derived from other parents and from independent demands. Example 10–5 continues the salamite example to demonstrate the role of the BOM file.

Developing the master production schedule and forecasting MPS requirements are cumbersome for planners if large numbers of products are in the BOM file. Therefore, the BOMs provided by the engineering department (called engineering bills) may require consolidation. The usual approach is to judiciously combine some engineering bills into modular bills and phantom bills (or super bills). The full approach, called restructuring the bills of materials, is often a valued step in MRP implementation; the method is somewhat complicated, however, and is reserved for advanced studies.[5]

Computer Runs.   MRP computer runs are usually weekly; a total regeneration of material requirements generally is performed over the weekend. Some companies use regenerative MRP processing every two or three days or even daily. An alternative to regeneration is net-change MRP. Net-change computer software is designed to update only items affected by a change in quantity or timing for a related item. Since not all part numbers need be regenerated, net change saves on computer time and on volume of output data presented to planners for review.

Scheduled Receipts and the Open-Order File

Another MRP factor is scheduled receipts. Returning to Exhibit 10–16, we see a scheduled receipt of 1,000, which is the gross-requirement quantity in week 4. A scheduled receipt represents an **open order** instead of a planned order. In this case, an order for 1,000 has already been released, for make or buy, and is scheduled to be delivered in week 4. Since the lead time is five weeks, the order would have been released, opened, and scheduled two weeks ago. (Remember, we're at time zero, the beginning of week 1.)

Let's examine the events that change a planned order into a scheduled receipt. The following table is a partial MRP for sal as it might have appeared on Monday morning two weeks ago.

Lead time = 5		1	2	3	4	5	6
Gross requirements							1,000
Scheduled receipts							
On hand	0	0	0	0	0	0	−0 ~~1,000~~
Planned order releases		1,000					

PP

Any time a planned order release appears in the first time-bucket, action to schedule the order is called for. Therefore, sometime on Monday the scheduler writes a shop order to make 1,000 grams of sal. The effect of scheduling the order is to remove it from the planned-order-release row and convert it to a scheduled receipt, as follows:

Lead time = 5		1	2	3	4	5	6
Gross requirements							1,000
Scheduled receipts							→1,000
On hand	0	0	0	0	0	0	0
Planned order releases		◌					

On the next MRP run, the scheduled receipt for 1,000 grams will be included. The order is shown as a scheduled receipt each week until the shop delivers the 1,000 grams. But the scheduler could cancel the order or change its quantity or timing. Also, the shop may successfully produce more or less than the planned quantity of 1,000 grams.

Referring back to the system flowchart of MRP computer processing in Exhibit 10–13, we see that MRP makes use of an open-order file, which holds data on open orders (scheduled receipts). Each time a scheduler releases a shop order or a buyer releases a purchase order, the order is noted in the open-order file. (Alternatively, item master file records may contain fields indicating if there is an open order for a given item.) When orders are received (or canceled), they are closed and removed from the file.

One step in an MRP computer run, usually after calculation of planned order releases, is to evaluate open orders. The computer checks to see whether quantities and timing for each order in the open-order file are still correct. The check may show that a certain open order is still needed, but perhaps a week later or in a different quantity; or perhaps the order is no longer needed at all. The system issues **rescheduling notices,** which highlight the difference between present requirements and open orders. If the open order is overstated, the shop scheduler or buyer will sometimes ignore the rescheduling notice and allow the order to be completed early or in a quantity in excess of current need, because rescheduling for every new requirement would be too disruptive for the suppliers or shops doing the work. (Order changes and rescheduling notices are normal; the disruption resulting from reacting to every rescheduling notice is often called system nervousness.)

Multiple Parents and Scrap Allowances

So far, we've examined simplified MRP examples. MRP is at its best, however, for complex product structures that can benefit from the computer's sorting powers. Exhibit 10–17 is a partial bill of materials for a bicycle. There is enough room to show only a sample of the bicycle's 300-odd component parts. The complete BOM breaks down into as many levels as are necessary to get to the purchased part. Take the breakdown of the front and rear wheels. Each wheel has a tire, an axle assembly, a rim assembly, 28 spokes, and 28 nipples; each spoke is fabricated (cut, bent, and threaded) from 11 inches of raw wire stock. The nipple is a second-level purchased item and the wire is a third-level purchased item. Spoke nipples and wire stock appear at two lo-

EXHIBIT 10–17   Partial Bill of Materials for a Bicycle

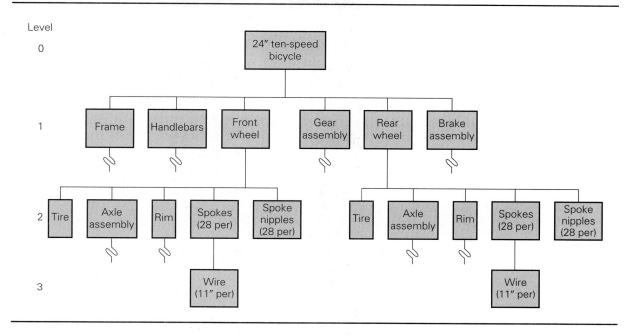

cations in the BOM; they also would occur in the BOMs for other bicycle sizes. The computer is efficient for totaling the quantities needed for parts occurring in multiple locations, which is a step in exploding the BOM. (Before computers and MRP were available, BOM explosion was done by legions of clerks using index cards and adding machines.)

Example 10–6 uses some of the bicycle components to show how MRP treats multiple parents and scrap calculations. In the example, netting with scrap allowance included is done as follows:

$$\text{Net requirement} = \frac{\text{Shortage amount}}{1 - \text{Scrap rate}} \qquad (10\text{–}2)$$

EXAMPLE 10–6:   MRP PROCESSING—BICYCLE SPOKE NIPPLES

Exhibit 10–18 shows generation of gross requirements for spoke nipples and their translation into planned order releases. Planned order releases for front and rear wheels are given for three sizes of bicycle: 20-inch, 24-inch, and 26-inch. Requirements for wheels would have been derived from master production schedules (level 0) for all bike models. Planned order releases for spoke nipples emerge after higher levels of MRP processing have been completed.

In the exhibit, orders for more than one parent are consolidated to become gross requirement for a next-lower-level part. The requirement for nipples in week 5 is based on 84 + 60 + 24 + 24 = 192 wheels. At 28 nipples per wheel, the gross requirement is 192 × 28 = 5,376. For week 6, the basis is 36 + 36 + 72 + 84 = 228 wheels: the gross requirement is 228 × 28, which equals 6,384. (Front-wheel and rear-wheel planned orders

Exhibit 10–18   **MRP Generation of Planned Order Releases—Spoke Nipple Example.**

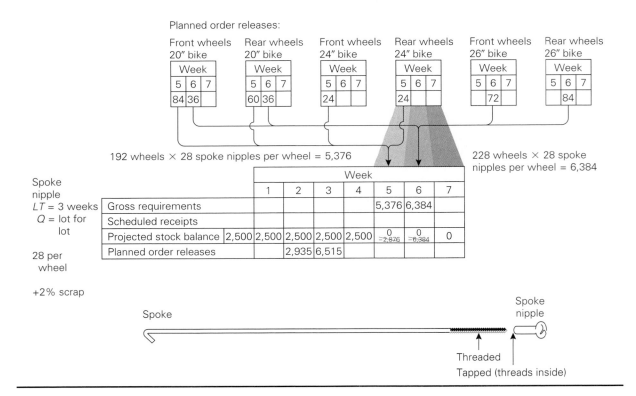

may be unequal, because there may be extra demand for one or the other as service parts, to make up for scrap losses, etc.)

The 2,500 nipples on hand at week 0 are projected to stay on hand (in stock) through four weeks. In week 5, 5,376 are needed but only 2,500 are available; there is a projected shortage of 2,876. The possibility of a shortage triggers the following: The MRP program subtracts the purchase lead time (*LT*), three weeks, from week 5, giving a planned order date of week 2. The lot size is lot-for-lot. Thus, from Equation 10–2, the computer calculates the planned purchase order size of 2,935 units, a quantity that covers the projected shortage of 2,876 and allows for a 2-percent scrap rate. Similarly, the projected shortage of 6,384 in week 6 is covered by a planned order back-scheduled to week 3. The order quantity (6,515) again allows for 2 percent scrap.

Note the treatment of the scrap factor. The planned-order-release amount includes the 2 percent so that the extra amount will be placed on order. Planned receipts do not include it, since 2 percent is expected to be scrapped.

Independent Demands for Component Parts

Independent demands for component parts may be entered into the item master file. The subset of MRP for handling independent demands is often called **time-phased order point (TPOP)**. TPOP requires that the independent demands be forecast since they cannot be computed; there are no parent demands from which to compute.

The main difference between MRP and TPOP is this: Dependent demands are calculated based on parent-item needs (MRP), while independent demands are forecast TPOP actually loses its identity when the independent demand is merged with demands derived from MRP; MRP takes over from there. Example 10–7 illustrates the method.

EXAMPLE 10–7: INDEPENDENT DEMANDS—BICYCLE SPOKES

For a bicycle manufacturer, most of the gross demands for spokes are dependent demands derived from planned orders for wheels. Some independent demands for spokes come from parts wholesalers and other bicycle manufacturers that do not make their own spokes.

The independent sources do not make their demands known very far in advance. Thus, independent spoke demand is forecast. The most recent forecast for 11-inch spokes is for 800 units. That quantity is used as the forecast for the next 52 weeks. Exhibit 10–19 shows the 800-per-week projection at the upper left. The upper right shows a dependent demand for 672 spokes in week 5; that demand is derived from MRP processing at the level of the parent item, 24-inch bike wheels.

EXHIBIT 10–19   TPOP—Spoke Example

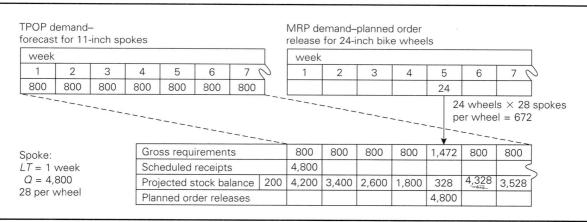

The two sources of demand merge into gross requirements for spokes. The independent-demand quantities, 800 per period, are extended directly; the single dependent demand of 672 is computed from the planned order of 24 wheels times 28 spokes per wheel. From this point, MRP logic takes over; the figure shows a net requirement in week 6 covered by a planned order release with a fixed quantity of 4,800 a week earlier.

Evolution of MRP

The logic inherent in MRP processing seems so straightforward that some students are prone to ask, "Why didn't manufacturers always use it?" The answer is also straightforward: MRP is a tool born of computer technology; the hardware needed for MRP in even a medium-sized company simply didn't exist until the mid–1960s and the software wasn't available until the early 1970s. The sharp growth in MRP applications occurred in the late 1970s. In its nearly three decades of life, however, MRP has evolved and its logic has been extended.

Closed-Loop MRP.   Early MRP systems were one-way streets. They fed plans to production associates but received no feedback as to the success (or lack thereof) in executing those plans. MRP generates valid schedules in that they are logical extensions of parent demand, but once orders are launched, some of the planning factors stray off course. Lead-time estimates can be wrong, quantities of items actually received can differ from quantities ordered, customer requirements can change, and new designs and changed part numbers can disrupt existing bill-of-materials and inventory-status files.

In closed-loop MRP, three general types of activities help restore order: close file control ensures that the data files from which MRP draws its information are accurate; production activity control routines provide the scheduler with timely updates as to the status of orders as they move through the plant; and rescheduling actions ensure that revised plans, based on updated information, are known to all (including customers and suppliers).

Distribution Requirements Planning.   Distribution requirements planning (DRP) extends MRP logic to independent demands from, say, company-operated distribution centers. Traditionally, finished-goods inventories were planned independently of manufacturing; each distribution center would place its order as needed to replenish its shelves. Under DRP, however, demand forecasts for finished goods at the distribution centers become entries to the manufacturing plant's master production schedule.

Since requirements are based on need, customer service levels improve even as overall inventory levels are reduced. For the manufacturer, early warning in the form of realistic needs captured on the master schedule aids production planning and helps prevent crises brought on by "suddenly empty" shelves at a distribution center.

While basic MRP is well defined (standard files and subroutines), the meaning and composition of MRP II is fuzzier (many possible configurations) and not easily illustrated with a few tables.

Manufacturing Resource Planning (MRP II).   Perhaps the most noteworthy extension of closed-loop MRP to date is manufacturing resource planning, or MRP II—which is intended to incorporate all resources of a manufacturing company. Early MRP II applications used the master production schedule to plan capacity, shipments, tool changes, design work, and cash flows. MRP II software vendors kept adding modules, however, to stay ahead of competitors. Maintenance management, quality, field service and warranty tracking, marketing support, and engineering change control are among the applications one might find in today's MRP II systems.[6]

But that's not all. Some packages incorporate a simulation module, enabling the computer to test prospective schedules before the company commits to a plan. A finite scheduling module, capable of incorporating capacity constraints into the planning mix, is also frequently available. And, to put these tools where they are most needed—in the hands of the operator—client/server technology, or distributed computing, brings MRP II to the desktop PC.[7] Some observers maintain that a fully configured MRP II system, such as we've described here, will continue to be cutting-edge technology for some time.[8]

Other Extensions of or Alternatives to MRP II.   MRP II, however, is attracting competition. Some of the emergent alternative systems attempt to establish better connections with customers and suppliers. **Enterprise resource planning (ERP),** for example, is a term coined by The Gartner Group of Stamford, Connecticut, and—though not revolutionary in concept—purports to ensure that planning decisions do consider both upstream and downstream members of the supply chain.[9] From published descriptions, however, ERP includes most of the modules attributed to a "loaded" MRP II system.

While MRP was fashioned for the manufacturing sector, and its partner DRP for distribution, there have been some efforts to extend it elsewhere. A promising example is MRP's use in hospitals. Many surgeries are elective and therefore scheduled in advance. Adding those to a history-based forecast of non-elective surgeries produces a master schedule, which could drive a computer routine that will plan the required medical devices, instruments, supplies, surgical rooms, staff, and so forth.

Another approach to hospital applications has been developed by researchers Aleda Roth and Roland van Dierdonck. In a research report, they describe their system, called hospital resource planning (HRP), and tests of its feasibility:

> We gathered longitudinal data from two hospitals, one 300-bed community hospital and one 1,100-bed teaching hospital. Our exploratory study indicated that while the concept of MRP II can be transferred to hospitals, the traditional MRP logic has shortcomings. HRP advanced prior research in three ways: (1) consideration of DRGs [diagnostic-related groups] as products with a bill of resources structure that simultaneously incorporates both capacity and materials resources, (2) implementation of a hospital-wide (versus a functional) planning and control system, and (3) gross-to-net requirements logic based on notions of treatment stages.[10]

Whether ERP, HRP, and other extensions of MRP II stick and flourish remains to be seen. They all, however, aim toward a similar set of benefits, discussed next.

Benefits of MRP and MRP II[11]

How valuable is MRP or MRP II? As to overall impact, respected authorities have differing opinions. The late Oliver Wight stated that, "MRP II results in management finally having the numbers to run the business." And when "everybody uses the same set of numbers," MRP II serves as "a company game plan."[12] George Plossl, however, has a different view: MRP II "ignores execution and control activities and has produced more confusion than benefits."[13]

In the narrow sense, the chief benefit of MRP/MRPII is its ability to generate valid schedules and keep them that way. A valid schedule has broad benefits for the entire company, including the following, roughly in order of importance:

1. *Improves on-time completions.* Industry calls this improving customer service, and on-time completion is one good way to measure it. MRP/MRP II companies typically achieve 95 percent or more on-time completions, because completion of a parent item is less apt to be delayed for lack of a component part.

2. *Cuts inventories.* With MRP/MRP II, inventories can be reduced at the same time customer service is improved. Stocks are cut because parts are not ordered if not needed to meet requirements for parent items. Typical gains are 20 to 35 percent.

3. *Provides data (future orders) for planning work center capacity requirements.* This benefit is attainable if basic MRP is enhanced by a capacity requirements planning (CRP) routine (discussed in Chapter 14).

4. *Improves direct-labor productivity.* There is less lost time and overtime because of shortages and less need to waste time halting one job to set up for a shortage-list job. Reduction in lost time tends to be from 5 to 10 percent in fabrication and from 25 to 40 percent in assembly. Overtime cuts are greater, on the order of 50 to 90 percent.

5. *Improves productivity of support staff.* MRP/MRP II cuts expediting ("firefighting"), which allows more time for planning. Purchasing can spend time saving money and selecting good suppliers. Materials management can maintain valid records and better plan inventory needs. Production control can keep priorities up-to-date. Supervisors can better plan capacity and assign jobs. In some cases, fewer support staff are needed.

6. *Facilitates closing the loop with total business planning.* That includes planning capacity and cash flow, which is the chief purpose and benefit of MRP II.

While these are impressive, it should be noted that JIT yields the first five benefits but much more so. Some firms combine the two approaches by overlaying JIT upon an existing MRP system; other firms treat JIT as a replacement for certain MRP subroutines (see the Contrast box, MRP Coverage).

Benefits of MRP/MRP II are offset somewhat by its complexity. Considerable time, training, preparation, and discipline are necessary in order to realize the promised benefits. The next technique, reorder point, does not offer those benefits, but it is simple.

Reorder Point (ROP)

Inventory timing with **reorder point (ROP)** is probably as old as humanity (maybe older; some animals, such as squirrels, also replenish low stocks). The ROP provides for replenishing stocks when they reach some low level. Let's look at some ROP variations.

Perpetual Inventory System

The classic use of the reorder point occurs in a **perpetual inventory system.** Perpetually—every time an issue is made—the stock on hand is checked to see whether it is down to the ROP. If it is, someone places an order. In the informal case, stock clerks perpetually examine the physical stock level itself. More formally, a records clerk or a computer examines the balance on a stock record.

Reorder points are part of our personal lives. We may reorder (go out to get) postage stamps when we have only three left, or we may buy a new half gallon of milk when there is about two inches left in the old container. Sometimes we get reminders from the manufacturer: the desk calendar or box of personal checks containing a reorder notice.

Two-Bin System

A version of the perpetual reorder point called the two-bin system is often used in small stockrooms. Two adjacent storage bins hold a single item, and users are told to withdraw from bin 1 first. The rule is this: When the first bin empties, place an order. The second bin contains the ROP, a quantity that covers the lead time for filling the order and allows for some additional buffer or safety stock.

MRP Coverage

Wide MRP Coverage	Reduced MRP Coverage
A goal of Class A MRP requiring	A goal of disciplined simplicity requiring
High record accuracy.	Exact stock placement and standard quantities.
All MRP subroutines in use.	Reduction of subroutines, except for data files.
All part numbers on MRP.	Migration of parts off MRP and onto JIT, regular-use parts first.

In Oliver Wight's 1970s-vintage classification scheme, Class A MRP is the most advanced level.

There are many variations. A colored sheet of paper may be inserted in a stack of forms on a shelf to show when the ROP (the second bin) has been reached. Indirect material, such as washers, screws, and nails, is often placed in trays on assemblers' workbenches; a painted line partway down inside the tray can designate the ROP. Transistors, diodes, and so on, are often stored in corrugated boxes on shelves; a small box in the larger box may be used to contain the ROP (the second bin). Exhibit 10–20 shows two component parts (left side and right side of a bin) controlled by a two-bin system at Upright-Ireland. At Upright, the two-bin system is an element of JIT, which covers virtually all of Upright's parts, bought or made. When an associate breaks into the second bin, that is the kanban signal to order another package.

The two-bin system works best when one person is in charge of the stockroom or is in charge of a daily check to see which items are down to the ROP. Otherwise, people can get too busy to note the need for an order; associates can blame each other if the second bin is emptied but no one has reordered.

In firms with partial computer control of inventories, a bar code strip can be affixed to bin 2. Then, when bin 2 is entered, it is easy to initiate the reorder. Just scan the bar code, which holds identifying data. Associates are less likely to forget to order when ordering is so simple.

ROP Calculation

Planners and buyers may set the reorder point (the quantity in bin 2) by judgment and experience or by an ROP formula. Judgment would tend to follow the concepts embodied in the basic ROP formula:

$$ROP = DLT + SS = (D)(LT) + SS \qquad (10\text{–}3)$$

where

ROP = Reorder point
DLT = Demand during lead time
SS = Safety stock (or buffer stock)
D = Average demand per time period
LT = Average lead time

EXHIBIT 10–20

Two-Bin (Kanban) System at Upright-Ireland

ROP calculation is simple, but it does require reliable numbers if it is to be trusted. The planner or buyer often uses recent averages for demand rate and replenishment lead time. Safety stock could be set judgmentally or by using a formula; more on how to do that after we consider two ROP examples.

EXAMPLE 10–8:   ROP CALCULATION—FUEL OIL EXAMPLE

Assume that a building heated by fuel oil consumes an average of 600 gallons per year and the average lead time is two weeks. Thus:

$$D = 600 \text{ gallons per year}$$

$$LT = 2 \text{ weeks}/52 \text{ weeks per year} = 0.04 \text{ year}$$

$$DLT = (D)(LT) = (600)(0.04) = 24 \text{ gallons}$$

Then, if desired safety stock is 40 gallons:

$$ROP = DLT + SS = 24 + 40$$

$$= 64 \text{ gallons}$$

Replenishment Cycle

In Example 10–8 an average demand rate of about 24 gallons is based on an average replenishment lead time of two weeks. Average values tend to smooth things out, masking the existence of stock outages and inventory peaks. Example 10–9 provides a more realistic picture of ROP replenishment cycles.

EXAMPLE 10–9:   REPLENISHMENT CYCLES FOR DISCRETE DEMAND—RADIATOR CAP EXAMPLE

Radiator caps are issued in discrete units; that is, you cannot issue half a radiator cap. (In contrast, a continuous item like fuel oil can be issued in fractions of a gallon). Exhibit 10–21 shows two replenishment cycles for radiator caps. The graph shows a stairstep de-

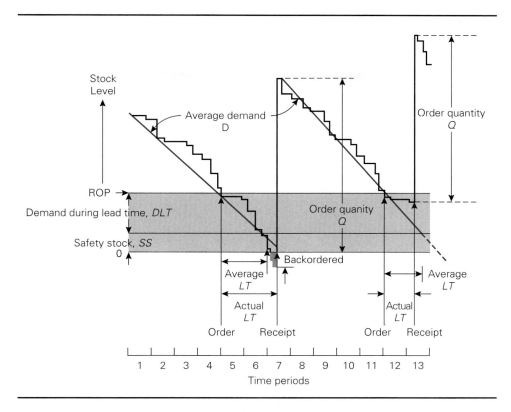

Exhibit 10–21

ROP Replenishment Cycles—Radiator Cap Example

pletion pattern. It also shows early and late order arrivals, including a case in which backordering occurs.

In the first cycle, radiator caps start out being issued at a slow pace (i.e., slower than past average demand). In the fourth time period there is a spurt, and at the end of the period stock on hand drops below the ROP. An order is placed. During lead time, stock issues begin slowly, then speed up in periods 6 and 7. All radiator caps are gone by the beginning of period 7, and orders still come in.

The shaded zone below the zero line indicates orders unfilled because of the stockout condition, caused by the combination of slow delivery (greater-than-average lead time) and a late spurt in demand.

The second cycle begins when the order arrives in period 7. The order quantity (lot size) brings the stock level up from zero to Q units, and the backorders are immediately filled, dropping the stock level somewhat. The stock depletion rate is about average through period 10. In period 11, demand for radiator caps surges. The surge continues into period 12, and it reduces stock to below the ROP. An order is placed.

This time, delivery is faster than average (see actual LT as compared with average LT), and there is little demand during the lead-time period. The result is little use of the DLT quantity and no use of the SS amount. Stock is high when the order quantity (Q) arrives. The order arrival pushes up the stock level to near the maximum possible, which is the ROP plus Q.

backorder
Order accepted when stock is out.

Periodic System

The ROP method of replenishment requires perpetual checking of the balance on hand. Why not just check the balance at fixed time intervals? The periodic system does just that. The regularity in order intervals makes the periodic system popular with retailers, who often set up a schedule of checking stock levels in slack periods each day, once a week, or perhaps monthly. Grocers, restaurants, gas stations, clothing stores, and auto parts stores are some of the many kinds of businesses that favor a periodic system.

Often the periodic system of timing orders is combined with maximum–minimum quantity criteria. For example, a grocery store might periodically re-order laundry soaps, with two days as the order interval. The maximum shelf space, and therefore maximum inventory, for one item—say, Whiter-White Detergent—might be four cases, and the desired minimum, one case. The periodic system works like this:

1. Check stock of Whiter-White on Monday, Wednesday, Friday, and so on.
2. If shelf stock is below one case, reorder enough to bring the stock as close to four cases as possible without exceeding that amount.
3. If stock is above one case, don't reorder.

Note that the minimum is really a reorder-point quantity used in conjunction with the reorder-point interval; the maximum governs what the lot size must be in order to bring stock up to the maximum level.

Buffer Stock (Safety Stock)

Factory people tend to call it buffer stock: a buffer between one machine and the next. To retailers and wholesalers, where reorder points are most common, it's safety stock.

Regardless of the system used for inventory timing, keeping customers well served is difficult. Consumption and output rates vary, and stoppages, accidents, and natural disasters sometimes disrupt operations. These difficulties lead managers to rely on protection in the form of buffer stocks, also called safety stocks.

Even well-run just-in-time operations and quick-response programs must rely somewhat on buffer stocks. Buffer stock, a special class of inventory, is like the spare tire in your auto or your homeowner's insurance policy: You hope you don't need it, but you don't dare operate without it. Buffer stock is expensive, however, and needs careful management.

In Chapter 8, we introduced the concept of offline buffer stock, which provides protection but does not consume throughput time. Sometimes it is appropriate to calculate the quantity of buffer stock; the calculation procedure and comments about its limitations round out our discussion of careful buffer-stock management.

Statistical Safety Stock

In retailing and wholesaling, safety (buffer) stock must be far greater than in dependent demand situations. Customers must be served, but their demands for a given item tend to be highly variable. Fortunately, demand variability and customer service can be expressed in numbers. Manipulate the two numbers (the desired customer-service level and the demand-variation level) in a certain way, and the result is a calculated statistical safety stock.

The first step is to decide on the desired customer **service level.** Among the many possible definitions of service levels, the following is popular: The percentage of orders filled from stock on hand, also called **fill rate.** That, plus its converse, the **stockout rate,** must equal 100 percent. For example, a planned service level of 0.98 means that customer orders would be filled 98 percent of the time, with a stockout the remaining 2 percent of the time.

Safety stock is calculated from service level by the following formula (assuming independent demands, normally distributed):

$$SS = z\sqrt{LT\,(SD)^2} \tag{10--4}$$

where

   SS = Safety stock

   z = Value from normal distribution table (see Appendix A), based on service level

   LT = Lead time

   SD = Standard deviation of demand

(Note: LT and SD must be stated in the same time units; for example, if SD is calculated based on variability over one-month time periods, LT must be expressed in months.) Example 10–10 illustrates use of the formula.

EXAMPLE 10–10:   SAFETY STOCK—LOAVES OF BREAD

Assume that mean demand for bread at your house is 100 slices per week and that demand varies by a standard deviation of 40 slices per week. The desired service level is 97.72 percent. It takes just one day to replenish the bread supply. How much safety stock should you carry? What is the reorder point?

Solution

All data must be in the same time units. Thus, replenishment lead time of one day is converted to 1/7 week.

   The service level, 0.9772, represents a probability: 0.50 (the left half of the area under the normal curve) plus 0.4772. We look for 0.4772 in Appendix A and find it where $z = 2.00$. From Equation 10–4:

$$SS = z\,\sqrt{LT(SD)^2}$$

$$= 2.00\,\sqrt{1/7(40)^2} = 30.2 \text{ slices.}$$

and, from Equation 10–3:

$$ROP = (D)(LT) + SS$$

$$= (100)(1/7) + 30.2 = 44.5 \text{ slices}$$

Perspective on Buffer Stock

Unfortunately, the statistical safety stock method omits factors that affect safety stock. One is the effect of lot size. In Chapter 8, we learned that large lot sizes act as buffer stock; if the lot size is very large, a calculated statistical safety stock will be insignificant (compared with the buffering effects of the large lots) and not worth calculating. Small lot sizes have the opposite effect, which suggests keeping larger safety stocks on hand than the calculated statistical quantity.

   In retailing and wholesaling, lot sizes normally are moderate, which means that the statistical model is valid enough. Exceptions are hard-to-get items or items from undependable suppliers. In those cases, the main concern may be with variable supply, but the statistical model accounts only for variable demand.

The same types of limitations restrict use of the statistical model in setting buffer stocks for semifinished factory materials and other dependent-demand items. The big problems are the variabilities in supply (the maker), which the statistical model does not address.

Other miscellaneous factors that affect buffer stock are

Cost. For very costly items, keep very little (even zero) buffer stock on hand. For low-cost items (washers, paper clips), keep perhaps as much as a year's worth.

Space. If the item is very bulky, keep the buffer stock small, and vice versa.

Consequences of a stockout. Sometimes a wide variety of options, such as substitute items, are available in the event of a stockout; in such cases, keep the buffer stock small.

Obsolescence. In high-tech industries, large buffer stocks mean large obsolescence costs; thus, keep buffer stocks small.

With so many factors not present in the model, how can the model be effectively used? To answer this question, let's consider a company that takes particular pride in its high service level. The centerpiece of Frito-Lay's corporate culture is its ability to provide its customers with a 99.5 percent service level.[14] Current-demand data (captured by barcode scanning or collected by Frito-Lay's 10,000 store representatives) go into company computers, which calculate demand, standard deviation of demand, safety stock, and reorder point for each product. Armed with computer listings of calculated ROPs for each item, product managers can decide whether to change any ROPs in light of other safety-stock factors such as cost and space.

Summary

Just-in-time processing helps providers deliver outputs cheaper, better, and faster. It not only cuts throughput time on average, but also reduces variation around the average. A bedrock tool of JIT is queue limitation devices. These include classical card kanban, labeled containers (where the item is uniform), unlabeled containers or kanban squares (which can be used for nonuniform items), timers (for queue-time limits), queue limit policies (less disciplined than physical limiters), colored indicators, electronic signals and automatic (e.g., electric) stop devices.

While queue limiters do not deal with service times, they place upper limits on waiting times, which in most cases consume far larger amounts of throughput time. Thus, queue limitation can eliminate variation to the point where customers can be given fairly certain delivery (or appointment) dates or times, with no need to speculate or negotiate.

A server employing queue limitation would normally begin with enough units, say, 10 kanban containers, to protect against delivery uncertainly or surges in demand. As delivery problems are solved or customer demands are smoothed out, the server then reduces units (kanban removal), which cuts throughput time.

Vending machines operate as pull systems. The customer's coin drop is the pull signal that actuates the serving mechanism. More common are push systems in which customers push forward on the server, or the producer pushes the parts on to the next process; the main concern is keeping busy, not fast service. Firms increase competitiveness by shortening queues, which makes processes act more like customer-pull systems.

While JIT/queue limitation has the feel of a pull system, material requirements planning (MRP) is usually considered a push system; it generates planned orders rather than responding quickly to customer pull signals.

In MRP, a master production schedule for many periods into the future is exploded into gross requirements for all component parts in the bill of materials. The item master file contains the current stock balance for each part, and projected stock balances are calculated for each future period. Where a negative projected balance is found, the computer backschedules (offsets for lead time) in order to plan an order in a quantity large enough to prevent the negative balance. Scrap allowances and independent demands for service parts can be included in MRP processing.

An extension of MRP called time-phased order point (TPOP) allows for blending independent demands (e.g., for service parts) with calculated demands based on parent-item requirements. Basic MRP just launches orders, but closed-loop MRP provides for production-progress data to be fed back to the computer, which then issues any needed rescheduling notices. By prudently acting on the notices, schedulers and buyers can keep make rates and use rates better coordinated with less risk of large residual inventories, more like the pull concept.

Another extension of MRP, distribution requirements planning (DRP), ties demands for distribution inventories to planning for manufacturing inventories.

The unique feature of MRP is not the explosion of bills of materials for items in the master schedule; that was done years before MRP was developed (the method produced a list of shortage items that the reorder point system failed to provide enough of). What is unique is that MRP plans far enough into the future to allow lead-time offsetting for ordering parts. People will trust MRP outputs only if the item master file and bill of materials, the key inputs, are accurate.

MRP is effective in that it plans material needs based on demand projections, not just to refill a stockroom shelf. MRP II extends MRP into the planning of almost any manufacturing resource, including cash flow, and provides a basis for ties to overall business planning. MRP II continues to evolve, but increasing complexity is also noticeable.

The oldest inventory-timing approach is replenishment by reorder point (ROP) methods. In the perpetual system, stock is replenished when it drops to a reorder quantity, the ROP. The ROP equals enough stock to cover average demand over an average lead time, plus some safety stock to protect against nonaverage surges in demand or lengthy lead times. In a periodic replenishment system, reorders are at fixed intervals rather than when stock gets low.

Statistical safety stock calculation employs standard deviation of demand, desired customer service level (service from stock), and lead time. The formula works where demand uncertainty is the dominant variable, as in retailing and wholesaling. Other businesses involve variabilities in supply, which makes the statistical method less useful.

Solved Problems

Problem 1

At Computer Services, Inc., small software jobs start at the desk of the chief analyst, who assigns each job to one of the 10 systems analysts. On average, a job sits in the chief's in-basket for 7 3/4 hours before the chief starts processing it. Average processing time is 15 minutes. In systems analysis, there typically are 60 active jobs. Is queue limitation (kanban) usable at either work center? Explain.

Solution 1   Queue limitation could be used in several ways. For the chief, the rule could be to have zero jobs in the in-basket (queue limit = 0) at the end of the day and stay late, if necessary, to meet the rule. Another possibility is to set the queue limit = 5; if the in-basket ever has more than five jobs, call for help from the most senior analyst.[15]

For the analysts, a general queue limitation policy is one possibility. For example, set an overall response ratio at 2 to 1, with no more than 20 jobs assigned to the 10 analysts. Stay late, borrow programmers for use as analysts, or subcontract work to avoid exceeding the ratio. A rule such as queue limit = 2 at each analyst's desk will yield the same overall ratio. It is hard to say whether the overall ratio or queue limit = 2 at each analyst's desk would work better.

The result of using queue limitation is to speed work through in much less total cycle time (but the same work content time per job). In the office, queue limitation forces people to start one job and finish it instead of starting many jobs, switching among them and stretching all of them out.

Problem 2   The same extruded plastic case is used for three different colors of highlighter felt-tipped pen, A, B, and C. Demand for each color for the next five weeks is as follows (numbers are in thousands):

	Week				
	1	*2*	*3*	*4*	*5*
A	10			10	
B	18		18		18
C	8	8	8	8	8

a. What is a plausible reason for demands for A and B to occur in alternate periods whereas demands for C occur in every period?

b. Calculate gross requirements for the plastic case. Then, given an on-hand balance of 70,000 at time 0, a lead time of two weeks, and an order quantity of 20,000, calculate planned order releases.

Solution 2   a. Demand for colors A and B appears to come from planned orders for a higher-level parent item, perhaps a package containing both colors of highlighter pen. Color C's demand could be independent, perhaps direct orders from a wholesaler or retailer.

b.

	Week					
	0	*1*	*2*	*3*	*4*	*5*
Gross requirements		36	8	26	18	26
Scheduled receipts						
Projected stock balance	70	34	26	0	2 ~~−18~~	16 ~~−24~~
Planned order releases			20	40		

Explanation: The projected −18 in week 4 requires a planned order of 20 backscheduled by 2 weeks to week 2. The projected −24 in week 5 requires a double lot size—40 instead of 20—backscheduled to week 3.

A wholesaler's computer records show the following for one of its inventory items:

$$\text{Mean monthly demand} = 8{,}000$$

$$\text{Standard deviation of demand} = 1{,}000 \text{ per month}$$

$$\text{Replenishment lead time} = 1 \text{ month}$$

If the desired service level is 95 percent, what is the statistical safety stock? What is the reorder point?

The service level, 0.95, represents a probability: 0.50 (the left half of the zone under the normal curve) plus 0.45. We find 0.45 in Appendix A where, by interpolation, $z = 1.645$. Then, from Equation 10–4:

$$SS = z\sqrt{LT(SD)^2}$$

$$= 1.645\sqrt{1(1{,}000)^2}$$

$$= 1{,}645$$

Next, compute mean demand for the lead time period:

$$DLT = 8{,}000 \text{ per month} \times 1 \text{ month} = 8{,}000$$

Then, from Equation 10–3:

$$ROP = DLT + SS$$

$$= 8{,}000 + 1{,}645 = 9{,}645$$

Review Questions

1. What is the role of the maker or provider under push systems and under pull systems?
2. Why is it desirable for the queue limit to be small? Why must it usually be larger than zero?
3. What types of kanban/queue-limitation signals might be used to trigger materials movement?
4. Under what circumstances would kanban removal be appropriate?
5. How might queue limitation be applied to patrons awaiting service?
6. How can queue limitation be made to work when the demand rate is highly variable?
7. What are the marketing and competitive advantages of queue limitation?
8. How does MRP differ from MRP II?
9. What is the role of the item master file in MRP?
10. How does an open order differ from a planned order?
11. How does DRP improve on the usual way in which distribution centers are managed?
12. What is the hazard in using the computer and MRP to reschedule whenever any manufacturing variables change?
13. What is closed-loop MRP?
14. Why is the ROP system considered a perpetual system?
15. Given a safety stock, what else is needed to arrive at a reorder point? Explain.
16. Contrast visual and records-based ROP.
17. To what extent can safety stock determinations be computerized? Does it depend on type of industry? Explain.
18. Is the periodic system simpler or more complex than the perpetual system? Explain.

Exercises

1. Sentrol, Inc., maker of premier sensor products for the security industry, employs nearly every kind of queue limiter in its plant operations, which has cut its average production throughput time to four hours. A remaining problem is cutting the time to refill assembly teams' kanban containers with purchased components from the stockroom next door. Most containers are about the size of a one-quart ice cream carton and hold lightweight resisters, wire sets, screws, and so on. It takes about 50 minutes for a stockroom associate pushing a trolley of full kanban containers to make a complete circuit around the assembly floor; the circuit includes collecting empty kanban containers.

   On a trial basis, a stockroom associate on roller skates (with crash helmet and knee pads) has been making the circuit, carrying two or three cartons at a time. Does this idea sound feasible? What would its advantages be? How would they be measured? Are there disadvantages?

2. Sentrol, Inc., maker of premier sensor products for the security industry (motion detectors, door and window entry detectors, etc.), receives hundreds of orders and other inquiries from resellers and final users by phone each day. Sentrol's customer strategy team has rejected the use of an automatic answering system. The team believes that good service requires real people answering the phones within four rings every time. The trouble is, the calls arrive unevenly, sometimes 5 per hour and sometimes 50 per hour. Is the customer strategy team's four-rings policy practical? If so, how can it be made to work? (Note: Four rings is an queue-limitation policy.)

3. An accounts payable office consists of three people. Their work flow includes passing piles of invoices among them in the process of authorizing payment. Recently, the average number of invoices on the three desks was 150 and the typical time an invoice spent in the office was three days. Select a response ratio, and explain how it might be used to improve the operation. What results might be expected?

4. A manufacturer of X-ray machines presently has partially completed machines scattered around the assembly areas, with only a few actually being worked on by the department's five assemblers. The units accumulate in assembly because parts and subassemblies from other departments arrive whenever the departments happen to complete them.

   a. Is the current system push or pull? Explain.

   b. Suggest an improved system.

5. Four ways to limit queues are (1) kanban squares, (2) special-purpose containers, (3) general-purpose containers with kanban (cards) attached, and (4) a powered assembly conveyor with no container or card necessary. Which of the four should be used in each of the following situations? Explain your answers.

   a. A book printer; books are printed and bound in a route through four different departments.

   b. Final assembly of 13-inch TV sets.

   c. Production of vitreous china products (sinks of all sizes, toilets, tubs, etc.); involves molding, glazing, firing in kilns, and so forth.

   d. Repetitive production of several different large, highly polished precision metal parts.

   e. Internal mail delivery in a large office building.

6. The following matrix shows partial MRP data for one component part. Scheduled receipts are missing, as is the planned-order-release row. Lead time is three weeks. A fixed order quantity (rather than lot-for-lot) is used.

	Week					
	0	1	2	3	4	5
Gross requirements		80	80	90	90	90
Scheduled receipts						
Projected stock balance	190	270	190	100	10	80

What fixed order quantity is used? When is a scheduled receipt due in? In what period is there a planned order release?

7. A partial master production schedule and material requirements plans for a bicycle manufacturer are shown in the accompanying figure.

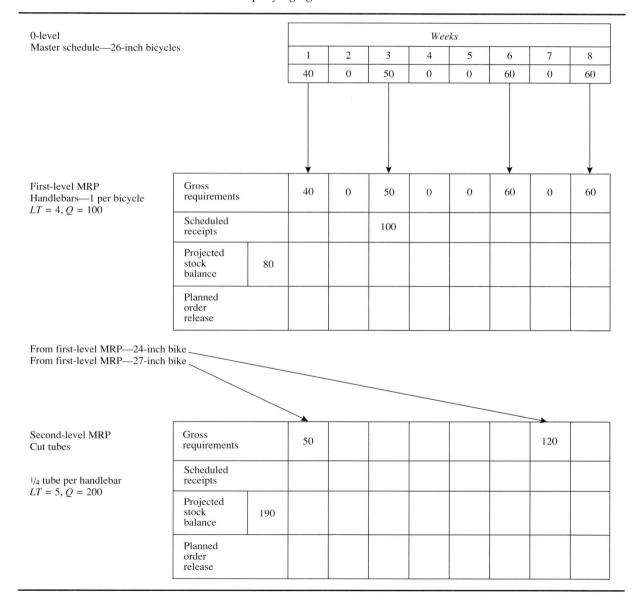

a. Complete the calculations of gross requirements, projected stock balances, and planned order releases for handlebars and cut tubes.

b. Recalculate the planned order release for cut tubing given a scrap allowance of 3 percent.

8. Six companies produce and sell irrigation equipment in the same region of the country. Company A has a reorder point system. Company B uses MRP, but only to launch orders. Company C has full closed-loop MRP. Company D uses MRP plus distribution requirements planning. Company E has an MRP II system (including DRP). Company F produces orders as they are booked, with each assembly triggering pull signals back through all processes and small kanban quantities of all parts kept on the plant floor. Discuss each company's likely competitive strengths and weaknesses.

9. Acme Wood Products Corporation makes wooden picture frames. The 10-by–12-inch size is made with three finishes: oak stained, walnut stained, and mahogany stained. The parts needed for final assembly and finishing for each frame are two 10-inch and two 12-inch wood pieces and four corner brackets. Inventory planning is by MRP. Lot sizes are 10,000 for wood parts and 5,000 for brackets.

a. Construct the BOM structure. You need not limit yourself to the given data.

b. What should go into the item master file? Be as specific as possible given the above data, but you need not limit yourself to these data.

c. Assume that for every oak-stained frame, two walnut-stained and three mahogany-stained frames are made. Also assume that gross requirements for 10-inch wood pieces in the next five weeks are 0, 600, 0, 240, and 300. Compute all parent-item gross requirements based on these gross requirements for the wood pieces (work backward).

d. Based on the gross requirements information from (c), compute the planned-order-release schedule for 10-inch wood pieces only. Assume a current on-hand balance of zero and a lead time of one week.

10. The following sketch shows the two main parts of a transparent-tape dispenser: molded plastic housing and roll of tape. A master production schedule for the dispenser is shown below the sketch.

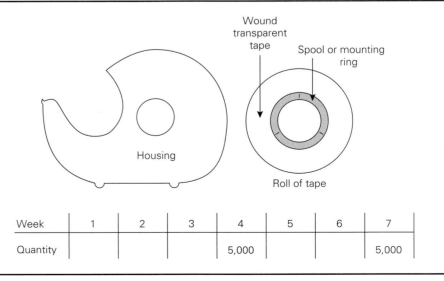

Week	1	2	3	4	5	6	7
Quantity				5,000			5,000

a. Draw a structured bill of materials for the tape dispenser. Include the main parts and one level of parts below that.

b. Assume that lead times are one week for the roll of tape and two weeks for the spool (mounting ring). Beginning on-hand balances are 0 for the roll of tape and 3,000 for the spool. Draw the MPS, with MRPs for the roll of tape and the spool below it. (Do not include housing and wound transparent tape.) Compute gross requirements, scheduled receipts (if any), on-hand balances, and planned order releases for the roll of tape and the spool. Use lot-for-lot order quantities (not fixed order quantities). Show your results in the usual MRP display format.

c. Explain your entries or lack of entries in the scheduled-receipts row for both the roll of tape and the spool.

d. Assume that the rolls of tape are sold separately as well as being a component of the tape dispenser. Make up a forecast of independent (external) demand for rolls of tape for each of the seven time buckets. Merge your forecast of independent demand with the dependent demand from the parent item. Also, assume an on-hand balance of 2,000 for the roll of tape and a scheduled receipt of 4,000 in week 2 for the spool. Recompute MRPs as in (*b*). What could explain the quantity 4,000 as a scheduled receipt in week 2?

11. Assume you are employed by a company that makes a type of simple chair (you decide on the chair's design). MRP is to be the method of inventory planning for the chair.

a. Draw a bill-of-materials structure for the chair. Briefly explain or sketch the type of chair.

b. Develop an 8-to 10-week MPS for the chair.

c. Develop MRPs for three or four of the chair's components, with the following restrictions:
   (1) Include level 1 and level 2 components (e.g., a chair arm might be level 1 and the raw material for making it level 2).

   (2) Make your own assumptions about lead times, order quantities, and beginning inventories.

Your answer should be realistic; no two students should have the same answer.

12. Follow the instructions of problem 11, but use a ball-point pen as your product.

13. Select a product composed of fabricated parts (not one referred to in the text explanation of MRP or in preceding MRP problems). In one page, develop an MPS for the product, plus a level 1 MRP for a major module and a level 2 MRP for a part that goes into the level 1 module.

a. Develop an 8-to 10-week planning period.

b. Draw the MPS at the top of your page, with time buckets for the two levels of parts MRPs lined up below it. The material requirements plans for the parts should include four rows: one for gross requirements, one for scheduled receipts, one for projected stock balance, and one for planned order releases. Make up the following data: realistic quantities for the MPS; beginning on-hand balances, lead times, and order quantities for each part (make one order quantity fixed and the other lot-for-lot); and one or more scheduled receipts based on a previous, already-released order (be careful about the timing and quantity of scheduled receipts).

c. For level 1 and level 2 parts, calculate the timing and quantities of gross requirements, scheduled receipts, on-hand balance, and planned order releases. Display results on your charts, and
   (1) Include a safety stock for one of the parts.

   (2) Include a scrap allowance for one of the parts.

(3) Include demands from an external source (rather than from parent planned order releases) for one of the parts.

14. Below are bills of materials for two sizes of kitchen knife. Two parts are common to both knives: rivets and 8-foot wood bars. Also, a 6-inch cut wood block is common to two different parents (handle, left, and handle, right) for the medium-size knife. Currently, there are no parts of any kind on hand or on order. Order quantities are lot-for-lot rather than fixed. The master schedule for the next seven weeks is given below.

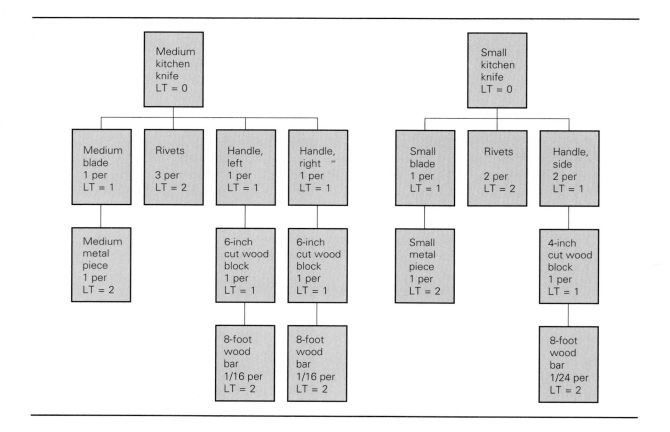

	Week						
	1	*2*	*3*	*4*	*5*	*6*	*7*
Small knife	0	0	0	0	1,200	0	960
Medium-sized knife	0	0	0	800	0	1,200	400

a. What is the first planned order release for rivets? Calculate quantity and week.

b. What is the total number of 4-inch cut wood blocks that should be ordered to cover MPS demand in weeks 1 through 5?

c. How many 8-foot wood bars should be ordered in week 3?

15. The following table shows partial MRP data for one component part. Lead time is two weeks.

		Week				
	0	1	2	3	4	5
Gross requirements		80	0	80	90	90
Scheduled receipts				70		
Projected stock balance	90					

a. If the order quantity is lot-for-lot (just enough to meet requirements), when should there be a planned order release?

b. If a scrap allowance of 10 percent is included in planned order releases, what should the planned-order-release quantity be?

16. Following is a list of inventory items that might be found in various locations in a hospital. For each item, pick what you feel are the two factors that should most influence safety stock for the item. Also, state whether the item should have a high, medium, or low safety stock as measured in weeks' supply. Explain

Toothpicks.	Pillows
Disposable hypodermic syringes.	Rare blood.
X-ray film.	Aspirin.
Coffee cups (pottery).	Soap solution for mopping floors.
Daily newspaper (for sale).	Prosthetic devices (artificial limbs).

17. A beer distributor reorders when a stock item drops to a reorder point. Reorder points include statistical safety stocks with the service level set at 95 percent. For MGD beer, the forecast usage for the next two weeks is 500 cases and the standard deviation of demand has been 137 cases (for a two-week period). Purchase lead time is one week (a five-day workweek).

a. What is the safety stock? How many working days' supply is it?

b. What is the ROP?

c. How many times larger would the safety stock have to be provide 99-percent service to MGD customers? How many working days' supply does the 99-percent level provide?

d. Statistical safety stock protects against demand variability. What other two factors do you think are especially important influences on size of safety stock for MGD beer? Explain.

18. Brown Instrument Company replenishes replacement (service) parts based on statistical reorder point. One part is a 40-mm thumbscrew. Relevant data for the thumbscrew are

Planned stockout frequency = One per year

Planned lead time = 1 week

Forecast for next week = 30

Batch size = 300

Standard deviation of demand = 25 (per week)

a. What is the reorder point? (Hint: Convert planned stockout frequency, in weeks, to service level.)

b. What would be the effect on ROP if lead time were four weeks instead of one? (Just discuss the effect; don't try to calculate it.)

19. An auto muffler shop reorders all common mufflers, and the like, every Tuesday morning. (Rarely needed mufflers are not stocked.) Two of the biggest-selling

models are muffler A and muffler B. Each is ordered if stock is below 3, and enough are ordered to bring the supply up to 10; under this reordering system, the average inventory of each is about 8. It takes two days to replenish.

A reorder-point policy with a service level of 90 percent is being considered as a replacement for the present policy. To see whether ROP would reduce costly inventories, the following data are provided:

	Muffler A	*Muffler B*
Item cost	$7	$39
Daily usage (average)	2	2
Standard deviation of daily usage	1.5	1.5

a. What kind of reorder policy is the present one? Are there names for it?

b. What safety stocks and ROPs would there be for mufflers A and B under a perpetual system?

c. Should the muffler shop go to a perpetual system? Stay with the present system? Devise a hybrid system? Discuss, including pros and cons.

20. One storeroom item has an average demand of 1,200 per year. Demand variability, as measured by standard deviation, is 25 (based on monthly calculations).

a. If the desired service level is 90 percent and the lead time is 2.5 months, what is the statistical safety stock?

b. The item is bulky, costs over $1,000 per unit, and is bought from a variety of suppliers. What effects should these factors have on the safety stock? Explain.

21. Star City Tool and Die has been using a certain 2-inch-square metal insert at an average rate of 200 per five-day week with a standard deviation of 125. Star City makes the inserts itself on its punch press. Only one day is needed to make more of them.

a. The insert is so critical that management wants the item to be available (in stock) 99.9 percent of the time. What is the statistical safety stock? What is the statistical reorder point?

b. The insert has been required for only the past six weeks and is inexpensive to make. Should these factors affect safety stock and reorder point? Explain.

22. Fuel oil is one source of heat in a northern university. Average fuel demand in winter is 6,000 gallons per month. The reorder point is 6,400 gallons, the average lead time is two weeks, and the order quantity is 8,000 gallons.

a. How many orders are there in an average five-month winter season?

b. What is the demand during lead time? What is the safety stock?

c. Draw a graph showing three replenishment cycles for the fuel oil. Construct the graph so that
(1) In the first cycle, delivery takes more than two weeks (with normal demand during lead time).

(2) In the second cycle, delivery takes less than two weeks (with normal demand during lead time).

(3) In the third-cycle, lead time is average but demand during the lead-time period is low.

Note: Since fuel-oil usage for heating is continuous rather than discrete, your line showing actual usage should waver downward rather than follow a downward stairstep pattern.

23. One of the products manufactured by a maker of hand tools is pliers. There are four parts, shown in the accompanying illustration. The status of each part at a given point is shown below the sketch; reference data are also given.

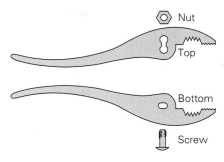

Item	Inventory Status	ROP	Q	LT
Nut	8,000 on hand, none on order	4,000	10,000	10 days
Top	2,200 on hand, none on order	2,000	5,000	10 days
Bottom	3,800 on hand, none on order	2,000	5,000	10 days
Screw	1,700 on hand, 10,000 ordered two days ago	4,000	10,000	5 days
Pliers	2,700 on hand, none on order	3,000	3,000	5 days

For the given data, the following partial table lists required ordering actions and resulting inventory status. Complete the table (determine the correct ordering actions and inventory statuses for the blank cells).

Item	Ordering Actions	Inventory Status
Pliers	Shop order for 3,000 to replenish low (below ROP) stocks.	2,700 in stock
Nut	Releases 3,000 from warehouse for pliers shop order.	5,000 in stock
Top		
Bottom		
Screw		

CASE STUDY

HYGAIN-TELEX

The HyGain-Telex plant in Lincoln, Nebraska, manufactures antennas. It currently has a U.S. Army contract for Model X32 antennas. The contract requires a production rate of 200 Model X32s per day. The contract quantity may be changed quarterly.

Chris Piper, the foreman, is collecting data for a JIT project. Piper has selected the X32 antenna base (not the whip part of the antenna, which is fairly simple) for the JIT project. Exhibit CS10–1 is a photograph of the base.

Case topics: Cycle-time-to-work-content ratio; pieces-to-work-stations ratio; distinction between preventive; maintenance and setup; frequency of delivery; kanban; statistical process control; total preventive maintenance; simplifying the schedule; partnership with customer; cellular manufacturing.

Manufacture of the X32

The X32 base, a cylinder 6 inches in diameter and 10 inches high, goes through several stages of manufacture. Piper's data collection involved the following basic production processes and standard times:

Mold the Lexan plastic base: Some holes are molded into the base by use of core plugs; 2.50 minutes.

Drill and tap (eight operations): Seven drill or tap operations, taking from 0.12 to 1.02 minutes; install helicoils, 1.82 minutes. (The eight operations include drilling a dozen more holes; half of the drilled and molded-in holes are tapped, and half are installed with helicoils, which are self-threaded inserts, a rather old technology.)

Assemble (epoxy) a "birdcage" (ferrite core, coaxial cable, etc.) inside the Lexan base: 1.78 minutes. (Note: The birdcage is produced as a subassembly, going through 12 operations.)

Foam the assembly: 2.61 minutes.

Paint: 1.82 minutes.

Flow Data

Piper thought that the place to start was between drill-and-tap and assembly. Drill-and-tap ran one shift, and assembly usually ran two shifts. Piper asked L. G. Smith, the industrial engineer, to find out the flow distance between processes, especially those two processes. Smith scaled off the distances on the factory blueprints and came up with a total flow distance of 1,296 feet, which breaks down as follows: from mold to drill-and-tap, 192 feet; from drill-and-tap to tank assembly, 144 feet; from assembly to paint, 480 feet; and from paint to final prep, 480 feet.

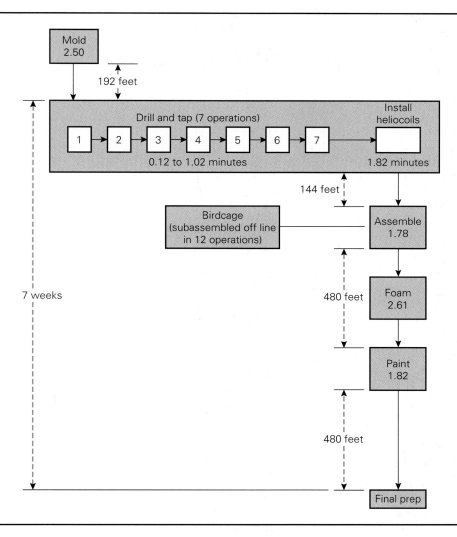

Piper wanted to be sure. "Are those prints current? he asked. Smith assured him that they were. Just to make sure, Piper got a tape measure and checked some of the distances; they were indeed correct.

For flow-time data, Piper went to Raul Nieves, the scheduler. Nieves pointed out that the flow time from molding to final prep had been "as short as about five days for a few lots, but we are quoting six weeks to marketing." Piper asked Nieves to come up with some sort of average. Nieves did so by putting pieces of colored tape on a few molded bases from several lots over the space of three weeks. The average flow time, found by noting how long it took for the taped units to get to final prep, was seven weeks. One week of that was the flow time from the start of drill-and-tap to assembly (see Exhibit CS10–2 for summary data).

Question 1. What is the ratio of actual production cycle time to work content time from the start of drill-and-tap to final prep? (Note: You will not need to be concerned with the issue of one or two shifts.)

Nieves also provided Piper with scheduling and unit-load data. Scheduling released work packets in lot quantities of 2,000. Drilled and tapped bases were forwarded to assembly by forklift truck, in wire-bound pallets holding about 400 bases. In other words, about five forklift trips were required to move one packet-release quantity to assembly.

Problems

At this point Piper called a meeting. Smith and Nieves were there, along with Karen Jones, manager of quality assurance; Bob Crane, an inspector; Doug Atkins, a drill press operator; and Ellie Olson, an assembler. Piper announced that the purpose of the meeting was to "brainstorm what can and maybe can't be done to reduce WIP and flow time" between drill-and-tap and assembly. Piper explained that the purpose was to improve and not look for blame. In that spirit, "please speak frankly."

Piper's first question was directed to Atkins: "Doug, there's no setup time on the drill press that you use for the X32—it's a dedicated tool, right?" Atkins said that it was.

"How about up time on the drill press? Is it reliable?" asked Piper. Atkins replied that the drill press itself was fine but that the tapping head with spindles in the taps was a problem sometimes: "They break, or the bushings loosen," which results in off-center taps or a marred surface around the outside. "Then I have to call maintenance to make adjustments or replace the head."

"About how many hours per month are you down waiting for them to make those adjustments or replacements, Doug?" Atkins estimated about five hours.

Ellie Olson was next. "Ellie, do you have any problems with the bases? Quality problems or running out of bases?" Ellie said that sometimes she did have to wait for the fork truck to bring another wire-bound; she estimated six hours of wait time per month.

The quality problems were the biggest headache, Olson felt, and she looked at Bob Crane, the inspector, for corroboration. Crane agreed that the defect rates were high, especially cracks and fractures around the helicoil inserts. Some, "maybe 5 percent," they thought, were minor defects that Crane or Olson let pass. Crane had figures on how many were defective but repairable and defective-scrapped: 2 percent repaired, 4 percent scrapped.

Karen Jones, quality manager, pointed out that their customer, the Army, had been rejecting an average of 7 percent in recent months. "I believe that the majority of the problems can be traced back to drill-and-tap," she stated.

Piper then asked if anyone knew how many bases were in work-in-process.

Nieves said he had just made a rough count; there were six wire-bounds full at drill-and-tap and eight and a half full at assembly.

Question 2. If 15 direct-labor employees are involved in the production of the Lexan base, what is the ratio of pieces in process to people who could work on them?

JIT Opportunities

At this point, the group began brainstorming on JIT opportunities. Here are some of the options they discussed:

1. Setup reduction (adjust and replace spindles/bushings) on the drill presses. To this suggestion, everyone nodded their heads, but no one commented pro or con.
2. Cut transit quantities. Nieves (scheduler) protested: "The fork truck drivers would be making more trips."
3. Adopt kanban. Nieves liked the idea.
4. Use process control charts in drill-and-tap. Everyone thought it was about time to do some of this.

Source: Adapted from Richard J. Schonberger, *World Class Manufacturing Casebook: Implementing JIT and TQC* (New York: The Free Press, 1987). Copyright © 1987 by Richard J. Schonberger. Reproduced by permission of The Free Press. The characters and some of the data in this case study are fictitious, but much of the process data are based on a real product at HyGain-Telex.

395

5. Adopt total preventive maintenance. This was Piper's (the foreman's) idea. The others showed little reaction; they seemed not to know what that meant.

6. Put in conveyors. Smith (the industrial engineer) offered that one; nobody challenged the idea.

7. Slash the buffer stock. Nieves suggested this, pointing out that inventory counting was a headache anyway. Olson was indignant: "I run out of bases too often as it is."

8. Get rid of the packet-release quantities. Smith suggested this but admitted that he did not know what kind of scheduling might replace the packet-release system.

9. Bring the design engineers in to come up with a better design of the base. Everyone smiled and nodded vigorously.

10. Expand the size of the task force (which they were calling themselves by that time), including a customer (Army) representative. This was Jones's suggestion, which was met by a couple of favorable nods.

11. Move a drill press into the assembly department. This was Smith's idea. Crane (inspector) said that "if we do that I won't have to inspect the bases—and I'm not complaining; it's a boring job."

The meeting broke up with plenty of ideas but no decisions.

Question 3. What should be done? Should all the ideas be implemented? None of them? A different set? What order? To what extent? What time period? What guidance and direction? Discuss each of the 11 options that came out in the brainstorming session.

For Further Reference

Books

Blackburn, Joseph D. *Time-Based Competition: The Next Battleground in American Manufacturing.* Burr Ridge, Ill.: Richard D. Irwin, 1990 (HD 9725.T57).

Hall, Robert. *Zero Inventories.* Burr Ridge, Ill.: Dow Jones-Irwin, 1983.

Japan Management Association, ed. *Kanban: Just-in-Time at Toyota.* Trans. David J. Lu. Portland, Ore.: Productivity, Inc., 1986 (originally published in Japanese in 1985) (TS157.T6913).

Lubin, Richard T. *Just-in-Time Manufacturing: An Aggressive Manufacturing Strategy.* New York: McGraw-Hill, 1988.

Monden, Yasuhiro. *Toyota Production System: Practical Approach to Production Management.* Norcross, Ga.: Institute of Industrial Engineers. 1983.

Orlicky, Joseph. *Material Requirements Planning.* New York: McGraw-Hill,1975 (TS155.8.O74).

Schniederjans, Mark J. *Topics in Just-in-Time Management.* Needham Heights, Mass.: Allyn & Bacon, 1993 (TS155.S3243).

Schonberger, Richard J. *Japanese Manufacturing Techniques: Nine Hidden Lessons in Simplicity.* New York: Free Press, 1982 (HD70.J3S36).

Wight, Oliver W. *MRP II: Unlocking America's Productivity Potential.* Williston, Vt.: Oliver Wight Limited Publications, 1981 (TS161.W5x).

Periodicals/Societies

APICS—The Performance Advantage (American Production and Inventory Control Society).

IIE Solutions (Institute of Industrial Engineers).

Journal of Operations Management (American Production and Inventory Control Society).

Journal of Purchasing and Materials Management (National Association of Purchasing Management).

Production and Inventory Management Journal (American Production and Inventory Control Society).

Target (Association for Manufacturing Excellence).

11 QUICK-CHANGE FLEXIBILITY AND LOT SIZING

Chapter Outline

Quick-Change Flexibility
> *Guidelines*
> *Quick-Changeover Projects*

Lot Sizing: Fundamentals
> *Lots and Throughput Times*
> *Lot-for-Lot Operations*
> *Economic Order Quantity*

Preference for Simpler Models

Lot Sizing under Attack
> *Transfer Lot Reduction*
> *Benefits of Smaller Lots*
> *New Economics of Lot Sizing*

Supplement: Economic Order Quantity: Theory and Derivations

> JIT processing of dishes at a restaurant would go like this: Clear a plate after patron finishes, take it away to wash and dry, and carry it back for placement on another table. Do the same, in turn, for each plate, fork, cup, and so on. Just-in-time it may be, and lean-and-mean (minimal investment in dishes), but efficient it is not.
>
> Good management requires handling dishes in lots, whether busing and cleaning them or setting tables. Serve customers as quickly as possible (pure just-in-time) but save up dishes for processing in non-JIT lots of some size. But what is the correct size?

*𝒫*RINCIPLES 2 AND 12:

Continuous improvement in lead time and flexibility. Cut changeover and startup times.

In this chapter, we consider various **lot sizing** models for part of the answer. Another part lies in the second principle of operations management: continuous improvement. One avenue is refined determination of the lot size itself. A related avenue is quick changeover flexibility, which makes smaller lots economical. Since quick-change flexibility is a basic goal of operations management (regardless of the lot-size issue), we consider it first.

Quick-Change Flexibility

How long does it take an Indy 500 pit crew to change four tires, fill the tank, clean the windshield, and squirt Gatorade into the driver's mouth? Fifteen seconds? Less? Regardless of how long, the workings of an efficient pit crew capture many concepts of quick-change teamwork and readiness.

Concern about changeover and readiness is not limited to pit crews. The Ritz-Carlton Hotel Company, a 1992 winner of the Malcolm Baldrige National Quality Award, for example, switched from independent room cleaning to team cleaning as part of an effort to reduce the time needed to prepare guest rooms. By more than meeting its goal of a 50-percent reduction in cleaning-cycle time, Ritz-Carlton made a significant reduction in the time guests had to wait at the front desk for check-in.[1]

From the famous racetrack in Indianapolis to the posh suites in some of the world's finest hotels, quick-change tactics are directly responsible for winning operational performances. The underlying concepts are simple and can be expressed as guidelines for action.

Guidelines

Although some businesses are famous for their quick changeover expertise (e.g., stage crews and airline caterers), most organizations give the matter scant attention. But elevated competition in many businesses demands quicker, error-free service and enhancing the firm's ability to continually reduce changeover and get-ready times. The training materials that address these concerns are based on a few guidelines (see Exhibit 11–1), which we discuss next.

A milestone achievement for a quick-changeover team is one-touch setup, meaning virtually no setup time; next best is single-digit setup (less than 10 minutes).

Changeover Avoidance.   Guideline one is the special case of a single service, product model, or type of customer that gets its own dedicated process. If, say, three quarters of McDonald's customers wanted a Big Mac and a medium Coke, the restaurant would set up a dedicated Mac-and-a-Coke line, with no flexibility or changeovers to worry about. All companies would love to have products that popular. The simplicity, low cost, and uniformly high quality of this mode of processing yields high profits and large numbers of loyal customers.

Be-Ready Improvements.   The next three guidelines provide natural, low-cost improvement projects for teams of associates.

Guideline two is doing all possible setup steps while the process is engaged on its previous product model, type of customer, or service. That minimizes the time the process is stopped and unproductive. Alternatively stated: Convert internal setup

Experience shows that the be-ready improvements can often cut changeover times by 50 percent or more.

Changeover avoidance:

1. A dedicated, single-purpose process.

Be-ready improvements—developed by teams of associates:

2. External (offline) steps performed while process is active.
3. Setup implements close, clean, in top condition, and ready.
4. For costly equipment, trained crew and clockwork precision.

Modifications—technical assistance on improvement team:

5. Eliminate/immobilize unneeded devices and adjusters.
6. Add positioners and locators.
7. Simplify/standardize software, equipment, fixtures, fasteners, and accessories.
8. Employ externally loadable magazines and work-element holders.

EXHIBIT 11–1

Quick Changeover, Setup, and Readiness Guidelines

setup or changeover
Timed from end of
previous productive
output to the start of
the next, including all
checks for quality and
adjustments to get it
right.

time (while the process is stopped) to external steps (done offline, while the process is running a prior job). At a laundromat, for example, have your next load sorted and the detergent and other additives measured out before the machine stops.

Exhibit 11–2A shows detailed analysis of setup steps on a packing machine at Microsoft, Dublin, Ireland. The analysis includes separate columns for steps to be done while the machine is stopped versus those to be done beforehand. Packaging machine changeovers are frequent because this plant duplicates and packages diskettes just in time for many Microsoft products in many different languages for the European market.

Guideline three (an extension of two) provides the discipline of "A place for everything, and everything in its place." Have you had to wait to sign something while a clerk looks for a 49-cent pen? Or has one, but it won't write? By contrast, an Indy pit crew is ready with gasoline hoses, tire-changing devices, and tires correctly positioned and in tip-top shape. And room-cleaning teams at Ritz-Carlton hotels have towels, linens, bar stocks, and cleaning supplies stocked and ready for use long before cleaning activities begin. Surgical teams in operating rooms, rescue team personnel, and fire fighters adopt the same kinds of readiness habits and discipline.

In some firms,
operators rig
pegboards on which to
hang tools. A shadow
board, with silhouettes
of tools painted on,
provides better
visibility.

In factories, readiness may include hanging precleaned and sharpened hand tools on "shadow boards" at the workplace: no fumbling through a drawer or tool box, or walking to a tool room. Exhibit 11–2B shows a shadow board holding four simple tools used by teams assembling instruction manuals at Microsoft's plant in Dublin, Ireland.

Where equipment is expensive—a race car, a surgical room, or a massive press line that stamps out automobile body parts—a sizable, well-trained changeover crew is justified. Guideline four is deftly applied, for example, in well-managed conference centers: Dozens of employees gather minutes before a conference ends, and quickly and acting in parallel, they dismantle the speaker's platform, remove water pitchers and other table-top items, fold and stack tables and chairs, clean the area, and set up for an evening banquet or wedding party.

EXHIBIT 11–2   Changeover Analysis and Shadow Board at Microsoft-Ireland

A. Setup steps

B. Shadow board

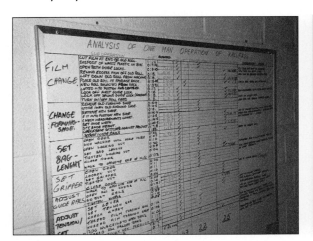

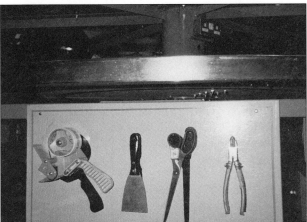

Too often the opposite occurs in factories of well-known companies, such as a $5 million packaging line for a headache remedy halted for four hours while one or two maintenance technicians make hundreds of adjustments, one by one (serially), for the next package size or type of tablet. The JIT movement has caused many manufacturers to change their human resource practices so that such expensive equipment can be set up efficiently.

Modifications.   Guidelines five through eight generally require that the improvement team call on an expert for technical assistance. Since the modifications may be costly, these guidelines would usually take effect after the be-ready guidelines (two through four).

Guideline five calls for eliminating or immobilizing devices and adjusters that come with the equipment or that were once part of the process but are no longer needed. For example, an overhead projector has a focus knob, but if the projector stays in the same classroom anchored to a table facing the same screen year after year, the focus adjustment unit is an invitation for unnecessary, non-value-adding

𝒫RINCIPLE 7

Develop human resources through cross-training.

Experience shows that following be-ready and modification guidelines can often cut total changeover time by 80 or 90 percent.

Into Practice

Quick Setup at. . .

Kentucky Fried Chicken

Quick-setup techniques are not limited to manufacturing plants. Associates at four Oklahoma City area KFC restaurants studied Shigeo Shingo's SMED (single-minute exchange of die) book and put it to use reorganizing the window service area. Changing from one order to another now involves no lifting, no bending, no more than two steps (down from six), easy reach-up-and-pull-down motions, and only two sizes of packer boxes. These changes, plus a few others (see related Chapter 5 discussion) cut window "hang time" delays, which customer surveys revealed were driving customers away. The four restaurants reduced average hang times from over two minutes to 60 seconds. In the year of the improvements, these restaurants enjoyed 17.5-percent growth in sales and 12.3-percent increases in productivity, as compared with declines of 3.0 percent and 0.4 percent in the same measures for the entire KFC district.

Source: Uday M. Apte and Charles C. Reynolds, "Quality Management at Kentucky Fried Chicken," *Interfaces*, May–June 1995, pp. 6–21.

General Mills

How do auto-race pit crews change tires and service cars so quickly? Some engineers from General Mills visited Nascar race tracks to find out. For one thing, according to General Mills' chairman Stephen W. Sanger, they learned that "you don't do anything that requires tools if you can figure out a way to do it without them. If you can put a handle on something instead of a wrench, you do it. And you don't do anything during a pit stop that you can do before."

Source: "General Mills Gets in Shape for Turnaround," *The Wall Street Journal*, September 26, 1995, pp. B1 and B4.

tampering and variable image quality. In one company, a conference room user had wound strapping tape around the adjustment knob at the right focus setting so that other users could skip the adjustment step.

Why not just order the projector with a fixed focal length to suit the room lay-out? Because it would be a costly special order, and the manufacturer would have to charge a higher price. Equipment designers usually include many adjustment features, which broadens appeal, increases demand, produces economies of scale, and lowers the price. After the sale, however, teams of users should work on re-moving or immobilizing unneeded adjustment devices.

Guideline six is the opposite of five: adding special features not usually pro-vided by the equipment manufacturer. For example, to make recycling easier, a team might come up with a plan to equip all the firm's pop machines with a bin that receives, crushes, and holds empty cans.

In manufacturing, setup teams frequently devise locator pins, stops, air-cushion glides, and guide paths that make it easier to change a mold or a die. Exhibit 11–3 shows huge "sleds" on rails, used for quickly and accurately mov-ing multi-ton dies in and out of stamping presses.

Guideline seven calls for simplified, standardized designs. Too many brands of word processors computers, typewriters, and drill presses (each obtained at a

EXHIBIT 11-3

Quick-Die-Change Equipment, GM Stamping Plant

Die-handling sleds on rails are among the quick-die-change innovations on this six-press tandem stamping line, for auto body parts, at this General Motors stamping plant in Pittsburgh. This plant was the winner in a nationwide competition, called the Die Change Challenge, clocking a single-digit die change at 9 minutes 41 seconds (compared with an average 23 hours at the same plant a few years earlier). The resulting plant flexibility was a key factor in a corporate decision to remove the Pittsburgh facility from GM's plant closure list.

Source: "Industry News," *Manufacturing Engineering,* July 1992, p. 24

bargain price) expand exponentially the array of supporting devices and sets of instructions needed for setup and changeover. Standardization also applies to accessories; for example, if all fastening bolts on a machine are the same size, only one size of wrench is needed in machine changeover.

The other part of this guideline is simplification, which should take place before standardization. Exhibit 11–4 shows three examples of how an accessory might be altered so that its use in a changeover takes much less time:

- A U-shaped washer can be slid against a bolt; no need to remove a nut first.
- Pear-shaped bolt holes allow the head of the bolt to slip through the large hole, then slide into the narrow slot for tightening.
- A bolt with cutaway threads may be inserted all the way down into a hole with similar cutaway threads; then, just a quarter turn of a wrench fastens the bolt tightly.

Quick-change teams worldwide have been trained to make use of these kinds of simplified devices.[2]

Guideline eight specifies having extra holders for the work elements, such as component parts, tools, or paper feedstock. Think of a fondue party where each person loads a backup fondue fork while having another already loaded fork in the hot oil.

Quick-Changeover Projects

The eight guidelines assist project teams organized specifically to improve readiness and cut changeover times. In practice, by cutting setup time, the project team usually also improves process consistency, quality, safety, maintenance, ease of operation, housekeeping, and other factors for the target process. Similarly, a team organized to reduce process variation will often also cut setup time. In other words, many of the goals of continuous improvement and competitiveness overlap and are largely inseparable.

This inseparability can be bothersome to veteran managers and technicians, who are used to seeing the work subdivided into many specialties and allocated to specialty departments: quality issues to a quality department, maintenance to a plant maintenance group, and so on. However, as we have reiterated throughout this text, superior companies have discovered the power of continuous improvement led by

$\mathcal{P}$RINCIPLE 15:

Improvement led by front-line teams

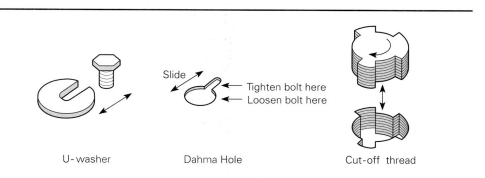

| U- washer | Dahma Hole | Cut-off thread |

Slide
Tighten bolt here
Loosen bolt here

EXHIBIT 11-4

Washer, Bolt Hole, and Threads Simplified for Quick Installation

Source: Adapted from Kiyoshi Suzaki, *The New Manufacturing Challenge: Techniques for Continuous Improvement* (New York: Free Press. 1987). p. 38.

ontrast

Setup/Changeover/Readiness Projects

No Viewpoint	Specialist Viewpoint	Broadened Viewpoint
Setups not viewed strategically.	Improvement talent and funds scarce, so focus only on bottlenecks.	Improve at all processes.
Process set up by outside experts.	Work speeding through setup at a non-bottleneck will just stall later at a bottleneck.	Improvement talent includes every associate; most improvements are low cost.
Once setup procedure is established and (sometimes) timed, it is permanent (no improvement).		Can't divorce setup from other process improvements going on.
		Each cut in setup time frees some labor and reduces startup problems.
		This year's slack process is next year's—or next week's—bottleneck.

---

teams of front-line employees, who call on experts only as needed and usually after several rounds of low-cost improvements have already been implemented. (See Contrast box.)

In organizations yet to reach this stage of all-employee involvement, responsibility for improvement projects may be housed in the specialty departments. Or front-line improvement teams are dominated by supervisors, managers, or outside experts. In such cases problem-solving talent is viewed as a scarce resource that should be directed toward highest-priority projects, such as setup/changeover improvement at bottleneck process. Some advisers maintain, as well, that quick setup on a non-bottleneck process will speed the work through that process only to be idled at a bottleneck. While that can be true in the short run, it is not a good reason for making quick setup a low priority for improvement-minded teams in non-bottleneck work centers.

Also, situations change. Today's non-bottleneck process is likely to become a bottleneck before long. Bottlenecks change with changes in markets, suppliers, products, and processes; and that rate of change accelerates when continuous improvement is taking place throughout the organization.

In inventory-intensive operations, the focus on quick setup is closely related to the goals of cutting lot sizes and throughput times, which we address in the remainder of the chapter.

> Add a second, low-cost machine at a bottleneck process (or use subcontracting) to eliminate the bottleneck.

Lot Sizing: Fundamentals

A **lot** is a group of items processed, transported, and/or tracked as a unit. In manufacturing, items within a lot are typically meant to be identical. In services, lot items may differ from one another to a greater degree, but they usually share a common flow sequence. In this section, we first see how lots form and examine the specifics of lot-size effects on throughput times. Then we explore benefits of lot-for-lot operations, look at examples of how lot sizing might be used, and conclude with an overview of lot sizing in practice.

Lots and Throughput Times

Often, people create lots purposefully, but on other occasions lots just seem to appear. The grouping of items into lots is a reality in both manufacturing and service operations.

Lots in Manufacturing.   In Example 10–4, "MRP for a Chemical Product—Fixed Order Quantity," the order quantity for salamite was deliberately set at 500 units. Justification for that lot size hinged on the economics of production; it goes something like this: Salamite is produced in a 500-unit vat, so whenever we issue a production order for salamite, the lot size will be 500 units, regardless of how many we actually need at the time. The higher the setup time and cost—that is, the *less* quick-change flexibility a company enjoys—the more sense this sort of thinking seems to make.

Lots in Services.   Lot sizing issues are also plentiful in the offices of Poge, Poge, Perry, and Wacker. In the mail room, Arvin accumulates about two hours' worth of incoming mail and faxes before distributing them to departments. In accounts receivable, Cheryl typically spends mornings on problem accounts. In the afternoon, she turns her attention to the ever-present pile of new invoices in her in-basket and completes as many as she can. Just before quitting time, she drops the finished invoices off at Jim's desk—in his in-basket—for subsequent processing. And so it goes throughout the company: Each employee sensibly accumulates a reasonable pile of items to work on before attacking the pile, and sensibly accumulates a reasonable load before passing it to the next stop.

Regardless of how or why lots are created, however, they can have adverse effects on operations and on customer service. First, lots generally increase throughput time. Exhibit 11–5 illustrates, using three different lot sizes, in a simple process that could fit either manufacturing or service situations.

Case 1, Six Pieces: In the first case assume that a lot of six pieces moves as a unit through the three-station process from left to right. In stations I and III, processing is sequential, one piece at a time. In station II, the entire lot may be processed simultaneously. For simplicity, assume processing time is two minutes at each station, and transport times between stations and to the final customer are each one minute. Therefore, each piece in the lot has a throughput time of 29 minutes, consisting of

- 6 minutes processing (2 minutes at each of the three stations).
- 3 minutes transport (1 minute for each of three transports).
- 10 minutes waiting time, station I (2 minutes for each of the other 5 pieces in the lot to be processed).
- 10 minutes waiting time, station III (again, 2 minutes for each of the 5 other pieces in the lot).

Case 2, One Piece: Suppose the lot size was one rather than six. The piece could move through the process to the final customer in nine minutes—no waiting at stations I and III for processing of other pieces.

Case 3, Ten Pieces: Now, let's go the other way, and increase the lot size, to say, 10 pieces. Piece processing times and transport times are unaffected, but total waiting

---

We've already noted some of the ways lot sizes affect operations. In Chapter 8, for example, we saw how lot size can affect work flows, quality, and costs.

throughput time
Time required to complete a processing sequence.

EXHIBIT 11-5

**Lot Size and
Throughput Time**

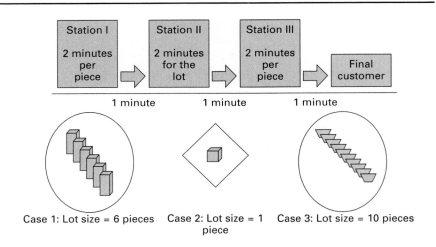

time increases from 20 minutes to 36 minutes, that is, 18 minutes each at station I and at station III. This waiting time—36 minutes when the lot size is 10—is attributable to our decision to process and transport work pieces in lots, and is referred to as **lot delay**.[3] Here, lot delay increases throughput time to 45 minutes (6+3+36).

Large lot sizes also increase throughput times in other ways. Examine Exhibit 11–5 again. Suppose a lot, *Y*, arrives at station III for processing, but must be held up while another lot, *X*, is being finished. Lot *Y* is undergoing **process delay.** Although the *occurrence* of this process delay might be the result of poor planning or schedule mix-ups, its *duration* will depend on the size of the lot being worked on in station III. So, a portion of process delay may also be attributed to lot sizes.

Let's summarize: In sequential processing environments, lots increase throughput times. Thus, the Poge, Poge, Perry, and Wacker employees are missing the consequences of their so-called reasonableness. Lot and process delays keep important messages from reaching recipients for a day or two. Then, the in-basket pile creates further delays. Lengthened throughput times for order processing drive customers to competitors. Moreover, delayed invoice processing creates unwanted disruptions in cash flow—customers can't be expected to pay until they know what they owe. Unfortunately, these inefficient practices are common in firms such as law offices, banks, insurance companies, government agencies, hospitals, and manufacturing companies. The necessary remedy? Cut process and transfer lot sizes—aim to smooth the flow of work. In Exhibit 11–5, the eventual goal might be to process one piece at station I then pass it on to station II while the second piece starts at station I.

But what about simultaneous processing situations, like station II in Exhibit 11–5 or the vat used to produce salamite in Example 10–4? As we see next, lots can cause a different kind of trouble in these cases.

Lot-for-Lot Operations

In **lot-for-lot processing,** demand drives lot sizes. More specifically, the lot size produced for a period equals the net demand for that period. As we saw in Chapter 10, lot-for-lot works well in the parent–component dependency chains of MRP. It is also an effective lot-sizing policy for JIT environments.

process lot:
Lot undergoing a value-adding transformation.

transfer lot:
Lot being transferred (moved) to the next value-adding transformation.

Furthermore, lot-for-lot may be passed down through several stages of supply: "The customer bought four premium tires, so we pulled four from stores, and they ordered four from our distributor, who ordered four from the manufacturer." With no batching into larger lots, orders are frequent. While this might cause order-processing costs to be high, inventories are low and supplier activities closely match real demand. Also, the synchronizing and smoothing effects of lot-for-lot, as compared with batching, stand out. Consider, for example, two sizes of canned food items, apple juice and apple sauce, and two layers of components going into those end products.

Exhibit 11–6A shows a smooth demand pattern for the four products at the canning level. The smooth pattern is carried downward to apple processing and to apple picking. An obvious benefit is the uniform workload for apple pickers, apple

---

EXHIBIT 11-6   Lot-for-Lot versus Batched Ordering

A. Lot-for-lot ordering

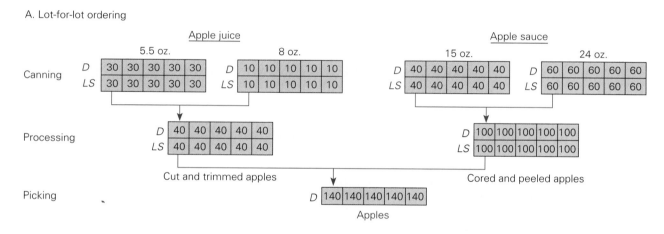

B. Batched orders

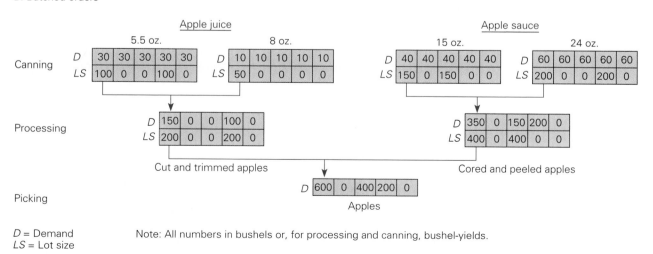

D = Demand   Note: All numbers in bushels or, for processing and canning, bushel-yields.
LS = Lot size

$\mathscr{I}$nto $\mathscr{P}$ractice

When Large Lots Are Required

Firms such as drug and medical-device manufacturers are required by government regulations to conduct lot-acceptance sampling inspections. This involves testing a statistical sample drawn at random from a larger lot. According to statistical sampling tables, as lot size increases, the percent sampled from the lot gets smaller; therefore, larger lots save on inspection costs. Thus, inspection department managers are motivated to delay sampling until a large lot accumulates.

However, this practice can be frustrating to other managers striving for the just-in-time ideal of making and forwarding items in small lots at the customer's use rate. Gradually, regulations and policies are being rewritten in favor of on-line process control, which is more effective in controlling quality than acceptance sampling, and more JIT friendly.

processing associates and equipment, and apple canning line operators and equipment; capacity planning is simple, and capacity may be kept uniformly busy, with little or no overtime or idleness.

The buying of cans, labels, boxes, sugar, and other ingredients and supplies is also uniform. Scheduling and purchasing may be greatly simplified, perhaps to the point where schedules are simply a daily rate, with no need for separate orders and order follow-up for each lot. Queue limitation and kanban might be easily introduced. When even demand is passed back to outside suppliers, they can pass it back through some of their own operations, thus cutting their costs, which can mean price reductions to our apple company.

In Exhibit 11–6B we see a much different pattern. The canning is done in batches, which are fixed in quantity and in excess of daily demand. Maybe somebody has decreed, "Let's can on Monday, Wednesday, and Thursday, and try to save Tuesday and Friday for maintenance on the canning line." But what may be good policy for canning certainly is not good for apple processing, which now has lumpy demands (150, 0, 0, 100, and 0 for cut and trim; 350, 0, 150, 200, 0 for core and peel).

Not to be outdone, processing also decides on fixed-batch lot sizes (200 and 400, respectively) that are larger than, and unsynchronized with, parent demands. Those lot sizes become an even lumpier demand pattern for the apple pickers (600 on Monday, none on Tuesday, 400 on Wednesday, 200 on Thursday, and none on Friday). If the pickers can find steadier work, they will surely leave.

This example makes a strong case for keeping lot sizes from growing (but see the Into Practice box for a qualified exception), and for trying to maintain the synchronization inherent in the lot-for-lot approach.

Economic Order Quantity

Unlike lot-for-lot ordering, which uses actual period demand, other lot-sizing models depend on demand forecasts, which are, in turn, often based on past average demand. The economic order quantity (EOQ) is such a model, and may be appropriate for management of a single inventory item. The reorder point, presented in Chapter 10, also depends on past average demand. While EOQ and ROP are sometimes studied as a set, we prefer to point out that EOQ may be used with a variety of order-timing methods, and in turn, ROP is usable with various lot-sizing methods.

In this section, two examples demonstrate how the EOQ might be applied. The first uses the basic model and the second incorporates quantity discounts.

A little rusty on EOQ formulas? The chapter supplement provides some help, as do end-of-chapter solved problems.

EXAMPLE 11–1:   ECONOMIC ORDER QUANTITY—BOOKSTORE

B. K. White, manager of Suburban Books, is thinking of purchasing best-selling titles in economic order quantities. White has assembled the following data:

Inventory on hand (books):	
Estimated average last year	8,000
Estimated average cost per book	$10
Average inventory value	$80,000
Annual holding cost:	
Rental: Building and fixtures	$ 7,000
Estimated shrinkage loses	700
Insurance	300
Total	$ 8,000
Annual capital cost:	
Capital invested (tied up in books)	$80,000
Interest rate	15%
Total	$12,000
Annual carrying cost (Annual holding cost + Annual capital cost)	
$8,000 + $12,000	$20,000
Carrying cost rate, I (Annual carrying cost ÷ Inventory value)	
$20,000/$80,000	0.25
Purchase order processing cost, S	$4 per order

Solution

Now White has the cost data needed to calculate EOQs. He selects his biggest seller as the first book to be ordered by EOQ—*Gone with the Wind,* which is enjoying a burst of renewed popularity in the store. The paperback recently sold at a rate of 80 copies per month and wholesales for $5 per copy. Thus, for the EOQ equation:

$$C = \$5 \text{ per unit}$$

$$D = 80 \text{ units/month} \times 12 \text{ months/year} = 960 \text{ units/year}$$

$$I = 0.25$$

$$S = \$4$$

Then, using equation S11-2 (from supplement),

$$EOQ = \sqrt{\frac{2DS}{IC}} = \sqrt{\frac{2(960)(4)}{0.25(5)}} = 78 \text{ copies/order}$$

The EOQ, 78 copies, is about one month's supply (78 copies/order ÷ 80 copies/month = 0.98 months/order); it is also $390 worth ($5/copy × 78 copies/order = $390 per order).

White's assistant, M. B. Ainsworth, cannot resist pointing out to her boss a fallacy in this EOQ of 78 copies. She puts it this way: "Mr. White, I'm not so sure that *Gone with the Wind* is the right book to order by EOQ. The EOQ is based on last month's demand of 80. But demand might be 120 next month and 150 the month after. Also, the average carrying cost rate, *I*, was based mostly on larger hardcover books, which cost more to store. Maybe we should use EOQ only on our stable sellers in hardcover. How about Webster's *New Collegiate Dictionary?*"

Users may employ variations on the basic EOQ to offset some of the model's limiting assumptions. One variation incorporates quantity discounts as Example 11–2 shows.

Example 11–2:   EOQ with Quantity Discount—Bookstore

B. K. White, manager of Suburban Books, has applied basic EOQ to *Gone with the Wind.* But he didn't allow for quantity discounts. Popular Publications, Inc., offers the following price breaks for *GWTW*:

Quantity Range	Price per Copy
1–48	$5.00
49–96	4.70
97 and up	4.40

Other data, from Example 11–1, are

$$I = 0.25$$

$$S = \$4 \text{ per order}$$

$$D = 960 \text{ units/year } (12 \times 80)$$

Solution:

Following the procedure from Example S11–2 in the supplement, White's first step is to calculate the EOQ using the best available price—$4.40 in this case:

$$EOQ_{4.40} = \sqrt{\frac{2DS}{IC}} = \sqrt{\frac{2(960)\,(4)}{(0.25)\,(4.40)}} = 84$$

Since 84 is not within the appropriate quantity range (97 or more), White computes the EOQ with the next price option, $4.70:

$$EOQ_{4.70} = \sqrt{\frac{2DS}{IC}} = \sqrt{\frac{2(960)(4)}{(0.25)(4.70)}} = 81$$

The order quantity, 81, is within the appropriate range of 49–96, so White is ready to calculate total annual cost, first at the EOQ of 81 and then at the order quantity that would allow him to take advantage of the next price break. Using equation S11–1 from the chapter supplement:

$$\text{Total annual cost} = \begin{array}{c} \text{Annual order} \\ \text{processing cost} \end{array} + \begin{array}{c} \text{Annual} \\ \text{carrying cost} \end{array} + \begin{array}{c} \text{Annual} \\ \text{purchase price} \end{array}$$

$$= \frac{D}{Q}(S) + IC\left(\frac{Q}{2}\right) + DC$$

$$\text{Total annual cost}_{81} = \frac{960}{81}(4) + 0.25(4.70)\left(\frac{81}{2}\right) + 960(4.70)$$

$$= 47.41 + 47.59 + 4,512 = \$4,607.00$$

$$\text{Total annual cost}_{97} = \frac{960}{97}(4) + 0.25(4.40)\left(\frac{97}{2}\right) + 960(4.40)$$

$$= 39.59 + 53.35 + 4,224 = \$4,316.94$$

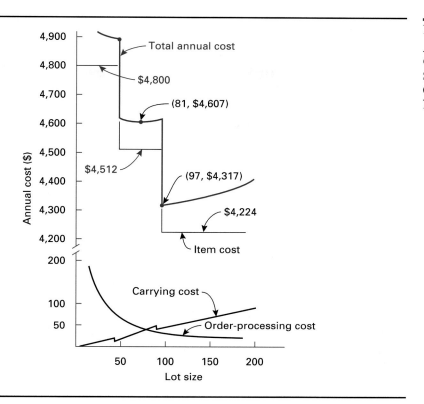

EXHIBIT 11-7

Annual Cost Graph of Lot Sizes with Quantity Discounts

Thus, the true economic order quantity is 97, since its total annual cost, $4,316.94, is less than the total of $4,607.00 for a quantity of 81.

The cost–volume pattern for *Gone with the Wind* has been clarified. Exhibit 11–7 is White's sketch of the cost–volume pattern. It shows that annual order-processing cost drops smoothly and is not affected by the quantity discounts. The annual carrying-cost line has two small bumps, one at each price break. The annual item cost plunges at each price break, and those effects are dominant in the makeup of total annual cost. The feasible EOQ of 81 at a unit price of $4.70 is not economical compared with the true economic order quantity of 97 at the $4.40 price break.

Preference for Simpler Models

There are more elaborate lot-sizing algorithms than those just discussed. The problem with some of the models that look good on paper, however, is that they require cost calculations for future periods, which means reaching into the future for a demand forecast. But we saw in Chapter 6 that forecasting accuracy drops the further into the future one projects.

Ready access to computers allows any of the lot-sizing models to be run dynamically; that is, lot sizes can be recomputed every time demand projections change. The effect, however, is unstable planned lot sizes. Ever-changing forecasting signals cause the entire inventory planning and control system to become nervous. Costs of replanning, rescheduling, and other shuffling of resources generally outweigh any apparent lot-sizing savings.

Thus, many feel that one lot-sizing method is as good as another. Historically, the simpler models, such as lot-for-lot and basic EOQ, have been preferred in business. The preference for simpler models continues today and probably will in the future, judging by the findings of a large-scale survey.[4] Researchers surveyed firms that provide MRP software to over 25,000 worldwide manufacturing locations. They found that lot-for-lot is the most commonly used lot-sizing technique, fixed-order-quantity is second, fixed-period-quantity is third, and EOQ fourth. The users' rationale for choosing the simple models includes (1) simplicity, (2) employee acceptance, (3) recognition that real-world conditions tend to deny any savings predicted by more complicated optimization models, and (4) realization that lot sizing is not nearly so important as taking steps to drive lot sizes down.

fixed-period-quantity
A lot-sizing model that sets order quantity equal to projected net requirements for a given time period.

Lot Sizing under Attack

Today, with just-in-time and total-quality-management zealots looking for waste under every rock, some rethinking about lot-sizing models is taking place. Instead of asking, What is the economic lot? the new question is, What must be changed to move toward piece-for-piece, or lotless, operations? As we consider that question, we must bear in mind that some of the business world and much of the nonprofit world still is not very JIT/TQM-minded, and therefore some of the fundamentals of lot sizing continue to have a useful role.

We begin our discussion of the pursuit of lotless operations by taking a look at reducing transfer lots. Next, we consider some of the benefits and methods of lot-size reduction and conclude with a synopsis of contemporary thinking about lot-sizing economics.

Transfer Lot Reduction

While process lot sizing has received plenty of attention, transfer lot sizing tends to be overlooked. Actually, though, much of the logic that supports process lot-size reduction (OM Principle 13) also applies to transfer lots.

The rationale for transfer lot-size reduction is simple. Recall from the discussion of Exhibit 11–5, we suggested an improvement target that went something like this: After the first piece is processed at station I, send it on—apart from the rest of its lot—to station II. Were the logic followed throughout the process, a rushed customer could receive output in nine minutes, before the process lot (now down to five pieces) had left station I.

In Exhibit 11–6A, lot-for-lot is the policy for process lots. The transfer lots, however, can be larger or smaller than the process lots. For example, the process lot of 140 bushels per day in picking might be transferred to processing in sub-lot quantities of 20 bushels every two hours, assuming two 7-hour shifts.

Large tour groups are often handled in much the same way. If a group of 100 college freshman are to tour the library, the tour leader will break them up into, say, five groups of 20, and stagger the start times as several tour guides lead the groups through the building.

Even with widespread use of E-mail, pagers, and mobile telephones, smaller transfer lots might also be good policy for the mail room clerk in the earlier chapter example. If the clerk made deliveries every 15 minutes instead of every two hours, the transfer lot size and the non-value-adding delivery delay would be reduced eightfold, greatly improving customer responsiveness.

Would delivery of mail every 15 minutes make sense? Would transfer of apples from the orchard to processing every two hours be reasonable? It depends on the distance, the content of the lot, and the mode of transport. A 15-minute delivery interval would make sense if all the offices were together on one floor of an office building. If the offices are geographically dispersed, maybe it's time to bring them together. It might make sense to form office cells with complete teams in the same room, thus avoiding the mail room for most internal document transfers.

For apples, a golf cart or other small vehicle might be efficient for delivering 20 bushels every two hours from orchard to plant. If competition requires cutting the transfer lots even more, how about a processing unit on the back of a truck, which follows the pickers through the orchards? Even some railroad freight haulers are striving for smaller lots; see the Into Practice box, Smaller Trains at Conrail.

To summarize,

*$\mathscr{P}$*RINCIPLE 6:

Organize focused cells.

1. The economic justification for cutting transfer lots is innovation-based reduction of handling costs, which is similar to reducing the cost of changeovers in the case of process lots.

2. Typical innovations involve simplifying the method of transfer (usually toward a less costly mode) and cutting transfer distances by moving people or processing units close together.

Benefits of Smaller Lots

For many years, experts advised manufacturers, wholesalers, and retailers to employ economic order quantity models in lot sizing. That advice was widely heeded, especially by professional managers. EOQ models became one of the most used of all management science tools.

However, many who once favored use of EOQ models now support the principle of driving lot sizes down continuously.[6] Benefits of smaller lots cut across departments and reach out to customers, and thus might not be apparent to an isolated inventory manager or model builder. They include the following:

1. Smaller lots get used up sooner; hence, defectives are caught earlier. This reduces scrap and rework and allows sources of problems to be quickly caught and corrected while the evidence of possible causes is still fresh.

2. Small lots decrease throughput time. As we've seen in this chapter, lot-size reductions directly reduce lot delay and indirectly reduce process delay.

$\mathscr{I}$nto $\mathscr{P}$ractice

Smaller Trains at Conrail

In a strategic shift, Conrail is putting fast freight movement, a requirement of its just-in-time customers, ahead of productivity. The key change is keeping trains shorter. "Although longer trains saved on crew and locomotive costs, they resulted in freight sitting in yards and missing connections."

Source: Daniel Machalaba, "Highballing Along: New Conrail Resembles a Growth Company." *The Wall Street Journal,* November 20, 1992.

3. With small lots, floor space to hold inventory can be cut and work stations can be positioned very close together. Then employees can see and talk to one another, learn one another's job (which improves staffing flexibility), and function as a team.

4. Small lots allow tasks to be closely linked in time. A problem at one work station or supplier firm has a ripple effect; subsequent operations are starved of inventory. Provider and user must treat the problem as a joint problem, and a team attack on such problems becomes natural and common.

5. Activity control is simplified, and costs of support staff, handling and storage devices, control systems, and so forth are reduced.

6. Most important, customers are served more quickly and flexibly, and that increases revenue and avoids the expense of attracting new customers when present customers exit.

The benefits become more pronounced as lot size decreases. The limit? An ideal lot size of one, requiring three key actions:

Contrast

Capturing Lot-Sizing Savings

Old Wisdom	New Wisdom
Space	
Storage space not easily converted, so smaller EOQ lots will capture capital-cost savings but not holding-cost savings.	Within a few months, space will be reemployed; until them, cordon it off and cease charging it as inventory-carrying cost.
Money	
Business plan may limit investment in inventory, so if EOQ calls for larger lots, financial policy may not allow them.	Follow Principle 13, ever smaller lot sizes, which further encourages simplifying and cutting costs of processing orders (e.g., via kanban and setup time reduction).
Price/Delivery	
Smaller lot sizes preclude taking advantage of quantity discount price breaks, so large purchase lots are a necessary part of operations.	Follow Principle 5 to establish partnerships with suppliers; negotiate favorable price and delivery schedules for mutual long-term benefit.
Staff	
People who process orders and set up processes may not be easily retrained/reassigned, so larger EOQ lots may fail to capture staff-reduction savings.	Follow Principle 7, cross-training all associates; also, if ordering is reduced, or "order-less" processing employed, buyers/order processors have more time for process improvement; setup people have more time to attack setup times and help train operators to set up their own jobs.

---

1. *Reduce setup and changeover costs.* Quick-change tools presented in this chapter point the way.
2. *Reduce order-processing costs.* Kanban, rate-based scheduling, blanket contracts, and customer–supplier partnerships help meet this goal.
3. *Sever ties between process lots and transfer lots.* This chapter showed the effects on throughput time, and later, in Chapter 14, we see how separation of process and transfer lots helps smooth job and batch operations.

In the past, OM students studied a host of lot-sizing models and then grappled with the realities—the difficulties in actually realizing any of the cost savings the models promised. Today, revised thinking about lot-sizing savings provides a sharp contrast, as the box, Capturing Lot-Sizing Savings, illustrates.

New Economics of Lot Sizing

Exhibit 11–8A illustrates the economic order quantity concept in graphical form. As continuous improvement programs grounded on the principles of operations management take effect, however, the factors which drive EOQ computations change.

First, drive down setup and order processing costs—the S in the EOQ formula's numerator—so that the cost of ordering frequently in small lots is not much more than ordering infrequently in large lots. How? For items produced in-house, engineer setup and changeover times downward, first to single-digit setup times and finally to one-touch setup. For purchased items, implement kanban, which simplifies ordering, and thus reduces order costs. Stable contracts with a few good (perhaps nearby) suppliers also serve to reduce ordering costs.

Second, annual carrying costs—expressed by the carrying cost rate, I, in the EOQ denominator—get a more thorough assessment than has been the case in the past. Today's value-oriented analysts are inclined to dig out more of the internal

---

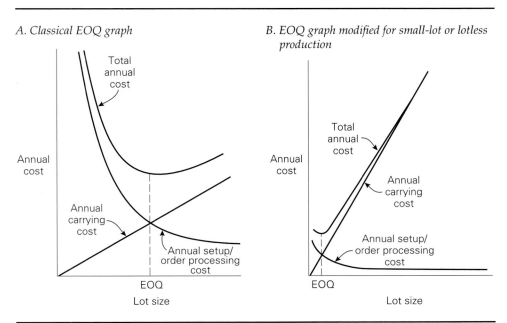

A. Classical EOQ graph

B. EOQ graph modified for small-lot or lotless production

EXHIBIT 11-8

Modifying the EOQ Concept

costs that truly stem from carrying inventory; the cost categories defined in Exhibit 8–2 guide their efforts. The magnitude of carrying costs increases further when they factor in the external costs of carrying large inventories—namely, customer- and quality-related costs associated with *not* reaping the six benefits of small lots defined in the last section. The result is a much steeper carrying-cost curve.

The effects of these changes are shown graphically in Exhibit 11–8B. The lower setup/order-processing curve, coupled with the steeper carrying-cost curve, acts to drive the economic order quantity to the left, that is, toward lower values. Efforts to define a theoretical minimum value for the EOQ are probably unwarranted. Practical people, at least, seem not to care. They have simply set forth a goal of continuous improvement—in large steps or small—toward piece-for-piece or lotless operations.

Summary

Just-in-time processing may be efficient as well as competitive, but sometimes it's necessary to process and transfer work in larger lots. By following the guidelines for quick changeover and setup, teams strive to continually cut process lots, toward the ideal of one unit.

The first guideline is changeover avoidance, via a process dedicated to one type of work. Three be-ready guidelines assist front-line improvement teams: convert internal changeover steps (while the process is stopped) to external, offline steps; keep setup implements close, clean, and in top condition; and, for costly equipment, employ a crew who do the changeover steps in parallel. Four modification guidelines, usually calling for technical assistance, are next: remove unneeded process adjustment devices, add needed positioners and locators to simplify and standardize equipment and accessories, and use externally loadable work holders and feeders.

Following the guidelines can often cut changeover times by 80 to 90 percent. Changeover time reduction usually carries with it improvements in process control and consistency, operability, and several other factors. Regardless of the main goal of an improvement team, other improvements are likely. Consequently, the old practice of parceling out improvement work in pieces to specialty departments is giving ground to broad-spectrum project teams. These teams may be formed of front-line associates, who call on specialists as necessary. Also, the view that setup time projects should target only the bottleneck processes is erroneous since associates should be at work on all kinds of process improvements in every process and since bottlenecks aren't fixed.

Lots exist in manufacturing and in services, and may be created without intention. Lot delay happens when pieces in a lot wait for other members of the lot to be processed. Process delay occurs when lot processing or transport is held up. Both increase throughput times.

The lot size, or quantity ordered, must be decided when an order is planned. Several orders may be grouped together (batched) to save on setup and order processing costs, but that increases inventory carrying costs (holding costs plus capital costs). Also, large orders or batches tend to result in unbalanced or lumpy workloads in processing. Thus, lot-for-lot ordering has some advantages.

Acting on a need for an inventory item generates an order-processing cost, mostly the cost of equipment setup for manufactured items and the cost of processing purchase orders for purchased goods. In addition to the cost of ordering inventory, there is the cost of having or carrying it. Carrying costs include foregone interest on capital tied up in inventory plus physical holding or storage cost.

At the economic order quantity (EOQ), annual order-processing costs equal annual carrying costs, and the sum of the two is minimized. Since the sum varies little on either side of the minimum-cost point, the EOQ may be treated as a fairly wide zone. EOQ computation requires four inputs: annual demand, order-processing cost rate, carrying cost rate, and unit cost of the item being ordered. Variations in the basic EOQ model include allowance for quantity discount and inclusion of a production-rate minus usage-rate adjustment.

Dynamic lot sizing may be used when real-world conditions change, but it tends to result in nervous operations. Although simpler lot-sizing models are preferred, there is a growing challenge to the basic assumptions of lot sizing. In particular, the just-in-time ideal is piece-for-piece, or lotless, production.

Operations with smaller lots are beneficial throughout the production process. Benefits include catching errors and correcting causes sooner, reducing throughput times, reducing inventory space to put front-line employees close together, linking operations more closely so that employees face problems jointly, simplifying the inventory management system, smoothing workloads, and becoming more flexible and quicker to respond to customer demand.

The new economics of lot sizing favors efforts to reduce lot sizes. The goal is lotless operations, and continuing improvement is the path.

Solved Problems

(Note: You may need to refer to the chapter supplement to solve these problems.)

Problem 1

A manufacturer of industrial solvents has been buying for its own use about 18,000 bottles of solution X4X annually for several years. The cost is $10 per bottle, and $100 is the approximate cost of placing an order for X4X. The firm uses a carrying-cost rate of 30 percent. Calculate the EOQ, the annual ordering cost, and the annual carrying cost for this item.

What would you expect to occur if lot sizes were made larger than the EOQ? Smaller? (Hint: Base your answer to these questions on Exhibit S11–2 in the chapter supplement.

Solution 1

The EOQ may be found using equation S11–2

$$EOQ = \sqrt{\frac{2DS}{IC}} = \sqrt{\frac{2(18,000)(\$100)}{(0.3)(\$10)}}$$

$$= \sqrt{1,200,000} = 1,095.45 \text{ bottles}$$

Equation S11–1 contains the annual ordering and carrying cost terms. Thus,

$$\text{Annual ordering costs} = \left(\frac{D}{Q}\right)(S) = \left(\frac{18,000}{1,095.45}\right)(\$100) = \$1,643.16$$

And

$$\text{Annual carrying costs} = \left(\frac{Q}{2}\right)(IC) = \left(\frac{1,095.45}{2}\right)(0.3)(\$10) = \$1,643.18$$

Thus, we see that at the EOQ, the annual ordering cost and the annual carrying cost are equal, the very slight difference due to rounding. Exhibit S11–2 shows the equality of the two costs graphically.

At any lot size other than the EOQ, the total annual cost will increase, as shown by the total cost curve in Exhibit S11–2. If the lot size were increased, we would expect carrying cost to increase and ordering cost to decrease. A lot size of less than the EOQ will result in a reduced carrying cost but a higher ordering cost. Overall, however, minor changes in lot size have minimal impacts on total inventory policy costs, so it makes sense to think of the EOQ as a zone or range of lot-size values.

Problem 2

T-Square, Ltd., an engineering firm, uses packages of plastic tape of different patterns, widths, and shading to create layouts and other design drawings. About 2,000 packages are consumed each year. The supplier, an office supply company, offers quantity discounts as follows:

Quantity/Order	Unit Price
1–99	$10.00
100–499	9.50
500 and up	9.00

T-Square uses a 35-percent carrying-cost rate and spends about $30 placing a tape order. Use the EOQ with quantity discount procedure, as demonstrated in Example 11–2, to determine the appropriate tape lot size.

Solution 2

First, calculate the EOQ for the lowest available price:

$$EOQ_{9.00} = \sqrt{\frac{2(2,000)(\$30)}{(0.35)(\$9.00)}} = 195.18$$

This value is not within the applicable quantity range (500 and up), so repeat using the next available price:

$$EOQ_{9.50} = \sqrt{\frac{2(2,000)(\$30)}{(0.35)(\$9.50)}} = 189.97$$

This value is within the appropriate range (100–499), so it is a possible EOQ.

Next, calculate the total annual cost associated with the only feasible EOQ, (approximately) 190 packages, using equation S11–1:

$$TC = \left(\frac{D}{Q}\right)(S) + (IC)\left(\frac{Q}{2}\right) + DC$$

$$= \left(\frac{2,000}{190}\right)(\$30) + (0.35)(\$9.50)\left(\frac{190}{2}\right) + (2,000)(\$9.50)$$

$$= \$315.79 + \$315.88 + \$19,000.00 = \$19,631.67$$

Now calculate the total cost if the lot size were made equal to the next quantity break point, 500 units in this case:

$$TC = \left(\frac{D}{Q}\right)(S) + (IC)\left(\frac{Q}{2}\right) + DC$$

$$= \left(\frac{2,000}{500}\right)(\$30) + (0.35)(\$9)\left(\frac{500}{2}\right) + (2,000)(\$9)$$

$$= \$120.00 + \$787.50 + \$18,000.00 = \$18,907.50$$

Since the total annual cost of ordering at the best quantity discount amount, 500 units, is less than that associated with the EOQ, the more economical lot size for T-square is 500 packages.

1. How can process changeovers be avoided entirely?

2. Who should lead the effort to convert internal setup time to external? Why?

3. How does Principle 7, involving cross-training, relate to quick changeover?

4. When should experts be called in to assist in a quick-setup project? What would the experts' role be?

5. What is lot delay? How does it differ from process delay?

6. How does the existence of lots affect throughput time? Illustrate with an example of your own creation.

7. Why is setup/changeover time reduction important for lot sizing?

8. Why does lot-for-lot tend to ease the problem of lumpy workloads?

9. Why are lumpy workloads a problem?

10. Explain how order-processing/setup costs and carrying costs relate to lot size.

11. In what sense is the EOQ a zone?

12. Why is construction of the ultimate EOQ model, with all costs included, an impractical goal?

13. What assumptions underlie the basic EOQ model? Are they realistic? Explain.

14. What benefits are associated with smaller lot sizes?

15. How may order-processing costs be cut in order to make it economical to buy in small amounts?

16. How does reducing lot sizes improve quality? Workforce communications? Problem solving?

17. If EOQs (for a lot-size reduction campaign) result in small lots and less inventory, will there be savings from emptying out storage space? Explain.

18. If process lots are unyieldingly large, is it practical to turn to transfer lots for improvement in responsiveness? Explain.

1. Clerks at your local post office must be prepared to sell stamps, weigh and post several types of letters and parcels, insure mail, and perform dozens of other operations. Find out about and discuss two of the quick-changeover guidelines that seem to be followed by post office clerks to enable them to quickly switch from one operation to another.

2. The chapter discussion of quick-change flexibility includes as an Into Practice box, "Quick Setup at Kentucky Fried Chicken and at General Mills." Review the example and relate each improvement to one of the eight guidelines for quick changeover listed in Exhibit 11–1. (Example: For General Mills, "You don't do anything during a pit stop that you can do before"; which of the eight guidelines does that statement refer to?) Discuss your answers.

3. From your own experience as a client or customer, give an example of especially good server readiness and especially poor server readiness.

4. Exhibit 11–3 shows die-handling sleds on rails along a stamping line, which presses a steel sheet between upper and lower dies into auto body parts (the steel goes into the first press for partial shaping, then into the next for more shaping, etc., for progressive shaping into the final part). Changeover time from, say, a fender to a door panel—an extreme changeover—is 30 minutes. The plant has several identically equipped stamping lines and racks containing dies for hundreds of different auto body parts that go to auto body repair shops (not to GM assembly plants).

   a. From the photo and this explanation, which of the eight quick-changeover guidelines have been followed? Explain.

   b. What would be necessary to reduce this type of changeover to single-digit minutes (which is the next goal at this GM plant) or less? (Hint: Carefully consider the eight quick-changeover guidelines.)

5. Exhibit 11–2B is a photo of four tools hanging on a shadow board just below the edge of a round table used for assembling instruction manuals for Microsoft software products. The location of these tools below the table edge might be an obstacle to reducing changeover time still further. Suggest an improvement that would cut changeovers further; cite the quick-changeover guidelines that apply to your improvement.

6. Would the comparison between lot-for-lot and batch (Exhibit 11–6) make sense if clients were being processed instead of apples? If so, develop a brief example and explain. If not, explain why not.

7. The master scheduling team at a plant producing steel chain is considering a lot-for-lot policy instead of batching into larger lots. The following is their partially completed analysis for three levels of chain making (final chain making, fed by fabrication of cut steel pieces, fed by purchased steel rods).

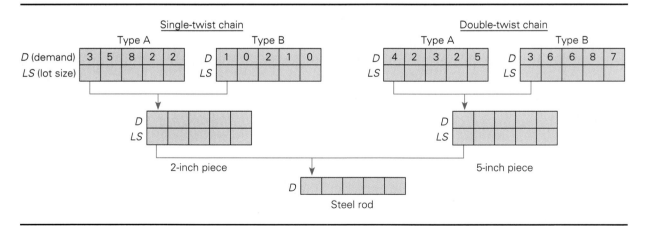

   a. Complete the lot-for-lot analysis, following the method of Exhibit 11–6A.

   b. Now construct a similar analysis, following the method of Exhibit 11–6B; assume a lot size of 10 for type A and 5 for type B single-twist chain making, 15 for type A and 20 for type B double-twist chain making, 20 for 2-inch-piece fabrication and 40 for 5-inch-piece fabrication.

   c. Does your analysis demonstrate the benefits of lot-for-lot in this example of uneven end-product (finished chain) demand? Discuss.

8. The provincial government uses massive quantities of computer printer paper, which it buys centrally. The purchasing department calculates an economic order

quantity based on an assumed carrying-cost rate of 30 percent per year. A box of printer paper costs $40, it costs $60 to process an order, and annual demand is for 36,000 boxes of paper.

   a. What is the EOQ?
   b. The buyer finds that 10 percent more than the EOQ would be a whole truckload. Should she order the extra 10 percent? Think about this carefully, and explain your answer.

9. Continental Plate and Boiler Company has one storeroom that holds various sizes of pipe and steel plate. Following are costs and other data associated with pipe and plate buying and storage:

Average inventory on hand	$1.5 million
Purchasing department wages and overhead	$33,000/year
Purchases of pipe and plate	$4.5 million/year
Number of purchase orders processed	500/year
Interest rate	18 percent per year
Depreciation on storeroom and its storage racks	$38,000/year
Overhead and expenses (including taxes and insurance to operate store (room)	$10,000/year
Storeroom salaries	$16,000/year

   a. What is the average cost of processing a purchase order (S)?
   b. What is the annual capital cost? Annual holding cost? What is the carrying cost rate (I)?
   c. What are some other, less tangible costs of carrying inventory? How might those costs affect inventory policy at Continental?

10. Maple Tree Insurance Company uses 2,000 boxes of staples per year. The boxes are priced at $3 in quantities of 0 to 99 boxes or $2.60 in quantities of 100 boxes or more. If it costs $15 to process an order and the annual carrying cost rate is 0.30, how many boxes should be ordered at one time?

11. A chemical plant consumes sulfuric acid in a certain process at a uniform rate. Total annual consumption is 25,000 gallons. The plant produces its own sulfuric acid and can set up a production run for a cost of $4,000. The acid can be stored for $0.60 per gallon per year, including all carrying costs (cost of capital as well as cost to hold in storage). The production rate is so rapid that inventory depletion during production may be ignored.

   a. What is the economic order quantity?
   b. How many times per year should the acid be produced?

12. A cannery buys knocked-down cardboard boxes from a box company. Demand is 40,000 boxes per year. The inventory carrying-cost rate is 0.25 per year, and the cannery's purchasing department estimates order processing cost at $20. The box company prices the boxes as follows:

   For a purchase of 100 to 3,999 boxes: $0.60 each (minimum order = 100)
   For a purchase of 4,000 or more boxes: $0.50 each

   a. Determine the economic purchase quantity (EPQ).
   b. Express your EPQ in months' supply, and then in dollars.

13. A manufacturer of wooden furniture carries in its warehouse only one type of inventory: lumber. Following are various costs that may or may not be associated with that inventory:

Rent on warehouse	$23,000/year
Wages and salaries, purchasing department	$80,000/year
Inventory taxes	$18,000/year
Cost of capital	14%/year
Value of average inventory on hand	$680,000
Insurance on warehouse contents	$3,500/year
Operating supplies, purchasing department	$1,400/year
Operating budget, production control department	$160,000/year
Expenditure on inventory	$3,400,000/year
Cost of a 12-foot, one-by-four-inch board	$1
Overhead, purchasing department	$25,000/year
Wages and salaries, warehouse	$48,000/year
Overhead, warehouse	$8,000/year
Miscellaneous expenditures, warehouse	$4,200/year

a. What is the inventory carrying cost rate (I) for the total inventory stored?

b. What is the average cost of processing a purchase order (S)? Assume that 3,000 purchase orders per year are processed.

c. What is the EOQ for one-by-four-inch boards? Assume that 30,000 of these boards are used annually.

d. What is the annual cost of capital invested in one-by-four-inch boards? (Ignore safety stock.)

14. A small company adopts buying by EOQs for all items in its stockroom. The EOQs show that many items formerly had been ordered in quantities far larger than their EOQs. The company has one buyer and one enclosed stockroom with one storekeeper.

a. What savings can the company expect to derive from its EOQ ordering? What potential savings may prove to be difficult to capture?

b. If the company adopts a full just-in-time effort, including flexible resource policies, how would that affect the answers to the questions posed in (*a*)?

15. For the first time, Ordinaire, Inc., has calculated economic order quantities for items carried in stock. The calculations show that, for years, the supplies stockroom has been ordering quantities that are too large and the direct material stockroom has been ordering quantities that are too small. The comptroller is convinced that adopting the EOQs will save over $100,000 per year in reduced inventory cost. Critique the comptroller's viewpoint. (Hint: What expected savings, if any, may fail to be captured?)

16. Among other things, Marksman Industries makes 10 different models of gun-cleaning rods. Presently, the 10 models are manufactured one at a time, each for about one week's worth of production (average). The schedule is supposed to provide enough of a given model during the week-long production run to satisfy about 10 weeks of consumer demand (it will not be made again for 10 weeks). The problem is that by the end of the 10-week cycle for a model, expected consumer demand may have changed. By the time of the next production run, Marksman may have run out of a given model or accumulated a large excess. How can Marksman be more responsive to actual consumer demand? Explain.

17. Federal Time Corporation makes and sells clocks. Plastic lenses for clock faces are molded in Federal's own facilities. One popular table model has an annual demand of 40,000 clocks; its lens costs $0.60 to make. Setup to mold the lens, consisting of inserting and clamping the correct mold in the injection-molding equipment, costs $80 per production run. (Setup time is about four hours.)

a. Federal has been using EOQ to determine number of lenses per production run. It uses an inventory carrying cost rate of 0.25 and the formula $EOQ = \sqrt{2DS/IC}$. What is the EOQ for this lens?

   b. The plant manager has become convinced that there are benefits in running lenses in much smaller lots than EOQs. The four-hour setup time must be reduced in order to make small lots economical. What kinds of improvements does Federal need in order to achieve single-digit setup? To achieve one-touch setup?

18. A well-known phenomenon in the semiconductor industry (making microprocessors and memory chips) is that fast processing of a production lot has a higher process yield than slow processing. (*Process yield* means number of good chips from a wafer—i.e., chips that pass electronic tests of quality.) The reason is that the wafers are susceptible to handling, dust, and other kinds of damage that are reduced if the production run is completed and the chips sealed over quickly.

   One semiconductor manufacturer has several models of memory chip to run, one at a time. A production run of a given model normally takes five weeks, but a few small, special runs have been completed in as little as two weeks, with high process yields. How can a manufacturer gain these advantages all the time instead of only in special cases?

19. A producer of precision instruments has initiated a just-in-time effort. One of its early achievements was reducing setup time on a milling machine for making a key component part. The old setup cost was $200; now it is $8. As a result, the new economic lot size is only 16 units, whereas the old one had been much higher.
   a. If the company is serious about obtaining full just-in-time benefits, what lot size should be run? Explain.
   b. What was the old EOQ? (Hint: Use the new EOQ along with the ratio of new to old setup cost. No other data are needed.)

For Further Reference

Books

Hopp, Wallace J., and Mark L. Spearman. *Factory Physics: Foundations of Manufacturing Management.* Burr Ridge, Ill.: Irwin, 1995 [TS155.H678].

Shingo, Shigeo. *A Revolution in Manufacturing: The SMED [Single-Minute Exchange of Die] System.* Portland, Ore.: Productivity Press, 1985.

Steudel, Harold J., and Paul Desruelle. *Manufacturing in the Nineties.* New York: Van Nostrand Reinhold, 1992 [HD9725.S68].

Suzaki, Kiyoshi. *The Manufacturing Challenge: Techniques for Continuous Improvement.* New York: The Free Press, 1987 [HD9720.5.S98]

Periodicals/Societies

Decision Sciences (Decision Sciences Institute).

Industrial Engineering Solutions (Institute of Industrial Engineers).

Journal of Purchasing and Materials Management (National Association of Purchasing Management).

Production and Inventory Management Journal American Production and Inventory Control Society).

SUPPLEMENT

ECONOMIC ORDER QUANTITY: THEORY AND DERIVATIONS

The economic order quantity (EOQ) is the number of units of a single item that should be planned whenever an order is placed so as to minimize the inventory management costs of that single item during a given time period, usually one year. In this supplement, we first address EOQ assumptions, take a look at categories of costs that arise in inventory management, and then put everything together to determine the EOQ and other related order quantities.

EOQ Assumptions

Like most models, the basic EOQ makes a few simplifying assumptions. While the real world never quite matches the assumptions, sometimes the matchup is close enough for EOQ concepts to be helpful. Assumptions that pertain to the *basic* EOQ model include

1. Demand is known and constant, without seasonality. Past demand is used to forecast future period demand.
2. Order processing (or setup) costs are known and constant—they don't vary with quantity ordered.
3. Cost per unit (e.g., purchase price or production cost) is constant; there are no quantity discounts or economies of scale.
4. The entire lot is delivered at one time (instantaneous acquisition). This is commonly the case for purchased goods, but not for items produced by the user.
5. The carrying-cost rate is known and constant. Total carrying costs are a linear function and depend on carrying-cost rate and quantity ordered.
6. The inventory depletion rate is constant throughout the order cycle; the average inventory equals one-half the quantity ordered.

Costs of Inventory

EOQ logic seeks to minimize three types of period inventory costs: order processing cost, carrying cost, and item cost.

1. Order Processing Cost.   In a given time period (say, a year), an item may be reordered once, twice, three times, or more, even daily in some JIT cases. If it is ordered once, the lot size is large enough to cover the whole year's demand; if ordered twice, a half-year's demand is the lot size; and so on.

The costs of processing an order include the clerical costs of preparing the purchase order or work order. If it is a purchase order, costs of order expediting and processing the invoice are included; if it is a work order, the main cost may be process setup cost. If S is the average cost of processing an order, Q is the lot size (quantity ordered), and D is the forecast annual demand for a given item, then

$$\frac{D}{Q} = \text{Number of orders per year}$$

$$S\left(\frac{D}{Q}\right) = \text{Annual cost of processing orders}$$

Forecast demand (D) could cover a period other than a year. For example, if D represents monthly demand, $S(D/Q)$ equals the monthly cost of processing orders.

2. Carrying Cost.   Carrying cost (discussed at length in Chapter 8) is the cost to finance inventory and hold it in idleness. Thus, carrying cost increases as number of idle units increases. If an item is reordered infrequently in large lots, its carrying costs will be large; if ordered often in small lots, its carrying costs will be small.

Total carrying costs per period divided by value of all inventory items yields what is known as the annual inventory-carrying-cost rate (I). Cost analysts may set one rate for all items carried in a given firm. To compute annual carrying cost for a single item, we need the unit cost (C) for the item. Then:

IC = Cost to carry one unit for one year

For any given lot size (Q), annual carrying cost equals annual cost to carry one unit times average number of idle units, ($Q/2$). Symbolically, for a given item we have:

$$IC\left(\frac{Q}{2}\right) = \text{Annual carrying cost}$$

Why is the average inventory equal to $Q/2$? Exhibit S11–1 illustrates the repetition of EOQ order cycles during the year. Inventory increases from 0 to Q (the EOQ) on receipt of each order. Demands during the order cycle reduce inventory from Q to 0. The average amount of inventory, then, is simply the average of the maximum amount (Q), and the minimum amount (0), or $Q/2$. (The mathematically inclined might prefer to make the point with a geometrical proof that triangles I and II in Exhibit S11–1 are identical.)

3. Item Cost.   Item cost comes into play, for instance, when the buyer may obtain price discounts by buying in quantity. But recall that an assumption of the basic EOQ model is constant item cost or price; it is unaffected by quantity ordered. The annual item cost, therefore, is annual demand (D) times unit cost (C). Though necessary for materials budgeting, item cost is mathematically removed from consideration in basic EOQ computations.

We may compute a total annual cost for the item by summing the order-processing costs, carrying costs, and item costs:

$$\text{Total cost} = TC = \left(\frac{D}{Q}\right)(S) + (IC)\left(\frac{Q}{2}\right) + DC \qquad \text{(S11–1)}$$

Basic EOQ Formula Derivation

Exhibit S11–2 shows a plot of the cost elements contained in equation S11–1 as they would vary with lot size. Item costs, independent of lot size, needn't be plotted. The EOQ is the order quantity that minimizes total annual costs—that is, where the slope of the total cost curve is zero. Also, as the vertical dashed line shows, annual order-processing costs equal annual carrying costs at the EOQ.

Thus, by taking the derivative of the total cost function with repect to Q and setting it equal to the slope (zero), we obtain an expression for the EOQ:

$$\frac{d(TC)}{d(Q)} = \frac{d\left[\left(\frac{D}{Q}\right)(S) + (IC)\left(\frac{Q}{2}\right) + (D)(C)\right]}{d(Q)} = 0$$

$$= -\frac{DS}{Q^2} + \frac{IC}{2} = 0$$

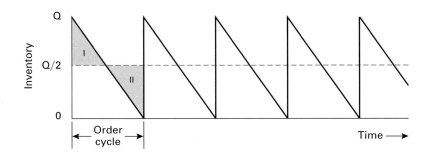

EXHIBIT S11–2

Graph of Annual Inventory Policy Cost and Lot Sizes

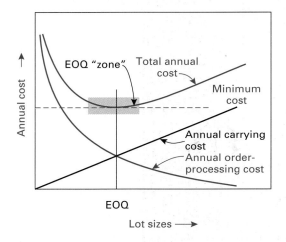

Rearranging the terms, we obtain

$$Q^2 = \frac{2DS}{IC}$$

By taking the square roots of both sides,

$$Q = \sqrt{\frac{2DS}{IC}} \qquad\qquad \text{(S11–2)}$$

Equation S11–2 is the classic EOQ formula. Example S11–1 demonstrates the computations, and Example 11–1 in the chapter illustrates how the EOQ model might work in practice. Before turning to extensions of the basic model, two practical reminders are in order:

EXAMPLE S11–1:   BASIC EOQ COMPUTATIONS

Annual demand for an item with a unit cost of $4.00 is 5,000 units. The carrying-cost rate is 50 percent, and it costs $100 to process an order. Compute EOQ and total annual inventory costs for the item.

Solution

EOQ is determined with equation S11–2:

$$EOQ = \sqrt{\frac{2DS}{IC}} = \sqrt{\frac{2(5,000)(\$100)}{0.5(\$4)}} = 707$$

Substitute values into equation S11–1 to obtain total annual inventory costs:

$$TC = \frac{D}{Q}(S) + IC\left(\frac{Q}{2}\right) + DC$$

$$= \frac{5,000}{707}(\$100) + (0.5)(\$4)\left(\frac{707}{2}\right) + 5,000(\$4)$$

$$= \$707 + \$707 + \$20,000 = \$21,414$$

- In Exhibit S11–2, a shaded zone contains the minimum cost point. In that zone, which is fairly large horizontally, total annual cost does not deviate much from the minimum. Thus, in a practical sense, EOQ may be thought of as a zone or range of lot sizes, rather than as an exact quantity.

- The total cost curve shown in Exhibit S11–2 reflects inventory *policy* costs only. In practice, item costs ($D \times C$), though not considered in *basic* EOQ determination, can be considerably more than the annual policy costs.

EOQ with Quantity Discounts

Sometimes the cost for purchased items varies due to quantity discounts—price breaks offered by a supplier for volume purchases. Item cost then becomes a relevant factor (along with annual carrying and order-processing costs) in total inventory costs. In the quantity discount situation, associates use equation S11–2 to compute an EOQ. But if the price break afforded at the next (larger) order quantity point reduces total annual costs, then that larger order quantity is the true economic order quantity. A procedure for finding the true EOQ and total annual inventory costs is[6]

1. With equation S11–2, compute the EOQ using the lowest offered price as item cost (*C*). If the EOQ falls within the quantity range that applies to the lowest feasible price, it is the true EOQ. Use equation S11–1 to find total annual costs.

2. If the EOQ falls below the lowest-price quantity range, use the next higher price as the value for *C* and recompute the EOQ. If the (newly) computed EOQ is not within the relevant quantity range for that price, move to the next higher price, and so on.

3. When the computed EOQ is within the appropriate quantity range, use equation S11–1 to find total annual costs at that order quantity and at the order quantity that would permit the next price break. The lower of the two costs identifies the true economic order quantity.

Example S11–2 explains the procedure and illustrates the computations. In the body of the chapter, Example 11–2 shows how EOQ with quantity discounts might be applied by a small business.

EXAMPLE S11–2:   EOQ WITH QUANTITY DISCOUNT COMPUTATIONS

Annual demand for an item is 5,000 units. The carrying-cost rate is 50 percent, and it costs $100 to process an order. Quantity price breaks are available as shown in the table below:

Quantity Range	Price per Unit ($)
0–99	4.00
100–499	3.80
500–999	3.60
1,000 and up	3.40

Compute EOQ and total annual inventory costs for the item.

Solution

First, use equation S11–2 to compute EOQ with the lowest possible price, $3.40, as the item cost:

$$EOQ = \sqrt{\frac{2DS}{IC}} = \sqrt{\frac{2(5,000)(\$100)}{0.5(\$3.40)}} = 767$$

Since the computed EOQ, 767, is not within the appropriate quantity range of 1,000 or more, move to the next price and recompute the EOQ:

$$EOQ = \sqrt{\frac{2DS}{IC}} = \sqrt{\frac{2(5,000)(\$100)}{0.5(\$3.60)}} = 745$$

This EOQ is within the applicable quantity range (500–999), so move on to computation of total costs. At the computed EOQ, equation S11–1 yields

$$TC_{745} = \frac{D}{Q}(S) + IC\left(\frac{Q}{2}\right) + DC$$

$$= \frac{5,000}{745}(\$100) + (0.5)(\$3.60)\left(\frac{745}{2}\right) + 5,000(\$3.60)$$

$$= \$671 + \$671 + \$18,000 = \$19,342$$

Total costs for the next price-break point—that is, order quantity of 1,000 at a unit price of $3.40:

$$TC_{1,000} = \frac{D}{Q}(S) + IC\left(\frac{Q}{2}\right) + DC$$

$$= \frac{5,000}{1,000}(\$100) + (0.5)(\$3.40)\left(\frac{1,000}{2}\right) + 5,000(\$3.40)$$

$$= \$500 + \$850 + \$17,000 = \$18,350$$

Thus, 1,000 is the true EOQ since total annual costs are less at that order quantity. Item cost reduction with the price break more than offsets the slightly higher inventory policy costs.

Economic Manufacturing Quantity

Basic EOQ is suitable for purchased items—an economic purchase quantity—in which the whole lot is usually delivered at one time. When an item is made instead of bought, the quantity ordered is available in trickles as it comes off the production line. This complicates figuring average inventory, on which annual carrying cost is based, and results in a modified EOQ formula. The modification may be called an **economic manufacturing quantity (EMQ)** formula.

EMQ formula also applies to the rare case in which a purchased lot is delivered in trickles, instead of all at once.

The EMQ calls for one new term, the production rate (P). P is measured in the same units as D (demand rate), typically in units per year. P must be greater than D in order for the demand to be covered. $P - D$ is the rate of inventory buildup; that is, producing at rate P and using at rate D. The difference equals the rate of increase in stock. (Some prefer to use weekly or monthly build-and-use rates, which work just as well in the EMQ model.)

To develop the model, consider that a lot is made in time T:

$$Inv_{max} = Q_{max} = \text{Build rate} \times \text{Time} = (P - D)(T)$$

Since Q_{max} is maximum planned inventory and $Q_{max}/2$ is average inventory,

$$\text{Average inventory} = \frac{Q_{max}}{2} = \frac{(P - D)(T)}{2}$$

The term T may be eliminated by substitution. The time needed to produce a lot, Q, is

$$T = \frac{\text{Quantity}}{\text{Rate}} = \frac{Q}{P}$$

Thus,

$$\text{Average inventory} = \left(\frac{P-D}{2}\right)\left(\frac{Q}{P}\right) \text{ or } \left(\frac{P-D}{P}\right)\left(\frac{Q}{2}\right)$$

And

$$\text{Annual carrying costs} = (IC)\left(\frac{P-D}{P}\right)\left(\frac{Q}{2}\right)$$

Using this expression for carrying costs to replace the carrying cost element in equation S11–1, again taking the first derivative with respect to Q, and rearranging the terms as we did when deriving the basic EOQ formula, we obtain

$$\frac{DS}{Q^2} = \left(\frac{IC}{2}\right)\left(\frac{P-D}{P}\right)$$

Or,

$$Q = \sqrt{\frac{2DS}{IC}\left(\frac{P}{P-D}\right)}$$

Alternatively,

$$EMQ = \sqrt{\frac{2DS}{(IC)(1-D/P)}} \tag{S11–3}$$

Differences between basic EOQ and EMQ may be shown graphically. Exhibit S11–3A shows the general pattern of usage and replenishment for basic EOQ. It looks like a ripsaw blade. The vertical line represents the increase in stock that occurs when the whole EOQ is received at one time (instantaneous replenishment). The downward-sloping line is the average demand rate (D). Maximum quantity ($Q_{max.}$) is equal to Q, and average quantity ($Q_{ave.}$) is equal to $Q_{max.}/2$.

Exhibit S11–3B shows the general inventory pattern for EMQ. It looks like a cross-cut saw blade. The upward-sloping solid line represents the rate of inventory buildup ($P - D$); the production rate (P) is shown as a dashed line for reference purposes. The downward-sloping line is the average demand rate (D). Maximum inventory ($Q_{max.}$) is not equal to Q;

EXHIBIT S11–3   **Basic EOQ and EMQ Replenishment Patterns**

A. Basic EOQ pattern of instantaneous replenishment

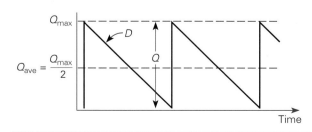

B. EMQ pattern of noninstantaneous replenishment

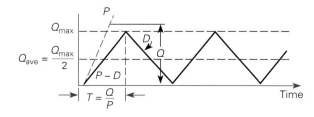

the stock level never reaches Q because some of Q is being used up (delivered) as it is being produced. $Q_{max.}$ is, instead, equal to $(P - D)(T)$ or $(P - D)(Q/P)$, as was shown earlier, and $Q_{ave.}$ equals half of $Q_{max.}$

Note that for otherwise equal conditions, EMQ is larger than basic EOQ. Inspection of the EMQ formula shows this to be mathematically obvious, because the factor $1 - D/P$ in the denominator makes the denominator smaller and the EMQ larger. The logical reason is that with EMQ there is less stock to carry since part of Q is used as it is produced; with less to carry, it is economical to produce a bit more per lot.

Example S11–3 illustrates the EMQ procedure, and Solved Problem 2 at the end of the chapter shows how EMQ might be put into practice.

Example S11–3:   EMQ Computations

Annual demand for an item produced in-house with a unit cost of $4.00 is 5,000 units. The carrying-cost rate is 50 percent, and it costs $100 to process an order. Production rate is 500 per week, and demand is constant throughout the year. Compute EMQ and total annual inventory costs for the item.

Solution

Constant demand translates into approximately 100 units per week ($5,000 \div 50$). Thus, the D:P ratio required in the EMQ formula denominator is 100:500, or 0.278. With this and other supplied information, equation S11–3 provides the EMQ:

$$EMQ = \sqrt{\frac{2DS}{IC(1 - D/P)}} = \sqrt{\frac{2(5,000)(\$100)}{0.5(\$4)(1 - 100/500)}} = 791$$

We determine total annual costs from equation S11–1; the carrying cost element is modified to reflect non-instantaneous acquisition of inventory:

$$TC = \frac{D}{Q}(S) + IC\left(\frac{P-D}{P}\right)\left(\frac{Q}{2}\right) + DC$$

$$= \frac{5,000}{791}(\$100) + (0.5)(\$4)\left(\frac{500-100}{500}\right)\left(\frac{791}{2}\right) + 5,000(\$4)$$

$$= \$632 + \$632 + \$20,000 = \$21,264$$

Associates at Aid Association for Lutherans Insurance Company (Appleton, Wisconsin) work together in multifunctional self-managed teams

Translating Planned Orders into Outcomes

IV

At precisely 12 noon, the entire insurance staff—nearly 500 clerks, technicians, and managers—piled their personal belongings on office chairs and said good-bye to fellow employees. Pushing the chairs along crowded corridors, crisscrossing and colliding at intersections, all 500 made their way to newly assigned work areas.[1]

That's the sound of moving day at Aid Association for Lutherans (AAL), an insurance company. But this moving day was different. Departments and sections weren't just changing offices; the organization structure itself was on the chopping block. The 500 employees were shaken out into 15 focused teams in two tiers. The top tier is five groups, each serving insurance agents in a different region. Within each group are three bottom-tier teams of 20 to 30 people, one team for new policies, one for claims, and one for services.

The do-si-do at AAL is an advanced kind of re-engineering, altering its form of organization, its mode of operations, and its facility layout. In TQM terms, AAL refocused itself on families of customers in the different sales regions. In OM terms, it metamorphosed from departments treating each insurance policy as a job to teams (e.g., one team focusing on policies, another on claims) working in more of a repetitive mode. Layout of the offices changed as well: from functional to product focused.

In parts I and II, the different operations modes and layout types were not significant issues. The part III opener showed how organizations differ from custom to commodity and intermittent to continuous. Now, in Part IV we zero in on these differences. Chapter 12 sets forth the mode and layout differences and deals with a few of the issues. Chapters 13, 14, and 15 present operations management approaches to planning, scheduling, and control for each of the operations modes: continuous and repetitive, job and batch, and project.

12 PROCESS SELECTION AND LAYOUT

Chapter Outline

Differentiating Operations
   Modes of Operations
   Focus

Mode Shifting
   From Custom to Commodity
   Extended Streamlining—Across
     Process Stages
   Trends in the Other Direction

Facilities Layout
   Layout Types
   U-Shaped Layout

   Layout Features

Layout in Action
   Layout and Re-layout
   Layout-Planning Steps
   Layout-Planning Example
   Computer Assistance in Layout
   Open Layouts

Case Study: Streamlined Patient
Transfers: Hours to Minutes

Case Study: Microsoft Corporation—
Dublin, Ireland

Experience is the best teacher, they say. Have you had enough experience, in your personal life if not work life, to relate to the full spectrum of operating environments? Perhaps so—as a trip to a shopping mall illustrates:

- Low on cash? The 24-hour automatic teller at the branch bank in the mall's parking lot, an example of *continuous service* operations, can solve that problem.
- A dedication plaque in a courtyard or atrium of the mall reveals its opening date, construction costs, and other information—reminders that the planning and building of a mall is a massive one-of-a-kind *project* that consists of many smaller operations.
- Inside the mall is a shop offering interior decorating services. Each decorating job, though smaller in scale, shares with the mall the uniqueness of a one-of-a-kind effort typical of *job operations*.
- We may stop for a soft drink, the product of a *continuous production* process at the manufacturer's plant. An accompanying cookie is the result of *batch* production in a bakery.
- *Assembly lines* or *cells* have provided the televisions and computers available in the electronics store and the shoes and clothing in the department store.

The mall trip yields examples of five modes of operations, elaborated on in this chapter. First we contrast these five modes of operations and the focus of each. Then, we consider how companies may metamorphose to an alternate mode in order to become more effective at serving their clientele. Key issues include product volume and variety, flexible response, and the physical layout of resources.

Differentiating Operations

Those who provide society with shopping malls, cookies, or decorating services share basic strategic aims emphasized in earlier chapters. The bedrock aim in each case is to improve all dimensions of customer service. Ways of managing the effort differ, however, depending on the mode of operations, its limitations, and its demands on management.

Modes of Operations

Exhibit 12–1 circumscribes three basic modes of operations. As the axes indicate, operation size and output volume are determining factors.

Projects, high and left in the Exhibit, are unique, large-scale endeavors. A project team typically spends months or years completing a single project, which, if large enough, may split into subprojects. Project output is one unit. If other similar projects follow, then each is a separate project. For example, a series of spacecraft-tracking stations built around the world might call for nearly identical facilities (antennas, communications, power supplies, and so forth). But each site is different: Climate, terrain, national policies and building codes, and other variables make each station's construction unique.

A **job** is a small-scale, small-output-volume effort; painting a room or performing surgery are examples. Like the project, a job may be one-of-a-kind, although jobs frequently provide a small volume of like units. For example, a job might call for installing two soccer goal nets or staining eight matching dining chairs.

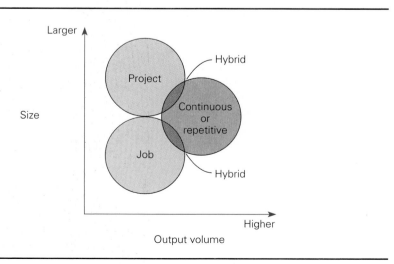

EXHIBIT 12–1

Types of Operations—Size and Volume Classification

When output volume must be higher, as with most consumer goods, **continuous operations** or **repetitive operations** are needed. Continuous and repetitive operations are together in one circle in Exhibit 12–1 because both have little variety, an issue we explore in the next section. But there are important distinctions between the two. Output from repetitive operations occurs in discrete units (e.g., production of circuit breakers or computer disks, or processing of insurance claim forms); by contrast, continuous output is not identifiable as a discrete unit; it flows or even pours (e.g., petroleum products from a refinery or electrical power from a utility).

The two overlapping areas in Exhibit 12–1 indicate hybrid operations. The upper one represents the special case when a large project consists of multiple nearly identical units, most likely produced at the same location. An example would be an order for 12 destroyer escorts by the navy. The lower overlap region represents larger-quantity job orders. For example, a welding business might receive an order to perform 500 identical welds.

In manufacturing, large-quantity job operations occur so frequently that they have their own name: **batch operations.** Companies that thrive on filling multipiece job orders are sometimes referred to as batch producers or batch processors.

Each mode of operations tends to have a different focus, as we see next.

Focus

The modes of operations differ along three dimensions: process overview, volume, and variety/flexibility. Exhibit 12–2 shows how different combinations of the three

EXHIBIT 12–2   **Operations Modes and Characteristic Focus**

Process Overview	Functional	Functional	Mixed	Product	Product
Volume	**Lowest (one item)**	**Very low**	**Moderate**	**High**	**Highest**
Variety/Flexibility	**Highest**	**Highest**	**Moderate**	**Low**	**Lowest**
1. Project.	Construction Computer network installation R&D effort				
2. Job.		Tool-and-die shop Repair services Portfolio review			
3. Batch.			Heavy equipment Printing services Cement mixing		
4. Repetitive.				Auto assembly License processing School registration	
5. Continuous.					Steel mill Brewery 24-hour laundry

dimensions line up into five characteristic areas of concentration or focus. Let's look more closely at each combination of focus and mode.

1. *Project.* Building construction, computer network installation, and research and development (R&D) are one-of-a-kind endeavors, commonly called projects. With large numbers of diverse activities in process at one time, operations management tends to be chopped up. An overview of the process sees functions (design, site planning, budgeting, etc.), rather than the end product itself. Keeping all these functions and their activities straight is a matter of good planning and control of project sequence and timing. Typically, resources—people and equipment—are quite flexible, since they must be able to adapt to the unique features of the given project and contribute differently as the project rolls along.

2. *Job.* The job mode spans the service sector and much of the manufacture of tooling and component parts. Volumes are very low: the few customers at a single table in a restaurant, a police officer on the job at a single traffic accident, a single TV set in for repair, a die set produced in a tool and die shop, or five assemblies of a certain circuit board. Though volumes are low, many different jobs are in various stages of completion at any one time. Managers overseeing the process tend to look at the functions (or departments) and their problems, more than the product (jobs) themselves.

The high variety of jobs in most service centers or job shops requires a high degree of flexibility in employees and facilities. With such high job variety, operations management can become chaotic. The management challenge is to reduce complexity of operations while still providing the sense of unique service that customers expect or the jobs require.

3. *Batch.* In common usage, batch may be anything from a pan of cookies in your kitchen, to a truck full of concrete, to a massive vessel of chocolate, raw rubber, or molten metal in a factory. Our usage is more restrictive. We consider small-scale baking at home to be a job; production in massive vessels is part of continuous processing. Batch processing falls somewhere in between. Moreover, it is intermittent (like job processing), but output consists of standard, familiar items. As befits its center position in Exhibit 12–2, the three characteristics of focus for batch processing are moderate, moderate, and mixed. In a commercial bakery, for example, bakers and their equipment have enough flexibility to produce several varieties of bread and cookies, perhaps a batch of each type daily; but grilling steaks or creating caesar salads is outside their skill range. Though batch processing shares some of the difficulties found in job operations, familiarity with the output mix precludes many of the surprises faced by job-processing associates.

4. *Repetitive.* In repetitive operations, variety is low, labor is trained for, and equipment designed for, a narrow range of applications, and output volume is high. The uniformity of processing and the continuity of it makes it natural to view repetitive operations as a whole product flow rather than a collection of separate processes or functions. Planning, scheduling, counting, and controlling is by the discrete unit or piece. Repetitive services include forms processing, registrations, and processing customers in a tanning salon. In manufacturing, the assembly industries—from automotive to consumer electronics—provide many examples.

*P*RINCIPLE 9:

Flexible, movable equipment.

*P*RINCIPLE 7:

Mastery of multiple skills.

5. *Continuous.* Continuous processors are often referred to as the process industry (short for *continuous-flow process*). Production of fluids, grains, flakes, and pellets, as well as the mining of ores, coal, and so forth, fit the category. Makers of small, discrete items (e.g., nails and toothpicks) are also sometimes considered part of the process industry. Planning, scheduling, and controlling such products is by volume, rather than by unit or piece. Output volume is very high, but variety is low. Like repetitive mode, managers view continuous processing in terms of products more than separable processes or functions. Labor and equipment are specialized, and the industry is capital intensive.

Both repetitive and continuous operations require elaborate advance planning, but have innate advantages in operation and control. Simple, rather inflexible rules and rigid standards govern operations. Sometimes it is possible to shift from other modes toward this mode of operations, thereby gaining simplicity and control. The mode shifting idea is our next topic.

Mode Shifting

City driving is harder on a car than highway driving. Mileage is lower, wear and tear is greater, and service is needed more frequently. In addition, the driver's time is wasted on stop-and-go traffic and in the time required for extra auto maintenance. To some extent, city drivers can emulate highway drivers—anticipate traffic light changes, avoid jack-rabbit starts and stops, and so forth.

Operations management is similar: Stop-and-go operations can cause extra waste, inefficiency, high cost, and so on. Like good city driving, astute management can shift irregular stop-and-go operations toward more of a streamlined steady-flow mode. The advantages are considerable. Some are apparent: higher efficiency, consistently higher quality, shorter throughput times, lower inventory, lower labor cost, simpler planning and scheduling, and fewer surprises.

Another kind of benefit of streamlining is more subtle and in the past often not exploited: gaining better visibility of whole products and processes for delivering them. Products are what customers buy, not functions, not separate tasks. Focusing on products, or on customers of those products, has strong appeal as a foundation of total quality management. In other words, today companies have an elevated interest in shifting from modes that dwell on functions to those that focus on products and customers. To better understand mode shifting—toward more product- or customer-focused, streamlined operations, we turn to some notable examples.

For an exceptional current example, see the end-of-chapter case study, "Microsoft Corporation—Dublin, Ireland," which demonstrates customer focus for both manufacturing and marketing.

From Custom to Commodity

The Part III opener placed the goods and services that we consume on a variety axis, as shown in the Exhibit on p. 174. At the high-variety end are custom items; at the other end are commodities.

At one time, all products were provided in the job-processing mode as custom items. For example, put yourself in Placerville, California, in 1849 during the gold rush. Suppose you have a toothache and are lucky enough to find a dentist in the camp. The dentist says you need a tooth filled. He melts down freshly panned gold from the South Fork River and fills your tooth by the light of a lamp burning the oil of a muskrat trapped near the same river. Of course, fuel and gold are commodities today, produced more or less continuously, but they were custom products made in the job mode in 1849.

As demand for any product expands, the low-volume job mode should give way to repetitive or continuous processing, which provides economies of scale. While this applies especially to manufacturing and inventory-related services, there are also examples from human services.

For example, one of the former Soviet Union's first, famed entrepreneurs (in the late 1980s) was Svyatoslav Fyodorov. Dr. Fyodorov's eye surgery clinics annually processed over 200,000 patients suffering from myopia, and were no less than assembly lines:

> Eight beds are arranged around a central axis like spokes in a wheel. A surgeon stands at the head of each bed, on which only the eye of the patient is visible. After each doctor finishes his portion of the task, the wheel makes one-eighth of a turn. The next doctors talk to each other through tiny microphones and headsets. Soft music plays in the background.[1]

Fyodorov accomplished the feat of shifting his specialty out of the job mode into repetitive processing. Other examples of mode shifting cut across process stages.

For a health care example, see the end-of-chapter case study, "Streamlined Patient Transfers: Hours to Minutes."

Extended Streamlining–Across Process Stages

Four and one-half decades before Fyodorov, John D. Rockefeller's oil wells steadily pumped product into Rockefeller pipelines and rail tanker cars, which forwarded the product to Rockefeller tank farms and retail stations. The continuous mode was virtually uninterrupted through three major process stages. Stop-and-go between stages is more typical in the petroleum business. Similarly, Andrew Carnegie's steel manufacturing empire included railroads and lake steamers that moved ore to the great furnaces and then to the finishing mills of Pittsburgh.

Today, one of the purest examples of streamlining across stages may be found in the coal fields of the Western United States. The output of lignite mines goes into trucks that drive a mile or so to giant electric power plants and dump their loads onto conveyors. Without stopping, the coal marches forward into furnaces that drive the generators that convert steam to electric power. Still without stopping, the electricity pulses through wires for immediate consumption by millions of users. The operation is continuous from coal through to someone's lamp or refrigerator.

Perhaps the most quoted accolade to the efficiencies of streamlined operations comes from a pioneer in the automobile industry. Ford Motor Company once transformed iron ore from its own mines into millions of identical Model T automobiles. As Henry Ford noted, "Our production cycle is about 81 hours from the mine to the finished machine in the freight car, or three days and 9 hours."[2]

Ford's other quotation: "They can have any color they want, so long as it's black."

Trends in the Other Direction

The products in these examples—gold, muskrat oil, eye surgery, petroleum, steel, electric power, and Model T Fords—could be provided in a more focused repetitive or continuous mode, as long as customers demanded little variety. Indeed, some of history's most skillful entrepreneurs were able to cultivate mass demand and keep it steadily supplied with relatively undifferentiated goods or services. But what happens when customers require variety?

Ford's repetitive-flow mode of manufacture began to unravel when customers started demanding variety: big cars and small ones, luxury models and sporty roadsters with rumble seats. Changing customer tastes affected producers. The auto industry, from assembly plants to parts makers to steel mills, moved well away from repetitive processing and adopted intermittent production—one model at a time, with long cycle intervals.

Must an organization choose between satisfying customers' needs for variety and enjoying the benefits of focused, streamlined operations? Exhibit 12–2 conveys the conventional view—that only low-variety, high-volume products are likely to reap those benefits. While that has been the common wisdom, today's more positive view is that companies with less continuous operations can share the wealth.

In addition to the preceding examples (and the end-of-chapter case studies), we've already presented a wide assortment of concepts and techniques for becoming more focused and streamlined. These have been discussed in the preceding five chapters: simplified capacity planning in focused businesses (Chapter 7), improved flow-control and quick-response techniques (Chapters 8 and 11), smoother order processing with reduced documentation (Chapter 9), and queue limitation (Chapter 10). The chapters ahead include other equally effective techniques. The Contrast box includes these points from earlier chapters in summarizing how contemporary firms shift themselves toward smoother, more streamlined modes of operation.

A single company, Toyota, deserves much of the credit for the new belief that companies can alter their presumed fate. Over four decades after Ford figured out how to produce automobiles repetitively, Toyota developed methods of doing the

Contrast

Variety, Volume, and Flow

High-Variety Characteristics

Conventional	**Contemporary**
Disruptive processing.	Smoothing out the disruptions.
Long setups/changeovers.	Reducing setup/changeover times.
Skills/equipment grouped by speciality.	Skills/equipment grouped by product/customer family.
Long transport distances.	Transport distances shortened by cellular organization.
Complex flow control.	Flow controls simplified via visual queue limitation devices.
Overtime and undertime for narrowly skilled employees.	Cross-trained associates moving to where the work is.

High-Volume Characteristics

Streamlined flow, a special case (opposite of high-variety processing).	Ideal is always to strive to behave like streamlined, high-volume processors.

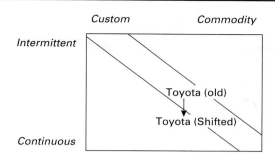

same thing but with a variety of models instead of "basic black." Its ability to process mixed models in a repetitive mode, in effect, moves Toyota downward on the product–process matrix displayed in the Part III opener, as the sketch above indicates. The shift is toward a more repetitive (continuous) mode, without much rightward movement toward commodity products.

The quest for more continuity without loss of variety, or more variety without loss of continuity, has become strategic and in some cases competitively vital. Frequently, however, the chief obstacle to be overcome is physical: Long flow distances between consecutive processes simply do not permit streamlined, product-focused operations. The facility layout responsible for the long flow distances must be changed.

Mode shifting captures much of the essence of business process re-engineering.

Facilities Layout

The operations management masterminds at the Arsenal of Venice in the fifteenth century understood the importance of layout.

> And as one enters the gate there is a great street on either hand with the sea in the middle, and on one side are windows opening out of the houses of the arsenal, and the same on the other side, and out came a galley towed by a boat, and from the windows they handed out to them, from one the cordage, from another the bread, from another the arms, and from another the balistas and mortars, and so from all sides everything which was required, and when the galley had reached the end of the street all the men required were on board, together with the complement of oars, and she was equipped from end to end. In this manner there came out ten galleys full armed, between the hours of three and nine. I know not how to describe what I saw there, whether in the manner of its construction or in the management of the workpeople, and I do not think there is anything finer in the world.[3]

layout
The physical organization or geography found at a facility; basic types include functional, product, cellular, and fixed position.

That description identifies the Arsenal of Venice as having a product layout. In this section, we examine basic layouts and their features.

Layout Types

There are four basic types of facilities layout:

1. **Functional layout.** The **functional layout** groups like facilities or functions together: human resource people in the HR department, sheet-metal equipment and people grouped in the sheet-metal shop, and so forth. The functional layout tends to emerge as small organizations grow

and functional groups appear (e.g., bookkeeping and accounting, sales and advertising, packing and shipping). Such a layout may facilitate use of common tools, files, utility hookups, and so on. Also, putting people with like functions together may create a climate for mutual support and learning. Functional layouts tend to go with the job-processing mode.

However, the functional layout has a substantial disadvantage: It puts distance between provider and customer. For example, the accounts receivable clerk usually has frequent business with the sales clerk, but the accounting and sales departments may be at opposite ends of the building.

2. **Product layout.** Facilities line up along the flow of the product in the **product layout.** The customer (next process) is adjacent to, or very near, the provider. Cafeterias, packing and shipping, and assembly lines are examples. Often, product layouts require substantial investment for lining up equipment and hooking up utilities along the flow path, which may be ill-advised if product volumes fall off or never materialize. The major disadvantage of product layouts, however, is in how they usually are managed. If associates along a flow line are allowed to do only one small job day in and day out, they can hardly be expected to grasp the overall operation or gain a sense of fulfillment. Their worth is diminished, boredom sets in, and morale drops. With cross-training and job rotation in flexible product-flow cells, however, those deficiencies fade.

3. **Cellular layout.** In the **cellular layout** the idea is to arrange labor, work stations, and equipment into work cells that process families of goods or services that follow similar flow paths. Cells perform better in concert with a number of complementary concepts: Deliberately design items to have as many common features as possible, locate high-use data and accessories within the cell, and cross-train cell operators. A cellular layout is similar to a product layout, although most people think of product layouts (flow lines) as handling only one or just a few products instead of a family. Cellular layout became one of the more important operations management concepts in the 1980s, partly because of its close association with just-in-time applications.

Cells are often the objective and the result when companies elect to break up functional layouts. For example, a company might form complete design, budget, and buy cells by relocating buyers and accountants next to product designers. Or a manufacturer might transfer a stamping press to where it can make and feed a single part to a using station on a production line. The photo in Exhibit 12–3 shows just that: A stamping press that just makes junction box brackets is positioned at the point of use (where the brackets are used on the line) in a General Electric dishwasher plant.

The cellular concept applies in human services as well (although the preferred term tends to be *team* rather than *cell*). The Into Practice box, "Moving Facilities for Moving Money," illustrates this for securities processing.

4. **Fixed-position layout.** In the **fixed-position layout,** it is the product whose position is fixed, and resources (people, machines, materials, and so on) must come to it. Construction is a good example. Another is the manufacture of items too large to be easily moved, such as aircraft and locomotives. Still others are patients in hospital beds, or an actor being dressed, made up, and coached before the performance.

*P*RINCIPLE 6:

Organize resources into multiple "chains of customers."

EXHIBIT 12–3
Point-of-Use Manufacturing

Junction box brackets stamped at the point where they are used.

Mixed layouts—two or more layout types in a single facility—are common, if not the norm. An example is a restaurant that sets up a buffet brunch line on Sundays. The patron has the choice of going through the buffet line or sitting down and ordering from the menu. A patron entering the restaurant may be thought of as raw materials; a patron leaving is finished goods. The operations are to transform a hungry patron into a fed one. The restaurant processes two types of patrons through two types of facilities layout. The buffet customer goes through a product or cellular layout (hard to narrow it down to one or the other). It is a flow line. The menu customer receives service in a fixed layout: Menu, waiter, food, drinks, and check come to the fixed position.

Exhibit 12–4 is a sketch of such a restaurant, identifying the product layout and fixed layout. It also shows that the restaurant includes a functional layout in

Into Practice

Moving Facilities for Moving Money

"Garbage—or something like it—was what the Bank of Boston found when it looked at its securities-processing business . . . which handles stock transfers, dividends and interest payments, pension plan administration, and related tasks—about 25 million transactions a year. It had six separate operations, each with its own mainframe, scattered over 11 locations. Work for one customer could shuffle through several systems—one for dividends, another for stock sales, a third for bond interest—costing time, labor, and money at each point.

"[Working with a consulting firm,] the bank put everyone in securities processing at one location with two computer systems and set up the work around its core process, moving money. Computer cables run across the ceiling like track lighting, allowing the bank to change the layout overnight. The idea was to mimic a just-in-time, flexible factory. Says senior vice president John Towers: 'We created a utility that could service all the product lines.' Productivity soared: After $2\frac{1}{2}$ years, with 17 percent fewer employees, the division does 80 percent more securities-processing business."

Source: Adapted from Thomas A. Stewart, "U.S. Productivity: First but Fading," *Fortune*, October, 1992, pp. 54–56.

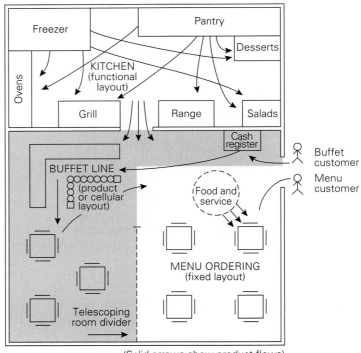

(Solid arrows show product flows)

the kitchen. There foods, not patrons, are the products being transformed. Functional areas include grill, salads, range, deserts, ovens, freezer, and pantry. Arrows show the jumbled flow patterns.

Compared with a single-layout facility, a mixed-layout facility is more difficult to plan, more costly to equip, and more troublesome to maintain. But it may be easier to keep busy because it offers a wider variety of products or services to an enlarged pool of potential customers.

U-Shaped Layout

The main feature of both flow lines and work cells is the close proximity of work stations, which speeds up flow and reduces in-process queuing. Usually, for even better results, the stations are laid out into a U shape. At least six advantages for cells or lines may result from **U-shaped layout.**

1. *Staff flexibility and balance.* The U shape allows one associate to tend several work stations adjacent or across the U, since walking distance is short. Also, more options for balancing work among personnel exist: As demand increases, labor may be added until every station in the cell is tended by an associate.

   Exhibit 12–5 shows a typical U-shaped layout for a manufacturer. As many as eight employees, or as few as one, might tend the machines, depending on demand. Also note that kanban squares link each station with its customer station.

2. *Teamwork.* Getting all staff into a cluster enhances teamwork and joint problem solving. Slowdowns or stoppages quickly ripple through the cell, and cell members form a natural team that must collectively solve the problems and get the process going again. Natural teams can hardly form, much less work effectively, if employees are strung out along long lines or dispersed and separated by walls of inventory.

3. *Rework.* When a mistake occurs, a common policy is to send the customer to the complaint department or the item to a separate rework group. But a tenet of total quality management is quality at the source, which calls for

PRINCIPLE 1:

Team up with the customer—the next process.

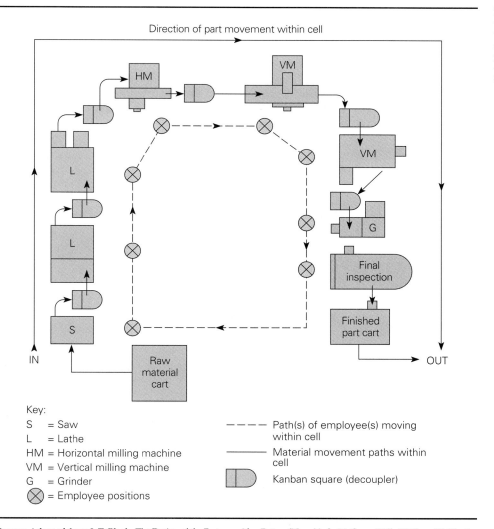

EXHIBIT 12–5

U-Shaped Layout— Manufacturing Cell

Direction of part movement within cell

Key:
S   = Saw
L   = Lathe
HM = Horizontal milling machine
VM = Vertical milling machine
G   = Grinder
⊗ = Employee positions

− − − − Path(s) of employee(s) moving within cell

——— Material movement paths within cell

Kanban square (decoupler)

Source: Adapted from J. T. Black, *The Design of the Factory with a Future* (New York: McGraw-Hill, 1991), p. 67. Used with permission.

correcting mistakes right where they occurred. In the U-shaped layout, the distance to return a mistake is short, making it easier to follow the TQM tenet.

4. *Passage.* A long, straight line interferes with travel of employees, customers, vehicles, and supplies. We object when supermarket aisles are too long, and people protest when a freeway cuts through a neighborhood. A long, straight production line may be a similar imposition.

5. *Work and tool distribution.* Since all stations in a U are immediately accessible from the center, it is easier to distribute materials, parts, instruction sheets, and so on. A single person may be able to handle distribution tasks while also tending a starting or ending station in the U. In unmanned cells, a robot at the center may distribute work and tools and also perform assembly operations.

6. *Linking with other U-shaped layouts.* The U shape provides many arrangement options for linking feeder and user cells. Exhibit 12–6 shows a linked-cell system consisting of final assembly, subassembly, and fabrication cells—all U-shaped. Each fabrication cell might resemble the one shown in Exhibit 12–5 and would provide a different parts family to the subassembly and assembly cells at the appropriate point of use. In a well-balanced system, fabrication cells would have the same degree of demand-mix and volume flexibility as the subassembly and assembly

---

EXHIBIT 12–6

Linked-Cell Manufacturing System

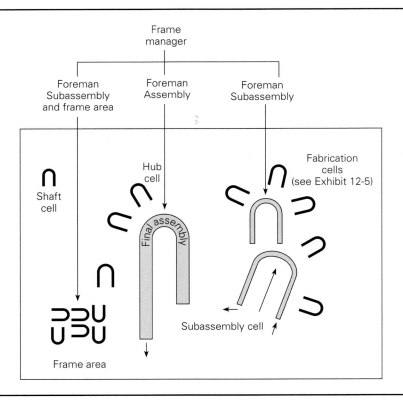

Source: Adapted from Richard J. Schonberger, "The World Class Manufacturing Company," Tape 4 of 12-tape videotape set, 1990; and J. T. Black, *The Design of the Factory with a Future* (New York: McGraw-Hill, 1991), p. 66. Used with permission.

cells. Note, also, the partial organization chart above the layout diagram: no functional departments. The management hierarchy is cellular to match the layout of facilities.

There are cases where these advantages of the U shape do not fully apply. For example, with a high degree of automation and few parts or tools to be handled, the teamwork benefits are absent. Also, a line processing wide sheets of steel, aluminum, glass, and so on, perhaps should run straight because transfer between machines is simpler if there are no changes in direction.

Layout Features

Some of the distinguishing features of the primary layout types are shown in Exhibit 12–7. It lists eight resource factors and the common treatments for each layout type.

The first factor, facilities arrangement, states the main differences among the layout types. They have already been discussed.

Type of operations is the second factor. Functional layout is dominant in job and batch operations; product layout is typical in repetitive and continuous operations. Continuous improvement calls for identifying all items that have the potential for more or less repetitive operations and to organize product layouts for those items. Cellular layout is suitable for small lots of first one part in a family and then another. Fixed layout is common in construction and industrial projects and for production of large-scale products (e.g., missiles and dynamos). Fixed layout may also apply to cases of special human services. For example, the resources come to the client or customer in surgery, grooming, feeding, and home TV repair.

Cost of layout/re-layout is third. In functional layout, machines, desks, and the like generally are not tightly linked; thus, functional layout usually is not costly. For a product or cellular layout, the cost is high if pieces of equipment are closely interlinked as in automated lines; the cost may be moderate if production is more labor intensive (i. e., one person hands work to the next). Fixed layout of a construction site requires temporary parking and storage space for operating resources, which

---

Exhibit 12–7   Resources and Layouts—Common Characteristics

Resource Factors	Types of Layout		
	Functional	*Product or Cellular*	*Fixed*
1. Facilities arrangement	Facilities grouped by specialty	Facilities placed along product-flow lines	Facilities arranged for ease of movement to fixed product
2. Type of operations	Job and batch	Continuous and repetitive	Construction and industrial projects; large-scale products, special human services
3. Cost of layout/re-layout	Moderate to low	Moderate to high	Moderate to low
4. Facility utilization	Usually low	High	Moderate
5. Type of operating facilities	General purpose	Special purpose	Mostly general purpose
6. Handling equipment	Variable path	Fixed path	Variable path
7. Handling distance	Long	Short	Moderate
8. Employee skill level	Skilled	Unskilled	Unskilled to skilled

usually are not costly. Fixed layout for goods production and for special human services may take more than just parking space; it may require a well-equipped bay for assembling a missile or aligning wheels, or a well-equipped operating room. The layout cost can be low if the facilities are mainly general-purpose hand tools, but can be higher (moderate) if special lighting, holding fixtures, work pits, and so forth, are involved.

Fourth is facility utilization. In functional layouts, facilities tend toward low utilization. That is not desirable, but it is typical because the job mix changes all the time and different jobs use different facilities. High facility utilization—little idleness—is a goal of product layout. Line balancing helps achieve it. Fixed layouts tend to have moderate facility utilization because the product mix is not very diverse.

The fifth factor is type of operating facilities. Functional layouts usually hold standard, general-purpose equipment, tools, handling aids, and so forth. Special-purpose facilities are worth investing in if the volume is high, as it normally is with product layouts. In fixed layouts, special products call for some special-purpose facilities, such as an overhead crane or a mounting fixture, but most of the facilities will be general purpose since production volume is not high.

Sixth is handling equipment. In functional layouts, variable-path equipment (hand-carry or on wheels) provides needed handling flexibility. Fixed-path handling equipment (conveyors, elevators, chutes, etc.) helps cut handling time in product layouts. In fixed layouts, a variety of resources come to the site from different places; hence, variable-path handling equipment.

Seventh is handling distance. Functional layouts stretch out over vast areas. In product and cellular layouts, the opposite is true. In fact, a purpose is to tightly cluster the facilities in order to cut distance and handling time. Fixed layouts are in between. The product stays put, but the resources do not flow to the product by fixed routes; resources move to the product from various locations over moderate handling distances.

The eighth factor is employee skill level. In functional layouts, employees tend to be skilled. Clerks, machinists, plumbers, computer operators, nurses, and accountants fit the category. If the skill is based on higher education or apprenticeship, the pay tends to be high; if based on vocational training, the pay tends to be moderate or low. Employees positioned along product layouts are often hired without a particular skill. Such employees may become adept, but they are classed as unskilled because they are easily replaced from an unskilled labor market. In fixed layouts, skilled craftspeople, such as carpenters and welders, often work alongside unskilled laborers, such as shovelers or riveters.

While many more operating-resource factors could be discussed, these eight are enough to show the basic nature of each layout type. Exhibit 12–7 is not intended as an if–then analysis device; that is, we would not conclude that if people are skilled, facility utilization is low, and so on, then a functional layout should be developed. There are better ways to plan the right kind of layout. We consider some of them next.

Layout in Action

Earlier discussion of basic layout types focused mainly on *what;* here we concentrate more on *how.* First, however, we examine the effects of operating environment on layout and, perhaps more important, on re-layout.

Layout and Re-layout

New facilities require new layouts. Existing facilities get out-of-date and require re-layout. The type of operating environment affects facility layout; we'll consider just four operating environments: mechanized production lines, labor-intensive production lines, job or batch production, and labor-intensive services.

1. In mechanized production lines, original layout planning had better be good because of the high cost of repositioning large machinery and related facilities. In a petrochemical plant, for example, the layout of tanks, chambers, valves, pipes, and other equipment is so much a part of the plant itself that major re-layout may never be feasible. In steel manufacturing, the cost of major re-layout is also enormous, and steel mills may close rather than retool and re-layout to improve efficiency, meet pollution control regulations, and so on. Power-train makers in the auto industry retool their automated transfer lines every few years, but the layout of retooled machines changes infrequently. In each of these examples, the initial layout choices restrict the firm's ability to respond to major changes in product line or technology for years to come.

2. Assembly lines (manual, not robotic) are less fixed. Assemblers and their tools are mobile. Thus, initial layout planning is not so critical; the focus is on re-layout, which has its own costs. These include costs of planning, line balancing, retraining, and rearranging benches, storage facilities, material handling aids, and large pieces of equipment.

3. Job and batch production often entails large machines and storage and handling aids. Re-layout may be attractive, however, because the equipment used tends to be general purpose, loosely coupled, and movable. A pump manufacturer in South Carolina has constructed a plant with very thick concrete floors so that heavy equipment can be moved anywhere. Exhibit 12–8 shows three versions of putting equipment on wheels for easy re-layout.

- Part A of the exhibit shows two large drill presses on casters, with detailed blowups of the casters and mountings themselves.
- Part B shows a combination assembly bench and material transport cart. It holds five cannisters in a plant producing self-contained breathing apparatus. The operation is laid out into several cells for assembly and test, and each cell provides floor space for one wheeled bench/cart.
- Part C shows a packing bench on wheels. It is used for packing the safety headgear shown in the background. Packers push the bench next to a machine printing customer logos on the hats or into aisles of a stockroom holding headgear so packing can take place there. Prior to development of the wheeled benches, headgear moved by fixed conveyor to a separate packing department.

*𝒫*RINCIPLE 9:

Flexible, movable equipment.

These kinds of devices for flexible layout and re-layout are important; otherwise the ability to change and continually improve may be thwarted. Symptoms of the need include bottlenecks, backtracking, overcrowding, poor utilization of capacity (including space), poor housekeeping, missed due dates, too much queue time, and a high or growing ratio of total cycle time to actual work content.

4. Labor-intensive services undergo frequent re-layout. Office employees may begin to "wonder where my desk will be on Monday morning." The desk may be

Exhibit 12–8

Equipment on Wheels

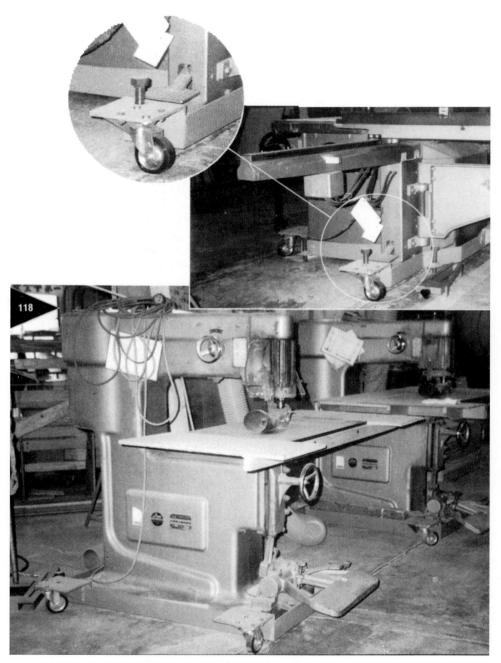

A. Machines on casters*

*Reprinted from Hiroyuki Hirano, ed., *JIT Factory Revolution: A Pictorial Guide to Factory Design of the Future* (Portland Ore.: Productivity Press, 1988), p. 118. English translation copyright © 1988 by Productivity Press. Reprinted by permission.

Exhibit 12–8
(concluded)

B. *Assembly bench/cart for self-contained breathing apparatus at Mine Safety Appliance Co., Inc. (Used with permission.)*

C. *Wheeled packing benches for safety headgear at Mine Safety Appliance Co., Inc. (Used with permission.)*

across town in newly rented office space. Physical obstacles are few; most offices can move overnight if telephone hookups can be arranged. With few physical problems, office re-layout commonly focuses on people and work climate.

Perhaps people and work climate should be central concerns in all layout and re-layout work. Certainly, many layout jobs are more complex than that faced by Woodsmith (see Into Practice box, "Re-layout . . ."), yet human needs often can be accommodated. We will see this in later sections as part of a detailed layout-planning example.

Layout-Planning Steps

In a complex layout situation, hundreds or thousands of jobs may be in progress at any given time. Repetitive, job, and project work may be included, with products and resources moving to work stations via many routings.

When routes are so diverse, how work areas are arranged in a building makes a difference. Dominant flow patterns from makers to customers are there among the apparent jumble of routings, and layout analysis helps to find those patterns.

One layout principle is to arrange work areas in the order of dominant flow. A goal is to get work or resources into, through, and out of each work center in minimum time at reasonable cost. The less time spent in the flow pattern, the less chance of collecting labor and overhead charges and the faster the immediate and final customers are served.

Other factors besides flows may be important. If so, the nonflow factors (e.g., teamwork) may be combined with flow data. The combined data will suggest

Re-layout: Employees Pitch In

When Woodsmith, a Des Moines–based publisher of catalogs for do-it-yourself carpenters, recently re-designed its offices, CEO Donald Peshke chose to forgo the use of outside contractors and instead asked each of the 35-person staff to do his or her own area. Peshke's goal was not so much to save money as to save time.

Outside installers would have required over a week to break down the office's movable wall panels and modular furniture and transform the office. With a Friday evening kickoff pizza party, the Woodsmith staff launched the week-end stint, and by Monday morning had the walls redone, furniture installed, and equipment relocated.

With help from a local Herman Miller dealer, each employee had designed a layout for his or her work area, deciding where to locate work surfaces and position computers, file cabinets, and other equipment. Peshke explained: "Our approach was to get them involved in the design so they'd understand what couldn't be done. They accept limitations a lot better that way, instead of the boss saying, 'This is what you're going to live with, like it or not.'" But the best part of the whole experience, according to Peshke, "turned out to be the camaraderie it developed."

Source: Robert A. Mamis, "Employees as Contractors," *Inc.*, November 1992, p. 53.

how close work areas should be to one another, and a rough layout can be developed. The next step is to determine the space requirements for a rough layout. The last step in layout planning is to fit the rough layout into the available space, that is, the proposed or existing building. Several layout plans can be developed for managers to choose from.

The layout planning steps just described are listed in Exhibit 12–9, along with planning aids usable in each step.

Layout-Planning Example

Example 12–1 demonstrates the layout planning steps. The method and some of the tools were developed by R. R. Muther, who calls the approach **systematic layout planning (SLP).**[4] SLP is respected for its practicality, is widely referenced, and is widely used. Though developed in an earlier era, SLP works well in support of a modern, customer-oriented approach to layout.

	Steps	Possible Tools
EXHIBIT 12–9		
Layout Planning—Steps and Possible Tools	1. Analyze work flows.	Flow diagram From–to chart
	2. Identify and include nonflow factors, where significant.	Activity-relationship (REL) chart Combined REL chart
	3. Assess data and arrange work areas.	Activity arrangement diagram
	4. Determine space arrangement plan.	Space relationship diagram
	5. Fit space arrangement into available space.	Floor plan Detailed layout models.

EXAMPLE 12–1:   LAYOUT PLANNING—GLOBE COUNTY OFFICES

Citizens' main contact with Globe County offices is in registering and licensing vehicles. Many people complain because the three county offices involved have not consolidated their services. On busy days there are waiting lines at all three offices. Many vehicle owners must visit all three, and it is common for a citizen to find out, after shuffling forward for awhile, that it is the wrong line.

The elected officials who run the three offices have decided to consolidate. Mr. Ross, a consultant, has been hired to conduct layout analysis using SLP.

Ross's analysis reveals that 12 activities are to be located in the available space and that four of those have significant flows: three service counters, plus the office copier (see Exhibit 12–10). The space requirements are based on careful measurement of desks, files, and so forth, plus use of widely available industry space standards (e.g., 300 square feet per auto in a parking lot).

Flow analysis. For those four activities, Ross gathers flow data, which he enters on a from-to chart (which resembles the distance chart found on many road maps), as shown in Exhibit 12–11A. Numbers above the diagonal represent flows of patrons from one activity to another; numbers below the diagonal reflect backtracking by patrons who find themselves in the wrong office, and round trips to and from the copiers.

Exhibit 12–11B is a conversion chart, which Ross develops for displaying from–to data in order of descending flow volume. Ross then judgmentally inserts horizontal lines that divide the flow-volume bars into five zones, labeled A, E, I, O, and U, which are the standard SLP symbols for flow volume.

Nonflow factors. Next, Ross lists nonflow factors, such as the need for employees to be near their supervisor, and rates them using the same five vowel designators. He combines flow and nonflow factors on an activity relationship (REL) chart, a segment of which is shown in Exhibit 12–12. (See Solved Problem for a more complete example.)

The REL chart is easy to interpret. The single A in the chart indicates that it is absolutely necessary for customer service people in the clerk and treasurer offices to be close together. Reasons are "work flow" (1), "employee sharing (between departments)" (3), and "share counter" (4). The same reasons apply to the E, for especially important, in the box connecting customer service counter people in the assessor and treasurer offices.

Activity arrangement. Now Ross converts the combined REL chart to an activity arrangement diagram, which shows the arrangement of all activities but without indicating requirements for space, utilities, halls, and so on (see Exhibit 12–13). In this diagram,

EXHIBIT 12–10   **Major Work Areas—County Offices**

Activity	Space Requirements (square feet)	Activity	Space Requirements (square feet)
1. County assessor's office:		3. County treasurer's office:	
a. Management	600	*i.* Management	420
b. Motor vehicle—counter*	300	*j.* Motor vehicle—counter-clerical*	1,600
c. Motor vehicle—clerical	240	4. Support areas:	
d. Assessors	960	*k.* Mail and copier*	240
2. County clerk's office:		*l.* Conference room	160
e. Management	840		
f. Recording and filing—counter	240	Total	7,520
g. Recording and filing—clerical	960		
h. Motor vehicle—counter-clerical*	960		

* Significant flows.

Source: This is adapted from a real case. Thanks go to Ross Greathouse of Greathouse-Flanders Associates, Lincoln, Nebraska, for providing original case data.

EXHIBIT 12–11

Flow Volume (People per Day)—County Offices

A. From-to chart

From	To	Clerk 1	Assessor 2	Treasurer 3	Copier 4	Totals 5
Motor vehicle counter— clerk	1		A 100	B (250)	D 30	380
Motor vehicle counter— assessor	2	C 20		A 100	D 10	130
Motor vehicle counter— teasurer	3	C 40				40
Copier	4	D 30	D 10			40
Totals		90	110	350	40	590

Types of product flow:

A Patrons licensing newly purchased vehicles.

B Patrons licensing same-owner vehicles.

C Patrons to wrong office— backtrack to correct office.

D Round trips to copier.

B. Conversion to vowel ratings on bar chart

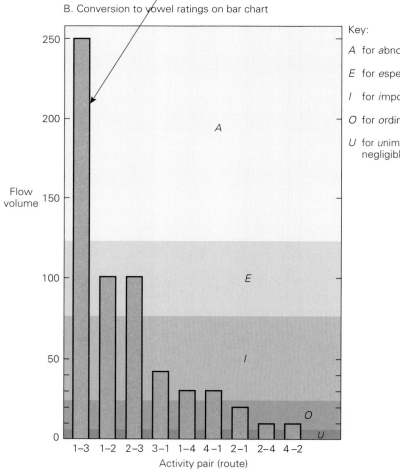

Key:

A for *a*bnormally high flow

E for *e*specially high flow

I for *i*mportant flow

O for *o*rdinary flow

U for *u*nimportant moves of negligible flow volume

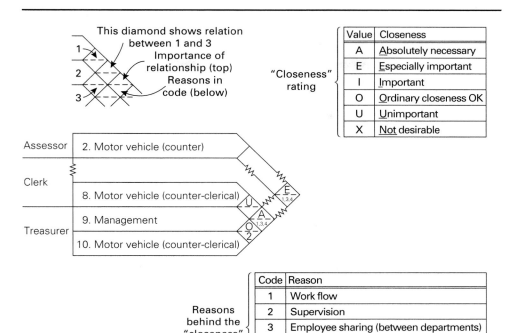

Source of REL chart form: Richard Muther and Associates, Kansas City, Missouri. Used with permission.

EXHIBIT 12–12

Combined Activity-Relationship (REL) Chart— County Offices

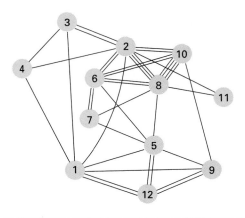

EXHIBIT 12–13

Activity-Arrangement Diagram—County Offices

number of lines between activities stands for flow volume: Four lines corresponds to an A rating on the REL chart, three lines stands for an E rating, and so forth. Distances between circles are set according to desired degree of closeness, as much as possible. Activities 2, 6, 8, and 10, at the core, are all service-counter activities, which earlier ratings showed should be placed close together.

Space arrangement. Ross's next-to-last chart (not shown) includes the space data from Exhibit 12–10. The result is a diagram that is in the generally rectangular shape of the

EXHIBIT 12–14   **New Layout and Motor Vehicle Licensing Counter**

A. Final layout—county offices

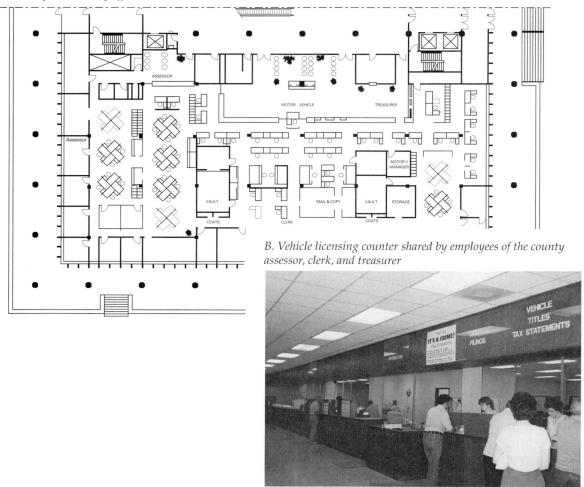

B. Vehicle licensing counter shared by employees of the county assessor, clerk, and treasurer

space into which the activities must fit; activity blocks are sized according to space needed. The space relationship diagram may be regarded as a rough layout. (See Solved Problem for an example.)

Layout into available space. Finally, Ross is ready to draw some final layouts, complete with walls, halls, aisles, and other needed elements.

Exhibit 12–14 shows what Ross might have developed. Part A is an actual layout of the county office renovation that is the basis for this example. Part B shows the main feature of that layout, the shared counter. The layout was developed by an architectural firm (though the systematic layout planning process, as presented here, was not fully used) and approved and implemented by newly elected Lancaster County officials in Lincoln, Nebraska.

The Globe County Offices example is fairly simple. In large, complex layouts, analysis within each activity area could include the full SLP treatment—that is, all the SLP steps. In later steps, various two– and three-dimensional models (manual or computer graphic) can be manipulated to produce workable layout options. In the Globe County example, we also glossed over all the trial and error usually involved in the diagramming.

Computer Assistance in Layout

Some of the drudgery can be avoided by using computer software in the search phase of layout planning. One program, called CORELAP (computerized relationship layout planning), uses closeness ratings from the REL chart (e.g., Exhibit 12–12) as inputs. It produces a single layout of rectangular-shaped departments; department lengths and widths are set forth in advance. The CORELAP algorithm maximizes common borders for closely related departments. CORELAP is flexible enough to be used for either office or plant layout.

A program called CRAFT (computerized relative allocation of facilities technique) requires an existing layout as an input. Its job is to improve the layout. CRAFT uses flow (from–to) data but not nonflow (REL-chart) data. Its main purpose is to minimize material-handling cost, which is a dominant concern in plant layout. CRAFT is usually not well suited for office layout, in which other matters besides work flow are important.[5]

Open Layouts

One of the special influences on office layout is the **open-office concept.** The concept eliminates many floor-to-ceiling walls and deemphasizes functional compartmentalization of people. One key advantage is that the open-office concept is more customer friendly, especially in establishments that are trying to promote customer service. By opening up to customers, providers remove some of the mystery or secrecy from their operations. Banks are good examples.

Other advantages of open layouts are that they foster better employee communications and provide flexibility for easy re-layout. Modular office furniture and movable, partial-height partitions aid in achieving these goals.

Open offices in Japan, where the concept is deeply ingrained, often are truly wide open. North Americans, in contrast, have emphasized maintaining a degree of privacy and cutting noise. Interior designers use wall carpeting, sound-absorbent panels, acoustical screens, fabric-wrapped desktop risers, and free-standing padded partitions. Office landscaping (use of plants) is also commonplace. In fact, plants are so prominent in the office of Mars (candy bars) in Veghel, Holland, that people there call it the office-garden concept.

Layout-planning expertise is also available from architectural firms and firms specializing in layout. Interior designers are likely to focus on appearance, atmosphere, light, and acoustics, mostly in offices (especially offices in which the public is met frequently). Layout specialists are more engineering oriented and likely to direct their efforts to material-flow factors; they tend to work mostly on factory layouts, where function rather than appearance is the main concern. Architects are helpful for new construction or major remodeling.

Summary

As associates transform orders into outcomes, the arrangement of their work-places and the accessories they use depend to a great extent on customers' volume and variety demands. Of specific interest in this chapter are modes of operations, operational focus, streamlining efforts, and facility layout.

Including hybrids, there are five basic modes of operations: project, job, batch, repetitive, and continuous: (1) Projects are large-scale, one-of-a-kind efforts that are usually managed as separate functional components. They vary highly from one to the next and among tasks within each project, thus requiring flexible resources. (2) Job operations are like small-scale projects. Typically, many jobs, high in variety, are in process at the same time. This requires flexible human and physical resources and fosters more managerial emphasis on functional resources than individual jobs. (3) Batch processing is also intermittent, but moderate in volume, variety, and required flexibility. Managerial focus is mixed: somewhat on the functions and somewhat on the products. (4) Repetitive operations occur when demand calls for high volume, but output variety is low. These conditions result in an emphasis on products (not separate functional resources), which are specialized rather than flexible. (5) Continuous processing requires highly specialized equipment and skills to provide a constant flow of largely undifferentiated output, which again puts the focus on products, not functions.

At one time, the common viewpoint was that mode of operations was a given; for example, offices were stuck in the job processing mode. The contemporary view favors retaining high-variety capability but otherwise shifting the mode toward more repetitive/continuous processing—to gain efficiencies and other advantages. Scattered historical examples of mode shifting, plus many current cases of doing so, demonstrate the possibility and benefits of the concept.

Layout is the physical organization or geography found at a facility; basic types include functional, product, cellular, and fixed position. The functional layout is accomplished by grouping like functions, tools, or facilities together; it tends to evolve as organizations grow. In product layout, facilities are arranged along the flow path of goods or services. Provider–customer pairs tend to be closer together. To create a cellular layout, employees arrange work stations and equipment into cells that process families of goods or services that follow similar flow paths. Cells may consist of manufacturing or service operations—for example, a cell team of an accountant, an engineer, and a human resource specialist. The fixed-position layout is used when the output—a product or a person receiving service—is stationary, and people, materials, and equipment must come to it. Mixed layouts, where two or more of the basic types occur within a single facility, are common, if not the norm.

U-shaped layouts are increasingly appropriate for product lines and work cells. Advantages of the U shape include greater staffing flexibility and teamwork, rework performed at the point of error, easier passage through the facility, smoother work and tool distribution, and simplified linkages between feeder and user cells.

Resource factors receive varying treatment under the different layout types. Arrangement, cost of layout and re-layout, utilization, type of facilities, handling equipment and distance, and general employee skill level are among the more noteworthy.

Systematic layout analysis (SLP) is a useful approach that usually begins with product and quantity analysis. The from–to chart shows flow volumes for products or resources that move in quantity; the activity relationship chart addresses nonflow factors. The analyst combines the charted data to form an activity arrangement diagram, which leads, in turn, to a space relationship diagram showing work-area requirements for each activity. Finally, the analyst fits the activities onto a floor plan, and the layout model is complete. SLP may be partially computer assisted and is suitable for offices as well as plants. A trend in office layout is toward openness rather than closed-off rooms. The interior designer's art as well as the science of flow analysis are important in office layout.

Solved Problem

The five departments of a warehouse with their approximate square-footage requirements and activity relationships are as follows:

DEPARTMENT	AREA (square feet)	ACTIVITY RELATIONSHIPS
1. Materials scheduling	1,000	
2. Packaging and crating	1,500	
3. Materials control supervisor	500	
4. Shipping and receiving	3,000	
5. Warehouse (storage)	6,000	
TOTAL	12,000 square feet	

a. Develop an activity arrangement diagram based on the REL chart data.

Solution

b. Develop a space relationship diagram for the five departmental areas.

c. Fit the five departments into a 100-foot by 150-foot building, and try to maintain 10-foot aisles between departments.

a. Activity arrangement diagram: *b.* Space relationship diagram:

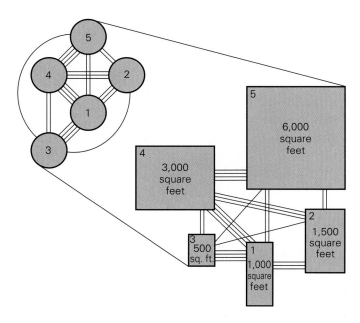

c. Following is a sample departmental layout in a 100-foot by 150-foot building, maintaining 10-foot aisles. (Note: Department 1 has more space than required; all others have the required amount.)

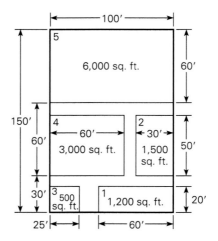

Review Questions

1. Explain the main differences among the basic modes of operations.
2. Explain how each of the following vary among the five modes of operations:
   a. Process overview.
   b. Variety/flexibility.
   c. Volume.
3. Are industries stuck in their conventional process mode? Why or why not?
4. What are streamlined operations? Cite four industries that tend to be among the less streamlined, and explain how they might be able to shift their operations mode, and why.
5. What is layout? Distinguish among the four major layout types.
6. What are the primary advantages and disadvantages of functional layout?
7. Suppose plant associates convert part of their facility from functional to cellular layout. What might be the advantages of such a move?
8. What kinds of goods and services are produced in fixed-position layouts? Why?
9. What is a mixed layout? Cite advantages and disadvantages of mixed layouts.
10. Why is the U-shaped layout well suited for cells or flow lines?
11. Discuss the ways in which U-shaped layouts help associates follow the tenets of TQM?
12. What is the origin of the data that go on the combined activity relationship chart?
13. How are degrees of closeness shown on the activity arrangement diagram? What determines sizes of blocks on the diagram?
14. How is the space relationship diagram converted to final layout?
15. How does office layout planning differ from plant layout planning?
16. What is the open-office concept? Is it desirable in all offices? Explain.
17. What are some interior-design variables? How are they related to the concept of layout?

1. For each of the following examples, try to determine the main kind of operation: repetitive or continuous, batch, job, or project. Discuss each.

Medical clinic.	Cafeteria.	Commercial fishing.
Crane manufacturing.	Book printing.	Grocery checkout.
Auditing.	Petroleum refining.	Farming.
Architecture.	Purchasing.	Mowing grass on campus.
Shoe repair.	Bottling.	Law practice.
Radio manufacturing.	Construction.	Welding shop.

2. Why does operations management tend to be more highly developed in repetitive than in job or project operations?

3. As organizations grow, their productive character may change—for example, from batch or job (custom) to repetitive or from project to repetitive. Describe how this might happen for a type of organization of your choice. Also describe the accompanying changes in the management of operations; that is, why would different kinds of planning and control models be called for?

4. Fifteen examples (three from each of the common modes of operations) are shown in Exhibit 12–2. Select one example, interview someone who works in your selected job environment, and prepare a report addressing the following:
   a. Describe the nature of the industry; the company or agency's mission; the volume, variety, and flexibility characteristics; and the process overview.
   b. From your interview results and your own observations and research, describe the various uses of any major tools or equipment used by the person you interviewed.
   c. Describe the layout of two primary areas (office, plant, cafeteria, laboratory, and so forth) in the facility in which your interviewee works. Discuss the appropriateness of the layout.

5. Some golfers occasionally need a sand wedge. Would such an item be a custom product or a commodity item? Discuss.

6. What is the basic layout of the college or university in which you are enrolled? What are the advantages of such a layout? The disadvantages?

7. The music and theater departments at State University will jointly present *The Sound of Music* at four locations around the state during the upcoming season. Two shows, a matinee and an evening performance, will occur at each site.
   a. What form of layout will this eight-performance effort require? (Hint: Don't rush to limit your options.) Explain fully.
   b. Discuss the effects of volume and variety. How would your response change if a different performance were to be given at each site?
   c. Fred and Freida, the production managers of the show, have asked you for ways in which they might streamline the entire effort. What would you suggest?

8. Greg Bailey and Greta Benson are executive partners at Bailey & Benson, Ltd., a CPA firm that specializes in personal taxes, estate planning, and other related accounting services for a small but growing number of wealthy clients. Both Greg and Greta feel that Bailey & Benson's reputation for high-quality custom services is largely responsible for their success.

   To help serve their growing client list, they have recently hired Haley Johnson and Harold Jones as junior associates. Haley feels strongly that a streamlining effort would help Bailey & Benson increase its efficiency and serve an even greater number of clients. She has a strong ally in Harold; he believes that greater use of high-quality software with state-of-the-art computer-generated standard forms is in the clients' best interests.

Greg and Greta have reservations. Can they streamline, as Haley puts it, and continue to provide custom service to discriminating clients? Discuss.

9. At Chicago's Lutheran General Health Systems, "sometimes miscommunication and mistrust led . . . staff to waste . . . expensive medications," such as $200-a-dose cancer-therapy drugs. "A study found nurses often would order a drug delivery for 10 AM if they really wanted it by noon because they feared the pharmacy wouldn't fill the order in time otherwise. But the pharmacy often surprised nurses, and a drug ordered for 10 AM would arrive then, two hours before it was needed. As a consequence, another dose would be ordered for noon, wasting the $200 dose.

"Last August waste from such practices cost Lutheran General $10,000 for one drug alone. According to one manager, 'Everyone was doing what they thought was in the patient's best interest. And in the days when you were dealing with aspirin tablets, such practices were fine. But with high-tech, high-cost therapies we have now, we cannot afford to do things the old way.'"[6]

Using concepts from the chapter, what should Lutheran General do? Explain.

10. For each of the following sellings, suggest which types of layout (functional, product, cellular, fixed, and mixed) are likely to apply. Some types may have more than one likely type of layout. Explain your choices briefly.

Auto assembly.	Military physical exams.
Auto repair.	Small-airplane manufacturing.
Shipbuilding.	Small-airplane overhaul and repair.
Machine shop.	Large airplane overhaul and repair.
Cafeteria.	Shoe manufacturing.
Restaurant.	Shoe repair.
Medical clinic.	Central processing of insurance forms.
Hospital.	Packing and crating.

11. Draw a layout of a dentists' office (group practice with three dentists). Label the areas as to whether they are functional, product, cellular, or fixed. Explain.

12. Develop an REL chart for a large discount or department store that you are familiar with. (You may need to visit the store for firsthand information.) Use the store's different departments as activities. Is the REL chart likely to be helpful in layout or re-layout of such a store? How about a flow diagram or a from–to chart? Explain.

13. Automatic Controls Corporation is building a new plant. Eight departments are involved. As part of a plant layout analysis, the activity relationships and square-footage needs for the departments are shown on the combined REL chart (combined flow analysis and nonflow analysis) on the next page.
    a. Develop an activity-arrangement diagram based on the REL-chart data.
    b. Develop a space relationship diagram for the eight departmental areas.
    c. Fit the eight departments into a 100-foot by 80-foot building in as close to an optimal layout as you can. Include aisles between departments on your layout.
    d. How necessary is the combined REL chart in this case? If it were not included in the analysis, what would the analysis steps be? Explain. (Hint: Note the pattern of reasons for relationships.)

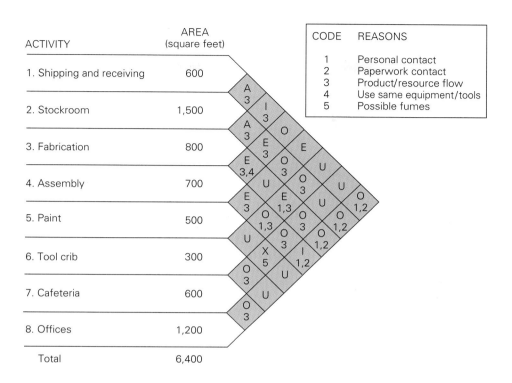

ACTIVITY	AREA (square feet)
1. Shipping and receiving	600
2. Stockroom	1,500
3. Fabrication	800
4. Assembly	700
5. Paint	500
6. Tool crib	300
7. Cafeteria	600
8. Offices	1,200
Total	6,400

CODE	REASONS
1	Personal contact
2	Paperwork contact
3	Product/resource flow
4	Use same equipment/tools
5	Possible fumes

14. Pharmaco, Inc., manufacturer of a drug line in liquid and tablet form, is considering moving to a new building. Layout planning is in process. The following data have been collected on material movements in the drug manufacturing process.[7]

	Unit Loads per Month	Move Distances (feet) in Present Building
Raw-Material Movements		
Receiving to raw-material storage:		180
1. Powder in drums.	800	
2. Powder in sacks on pallets.	1,100	
3. Liquid in drums.	100	
4. Controlled substance (heroin) in cans in cartons.	10	
5. Empty bottles in cartons on pallets.	8,000	
6. Water piped into granulating and liquid mixing (gallons).	3,000	
In-Process Movements		
Raw-material storage to granulating:		410
7. Powder in drums.	800	
8. Powder in sacks.	1,000	
9. Controlled substance in cans.	50	

(continued)

(concluded)

	Unit Loads per Month	Move Distances (feet) in Present Building
Raw-material storage to liquid mixing:		300
10. Powder in sacks.	100	
11. Liquid in drums.	100	
12. Controlled substance in cans.	10	
13. Granulating to tableting (granules in drums).	1,500	290
14. Tableting to fill and pack (tables in tubs).	6,000	180
15. Liquid mixing to fill and pack (gallons piped).	4,000	370
16. Raw-material storage to fill and pack (empty bottles).	8,000	260
17. Fill and pack to finished storage (cartons of bottles and of tablet packs on pallets).	10,000	320

> *a.* Convert the given flow-volume data to a vowel-rating scale; that is, identify which activity pairs (routes) should be rated A, E, I, O, and U.
> *b.* Develop an activity arrangement diagram.
> *c.* The layout planners see little need for a from–to chart or an REL chart. Explain why.

15. The SLP example (Globe County Offices, Example 12–1) includes only a partial combined REL chart (Exhibit 12–12) and omits the space-relationship diagram. Using the given data in the example, follow the method of the Solved Problem and
    a. Construct a complete combined REL chart to include all offices. (Use your best judgment along with available information in the example to assign "closeness values" and likely "reasons behind the closeness values.")
    b. Construct a space-relationship diagram based on the activity-arrangement diagram (Exhibit 12–13) and given space requirements (Exhibit 12–10).

16. The woodshop building of E-Z Window Company is undergoing major re-layout in order to reduce backtracking and decrease flow distances. A flow diagram of the frame-manufacturing operation and an REL chart for nonflow factors in the operation is shown on the next page.
    a. Construct a from–to chart based on flow-diagram data. What is the meaning of the notation that quantities are in unit loads? Explain by referring to a few examples on the chart.
    b. What proportion of total flow on your from–to chart represents backtracking? How does that proportion depend on your chosen order of listing activities on the chart? What does your chosen order of listing activities imply about the final layout arrangement?
    c. Convert the flow volume data in your from–to chart to a vowel-rating scale; that is, identify which activity pairs (routes) should be rated A, E, I, O, and U.
    d. Combine your vowel-rating data representing flow volumes with the non-flow-factor vowel ratings on the REL chart. Express the result in a new, combined REL chart.
    e. Convert your combined REL chart into an activity-arrangement diagram.
    f. Develop a space-relationship diagram for the eight activity areas.
    g. Fit the eight activity areas into a square building without allowances for aisles, and so on. Make your layout as nearly optimal as you can.

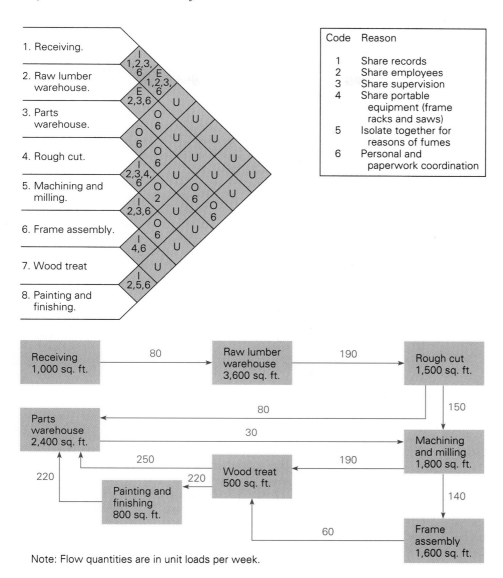

Code	Reason
1	Share records
2	Share employees
3	Share supervision
4	Share portable equipment (frame racks and saws)
5	Isolate together for reasons of fumes
6	Personal and paperwork coordination

Note: Flow quantities are in unit loads per week.

17. Examine the "Principles of Operations Management" (Exhibit 2–3 in Chapter 2). Which principles seem most directly affected by layout and re-layout decisions? Discuss.

CASE STUDY

STREAMLINED PATIENT TRANSFERS: HOURS TO MINUTES

The process of admitting patients to Northwest Hospital's Transitional Care Unit (TCU) was cumbersome. It took 6 to 12 hours just to get the necessary approvals when a physician referred a patient to the TCU. Then the patient's chart had to be reviewed, which was delayed until the next day. Thus, it took at least 24 hours and often 48 hours for the patient finally to be moved to the TCU.

"Five people evaluated each patient" because, explained Gayle Ward, assistant director of nursing, "there were two different philosophies" for admission. One centered on control of patients and payments, the other on smooth management of evolving patient care. Because of the cumbersome admissions procedure, some physicians had become reluctant to refer patients; the TCU's beds were underutilized, and the unit had become a financial problem for the hospital.

Thus, the TCU admission process was ripe for improvement when TCU's total quality management training program began in July of 1992. In conjunction with training in the quality sciences by an outside consultant, a project team was formed composed of Becky Larson from care management; Matt Quaterman, admissions coordinator; Rebecca Pelroy, from TCU billing; Pat Ford, utilization review coordinator; and the acute care case managers, Jo Croot and Gayle Ward. The team developed a process-flow diagram for the admissions process and then "streamlined it by eliminating complexity and rework. The staff didn't think [the new process] would work."

Jo said, "Give me one week. . . . That first day I had about 40 calls and messages with questions about the process. I kept saying, 'Stick to the diagram.' We started turning referrals around from six hours to less than one hour and filling beds as soon as they became empty."

Within two weeks, the new process of relying on the judgment of the case managers rather than on the several review stages was working. It reduced the admissions workload by eight hours a day for Jo and her staff. Delays for hand-carrying of paperwork were also eliminated. "We do almost everything by phone [and let the] paperwork catch up." Admissions that once took as long as two days were cut to 20 minutes. "Physicians are happier with the service, beds fill quicker, there are more admissions from outside the hospital, and the evening shift is also admitting patients."

The streamlined procedure has exposed underlying stumbling blocks, according to Jo Croot. After implementation, however, Jo had continued to feel frustrated by the number of referrals that were refused admission. "I tracked down the reasons why and made a bar chart." Her chart, tracking 51 such refusals, showed the following:

- One patient was admitted instead to the rehabilitation unit.
- One was sent instead to an outside gero-psychiatric unit.

- Two had no insurance.
- Two had died.
- Twenty-five had been discharged directly to their homes.
- Twenty had been placed in some other nursing home, hospital, or other facility.

The study confirmed that "these 51 referrals were appropriately screened and placed elsewhere by our case managers." Thus, by her bar chart, Jo had developed the evidence that the new admissions process was not only quick but also producing correct (high-quality) referral decisions.

Case topics: Streamlined processing in human services; flow charting; multifunctional teamwork; bar chart; quality health care.

Case Questions

1. Two competing philosophies were at work under the old TCU admissions process; the "smooth management of evolving patient care" one seemed to win out under the new approach. Does the makeup of the project team suggest that outcome? Is it reasonable to expect that proponents of both philosophies will come to appreciate the new procedure? Discuss.

2. Are the human reactions to the new process (staff doubt that it will ever work, the 40 calls that Jo got the first day and so forth) normal? Why? In this case, positive changes were apparent almost immediately. But what might have happened if those changes were much slower in developing? Was Jo wise to suggest rapid results when she said, "Give me one week?" Why?

3. Jo's chart is offered as evidence that the streamlined TCU admissions procedure produces quality admissions decisions. Do you agree? Why or why not?

Source: Adapted from Jodi B. Torpey, *Northwest Hospital Quality Case Studies* (Seattle: Quality Health Systems of America, 1992), pp 48–54. Used with permission.

MICROSOFT CORPORATION—DUBLIN, IRELAND[8]

Introduction

Microsoft grew exponentially in the 1980s to become the world's leading software company. Its market value of $21 billion exceeded even that of General Motors. Founded by Chairman Bill Gates in 1975, Microsoft emerged in the 1990s, according to *Business Week,* "as clearly the most important single force in the entire computer industry."

The company introduced 48 new products in 1992, including well over 100 international versions. Most phenomenal of all was the introduction of Microsoft Windows 3.1. Now running on more than 12 million systems worldwide, Windows has become the fastest selling graphical user interface ever. In the two years since its introduction, these figures represent a new customer every 10 seconds. Other leading software products include Microsoft Word, Excel, Powerpoint, and Project. The company's manufacturing facilities are located in Bothell, Washington, (serving North America and the rest of the world), Nunacao in Puerto Rico (serving North and South America), and Dublin, Ireland (serving Europe).

Competing from the Periphery—Microsoft Ireland

Microsoft Ireland, located in Dublin since 1985, is the European manufacturing base of Microsoft Corporation. The 80,000-square-foot facility employs 350 people. From there, the company supplies software packages to all major European markets, with Britain, Germany, and France accounting for in excess of 60 percent of all sales.

Providing logistics service support to the European marketplace from a detached island location has freight and time-to-market disadvantages. Crowley[9] documents the problems encountered by exporters located in peripheral countries such as Ireland. They include the following:

- Ireland has a small open economy that is further split into two sub-economies. Port and shipping terminal investments must therefore be highly concentrated to gain economies of scale sufficient to be competitive.

Case topics: Customer focus; just-in-time; quick setup; cells; supplier partnership; pay-for-skills; inventor; distribution.

- Ireland is an island and, since the opening of the England–France channel tunnel, the only European Union member without a land-link to Europe.
- Ireland is remote from the center of gravity of the single European market when compared with the other member states. Hence the role of logistics is proportionately higher for Irish industry.
- Ireland is impeded geographically from the European mainland by Britain, so single-mode, straight-line routings cannot be followed to central European markets.
- Ireland lacks an abundance of raw materials, which "doubles" its logistical demands; that is, industry must both import raw materials and export finished goods.

These five handicaps work out to estimated transportation costs for Irish exporters to the European mainland of over 9 percent of export sales value, or twice those incurred by other European member states. Additional logistics overheads add to the competitive disadvantages faced by Irish exporters.

Manufacturing on the Periphery: Microsoft Ireland, 1985–88

When initially established, the plant had direct responsibility for manufacturing and shipping to the United Kingdom and European destinations. Marketing, customer service, and technical support was provided by each national sales subsidiary, of which there were 13 in Europe. The manufacturing process at Microsoft Ireland was, and still essentially is, a two-stage one. The first stage was duplication of software packages from master disks. The second was assembly of the finished software package. Assembly was labor intensive, consisting of placing the duplicated disks, labels, manuals, license agreement, and packing materials in the appropriate carton; and then shrink-wrapping the carton prior to shipment.

Initially, Microsoft operated like most other manufacturers: long production runs, large inventories, lengthy setup times, quality-control problems, and multiple suppliers. From a total product range of 280 products, high-volume lines such as Word would be produced in batches of 10,000 units once a week, with lower-volume lines being assembled just once a month. The primary objective was minimizing costs associated with long setup times. This called for bulk deliveries of raw materials from suppliers and required a warehouse of 40,000 square feet capable of housing eight weeks of inventory with associated storage costs. At the end of a production run, the finished goods were moved back to the finished-goods warehouse where they awaited shipment. Delivery to customers occurred at the end of the month. This approach resulted in a three-week order cycle and lent itself to stockouts, inasmuch as production capacity was locked into a given line for considerable periods of time.

The structure of the distribution channel at this time was typical of the industry. Microsoft Ireland would ship large batches intermittently to the warehouses of the 13 sales and support subsidiaries around Europe who were responsible for onward logistics. For example, Microsoft Ireland shipped product directly to the U.K. subsidiary's warehouse. From there, Microsoft UK would ship to a mix of about 200 distributors and dealers using contract delivery for large distributors and couriers for small orders to dealers. Backorder rates were typically in the order of 15 percent of total sales.

Journey to Lean Production, 1988–90

In 1988, Microsoft Ireland decided to confront these problems of working capital tied up in inventory, quality, and product availability. They employed a consulting firm, World Class International (WCI). WCI's studies showed that on average, Microsoft's composite lead time was 151 days: 60 days in raw material, one day in work-in-process (WIP), and 90 days in finished goods. Moreover, the product received value for only four minutes (the time it took the package to be assembled) during a normal production run. Faced with a response ratio of 151 days to four minutes, the company's reaction was immediate: Emphasizing throughput time, the new policy would be to produce smaller lots more frequently. The object was to receive supplies daily and build (assemble) daily. The consultants and Microsoft identified four critical dimensions in the implementation process:

Question 1.   With just one day of WIP, can Microsoft Ireland be considered a just-in-time (JIT) producer? A world-class manufacturer?

Supplier Reduction.   The company's supplier base included indigenous printing companies (manuals), packaging manufacturers, disk manufacturers, and freight forwarders. Microsoft decided to initiate a process of selecting a reduced number of strategic partners. In return for providing its suppliers with a long-term commitment, standardization of product design, and rolling sales forecasts, cost reductions would be shared 50–50 between Microsoft and the supplier. Microsoft received assurances with regard to mutual cost reduction and daily deliveries. These commitments were based not on legally binding contractual agreements but rather on "gentlemen's agreements" coupled with quarterly reviews. The strategic partnership effort reduced the supplier base by 70 percent, which significantly lowered transaction and communication costs. Raw-material inventories were also reduced by 70 percent.

Cut Production Batch Sizes in Half.   To facilitate shorter production runs, lower inventories, and assembly of all products on a JIT basis, setup times had to be dramatically reduced. In assembly, setup was taking 35 minutes. This involved clearing out the previous job after checking (counting) it; then ensuring that all the disks, manuals, and packaging were available at the appropriate work stations on the 30-foot-long assembly line.

The first improvement occurred while the plant was still underutilized. While some assemblers were completing one job, others prestaged the next job on a second idle assembly line located parallel to the first. But as the plant got busier, the second assembly line was needed for production. A different way of achieving quick setup was needed. The company came up with an imaginative and novel approach in which its 30-foot-long assembly lines would be replaced.

The classic JIT configuration—a U-shaped line in which all assemblers would be in close proximity—was attractive. However, Jim Gleason, production manager, thought that for this process a completely round carousel configuration would work even better. Plant manager Brian Reynolds liked the idea but suggested making it a dual-level carousel. With two levels, while operatives assemble from one level of the carousel, teammates who have completed their tasks for that run set up the other carousel level for the next production run. Their creation is shown in Exhibit CS12–1. The simple tools used in the setups (scissors, tape dispenser, etc.) were placed on easy-to-see shadow boards, an example of which is shown in the photo in Exhibit 11–2B (previous chapter).

In addition to eliminating setup time, quality control improved: In a production batch of 10 units, it became immediately obvious at the end of the process if any disks or manuals

Exhibit CS12–1   Dual-Level Carousel Assembly Tables

were not included in the carton, as they would remain highly visible on the carousel. By producing in smaller batches, quality problems were immediately and clearly identified.

A major piece of equipment in each cell is a Kallfass packaging machine, which shrink-wraps packages of disks. In Chapter 11, Exhibit 11–2A shows the kind of detailed analysis undertaken to cut changeover time on the Kallfass. This analysis is the work of the machine's operator. Changeover time, progressively reduced from 35 minutes to one minute, was plotted on a large trend chart near the Kallfass.

Question 2.   What kinds of changeover improvements would be appropriate on the Kallfass machine?

Employee Involvement.   Overcoming resistance to change on the shop floor required radical changes in the way people were managed. Managers identified employees who they felt would be suitable facilitators in training operatives in JIT/TQM techniques. Considerable resources were devoted to company training.

For example, management recognized the Kallfass operator's talents and bestowed upon him the extra assignment of running training classes in quick setup for other plant personnel. During a plant visit, one of the case writers saw a wall notice announcing the next class and listing who would be trained; plant manager Reynolds' name was included on the list.

At first the company did not offer more pay for additional skills. Within a year, however, it became clear that the expansion of employee skills was paying big dividends. As a result, a revised compensation system would pay on the basis of number of new skills employees acquire. In the new system, employees certified as "world-class operators" would receive 5 percent more pay, first choice of jobs, and opportunities to work on engineering and other projects.

The training was also geared toward development of quality-focused teams that used brainstorming to improve manufacturing processes. Emphasis on continuous improvement yielded 3,700 employee suggestions in the first two years of operation, an annual rate of over 5 per employee.

Focused Factories.   Plant layout and organization was still another target for improvement. Microsoft Ireland would employ the focused-factory concept, pioneered by Skinner[10] in the 1970s. Skinner maintained that a plant would perform better if it limited itself to a focused number of tasks, processes, or products. Initially, Microsoft established focused cells around common product families, such as Windows or Excel. As business expanded, the number of such cells grew from 1 to 10.

While the results were good, managers later decided on a different object of focus: customers. Since the geographic destinations of the software packages were language related, four focused "factories within the factory" were introduced: one (Euro) for English-language customers, a second for Germany, a third for France, and the fourth for the rest of Europe (several languages). Referring again to Exhibit CS12–1, we see a typical layout for one of the four focused units along with a photo of a cell within the unit.

The focused factories deal with the customers of specific geographic markets. Each has its own independent manufacturing cells, complete with production equipment (duplicating machines and carousels) and work teams (see Exhibit CS12–2). Each of the four cells in the French factory includes a Kallfass shrink-wrap machine. The other focused factories do not include shrink-wrap, inasmuch as customers in the other markets have accepted reduced packaging.

Prior to 1988, Microsoft-Ireland had 42 major suppliers. A supplier-reduction campaign reduced that to 11 suppliers, 4 of which were print shops. It was not possible to cut to just one printer, because none in Ireland had enough capacity to handle all of Microsoft's demand. Also, with the work split among four printers, each focused factory could then have its own printer, specializing in the language of that factory. The printer for the French-focused factory is good at running larger lots. In contrast, the printer for the multilingual factory has learned how to run small lots (e.g., 300 units). The following contributed to making small lots feasible:

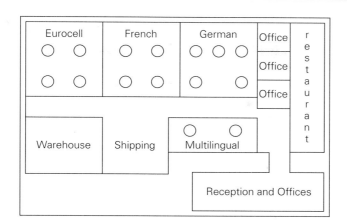

- The printer placed a folding machine right next to each printing machine—instead of all folding machines in a separate department.

- Quick-drying inks eliminate the need to allow time for ink to dry before folding (which overcomes a reason why printers often claim not to be able to offer quick response).

- Earlier, Microsoft had standardized page sizes, which eliminates the need for the printer to reset machines for different sizes.

- Microsoft had the printer equip its machines with blank-page detectors, which eliminates a critical quality control problem—and time-consuming inspections and rework.

The national flags of the destination markets were in evidence at each focused factory, making it easy to see where to deliver. With this kind of simplification and with each cell maintaining direct contact with and deliveries from its own suppliers, paperwork and administrative costs plunged. Within months, cost of goods sold had been reduced by 25 percent, while inventory levels in the plant had been cut by 75 percent, and customer lead times reduced to one day.

Question 3.   Which is best for Microsoft Ireland, focus by product family or focus by language group? Discuss.

Changes in Channel Structure in the United Kingdom

As the radical changes in operations in the Dublin plant were beginning to pay off in improved manufacturing performance, other developments and changes began to emerge in the channels of distribution.

Relocation of Microsoft UK's Headquarters.   In the 1980s, Microsoft operated a single distribution center (DC) in the United Kingdom, plus five more DCs in five other European locations. The distribution centers, in turn, served many large and small distributors and dealers.

In 1990 Microsoft UK (the sales and service subsidiary in Britain) was in the process of relocating to a new site at Winnersh in the southeast of England. As there was a lack of suitable warehousing space at this new headquarters, the parent company felt it was now opportune to evaluate the future warehousing requirements for the United Kingdom. There was some concern that the phenomenal growth rates in the industry could lead to customer-service and cost problems. As a result, the company decided to evaluate separating the warehousing function from the marketing and technical-support functions currently performed by Microsoft UK.

Emergence of a Low-Cost Channel of Distribution.   Approximately nine major distributors accounted for 80 percent of Microsoft's business in the United Kingdom. The remaining 20 percent included some 200 smaller dealers, educational establishments, and original equipment manufacturers. A notable feature of the industry is that channel structure has been historically based on computer hardware. In the mid–1980s, distributors concentrated on the sale of PCs, which offered high profit margins. However, this situation changed considerably in the 1990s as low-cost equipment began to appear on the market. The mystery surrounding the use of PCs began to evaporate with the spread of interface software such as Windows. Hardware manufacturers now began to use more direct forms of distribution to retailers as lower-cost distribution channels became the norm. Direct marketers such as Dell and Gateway developed mail and toll-free telephone ordering. Ever narrowing margins on PCs became less attractive to major distributors, and their primary focus shifted to sale of software products and ancillary hardware such as printers.

From Lean Production to Lean Logistics: Channel Implications, 1990–92

In light of these developments, Microsoft Europe managers felt it was timely to examine logistics strategy. Main issues were warehousing and structure of the channels of distribution. Following a comprehensive analysis of options, the decision was to relocate the U.K. distribution hub to the manufacturing facility in Dublin. While this might appear to have been a very radical decision, given the longer distribution distances, it considered the broader issue of logistics and channel strategy, rather than simply warehouse location. Rationale for selecting the Microsoft-Ireland location included the following:

- Rate-based manufacturing raised significant implications for logistics: The ability to manufacture each product daily offered the opportunity to deliver principle products daily.
- Locating the U.K. warehouse in Dublin facilitated "one-touch inventory"; that is, once finished goods were shipped from the production line in Dublin (one touch), there were no further intermediate stocking (touching) points at Microsoft UK.
- A more direct low-cost channel structure emerged. The company's distribution network in the United Kingdom was reduced from 200 geographically dispersed dealers down to just nine major, concentrated distributors.
- Implementation of lean production with just-in-time supplier deliveries released 40,000 square feet of space formerly used for warehousing purchased materials. This space at the Dublin site could now be used as the distribution hub.

Managing Service Logistics from the Edge

Managers at Microsoft Ireland were aware that relocation of the U.K. distribution warehouse to Dublin presented a number of interdependent challenges, which included

- *Control of inventory and customer service levels.* A major factor to be considered was the perceived loss of control by Microsoft UK over the entire distribution function. Concern had been expressed about separating the sales and warehousing functions and effects on customer service levels in Britain.
- *Loss of visibility.* Other concerns revolved around Microsoft UK's loss of visibility of inventory levels for all stockkeeping units. Not being able to actually see the

inventory creates feelings of discomfort. The need was for some means of counterbalancing this fear factor with a comfort factor.

These concerns led to development of a phased implementation plan: Microsoft UK would initially define customer service measures and levels. Providing a comfort factor, daily E-mail updates would flow between Ireland and the United Kingdom. Finally, any manufacturing–marketing interface difficulties relating to customer service would be addressed at weekly problem clinics at the U.K. headquarters.

Within a year, the impact of lean logistics (relocation, direct shipment, and one-touch inventory) on performance was as significant as had been achieved earlier though world-class manufacturing. In a marketplace where rapid product introductions and revisions mirrored the importance of time-based competitive strategies, the company was able to record the following improvements in logistic performance:

- Delivery lead times were cut to one day for principle products. For slow sellers, customers were each given a certain day of the week that they would receive delivery.

- Inventory savings of over $4 million were achieved in the first year of operation.

- Backorder levels fell from 15 percent to just 5 percent of total orders.

Furthermore, from Microsoft UK's perspective, more time and resources were now available to devote to their core competency: marketing and technical support.

Conclusion

The case study illustrates synergistic effects of world-class manufacturing and distribution. While logistics decisions have often been a source of conflict between marketing and manufacturing, Microsoft's experience shows that mutually beneficial results are possible. A key to success is trust: The sales and service subsidiary gained confidence that logistics could not only effectively be managed by manufacturing but effectively managed from a peripheral location.

The case also illustrates the interaction between distribution-channel developments and the management of logistics. A wide range of distribution channels must be serviced by Microsoft, each requiring different approaches. These channels are far from being static, so flexible strategies are necessary. Indeed, Stern et al.[11] argue that, ultimately, organizations like Microsoft "instead of merely watching their channels develop organically or playing the reactionary game of catch-up, must think creatively about how they can deliver superior value to their customers." Increased product customization will drive the concept of "tailored channels," which in turn will drive logistical differentiation. And it is logistics, La Londe and Powers[12] contend, that will ultimately integrate the product-service chain in the next century.

Question 4. In the light of the Stern et al. statement, what's next? That is, what new manufacturing-logistics initiatives might be expected for Microsoft Corporation?

For Further Reference

Books

Apple, James M. *Plant Layout and Material Handling.* reprint ed., Melbourne, Fla.: Krieger, 1992 (TS155. A58).

Black, J. T. *The Design of the Factory with a Future.* New York: McGraw-Hill, 1991.

Hales, H. Lee. *Computer Aided Facilities Planning.* New York: Marcel Dekker, 1984 (TS177.H35).

Harmon, Roy L. *Reinventing the Factory II.* New York: The Free Press, 1992 (HD56.H37).

Konz, Stephan A. *Facility Design.* 2nd ed. Scottsdale, Ariz.: Publishing Horizons, 1993 (TS177.K66).

Molnar, John. *Facilities Management Handbook.* New York: Chapman & Hall, 1983 (TH151.M59).

Schonberger, Richard J. *Building a Chain of Customers.* New York: The Free Press, 1990 (HD58.9.S36).

Steudel, Harold J., and Paul Desruelle. *Manufacturing in the Nineties*. New York: Van Nostrand Reinhold, 1992 (HD9725.D68).

Periodicals/Societies
APICS: The Performance Advantage (American Production and Inventory Control Society).

Industrial Engineering Solutions (Institute of Industrial Engineering).
Industry Week.
Production and Operations Management Journal (Production and Operations Management Society).
Office.
Today's Office.

MANAGING CONTINUOUS AND REPETITIVE OPERATIONS

13

Chapter Outline

> "Keep it clean. Keep it cold. Keep it moving." This simple formula for success in his business comes from Paul Nelson, Production Manager of Vitamilk Dairy, Seattle, Washington. To follow this script, Vitamilk trucks its product direct to retail stores. In contrast, dairies in most cities ship to distribution centers, which later load it into delivery trucks going to the stores. This means final customers will be using products that may be days less fresh.

For the lay person, high-volume operations conjures up images of products zipping down long conveyorized assembly lines or of liquids flowing continuously from vats through a maze of pipes until forced through nozzles into bottles or cans. The Vitamilk plant captures both images: vats and pipes for the early processes (e.g., pasteurization and processing into such products as yogurt, ice cream, and powdered milk) and conveyors drawing the containers past filling and capping stations. The bigger picture includes keeping the product moving all the way to the retailers.

As noted in Chapter 12, the process industry consists of companies that produce fluids and powders (e.g., Vitamilk Diary), plus pellets, grains, ores, and other commodities in continuous fashion. Its close partner, repetitive operations, provides widely used consumer goods and industrial components. Though continuous and repetitive operations are related, they differ in several ways, including some that affect operations strategy. In this chapter, we examine the kinship and differences along with key management issues.

Process Industries—and Hybrids

There are not many purely continuous process industries. Perhaps the one that comes closest is electric power generation. In Wyoming's coal fields, giant shovels dump lignite into huge trucks that move trainlike to dump their loads onto conveyors that carry the fuel into the furnaces of a 500 megawatt energy plant. The coal burns and the turbines spin, generating the power that flows through wires to a million homes and businesses. Nothing stops. The output is not stored. The same goes for hydroelectric power, minus a few steps.

Far more common is hybrid processing: both continuous and repetitive in the same plant. Typically, the front end is continuous—raw materials start as flows—but the end products emerge as units. In candy factories, for example, sugar, chocolate, water, and other ingredients flow in, and cartons of candy bars or boxed candy come out. Potatoes, salt, vegetable oil, and so forth, flow into a potato chip plant, and cartons of sacked chips emerge. Sugar, water, flavoring, and active ingredients flow into a drug-producing plant, and out come boxes of bottled cough medicine. Exhibit 13–1 illustrates typical production of food items. Continuous flow of dough through the mixing stage gives way to individual pieces for subsequent freezing and packaging in highly repetitive fashion.

A critical operations strategy for the hybrids is streamlined processing in both the continuous and repetitive stages. Sometimes, however, the market, the competition, equipment, and other factors gang up to push a firm away from streamlining. The Pepperidge Farm division of Campbell Soup is an example.[1] Pepperidge's dilemma was the same as that of many food processors: a growing variety of products and package sizes and types vying for too few production lines. The schedule

Exhibit 13–1

**Typical
Production of
Food Items**

Pepperidge Farm cookie line. (Used with permission.)

for any given product was intermittent with long intervals between production runs—a far cry from streamlined, continuous flows.

One solution was faster changeovers from production of one product to another. This would allow more frequent production of all items. Pepperidge scoured the world to find equipment that could be quickly changed over. They installed new equipment that allowed a single plant to produce nearly 10 times the number of products per day as the old. With more frequent production—more continuous—the company moved closer to synchronizing baking with store sales. Bake-to-store cycle times for cookies and breads were roughly halved. This is a sizable competitive advantage, since the product on the shelf is fresher. Thus, the operations strategy of becoming more streamlined dovetailed with the business strategy of gaining competitive advantage from providing fresher products closer matched to sales rates.

This strategy applies not only to Pepperidge. It has general application in the process industries. The Pepperidge success formula, plus other factors critical for continuous processors are our next topic.

*P*RINCIPLES 9 AND 12:

Use simple, flexible equipment. Cut changeover times.

Key Success Factors

> The Cypress Plant was built with quality, just-in-time, and total employee involvement in mind; the plant was designed internally, and those who designed it run it. All associates are cross-trained on every task, and a weekly job rotation includes every facet of the plant. Obvious benefits include flexibility and enhanced problem solving. Rapid response to customer requirements has been attained through an 80 percent reduction in changeover times, receipt of materials in the exact (containerized) quantity needed and at the point-of-use, process streamlining, buffer inventory reductions, and quick-response shipping. Brainstorming, partnerships with suppliers, benchmarking, and elimination of non-value-adding steps are other activities contributing to success.[2]

These comments, describing Milliken & Company's Cypress chemical plant in Blacksburg, Virginia, show that many of the themes of this book apply to the chemical industry, too. Success in chemicals, as in other businesses, comes from giving customers quality, flexibility, and responsive just-in-time service with short cycle times and eliminating wastes to drive down costs.

Chemical companies and other process-industry organizations, however, have their own ways of pursuing the general success formula. Exhibit 13–2 identifies key success factors that apply especially to process-industry operations. Each is explained next in two parts: the success factor and contemporary examples of how to apply it.

Capital Investment and Process Design. Usually continuous processors are capital intensive. Their plants bristle with high-cost automation. Often, competitive advantage comes from having the most modern equipment and from keeping it running close to 168 hours per week. (Twenty-four hours a day times seven days equals 168 hours a week.) Since this strategy—keep the plants running—tends to produce excessive inventories of certain items, it calls for a companion strategy in sales and marketing: Promote, advertise, and cut deals to move the inventory.

Application. Equally important is for the plants to be designed for fail-safe, high-yield operation. Multifunctional product–process design teams can apply their breadth of experience to this goal. Milliken's Cypress plant, designed with operator involvement, is a case in point. The plant features two separate reactor groups, one for large orders and the other for small ones. Conventionally, chemical plants have a

EXHIBIT 13–2

**Success Factors
for Process
Industries**

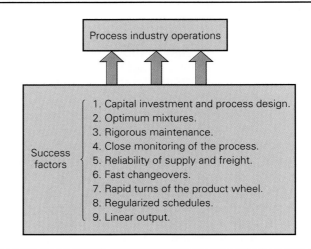

single large reactor group, which forces dominant products to compete for processing time with small-volume products. Customer service on both large and small orders suffers.

Optimum Mixtures.   Some process industries rely heavily on linear programming for finding optimum (best) mixtures of ingredients. An example is production of pet food and livestock feed. Product planners use LP to select the lowest-cost mix of ingredients that will meet nutrition and other standards. Since volumes are usually large, savings of a few cents per bag can add up quickly.

Application. Optimizing the mix begins in preproduction planning. Product-development teams search for better ingredients and involve suppliers in process and materials improvement. Sourcing teams aim for supplier certification.

Rigorous Maintenance.   An equipment breakdown idles an entire process. In the case of a food or drug company, for example, a whole mixing or bottling line may shut down. When the product is perishable, avoiding breakdowns is all the more critical; perishability disallows buffer stocks between process stages as protection against breakdowns. The process itself must be capable and well maintained.

Application. The highest form of process maintenance is called total preventive maintenance (TPM) and involves every operator. A goal is to eliminate costly downtime caused by equipment malfunctions and failures. TPM practices include absolute cleanliness and orderliness, regular calibration of measurement tools, and prefailure replacement of components. (More on this in Chapter 17.)

Close Monitoring of the Process.   In the process industries, federal law or industrywide standards often govern product quality, purity, sanitation, and waste. Process monitoring must be rigorous to ensure that standards are met and products are safe and salable.

Application. Much of the monitoring may be automated. Programmable logic controllers, a rugged, special-purpose type of computer processor, guide much of the monitoring. (See Into Practice, "PLCs at La Victoria.") Just as important are operator uses of data-based tools for discovery of malfunctions and root causes and their rapid correction.

PLCs at La Victoria

"K.I.S.S.—Keep It Simple Son!—that is what I tell myself," grins Wes Guthrie, purchasing expediter at La Victoria Foods. La Victoria's single plant in City of Industry, California, produces salsas, jalapeños, nachos, and tomatillo entero.

"The simpler it is in a food plant the better efficiency you have because there is less to break down. . . . When the chiles are here and when the tomatoes are here, we have to run. We cannot have a plant breakdown. . . . None of this raw produce keeps."

Maintenance superintendent Andy Zamberlin notes that when he came to La Victoria 13 years before, the place was a nightmare. It had "too much complicated machinery such as stop/starts, electric motors, and electric eyes that just did not run right."

Zamberlin and his staff eliminated much of assorted, conventional electro-mechanical automation controls. Today, "almost all of La Victoria's equipment is run by PLCs (programmable logic controllers).

Several PLCs control the batching process. Several control the filling process. Some control the steam process, which is the 'breaking' or peeling of the tomatoes. Others control the fillers themselves. . . . These are programmed so that the drive motors are in step with the capping machine so they do not speed one up and slow one down."

But, Guthrie points out, their kind of process control requires a good deal of human involvement. "We've got tomatoes of different sizes and textures. They might be mushy, they might be hard, they might not peel. . . . There are so many variables." Therefore, Guthrie points out, "These PLCs have to be user controllable. You program parameters, but the operator has to be able to control it."

Source: Blake Svenson, "Keeping It Simple to Reduce Spoiled Efficiency in the Food Industry," *Industrial Engineering,* June 1992, pp. 29–32.

Reliability of Supply and Freight.   This includes selection of a plant site close to markets and supplies of materials. Raw materials are the lifeline of process industries. Thus, regardless of plant location, the freight haulers bringing in material must be reliable. Stockpiling as protection for shaky supply or freight is a limited option. Most of the process industry produces in such large volumes that even a few days' supply of ingredients would make a mountain.

Application. Strong supplier relations are critical. The quest is for partnerships with a few good suppliers. Ideally, they deliver just in time direct to points of use closely synchronized with production schedules. For disaster protection, it may be best to store extra stock offline where it will not interfere with the continuity and speed of flow. (Offline buffer stock was discussed in Chapter 8.)

Fast Changeovers.   Producing different blends and container sizes requires changing production lines. Some line changeovers take several days, which may include completely cleaning out all equipment. Fast changeovers make it easier to fit more jobs, large and small, into the schedule in a given time period.

Application. The guidelines for quick changeover (Chapter 11), perfected for sheet-metal fabrication and machining, apply as well in the process industries. Flexible, cross-trained associates participate in changeover improvement projects and also execute the improvements. An objective is to schedule more products per time period closer to actual demand patterns. Example: Monsanto Plastics in Cincinnati cut its time to change color in its plastic products from 10 to 12 hours to

1 ½ hours. The method was to prepare a duplicate color module offline, then stop the process to quickly swap the color modules.

Rapid Turns of the Product Wheel.   Many companies in the process industries produce assorted products on a single high-capacity production line. Figuratively, the assortment arranges itself on what industry people call the **product wheel.** See Exhibit 13–3. Make the first product, change the process, make the second, change, and so on around the wheel. **Product wheel turn time**, therefore, is the required production cycle time for any member of the product family. Conventionally, companies turn the wheel slowly. That is, they produce huge quantities in long production runs between changeovers. Their aim is to increase the ratio of production time to changeover time. The downside is that customers wanting product E must wait through production runs of products A through D. A more customer-sensitive practice is to speed up the wheel turns.

Application. The usual practice produces large amounts of inventory out of synch with demand rates. While a faster wheel turn reduces equipment utilization, it also cuts lot-size inventories. Speeding the wheel thus may be cost neutral. Example: At Esso Chemical's Sarnia, Ontario, plant (producing polyvinyl chloride, polyethylene, etc.) the wheel turn time was reduced from 80 days to 30. Quicker changeovers paved the way.[3]

DuPont has developed a method of calculating wheel turn time.[4] Data required are downtime attributable to changeovers, outage time, production rate, and demand rate. The DuPont formula is

$$W = \sum C \Big/ \left(1 - O - \frac{\sum D}{P}\right) \qquad (13\text{--}1)$$

where

W = Wheel turn time

C = Downtime attributable to changeovers (not including changeovers done off line or "on the fly")

O = Outage time, as a decimal

P = Production rate, expressed as a composite average for all products represented by the wheel

$\sum D$ = Average quantity demanded (ordered), summed up for all products on the wheel, for a given time period

EXHIBIT 13–3
Product Wheel

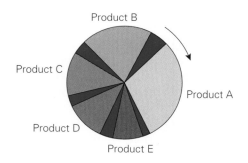

Note: The wedges between products represent process changeovers.

Source: Adapted from Wayne K. Smith, James L. Ingraham, and David M. Rurak, "Time and Pull: A DuPont Case History," *Target* (January/February 1993), pp. 27–42.

Assumptions: Production rate P must exceed demand rate D, and outage O plus the composite demand-to-production ratio ($\Sigma D/P$) must be less than 1.0.

Finding the wheel turn time is important for product scheduling. It is even more important for salespeople, who need the information for order promising to customers. An example demonstrates the calculation.

EXAMPLE 13–1   WHEEL TURN TIME, EXTRUDER
_____

Given:
A DuPont plant operates an extruder 24 hours a day. The following are characteristics of the operation:

- Five products varying in color from white (A) to black (E).
- 15-minute changeovers (done on the fly while extruding continues) between colors.
- An eight-hour cleanout between E (black) and A (white).
- 8-percent outage for maintenance.
- 5-percent operator unavailability (breaks, meetings, etc.).
- Required to be produced and shipped daily: 20,000 pounds.
- Production rate of 1,000 pounds per hour or 24,000 pounds per day.

What is the wheel turn time?

Solution

Omitting the 15-minute changeovers, since they are on the fly and do not affect $\sum C$, we have,

$$\sum C = \text{Sum of the changeover times} = 8 \text{ hours}$$

$$O = 0.08 + 0.05 = 0.13$$

$$W = 8 \text{ hours} / [1-0.13-\left(\frac{20,000}{24,000}\right)] = 219 \text{ hours or about 9 days}$$

Thus, sales must allow for up to nine days production cycle time in making order promises to customers.
_____

Regularized Schedules. Dominant products (say, the 10 most popular of 200 fabrics woven in a textile plant) deserve special treatment. One approach is to fit these products into regularly scheduled processing time slots based on average demand rates. A regularized schedule provides predictable output forward in the chain of customers and stable materials usage for the supply chain. Nondominant products do not have enough volume to make this approach feasible; thus, those products (the other 190 fabrics) may be scheduled irregularly as demands dictate.

Application. This may call for two scheduling systems in a single plant. One is for dominant products based on demand rates. (The rate is usually a smoothed representation of actual up-and-down demand patterns.) The second is for low-volume, high-variety products. At Milliken's Cypress plant the separate reactor group for large orders provides an ideal situation for scheduling to a rate.

Linear Output. A goal for the process industry is exceptional predictability of output, linear with the schedule. A regularized schedule provides a plan. On the execution side, the company must achieve stable yields per production run. In the process industries, yield means percentage of planned output actually achieved.

Say that a fabric producer achieves a yield of 95 percent in one production run, 70 percent in the next, and then 98 percent. This yield pattern is decidedly unstable, which causes supply and demand problems both forward to the customer and backward through the supply chain.

Application. The process industries tend toward a fixation on maximizing output volume. Often rather little attention is paid to **linearity.** (Linearity means make to a number—the demand rate—and stop, rather than "Let's see how much we can make today.") Over-committing equipment and people usually dooms linearity. The antidote is to put some slack in the schedule; that is, schedule production for somewhat less than 168 hours a week. This provides time to address likely process problems and to allow time for process maintenance. While slack scheduling may seem to reduce output, it can often increase average output by eliminating causes of severe stoppages.

Conventional practice in the process industry gives emphasis to items 1 through 5 in Exhibit 13–2. Recently, companies have begun to address item 6, quick changeover, and item 7, its companion, fast wheel turns, as well. Few companies, however, have paid heed to items 8 and 9, regularized schedules and linearity, which we consider in more detail next.

Regularized Scheduling and Linearity

Despite the razzle-dazzle of new high-technology equipment, improvement in continuous processing and high-volume repetitive operations often hinges on better scheduling and on greater accuracy in providing the scheduled amount (hitting the target) consistently. Proven techniques for accomplishing these and other aims include processing with regularized schedules and linear output. To fully appreciate their usefulness, the negative consequences of irregular schedules and output need to be understood.

Consequences of Irregular Processing

The bar chart in Exhibit 13–4 represents what a typical process-industry production schedule for item X might look like. Item X is one model or size in a family of products. It might be standard-size 60-watt light bulbs; 8-oz. cans of tomato sauce; type-AAA batteries; rolls of 35 mm 24-exposure, 100-speed color film; twin-bed-size white percale sheets; 3.5-inch Brand Z floppy disks; half-gallon cartons of

---

EXHIBIT 13–4

Schedule, in Work Shifts, for Item X

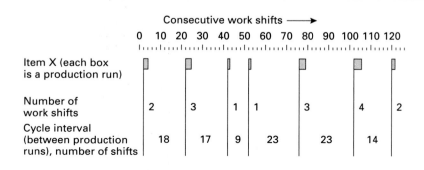

cherry nut ice cream; bottles of 50 decongestant tablets; or four-by-eight-foot sheets of 3/8" plywood.

The exhibit follows the tendency to schedule not in pieces or volume but in work shifts. Now, notice the variabilities. The number of shifts (length) of each production run varies: 2, 3, 1, 1, 3, 4, and 2. The interval between production runs also varies: 18 shifts, then 17, 9, 23, 23, and 14. Between production runs, other models of the same basic product occupy the schedule: other types or sizes of light bulbs, canned tomato products, batteries, and so on. Normal sales variations, special marketing promotions, and the end-of-the-month push to meet a sales quota cause demand variability, to which the production schedule must react.

Output is another source of variability not shown in Exhibit 13–4. In the process and high-volume assembly industries, the schedule is reasonably definite as to number of shifts but often rough as to units. For example, consider the first bar in Exhibit 13–4, a production run of two shifts. If Item X is standard 60-watt light bulbs and an average of 10,000 can be produced in a shift, the bar is interpreted as follows: The production run is two shifts, which might yield 20,000 bulbs. But the yield varies. If all goes well 20,400 may be produced, but on a poor day, only 18,500. Once in a while there will be a serious equipment or raw-material failure, and output may be only 8,000. Production of only 8,000 risks a stockout and lost sales; thus, 60-watt bulbs will need to be fitted into the schedule again quite soon. The whole schedule gets adjusted now and then for such reasons. (See Into Practice box, "Irregular Output: From Record High to New Low," for still another cause of variability.)

Overtime or extra shifts are a possibility if the plant is not running at or near full capacity. Traditional accounting systems, however, can nudge manufacturing managers into making poor decisions. They may run costly equipment near to full capacity and skimp on maintenance, inviting later stoppages. If sales fall, managers may lower capacity (shut down a production line) just to ensure that the accounting records show high capacity utilization without large cost variances.

To sum up, irregular production intervals, run times, and output release clouds of uncertainty. Since sales is uncertain about how much product to expect from operations, it tries to keep protective, and costly, buffer stocks in the distribution system. The greater costs are at the supplier side: What supplies of all the

Irregular Output: From Record High to New Low

At a South African brewery senior management keenly watched the weekly production total (amount of beer packaged). When the total hit a new record, management threw a "barbey" and beer party for all employees. So employees would occasionally summon a special effort to achieve that. But, "in the week following the record, everyone was so tired that they approached new lows. Management was stimulating their own instability."

_____

Source: Tongue-in-cheek report from Dr. Norman Faull, partner in the Faull and van der Riet consulting firm, specializing in consulting for brewing, paper-making, and other process-industry businesses. Their approach is built around the "success factors for process industries" in Exhibit 13–2.

ingredients should be kept on hand? When and how much should each supplier deliver? How can suppliers ever achieve regular production schedules and thereby hold down their wasteful buffer stocks and costs? Irregularities pass backward through all prior stages of supply and production.

Something must be done. There is a crying need for regularity and stability.

Regular-Slot Processing

Giving the stars in the product line regular slots in the schedule is one fairly easy way to gain some regularity and stability. The stars are the models or sizes that sell in some quantity every day and earn a high proportion of total revenue. If they sell every day, the ideal is to make some every day, from 8 to 9 AM, perhaps. The slots should be equal in hours of run time, should be changed when the demand rate changes, and should be spaced at regular intervals.

The superstar (the number-one revenue earner) gets first claim at regular slots in the schedule; some of the starlets follow. The following example illustrates.

$\mathcal{P}$RINCIPLE 2:

Reduce variability.

EXAMPLE 13–2:   REGULAR-SLOT SCHEDULING, PHOTOGRAPHIC FILM

Jmart contracts to buy its branded photographic film from a major film manufacturer. Jmart has informed the manufacturer that past service on fast-moving film products has been unsatisfactory. The three products are 100-, 200-, and 400-speed 35 mm 24-exposure film. After some soul-searching, a planning team at the factory has developed a response. It will adopt regular-slot scheduling for the three products of concern by Jmart, its most important customer. These are its top three products, representing about 15 percent of total production volume. Seventy-seven lesser products account for remaining production volume.

The present schedule, in shifts per production run, is like that shown in Exhibit 13–4: Cycle intervals and production shifts per run are both irregular. The new schedule is shown in Exhibit 13–5. The superstar product, 100-speed film, is in the schedule for 1½ shifts out of every 10 and at a regular interval of every 10 shifts. The 200-speed film's schedule is 1 shift out of every 20, and 400-speed's schedule is 1 shift out of every 40. Those production-run lengths and cycle intervals were not set capriciously. They are based on recent average demand from Jmart plus other customers together with information about average production rates per shift. The plan for the 77 other products is to fit them into the schedule irregularly, as in the past.

EXHIBIT 13–5

Three Products with Regularized Schedules

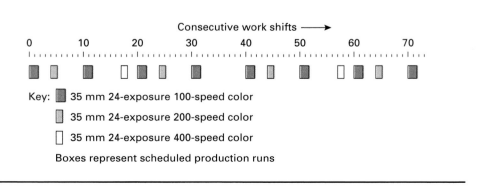

Consecutive work shifts ⟶

Key: ▓ 35 mm 24-exposure 100-speed color

　　　 ▨ 35 mm 24-exposure 200-speed color

　　　 ▯ 35 mm 24-exposure 400-speed color

Boxes represent scheduled production runs

In Example 13–2, we were told that regular-slot scheduling yields a production interval for 100-speed film of 10 shifts and that meeting the production rate requires 1½ shifts of capacity each production run. We were not told how to compute those numbers, which is our next topic.

Takt Time and Capacity Determination

In regular-slot scheduling, the demand-driven production interval, called **takt time,** is calculated as follows:

$$\text{Takt time} = \frac{\text{Available time}}{\text{Customer demand rate}} \qquad (13\text{–}2)$$

Takt time is the maximum interval between successive production units that will still allow the producer to meet a given demand rate. Takt time is the inverse of the minimum allowable production rate and—by itself—is independent of both

- Actual or possible production time.
- The amount of capacity needed to meet the customer demand rate.

Equation 13–3 employs the computed takt time plus a given per-unit cycle time in order to determine amount of capacity needed:

$$\text{Modules of capacity needed} = \frac{\text{Cycle time}}{\text{Takt time}} \qquad (13\text{–}3)$$

The following example employs both formulas.

EXAMPLE 13–3:   DETERMINING TAKT TIME AND NEEDED CAPACITY

An automatic machine at Writing Materials, Inc., produces cuneiform writing instruments in a one-shift-per-day operation. Customer demand is 2,700 pieces per 450-minute day (a 480-minute shift, less 30 minutes for breaks). Cycle time per piece is 20 seconds. What is the takt time, and how many modules of capacity are needed to meet customer demand?

Solution

From equation 13–2,

$$\text{Takt time} = \frac{450}{2,700} = 0.167 \text{ minutes per piece, or 10 seconds per piece}$$

From equation 13–3,

$$\text{Modules of capacity} = \frac{20 \text{ seconds}}{10 \text{ seconds}} = 2 \text{ modules}$$

This result means that the company needs two automatic machines, each producing at 20-second cycle time rate. An alternative is increasing to two shifts per day on the single automatic machine.

Linearity

Regular slots improve predictability, but yield per run still can be quite variable. In many cases, regular schedule slots should be combined with a policy of linear output. That means setting an attainable output target, running production until it is achieved, and not allowing overproduction.

linearity index
Measure of consistency in hitting output target quantity, expressed as a percentage.

No matter how attainable the target quantity is supposed to be, it cannot be met every time. A good way to monitor degree of success is with a linearity index.[6] The index equals 100 percent minus the mean percent deviation, which is the sum of absolute percentage deviations from schedule quantity divided by number of production runs. Mathematically, it is

$$L = 100\% - \frac{\sum |D|}{N} \qquad (13\text{--}4)$$

where

L = Linearity index

D = Deviation from schedule quantity as a percentage of schedule quantity per run

N = Number of production runs

Typically, associates calculate the index monthly, and number of production runs (N) equals number of working days in the month. Calculation of the index is more simply illustrated, assuming only one production run per week, in Example 13–4.

EXAMPLE 13–4:   CALCULATION OF LINEARITY INDEX

Given:
500 units of a certain model of a product are to be run one shift a week on Mondays. Actual production last month was 500, 490, 510, and 500. Compute the linearity index for the month.

Solution:
The deviations from schedule, in units, are 0, −10, +10, and 0. To convert to percent, associates divide each deviation by the schedule quantity per run, 500. That yields 0, −2, +2, and 0 percent, respectively. By equation 13–4 (ignoring minus signs, since the sum of the absolute deviations is used),

$$L = 100\% - \frac{\sum |D|}{N}$$

$$= 100\% - \frac{0\% + 2\% + 2\% + 0\%}{4} = 99 \text{ percent}$$

The linearity index mathematically reflects that any deviation, over or under schedule, is undesirable; both over- and underproduction cause problems for suppliers and uncertainty for users. In Example 13–4, the shortfall of 10 units in week 2 was made up by deliberate overproduction of 10 in week 3 to get back on target. (The index does not reward getting back on target. However, an alternate form of the index, calculated based on a cumulative schedule, does encourage getting back on schedule; the cumulative basis might be useful in some cases.) Note too that the index will always be 100 percent if the schedule is met every time.

At some Hewlett-Packard plants, linearity is calculated for every product and every production line every shift every day. (See photo in Exhibit 13–6.) The average of daily results yields a monthly linearity index, which is posted on a graph for all to see.

Is perfect (100-percent) linearity the goal? Not exactly. If it were easy to be linear every day, that would indicate fat: excessive materials, people, or equip-

EXHIBIT 13–6

Linearity Chart at H-P Vancouver

An early version of the linearity index at a Hewlett-Packard printer plant, Vancouver, Washington. Row totals are the sum of hourly printer completions, by date (September) and shift.

ment. For a high-tech company like Hewlett-Packard, the linearity pattern over successive models might take the shape of a rip saw: In the first week after release from engineering, production-line linearity is poor, say, 65 percent. Things go wrong and stop production for a time. In the next few weeks, as problems get ironed out, linearity rises. After a time, linearity approaches 95 percent or higher, though sometimes production associates must come in on weekends to make up for a bad day or two during the week. Then, just as everyone is settling into a routine, engineering releases a new model. Linearity plunges, and the cycle repeats.

The linearity index is usable in continuous processes, but it seems to have been first used in repetitive operations, our next topic.

Repetitive Operations

Once the product's state changes from continuous flow to discrete units, we call it repetitive rather than continuous. Of course, a good share of the world's products are discrete from start to finish. In producing discrete units, a worthy goal is to increase repetitiveness and get away from lots.

The repetitive mode encompasses more than just manufactured products. High-volume financial, postal, transport, and clerical operations also are in the repetitive category. See the Into Practice box for an example from banking.[7]

Repetitive operations offer a wealth of targets for continuous improvement. One vital factor is good facility layout, as discussed in Chapter 12. Building upon good layout are the nine factors listed in Exhibit 13–2. Though presented as success factors for the process industries, they generally apply in repetitive operations as well. Fast changeovers, regularized schedules, and linear output—numbers 6, 8, and 9 in that exhibit—are especially relevant in the repetitive case.

In addition to the nine factors from Exhibit 13–2, we add five more that are uniquely important in repetitive processing. These five are listed in Exhibit 13–7 and considered more fully below.

EXHIBIT 13–7

Repetitive Operations Improvement Factors

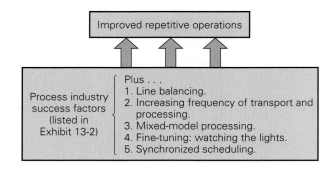

Process industry success factors (listed in Exhibit 13-2)

Plus . . .
1. Line balancing.
2. Increasing frequency of transport and processing.
3. Mixed-model processing.
4. Fine-tuning: watching the lights.
5. Synchronized scheduling.

Improved repetitive operations

Into Practice

Transit Banking at First National Bank of Chicago

They come to O'Hare International in aircraft ranging from jumbo passenger planes to chartered two-seater pleasure craft. In trays, boxes, and bags, they head into the city by truck. Their destination is a block-square, 57-story downtown building on Dearborn between Madison and Monroe: First National Bank of Chicago.

The cargo is checks, some 3 million per day. First Chicago (as it often calls itself) performs contract check clearing for some 12,000 coast-to-coast businesses. A big customer, in, say, Los Angeles—Wilshire Petroleum, perhaps—accumulates checks drawn on banks from all over the country every day. Wilshire wants its money fast. First Chicago has the horsepower—and nearby access to 24-hour-a-day O'Hare airport—to get the job done.

First Chicago clears checks round the clock, seven days a week. Six major deadlines per day dictate cyclic activity for the staff in the Deposit Services department. The deadlines and per-check prices are negotiated with customers. In some cases the deadline is just one hour after receipt of the checks. Processing is in four stages: receiving (including unwrapping and encoding, using 80 encoding machines), sorting (using nine high-speed reader-sorters), wrapping, and final posting. Crews of cross-trained employees migrate from receiving early in the day to wrapping later on. Nearly 200 full- and part-time employees keep the checks moving—and customers happy.

Line Balancing

After a product or cellular layout has been developed, task assignments must be divided among the work stations. Dividing the tasks evenly results in a balanced line. When products or processes change, line *re*balancing becomes necessary. Even simple line-balancing analyses can become quite detailed, and we reserve most of the procedural specifics for an example later in the chapter. Here, we focus on a general overview of line balancing.

Part of **line balancing** analysis is determining number of work stations or number of assemblers, or both. This requires a specified demand rate and data on time standards, work methods, and process flow. Industrial engineers are often the analysts in charge of such information.

To illustrate, suppose demand is such that a line is to provide a unit of work every 3.5 minutes (the takt time). The analyst wants to assign each work station precisely 3.5 minutes of work. That balances the workload, and it synchronizes tasks so that each pass to the next station occurs just as the assembler completes the task and is ready for the next piece. That 3.5 minutes is the desired **station cycle time.**

Perhaps time standards show that the total **work content time** to make one unit is 35 minutes. Then, with each station working 3.5 minutes, 10 work stations are needed.

For a piece having 35 minutes of work content, the throughput time is unlikely to be 35 minutes. Handling among stations and various delays may add time. Also, there may be small buffer stocks between some processes. For example, most high-volume production lines assembling TVs, cameras, videocassette players, keyboards, and the like have several units between stations. If there are two idle units between stations for every one being worked on (a 3:1 pieces-to-stations response ratio), the throughput time is 3 times 35 minutes, or 105 minutes. That is, a unit gets 3.5 minutes of work at station 1, then waits for 7 minutes. It gets 3.5 minutes more work at station 2, then 7 minutes' wait time, and so on, through 10 stations. Raw material enters every 3.5 minutes, but each unit spends 105 minutes in the system. The production rate is 17.14 units per hour (60 minutes/hour ÷ 3.5 minutes).

In this situation, an obvious improvement target is the difference between the throughput time of 105 minutes and the work content time of 35 minutes. The extra 70 minutes is non-value-adding waste, measured as delay time. Eliminating that waste cuts inventory, floor space, time lag until discovery of errors, and time to effect design and demand changes. It also brings about closer dependencies between each provider–customer pair, which creates a better climate for teamwork. The narrow efficiency approach to improvement focuses on work content times and employs methods and time study. The broader effectiveness approach concentrates especially on the non-value-adding delays.

Increasing Frequency of Transport and Processing

There are numerous examples of businesses that achieve roughly repetitive operations in final assembly but are far from it in earlier processes. The term *roughly repetitive* allows for variety within limits. In a Mr. Steak restaurant, the cook who grills steaks has a repetitive job, but the steaks vary in size and quality of meat. Routine purchase orders (POs) in a purchasing department are similar. Each PO is slightly different, but processing them is basically a repetitive operation. In the first case, the preceding process is in lots, not repetitive—purchased lots of steaks. In the second, both the preceding and next operations are in lots—batches of incoming requisitions (requests to buy) received by internal mail and batches of outgoing mailed purchase orders.

Is there room for improvement? Often there is. If a Mr. Steak restaurant currently receives steaks every three days, improvement would be receiving in smaller (more repetitive) daily amounts. Obvious advantages are less cold storage, better control of aging, and less forecast error. In the case of POs, a modern improvement is electronic communication. Receive requisitions by e-mail. Send orders to suppliers electronically via electronic data interchange or facsimile, one at a time, immediately as needs are known. That gets the supplier working on the order sooner.

Steaks and POs have what are called shallow bills of materials. (For grilled steaks there are just two BOM levels: raw and grilled.) Many products with deep BOMs are, like steaks and invoices, roughly repetitive in the last process, final assembly, but not in earlier processes (lower levels on the BOM). Examples are cars, trucks, tractors, and small aircraft. In final assembly, each successive unit may have its own set of options, but the assemblers perform almost the same operations over and over.

For such products, a way to improve operations is to extend the repetitiveness backward into subassembly, fabrication, and purchasing. The easy way is to cut transfer-lot quantities: smaller loads moved more frequently, ideally with the discipline of kanban. Next, cut process lot size and cycle interval (interval between production runs); this often requires reducing setup or changeover times. (When the transfer-lot quantity is one unit, that is as repetitive as is possible for a certain production run or lot.) These topics were addressed in Chapters 8 through 11 and need no further discussion here.

Mixed-Model Processing

mixed-model processing
Short cycle–interval production of a variety of types, sizes, or models of a product family on the same line or within a single cell.

The production schedule interval for the film in Example 13–2 was shown in work shifts, such as 10, 20, and 40. Schedules can be repetitive in much longer or shorter cycle intervals. A very short cycle interval (a day or even a few hours) may call for mixed-model processing.

Consider the irregular, long cycle–interval schedule for products L, M, and N shown in Exhibit 13–8A. The boxes represent production runs; they vary in duration, as do the intervals between them. For example, in February and March, nearly two months pass between production runs of product N. Suppose that L, M, and N are standard products that enjoy regular, perhaps daily, sales; thus, they show good potential for repetitive regularized production.

Exhibit 13–8B shows a regularized repetitive schedule with a fairly short cycle interval (one day) between repetitions. Let's examine how a scheduler might de-

EXHIBIT 13–8

Irregular, Repetitive, and Mixed-Model Schedules

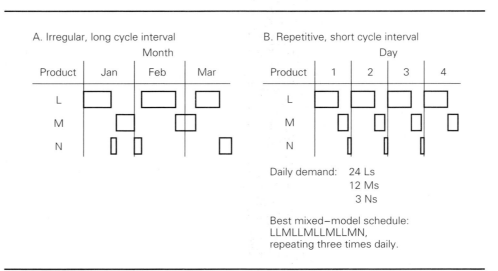

A. Irregular, long cycle interval

Product	Jan	Feb	Mar
L			
M			
N			

B. Repetitive, short cycle interval

Product	1	2	3	4
L				
M				
N				

Daily demand: 24 Ls
12 Ms
3 Ns

Best mixed–model schedule:
LLMLLMLLMLLMN,
repeating three times daily.

termine the mixed-model processing cycle. The objectives are to match production to demand with a regularized schedule that gives star products priority status.

Assume that daily sales average 24 Ls, 12 Ms, and 3 Ns, for a total of 39 units. First, reduce those requirements to the minimum ratio; dividing each demand amount by 3 yields 8, 4, and 1. Second, sum the minimum ratios, obtaining the number 13. That becomes the number of units in the repeating processing cycle. That is, every cycle will contain 13 units; 8 will be Ls, 4 will be Ms, and 1 will be N. To meet daily demand, the cycle will repeat three times each day. Third, find the mix of the 13 units that is most repetitive, minimizing the interval between production of each type of product.

This last step might require trial and error, but one or two simple passes may suffice. Consider two possible solutions that meet the daily demand requirement:

1. LLLLLLLLMMMMN—Repeat three times per day. Assessment: Not repetitive within cycle; must wait through up to five units for next L, up to nine units for next M.
2. LLMLLMLLMLLMN—Repeat three times per day. Assessment: Repetitive within cycle, four repeating triplets followed by singleton; maximum wait to next L is two units, and maximum wait to next M is three units. (This is the best schedule for this product mix.)

One advantage of going to the lowest-ratio, most-repetitive mix is that it allows providers of component parts to consider low-capacity processes and cheap equipment. Assume that the products L, M, and N in Exhibit 13–8 are (respectively) 24-, 20-, and 18-inch bicycle wheels, which are made from cut metal strips. If the whole day's requirement of each size is cut in one batch, what cutting equipment is appropriate? A good choice might be a costly, semiautomatic cutting machine that takes an hour to adjust for length changes (setup) but then cuts pieces fast.

On the other hand, if production of each size wheel is spaced out in the lowest-ratio model mix, the need for cut metal strips is also spaced out. Instead of the costly, high-speed cutter, why not use a simple band saw? It is much slower, but it takes virtually no time for a length change, and the low-ratio mixed-model schedule requires many length changes per day. In our example, the band saw would cut two 24-inch strips, one 20-inch strip, two 24s, one 20, two 24s, one 20, two 24s, one 20, and, finally, one 18-inch strip. That 13-unit sequence repeats two additional times throughout the day, exactly matching demand at the next processes, which are rim forming and wheel assembly.

What if the high-speed cutter is already owned and the producer, as part of a continuous improvement effort, is changing the schedule from a daily batch to lowest-ratio mix? An attractive option is to treat 24-inch wheels as the star. Set up the high-speed cutter permanently for that length and cut two at a time intermittently throughout the day. This has the advantages of speed, no more one-hour length changes, and perfect stockless synchronization with the next process. Buy a band saw, if one is not already owned, to cut the 20- and 18-inch lengths.

The benefit of being able to use cheaper, simpler equipment as a result of low-ratio mixed-model scheduling may seem small, or rarely applicable. Not so! Toyota Motors has followed this scheduling and frugal equipment policy (capital expenditure avoidance) perhaps more extensively and longer than any other manufacturer. As a result, Toyota finds itself with massive retained earnings.

Thus far, our discussion of mixed-model processing has been limited to issues and benefits associated with scheduling. Line-balancing algorithms have also been

There are two levels of repetition in mixed-model processing: (1) cycle repetition during the processing period (day or shift) and (2) repetition within the cycle itself.

*P*RINCIPLE 9:

Look for simple, flexible, low-cost equipment.

developed for mixed-model assembly lines. For example, in a mixed-model doll clothing line, male dolls, female dolls, large dolls, small dolls, and so forth, may be clothed in a mixed sequence.

Mixed-model line balancing involves (1) determining the sequence of products (model numbers) moving down the line and (2) balancing the line. Some line-balancing methods allow for restrictions and special conditions: subassembly lines that feed main lines, distance and direction requirements, safety needs, special groupings of elements, zoning restrictions, maximum and minimum conveyor speeds, and so forth.

Example 13–5 illustrates some factors involved in mixed-model line balancing.

EXAMPLE 13–5:   MIXED MODELS—BORING HOLES IN PUMP HOUSINGS

A machine center bores holes in pump housings. It used to take twice as long to set up and run a lot of large pump housings as it did small housings. After a vigorous improvement effort, the setup times are now nearly zero for either size of housing. With negligible setup times, it seems reasonable to run mixed models down a mini-production line composed of machines that bore the holes.

The schedule calls for 22 large (L) and 88 small (S) pump housings per day. Run times are 12 minutes per large unit and 2 minutes per small unit. What cycle of mixed models will produce the scheduled quantity with balanced production?

Solution

Model sequence:	L	S	S	S	S	L	S	S	S	S	. . .
Operation time:	12	2	2	2	2	12	2	2	2	2	. . .
			20					20			

This cycle takes 20 minutes and repeats 22 times per day. The production requires 20 × 22 = 440 minutes out of a 480-minute workday, which leaves 40 extra minutes for problem solving, equipment care, and so forth.

Fine-Tuning: Watching the Lights

Line balancing seems precise and accurate, but it isn't. A good typist can type twice as many words per minute as an average one. Similarly, a good welder, solderer, or painter can work twice as fast as an average one. In a line balance based on standard pace, the fast people will not have enough to do and the slow ones will have trouble keeping up. Fine-tuning is needed. The supervisor or operating team will see who the slower and less experienced ones are and can fine-tune by reassigning some work elements from slower to faster people. A novel method called watching the lights serves to make fine-tuning a bit easier.

It is fairly common for trouble lights to be mounted above production lines to alert troubleshooters and supervisors when there is a slowdown or line stoppage. Typically, a red light signals shutdown and a yellow signals trouble. Yellow lights may also aid in fine-tuning the line balancing. Here is how it works:

1. A new production schedule is issued, rough line balancing takes place, and work begins.
2. Anyone who has trouble keeping up will turn on the yellow light frequently. Those who have no trouble keeping up will not turn on their yellow lights. The message to the supervisor and team is clear. Take a few

small duties away from those with too much to do and reassign them to those whose lights have not been coming on. When everyone's yellow lights are coming on at about the same frequency, the line is balanced, and no one is pushed into making errors out of haste.

3. With the line balanced, yellow lights no longer suggest line imbalance; they indicate trouble. For the remaining days or weeks of the schedule, the problem signaled by a yellow light is recorded so that there are good data for problem solving.

When industry veterans first hear about this approach, they tend to be dubious or full of questions: "But some people will have much more to do than others. Is that fair? Won't the faster operators complain? Or won't they deliberately go slow and push the yellow button in order to avoid getting more tasks to do?"

The first question is not so hard. It is true that the fast people will end up with more tasks to do, but surely that is more fair, not less. The system should not mask the abilities of the fast employees, nor should it unduly pressure the slower ones. There will be complaints from some of the faster people. The complaints may be resolved in two ways:

1. Give the faster employees bonuses, incentive pay, merit wage increases, pay for knowledge, or special training or other rewards.
2. Evolve a performance appraisal approach that rewards for problem solving, quality control, and work improvement. These activities focus on innovativeness, leadership, and communication skills. Make sure that enough labor is available to make it possible to meet the schedule every day and on most days still allow time for problem solving, quality control, work improvement, and maintenance.

Synchronized Scheduling

As we have seen throughout this chapter, streamlined operations require changes in scheduling. The ultimate is to let a final assembly schedule serve as the schedule for all major assemblies, which in turn would serve as the schedules for fabricated parts, and so on, back to purchased parts and beyond. That ideal is perfectly synchronized scheduling. It involves meshing the timing of delivery or production of an item with the use rate of the next item at the next higher process level. Synchronizing delivery with usage is good; synchronizing operations and delivery with usage is even better: Make one, deliver one, use one.

Synchronizing is attractive for repetitive processors, less so for continuous. (As noted earlier, in continuous processing, producing up to the full 168 hours a week tends to be a foremost strategy: Keep the costly plant facilities busy.) Repetitive production is often labor intensive. People are highly flexible (except when it comes to working late shifts, which they dislike). So why not harness labor flexibility to closely match variable demand patterns? This makes more sense than pursuing a strategy of running full tilt 168 hours a week.

As an example of synchronization, consider what happens to a written sales order sent in to a home office for action. Typically, the value-adding action is hard to find amid all the order-processing delays. The order may spend two days in central sales, two in accounting for a credit check, three in order filling and packing, and finally one more in shipping. And we should probably add a day for passage through the company mail room between each action activity. The total throughput time in this out-of-sync, snail-paced operation is about 11 days.

One way to synchronize these operations would be requiring each office to process this hour whatever came in last hour, mail service included. That cuts throughput time from 11 days to seven hours!

As an example of synchronization in a factory, imagine a plant that makes blue jeans. Suppose the schedule for the next two hours calls for the sewing machines (final assembly) to sew stovepipe-cut 28-inch-waist and 30-inch-length jeans. Then, the schedule for the next two hours in the cutting room should call for cutting fabric for the same size and style. Cut one pattern, send it forward, and immediately sew it. If zippers, thread, labels, and rivets are also on the same schedule, the schedule is highly synchronized. While there may still be some idle inventories (e.g., because of delivery problems, potential stoppages or defects, or difference in process speeds), none result from mismatched schedules.

Of course, one way to get synchronization is to relocate far-flung processes into a cell. Examples are an order-processing cell in which orders are passed from desk to desk in one room or a blue jeans cell complete with cutting, sewing, and packaging.

Line-Balancing Example

Any of several line-balancing methods may be used in the rough, or initial, balancing stage. They include trial and error, as well as heuristics, algorithms, and mathematical models. Computer programs are available for many of the algorithms and models; study of those tools is reserved for more specifically focused texts. Here, we look at a manual heuristic line-balancing procedure, which begins, like other line-balancing methods, with a precedence diagram.

Precedence Diagram

The **precedence diagram** charts the work elements and their required sequence. To get the work elements, the entire process is divided into tasks and subtasks. This division of labor is carried down to where a task is assignable to a single station.

One popular type of precedence diagram shows the earliest stage of production where each work element may be done. Element durations, numbers, and sometimes descriptions go on the diagram; arrows show which elements must come before which others.

Example 13–6 demonstrates precedence diagramming. The assembly task is clothing a male doll. In real doll making, all of the work elements for such assembly would probably be done by a single assembler because the element times are very short. But for the sake of illustration, we shall assume progressive, rather than autonomous, assembly. Precedence diagramming can allow for a variety of special restrictions, but this example is kept simple.

EXAMPLE 13–6:   PRECEDENCE DIAGRAM FOR LINE BALANCING—DOLL ASSEMBLY[8]

A toy company is coming out with a new male doll. The doll is to be clothed on an assembly line, with different items of clothing put on at different stations. The company wants a balanced assembly line.

Methods engineers have broken up the whole job into 13 separate items of clothing, each of which is a work element, with element times as follows:

Element	Element Time t (in 0.01 minutes)
A. Put on undershorts.	10
B. Put on undershirt.	11
C. Put on left sock.	9
D. Put on right sock.	9
E. Put on slacks.	22
F. Put on shirt.	42
G. Put on left shoe.	26
H. Put on right shoe.	26
I. Put on belt.	30
J. Insert pocket items (wallet, keys, and handkerchief).	20
K. Put on tie.	63
L. Put on coat.	32
M. Put on hat.	6
Total work content time, $\sum t$,	306

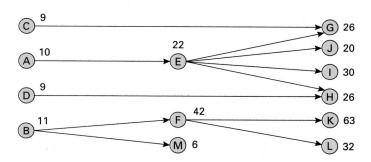

Exhibit 13–9

Precedence Diagram— Clothing a Doll

Solution

Using the elemental data, associates develop the precedence diagram shown in Exhibit 13–9. Work elements are in the circles and element times are beside the circles. Four elements (A, B, C, and D) have no predecessors and can be started any time. No other elements may begin until their predecessors have been completed.

Line-Balancing Analysis

Once the precedence diagram has been completed, actual line balancing may begin. A perfectly balanced line has zero balance delay, which means no wait time at any work station. **Balance delay,** d, is

$$d = \frac{nc - \sum t}{nc} \tag{13–5}$$

where

n = Number of work stations

c = Station cycle time

$\sum t$ = Total work content time for one unit

The result of a line-balancing study is a certain number of work stations, each assigned to one person or piece of equipment. The goal is not a balanced line that produces as much as possible. Rather, it is a balanced line that produces to the demand rate, no more, no less. The following is an easy-to-use heuristic line-balancing method:

1. Develop the precedence diagram.
2. Determine the station cycle time (c) that will yield the per-shift output required to meet demand. The formula is

$$c = \frac{\text{Available production time per day}}{\text{Required output per day (in units)}} \tag{13-6}$$

3. With the station cycle time (c) as an upper limit, find the minimum number of stations (n) using the formula

$$n = \frac{\text{Total work content}}{\text{Cycle time}} = \frac{\sum t}{c} \tag{13-7}$$

4. Develop the first work station by assigning elements, one at a time, to it until the sum of the element times equals the cycle time, or until no feasible elements remain under the precedence restrictions. The rule is, give preference to elements that have the largest element time. (An alternate rule, not so applicable for this simple precedence diagram, is assign elements that have the most following elements.) Repeat for the second work station, the third, and so forth, until all work elements have been assigned to a station.
5. Calculate balance delay, based on minimum station cycle time, and evaluate. If unsatisfactory, investigate possibilities for altering the process technology to allow more flexibility in balancing the line.

The following example demonstrates this line-balancing method using the doll assembly data from Example 13–6. As will be shown, perfect balance (zero balance delay) is not necessarily ideal.

EXAMPLE 13–7:   BALANCING A DOLL ASSEMBLY LINE

The sales plan requires an output rate of 450 dolls per day on a one-shift-per-day assembly line. Total assembly time per day, allowing for breaks and other activities, is 420 minutes. How many work stations should there be, and which work elements should be assigned to each station to yield a well-balanced line?

Solution

1. Precedence diagram. Given in Exhibit 13–9.
2. Station cycle time. In the numerator, convert minutes to hundredths of a minute.

$$c = \frac{\text{Production time}}{\text{Required output (in units)}} = \frac{420 \text{ min} \times 100}{450 \text{ dolls}} = 93.3 \text{ rounded to } 93$$

3. Minimum number of work stations. Express both numerator and denominator in hundredths of a minute. Total work content ($\sum t$) is 306 hundredths of a minute (from Example 13–6). Then,

EXHIBIT 13–10

Balancing Procedure and Results

A.   *Line-Balancing Steps*

Element Assigned	Element Time (in 0.01 minutes)	Remaining Unassigned Time (in 0.01 minutes)	Permissible Remaining Elements	Task with Greatest Element Time
Start		93	A, B, C, D	B
Station 1 B	11	82	A, C, D, F, M	F
F	42	40	A, C, D, L, M	L
L	32	8	M	M
M	6	2	None	
Start		93	A, C, D, K	K
Station 2 K	63	30	A, C, D	A
A	10	20	C, D, E	C or D
C	9	11	D	D
D	9	2	None	
Start		93	E	E
Station 3 E	22	71	G, H, I, J	I
I	30	41	G, H, J	G or H
G	26	15	None	
Start		93	H, J	H
Station 4 H	26	67	J	J
J	20	47	None	

B.   *Results: Four Work Stations*

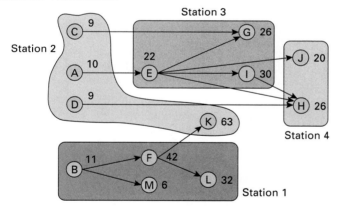

$$n = \frac{\Sigma t}{c} = \frac{306}{93} = 3.3 \text{ rounded to 4 stations}$$

4. Assign work elements to create work stations. Exhibit 13–10 shows how the procedure allocates work elements to the four work stations.

5. Balance delay. All work stations have remaining unassigned times. We can reduce station cycle time by the minimum amount of this unassigned time, which in this case is 2 at the first and second stations. So the minimum station cycle time (*c*) is 93 − 2 = 91. Then,

$$d = \frac{nc - \Sigma t}{nc} = \frac{(4 \times 91) - 306}{4 \times 91} = 0.159$$

The 0.159 balance delay indicates 15.9-percent idleness among the four stations, mostly concentrated at station 4. Also, the plan has the assemblers completing the scheduled 450 dolls in 409 minutes (calculation: $91 \times 450/100$), which is 11 minutes less than the planned 420-minute day. What should be done about the idleness and the extra time?

One answer is to make good use of the balance delay: A single person at station 4 could load the pocket items. This would take only 20 hundredths of a minute (12 seconds) in each cycle of 306 hundredths of a minute (3.06 minutes). It might be a good job for a team leader. With so light a task, the leader would have time to help others, coach new employees, record data, perform inspections, fetch materials, and so forth. Alternatively, seek to improve the balance by shifting certain elements from work stations 3 and 4 to 1 and 2. (Various other heuristics, not included in this book, are available for seeking to improve upon a line-balancing alternative.) The extra 11 minutes per day provides extra time for employee projects, training, and so forth. What should not be done is use the 11 minutes to eke out more production, which would just be overproduction (if the customer demand rate is correct).

Line Balancing in Perspective

The heuristic method yields good, but not necessarily optimal, results, and development of optimizing algorithms and models continues. Though a variety of line-balancing computer software is available to ease the computational burden, manual heuristic and trial-and-error line balancing efforts are widespread.

For one thing, line balancing is not easily reduced to simple models or algorithms; there are simply too many choices, given the flexibility and variability of humans. Employees can run one machine or several, push a broom or wield a paintbrush between machine cycles, handle machine setup and inspection duties or leave those chores for special crews, speed up or loaf, stay at their work or wander off, fix broken equipment and suggest improvements or leave it up to the specialists, and file documents or sit around waiting for file clerks to do it.

*P*RINCIPLES 1 AND 13:

Get to know the customer. Operate at the customer's rate of use.

How can balance be designed into a process with those uncertainties? The answer is: One can design only a roughly balanced line. Supervisors and the work group itself need to fine-tune it and redo it often as customer demand rates change.

Scope of Application

The techniques of transforming irregular operations into repetitive, synchronized operations apply not only to high-volume production; they may also apply to building, say, one ship every two weeks or one passenger aircraft every three days. If each ship or plane is a special order for a different customer, that is only a partial obstacle to repetitive operations. In manufacture of ships and planes, thousands of parts are the same from unit to unit and are therefore unaffected by special orders. Those thousands of standard parts may be made to highly repetitive schedules—repeating only every two weeks or every three days—with some levels synchronized with the level directly above. The massive problem of scheduling all those parts thus can be partly simplified, and some flows of parts can be put on kanban.

One of the most pressing needs in operations management is extending the benefits of continuous and highly repetitive processing (the stuff of this chapter) into job and batch operations. We take up that challenge in the next chapter.

Summary

Process-industry companies are often hybrids: They have continuous operations in early production stages and repetitive operations in later stages (e.g., packaging). Though the process industries share many of the same success factors as other modes of operations, they have their own critical ones as well. Conventional process-industry concerns include having top-notch technology, optimum mixtures of ingredients, rigorous plant maintenance, close process monitoring, and reliable supply and freight. More recently, progressive companies have also paid heed to fast line changeovers, which make it economical to run smaller lots more closely synchronized with customer demand rates. A complementary pursuit, where a single line must produce a sequence of products, is rapid cycling through all of the products (metaphorically, turning the product wheel rapidly).

A common remaining weakness among continuous processors is high variability of output, which adversely affects both the customer chain and supply chain. Companies have been slow to take their medicine on this issue. Usually, they can reduce variability by regularizing schedules for top-selling products. For those products on a regular, rate-based schedule, the goal is linearity against the schedule. A useful measure of performance is the linearity index, where perfect (100-percent) linearity is meeting the rate exactly every day.

In the repetitive mode, a common weakness is failure to carry the repetitiveness through all processes. For example, final assembly may be repetitive and synchronized well to customer demand rates, but fabrication and purchasing may be in large lots. Ways of extending the repetitiveness include some of the same factors as for continuous processing. Besides those, the repetitive processor may increase frequency of transport and freight, produce to a repeating mixed-model schedule, and synchronize schedules for all stages to the average daily demand rate.

In addition, where assembly is sequential (progressive from work station to work station), an improvement method is called line balancing: Achieving a good balance of work among the work stations. (On the other hand, some repetitive processing is autonomous: A single person performs the complete sequence of tasks.) Line balancing may be done roughly using average data, but then fine-tuning needs to be done, and redone as conditions change. A simple but effective way to do the fine-tuning employs trouble lights: When an assembler has trouble and turns on a light, that either flags a process problem needing solution or it shows that the assembler has too many tasks assigned. If the latter, it's time to rebalance the line.

A goal in mixed-model scheduling is achieving the lowest-ratio, most-repetitive mix. For example, 10 units of product A and 5 of B reduces (lowest ratio) to 2 A's, 1 B, 2 A's, 1 B . . . repeating five times (most repetitive mix). This mix may be passed back to earlier stages that can synchronize their schedules to the same mix, which greatly reduces in-process inventories. In addition, a lowest-ratio schedule can lead to simpler, less-costly equipment that does not have to run very fast.

While there are computer routines that can assist in line balancing, manual heuristic methods can do quite well if the process is not too complex. Most line-balancing procedures start with a precedence diagram showing the required sequence of assembly and giving the station cycle time for each work element. The analyst then follows certain rules in grouping elements into work stations. A perfectly balanced line has zero balance delay. However, a line that is not well balanced (high balance delay) is not necessarily a problem, since anyone on line who has free time between cycles usually can fill in with other work, such as record keeping.

Solved Problems

Problem 1

The accompanying table shows 22 working days of production against a regularized schedule for a somewhat new product. The schedule rate, seven per day, was set on the 15th of the prior month. It gets changed in midmonth only when actual orders are greatly deviating from plan, as happened on August 22 to 26. Calculate the linearity index.

Date	Working Day	Pack Schedule	Actual Pack	Comments
8–1	1	7	3	No card cages
2	2	7	3	
5	3	7	10	
6	4	7	11	
7	5	7	4	Door latch problems
8	6	7	9	Two people short
9	7	7	9	
12	8	7	1	No drives
13	9	7	5	Rework required
14	10	7	4	Rework required
15	11	7	5	Rework required
16	12	7	6	Rework required
19	13	7	10	
20	14	7	7	
21	15	7	10	
22	16	0	0	No orders
23	17	0	0	No orders
26	18	0	0	No orders
27	19	7	5	
28	20	7	2	
29	21	7	3	
30	22	7	1	

Solution 1

Step 1: Insert working columns for calculation of absolute deviation (ignore minus signs) and percent deviation:

Working Day	Pack Schedule	Actual Pack	Absolute Deviation	Percent Deviation
1	7	3	4	4/7 = 57%
2	7	3	4	4/7 = 57
3	7	10	3	3/7 = 43
4	7	11	4	4/7 = 57
5	7	4	3	3/7 = 43
6	7	9	2	2/7 = 29
7	7	9	2	2/7 = 29
8	7	1	6	6/7 = 86
9	7	5	2	2/7 = 29
10	7	4	3	3/7 = 43
11	7	5	2	2/7 = 29
12	7	6	1	1/7 = 14
13	7	10	3	3/7 = 43
14	7	7	0	0/7 = 0
15	7	10	3	3/7 = 43

(continued)

(concluded)

Working Day	Pack Schedule	Actual Pack	Absolute Deviation	Percent Deviation
—Omit zero schedule days—				
19	7	5	2	2/7 = 29
20	7	2	5	5/7 = 71
21	7	3	4	4/7 = 57
22	7	1	6	6/7 = 86
Total = 19 working days				Total = 845%

Step 2: Calculate the linearity index (L):

$$L = 100\% - \frac{845\%}{19} = 100\% - 44.5\% = 55.5\%$$

Consider the following elemental precedence diagram (element times are in units of 0.01 minutes):

Problem 2

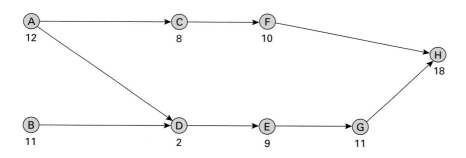

a. What would be the cycle times for a line with one work station (autonomous production)?
b. What would be the maximum daily capacity of such a line assuming 420 minutes of work time per day?
c. What is the shortest possible cycle time?
d. Assuming we used this shortest cycle time, what would daily line capacity be?
e. Plan a balanced line for the assembly operation using a cycle time of 0.29 minutes. Compute the balance delay for your solution. What will be the approximate capacity of the line assuming a 420-minute workday?

a. With one work station, the sum of the element times would be a reasonable estimate for the cycle time. In this case, the sum is 0.81 minutes.
b. With 420 minutes of available work time per day, the maximum capacity possible with a cycle time of 0.81 minutes would be: 420/0.81 = 519 units.
c. The shortest possible cycle time equals the time of the longest element, or 0.18 minutes. We would not necessarily want to use this as the cycle time, but it is possible to do so.
d. For a station cycle time of 0.18 minutes and 420-minute workday, the maximum capacity may be obtained by transposing equation (13–6) to

Solution 2

$$\text{Output} = \frac{\text{Production time}}{c} = \frac{420}{0.18} = 2{,}333 \text{ units}$$

e. Line-Balancing Steps

	Element Assigned	Element Time (in 0.01 minutes)	Remaining Unassigned Time (in 0.01 minutes)	Permissible Remaining Elements	Task with Greatest Element Time
Start			29	A, B	A
Station 1	A	12	17	B, C	B
	B	11	6	D	D
	D	2	4	None	
Start			29	C, E	E
Station 2	E	9	20	C, G	G
	G	11	9	C	C
	C	8	1	None	
Start			29	F	F
Station 3	F	10	19	H	H
	H	18	1	None	

Since remaining unassigned time at work stations 2 and 3 (the most nearly balanced stations) is 1, station cycle time may be reduced; that is, $29 - 1 = 28$. Then,

$$\text{Balance delay } (d) = \frac{nc - \sum t}{nc} = \frac{3(28) - 81}{3(28)} = 0.036$$

Line capacity $= 420/0.28 = 1{,}500$ units per day

Review Questions

1. Differentiate between continuous and repetitive operations. Give examples of industries where we might find both types in the same facility.

2. What are key success factors in the process industry? How might continuous improvement be obtained for each factor?

3. What is regularized processing?

4. What is the advantage in changing from a schedule of making each star product once a day to a minimum-cycle, mixed-model schedule?

5. What kinds of technological obstacles stand in the way of synchronized operations? Give an example other than those in the chapter.

6. In the process industries, what have been the success factors for operations in the past? What are more recent success factors?

7. In continuous operations, production usually is scheduled in shifts rather than units. Does this change under the concept of regularized scheduling?

8. Can a schedule of 5,000 different parts or models be regularized? Explain.

9. Explain the linearity index.

10. What, if anything, can be done if the goal is to synchronize schedules for multiple process levels but some processes have very long setup times?

11. How is synchronized production related to mixed-model production?

12. Can the concepts of regularized, synchronized schedules be applied to low-volume production? Explain.

13. How do the following terms differ? (*a*) cycle time, (*b*) work content time, (*c*) throughput time.

14. What is the purpose of determining balance delay?

15. What is meant by a mixed-model line? Are there any special problems associated with balancing a mixed-model line? Explain.

16. What does the phrase *watching the lights* refer to? How can it lead to increased productivity?

17. Which principles are especially relevant to the concepts in this chapter, and why?

Exercises

1. In the chapter discussion of repetitive processing, refer to the box entitled, "Transit Banking at First National Bank of Chicago." Which of the success factors discussed in the chapter apply well to the bank's processing? Explain.

2. In the following industries, which stages of processing are best considered as continuous flow and which as repetitive? Discuss.
   a. Soft drink manufacturer.
   b. Aspirin tablet producer.
   c. Breakfast cereal producer.
   d. Nursing care for hospitalized patient.
   e. Banking (account maintenance).

3. Modesto Farms operates a high-volume cannery for tomato products: canned whole tomatoes, tomato sauce, tomato paste, and the like. Discuss three vital success factors in the area of manufacturing for this company. Be as specific as you can, even though you have to speculate on the nature of this type of company.

4. Detergent is manufactured in a continuous process through a network of pipes, vessels, and pressure chambers. First, petroleum is distilled into paraffin, which is oxidized and then catalytically hydrogenated under pressure to form fat alcohols. Sulphuric acid is added, and water cools the mixture to yield fat alcohol esters. Bleaching agents and alkalies are injected, and an emerging paste of fat alcohol sulphate is processed through a "spray tower" into finished detergent. Discuss two vital manufacturing success factors for a detergent manufacturer; be as specific as you can.

5. Edsom, Inc., a maker of keyboards for computer products, has a department in which instruction manuals are assembled into three-ring binders and another in which the pages are printed. There are four stages of production for the complete binders:
   a. The print shop slices large sheets of paper to size. It prefers to run as many jobs as possible on a recently acquired heavy-duty slicer, which runs faster than two older model slicers still in the shop. All the slicers require some setup time for any job.
   b. The printshop prints pages for manuals. Because of long setup times, print jobs for manuals compete with other print jobs for slots in the schedule.
   c. A high-speed collator collates the pages. The collator, a dedicated machine in the assembly department, is only used for manuals.
   d. Human assemblers open binders, insert sets of pages, and close binders.
       Elsewhere in the plant, the keyboard assembly line runs to a daily rate and achieves nearly perfect linearity.

   Can the four stages of manual production be synchronized to the assembly rate for the keyboards? Should they be synchronized? Discuss fully, giving an example with sample numbers.

6. Building A delivers several kinds of bulky component parts to building B four miles away. The components are made in three production stages in building A.

Setup times on some of the equipment and parts assembly lines have been driven down nearly to zero. Building B houses final assembly and packing, each with negligible setup time from model to model of the family of end products.

Can five production stages in two buildings, plus deliveries between, be completely synchronized to the sales rate? Is a fully mixed-model synchronized schedule feasible?

7. Line 1 at the East Texas plant of Feast Frozen Foods has been troublesome. Its average production has been 5,000 12-ounce packages of frozen vegetables per shift, which is equal to average sales. But the variation around the average has been unacceptable. For the 10 shifts last week (a typical week), output was 4,728, 4,980, 5,009, 4,822, 5,860, 5,121, 5,618, 4,899, 4,620, and 4,900.

About 35 percent of line 1's output consists of Feast's top-selling product, frozen young peas. A production run of peas usually is one shift, but sometimes a half-shift run is scheduled; peas are packaged three or four times per week. The other 65 percent of production is split among 17 other products. Recently, the line 1 crew has been working overtime on about half its shifts. Changing the speeds of the tray-filling and packaging equipment is no problem.

a. Calculate the linearity for last week.

b. Recommend a plan for increasing predictability of output on line 1.

8. Faiko Time Company produces grandfather clocks. Customers (mostly retailers) can select from over 100 styles of fine wood and glass outer enclosures, which are made in Faiko's wood and glass shops. In contrast, only three types of clock mechanisms can be ordered; these are assembled in another Faiko shop.

The past two week's production orders have been as follows, in numbers of clocks ordered each day: 8, 9, 5, 7, 7, 9, 7, 4, 6, 10. Can Faiko adopt a workable production plan with a regularized production schedule and linear output? Explain why, why not, or to what extent.

9. Almost Blind Co. (ABC) produces metallic blinds for windows in 10 basic colors. The basic process is an extruder, on which color changes take an average of 40 minutes. Since the extruder is a very high-cost machine, ABC runs it seven days a week, 24 hours a day, except for daily maintenance averaging 30 minutes. ABC must produce and ship daily; recent daily amount shipped (including all 10 colors of blinds) has been averaging 1,600 lineal feet. The extruder's production rate is 100 lineal feet per hour. Determine the wheel turn time for the extruder and comment on its uses.

10. Conduct an investigation to determine three different kinds of products that would be produced sequentially in a version of the product wheel. Explain your choices.

11. A bicycle manufacturer has implemented a schedule of assembling every bike model every day (instead of long production runs for individual models). Can it use the same repetitive daily schedule in making handlebars, frames, and wheel assemblies? If so, can the repetitive schedule extend downward to tires, wheels, and spokes? Can it go further downward to wire extruders that make reels of spoke wire and to the steel plant that makes the commodity steel that is drawn into wire? Discuss the possibilities, obstacles, and benefits.

12. As a first step in a line-balancing analysis, the precedence diagram on the next page has been developed. All units are in 0.01 minutes.

a. Calculate $\sum t$. What station cycle time is required for a daily demand of 500 units? What is the minimum required number of work stations? Assume a workday of 430 minutes.

b. Balance the line as best you can, and calculate the resulting balance delay. If the delay is excessive, what is your advice (options include seeking a better balance or living with the imbalance)?

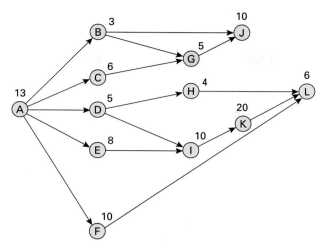

13. The processing of worker's compensation claim forms in a state office is being organized as a production line. Work elements have been divided as far as possible and have been organized into the following precedence diagram. (All element times are in minutes.) If the line must process 50 claims a week, what is the best way to balance the line? The state allows 40 minutes in an eight-hour workday for coffee breaks.

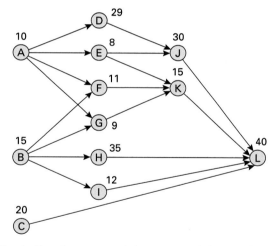

14. Crow's Eye Foods, Inc., has patent rights to a special type of segmented dish for perfect warming of foods in a microwave oven. The dish permits Crow's to launch a new line of frozen breakfasts. Crow's kitchens are planning for the first breakfast: two strips of bacon, one egg, and two slices of buttered toast.
    a. Develop a precedence diagram for use in balancing the production line for this breakfast. Make your own (reasonable) assumptions about work elements and element times. Explain your diagram.
    b. Make an assumption about demand and production time. Then, balance your line.

15. Zeus, Inc., makes three models of personal computers: large, medium, and small. One purchased part is an internal cooling fan: a large fan for the large computer, medium fan for the medium, and small fan for the small. Zeus produces and buys components purely just-in-time. The end-product schedule calls for producing one large, two medium, and four small computers every 10 minutes during the day, and the schedule is frozen for four weeks into the future. Suppliers deliver component parts (such as fans) once a day.

     a. What are the advantages of the daily mixed-model delivery schedule for the fan supplier? (One supplier provides all three sizes.)

     b. During one five-day period, Zeus has trouble meeting its daily schedule, falling short by 30 units the first day, 5 units on the second, 2 on the third, 25 on the fourth, and 8 on the fifth. What difficulties does this create for the just-in-time supplier?

     c. Zeus's schedule works out to 48 large, 96 medium, and 192 small computers per eight-hour day. What is wrong with the schedule (a possible contributor to the schedule problems described in part *b*)?

16. A production line assembles two models of hair dryer: standard (S) and deluxe (D). Each S requires 4 minutes of assembly time and each D 12 minutes. Marketing sells twice as many Ss as Ds. Develop a mixed-model sequence for the two dryers. Make it as well balanced as possible. What is the cycle time, and how many times can it repeat in a 480-minute day?

17. Parts A and B must be heat treated. The heat-treat time for part A is 5 minutes; for part B, it is 10 minutes. The schedule calls for 36 As and 12 Bs per day. Develop a balanced mixed-model sequence for the two parts. How many hours will it take to produce the scheduled amount?

18. Demand for a certain product averages 250 units per day. The product is made and sold in three styles; recently the split among them has been as follows: style 1, 60 percent; style 2, 30 percent; and style 3, 10 percent. Devise a mixed-model schedule with minimum cycle interval for this product line.

19. Find the lowest-ratio mixed-model schedule for four models of computer tables, where daily market requirements are 6 model Ds, 18 model Es, 12 model Fs, and 24 model Gs.

20. When production volume is high and product variety low, dedicated production facilities may be used to run a streamlined make-to-a-number operation. What can be done to streamline production of medium-volume products?

21 In a hospital, customers arrive irregularly. Are there any processes in a hospital that can escape from that basic customer-driven irregularity and get onto a repetitive schedule? Discuss, including any possible benefits.

22. In a department store, customers arrive irregularly. Are there any processes in a store that are important to customer service but that can be put onto a regularized schedule? If so, what are the benefits?

CASE STUDY

GETTING READY FOR MIXED-MODEL PRODUCTION AT KAWASAKI MOTORS USA

Mixed Models in Motorcycle Assembly

In September 1981, a Japanese management team replaced the American plant manager at the Kawasaki motorcycle plant in Lincoln, Nebraska. One goal of the new managers was to convert the main motorcycle assembly line to mixed-model production. The line had been running production lots of at least 200 of each model between line changeovers.

    Case topics: Preautomation; Mixed-model assembly sequence; Benefits of mixed-model assembly when sales are falling; Benefits of setup time reduction on presses.

    Source: From the *World Class Manufacturing Casebook: Implementing JIT and TQC*. New York: The Free Press. Copyright © 1987 by Richard J. Schonberger. Reproduced by permission of The Free Press.

The conversion was expected to take about three months. It required two kinds of exacting preparation:

1. *Identification:* All parts, tools, cartons, racks, and so forth, had to be clearly labeled so that an assembler would be able instantaneously to identify and select the right one. With a different motorcycle model next on the conveyor, delay in identifying it and all of the parts and tools to go with it would be intolerable. A color-coding system was devised so that, for example, all items related to a KZ650 motorcycle would be labeled with a gummed red dot. Even the position of the colored dot on the carton, part, or tool had to be precisely designed.

2. *Placement.* Engineers, material controllers, foremen, and assemblers all pitched in to devise exact locations for all parts and tools at work stations along the assembly line. The assembler, on seeing what the next model of motorcycle is, should be able to reach for the correct parts and tools blindfolded. Better racks, containers, and holding fixtures were designed to feed parts and hold tools in the right positions.

The preparations (which today we would refer to as preautomation) were successful. On January 1, 1983, the main assembly line fully converted to mixed-model production.

At that time, the production volume was at about 200 motorcycles per day. That 200 might consist of the following models: 100 KZ440s, 60 KZ650s, and 40 KZ1000s.

Question 1. For that mixture, what is the lowest-ratio mixed-model assembly sequence?

Question 2. Would there be any benefits of mixed-model assembly in a period when motorcycle sales were falling and excess bike inventories were building up in the distribution system (as in 1982)?

Mixed Models in Motorcycle Parts Fabrication

The main subassembly made in the Lincoln plant is motorcycle frames. The frame parts are formed from steel tube stock, and the parts are welded together into frames.

At one time frame parts were punched out on punch presses in lots of thousands at a time. The large lots were economical because it typically took half a day or so to move a heavy die into place on a large-size punch press and to get all of the die adjustments and machine controls just right. Part of the setup time was running off trial pieces, inspecting their dimensions, changing settings, running and inspecting a few more, and so forth.

In 1980–1981, the presses were modified for quick die changes and adjustments. Common roller conveyor sections were welded to form a carousel around the punch press; all dies were shimmed up so they had standard "shut heights"; and insertion and fastening were simplified. A dozen or more dies could be lined up around the carousel conveyor in the morning, and each die could be quickly and precisely rolled into place during the day in shifting from one frame part model to another (see Exhibit CS13–1). The changes cut average setup time to under 10 minutes (including zero inspection time). Instead of running thousands of a model between setups, it became economical to run in lots of 200, 100, or perhaps 50; while that is not the one-piece-at-a-time mixed-model ideal, it comes close.

But Kawasaki wanted to achieve the ideal: one-touch setup and one-piece-at-a-time production. That was accomplished for high-use frame parts in the summer of 1982. To achieve one-touch setup, large general purpose punch presses were replaced with small special-purpose screw presses. Each screw press has a die permanently built in so that there is no die change time and therefore no setup time—a dedicated machine. The small screw presses apply pressure slowly rather than punch suddenly, but their slowness is more than offset by the zero setup time. With dies exactly positioned, defective parts are much less likely. The screw presses were relocated to the welding shop, where a welder can set up several screw presses to make several different frame parts; as each part is completed, the welder may immediately weld it onto the growing frame. There are no

EXHIBIT CS13–1

**Carousel
Conveyor on
Punch Press**

lot-size inventories. Much of the punch press shop has been abolished, since welders now make each part as they go.

Question 3. What kinds of resource costs did Kawasaki reduce through their way of first achieving single-digit setup and then one-touch setup?

For Further Reference

Books

Harmon, Roy L. *Reinventing the Factory II: Managing the World Class Factory.* New York: The Free Press, 1992.

Harmon, Roy L., and Leroy D. Peterson. *Reinventing the Factory: Productivity Breakthroughs in Manufacturing Today.* New York: The Free Press, 1990 (HG56.H37).

Schonberger, Richard J. *World-Class Manufacturing: The Next Decade: Building Power, Strength, and Value.* New York: The Free Press, 1996.

Shingo, Shigeo. *Non-Stock Production: The Shingo System for Continuous Improvement.* Portland, Ore.: Productivity Press, 1988 (TS155.S45613).

Stephanou, S. E., and F. Spiegl. *The Manufacturing Challenge: From Concept to Production.* New York: Van Nostrand Reinhold, 1992 (TS155.S775).

Periodicals/Societies

Assembly Engineering.
Chemical Processing.
Industry Week.

C H A P T E R

MANAGING JOB AND BATCH OPERATIONS

14

Chapter Outline

"If the [flight] schedule doesn't work, nothing else can work," says David Siegel, a scheduling expert at Continental Airlines. To get a workable schedule, Continental had to force cooperation between marketing, which makes up the schedule, and operations, which flies the schedule. Previously, the two departments "never talked," says Greg Brennerman, chief operating officer for the airline. Marketing would change the schedule so often that the airline could not publish a timetable for several years. Moreover, marketing never consulted with operations as to the feasibility of each schedule.

"We were really just shooting our foot off in the past," says Deborah McCoy, a captain flying DC–10 aircraft and senior director of operational performance. "We knew what was wrong and we were very frustrated."

The new cooperative scheduling effort involved teamwork between marketing and operations. The teams studied the most common connections at its hubs and grouped those flights' gates and times close together. They found insufficient gate times and flying times on some flights and too much on others and made the proper adjustments. Those changes, plus various operational improvements and monetary incentives nudged Continental's on-time performance record up from near the bottom, according to the U.S. Department of Transportation, to near the top. As a bonus, Continental has been able to schedule and fly more flights per day with the same aircraft and crews. "Being on time makes you more productive," says Mr. Brennerman.[1]

Even though airlines usually fly repetitive schedules from city to city, the crews and support staff see each flight as a unique job—and often, as an obstacle course standing in the way of on-time performance. In this chapter we continue our study of operations environments, but shift the focus from continuous and repetitive processing modes to intermittent ones—specifically, to jobs and batches.

The Job Domain

Much of life's work consists of **jobs**—activities requiring allocation of a somewhat predictable collection of resources to a moderately discrete task, and having a defined end point and relatively tangible results. The job mode of operations covers nearly all human services, most office work, and the vast array of industrial job shops; a widespread, diverse, and hard-to-manage domain. This section narrows our focus and highlights key concerns, suggests a strategy for improving job management, presents a job operations system overview, and concludes with an example.

Focus and Concerns

The job environment has been intensively studied, and a bountiful terminology relates to it, especially in the manufacturing sector.[2] The vocabulary grows when we include the service sector. We needn't concern ourselves with most of these terms at this time, but a few are necessary to define the scope of our study. In particular, we must address output volume, task magnitude, and task variety.

Output Volume.   A job might yield a single unit of output, a dozen units, or even a few thousand. When output consists of multiple units, we refer to it as a **lot** or job lot. A **batch** is a certain type of job lot, usually a standard lot size or container quantity. Batch processing involves mixing a prescribed set and quantity of ingredients to create the desired output, typically measured by volume or weight: a yard of concrete, a pound of butter, or a liter of sulfuric acid. We treat jobs, batches, and lots together because they require similar management. For convenience, we use the term *job* when referring to any of these low-to-moderate volume modes of intermittent processing.

Lots and effects of lot size have been discussed in Chapters 8 and 11.

Task Magnitude.   When a job is expected to last for many months or years and calls for large commitments of resources—many people assigned to the team, dedicated facilities and equipment, big budgets, and so forth—we call it a **project** and manage it with special tools discussed in Chapter 15. So, in this chapter, we're not concerned with the very-large-scale efforts. Though smaller than a project, a job still requires a certain level of effort; it must encompass the whole work activity needed to fill some customer's request. That request is an **order**—perhaps called a service order, job order, work order, or shop order. In practice, the work needed to complete an order—the transformations of inputs into outputs—is carried out in a series of steps called **operations.** Not only is an operation one step in a job sequence, it is a step that almost always requires a new setup or changeover. Thus, orders, operations, and setups *are* very much a part of our concern in this chapter.

The order fulfillment sequence was discussed in Chapter 9.

Task Variety.   Variety—the typically large number of variables one must control—is what makes job management difficult. Consider these jobs: A broken fence repaired, six photostat copies made, 20 tennis rackets strung, a process flowcharted, a patient's disease diagnosed and treated, a computer program written and tested, and a training program delivered. The first three jobs are simple enough; the last four, on the other hand, could require considerable resources, get quite complicated and time-consuming, and produce a combination of tangible and intangible results.

Irregular and/or inconsistent colors, sizes, styles, and materials; varying lot quantities, process steps, waiting and setup times; changing regulations; special requests; and heightened customer expectations are among the many nuances that add spice to job operations. Managing such a jumble of jobs requires a concerted effort—and the right approach.

Managing Jobs: A Dual Approach

Successful job-operations management occurs when people focus attention on two broad sets of activities:

1. *Job planning, scheduling, and control.* This approach, grounded in information systems, has been highly developed, especially in North America. It essentially follows the dictum that job settings are complex, so people need sophisticated tools to manage them. Computerized work planning and scheduling, resource management, factory floor activity control, and simulation of planned operations are key components of these systems.

2. *Simplification, focus, elimination of non-value-adding steps, and streamlining of value-adding steps.* This approach, on the other hand, entails less information system support. Following the logic that job environments need not be as complicated as they have become, this strategy reduces the number of variables to be managed *and* reduces the variation in those (variables) which can't be eliminated.

The two approaches need not be mutually exclusive; it is not, for example, a "high-tech" versus "low-tech" contest. For one thing, information-system technology plays a significant role in what is sometimes called **agile manufacturing,** a streamlined, focused approach that is sensitive to diversity of customer requirements (See the Into Practice box, "Custom Jeans. . . "). But good technology is expensive, and should be focused on those activities where it can return value. High technology works better—giving customers the responsive service they deserve—when preceded by simplification and elimination of non-value-adding steps. Such an approach usually turns out to be more prudent financially, as well.

Second, job management does not boil down to a static one–two sequence: simplify, then schedule and control. Rather, it needs to be an iterative process of continuous improvement. For example, although Levi Strauss has streamlined its ordering, production, and distribution process for custom jeans, the pants still cost $10 more and require three weeks for delivery—two obvious targets for improvement that further rounds of simplification and better scheduling can address. And we must not forget those customers who prefer the immediate gratification and perhaps lower price of off-the-shelf clothes. The bulk of Levis still get made "the

*𝒫*RINCIPLES 5 AND 12:

Cut number of operations. Cut setup times.

Into Practice

Custom Jeans from Agile Manufacturers

According to Mike Cantwell, national director for manufacturing/distribution at Chicago-based Grant Thornton Consultants, "The early twenty-first century will be the age of customer service-driven manufacturing." Cantwell and his colleagues Mark Livingston and Lawrence Baye see agile manufacturing—the ability to be supremely responsive to customers' changing demands for customized products—as an essential strategy for survival.

"Agile manufacturing recognizes that customers are not just buying product from you, but buying flexibility and service," says Livingston. "You change your operation to suit what they want."

A case in point is Levi Strauss & Co. At selected company-owned stores, a sales associate uses a personal computer to electronically fit the customer and transmit the measurement data to a computer at the factory. It, in turn, directs a robot tailor to cut the fabric.

"For about $10 more than the cost of jeans off the shelf, you can have a customized pair in three weeks," says Baye.

Source: "Customer Service-Driven Companies to Dominate Manufacturing in the 21st Century," *Manufacturing Issues* (A Grant Thornton LLP Publication), Summer 1995, pp. 1–3.

regular way," and the company faces the challenge of improving the agility of those operations as well.

Before proceeding with detailed discussions of the two broad approaches, we need to know more about the job operations system and its variables. We turn to that issue now and examine scheduling, control, and simplification later in the chapter.

Job Operations Systems Overview

Any time a story about superior customer service appears, we wonder how the provider accomplished the feat. When a Levi Strauss retail sales associate sends customer measurements directly to a production-facility cutting room, for example, what gets bypassed? That is, what parts or jobs in the "normal" scheduling process are declared nonessential in such instances? Or, is every job still accomplished, but faster, say by cutting out or streamlining some wasteful operations?

Answers to these questions begin by examining just what it takes to plan, and control jobs. Exhibit 14–1 shows a general job-processing sequence applicable to manufacturing or service operations, along with the chapter(s) that contain material relevant to each step. First, the master scheduling committee (or person) positions the work in a master schedule or appointment book, sometimes with other similar work. Inventory and work-flow planning, as necessary, come next. Even in pure services, some inventory actions are generally needed so that the job will not be halted for lack of a certain item—say, a special tax form.

If all required inventories are on hand or due in, scheduling at a detailed job-by-job level may take place; for a multi-operation job, this may involve a scheduler's putting start and completion dates on each operation. In the dispatching step, jobs in progress get positioned one more time; dispatching is what we call prioritizing jobs in queue at a given work center. Finally, during or after the transformation, comes reporting and corrective control.

Well-known use of dispatching: Phone for a taxi, and a dispatcher assigns you to a cab, or a cab to you.

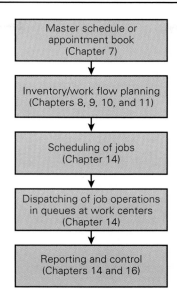

Exhibit 14–1

Job Planning, Scheduling, and Control

From Exhibit 14–1, we see that scheduling takes place at multiple levels, from master scheduling to job dispatching. It can go even lower, on down to the operations level. We consider the distinction between jobs and operations next.

Introductory Example: Jobs and Operations

Example 14–1 describes some of the details associated with even a relatively simple manufacturing job.

Example 14–1   Jobs and Operations—Bookcase Example

Upon appearing on the master schedule, an order for production of a certain model of bookcases triggers the explosion of the bookcase bill of materials (BOM) into component parts. These parts are dependent demand items, one of which is the shelf. If adequate shelf inventory does not exist and is not anticipated in the form of scheduled receipts, an order will be launched to produce shelf net requirements. Executing that order involves planning, scheduling, and controlling one job through the several operations required for its completion.

Chapter 10 describes BOM explosion and order positioning.

Exhibit 14–2 shows Job Number 4444, calling for production of 10 units of the shelf, part number 777. The job consists of a five-operation sequence. The figure shows the operations, numbered 10, 20, 30, 40, and 50, and the inventory conditions between them. Each operation takes place at a separate work center, including the stockroom, so the job routing requires inventory movement *and order tracking and control* through five centers.

As depicted in Exhibit 14–2, the actual job sequence is straightforward: Operation 10: Withdraw boards from the stockroom. Operation 20: Saw boards. Operation 30: Plane boards. Operation 40: Sand boards. Operation 50: Apply finish to sanded boards. The result is 10 finished shelves, component parts that go into the next higher-level item on the BOM for the bookcase.

EXHIBIT 14–2

Job and Operations for 10 Bookcase Shelves

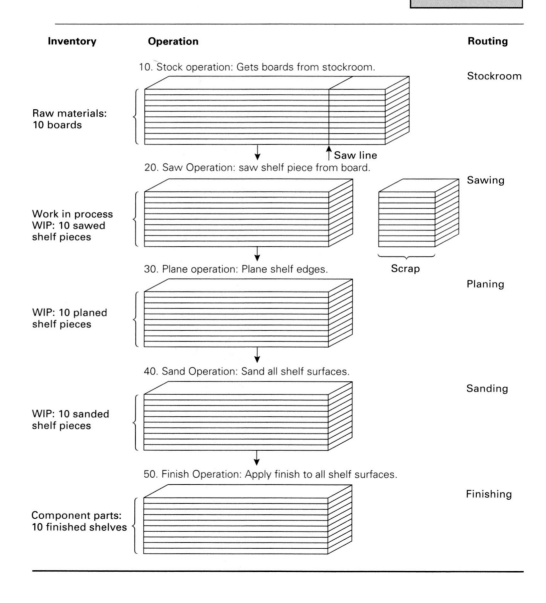

What we cannot see in Exhibit 14–2 are the troublesome realities of job environments: Each operation requires setup time; installing the proper saw blade, setting the depth of cut on the plane, and so forth. And, after each operation, work-in-process inventories form and sit idle, ready for transport to the next work center. We don't see the queues of other jobs waiting their turn at each work center—for example, orders for frames or cabinets. Also, routings vary; some jobs might require only sawing and planing before they are shipped out. Although we note the intentional scrap—the excess trimmed from boards—at the sawing operation, we don't see piles of unintentional scrap that happen when tools get dull, machines get out of alignment, specifications change, or instructions and other order-documentation paperwork get mixed up. Nor do we see the stacks of jobs returned for rework.

Finally, we do not see the human interactions. A dispatcher might be available to help the wood shop supervisor schedule and control operations—identifying "hot" jobs that are holding up work in assembly areas halfway across the plant. But, the due date for the entire shelf job, we are reminded, was set days or weeks earlier by a scheduler in a distant production control office.

The bookcase example exposes a few of the common complications in job management: multiple routings, setups, moves, queues, inventories, scrap, maintenance, and capacity management.

In a nutshell, many variables require attention, and the information system gets bogged down keeping track of problems. On the other hand, each complication is an improvement target—again, something we take up later in the chapter. At this time, let's focus on what is often the biggest complication of all—scheduling.

Scheduling

In common usage, the word schedule usually refers to a completion time or date and perhaps to a start time, as well. Master schedules—the first level of job scheduling mentioned in Exhibit 14–1—state the quantity needed and the completion day, week, or month, but usually not start times. We addressed master scheduling in Chapter 7. Detailed scheduling, at the job, component, or operation level, is our concern here.

We begin with a brief discussion of output versus resource scheduling, move on to address lead time and work in process, which are two basic causes of job scheduling problems, and conclude with examples of basic scheduling tools and techniques.

Output and Resource Scheduling

Actually, detailed-level scheduling in job environments involves more than deciding about needed completion dates and possible start times for the jobs and operations themselves. In those instances, we are usually fitting potential outputs to resources; schedule Job ABC to work center XYZ on such-and-such date. In some cases, however, it makes more sense to talk about scheduling the resource; for example, surgery suite C has been scheduled from 0800 to 1100 on Thursday.

In services, reservations serve as advance schedules. A reservation often more clearly defines the resource to be used than does an appointment. A reservation might even equate to a presale of the resource: reservations for cruises or no-refund airline tickets. In both manufacturing and services, however, the main concern is that the schedules for jobs and operations stay in sync with schedules for the resources needed for transformations.

Lead Time

Lead time, as cycle time is generally called in MRP and production-control circles, is the elapsed time required to perform a task or job. We get an idea of the trouble caused by lead time when we consider its components or elements and the uncertainty associated with it.

Lead Time Elements.   In job operations, lead time to produce or deliver something or provide a service usually contains much more delay time than actual work; that is, the part, client, or document spends far more time idle than being processed. In manufacturing, according to Orlicky,[3] the elements of production lead time for a given part are as follows, in descending order of significance:

1. Queue time.
2. Run time or service time: value-adding time during which the item is being produced or the service is being delivered.
3. Setup time.
4. Wait time (wait for instructions, transportation, tools, etc.).
5. Inspection time.
6. Move time.
7. Other.

Orlicky and others maintain that queue time (the first element) in metal fabrication shops normally accounts for about 90 percent of total lead time. It's often the same for customers buying tickets or paying tolls. Other delays (items 3 through 7 in the above list) take up part of the remaining 10 percent, which leaves run time (value-adding operations) with a very small percentage of total lead time.

Lead-Time Uncertainty.   Run time may be precisely measured using standard time techniques described later in Chapter 16. But queue time for an average job is hard to predict because the average varies with the changing mix of jobs in the system. Queue time for a particular job is even harder to predict, because the job may queue up at several work centers as it completes its routing. Therefore, some schedulers have a habit of simply adding a fixed number of days for queue time and other delays.

Dynamic scheduling is another option, the complexity of which requires that the system be computerized. In this approach, queue time includes an extra allowance for current or projected congestion. One simple measure of congestion is the number of open job orders, which the computer can find in the open-order file. Another is the number of operations in all open jobs, which demands access to routing data in addition to the open-order file.

Largely due to queue-time uncertainty, total lead time is also hard to predict. Accurate estimates of lead times, and therefore accurate schedules are likely only when work centers are uncongested; only then can the typical job sail through without long and variable work-center queue times. Two questions come to mind: First, with so much uncertainty and use of fudge factors in estimating lead times, is it possible to do a reasonable job of scheduling job operations anyway? Second, what can we do to improve the accuracy of lead-time estimates?

The answer to the first question is yes. In closed-loop MRP, work flows are monitored and schedulers and dispatchers are kept informed of job movement. If they discover that lead-time estimates—and therefore the schedules based on those lead times—are wrong, they can make adjustments; perhaps the scheduler changes the due date for a job, or maybe the dispatcher adjusts priorities for releasing jobs into work centers.

The answer to the second question, can we improve lead-time accuracy, is also yes. Since more accurate lead-time estimates depend on having less shop congestion, the solution is to reduce that congestion; that is, reduce work in process.

Work in Process

The work-in-process (WIP) problem is attacked directly with just-in-time techniques.[4] But the evils of WIP were receiving attention in Western industry well before JIT found its way across the Pacific. For 20 years or more, production-control books and dinner speakers at professional meetings for production-control people preached the following benefits of keeping WIP low:

1. *Service.* Low WIP means less queue time and quicker response to customers; also, with less queue time there is less uncertainty in the schedule and customers may be given better status information.
2. *Forecasts.* We know that forecasts are more accurate for shorter periods into the future—that is, for the shorter lead times that result from smaller amounts of WIP.
3. *Production-control work-force.* Less congestion means less need for control by expediters and dispatchers.
4. *Floor-space and inventory costs.* These are lower when fewer jobs are in process.
5. *Customer satisfaction.* Customers are happy when they don't have to wait in long lines (here the customers are the WIP). They get angry and may take their business elsewhere if lines get too long. Manufacturers have it easier, since inanimate parts waiting for machine time are unable to express anger.

Despite the advantages of low WIP, it can also make managers nervous and fearful that some work centers will run out of work. Each job in the work stream usually will require different operation times at each work center it visits. This causes work to pile up and overload some work centers and, potentially, underload others. As the job mix changes, and it often changes quickly, the pattern of over- and underloading changes. The scheduler is under pressure to overload on the average in order to hold down the number of underloaded work centers. Supervisors get nervous about cost variances when workloads get low.

*𝒫*RINCIPLE 11:

Cut wait time and inventory.

Having taken a look at job scheduling difficulties created by lead times and work in process, let's turn our attention to some basic scheduling tools. We start with the venerable Gantt Chart.

Gantt Charts

Henry Gantt's name is attached to a family of widely used scheduling charts. A few examples appear in Exhibit 14–3. In the basic **Gantt chart** form, much like Exhibit 14–3A, vertical divisions represent time, and horizontal rows, the jobs or resources to be scheduled. Lines, bars, brackets, shading, and other devices mark the start, duration, and end of a scheduled entity. The purpose of the charts, as with any visual aid, is to clarify, improve comprehension, and serve as a focus for discussion.

EXHIBIT 14–3

Common Forms of Gantt Charts

A. Schedule for machine

Scheduled computer jobs	M	T	W	T	F	S	S	M	T	W	T	F	S	S	M	T	W	T
Payroll			▪							▪							▪	
Accounts receivable					▪							▪						▪
MRP					▪						▪							

B. Schedule for space

Classroom schedule	(Monday) Hour							
	6	7	8	9	10	11	12	1
BA 101				MGM 331	ACCT 101			MGM
BA 102			ECON 205		ECON 400		FIN 394	

C. Schedule for labor and/or customers

	Dentist's appointments
Mon. 8:00	Mrs. Harrison
8:30	↓
9:00	J. Peters
9:30	Steve Smith
10:00	
10:30	
11:00	↓

The charts in Exhibit 14–3 are for scheduling three different resource types: equipment, space, and line employees. Each also identifies the jobs to be performed by the resources. Note too that each is a services example. While Gantt's original chart was for the control of repetitive manufacturing, today simpler forms of Gantt charts are more widely used in services, where routings are short and queues have few chances to form.[5]

In goods production, Gantt charts may be usable if

1. *There are not many work centers.* With many work centers, a carefully developed Gantt display of schedules tends to be a piece of gross fiction, because queuing effects (discussed earlier) make lead times unpredictable. Keeping the chart up-to-date under such conditions would be time-consuming and pointless.

2. *Job times are long—days or weeks rather than hours.* One example is a construction project. Drywallers, painters, cement crews, roofers, and so on, may each spend several days or weeks at a work site. With such a long job time, a schedule on a Gantt chart will hold still and not become instantly out-of-date as it would with very short jobs.

3. *Job routings are short.* In parts manufacturing, routings can be long. A single job may pass through 5, 10, or even 15 work centers, with

unpredictable queue time at each stop. With so much unpredictability, the Gantt schedule is not believable and thus not worth displaying.

Sometimes a Gantt chart is used for both scheduling and schedule control. This is especially the case in maintenance work. Examples are renovation, major maintenance, and extensive overhauls; nonmaintenance examples in which Gantt control charts might be used include computer systems analysis and programming projects, as well as computer program maintenance.

Exhibit 14–4 shows a Gantt control chart for renovation work. Part A is an initial schedule for three crews. An arrow at the top of each chart identifies the current day.

Exhibit 14–4B shows progress after one day. The shading indicates amount of work done, which probably is estimated by the crew chief, in percent of completion. Two-thirds of the first paint job was scheduled for Monday, but the paint crew got the whole job done that day. While the paint crew is one half-day ahead of schedule, drywall is one quarter-day behind. Carpentry did Monday's scheduled work on Monday and is on schedule.

Exhibit 14–4C for Tuesday shows painting falling behind, drywall on schedule, and carpentry ahead.

Maintenance is a service. Thus, it's not surprising that maintenance, like other services, may benefit from Gantt scheduling.

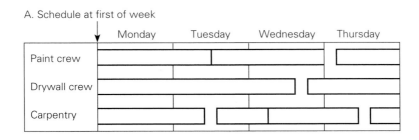

A. Schedule at first of week

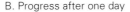

B. Progress after one day

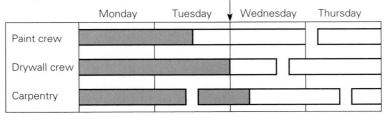

C. Progress after two days

Exhibit 14–4

Gantt Control Chart— Renovation Work

So that they are easy to adjust, schedule boards often use velcro or magnetic strips, pegs, plastic inserts, and the like to block out schedules and to show progress. Such boards are common in construction offices, project managers' headquarters, maintenance departments, retail stores, and restaurants.

The visual display offered by Gantt charts is a plus. But when things get complicated—for example, when there are many jobs, many routings, many work centers, and so forth—visual charts must give way to number- and word-based schedules. Also, while Gantt charts may be constructed from a need date backward or from a start date forward, backward scheduling is more likely to be the case in complex job settings. We take up these and related issues next.

Forward and Backward Scheduling

For services offered on demand, the customer need time is typically "as soon as possible" (ASAP is the well-known abbreviation). Using **forward scheduling,** the scheduler begins with the current time or date or with some other planned starting date, adds the successive duration times for various job operations, and arrives at an anticipated order completion date.

For services provided by appointment, **backward scheduling** may be used. An example is deliveries of checks and deposit slips from a small bank to a larger bank's computer service center. The service center may require delivery by 9 PM each day. If so, each delivery stop is backward scheduled; that is, the scheduler successively subtracts operation and transport times from 9 PM. The resulting schedule might appear as shown in the accompanying diagram.

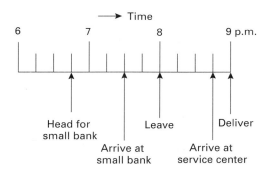

Backward and forward scheduling may be used in tandem. A scheduler might be asked to estimate the earliest date on which a job can be completed, which calls for forward scheduling. The date of need could be beyond the calculated earliest completion date; backward scheduling might then be used to determine the scheduled start date.

Goods producers, wholesalers, and retailers also use both forward and backward scheduling. Generally, inventories that are replenished by reorder point (ROP) are forward scheduled. Goods needed for a parent item or for a special event such as a wedding may be backward scheduled from the date of the net requirement—the MRP approach. Actually, in most MRP systems the planned-order-release date is not the scheduled start day. The computer backward schedules to determine the start *week,* which the scheduler uses to calculate the start *day.* Example 14–2 illustrates.

EXAMPLE 14–2   SCHEDULING A SHOP ORDER—QUIDCO, INC.
_____

The weekly MRP run at QUIDCO, Inc., shows a planned order in the current time bucket for part number 1005CX. The part is due on Monday of time bucket (week) 3, which is shop calendar date 105 (see Exhibit 14–5A).

The inventory planner validates the need for the order and the order quantity and timing. He decides that it should be a make rather than a buy order and therefore requests a shop order.

The scheduler finds the part number in the routing file, and the routing and time standards for each operation on a PC monitor. She prepares a shop order using the data from the routing file (see Exhibit 14–5B). She uses backward scheduling, along with QUIDCO's rules for computing operation lead times:[6]

1. Allow eight standard hours per day; round upward to whole days.
2. Allow one day between operations for move/queue time and other delays.
3. Allow two days to inspect.
4. Release shop order to the stockroom five days before the job is to be started into production.
5. All dates are treated as end of the eight-hour day.

She begins backward scheduling with the due date, 105, in the lower right corner. That is the finish date for the last operation, inspect. She subtracts two days for inspect and one day between operations, which makes 102 the due date for the finish operation. Finish takes 9.4 standard hours [0.4 + (0.18 × 50 pieces)], which rounds upward to two days. Subtracting that plus one day between operations equals 99 as the due date for the bend operation. Finally, she subtracts one day (6.7 hours rounded upward) for bend, five days for stockroom actions, and one day between operations, which makes day 92 the release date. The scheduler therefore holds shop order 9925 in her *hold-for-release* file on Monday and Tuesday (days 90 and 91) and releases it on Wednesday (day 92).

A shop calender of consecutively numbered workdays, omitting weekends and holidays, is common among manufacturing firms, because it makes computation easy.

A. MRP Listing of Planned Orders Due for Scheduling

Week of 90
Orders Planned for Release This Week
QUIDCO Inc.

Part Number	Due Date
0052X	110
0077AX	115
.	.
.	.
.	.
1005CX	105
.	.
.	.
.	.

B. Shop Order, Backward Scheduled

Shop Order Number 9925
Part Number 1005CX   Quantity: 50   Release Date: 92

Operation	Description	Work Center	Setup	Cycle Time	Standard Hours	Finish Date
20	Bend rod	16	4.2	0.05	6.7	99
30	Finish rod	85	0.4	0.18	9.4	102
40	Inspect rod	52				105
					Due Date:	105

EXHIBIT 14–5
Generating Shop Order from Current Planned Order Listing

A week goes by. The inventory planner notifies the scheduler that part number 1005CX has a new need date: the week of 110 instead of 105. (The latest MRP run informed him of the later date.) The scheduler recomputes operation due dates as follows:

$$
\begin{aligned}
\text{New job due date} = \text{Inspect due date} = \text{Day} \quad & 110 \\
\text{Less inspect time} = \quad & \underline{2 \text{ days}} \\
\text{Day} \quad & \overline{108} \\
\text{Less move/queue time} = \quad & \underline{1 \text{ day}} \\
\text{Finish due date} = \text{Day} \quad & \overline{107} \\
\text{Less finish time} = \quad & \underline{2 \text{ days}} \\
\text{Day} \quad & \overline{105} \\
\text{Less move/queue time} = \quad & \underline{1 \text{ day}} \\
\text{Bend due date} = \text{Day} \quad & \overline{104}
\end{aligned}
$$

The scheduler enters the three new operation due dates into the computer. The computer uses the new dates in printing out a daily dispatch list. Copies of the list go to the three work center supervisors to tell them about the changes in operations due dates.

In the QUIDCO example, we had the scheduler performing the backward scheduling manually, which helps illustrate the procedure. Obviously, in a real setting computers perform computations of this nature, following any prescribed set of lead-time rules. Also, under the influence of time-based competition, more companies are having MRP systems plan in days rather than weeks; schedulers may then plan in hours rather than days. The net effects are faster throughput and lower WIP, both acting to strengthen the financial posture of the firm.

Although the QUIDCO example provides details about scheduling a single job, what happens when several jobs need to be scheduled into the same work center at the same time? How does one determine the best sequence? Some sort of system for prioritizing is required. That is our next topic.

Work flow drives cash flow; speed up the former to speed up the latter.

Priority Rules

Priority systems come into play when multiple jobs or operations, typically in a queue, are competing for the same capacity. In retail settings, the priority system is simply first come, first served. In this democratic system, customers are considered homogeneous, one is not more important than another. First come, first served runs itself; no need to pay someone to pick and choose among customers.

Personal service settings might use first come, first served for their walk-in customers, while at the same time giving priority to customers with appointments. The priority rule is a simple one, but some differentiation among customers occurs.

Are wholesalers, factories, and offices blessed with such simplicity? Yes, but only if work can be processed quickly enough, with no queuing or other delays at each work center. If jobs can be processed or if wholesale or factory orders can be filled in, say, a day or less, the company probably will elect just to handle them as they come in. An exception might be an urgent job, which can receive high-priority treatment, such as hand carrying.

Some jobs shops (wholesalers, offices, labs, and so forth, as well as factories) are striving for delay-free processing but are still far from it. If it takes many days or weeks to process an order, the orders may need to be sorted by priority. Factors to consider in setting priorities for jobs include

1. Customer importance.
2. Order urgency.
3. Order profitability.
4. Impact on capacity utilization.
5. Shop performance.

Customer importance, order urgency, and order profitability are rather self-explanatory, and need not be further discussed. The fourth factor, impact on capacity utilization, often requires somewhat detailed analysis of capacity, work load projections, and activity control. We will leave those topics for more advanced studies. That leaves the final factor—shop or system performance.

Earlier, we saw that long lead times and facility congestion, in the form of work in process, are key variables that reduce the responsiveness of job operations. It comes as no surprise, therefore, that schedulers aim at reducing WIP and speeding up the flow of jobs through the system. Thus, average throughput time and average number of jobs in the system—as an indicator of WIP levels—are popular performance indicators. Emphasis on customer service adds another indicator—usually some measure of lateness, such as average time late. Several prioritizing rules exist to help the scheduler pick a job sequence that best meets one or more of these performance criteria. We shall consider four of the most popular:

- *First come, first served (FCFS).* This rule has been discussed within the context of retail operations. In service or manufacturing, the scheduler releases jobs in the order they arrive at the work center.
- *Shortest processing time (SPT).* Under the SPT rule, the scheduler prioritizes jobs in order of their required processing times; the job with the shortest time goes first.
- *Earliest due date (EDD).* Here, the customer with the earliest need date gets the priority, regardless of job arrival order or processing times.
- *Least slack (LS).* Defined as time remaining minus work remaining. The job with the least slack is released first.

Example 14–3 illustrates how these rules work.

EXAMPLE 14–3:   SCHEDULING MULTIPLE JOBS FROM A QUEUE

Five jobs are in a queue waiting to be released into a work center. These jobs, their required processing times, and their due dates are given in the table below. They are listed in the order of their arrival at the work center.

Job	Required Time (days)	Due Date (days hence)
A	3	5
B	6	8
C	2	6
D	4	4
E	1	2

Determine the proper job sequence using each of the following prioritizing rules: FCFS, SPT, EDD, and LS. For each solution, compute the average throughput time, the average number of jobs in the work center, and the average late time.

Exhibit 14–6

Job Scheduling

A. First-come-first-served (FCFS) rule

Job	Required time (days)	Due date (days hence)	Processing Period (start + req'd)	Completion Date	Days Late
A	3	5	0 + 3	3	0
B	6	8	3 + 6	9	1
C	2	6	9 + 2	11	5
D	4	4	11 + 4	15	11
E	1	2	15 + 1	16	14
Sums	16			54	31

Average throughput time = 54 ÷ 5 = 10.8 days.
Average number of jobs in the work center = 54 ÷ 16 = 3.38 jobs.
Average number of days late = 31 ÷ 5 = 6.2 days.

B. Shortest processing time (SPT) Rule

Job	Required Time (Days)	Due Date (days hence)	Processing Period (start + req'd)	Completion Date	Days Late
E	1	2	0 + 1	1	0
C	2	6	1 + 2	3	0
A	3	5	3 + 3	6	1
D	4	4	6 + 4	10	6
B	6	8	10 + 6	16	8
Sums	16			36	15

Average throughput time = 36 ÷ 5 = 7.2 days.
Average number of jobs in the work center = 36 ÷ 16 = 2.25 jobs.
Average number of days late = 15 ÷ 5 = 3.0 days.

C. Earliest due date (EDD) rule

Job	Required Time (Days)	Due Date (days hence)	Processing Period (start + req'd)	Completion Date	Days Late
E	1	2	0 + 1	1	0
D	4	4	1 + 4	5	1
A	3	5	5 + 3	8	3
C	2	6	8 + 2	10	4
B	6	8	10 + 6	16	8
Sums	16			40	16

Average throughput time = 40 ÷ 5 = 8.0 days.
Average number of jobs in the work center = 40 ÷ 16 = 2.5 jobs.
Average number of days late = 16 ÷ 5 = 3.2 days.

D. Least slack (LS) rule

Job	Required Time (days)	Due Date (days hence)	Slack (days)	Processing Period (start + req'd)	Completion Date	Days Late
D	4	4	0	0 + 4	4	0
E	1	2	1	4 + 1	5	3
A	3	5	2	5 + 3	8	3
B	6	8	2	8 + 6	14	6
C	2	6	4	14 + 2	16	10
Sums	16				47	22

Average throughput time = 47 ÷ 5 = 9.4 days.
Average number of jobs in the work center = 47 ÷ 16 = 2.94 jobs.
Average number of days late = 22 ÷ 5 = 4.4 days.

Performance Dimension	FCFS	SPT	EDD	LS
Average throughput time (days)	10.8	7.2	8.0	9.4
Average number of jobs in the work center	3.38	2.25	2.5	2.94
Average time late (days)	6.2	3.0	3.2	4.4

**EXHIBIT 14–7
Summary Table—
Scheduling with
Priority Rules**

Solution

The first column in Exhibit 14–6 parts A through D shows the correct job sequence under each of the priority rules. In each table, the column "Processing Period" shows the time a particular job will be worked on. For example, In Exhibit 14–6A, Job A will be accomplished in the first three days, then Job B will require the next six days and be completed on day 9; Job C is next, requiring two days ending on day 11, and so on. In Exhibit 14–6D, the solution under the least-slack rule, we've inserted an extra column to show the slack time. (Again, slack is available time minus required time.) The lower portion of each table contains expected shop performance figures—average job throughput time, average number of jobs in the work center, and average number of days late.

The summary table, Exhibit 14–7, compares performance of the four prioritizing rules in this problem. Shortest processing time (SPT) outperforms the other priority rules in all three of the performance dimensions.

Research has shown SPT to be a good rule to follow for job scheduling if a job queue has already formed, as is the case in Example 14–3. It will often minimize the average throughput time and result in the lowest average number of jobs in the system. Why, then, doesn't SPT become gospel? The answers lie in a deeper understanding of actual job operation settings.

• But contrary results in Blair J. Berkley, "Simulation Tests of FCFS and SPT Sequencing in Kanban Systems," *Decision Sciences* 24, no. 1, 1993, pp. 218–27.

First, scheduling occurs each day or perhaps each shift. As new jobs come along, the queue composition changes. Re-application of SPT would serve to keep longer jobs in lower priorities; they get delayed even further. Customers lose patience. Second, a queue must already exist in order for SPT to be applied. If we keep queues from forming in the first place, FCFS becomes the only practical scheduling rule. Third, SPT is fine as long as performance of one work center is the concern. But if jobs must meet up with other outputs later in an assembly sequence, for instance, EDD might be preferred.

Job-level scheduling, what Example 14–3 is all about, is the second level of scheduling addressed in Exhibit 14–1 (the third box in the figure). Still, many companies find it necessary to schedule at an even more detailed level—operations dispatching.

Operations Dispatching

Recall our discussion of lead-time uncertainty. Since SPT relies directly on knowledge of processing times (as does the LS rule, for that matter), its credibility drops as the possibility of processing-time uncertainty increases. When jobs contain long routings and therefore many operations, *job* processing times are really aggregate estimates that combine the individual times associated with the operations that make up those jobs.

For example, a scheduler might use SPT to release the bookshelf job described in Example 14–1 into the gateway work center—the stockroom in this case—based on its priority position in a job queue. Suppose many other jobs are currently in process, and several have routings that demand time at the planing work station. Quite possibly, a queue forms. Priority rules might also be employed to dispatch work through planing—a third level of scheduling and reflected as the fourth box in Exhibit 14–1.

Sometimes, the job scheduler also handles dispatching, but in complex settings, another individual, called a *dispatcher,* performs the work. In addition to managing **hot-list jobs,** orders for parts not available but needed immediately for open jobs currently in process on the shop floor, dispatchers often handle the **daily priority report** (also called the *dispatch list*).

A different priority report goes to each work center supervisor every day, only for jobs already in progress, not for those still in a planned-order state. Priorities are established by using one or more of the priority rules we considered for job scheduling. To illustrate, this time using the least-slack (LS) rule, let's assume that on day 101 four jobs are in queue at work center 16, which is the punch press center where metal is punched. Consider the data shown in Exhibit 14–8A (the first shop order, 9925, is from the QUIDCO example of Exhibit 14–5; recall that operation due dates are derived by back scheduling from the job due date). The slack for the four jobs is given in Exhibit 14–8B, which is roughly in the form of a daily priority report for work center 16. In the figure, slack values show that shop order 9925 is four days behind, 9938 and 9918 are each two days behind, and 9916 is two days ahead; the jobs should be run in work center 16 in that order.

In job operations, dispatching and related activities occur at the junction where planning and scheduling give way to control activities—keeping work moving on schedule and taking corrective action when required. The next section addresses other aspects of control.

A hot-listed job getting priority dispatching at a single work center may also be a hot job being expedited (e.g., hand-carried) through many work centers.

EXHIBIT 14–8

Planning Data and Priority Report for Work Center 16

A. Planning and routing data

Shop Order	Move/Queue Time	Punch Press Processing Time (Setup + Run)	Operation Due Date
9925	1 day	6.7 hours, or 1 day rounded	Day 99
9938	1 day	15.8 hours, or 2 days rounded	Day 102
9918	1 day	1.8 hours, or 1 day rounded	Day 101
9916	1 day	0.8 hours, or 1 day rounded	Day 105

B. Daily priority report, by operation slack

Shop Order	Demand Time (Due Date − Today)	Supply Time (Move/Queue + Processing)	Operation Slack
9925	99 − 101	1 + 1	−4
9938	102 − 101	1 + 2	−2
9918	101 − 101	1 + 1	−2
9916	105 − 101	1 + 1	+2

Job and Operations Control

Too many variables to manage—the main problem with job and operations scheduling—also makes controlling in these environments more difficult. As mentioned above, much of what dispatchers do to smooth and redirect work serves as control activities. Steps at better control can begin earlier, in the planning stage—when work is loaded onto (i.e., assigned to) work centers. Other actions include capacity control and activity control.

Work Center Loading

> *Scheduler:* "In a nutshell, what is your advice on how we should load your work centers?"
> *Supervisor:* "Keep' em busy. But not too busy."

The above exchange describes one concern of schedulers: loading the work centers. Whereas a multifunctional team plans overall capacity in light of predicted aggregate workload (Chapter 7), the scheduler (a role sometimes retained by supervisors) has the task of fitting jobs into the schedule so as not to overload or underload work centers day to day and week to week. In some companies, especially those that have implemented material requirements planning, the scheduler may perform loading with the aid of an MRP subroutine, capacity requirements planning.

loading Assigning workload to a work center.

Capacity requirements planning (CRP) is a computer-based method of revealing work center loads. A CRP run requires three inputs. One is planned order releases for component parts. Planned order releases are calculated by the computer in an MRP run (see Chapter 10). The second is open orders for component parts. These are orders released by scheduling (or purchasing) in an earlier period and still in process. The third input is routing data that tell which work centers each component-parts order goes through and how long it takes. Both the open-order file and the routing file must be computerized in order to run CRP.

Schedulers would want to apply CRP where it can do the most good: to work centers that have trouble achieving planned output, thus becoming bottlenecks. CRP projections in those work centers can warn of insufficient capacity far enough in advance for schedulers to do something about it. There is little sense in asking the computer to run CRP projections for all work centers and for 52 weeks into the future, because the real problems are in the near future and likely only in certain work centers. Common corrections include training new operators, shifting labor to new jobs, layoffs, subcontracts, and so on. With CRP's potential to alert managers so as to keep work center capacities reasonably close to planned loads, the usual chaotic atmosphere in the job shop may give way to reasonable order and tranquility.

Capacity Control

While capacity planning deals with blocks of jobs and capacity grouping, **capacity control** operates at the level of single jobs and single work centers. The capacity control problem is to make on-the-spot capacity adjustments in order to get a certain job through. Special capacity adjustments may stem from the press to get one or more hot jobs through the system. One way, considered here, is for expediters to push the work through. Another way, discussed in the final section of the chapter, is to select from a range of tools that simplify the processing or the handling so that special push activities are unnecessary—in other words, solve the root causes.

When a job is late or a key customer is getting impatient, our usual reaction is to **expedite:** do whatever is necessary to push the job through and never mind the chaos and interruptions that might ensue. In almost any line of work, unexpected hot jobs and processing obstacles make expediting necessary at least once in a while.

In the complex case of dozens, or hundreds, of jobs in process at any given time, the job mixture will generally include many nonurgent jobs along with a few hot ones. The scheduler's tendency (and the firm's policy) is to let the less urgent jobs or customers wait and push the hot jobs through via some form of expediting. In formal systems, sometimes people called *expediters* may physically move jobs along, mustering whatever resources are necessary and pushing aside any less-important work.

It's easy to see how this system works in the case of an emergency patient at a clinic or hospital. Medical staffers simply make a triage judgment as to criticality and process more-critical patients before others who had earlier positions in the queues.

Activity Control

The workplace is out of control if it is choked with partly completed jobs. That is true for a restaurant, clinic, or bank as well as for a goods producer. In Chapter 7, we studied production/capacity planning and master scheduling, which help to keep an overall balance between workload and capacity, and in the preceding section we considered work center loading concepts. There are two steps to be taken in the quest for balanced loads in work centers. Dispatching, discussed earlier, is one. The other involves input control of work releases into either gateway or bottleneck work centers. Together, these activities make up **activity control**—sometimes called **shop floor control.**

The first half of the scheduler's job is to set due dates for each operation and a release date for the whole job. The second half is to release orders in trickles so as not to overload the work centers. This is often referred to as **input control.** Two techniques of input control are load leveling and firm planned order.

Load Leveling.   The scheduler typically maintains some form of hold-for-release file. The file contains jobs with a mix of priorities. It may also include orders that were due for release on a previous day but were withheld because something (e.g., instructions or materials) was missing, or in order to avoid overloading certain work centers. The scheduler is attempting input **load leveling;** as the term suggests, the purpose is to release a level load, which is a mix of orders that neither overloads nor underloads a work center. Load leveling works well only for gateway work centers, those at the input end of the operation sequence. The foundry that produces castings is a common gateway in metal fabrication, a component sequencing machine used in printed circuit board assembly may be a gateway in electronics, and order entry or customer arrival is a gateway in many service businesses.

A scheduler could, with computer help, work up a schedule to level not only gateway but also downstream work centers. But it won't work. Variable queue times at later work centers get in the way, so that later operations are unlikely to follow the schedule closely enough for the loads to remain level.

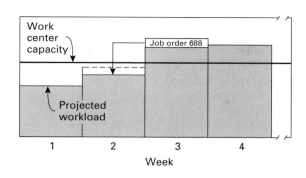

Exhibit 14–9

**Firm Planned
Order for Load
Leveling in
Gateway Work
Center**

*Action taken: Job order 688 is scheduled as a firm planned order in week 2 instead of week 3, its
MRP-generated date of need.*

Firm Planned Order.   The **firm planned order** is an MRP tool that may be used to
overrule the automatic rescheduling feature of MRP and thus help in load leveling. A
firm planned order may be scheduled earlier than the actual need to get the order into
a gateway work center in a slack (underloaded) week (see Exhibit 14–9). To invoke
the firm planned order, the scheduler instructs the computer to flag a particular
planned order and move it to a given time bucket. In the figure, planned order 688 is
moved from week 3, its calculated date of need, to week 2, which helps level the load
imbalance in weeks 2 and 3. The next MRP run will not reschedule the flagged job
back to its need date. It will issue a reschedule message, which may be ignored.

   The firm planned order may also be used to move a job to a later week. There
is no point in going far into the future, however, since conditions will change the
future before it arrives.

   These control tools, along with the planning and scheduling actions considered earlier in the chapter, create a complex system that itself resists control.
Efforts to simplify job and batch operations, thus making the system easier to manage, are the next topic.

Simplification: Reduction of Variables

Criss-crossed flow paths, high error rates, piled-high in-baskets, bulging stock
rooms of items not needed yet, shelves full of thick instruction manuals, frequent
rescheduling, high overtime and undertime costs, poor on-time service rates, long
cycle times, and large backlogs: These are symptoms of overly complex job operations and high-cost, ineffective attempts to cope.

   Assorted antidotes are available. We first consider ways to ease the related information processing burden, and then review an assortment of simplification
methods discussed in other chapters.

Paperless and Visual Systems

Each of the planning and control topics addressed in this chapter puts more computer transactions and paperwork into the system. Will the product or client get
lost under piles of paper? Sometimes it seems that way.

*P*RINCIPLE 16:

Cut transactions and
reporting.

Advanced communications and computer technology can create a paperless office or plant. A few such facilities already exist. Data-entry terminals in planning offices or, better yet, in customers' own facilities, display screens in work centers, bar codes on all parts containers or mail-distribution tubs, and bar-code readers to track the work flow all help make paper reduction possible. The scheduling and activity control procedures may be just as described above. The difference is that job orders, priority reports, and other notices and files are called up on screens instead of from printed pages.

Another way to deal with transactions and paper is to create the visual office or plant. It is not hard to conceive of this for repetitive or continuous operations. No data screens are needed to tell people what to do when the same work units follow the same flow path sometimes pulled by conveyors.

Can the scheduling and dispatching paper possibly be eliminated in a job shop? The answer is yes, at least partly. One documented case is the Hewlett-Packard 9000 computer work station.[7] H-P calculates that the 9000 series can be produced in 6 million different configurations. All production is to fill customer orders, which are small and in diverse configurations. The H-P plant eliminated job orders, ceased using MRP on the shop floor, and adopted visual kanban. MRP is still used for exploding customer orders into components. The exploded customer order goes to final assembly and is also used in planning orders for purchased parts.

All printed circuit-board assembly and major-module assembly and testing are triggered visually. Very small amounts, often one unit, of each partially completed item are stored in slots or shelves on racks in the work centers. When a customer orders a certain configuration of the finished item, final assembly pulls major modules (keyboards, logic units, and power cords) from nearby shelves. That authorizes major module assembly to make one more of each module to refill the emptied shelf spaces. Module assemblers withdraw components, such as circuit boards, from nearby slots. The empty slots visually authorize test operators to pull untested circuit boards from one rack, test them, and place them in the other rack to fill the emptied slot. The visual signal to make another item to fill a slot winds back through 11 production stages to the stockroom holding purchased items.

A few differences between visual and written work authorization are summarized in Exhibit 14–10. Note that the written system may include a job order, a pick list, and a priority report. The visual system may require an identification card in a slot, but that is fixed information, not transactions generated for each job; process instructions are also fixed information.

Often, the visual system can be used for some but not all items and processes. For example, in aircraft production, it would make no sense to keep an extra huge wing in a shelf and then trigger production of the next wing when the shelf empties. A schedule, not an empty shelf, should authorize the production of a wing. The components that go into the wing are another story. Finished units of common struts, fabric pieces, cable lengths, wire assemblies, and other wing parts could be kept in kanban racks near the wing assembly area. Removal of a strut or other piece from a shelf may then visually authorize production of another unit to refill the shelf.

The visual system for job shops and offices is not yet in wide use, but its potential for application is almost limitless. The case study at the end of Chapter 9, "The Office Goes Kanban at Boeing," illustrates. The visual system is potent because it copes with the explosive growth of overhead costs, especially those of processing transactions and of material handling and storage.

	Visual	*Written*
Work in process	Exact small quantity located next to work center	Large shelf space in stockroom; may be full, partly full, or empty
Delivery	Empty slot tells associate to get next unprocessed unit from rack; cards identify units in rack spaces	Written job order is transformed into pick list; tells stockroom what items to pick and deliver to work centers
Dispatching	Emptiest slot is next job	Daily priority report tells work center the order of working on the jobs in queue
Process instructions	In a file at the work center	Part of work package accompanying the job order

EXHIBIT 14–10

Work Authorization in Job Operations

Other Antidotes

Complementing the shift toward simpler information processing are other complexity antidotes that have been discussed in other chapters. They are reviewed below in two groups, one general and the other specific to this chapter's topics. Also see the Contrast box for a broad comparison of approaches.

General Simplifications.   These general items apply to all kinds of operations but are especially valuable in job and batch operations where complexity problems tend to be severe.

- Get focused: Strategically limit the variety of businesses per organizational unit (Chapters 1 and 2).
- Reduce, simplify, and standardize designs for the line of goods and services (Chapter 4).
- Control processes at the source, rather than discovering mishaps downstream (Chapter 5).
- Stay tuned to the pulse of the market via comprehensive demand forecasting (Chapter 6).
- Employ a cross-functional master planning team to plan capacity and master schedules so that demand and supply are a reasonably close fit (Chapter 7).
- Adopt quick-response and just-in-time flow controls to remove sources of non-value-adding delay and stay close to the actual demand changes (Chapter 8).
- Cut to a few good supplier-partners (Chapter 9), thus shrinking purchasing complications.
- Adopt simple queue-limitation and kanban flow controls (Chapter 10), thereby avoiding flow-control transactions.
- Cut job, lot, and batch sizes so that materials are ordered or produced based on current demand, thus avoiding problems of having too many of the wrong items and being out of the right ones (Chapters 8 and 11).

Special Simplifications.   The following items relate to expediting and capacity/activity control.

Contrast

Getting the Hot Jobs Done

Expediting

- Expediter selects hot jobs from overdue list; uses lot splitting, overlapping, hand-carry, air freight, "cannibalization" of other jobs, and so forth, to push hot jobs through.

Planning

- MRP creates planned orders.
- CRP identifies capacity shortfall.
- Scheduling/rescheduling assigns dates.
- Dispatching reprioritizes— latest jobs first.

Simplifying

- Quick setup so that hot jobs scarcely disrupt.
- Cells process similar jobs with natural overlapping and few transactions.

- Cut changeover and setup times (Chapter 11) so that lot splitting into smaller transfer lots does not elevate costs.
- Position facilities the way the work flows, thus avoiding long, jumbled flow paths (Chapter 12). A hot job then may go directly to the cell or flow line that is focused on similar items (goods, documents, or human services), where it may fit right in without special paperwork, setups, handling, or disruption.
- Keep physical resources in tip-top working condition (Chapter 17), thereby avoiding stoppages and rescheduling.
- Where there is flow distance to span (e.g., to and from a cell or in the absence of cells), downsize to lower-cost handling methods so that expediting is still affordable (Chapter 17). This final simplification may be illustrated with reference to forklift trucks and kanban on roller skates.

Forklift Trucks and Roller Skates

Forklift trucks are everywhere in industrial job shops. They can move loads of thousands of pounds. Since they can move very large loads, they do. Crates, pallets, and boxes are piled high, and the forklift moves the highly piled loads. In the late 1970s, Western visitors to Japan saw similar industrial job shops that made little use of forktrucks (except on receiving and shipping docks). In the 1980s, forktruck removal became popular sport in some companies; see Into Practice, "Reducing Forklift Trucks at Emerson."

The economics work as follows. Forktrucks, with their batteries and high battery-charging costs, are expensive. They require wide aisles, create safety hazards, and run into things and cause damage. If average transport loads are reduced, say, fivefold, simple wheeled carts will usually be strong enough. Wheeled carts moving one-fifth of the former load sizes would have to make five times more trips. The total handling cost may be less, however, because of the eliminated direct and indirect costs of the forklifts. Thus, forktruck removal may pay for itself even without the benefits of reduced delays and WIP inventories, which go down nearly fivefold as well.

Reducing Forklift Trucks at Emerson

William Rutledge, then executive vice president of Emerson Electric Company, knew what to do about the firm's heavy use of forklift trucks and the piles of inventory they thrive on. At a company meeting in 1986, he told all his division presidents that hence- forth corporate headquarters was charging a license fee for every new forklift: $5 for the first truck, $50 for the second, $500 for the third, and so on. The division presidents thought Rutledge was being facetious, but his point was clear!

Better yet, how about roller skates? That's the method of delivering small kanban quantities of parts to assembly cells at Sentrol, Inc. (see Exhibit 14–11). This producer of a premier line of sensors for business and home security (detection of glass breakage, motion, smoke, etc.) has fully implemented cells and kanban, which has driven average throughput times down from in excess of 10 weeks to about four hours. The perimeter of Sentrol's assembly floor is marked off with a painted pathway for the skater, who wheels around picking up empty kanban boxes, taking them to the adjacent parts storeroom, and skating back with full containers. While a forktruck driver or stock clerk pushing a trolley might make the rounds two or three times a day delivering large transfer quantities, Sentrol's skaters cover the entire floor several times per hour conveying small JIT quantities. Sentrol's skater position is highly sought after in the Portland, Oregon, area where the company is located.

Reforming the Job Shop: An Example

In this chapter, we have examined a sophisticated, many-faceted system of managing complex job operations, a system perfected in North America, largely in the 1970s. We've also emphasized simplification, an approach that is highly attractive in view of the high costs and complexity of job operations. We end

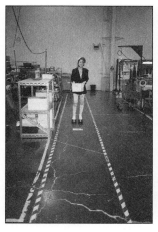  

EXHIBIT 14–11

Skater with Kanban Parts Containers, at Sentrol, Inc.

Left: Picking up empty container. Middle: Emerging from stock room with full container. Right: Dropping off full container.

this chapter by elaborating upon that message via a real-life summary (see Into Practice, "Reforming the Job Shop") of what can be done to improve a job shop. The message applies as well to job-oriented offices and, to some extent, human service operations.

Into Practice

Reforming the Job Shop

In the summer of 1985 [Schlumberger's Houston downhole sensors (HDS) division] was struggling. Operations were costly, chaotic, and falling short of acceptable standards. Customers were dissatisfied. About 15 percent of the logging tools produced by HDS failed on final acceptance test. Most products were built to schedules established far in advance, but on-time delivery was no better than 70 percent. The average lead times exceeded 12 months. Senior management was also dissatisfied. Cost of sales was unacceptably high, and the plant was bulging with inventories. WIP alone averaged five months of output.

What explains the chronic and intractable problems afflicting job shops? The answer lies in the manufacturing philosophy. At HDS, most products were batched for final assembly and tested in lots that usually represented two or three months' requirements. Therefore, lead times on orders were at least two to three months (in reality much longer) even though many logging tools could be assembled and tested in two weeks.

So why batch? Because management wanted to be as efficient as possible, with efficiency defined as minimizing direct labor charges. Batching generated short-term savings in virtually every phase of the production process. Setup costs are a good example. Parts needed for final assembly must be "kitted" in a warehouse before arriving at the assembly area. Management believed that pulling kits in large lots, rather than as orders arrived, saved money. Batching also meant that workers had to learn how to assemble and test a product only once per batch. Batching minimized the unit costs of configuring test equipment and debugging completed products. Finally, moving products in large batches was combined with the use of queues to smooth work flows and adjust to ever-present parts shortages. Batching in effect, allowed all the factory's workers to be busy all the time.

In the long term, however, batching becomes a big obstacle to the very efficiencies it seeks to achieve.

The long-lead-time, large-lot, long-queue philosophy invariably results in split lots, broken setups, lost and defective parts, late deliveries, and large WIP. The results are visible in job shops everywhere: the monthly hockey stick shipments, where a large volume of product leaves the factory at the end of each measurement period; relaxation of quality standards under pressure to make quotas; secret high-rework jobs hidden in WIP; ever-changing production priorities; and daily crises on the shop floor.

We believe the real solution lies in eliminating batching, smoothing, and artificial economies of scale, and organizing a job shop that can quickly and efficiently "change over" from one product to another without incurring large delays and cost penalties.

HDS adopted such a production philosophy. It emphasizes shorter lead times (down from an average of three months to two weeks today), small to nonexistent queues, low inventories, and quick recognition and correction of defects.

Getting control over the shop floor has allowed us to slash overhead. In the summer of 1985, 520 of the division's 830 employees were salaried or indirect personnel. The overhead count now stands at 220 employees. The largest reductions came from three departments—quality control; shipping, receiving, and warehousing; and production control (expediters, dispatchers)—whose roles diminish as quality and on-time performance improves.

These dramatic results did not require large capital expenditures. The management team initially cut the capital budget by 50 percent; annual spending has since run at less than half of depreciation. Those results did not require sophisticated computer applications. In fact, we turned off our shop floor computer, adopted a manual floor-control approach, and canceled a $400,000 automation project.

Source: Adapted from James E. Ashton and Frank X. Cook, Jr., "Time to Reform Job-Shop Manufacturing," *Harvard Business Review*, March–April 1989, pp. 106–11. Used with permission.

Summary

Much of life's work consists of jobs. Job and batch operations constitute a widespread, diverse, and hard-to-manage domain. Successful job operations management requires a dual approach—good planning, scheduling, and control systems and efforts to simplify, focus, and streamline the job environments. Historically, managers have placed too much emphasis on the former and too little on the latter. A primary target of the simplification efforts is to reduce the number of variables in job and batch systems, so modern scheduling and control tools can be focused on value-adding activities.

Job orders may subdivide into operations, each requiring a setup and each performed in a different work center. Scheduling at the operation level (work in queue at a work center) is called dispatching.

Because of variable queues, lead time to complete a job is often a question mark. The more congestion on the floor (e.g., WIP), the more uncertain the lead time. Schedulers can help by (1) controlling releases of orders (input control), and (2) employing the firm planned order feature of MRP in order to level work loads in gateway work centers. While on-demand services and stock replenishment may be forward scheduled, appointments and future orders (including those planned by MRP) are usually backward scheduled.

Appointments and scheduled jobs and operations should dovetail with schedules for operating resources: labor, equipment, tools, materials, and space. In services, it is sometimes helpful to display schedules on visual Gantt charts; Gantt control charts are used to plot status of work, especially in maintenance, construction, computer programming, and so forth.

In more complicated settings such as those employing MRP, backward scheduling sets job start dates by subtracting lead time from desired completion dates. Forward scheduling may be used in tandem with backward scheduling, such as when a scheduler is asked to estimate a completion date.

When multiple jobs or operations are waiting in a queue for release into the same resource (e.g., office, cell, or machine center), priority rules allow the scheduler or dispatcher to release work in a sequence that better meets desired performance objectives. Common priority rules include first come, first served (FCFS), shortest processing time (SPT), earliest due date (EDD), and least slack (LS). Dispatchers also perform control activities; they manage hot lists and handle daily priority reports, often with computers monitoring work flow.

Job and operations control activities include work-center load monitoring, perhaps using capacity requirements planning (CRP) subroutines; capacity control, including the option of job expediting; and activity control, employing tools such as input control, load leveling, and the firm planned order.

Simplification efforts have been underway in leading companies for several years, and a family of principles and techniques has emerged to guide managers in these efforts. For example, paperless work authorization is possible. Visual kanban-like systems go a step further by eliminating the need for some written work authorizations and flow tracking.

Solved Problems

Problem 1   The framing department has an order for 20-pound frames. The operations and standard times for producing one frame are:

Operation	Standard Time
Cut	4 hours
Weld	8 hours
Grind	3 hours
Finish	18 hours

a. If it is a hot job, how quickly (in eight-hour days) can it be completed allowing one extra day for material movement and delays?

b. The MRP system sets lead times for component parts by a formula: standard hours times five, plus two weeks, rounded upward to full weeks. What lead time does the MRP system use?

c. The above two answers are far apart, but both may be fairly realistic. Explain what happens when a planned system accommodates both.

Solution 1

a. Total work content $= 4 + 8 + 3 + 18 = 33$ standard hours
$= 4.125$ days, rounded up to 5 days

   Total expedited lead time $= 5 + 1$ extra day
$= 6$ days

b. From (*a*)

   Total hours $= 33$ hours

   Then

   Lead time $= (33 \text{ hours} \times 5) + 2$ weeks
$= 165$ hours (or 4.125 weeks) $+ 2$ weeks
$= 6.125$, rounded up to 7 weeks

c. The MRP system must back schedule using normal time estimates. The result is a fairly realistic week of need, seven weeks prior to the week due for the frame order. It is nearly eight times greater than the expedite time of six days, which is to be expected since in conventional job shops work spends most of its total lead time in various kinds of delay. The few hot jobs interrupt the routine ones, causing the latter to be delayed still more. (While that situation has been normal in job shops, simplified operations management systems are eliminating delays in some companies.)

Problem 2   Today is day 11 on the shop calendar, and three jobs are awaiting processing in work center 67, as shown in the following table:

Jobs in Work Center 67	Scheduled Operation Start Date	Scheduled Operation Due Date
A	12	18
B	8	16
C	13	17

Calculate operation slack for the three jobs. Arrange the jobs in priority order, and indicate which should be done first.

Solution 2   Slack is equal to available time minus required time, where

Available time = Operation due date − Today's date

and

Required time = Scheduled due date − Scheduled start date

Then

Job	Available Time (Due − Today)	Required Time (Due − Start)	Operation Slack (Available − Required)
A	18 − 11 = 7	18 − 12 = 6	7 − 6 = +1
B	16 − 11 = 5	16 − 8 = 8	5 − 8 = −3
C	17 − 11 = 6	17 − 13 = 4	6 − 4 = +2

First:	B
Second:	A
Third:	C

Review Questions

1. Why is simplification relevant in managing job operations?

2. Distinguish among scheduling, dispatching, and loading.

3. What is the difference between a job and an operation?

4. Why is it hard to estimate production lead time accurately?

5. Why is it important to minimize work-in-process inventory?

6. Contrast backward and forward scheduling.

7. Explain how a due date for a shop order may be translated into finish dates for each operation in the job.

8. What are the uses of Gantt charts?

9. Under what conditions are priority rules needed in scheduling?

10. What priority rule are you likely to find in retail settings? Why?

11. How might a scheduler gauge the amount of WIP in a job operations environment?

12. Explain the rationale for each of the following prioritizing rules: FCFS, SPT, EDD, and LS.

13. What is a daily priority report? To whom is it directed?

14. How do CRP reports get produced, and what are they used for?

15. Why should a scheduler avoid the temptation to have computers balance loads at distant downstream work centers?

16. How does the firm planned order help ensure that the right amount of work is released by the scheduler?

17. Compare the paperless and visual systems.

18. How does the admonishment "get focused" relate to improving job and batch operations?

Exercises

1. A manufacturer of stereo speakers produces five main types of high-quality speaker. The company considers itself a job shop. The single production line produces lots of each type of speaker on an irregular schedule. Price competition has been severe, and the company's profits have eroded. A conglomerate is buying the stereo manufacturer and intends to invest a considerable amount of cash to improve production control and cut production costs. What should the money be invested in?

2. An advertising agency has 12 departments. Every small ad job must pass through at least 6 of them, medium-sized ads through 9 of the departments, and large ads for major clients through all 12 departments. Typically, over 100 ad jobs (each a separate ad for a separate customer's product) are in process at any one time. Most are late, a contributing reason why the agency has lost a few long-standing clients. What should be done to improve on-time performance?

3. A scheduler at QUIDCO, Inc., is working up a schedule for making 20 of part number 0077AX. The inventory planner advises that the order be released this week, week of day 90, and that the order is due on the week of day 115, when it will be needed to go into a parent item. QUIDCO employs closed-loop MRP.
   a. How would the inventory planner have determined the week due and the week of release? If the inventory planner has determined these dates, doesn't that constitute rescheduling and eliminate the need for the scheduler to do anything? Discuss.
   b. The A in the part number signifies a costly item. For A items, the following rules are used for computing operation lead times:
      (1) Allow eight standard hours per day: round upward to whole (eight-hour) days.
      (2) Allow no time between operations. A items receive priority material handling.
      (3) Allow one day to inspect.
      (4) Release the job to the stockroom four days before it is to be started into production.
      (5) All dates are treated as end of the eight-hour day.

      Schedule a shop order for the item, assuming that the part goes through three operations plus inspection. You make up the setup times and operation times such that the schedule will fit between days 90 and 115. Explain.
   c. Compare the operation lead-time rules for part number 0077AX with the rules in Example 14–2 for part number 1005CX. Why should a more expensive item have different lead-time rules? (Hint: WIP has something to do with it.)
   d. A week passes. Inventory planning notifies scheduling that part number 0077AX is now due (to go into a parent item) in the week of day 120 instead of 115. The shop order, along with a planning package (blueprints, job tickets etc.), has already been released. There is no need to issue new paperwork, because QUIDCO has a computer-produced daily dispatch list for each work center. Least slack is the dispatching rule. The scheduler merely gets on a terminal and inputs updated scheduling information. Explain how that information would be used in generating dispatch lists. Also, explain how the dispatch lists serve the purpose of adjusting for the new due date.

4. The maintenance department has two renovation orders that are being scheduled. Order 1 requires these three jobs or tasks: 14 days of wiring, 7 days of drywall work, and 9 days of painting. Order 2 takes five days of drywall followed by six days of painting.
   a. Draw a Gantt chart showing the workloads (backlogs) for each of the three jobs (wiring, drywall, and paint).

     b. Draw a Gantt chart showing the two orders back-scheduled, the first with completion due at the end of day 35 and the second due at the end of day 14.

     c. Draw a Gantt chart with the two orders forward scheduled. In what situation would forward scheduling for these three trades be useful?

5. Four jobs are on the desk of the scheduler for a firm's minor construction department. Each job begins with masonry, followed by carpentry and wiring. Work-order data are as follows:

Work Order	Estimated Task Time—Masonry	Estimated Task Time—Carpentry	Estimated Task Time—Wiring
58	2 weeks	3 weeks	$1\frac{1}{2}$ weeks
59	1 week	$1\frac{1}{2}$ weeks	1 week
60	3 weeks	2 weeks	3 weeks
61	5 weeks	$\frac{1}{2}$ week	$1\frac{1}{2}$ weeks

     a. Prepare a Gantt chart scheduling the four jobs through the three crafts (crafts are rows on your chart). Use first come, first served as the priority rule for scheduling (first *job* first—the whole job). Assume that a craft cannot divide its time between two work orders. How many weeks do the four jobs take?

     b. Repeat (*a*) but use the shortest processing-time rule instead of first come, first served. Now how many weeks are required?

     c. Three weeks pass. The following progress is reported to the scheduler:
         Masonry completed on WO 58.
         Masonry not started on WO 59, 60, or 61.
         Carpentry half completed on WO 58.
     Show the progress on a Gantt control chart (using part *a* data).

     d. In this problem situation, each shop is fully loaded as the jobs are sequenced and scheduled. It is finite-capacity loading. What is there about minor construction work of this kind that makes scheduling and loading so uncomplicated (relative to job-lot parts fabrication)?

6. The following Gantt chart shows a scheduled project task and progress as of a given date:

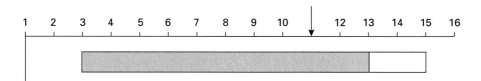

     a. What is the present date, and what is the percent of completion for the task? How many days ahead or behind schedule are shown?

     b. Redraw the chart as it will look tomorrow if the entire task is completed. How many days ahead or behind schedule does your chart represent?

     c. Saturdays and Sundays are not worked and are not identified on the chart. Explain how the dating system treats holidays.

7. Open Air Furniture Company makes patio furniture. There are just three work centers: rough saw, finish saw, and assemble.

     Production control keeps track of total workloads for use in short-term scheduling and capacity management. Each week's component-parts orders are translated into machine hours in rough saw and finish saw and into labor hours in assembly. Current machine-hour and labor-hour loads are as follows:

	Rough Saw	Finish Saw	Assemble
Current week	270	470	410
Week 2	40	110	100
Week 3	—	40	50
Week 4	—	30	15
Weekly capacity	150	225	190

    a. Is operations dispatching likely to be required at any work centers? Explain.

    b. Is this the type of firm that is likely to rely heavily on expediting? Explain.

8. The following chart shows projected loads for one work center:

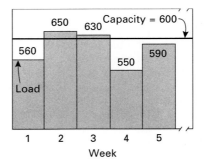

    a. What may the scheduler do to help correct the imbalance between load and capacity in some weeks? Discuss, including any limitations or difficulties in correcting the imbalance.

    b. How would the load report be produced?

9. On day 280, the daily priority report for the nickel-plating work center includes job number 2228. That job is due out of plating on day 279, and its planned run time is one day. If an additional day is allowed for move and queue time, what is the operation slack? Show your calculation. How should these calculated results be interpreted?

10. Jerrybuilt Machines, Inc., uses the least-slack priority rule. On shop calendar day 62, the following shop orders will be in work center 30:

Shop order	Move/Queue Allowance	Operation Time	Operation Due Date
889	2 days	3 days	68
916	2 days	1 day	64
901	2 days	1 day	69

Calculate the slack for each shop order, and arrange your calculated results in list form as they would appear on a daily dispatch list.

11. Five jobs are in a queue waiting to be released into a work center. These jobs, their required processing times, and their due dates are given in the table below. They are listed in the order of their arrival at the work center.

Job	Required Time (days)	Due Date (days hence)
A	5	7
B	7	10
C	10	11
D	3	8
E	6	7

Determine the proper job sequence using each of the following prioritizing rules: FCFS, SPT, EDD, and LS. For each solution, compute the average throughput time, the average number of jobs in the work center, and the average late time.

12. Five jobs are in a queue waiting to be released into a work center. These jobs, their required processing times, and their due dates are given in the table below. They are listed in the order of their arrival at the work center.

Job (days)	Required Time (days)	Due Date (days hence)
A	3	6
B	6	10
C	2	9
D	4	7
E	1	2

Determine the proper job sequence using each of the following prioritizing rules: FCFS, SPT, EDD, and LS. For each solution, compute the average throughput time, the average number of jobs in the work center, and the average late time.

13. The following data apply to three shop orders that happen to end up in the same work center on day 120:

Shop Order	Preceding Work Center	Completion Date (day moved to next work center)	Next (current) Work Center	Queue Time plus Run Time in Work Center 17	Date Due Out of Work Center 17
300	28	119	17	3 days	122
310	14	117	17	2 days	123
290	13	118	17	1 day	121

Moves from one work center to another take virtually no time. Calculate operation slack for the three jobs, and arrange them in priority order, first to last.

14. On day 12, shop order number 222 is in the blanking work center; it requires two days in blanking (including all waits, setups, moves, etc.) and is due out of blanking on day 15. Also on day 12, shop order 333 is in the same work center; it requires three days in blanking and is due out on day 17. Finally, on day 12, shop order 444 is in the work center; it requires one day and is due out on day 12.

    Determine which order should be run first, which second, and which third. Calculate slack for each order to prove your answer. What is the meaning of the slack value you get for order 444?

15. For *a*, *b*, and *c*, explain the applicability and describe a suitable approach to (1) scheduling, (2) dispatching, including a priority control rule, and (3) expediting.

a. Getting a driver's license, four stops: written test, driving test, photo, and payment of fee and receipt of license.

b. Getting your car repaired at a large auto dealer: wheel alignment, electrical system, and installation of a new bumper.

c. Manufacturing of a wide variety of models of metal office furniture, all models passing through four manufacturing areas: metal shop for cutting and forming the component parts, welding, painting, and final assembly.

16. A central sales office has seen its expediting (hand-carried orders) increase from 2 to 5 to over 10 percent in the last two years. Nonexpedited orders take at least a week to be processed. Suggest improvements in the priority and order-processing system.

17. The city planning department processes all requests for building and construction permits. The permit process, involving eight departments, has been unsatisfactory, and the mayor has appointed a new planning department administrator, who has stated his intention to install a computer system for logging and tracking the flow of all orders. The assistant administrator is arguing against the plan. She says it will be costly, add no value, and may not work. Elaborate upon her argument, including suggestions for an alternative approach.

CASE STUDY

5 MINUTES, $5—SEAFIRST BANK

We know your time is valuable. That's why we guarantee you won't wait in a teller line for more than five minutes. If you do, we'll give you either $5 cash or a coupon redeemable for $5.

That message is posted beside a clock where customers line up at each of the 270-odd branches of Seafirst Bank. (See Exhibit CS14–1; it shows Seafirst's quick service guarantee.)

Terry Mix, executive vice president and head of branch banking, recalls how it all came about in 1989. The inspiration came from then-CEO Luke Helms, "a visionary" who now heads all 2,000 branches of the Bank of America located in 10 states. (Seafirst is a Bank of America subsidiary.) Helms directed that Seafirst change to "a retail focus and a service product." He hand-picked a steering committee of about 12 people who developed the plan

EXHIBIT CS14–1

Customer Waiting for a Teller beside a "5-Minute Service" Clock

over a two-week period of "day-and-night" sessions. Mix, then a regional manager, was one of the 12. The committee's recommendations were fourfold:

1. 24-hour phone access to a centralized customer service department.
2. Saturday banking.
3. Open until 6 PM.
4. 5 minutes, $5.

Helms approved the recommendations, but wanted a name for it. The steering committee spent all night on the matter and came up with it: Excel Service. It took only a few weeks to put Excel Service into effect. Implementation involved nearly every Seafirst manager and staff professional. Saturday banking, open until 6 PM, and the $5 promise went into effect on March 1, 1989. Twenty-four-hour phone service, requiring extensive computer software development, went on-line on the same date. Seafirst's central computer system provides database and processing for the entire Excel Service program. It includes an IBM 3090 class mainframe, driving an Olivetti proprietary server, linked by a local area network to all the branch bank teller stations. The server uses a Unix operating system with all data written to mirrored disks, which provides full recovery if one disk is down. If the mainframe or network goes down, the server can still process transactions, but without access to the database.

Of Excel's four elements, the fourth is unique. The remainder of this case study concerns just that element.

Question 1. Assess Seafirst's approach to designing and implementing the new service package.

5 Minutes, $5—How Does It Work?

Terry Mix was asked how the branches are able to hold down the $5 payouts, given the volatility of demand (customer arrivals). "For one thing," Mix explained, "the information systems department uses a historical forecasting model. Every branch's transactions with a customer are tied to IS's central computers. So a computer database keeps track of all customer arrival/service patterns." Each week the computer prints a histogram report of the branch's transaction activity for the previous week. The service manager at a branch can staff accordingly, bringing in extra staff from a pool of casual employees when needed. "But, of course," Mix added, "sometimes a whole busload of customers will arrive at a branch. What do we do then? We pay."

Joe Zavaglia, senior vice president and manager of Seafirst's 36 Metropolitan District (which includes 36 branches), was asked the same question. Zavaglia also mentioned the monthly report, which lists average customer arrivals hour by hour for each day of the

5 Minutes, $5: Origins

Betty Lattie, senior vice president and manager of Corporate Affairs at Seafirst, traces the 5 minutes, $5 idea to her former employer, San Francisco's Wells Fargo Bank, in 1987. A Wells Fargo engineer directed the implementation, which took nearly a year. He taught queuing theory to managers in all the branches. Then he devised a method of collecting data on customer waiting times: The last person in line gets a slip of paper with the current time on it and turns it in to the teller, who time-stamps it. Knowledge of queuing theory, plus the data on actual customer waiting, helped the $5 program gain acceptance.

week. But the key is Seafirst's customer service managers, one for each branch bank, who get to know their markets and schedule employees accordingly.

In his experience, Zavaglia noted, "It takes four to six months for a new customer service manager to become familiar enough with the market to reduce $5 payments." One time, in reviewing a monthly report, he noticed high payouts for one of the branches, even though the manager had been there quite a while. Zavaglia asked for an hour-by-hour, day-by-day listing of customer activity along with $5 payments. It showed that the problem was poor staff scheduling. Joe went over the listing with the manager, who changed the way she had been scheduling. Soon the payouts dropped down to normal.

In Zavaglia's metropolitan district, however, payouts are sometimes hard to avoid. "Noncustomers, [e.g., homeless or jobless people] have sometimes been a problem," Zavaglia stated. "A group who just received their welfare checks might head for a Seafirst bank together and overload the tellers to get their $5. I've overhead people in the teller lines saying, Well, where will we eat today [on our $5], Burger King or McDonald's?" In one case, in the Broadway district, an item in an alternative newspaper said "go get your $5 from Seafirst bank." Someone posted the item on a signboard, and the rush was on.

Seafirst's payout method is to give the customer a $5 check. In machine-writing the check, the teller captures the date, time, and customer's name, which go into the bank's database. In contrast, ANZ Bank in Australia credits the customer's account for $5 (Australian). ANZ appears to be the third bank in the world to have a cash payout for waiting. This apparently followed a visit by ANZ representatives to Seafirst in Seattle, which Zavaglia recalls.

Question 2. Which is best, payout by check or payout by crediting a checking account?

Two more Seafirst staff were asked about the $5 payouts: Jill Petkovits, customer-service manager, at the Olive Way branch adjacent to Seattle's main shopping district; and one of her tellers, January Colacurcio. Each branch has one customer-service manager, whose duties include supervising the tellers.

Petkovits had been a customer-service manager for 12 years: 2 years initially, then a few years home with kids, and now back in the bank for the last 10 years. She said that her total staff is composed of five full-time tellers, and five casual staff. "The casuals work two to five days and usually less than 17 hours a week. Mondays and Fridays are busy, so we will have casuals here then." Petkovits said that she reschedules staff every week, one week ahead of time. Schedules are usually set for the week, although sometimes, if someone gets sick, she tries to bring in a casual employee on an unscheduled basis. When asked what she thinks of the 5 minute, $5 program, she replied, "It relieves frustration for the customer."

Colacurcio is full time in the summer and casual, averaging about 20 hours a week, in the school year. She majors in social science–education at the Seattle Pacific University and has been a teller for just over two years. When asked of her impression of the $5 program, Colacurcio said, "Most days I don't pay out at all. Then there might be two or three on the same day. But really it doesn't affect me too much." She was also asked what she and her associates do during lulls when there aren't any customers. "We do catch-up things, like counting and banding bills. If there's time, Jill might have us file signature cards or file microfiche."

While waiting for a lull to talk to Petkovits and Colacurcio, the casewriter thought, at one point, that the customer queue had grown to where payouts would surely be necessary. Zavaglia counted 11 customers and four tellers and stated that payouts were not likely. His rule of thumb: three customers or less in line for every teller is adequate. To check, Zavaglia timed the last person in line, a woman wearing a billed cap. She made it to a teller in about three minutes.

Question 3. What principle(s) does the $5 program follow? Explain.

Measuring Customer Service

The whole reason for the $5 program is to improve customer service, which Joe Zavaglia says is a rather new concern in banking; "Before about six years ago, banks didn't measure customer service. Now we evaluate our tellers, who have 80–90 percent of client contact, on three main factors:

1. *Balancing.* They self-balance, and also are evaluated on this by the customer-service manager.

2. *Good customer service.* Outside shoppers—from an outside firm called Genesis—rate their experiences with the tellers. They do this about every 90 days for large branches, and every six months for smaller ones. In addition, on a monthly basis Seafirst sends out customer survey forms to a random sample of new accounts.

3. *Referrals;* that is, referring customers to other Seafirst services, such as its bill-payer service ("Did you know you could do this by phone?"). The customer-service manager evaluates each teller on this factor.

Zavaglia sees structural changes at Seafirst as having an impact on service. "Back office clerical work has been centralized. This frees the branches to focus on customer service." On the second floor of the Olive Way branch, where Zavaglia maintains his district offices, "Nineteen years ago there were 120 people. This includes two full-time cooks. Now there are only about 20 people."

Zavaglia has been pleasantly surprised by a side benefit of the $5 program: It provides an objective way to measure customer service (speed of service delivery). "We just look at total amount paid out." He recalls, however, an alternate method of providing fast service, which was used at Security Pacific Bank, his employer before Security merged with Seafirst in April, 1992. The goal was four minutes to see a teller. To help achieve that, "floor managers" walked teller lines at busy times. They asked people in line if they had their checks or deposit slips made out and so forth, which then speeded up service delivery at the teller windows.

Question 4. Compare the effectiveness of measuring customer service by total amounts paid out versus outside shoppers and customer surveys. Compare, also, the $5 payout method versus the floor manager method.

Rallies

Zavaglia notes that his metropolitan region differs from Seafirst's other regions in one notable respect: much greater cultural diversity. This makes customer service a particularly interesting issue for these branches. For example, he explains, "In some cultures making eye contact is bad manners; when we hire from that culture, it then is difficult for that teller to maintain eye contact, which may be perceived poorly by a client from another culture."

To help get his diverse people united, Zavaglia, who has a master's degree in educational psychology, had instituted monthly sales rallies in a large open area outside his second floor office. Those rallies brought all the region's salespeople together for fun, awards, and togetherness.

One customer-service manager said, "Why not do this for the rest of us?" Zavaglia thought it was a great idea. "So we now hold quality rallies for all tellers and customer-service managers and staff every 90 days. We hold them at one of the branches after work. We invite families, too, since some employees must pick up kids from day care centers."

The rallies feature pizza and soft drinks and present four kinds of awards for the quarter:

1. Top balancers—those with a perfect balancing record for the 90-day period.

2. Top service scores.

3. Top referrers—if there has been a new "campaign" (e.g., a new service offered by the bank, such as telephone bill-paying) that clients needed to be aware of.

4. Impact player. Peers select the associate who has had the biggest impact—one for each branch for a total of 36 awards.

"We bring in a guest speaker for each rally. One was [former Seattle SuperSonic basketball player] Freddie Brown. Others include Seafirst's CEO, president, and head of customer service. Having families on hand is important to our people. It's especially meaningful to see a family member receiving an award" in some of the cultures that Seafirst's staff are a part of.

"Historically, this region has had the poorest customer service scores of all of Seafirst's regions [attributed partly to cultural diversity]. Before we started the rallies, our region scored eighth. . . . Now we're ranked third."

Question 5. To what principle(s) do the rallies relate?

For Further Reference

Books

Fitzsimmons, James A., and Robert S. Sullivan, *Service Operations Management*. New York: McGraw-Hill, 1982 (HD9980.5.F55).

Melnyk, Steven A.; Phillip L. Carter; David M. Dilts; and David M. Lyth. *Shop Floor Control*. Burr Ridge, Ill.: Richard D. Irwin, 1985.

Plossl, G. W., and O. W. Wight. *Production and Inventory Control: Principles and Techniques*. Englewood Cliffs, N.J.: Prentice-Hall 1967 (HD55.P5).

Vollmann, Thomas E.; William L. Berry; and D. Clay Whybark. *Manufacturing Planning and Control*, 3d ed. Burr Ridge, Ill.: Richard D. Irwin, 1992 (TS176. V63).

Wight, Oliver W. *Production and Inventory Management in the Computer Age*. Boston: CBI Publishing, 1974 (TS155.W533).

Periodicals/Societies

Decision Sciences (Decision Sciences Institute), an academic journal.

Production and Inventory Management (American Production and Inventory Control Society).

Journal of Operations Management (American Production and Inventory Control Society), an academic journal.

IE Solutions (Institute of Industrial Engineers)

C H A P T E R

MANAGING PROJECTS

15

Chapter Outline

Projects and Strategy
Projects: Vehicles for Improvement
Environmental Impact

Project Management: Teamwork and
Organization
High-Performance Teamwork
Project Organization Structures
Information Sharing

Project Representation
Work Breakdown Structure
Network

Phased PERT/CPM
Project Planning and Sequencing
Time Estimating and Critical Path
Project Scheduling
Reporting and Updating
Fitting PERT/CPM to the Situation

Continuous Improvement in Projects
*Network Simulation and the Always-
Late Syndrome*
Combating Project Uncertainty

"Concorde was the first of an important new breed of aerospace projects: those built through international cooperation [i.e., Britain and France, 1962–1973]. It was a huge technology-push 'spearhead' project, whose basic requirement was simply to carry passengers safely and supersonically. Its development represented a continual struggle to reconcile two entirely different requirements: sustained supersonic flight and subsonic approach. Its cost escalation and schedule delays were huge. This occasioned much public criticism and governmental chagrin. The British governmental psyche was so traumatized that its response to suggestions for high-risk major projects for many decades subsequently was invariably one of nervous disinclination.

"In the end, Concorde proved to be a commercial disaster for its developers . . . a technological triumph yet a plane designed on the massive misconception that speed was the principal criterion for airliner success; an aircraft project that was set up with no regard to the most basic rules of project management, such as a clearly identified owner organization, and one which experienced severe problems of design and technology mismanagement; a project whose chances of success were severely compromised by the two external factors of changes in fuel prices and environmental opposition."[1]

The opening comments on the Concorde come from Peter Morris in his 1994 masterwork, *The Management of Projects*. Morris calls the discipline "deceptively simple."

545

It is, he says, "*integrating* everything that needs to be done (typically utilizing a number of special project management tools and techniques) as the project evolves through its *life cycle* in order to ensure that all objectives are achieved."[2] He notes, however, that while project management "is now comparatively mature, and recognized by thousands if not millions of managers as vitally important, it is in many respects still stuck in a 1960s time warp." By that, Morris means that practitioners and academics mostly take a tools and techniques view of the subject. "Few address the larger, more strategic issues that crucially affect the success of projects."[3]

project Large-scale, one-of-a-kind endeavor; employs large amounts of diverse resources.

This third and concluding chapter in our study of types of OM environments examines the complex, unique nature of projects. We shall consider, in order, six aspects of effective project management:

1. Strategic implications of projects.
2. High-performance project teams.
3. Project organization structures.
4. Information sharing.
5. Tools and techniques.
6. Combating project complexity.

Projects and Strategy

Morris's assessment of the current lack of strategic focus in much of project management is noteworthy on two fronts: First, contemporary organizations have a crucial need for projects *as vehicles* for accomplishing strategic objectives. Second, failure to consider the overall strategic impact of a particular project on the organization's environment is nothing short of negligence, especially in this era of heightened social awareness of corporate conduct.

Projects: Vehicles for Improvement

Numerous large-scale activities that successful companies must pursue in order to meet strategic objectives call for project management. Projects demand large resource inputs, they incorporate countless value-adding operations, and their effects (ought to) cut wide swaths across organization departments.

For example, we recall a point from Chapter 3's discussion of benchmarking: Robert Camp identifies the targets of process-based benchmarking as business-wide processes that contribute most to company goals.[4] Camp goes on to list an array of 28 tools and techniques, old and new, that Xerox uses in its 10-step benchmarking efforts. Project management—the only technique to span all 10 steps—ties the whole system together.[5] ISO 9000 registration is another popular, large-scale effort of widespread organizational impact; it, too, demands project management (see the Into Practice box, "Project Management Applied. . .").

Later in this chapter, we consider a small-scale construction example, and in Chapter 4, we examined issues relating to product design and development. We could also make strong cases for project management in many other facets of contemporary operations management: developing quick-response systems

Project Management Applied—ISO 9000 Registration

Skillful management of a project—that's what ISO 9000-series registration is all about. AT&T Global Information Systems' Network Products Division achieved ISO 9001 registration in 13 months after approval of its registration project plan.

Addressing the early planning stages, David S. Huyink, project manager of the AT&T effort, and Craig Westover, who conducted the project's early benchmarking efforts, contend that ISO 9000 project planning must put a ". . . boundary around the process. . . . your documented project plan defines the system. It defines the output (ISO 9000 registration), it defines the process (the actions the organization must take to achieve registration), and it defines the input (the resources required to support the necessary and sufficient actions)."

Source: David Stevenson Huyink and Craig Westover, *ISO 9000: Motivating the People, Mastering the Process, Achieving Registration!* (Burr Ridge, Ill.: Irwin Professional Publishing, 1994), pp. 52 and 280.

(Chapter 8), supplier partnership networks (Chapter 9), quick-changeover projects (Chapter 11), and facility and process re-layout efforts (Chapter 12). In sum, whenever the task at hand is relatively large, complex, or inclusive, operations managers and their colleagues throughout the firm ought to be thinking project.

Environmental Impact

Projects are expensive; they're big and they invite internal and external scrutiny. Inside the organization, favorite projects can get the lion's share of resources; employees not on a high-impact project team may feel slighted, perhaps with good reason. Early in the project planning sequence, managers must ask, How will this project affect the organization as a whole? External scrutiny occurs when outsiders ask similar questions about the project's impact beyond the organization's boundaries.

Like the MRP systems discussed in Chapter 10, project management tools (considered later in this chapter) are products of the computer era, with formative development paralleling the rise of business computing in the 1960s. Morris observes that many of these early (1960s) projects experienced difficulties because interest was drawn to the excitement of developing the computer tools. Little attention went to management issues like technical uncertainly and contract strategy, or to the emergence of a new class of external factors such as community opposition and environmental impact.[6]

But after a decade or so, evidence suggesting the need for a broader outlook by project managers had begun to accumulate. Morris notes:

The projects of the early-to-mid-1970s were in fact pointing to a much fuller view of projects management, i.e., that

(a) The impact of projects on their environment is an essential dimension of their chances of success.

(b) This "environmental" impact is measured along several dimensions—economic, political, community, ecological.

(c) Therefore, those responsible for the initiation or accomplishment of such projects should strive to influence the project's chances of success along these "external" environmental dimensions, as well as ensuring that the internal project management functions are being carried out effectively.[7]

By the 1980s, large-scale growth in the project form of management in most companies stretched experienced project managers and their tools thin. As a result, project management is back in the limelight in the research community, as well as in the business world. Main advances lie not so much in tools and techniques as in strategies, organization, and human resource management. These developments may still be midstream. However, many companies have measurably improved their project management processes—enough so, for example, to have cut average project completion times by half or more. While the full story of project management effectiveness probably has not yet been written, we spell out what we know of it in the rest of the chapter.

Project Management: Teamwork and Organization

As in many other aspects of operations management, high-performance teamwork deserves a prominent place in effective project management. Teamwork performance, in turn, is affected by how the project is organized and by the flow of information.

High-Performance Teamwork

*P*RINCIPLE 1:

Team up with next and final customer.

Coincident with increasing reliance on projects to carry out company strategies, more and more people appear to be spending more and more time in project work. That includes early and continuing involvement of people who formerly had late involvement or no involvement in new-product projects: suppliers; customers; quality specialists; equipment, tool, and materials people; front-line supervisors and associates; and others. Including these people greatly improves the quality of project outcomes, especially if they collect data on mishaps and hold team meetings to improve processes and prevent the mishaps from happening again. Improved project quality is reflected by less project rework and scrap, in addition to speeding up project completion.

While broad representation on project teams is desirable, more people working more hours on a single project may not necessarily lead to quicker project completion time (see the Into Practice box, "The More the Messier").

The diverse members of the project team may split their time and allegiance between the project and their functional organization unit. For example, an accountant may handle accounts receivable most of the time, but help the project team with cost estimating, as needed. Associates in operations may attend some project meetings to look for operational weaknesses of the proposed design, but spend most of their working hours on the front lines.

Project Organization Structures

Amount of time that people spend on projects versus working in their functional departments is partly determined by positioning in the organization. The extent of project emphasis in the organization structure can range from zero to total. Three degrees of project organization are shown in Exhibit 15–1, numbered 1 through 3;

𝒥nto 𝒫ractice

The More the Messier

Marvin Patterson, director of corporate engineering at Hewlett-Packard Company, offers evidence on the drawbacks of having too many people on a project team:

> We observed this. . . in the completion of two projects sequentially. [The first was] a project requiring 127 new mechanical parts [and] six mechanical engineers over a period of three years. In a follow-up project, a low-cost roll of the same product, the task was to reduce the number of

mechanical parts by two-thirds, thereby reducing the manufacturing costs. That job took 17 [mechanical engineers] four years. What happened? When we asked, the answer came back, "We had so many meetings, we had to talk so much to coordinate the design over 17 people, that the communications burden became onerous."

Source: Marvin L. Patterson with Sam Lightman, *Accelerating Innovation: Improving the Process of Product Development* (New York: Van Nostrand Reinhold, 1993), pp. 184–85 (TS176.P.367).

they are flanked by two nonproject forms, numbered 0 and 00. The five structures are explained below.

0. *Pure functional organization.* In this structure there is no project activity; everyone in every functional department is engaged in ongoing operations. In some slow-to-change organizations, such as a government agency out of the public eye or a monopolistic business in a remote area, this lack of projects (other than occasional renovation and remodeling) may persist for years.

1. *Project coordinator.* This is the weakest approach to project management: A coordinator has a short-term assignment but no project budget or staff. The project coordinator's limited activities revolve around arranging meetings, working out schedules, and expediting. The effective coordinator tries to achieve teamwork by working closely with liaison people in the functional organization, where the real power rests.

2. *Product/commodity/brand manager or project engineer.* This second project form involves a career-track manager or engineer, sometimes with a small staff and limited budgetary authority. Responsibility is for an evolving product family (e.g., commercial loans), brand (e.g., Yellow Pages), or succession of small engineering projects (e.g., civil engineering/construction). To be effective, the management or project engineering team must develop and work closely with a cohesive processing team of associates from the functional base, where most of the work is performed.

3. *Autonomous project management team.* Here, the project manager has money to hire a full team out of the functional base or from outside the firm to perform the work in its own space with its own equipment and other resources. The project manager is usually a high-level person who may even outrank the functional managers. Newer versions of this form of project management have been called "tiger" or "bandit" teams because of their aggressive, focused approach and disregard for practices standard in the rest of the firm. After completion of the project, the team disbands or its members join new project teams.

Exhibit 15–1

Project Management Organization Structures

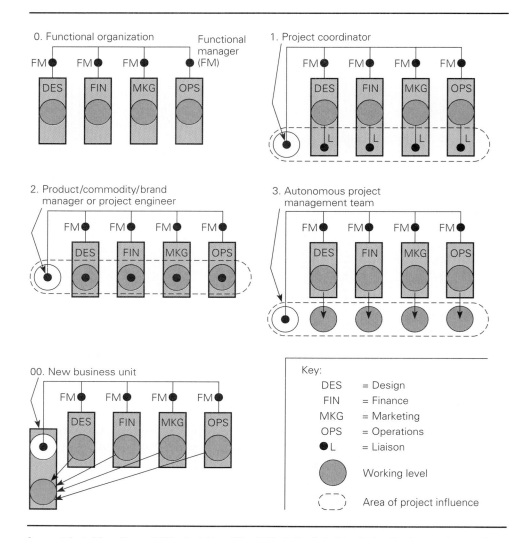

0. Functional organization

1. Project coordinator

2. Product/commodity/brand manager or project engineer

3. Autonomous project management team

00. New business unit

Key:

DES	= Design
FIN	= Finance
MKG	= Marketing
OPS	= Operations
●L	= Liaison

Working level

Area of project influence

Source: Adapted from Steven C. Wheelwright and Kim B. Clark, *Revolutionizing Product Development: Quantum Leaps in Speed, Efficiency, and Quality* (New York: The Free Press, 1992), p. 191 (HF5415.153.W44).

> 00. *New business unit.* Occasionally a super project is established as, or grows into, a separate division or business unit. In effect, it becomes a minicompany. As such, it may devolve into an ordinary functional organization, with no special project emphasis.

The three project management types in Exhibit 15–1 are general categories, not an exhaustive list. There are other ways to organize, staff, and fund projects, and many companies devise their own variations. See, for example, Chaparral Steel's three approaches (Into Practice box), which are variants of the three project management forms in Exhibit 15–1.

Any form of project management can greatly benefit from high-performance teamwork. However, a weak project structure can make that teamwork more difficult. A very strong project structure, such as the autonomous form in Exhibit 15–1, might seem to be synonymous with a high degree of teamwork. Not

$\mathscr{I}$nto $\mathscr{P}$ractice

Three Types of Projects—Chaparral Steel

Wheelwright and Clark's research suggests that most companies force-fit a standard approach to all projects, which leads to underpowered big projects and overkilled small ones. Chaparral Steel (which appears often on lists of world-class companies) avoids these problems by having three different project management approaches:

- Incremental projects in the $100,000 to $200,000 cost range lasting about two months. These projects (40 or more likely to be in progress on average) are performed by functional subgroups and a lightweight project manager.
- Platform projects in the $500,000 to $1 million range requiring 12–24 months to complete. These

projects (three to five under way on average) are led by heavyweight project managers, who usually have moved from a department head position and will return to that position after project completion.
- Major advanced-development projects in the $3 million to $5 million expenditure range requiring three to five years to complete. These projects (usually only about two in progress at any given time) are led by one of seven general foremen.

Source: Adapted from Steven C. Wheelwright and Kim B. Clark, *Revolutionizing Product Development: Quantum Leaps in Speed, Efficiency, and Quality* (New York: The Free Press 1992), pp. 216–17 (HF5415.153.W44).

so. That form has long been common in defense and aerospace; nevertheless, in most cases managers divided up most of the work by functional specialty. Projects proceeded slowly one stage at a time instead of simultaneously using cohesive teams. The influence of total quality management may be instrumental in correcting this weakness.

Project teams organized in any of the project management forms in Exhibit 15–1 may look outside the firm for team members. Outside teams could include fully staffed supplier or customer projects; for best results, the inside project group should establish cross-memberships with the outside project teams.

An excellent example of a company that gets maximum service from outside project teams is McDonald's Corporation. Out of a long string of McDonald's products that met its requirements for quality, speed, efficiency, production in a squeezed space, popularity, and profit, only one, the Quarter Pounder, was developed by an inside project team. All the rest were developed by franchised restaurant owners (the customers of McDonald's Corp.) and hard-charging, innovative suppliers.

One of McDonald's successes, Chicken McNuggets, was launched in 1980. The basic nuggets idea emerged after an inside project team had spent 10 years working toward a chicken product. But the nuggets still had to be developed. Bud Sweeney, an account executive at Gorton's (the frozen fish company) came to the rescue. On loan from Gorton's, Sweeney organized and led a chicken SWAT team (like a tiger team), which found help from several sources. Gorton's provided the unique tempura coating. McDonald's product development and quality assurance people handled specifications and test marketing. A chef on loan from a Chicago hotel came up with four dips. Keystone Foods, a frozen beef patty supplier, developed production lines to debone chicken and equipment to cut it into random-looking chunks. And Tyson Foods, a chicken processor, developed a special new breed of bird, called Mr. McDonald, that was almost twice the weight of an ordinary fryer, which made deboning easier.[8]

Information Sharing

Members of the project team can do little without information, which may be likened to raw materials in a factory. However, sharing information goes against the grain of most people in Western cultures. An individualistic attitude prevails: "My expertise, my experience, and my information is my strength, and I'll keep it for myself".

While we applaud the Western spirit of individualism—a healthful source of innovation—we do not want team members to withhold information from other team members. Information is power, and project teams with wide access to information, including each other's, are powerful and effective.

But what is the mechanism for pulling knowledge out of people's heads, personal files, desk drawers, and other hiding places? Can the Far East, where the culture is group oriented instead of individualistic, provide answers? Perhaps so. Jeffrey Funk details systematic procedures for information sharing at Mitsubishi Electric Company in Japan, based upon his two-year assignment working as a project engineer at that company.[9] Every scrap of information gleaned from visits to libraries, customers, trade shows, conferences, committee meetings, and so forth, is required to be written up and inserted into common files, fully cross referenced. Newly hired engineers at Mitsubishi spend a good deal of their orientation period getting to know the filing system and the rules for its use.

Principle 3:

Gain unified purpose via shared information.

Once such a system is established, it is easy for its users to identify anyone who fails to feed it. Peer pressure can shape behaviors for the common good. The box, "Ownership of Information," sums up these points about team ownership of information in contrast to private ownership.

At Mitsubishi, the information generally went into common file cabinets. The concept applies equally well to computer files. Patterson describes a project team at three geographically disbursed Hewlett-Packard sites: Waldbronn, Germany; Avondale, Pennsylvania; and Palo Alto, California. Each group was working on different parts of an operating system software project.

> The Palo Alto group agreed to maintain the current version of the total operating system and make it remotely accessible to the other sites through a WAN [wide-area network]. The next version. . . would then. . . be made available for remote access. Within minutes both the Avondale and Waldbronn teams would have the current system running at their sites, and development could continue with all teams once again synchronized. This development effort progressed well and resulted in a successful product.
>
> In contrast, an earlier effort, before the age of WANs, attempted. . . the same thing through shipment of magnetic tapes. Shipment delays and time lost passing through customs hampered engineering efforts immensely. Engineers in the three sites were

Contrast

Ownership of Information

Private Property

Task-related information retained by the holder of the position in the holder's personal space. Experience and training belong to the individual.

Team Ownership

Task-related information, experience, and training belong to the team and the company and should reside in files easily accessible to all team members.

only rarely working with the same version of the operating system. Often as not, recently designed code would prove to be incompatible with operating system updates that had been two weeks or more in transit.[10]

The information sharing referred to so far is mainly what is used to create project outcomes: raw and semifinished information transformed by the project team into completed software, product designs, process specifications, architectural plans, and so forth. Besides the *operating information*, the project group must manage project *planning and control information*, our next topic.

Project Representation

The size and complexity of project operations translate into a sizable project management task. A set of tools and techniques having the abbreviations CPM and PERT is tailor-made for the job.

The **critical path method (CPM)** was developed by Catalytic Construction Company in 1957 as a method for improving planning and control of a project to construct a plant for Du Pont Corporation. CPM was credited with having saved time and money on that project, and today it is well known and widely used in the construction industry.

The **program evaluation and review technique (PERT)** was developed in 1958 by Booz Allen & Hamilton Inc., a large consulting firm, along with U.S. Navy Special Projects Office. PERT was developed to provide more intensive management of the Polaris missile project—one of the largest research and development projects ever undertaken. Nevertheless, it was completed in record time, about four years. PERT got much of the credit and soon was widely adopted in the R&D industry as a tool for intensive project management.

A few early differences between CPM and PERT have mostly disappeared, and it is convenient to think of PERT and CPM as being one and the same, going by the combined term PERT/CPM. The construction industry still calls it CPM, and R&D people, PERT; a few other terminological differences are noted later.

PERT/CPM begins with the work breakdown structure and the network, graphical models that represent (model or mimic) the project itself.

Work Breakdown Structure

The **work breakdown structure** is for a project what the bill of materials is for a job. It is a representation of the building-block structure of the end product: major project modules, secondary components, and so on. To illustrate, we shall use a familiar example: home construction. We'll make it a luxury home, since building ordinary houses is so routine as to be more like repetitive than project operations.

A work breakdown structure for building a house is shown in Exhibit 15–2. Part A is a preferred way to develop a work breakdown structure; the planning team breaks down the project into tangible ends or outputs at levels 2 and 3. Part B is a functional-oriented way to draw it that is not recommended. The functional-oriented chart does not have tangible products whose completion may be assigned as a unit to a single manager or team. Carpentry, for example, is a function that results in several tangible outcomes: forms for footings, the house's frame, finished cabinets, and so forth. Painting, landscaping, and masonry also are found throughout the project and also result in several clearly identifiable outcomes. When the project

EXHIBIT 15–2

Work Breakdown Structures for a House-Building Project

A. Recommended: Output-oriented work breakdown structure

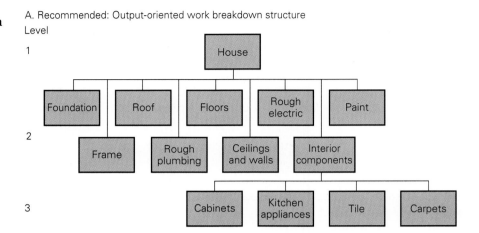

B. Not recommended: Functional-oriented work breakdown structure

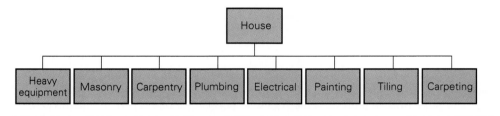

𝒫RINCIPLE 1:

Know the customer.

is delayed or resources are idled, painters can conveniently blame carpenters, and so forth. If managers supervise given parts of the *project,* instead of each craft or function, the managers may work to secure cooperation from the various crafts. The idea is to get each craft closely connected to a customer, the next craft, in a joint effort to complete a segment of the house correctly with no delays or wasted resources.

Network

A project consists of dozens, or even hundreds or thousands, of related tasks that must be performed in some sequence. PERT/CPM requires the sequence to be carefully defined in the form of a project **network** (see Exhibit 15–3). The starting and ending nodes of the network are joined by a series of arrows and intermediate nodes that collectively reveal the sequence and relationships of the project tasks.

Networks facilitate project management in at least two ways. First, the immensity of most projects makes it hard to remember and visualize the day-to-day and task-level activities, but a computerized network model remembers with ease. Second, the network aids in managing a large project as a system, consisting of subprojects (subsystems), sub-subprojects, and so on. For example, two of the successive nodes in Exhibit 15–3 could represent the start and end nodes of a subproject, for which a separate, more detailed network could be drawn. Alternatively, the network in Exhibit 15–3 might represent one subproject in an even larger project.

Although networks are valuable project management tools, they must be kept in perspective. First, as the project unfolds, initial planning networks go by the wayside; in large projects, hundreds of network changes can occur every month.

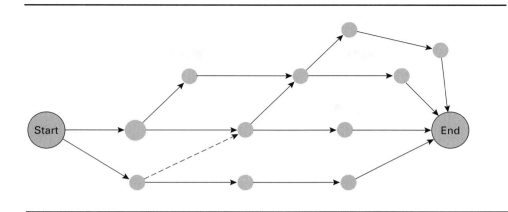

EXHIBIT 15–3
**A PERT/CPM
Network**

Second, just as forecasts are more dubious for distant time periods, time estimates and even sequencing for distant network activities are at best educated guesses. Detailed analysis of an initial planning network—especially of its latter portions—is often unwarranted. Drawing again from the work of Morris:

> One pattern that has emerged for virtually all projects is that once "downstream implementation" begins—after project definition is basically completed and contracts for implementation are let—the amount of work and management control and coordination will increase substantially.[11]

This shift from planning to control and coordination puts project managers in the driver's seat. If they don't like what the network shows about the project status, they shuffle resources or acquire new ones to move the project in a direction more to their liking. After all, they're managing the project, not the network.

Phased PERT/CPM

Once the project team gets the PERT/CPM models built, members may use the models for capacity planning, task sequencing, projecting completions, identifying most-critical tasks, simulating project change alternatives, scheduling, and controlling. These multiple uses of PERT/CPM tend to group into four phases of project management:

1. *Project planning and sequencing.* Activities in this phase resemble product/service design, process planning, and routing activities in repetitive and job operations.
2. *Time estimating and path analysis.* Time estimating for projects is like time estimating for job operations, but path analysis is unique to project management.
3. *Project scheduling.* Scheduling projects has some elements of both repetitive and job scheduling. But since a project is a single complex endeavor, schedulers must contend with many scheduling dependencies.
4. *Reporting and updating.* Treating the project as a single, large unit of work permits project managers to intensively control using the management-by-exception principle.

management-by-exception Tightly manage what is straying off course—the exceptions—and ignore the rest.

When the team employs all four phases, PERT/CPM is more than just tools and techniques. It becomes a management system, with each of the four phases as subsystems. While most projects are not complex enough to warrant the expense of the full system treatment, very large scale projects often qualify. We examine each of the four subsystems next.

Project Planning and Sequencing

In the first subsystem, the project management staff holds meetings with those who will be carrying out the project tasks. Together, in one set of meetings, they develop the work breakdown structure; from that, in a second set of meetings, they complete the network. Using the work breakdown structure of Exhibit 15–2 as our example, we'll proceed with the second set of meetings of the project staff and front-line construction people.

Task Lists, Network Segments, and Whole Networks.   Exhibit 15–4 shows how the project staff gets started on network development: Starting with one of the bottom-level elements of the work breakdown structure, they ask the front-line experts to make lists of tasks necessary to complete the element. Part A shows three of the project elements (cabinets, kitchen appliances, and tile) with tasks listed underneath each. Connecting the tasks into a logical sequence, forming a network segment as shown in Part B, is next. Kitchen wall cabinets go up early, since they are easier to install if the lower cabinets are not in the way. Floor cabinets are installed with gaps for the range and dishwasher, which are put in place next. Kitchen tile is laid after the kitchen cabinet and appliances have been installed; if laid sooner, the tile might not butt closely against the cabinets and appliances and also might get marred. Bathroom tile follows the bathroom vanity for the same reason. Since there appears to be no reason why the hood/fan and the hall tile should come either before or after the other tasks shown, the project staff temporarily draws them unlinked to other tasks. Later, when they put the full network together, they'll find the logical place in which to fit the hood/fan and hall tile.

The rectangles numbered 1, 2, and 3 in Exhibit 15–4B are not essential; they merely show craft groupings. Later, during scheduling, each craft may use Gantt charts to show when its project tasks occur. Note that it would serve no purpose to group all kitchen activities together, all bathroom activities together, and so forth; the kitchen is a room, but it is neither a product to be separately managed nor the responsibility of a separate craft. More important than the craft groupings in the rectangles are the dashed lines between the rectangles. They signify connections between the task of one craft and the task of the following craft.

Finally, the project staff combines the network segments into the full project network. Exhibit 15–5 is the result, except that, for study purposes, we've simplified it; for example, this house has no tile, carpets, or bathroom vanity. This completes the first subsystem. The project management staff has a reasonable representation of the sequence of project activities. It is a useful tool for coordinating and monitoring completions.

Networking Conventions.   A few rules and conventions of networking follow.

1. *One destination.* A PERT/CPM network (except segments) has only one start event and one end event. (In Exhibit 15–5, these are numbered 1 and 18.) To bring this about, all arrows must progress toward the end, and there can be no doubling

EXHIBIT 15–4

**Translating Task
Lists into
Network
Segments**

A. Task lists for project elements

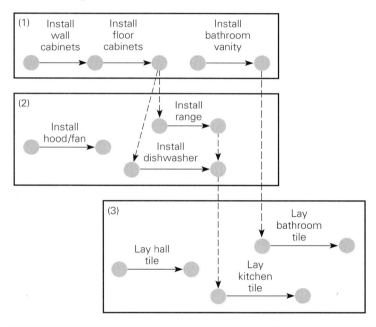

Cabinets (1)	Kitchen appliances (2)	Tile (3)

Install kitchen
wall cabinets
Install kitchen
floor cabinets
Install bathroom
vanity

Install range
Install dishwasher
Install hood/fan

Lay kitchen tile
Lay bathroom tile
Lay hall tile

B. Network segments

(1) Install wall cabinets — Install floor cabinets — Install bathroom vanity

(2) Install hood/fan   Install range   Install dishwasher

(3) Lay hall tile   Lay bathroom tile   Lay kitchen tile

Source: Adapted from Fred Luthans, *Introduction to Management: A Contingency Approach* (Richard J. Schonberger, contributing author) (New York: McGraw-Hill, 1976), p. 88 (HD31.L86). Used with permission.

back or loops. (However, doubling back and loops *are* allowed in a variation called graphical evaluation and review technique, or GERT.) Exhibit 15–6 shows those two no-no's. In large networks, it is common to make a few such errors inadvertently—for example, an arrowhead carelessly placed at the wrong end of a line. That results in wrong data on computer records. Most PERT/CPM computer packages detect such errors and print error messages.

2. *Event completion.* A network *event* stands for the completion of all activities leading into it. Further, in PERT/CPM logic, no activity may begin at an event until all activities leading into that event have been completed. For example, consider event 8 in Exhibit 15–5, completion of rough electrical and plumbing, plus cooling and heating, presumably including an outdoor cooling compressor. We could question that network logic because it says that the next activity (after event 8),

event (node) Point at which one or more activities (tasks) are completed, and, often, at which others are started; consumes no time or resources but merely marks a key point in time.

Exhibit 15–5   **Network for House Construction**

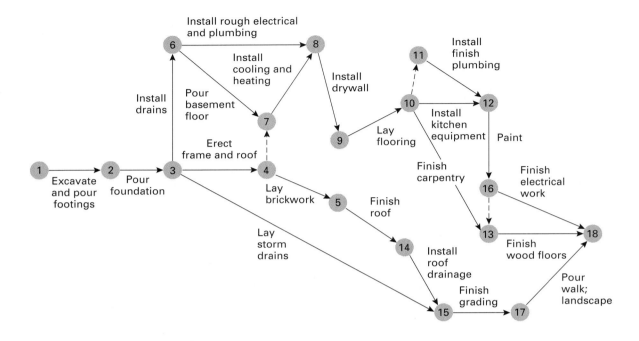

Source: Adapted from Jerome D. Wiest and Ferdinand K. Levy, *A. Management Guide PERT/CPM* (Englewood Cliffs, N.J.: Prentice-Hall, Inc., 1969), p. 16. Used with permission.

install drywall, depends on completion even of the outdoor compressor. In fact, the drywall is intended to cover up only the interior rough work. To reflect that intention, the segment of the network in the event 8 vicinity would need to be drawn differently, with activities relabeled. Since this would make the network more complex, we shall leave it as is.

Let us generalize to make an important point: Network logic should accurately reflect intended project-flow logic! Typically, managers who spend extra time and effort in network creation are rewarded during project implementation.

3. *Dummy activity.* A **dummy activity** is a dashed arrow; it takes no time and

activity (arrow) Basic unit of work in a project.

consumes no resources. Four of the five dummies in Exhibit 15–4 merely connect subnetworks. The project staff will probably omit them when the full network is drawn.

In Exhibit 15–5, two of the three dummies, 4–7 and 16–13, are necessary for project logic. Activity 4–7 is there to ensure that both 3–4 and 6–7 precede 7–8 but that only 3–4 precedes 4–5. The logic is as follows. We want cooling and heating to be installed on top of a basement floor (6–7) and through holes drilled in the frame (3–4). We want brickwork to go up against the frame (3–4), but it need not wait for a basement floor (6–7) to be poured. The dummy, 4–7, decouples the two merging and the two bursting activities to correctly show the logic. There is no other way to show it. Dummy activity 16–13 has the same purpose.

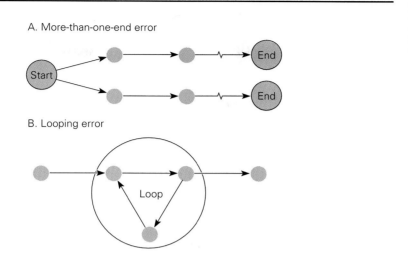

EXHIBIT 15–6
Networking Errors

A. More-than-one-end error

B. Looping error

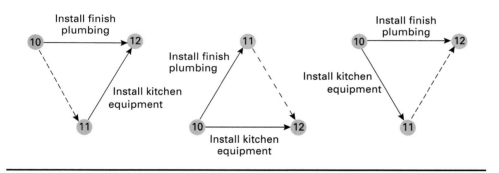

EXHIBIT 15–7
Use of a Dummy Activity

Install finish plumbing

Install kitchen equipment

Install finish plumbing

Install kitchen equipment

Install finish plumbing

Install kitchen equipment

Dummy activity 10–11 exists only to avoid confusing the computer, if the network is computerized. The problem is that two different activities occur between events 10 and 12. In Exhibit 15–5 an extra event (11) creates a dummy activity, 10–11. This ensures that "finish plumbing" and "kitchen equipment" will have unique numbers. Three equivalent ways to do this are shown in Exhibit 15–7.

4. *Event numbering.* Most computer software for PERT/CPM does not require that event numbers go from smaller to larger. Larger to smaller (e.g., 16 to 13 in Exhibit 15–5) is all right, because the *from* event (16) is entered into the predecessor field in the computer record and the *to* event (13) into the successor field. Thus, the computer has no difficulty keeping the sequence straight.

5. *Level of detail.* Every activity in Exhibit 15–5 could be divided into subactivities. In addition to the burden that more activities impose, however, there is no need to plan for a level of detail beyond what a manager would want to control. On the other hand, there should be enough detail to show when one activity should precede another.

6. *Plan versus actual.* The network is only a plan; it is unlikely to be followed exactly. For example, maybe walks and landscapes will get poured (17–18 in Exhibit 15–5) before finish grading (15–17). Or maybe money will run out and

PERT/CPM computer software identifies activities and their sequence by predecessor and successor event numbers—for example, dummy activity 10–11 goes *from* 10 *to* 11.

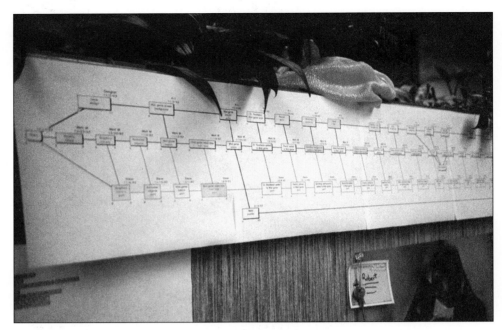

Networks are sometimes used even for small projects in small firms. This one is for a project under development at Bright Star, a 15-person company specializing in children's educational computer software.

Also, activity-oriented networks in this chapter are activity-on-arrow (or on-arc), in which the task is represented by the arrow (arc). Some people prefer activity-on-node networks, in which the node or circle represents the task and the arrow just shows sequence.

finish grading will be cut from the project. Thus, the network is not an imperative, and it is not violated when not followed. The network is just a best estimate of how the project team expects to do the project. A best estimate is far better than no plan at all and can even have value in small projects; see the accompanying photo of a network on display at Bright Star, a division of Sierra On-Line.

Events and Milestones.   Most of the network examples in this chapter are activity oriented. It is a form that front-line people can relate to; that is, it describes the work activities themselves. Upper managers are more interested in completions, or *events,* and an event-oriented network that they can use to review project completions. The project staff creates the event-oriented network from an activity-oriented network.

Exhibit 15–8 shows two forms of event-oriented networks. Exhibit 15–8A is a segment of the construction-project example stated as an event-oriented network. Nodes are drawn large in order to hold event descriptions. Descriptions use present-tense verb forms in activity-oriented networks but past-tense forms in event-oriented networks. For example, "pour basement floor" becomes "basement floor poured" in Exhibit 15–8A. At merge points (nodes where two or more activities converge), the event description can get cumbersome. For example, event 8 is "rough plumbing, cooling, and heating installed."

Networks for big projects may include tens or even hundreds of thousands of events. Upper managers surely do not care to review the project event by event. Instead, project managers commonly create a summary network for upper managers. The summary network may be limited to certain key events, called **milestones.** As an example, events 4 and 10 in Exhibit 15–8B are shown to be a condensation of a five-event segment, events 4–7–8–9–10, from Exhibit 15–8A. The best way to construct a milestone chart is to make milestones out of events that signify the end of major project stages. In house construction, most people would think of completion of framing and completion of rough interior work as major stages; these are milestones 4 and 10 in Exhibit 15–8B.

Some sequential accuracy is lost in condensing a network. For example, milestone event 4 subsumes events 2 and 3 (from Exhibit 15–5). But in cutting out event 3, two branches of the tree at that point—branches 3–6 and 3–15—are unceremoniously chopped off, as shown in the following illustration. From an upper-management perspective, however, the inaccuracy is of little concern.

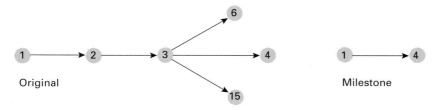

Time Estimating and Critical Path

The second subsystem involves putting time estimates on each network activity so that the project management team can identify critical and slack paths through the network. Critical path activities warrant intensive management; slack path activities usually do not.

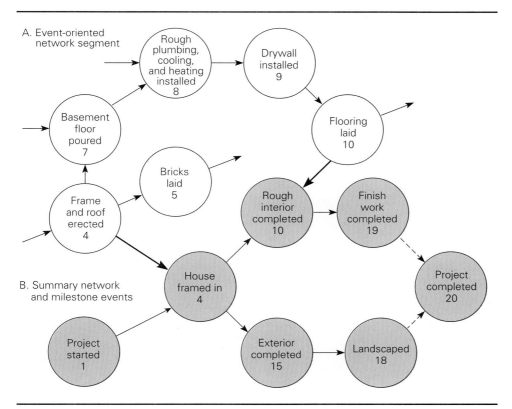

EXHIBIT 15–8

Events and Milestones

Activity Times.   It is harder to accurately estimate times for projects than for repetitive and job operations because of project uncertainly and task variability. Engineered time standards are unlikely for project activities, except for those that tend to recur from project to project. Instead, the project manager obtains technical estimates from those in charge of each project activity.

technical estimate
A type of historical, nonengineered (not carefully defined and timed) time standard; see Chapter 16.

The human tendency to pad time estimates in order to arrive at a more attainable goal is somewhat counteracted in construction projects. Typically, enough experience and historical data exist to keep estimators honest. Unfortunately, that is not always the case with research and development projects.

R&D projects often include advanced, state-of-the-art activities; historical benchmark data are scarce. Because of this, PERT, the R&D-oriented half of PERT/CPM, was originally designed with a special statistically based routine. PERT project managers asked not for one activity time estimate but for three: a most likely, an optimistic, and a pessimistic estimate. Next, the three time estimates were converted into most likely times and variances, and the probability of completing any given event by a given data could be calculated.

As early as 1961, when NASA adopted PERT, it dropped the requirement for three activity time estimates.

The technical logic of the statistical procedure has been confounded in practice by human behavioral tendencies. First, for an activity never done before, it is hard to pry one time estimate out of people, much less three. A request for three estimates may result in drawn-out discussion of the definitions of *most likely*, *optimistic*, and *pessimistic*. Second, the estimators for R&D activities often are scientists, engineers, and other professionals. They tend to be strong-willed and unafraid to withhold their cooperation. If pressed to provide three estimates, they may give meaningless ones such as 5–10–15 or 8–10–12.

For these reasons, the PERT three-time-estimating procedure has mostly fallen into disuse. Today, in both PERT and CPM, a single best estimate is the norm, where *best estimate* is defined simply as how long the activity is expected to take under typical conditions and with normal resources.

Path Analysis.   The most time-consuming path is the **critical path.** The path is time critical because a delay in completing any of its activities delays the whole project; see Into Practice, "Turkey Time." We continue the house construction exercise to demonstrate path criticality.

Turkey Time

John Battle, scion of an Old South political family and holder of a graduate degree in literature, was construction boss of the 62-story AT&T Gateway Tower in Seattle. "Estimates are done in heaven," says Battle. "The project is run in hell."

Battle likens the critical path to the turkey at a Thanksgiving dinner. Almost any other item on the menu can be done too soon, too late, or not at all, and its effect on the dinner will be marginal. But if the turkey gets delayed, so does dinner.

The critical elements on the path toward Gateway's completion included the "digging and pouring of the foundation, erection of the frame, installation of the elevators, application of the granite and glass skin, and. . . the testing of all the electrical, mechanical and safety systems."

Source: Adapted from Terry McDermott, "High Rise: When a Tower Goes Up, Risk Is as Substantial as the Steel Itself," *Sunday Seattle Times and Post-Intelligencer,* March 25, 1990.

EXHIBIT 15–9   Path Analysis

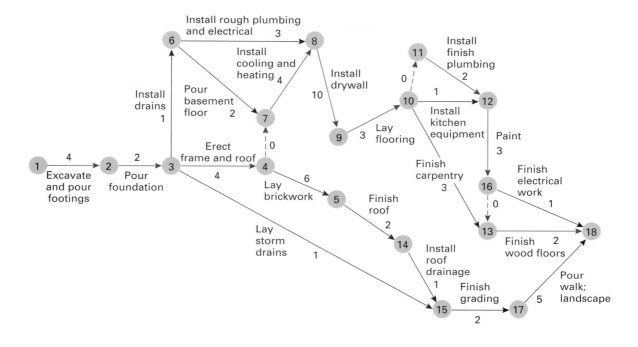

Path Number	Paths	Path Time
1	1–2–3–6–8–9–10–11–12–16–18	29 days
2	1–2–3–6–8–9–10–11–12–16–13–18	30
3	1–2–3–6–8–9–10–12–16–18	28
4	1–2–3–6–8–9–10–12–16–13–18	29
5	1–2–3–6–8–9–10–13–18	28
6	1–2–3–6–7–8–9–10–11–12–16–18	32
7	1–2–3–6–7–8–9–10–11–12–16–13–18	33
8	1–2–3–6–7–8–9–10–12–16–18	31
9	1–2–3–6–7–8–9–10–12–16–13–18	31
10	1–2–3–6–7–8–9–10–13–18	31
11	1–2–3–4–7–8–9–10–11–12–16–18	33
12	1–2–3–4–7–8–9–10–11–12–16–13–18	34
13	1–2–3–4–7–8–9–10–12–16–18	32
14	1–2–3–4–7–8–9–10–12–16–13–18	33
15	1–2–3–4–7–8–9–10–13–18	32
16	1–2–3–4–5–14–15–17–18	26
17	1–2–3–15–17–18	14

Paths 6–11: Nearly critical paths

Path 12: Critical path

Paths 13–15: Nearly critical paths

The house construction network of Exhibit 15–5 is reproduced in Exhibit 15–9, with estimates for each activity added. Path durations are given below the network. Although this network is very small, for illustrative purposes, there are still 17 paths to add up. Computers are efficient at adding path times, and path analysis subroutines are basic in PERT/CPM software.

In the figure, path 12 is critical, at 34 days; it is shown in contrasting color in the network. Several other paths—6, 7, 8, 9, 10, 11, 13, 14, and 15—are nearly critical, at 31 to 33 days. The critical path and nearly critical path activities deserve close managerial attention. Other activities have more slack or float time and need not be managed so closely. The more slack, the more flexibility managers have in scheduling activities.

Activity Slack.   Calculating slack time by comparing the critical path with noncritical paths seems fairly simple, at least in the networks discussed thus far. However, it becomes tedious, even impossible, for larger, more realistic project networks. Consequently, a three-step algorithm has been developed for finding slack time.

First, we continue with our house construction example to gain an intuitive feel for the concept of slack, especially as it pertains to paths and activities. Then, we can use the three-step algorithm to formally calculate slack for activities in a network segment.

In Exhibit 15–9, paths 7, 11, and 14 take 33 days, or 1 day less than the critical path. This means that relative to the critical path, paths 7, 11, and 14 contain a day of slack (in PERT lingo) or float (in CPM lingo). The day of slack applies not to the whole path but just to certain path activities. Consider path 7 first.

Path 7 is identical to critical path 12 except in the segment from event 3 to event 7. The critical path segment from 3 to 4 to 7 takes four days; the slack path segment from 3 to 6 to 7 takes three days. Activities 3–6 and 6–7 are said to have one day of slack. This means that 3–6 or 6–7 (but not both) could be delayed by one day without affecting the planned project duration. By like reasoning, activity 16–18 on path 11 and activity 10–12 on path 14 have a day of slack.

Slack analysis is complicated when an activity is on more than one slack path segment. Activity 3–6, for example, is on slack path segments 3–6–7 and 3–6–8. Segment 3–6–8 takes four days as compared with eight days for critical path segment 3–4–7–8. It may seem that activities 3–6 and 6–8 have four days of slack and that either could be delayed four days without affecting the planned project duration. But we learned above that activity 3–6, on slack segment 3–6–7, may be delayed no more than one day. Slack on 3–6 is therefore one day, not four days; the larger value is rejected. Activity 6–8, however, does have four days of slack.

The formal calculation of slack time may, in three steps, now be demonstrated for the activities shown in Exhibit 15–10.

1. *Earliest start and earliest finish.* Each activity has an **earliest start (ES)** and an **earliest finish (EF)** time, expressed in days for our project. They are determined by a forward pass through the network. We begin with activity 1–2 and set its *ES* to zero, the start of the project. The *EF* for an activity is equal to its *ES* plus its duration, *t*. Thus, the *EF* for activity 1–2 is

$$EF_{1-2} = ES_{1-2} + t_{1-2} = 0 + 4 = 4 \text{ (or day 4)}$$

The *ES* for each successive activity is equal to the largest *EF* of all predecessor activities. We see that node 2, the origin of activity 2–3, has but one predecessor: activity 1–2. Therefore, the *ES* for activity 2–3 is equal to the *EF* for activity 1–2 and has a value of 4. Continuing, we find the *EF* for activity 2–3 as follows:

$$EF_{2-3} = ES_{2-3} + t_{2-3} = 4 + 2 = 6$$

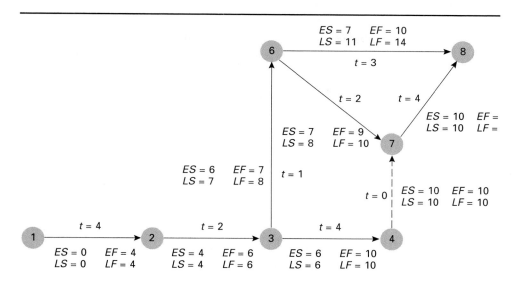

EXHIBIT 15–10

**Calculating
Activity Slack—
Summary Table**

Activity	(LF − EF)	(LS − ES)	Slack	
1–2	(4 − 4)	(0 − 0)	0	Critical activity
2–3	(6 − 6)	(4 − 4)	0	Critical activity
3–4	(10 − 10)	(6 − 6)	0	Critical activity
3–6	(8 − 7)	(7 − 6)	1	
4–7	(10 − 10)	(10 − 10)	0	Critical activity
6–7	(10 − 9)	(8 − 7)	1	
6–8	(14 − 10)	(11 − 7)	4	
7–8	(14 − 14)	(10 − 10)	0	Critical activity

Critical path: 1–2–3–4–7–8
Critical path duration: 14 days

Exhibit 15–10 shows the remainder of the *ES* and *EF* values. The largest *EF* (14 in this case) is taken as the project duration, which is also the duration of the critical path.

2. *Latest start and latest finish.* Each network activity also has a **latest start (LS)** and a **latest finish (LF)** time, again expressed in days for our project. Values for *LS* and *LF* are found by a backward pass through the network. Beginning at node 8, we use the project duration ($EF_{7-8} = 14$) as the *LF* of all activities ending on node 8. Then we find the *LS* for each activity by subtracting its duration *(t)* from its *LF*. For example, the *LS* for activity 7–8 is

$$LS_{7-8} = LF_{7-8} - t_{7-8} = 14 - 4 = 10 \text{ (or day 10)}$$

And for activity 6–8

$$LS_{6-8} = LF_{6-8} - t_{6-8} = 14 - 3 = 11$$

As we move backward through the network, each successive activity has its *LF* defined as the earliest *LS* of all activities that immediately follow. For example, the *LF* of activity 3–6 is 8, since 8 is the smaller of the *LS* values for activities 6–7 and 6–8. Exhibit 15–10 shows *LF* and *LS* values for the remaining activities.

3. *Slack calculation.* Slack for each activity is simply $LS - ES$ or $LF - EF$.

Negative Slack.   If LS is less than ES, negative slack results. Negative slack means the activity is late. Not only is this possible, it is almost the norm, at least for critical path activities. It is so rare for projects to be on time that *The Wall Street Journal* published a front-page story some years ago with headlines proclaiming that a certain large construction project was completed on time. (The project was the domed stadium in Pontiac, Michigan, which also met targeted costs!)

Suppose that in Exhibit 15–10 the due date had been day 11. For activity 7–8, for example, computations reveal

$$LS_{7-8} = 11 - 4 = 7$$

$$\text{Slack}_{7-8} = LS_{7-8} - ES_{7-8} = 7 - 10 = -3 \text{ (negative slack)}$$

Each of the other critical path activities would have slack of -3 days, which means the project is three days late while still in the planning stage! Two clear options exist. First, the schedule could be relaxed—push out the due date to 14, for example—to avoid negative slack at the outset. Second, and often the case with large projects, the project could start out late with hopes of catching up.

Slack-Sort Computer Listing.   The most common PERT/CPM computer output is a slack-sort report of all project activities. Slack sort means sorting or listing activities in order of their degree of slack. Critical path activities have the least slack and therefore appear first; near-critical activities, usually from more than one path, appear next; and so on.

Exhibit 15–11 illustrates this, again using the house-building example. Note that the top activities have negative slack and are most critical. Bottom-most activities are least critical; the last one, activity 3–15, has $+17$ days of slack, which means that it may be delayed 17 days without affecting the project due date.

The slack-sorted computer listing helps a manager more than a network does. Indeed, most managers rely on this type of listing and never need to see a network.[12]

Project Scheduling

The time data generated in the second PERT/CPM phase is a required input for the third phase, project scheduling. The first step is to compare the projected project duration with allowable duration. If projected duration fails to meet company commitments, choices have to be made before the schedule is set in concrete. Company managers may consider spending more on resources to **crash** the network, literally buying some project time reduction. Managers will want to examine cost and time options provided by the project management staff. Crashing and the time–cost trade-off procedure are explained next, followed by discussion of final project and work center scheduling.

Crashing and Time–Cost Trade-Offs.   If managers elect to spend more on resources to cut project time, they had better apply extra resources to critical path activities since that path determines project completion time. As the critical path is crashed, new critical paths may emerge. The cost to further reduce the project du-

Exhibit 15–11

Computer Listing for Path Analysis

	Slack-Sorted Activity Report				
Activity Number	Description	Time	Earliest Start	Latest Start	Activity Slack
1–2	Excavate, pour footings	4	0	−3	−3
2–3	Pour foundation	2	4	1	−3
3–4	Erect frame and roof	4	6	3	−3
4–7	Dummy	0	10	7	−3
.	.	.	.	.	.
.	.	.	.	.	.
13–18	Lay flooring	2	32	29	−3
3–6	Install drains	1	6	4	−2
6–7	Pour basement floor	2	7	5	−2
10–12	Install kitchen equipment	1	27	25	−2
16–18	Finish electrical work	1	32	30	−2
10–13	Finish carpentry	3	27	26	−1
.	.	.	.	.	.
.	.	.	.	.	.
15–17	Finish grading	2	19	24	+5
17–18	Pour walks and landscape	5	21	26	+5
3–15	Lay storm drains	1	6	23	+17

(Critical path brackets activities 1–2 through 13–18)

ration may then involve extra resource costs to reduce activity times on multiple paths. The analysis can get complicated.

If resource costs are inconvenient to collect, the choice of which critical path activity to crash is not clear-cut. Crashing an early activity on the critical path may seem wise because the reduction will apply to other paths that could become critical later; but money spent early is gone. The opposite wait-and-see approach seems wise for another reason: Perhaps some critical path activities will be completed earlier than expected, thus averting the need to crash at all; but if that does not happen, late options for crashing may be few and costly.

When it is convenient to collect resource costs, the project team may employ time–cost trade-off analysis, which we explain using the small network and related data of Exhibit 15–12. The critical path is B–D–E, eight days long, at a cost of $390. Project managers need not accept this plan. They may want to spend more money for extra shifts, air freight, and so on, to reduce the time required to complete various tasks. For example, activity A costs $50 to do in three days (normal), $75 to do in two days (paying for overtime, perhaps), and $100 to do in one day (paying still more, perhaps for extra shifts). The linear assumption, $25 for each day reduced, is generally accurate enough for planning purposes.

The normal and crash costs are often engineers' or managers' estimates based on established direct labor and overhead rates; a careful cost accounting estimate may not be necessary. Also, the estimates may be incremental rather then full costs.

The method of calculating average cost per day may be expressed as a formula:

$$\text{Cost per day} = \frac{\text{Crash cost} - \text{Normal cost}}{\text{Normal time} - \text{Crash time}} \qquad (15\text{–}1)$$

Exhibit 15–12

Network and Time–Cost Data

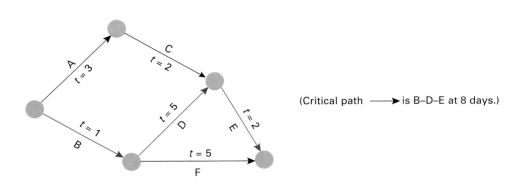

(Critical path ———▶ is B–D–E at 8 days.)

Activity	Normal		Crash		Cost per Day
	Time	Cost	Time	Cost	
A	3	$ 50	1	$100	$25
B	1	40	1	40	—
C	2	40	1	80	40
D	5	100	3	160	30
E	2	70	1	160	90
F	5	90	2	300	70
		$390			

Source: Adapted from Fred Luthans, *Introduction to Management: A Contingency Approach* (Richard J. Schonberger, contributing author) (New York: McGraw-Hill, 1976). p. 378 (HD31.L86). Used with permission.

For activity A, the calculation is

$$\frac{\$100 - \$50}{3 \text{ days} - 1 \text{ day}} = \frac{\$50}{2 \text{ days}} = \$25 \text{ per day}$$

Cost per day for each of the other activities is calculated the same way. Activity B cannot be crashed and thus does not have a cost-per-day entry.

The question is: If it costs $390 to do the project in eight days, what would it cost to do it in seven? If we should pick the lowest total in the cost-per-day column, $25 for A, we would be wrong. Spending $25 more on A would reduce A from three to two days, but it would not affect the eight-day projected duration. A critical path activity—B, D, or E—must be selected. B is out because its crash time is no better than its normal time. The choice between D and E favors D, at an extra cost of $30, as opposed to $90 for E. Thus, doing the project in seven days requires $30 more for a total cost of $420.

The next step is to investigate doing the project in six days. But the above reduction of D to four days results in two critical paths, B–D–E and A–C–E, both seven days long. Reducing the project duration to six days is possible by crashing A and D together at a cost of $55, D and C together at $70, or E alone at $90. The first option is cheapest; thus, it is selected, bringing the total project cost up to $475.

Next, try for five days. After the above step, all paths are critical at six days. The only choice (since B and D are already crashed to their minimum times) is to crash E and F by one day. The added cost is $160, with a total project cost of $635. No further time reductions are possible, since the B–D–E path is fully crashed.

If this were a construction project with a penalty of $100 for every day beyond a six-day project duration, alternative 3 below would look best since it has the lowest total cost, $475.

Alternative	Time (days)	Construction Cost	Penalty Cost	Total Cost	
1	8	$390	$200	$590	
2	7	420	100	520	
3	6	475	0	475	◄—Minimum
4	5	635	0	635	

Time–cost trade-off analysis originated with the CPM people in the construction industry. (For a construction example, see Into Practice, "Bridging the Profit Gap.") It remains more suited for use in construction projects than in R&D efforts for at least two reasons. First, costs and times are easier to estimate in construction. Second, the frequent use of late penalties in construction projects serves as extra incentive for managers in construction to consider time–cost trade-off analysis.

In less-certain project environments (R&D, information systems, disaster relief, etc.) the need to crash projects is just as great as in construction. While the time–cost trade-off procedure is generally not appropriate (the cost uncertainty problem), there are several other approaches for crashing; discussion of them is reserved for the final section in the chapter.

Event Scheduling.   Event scheduling, the assigning of dates to events in the final network, follows selection of a time–cost alternative. Final activity times, with holidays and weekends considered, form the basis for event dates. An event-dating subroutine in PERT/CPM software accepts as input the planned date of the first event and computes the others. A typical listing shows time-earliest (TE) and time-latest (TL) to complete each event and event slack $(TL - TE)$.

Into Practice

Bridging the Profit Gap

"At the rate of one a day, crews racing to rebuild the Mercer Island bridge have started sinking giant pontoon anchors weighing up to 300 tons each to the bottom of Lake Washington.

"Hundreds more workers at waterfront sites on Commencement Bay in Tacoma and on the Duwamish Waterway in Seattle are assembling the first pontoons, four of which are longer than a football field and so massive they'll have to be floated from their cradles on a high tide."

What's the rush? For General Construction Company and its partner, Rainier Steel Inc., the hurry is "about a $6 million bonus for finishing the job a year ahead of schedule. The state has agreed to pay the joint venture $18,500 a day for every day it finished early. . . . The bonus money 'is the majority of the profit on the project,' according to Scott McKellar, General Construction's vice president of operations."

Source: Adapted from Mark Higgins. "Ready, Set, Build: Crews Race to Finish Bridge Ahead of Schedule," *Seattle Post-Intelligencer*, Monday, May 26, 1992.

A normal complication in project scheduling is meshing project schedules with work center schedules. Each subcontractor, department, or work center involved in a given project is likely to be in on other projects, jobs, and repetitive operations. Fitting work center activities into project networks and fitting project activities into work center schedules is a tricky balancing act.

Exhibit 15–13 illustrates this concern. The work center, a grading crew, has developed a Gantt chart showing three upcoming activities that are on the PERT/CPM networks for three different projects. The activities are identified in their respective networks (the project managers' schedules) and on the work center schedule, which is the work center manager's concern. Consider activity 9–10 in project X, finish grading of city lot 2012. Obviously the project manager would like the grading crew on the job site at the right time. If activity 9–10 is a critical path activity, any delay on the grading crew's part will affect project X's completion. Any delay will also reflect negatively on the project X manager's performance, especially if late penalties are assessed.

The work center manager, on the other hand, strives for utilization of the work center's resources. After the grading of lot 2012, the work center manager might wish to proceed immediately to lot 8099 to avoid any work center idle time. The manager of project Y would probably have to veto the idea, however, if the predecessor activity for activity 16–17 (lot 8099 grading) has not been completed. Suppose the predecessor activity, shown as 13–16 in the project Y network, is removing a dead tree. Even the work center manager would agree with the project

EXHIBIT 15–13   **Decomposition of Network Activities into Work Center Schedules**

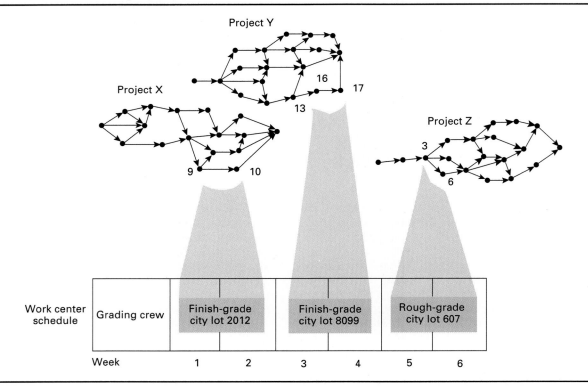

manager's logic: Grading simply cannot begin. Is the grading crew to remain idle for several work days?

Another common problem is when project schedules create demand for work crews to be in two places (perhaps on two projects, each with a different manager) at the same time. Suppose the manager of project Z decides to advance the schedule for activity 3–6, grading of city lot 607, by one week (five workdays). Obviously this will create a problem on the work center schedule during the fourth week. These kinds of conflicts are common and require compromise.

Reporting and Updating

Reporting and updating is the fourth and final subsystem. It extends PERT/CPM management beyond planning and scheduling and into the project control phase. PERT/CPM control revolves around periodic reports, which generally are issued every two weeks or monthly.

Exhibit 15–14 shows a typical reporting scheme. The partial network at the top of the figure divides into monthly reporting periods. At the end of each reporting period, event completion data go to the project management staff, who prepare them for entry into the computer. In Exhibit 15–14, the current month is February and February-planned events 1, 2, 3, 5, and 6 have been completed. A data-entry record is prepared for each; on the first record, for example, an 01 is placed in the event field and the completion date, 020497 for February 4, 1997 is entered in another field.

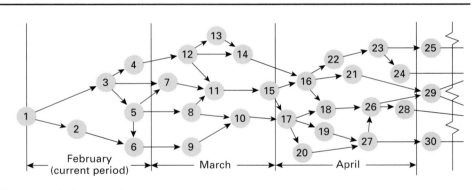
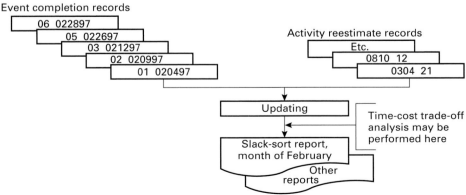

Exhibit 15–14

PERT/CPM Periodic Reporting

Event 4 was scheduled for February, but no notice of completion has been received. Instead, the project manager has received an activity reestimate notice. The first reestimate record shows the activity 03–04 (without the dash) in the key field, and places 21 (days), the new time estimate, in another field. The reestimate pertains to why event 4 has not been completed: Event 3, completed on February 12, plus 21 days for activity 3–4, pushes the planned completion date for event 4 into March. Future activities may also be reestimated, as 08–10 has been in Exhibit 15–14.

With event completions and activity reestimates as inputs, the computer updates the PERT/CPM network. A new slack-sort report is produced, showing the new slack status of each activity. The report is like Exhibit 15–11, except that it gives start and due dates for events. The report tells all parties about the new project schedule for all events. Other reports may be printed—for example, a report listing activities by work center (or department or subcontractor); various resource, budget, and cost reports; and summary (milestone) reports for upper mangers. Some of the reports get wide distribution, and in most firms those responsible for activities completed late must explain why.

Replanning is inherent to control. It is possible to rerun a time–cost trade-off analysis each month after the network has been updated, using event completion data and activity reestimates. Without this analysis, the computer will replan (reschedule) all events anyway, but without considering using more or less resources on given activities.

Major replanning may also occur by altering the network. The project staff may add or subtract activities and may change the sequence. All that is required is adding, removing, or changing a few records. The ease of making such changes is a key asset of PERT/CPM, because project uncertainty demands planning flexibility.

Fitting PERT/CPM to the Situation

PERT/CPM is expensive. Fully computerized PERT/CPM may eat up an additional 2 or 3 percent of total project cost, because it is not a replacement for conventional management. Conventional forecasting, scheduling, inventory control, quality control, budgeting, and so forth, are still done in each functional area (e.g., department or work center). A project management group and PERT/CPM systems hardware and software are additional costs.

Some organizations have tried out and abandoned PERT/CPM because it seemed not to pay for itself. In some cases, the problem is in trying to apply fully computerized PERT/CPM to small-scale projects. Exhibit 15–15 reemphasizes a point partially made early in the chapter: PERT/CPM consists of distinct and separable subsystems. The exhibit further suggests that only projects that are grand in scope warrant the full PERT/CPM treatment. At the other extreme, projects of modest scope may justify the expense of only the first subsystem.

Project scope is expressed in Exhibit 15–15 in terms of four characteristics: size, uncertainty, urgency, and complexity. Size and urgency are self-explanatory. Project uncertainty is of two types:

1. Task uncertainty: doubts about what is to be done.
2. Time uncertainty: doubts about activity time estimates.

Similarly, complexity may be thought of in two ways:

1. Organizational complexity: many organizations involved in the project.
2. Activity complexity: many activities in progress at the same time.

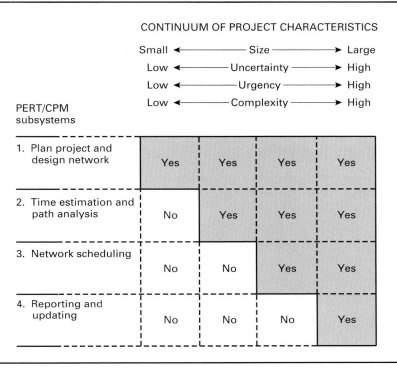

Exhibit 15–15

Matching PERT/CPM Subsystems to Project Scope

To illustrate, consider the kinds of construction projects managed by a typical (for the United States) Army Corps of Engineers district: dams, man-made lakes, dredging, channel straightening, levees, bridges, and riverbank stabilization, to name a few. The district may have perhaps 100 projects in progress at a given time.

A project such as a major dam may be only moderately urgent and uncertain, but it is likely to be very large and complex. In sum, the project characteristics seem to be far enough to the right in Exhibit 15–15 to warrant full, computer-based PERT/CPM, including all four subsystems (four yeses in the exhibit). Without computer-based scheduling, reporting, and control, coordinating the many simultaneous activities of the numerous participating organizations might be chaotic.

Most bridge construction jobs are much smaller and less complex. For such intermediate-scope projects, the project engineer probably should design networks, conduct path analysis, and perhaps use a computer to schedule project events, which may include time–cost trade-off analysis (two or three yeses). But subsystem 4, reporting and updating, may not be warranted. It is the costliest subsystem to administer; it probably costs a lot more than subsystems 1, 2, and 3 combined. A typical bridge is not so urgent as to require the tight time controls of subsystem 4.

Channeling and riverbank stabilization projects are still less urgent and rarely are large, complex, or uncertain. The project engineer may expend a small amount of time, effort, and cost to accomplish subsystem 1, designing PERT/CPM networks (one yes, left column of the figure). The benefits (seeing who has to do what and in what order) are large for the modest cost. There seems little reason to perform path analysis and the other subsystems.

In R&D projects, the model seems equally valid. Designing a major aircraft, such as the Boeing 777 or the Concorde, is a project of massive scope and urgency as well, in view of the capital it ties up. Full PERT/CPM is easily justified. Redesign of a horizontal stabilizer for an existing aircraft, on the other hand, is a modest project; subsystem 1 may be sufficient.

While the logic of this situational approach to the use of PERT/CPM is clear, many managers have not followed it. Attempts to view PERT/CPM as a single indivisible system for use in every project result in disappointment. In such instances, the source of failure is not the PERT/CPM technique.

Continuous Improvement in Projects

The high degree of complexity and uncertainty inherent in project work is good reason for stressing continuous improvement in project management. Part of the problem is chronic project lateness.

Network Simulation and the Always-Late Syndrome

Calculating critical paths is methodical and easily performed on a computer. Unfortunately, the method treats each path independently of all others. It fails to allow for time variation, which affects all event completion times and the total project duration. It is easy to prove by Monte Carlo simulation that the deterministic critical path time understates the likely project duration.[13] Exhibit 15–16 illustrates.

EXHIBIT 15–16

Effects of Variable Activity Times on Project Duration

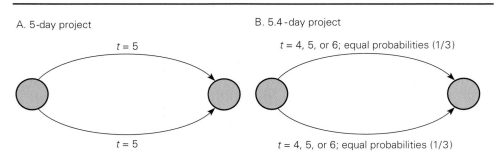

A. 5-day project

$t = 5$

$t = 5$

B. 5.4-day project

$t = 4, 5,$ or 6; equal probabilities $(1/3)$

$t = 4, 5,$ or 6; equal probabilities $(1/3)$

Possible Time Combinations for Network B

	Top Path	Bottom Path	Project Duration	
1	4	4	4	
2	4	5	5	
3	5	4	5	
4	5	5	5	
5	4	6	6	Mean = 49/9 = 5.4 days
6	5	6	6	
7	6	6	6	
8	6	5	6	
9	6	4	6	

The exhibit presents the simplest possible project: two activities occurring at the same time. (A single activity is a job; multiple activities going on simultaneously are a key distinguishing feature of a project.) In Part A, both paths are critical at five days; thus, it is a five-day project. In Part B, the mean or expected task time on each path is still five days. Yet, as the table shows, the simulated mean project duration is 8 percent greater at 5.4 days. In the table, we simulate the variability (four, five and six days) by considering all time combinations and allowing equal chances for each time value on each path. For each combination the higher path time is the project duration, which pushes the expected (mean) project duration up to 5.4 days.

With more variability, the expected project duration increases further. For example, if the path time is 3, 4, 5, 6, or 7, each equally probable, expected duration by simulation is 5.8 days, or 16 percent greater than the critical path time. If more paths are added, expected project duration also goes up. As a general rule, then, the more parallel paths and the more variable the activity times, the more project duration is in excess of the simple critical path time. This provides a mathematical explanation of why projects tend to be late.

Even though the critical path understates reality, it is widely used for the following reasons:

1. Path addition is cheaper to use and simpler to understand than Monte Carlo simulation.
2. Activity time estimates are rough anyway, and there are diminishing returns in more rigorous analysis of rough data.
3. It is difficult to know what to do with simulated network data. How should it change project management?

Despite these reasons, managers should realize that critical path analysis does understate project reality. Caution is the key word in its use.

Combating Project Uncertainty

We have just proved by simulation that projects are likely to be late. Still, the project management staff can work toward reducing the lateness by controlling its causes. Basically, the causes have to do with unnecessary project complexity and uncertainty. The *unnecessary* category includes having the wrong size and type of project management team and lack of information sharing (common files), topics discussed earlier in the chapter. Related factors are high turnover of team members, poor communication, task unfamiliarity, and too many changes.

Project teams typically disband when the project ends. Team members scatter to the four winds. Some join new teams with new members and others return to a functional home, such as the mortgage loan department or human resources. Each time a new project forms, it takes weeks or months for team members to become well-enough acquainted to be able to work well together. Through at least the early project phases, communication is poor, even when the team is multifunctional and working concurrently. Since the skills of each team member are not fully known, members get placed in the wrong assignment and later are moved one or more times in an effort to get a better matchup of needs and skills. Instability hampers effectiveness.

*P*RINCIPLE 11:

Cut start-up time.

To avoid these common problems, some firms are keeping team members somewhat intact from one project to the next. For example, Florida-based Harris Corp. does this in its government systems division. The division has established four project teams, each for a different series of its high-tech electronic products. Each team has a project manager, a project specialist, a material planner, a buyer, and front-line associates. The project manager and project specialist have complementary skills, one usually being an electrical engineer and the other a mechanical engineer. As one government contract winds down, the team gets started on the next contract, taking it from concept through completion.

Examples of other means of controlling causes of lateness are drawn from other chapters:

$\mathcal{P}$RINCIPLE 10:

Eliminate error and process variation.

- *Total quality management.* Effective project management includes collection of data on mishaps, followed by improvement projects to develop solutions to prevent those mishaps on following projects. Every team member should be involved. Continuous improvement seems to be late in gaining a foothold in project management, even though project work is badly in need of it to combat uncertainty and lateness. A probable reason, ironically, is that since projects are usually late, team members resist taking time to collect data and concern themselves with future projects, another project team's problem. If project teams stayed somewhat intact from project to project, they would probably have more incentive to improve the process.
- *Design guidelines* (from Chapter 4). These guidelines call for using standard, already proven designs. This reduces not only complexity but also project uncertainty. That is, with standard designs, activity time estimates will have lower margins of error, making critical-path estimates more accurate.
- *Benchmarking* (from Chapter 4). Project managers are no different from any other manager when it comes to using ideas from "the best." Even when the overall project is blanketed in uncertainty, there are usually many activities or even subprojects that can be speeded up by applying ideas garnered from benchmarking clearinghouses or from direct benchmarking efforts.
- *Quick-response techniques* (from Chapter 8). Project logistics can be mind boggling. The grand scale of operations associated with projects affords ample opportunities for time (and cost) savings through quick-response programs.
- *Supplier partnerships* (from Chapter 9). Relying on unknown and perhaps unreliable suppliers can add significantly to project duration. Though projects are complex—often requiring materials and knowledge from diverse sources—buying from established performers reduces risk.

Summary

Contemporary organizations need to rely on projects in order to accomplish large-scale, complex undertakings that are crucial to meeting strategic objectives. Due to their magnitude, however, projects invite scrutiny from organizational insiders and from the public at large. The impact of projects on their environment—

economic, political, community, and ecological—is an essential dimension of their chances for success.

As product life cycles shrink and continuous improvement expands, more people will spend more time on project teams. Getting projects done quickly and well requires compact, multifunctional teams working in the simultaneous mode.

Project leadership may range from a one-person project coordinator, to a small team responsible for a succession of brands or small projects, to a fully-staffed, autonomous pure project management team with its own budgetary authority.

Some of the more effective project management taps the expertise of suppliers and customers, either by including them on internal project teams or by encouraging project work from outside the organization. Since project teams feed on information, every scrap of information—from team member investigation, training, or experience—should be filed and cross-referenced for easy access by other project associates. The Western tendency for individuals to horde information is an obstacle to be overcome.

Some project information may be organized for development and use in proven project planning and control models, specifically, the program management and review technique and the critical path method (PERT/CPM). Both are based on a sequence chart called a network.

PERT/CPM consists of four subsystems: designing the network, path analysis, scheduling, and reporting and updating. In designing the network, the project team begins with planning project goals; the project plan may be displayed as a work breakdown structure. Task lists are then created and arranged into networks. Networks are activity oriented for lower managers and event oriented for high-level managers.

The project manager may collect time estimates for each network activity. Activity times for each path through the network may be added up, and the sum for the most time-consuming path, called the critical path, is the estimated project duration. Path analysis also includes determining slack for each activity. Slack is the amount of time that an activity may be delayed without making the whole project late. Negative slack occurs especially on the critical path whenever an activity is late.

The project scheduling subsystem is aimed at determining due dates for each network event. If forward scheduling yields a late project completion time, certain activities may be crashed (cutting activity time). Crashing is done by spending more for resources—for example, overtime. Time–cost trade-off analysis yields combinations of project times and costs. One time–cost alternative is selected, and the selected times are the basis for scheduling network events. Finally, organizations having a role in more than one project must fit in the scheduled project tasks so that their capacities will be properly used.

The reporting and updating subsystem may come into play after the work begins. Reports are usually biweekly or monthly. A basic report displays slack time for each activity; it lists most critical activities first, then next most critical activities, and so forth. The reports are valuable for replanning and rescheduling.

Each of the four PERT/CPM subsystems is more costly than its predecessor. All four should be used only if project size, uncertainty, urgency, and complexity are sufficient to justify the cost.

Projects are chronically late. Monte Carlo simulation of a project network will show that the deterministic critical path understates the likely project completion time because activities taking more time than predicted become additive rather than being counterbalanced by activities taking less time than predicted.

The complexity, uncertainty, and lateness tendencies of projects make them attractive candidates for continuous improvement and total quality management. Also, to combat complexity and uncertainty, project teams should, where possible, stay somewhat intact from project to project; and should utilize standard designs, supplier partnerships, benchmarking, and quick-response techniques.

Solved Problems

Problem 1   If there is negative slack of three days on the upper path for the network shown
  a. Will the project be completed on time?
  b. What is the slack on the lower path?
  c. Is there any need for crashing? Explain.

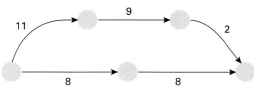

Solution 1   While the problem may be solved with the aid of *ES/EF/LS/LF* calculations, there is no need to do so for this uncomplicated network (it is uncomplicated in that the upper and lower paths each lead straight from first to last event with no interconnections). Further, avoiding the mechanical *ES/LS/EF/LF* tables forces us to think about what the critical path, the project schedule, and slack really mean.
  a. simple addition yields total duration on the two paths:

  Upper path: $11 + 9 + 2 = 22$ days

  Lower path: $8 + 8 = 16$ days

  Since the lower path is less time-consuming, the upper is the critical path. And when there is negative slack on the critical path, that means the project is late, in this case, by 3 days.
  b. Since slack on the upper path is -3 and its duration is 22 days, that means that the project's scheduled completion is in 19 days. Since the lower path takes 16 days, and 19 days are available in the schedule, slack on the lower path is $+3$ days.
  c. The top path is late by three days and thus must be crashed by three days; the bottom path takes three days less than the schedule calls for and thus does not need crashing.

Problem 2   Exhibit 15–17 shows a project network with activity times given in weeks.
  a. What are the paths in the network? What is the critical path? Its duration?
  b. Compute the *ES*, *EF*, *LS*, and *LF* times and the slack for each activity.
  c. Use the data in the time–cost information table to select appropriate time–cost alternatives for reducing the project duration by:

  (1) One week.
  (2) Two weeks.
  (3) Three weeks.

Solution 2   a. In this simple network, it is easy to identify all paths. (In more realistic networks, the task becomes impossible to accomplish without a computer.) Paths in this example network are:

EXHIBIT 15–17   Project Network with Activity Times

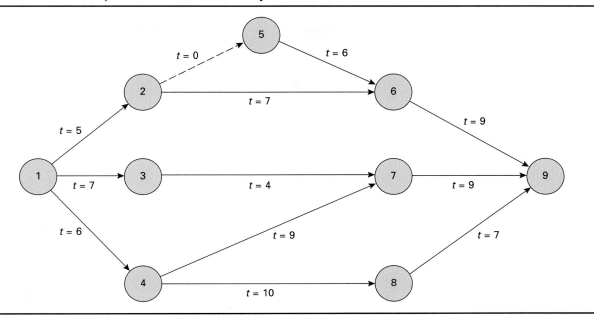

1–2–5–6–9	20 weeks' duration	
1–2–6–9	21 weeks' duration	
1–3–7–9	20 weeks' duration	
1–4–7–9	24 weeks' duration	(critical path)
1–4–8–9	23 weeks' duration	

b. The following table contains the information requested in *b:*

Activity	Duration (weeks)	ES	EF	LS	LF	Slack
1–2	5	0	5	3	8	3
1–3	7	0	7	4	11	4
1–4	6	0	6	0	6	0*
2–5	0	5	5	9	9	4
2–6	7	5	12	8	15	3
3–7	4	7	11	11	15	4
4–7	9	6	15	6	15	0*
4–8	10	6	16	7	17	1
5–6	6	5	11	9	15	4
6–9	9	12	21	15	24	3
7–9	9	15	24	15	24	0*
8–9	7	16	23	17	24	1

Notes: Activity 2–5 is a dummy, required to clarify the network because there are two separate activities between nodes 2 and 6.

Critical activities, marked with an * are determined through slack analysis. Recall that *LF* − *EF* = *LS* − *ES* = Slack.

ES for activity 6–9 is the larger of the *EF* for 2–6 and the *EF* for 5–6. Of these values (12 and 11, respectively), 12 governs. The *ES* for activity 7–9 is determined in the same manner.

LF for activity 1–2 is the smaller of the *LS* for 2–5 and the *LS* for 2–6. Of these values, 9 and 8, 8 is used. The *LF* activity 1–4 is found by comparing the *LS* values for activities 4–7 and 4–8.

c. The time–cost information for the project is contained in the following table:

Activity	Normal Duration (weeks)	Normal Cost ($)	Crash Duration (weeks)	Crash Cost ($)	Crash Cost ($/week)
1–2	5	800	3	1,100	150
1–3	7	950	3	2,150	300
1–4	6	600	4	1,400	400
2–5	0	—	0	—	—
2–6	7	1,100	5	1,500	200
3–7	4	750	4	750	—
4–7	9	1,600	8	1,800	200
4–8	10	1,000	9	1,300	300
5–6	6	1,300	4	2,200	450
6–9	9	2,000	8	2,500	500
7–9	9	1,500	7	2,000	250
8–9	7	900	5	1,600	350

(1) In order to achieve a one-week project time reduction, one of the critical activities (1–4, 4–7, and 7–9) must be crashed. Of the three, activity 4–7 has the lowest weekly crash cost, $200, and is therefore our selection.

(2) The two-week reduction cannot be found by considering only the *original* critical path. After 4–7 is crashed one week, there are *two* critical paths: 1–4–7–9 and 1–4–8–9. Also, note that 4–7 may not be crashed further. Since both (new) critical paths must be reduced in order to shorten the project, we might consider crashing 7–9 and 4–8 one week each. This costs $250 + $300 = $550, which is cheaper than the $600 cost of crashing 7–9 and 8–9.

Another alternative is to crash activity 1–4, which has the admirable effect of reducing time on both of our critical paths. While activity 1–4's crash cost seems high at $400, in this case it is a bargain, since it beats the $550 cost of crashing 7–9 and 4–8. Thus, our choice is to crash activity 1–4.

(3) Again look at activity 1–4. It may be crashed a second week for an additional $400. That should be done to obtain the desired three-week reduction in project duration.

Review Questions

1. Why are projects the vehicle of choice for accomplishing certain strategic objectives?

2. What does Morris mean by a project's "environmental impact"? Explain.

3. Why should project teams not work in the serial mode?

4. Will the addition of more associates on the project team reduce the project completion time? Explain.

5. What type of project management organization and leadership is likely for management of a pharmaceutical company's line of headache remedies? Why?

6. In development projects, how can the ideas of suppliers and customers be effectively incorporated?

7. Private ownership is basic in our Western society. How might that right affect information needed by a project team?

8. Why is a functional-oriented work breakdown structure not recommended?

9. How is a work breakdown structure translated into a PERT/CPM network?

10. Why must there be dummy activities in networks?

11. Why is the network an incorrect way to display activities (or tasks) occurring in repetitive production?

12. Why has the three-time-estimate (for each activity) procedure proved counterproductive?

13. Why might a project manager prepare both an activity-oriented and event-oriented network for the same project?

14. What is done with time estimates in PERT/CPM?

15. What is the purpose of path analysis in PERT/CPM?

16. What is a critical path?

17. Where and under what conditions is negative slack likely to occur?

18. For what is a slack-sort report used?

19. Why is it often sufficient for a project manager to develop a network but not carry the PERT/CPM technique any further?

20. What data are needed to perform time–cost trade-off analysis, and where are the data obtained?

21. In a time–cost trade-off analysis, why is it necessary to check to see which paths are critical after every change?

22. How are PERT/CPM data translated into scheduled jobs or tasks? Why might those scheduled task dates cause conflict for those who are to do the work?

23. Given the uncertainties inherent in R&D and construction projects, how can PERT/CPM adapt?

24. Why is PERT/CPM costly to administer?

25. Why is the deterministic critical path likely to understate the project duration?

26. How can project management teams combat project complexity and uncertainty?

Exercises

1. Which of the five project management organizational structures shown in Exhibit 15–1 would be suitable for each of the following? Explain your answers.
   a. Putting on a world's fair.
   b. Remodeling a branch bank.
   c. New-car contracting for a major rental-car agency.
   d. Dietary planning for Meals on Wheels (meals for the homebound elderly or disabled).
   e. A curb-and-gutter project in a city.

2. Contact a local construction company, information systems company (or department), public works agency, market research group, advertising agency, or research and development department (laboratory).
   a. Find out what form of project management is in dominant use and why.
   b. Find out if PERT/CPM is used, and which subsystems, and why.

3. Develop an output- or outcome-oriented work breakdown structure for a nonconstruction project of your choice. (Examples are a market research project, a political campaign, a disaster-relief project, a research and development project, and a large-scale, computer-based information system development.) You may

need to speculate about the nature of your chosen project if you have not had actual experience in a large project. In addition to drawing the work breakdown structure, explain the nature of your project. Show part of at least three levels on your structure.

4. Explain the purpose of activity 16–13 in Exhibit 15–5.

5. You and several others have been appointed as a planning committee by the president of your social organization. Your committee has decided that in order to obtain additional funds for operating expenses, you will produce a play or a variety show. You have been asked to submit a plan for the next meeting. The plan is to include all the activities or tasks that will have to be accomplished up to the opening of the show. Publicity, tickets, printed programs, and so on, as well as staging for the production, should be part of the plan. The committee has already decided that the scenery will be constructed in a member's garage and that the costumes will be rented.

   To facilitate presentation of the plan, draw a network diagram of about 30 activities. Include brief descriptions of the activities.

6. A manufacturer of CD players buys disk magazines from outside contractors. A new contract is to be awarded for a new style of disk magazine. The company has developed an activity-on-node network for the project. The accompanying network includes an initial contract for magazine development and a second contract for magazine (assuming that the disk magazine tests are OK) for production. Redraw the network in the activity-on-arrow form.

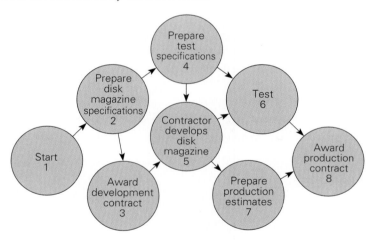

7. The manager for a project to develop a special antenna system is preparing a PERT-based project plan. Data for the plan are as follows:

Activity Number	Description	Expected Time (days)
1–2	Design frame	4
1–3	Procure mechanism	5
2–4	Procure parts	1
3–4	Dummy	0
3–7	Determine repair requirements	4
4–6	Assemble	2
4–7	Hire maintenance crew	3
6–7	Test	1

a. Draw the network.

    b. Compute and indicate the critical path.

    c. Compute slack times for all activities, assuming that the project is scheduled for completion in the number of days on the critical path.

    d. Five working days have passed, and status data have been received, as follows:

        (1) Activity 1–2 was completed in five days.

        (2) Activity 1–3 was completed in four days.

        (3) Activity 4–6 has been reestimated at four days.

    Based on the data, recompute the critical path and slack on all of the remaining project activities. (Assume no change in scheduled project completion dates.)

8. Aeropa, Inc., has a contract to develop a guided missile. A PERT/CPM network and activity times are given in the following illustration. Times are in weeks.

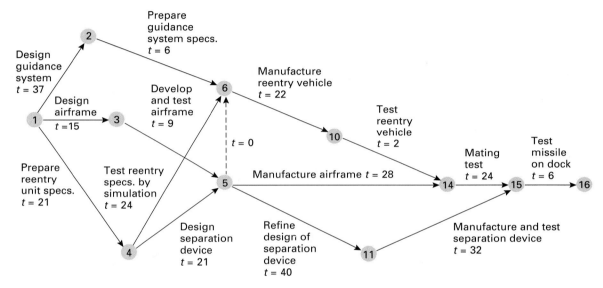

    a. Compute *ES, LS, EF, LF,* and slack for each activity. Assume that slack = 0 on the critical path. Identify the critical path activities and the critical path duration.

    b. Draw a condensed event-oriented network with only five milestone events. The five events should be designated as follows: 1. Start. 5. Shell specs completed. 6. Guidance specs completed. 14. Modules completed. 16. Missile tested.

        Put activity times on the arrows between your events. Compute ES, LS, EF, LF, and slack for each activity. Verify that the critical path duration is the same as in (*a*). What activity time goes on arrow 1–6? Explain the difficulty in deciding on a time for this activity.

    c. Assume the following project status at the end of week 50:

Activity	*Actual Duration*
1–2	39
1–3	17
1–4	20
2–6	7
3–5	9
4–5	28
4–6	20

No other activities have been completed.

Develop a slack-sorted activity report similar to Exhibit 15–11 for the project as of the end of week 50. What is the new projected project duration?

9. The following data have been collected for a certain project:

Activity		Normal		Crash	
Predecessor Event	Successor Event	Time (days)	Cost ($)	Time (days)	Cost ($)
1	2	6	250	5	360
2	3	2	300	1	480
2	4	1	100	1	100
2	5	7	270	6	470
3	4	2	120	1	200
4	5	5	200	1	440

    a. Draw the network.

    b. Compute and indicate the critical path and the normal project cost.

    c. Compute slack time for each activity in the network, using 12 days as the project due date.

    d. Perform time–cost trade-off analysis, crashing down to the minimum possible project duration. Display each time–cost alternative.

10. Normal and crash data for the accompanying network are given below. Compute all time–cost options. Which is best if there is a $40-per-day penalty for every day beyond a seven-day project duration?[14]

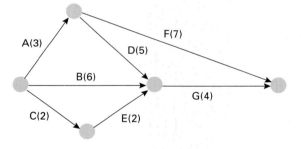

Activity	Normal		Crash	
	Days	Cost	Days	Cost
A	3	$ 50	2	$ 100
B	6	140	4	260
C	2	25	1	50
D	5	100	3	180
E	2	80	2	80
F	7	115	5	175
G	4	100	2	240
		$610		$1,085

11. *a.* For the accompanying network, what is the critical path and expected project duration? What is the second most critical path and its duration?

    b. What can the largest time value for activity 3–4 be to ensure that it is not a critical path activity? (Ignore the present time of five days for that activity in answering the question.)

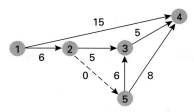

12. a. For the accompanying network, if there is slack of +6 on the upper path, what is the slack on the lower path?
    b. If the slack is −4 on the upper path, what is the slack on the lower path?

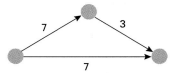

13. a. For the accompanying network, if there is slack of +5 on the lower path, what is the slack on the upper path?
    b. If there is slack of +1 on the upper path, what is the slack on the lower path?

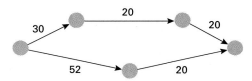

14. a. For the accompanying time-and-cost table, what is the least costly way to reduce the project time by one day? (You may wish to draw the network for better visualization of the problem.)
    b. What is the least costly way to reduce the expected project duration (i.e., crash the project) by three days?

	Normal		Crash	
Activity	*Time*	*Cost*	*Time*	*Cost*
1–2	2	$10	1	$15
2–3	6	8	5	18
2–4	2	15	1	21
2–5	8	30	6	52
4–3	2	7	2	7
3–5	3	21	1	33
1–5	8	20	5	41

15. *a.* For the accompanying network and time-and-cost table, what is the least costly way to reduce (crash) the project by one day?

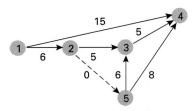

b. What is the fastest the project could be done if you used crash times?

	Normal		**Crash**	
Activity	*time*	*Cost*	*Time*	*Cost*
1–2	6	$100	5	$205
1–4	17	200	12	600
2–3	5	100	4	190
3–4	5	150	3	360
5–3	6	80	5	185
5–4	8	300	7	360

16. A number of project types are listed below, ranging from small and simple to grand. As indicated in Exhibit 15–15, modest projects warrant only the first PERT/CPM subsystem, whereas grand projects justify all four subsystems; in-between projects warrant subsystems 1 and 2 or subsystems 1, 2, and 3. Decide which subsystems should apply for each project listed. Explain each.
    a. Computer selection and installation for company of 200 employees.
    b. Moving the computer facility for a large bank to a new building in a major city.
    c. Moving the computer facility (same size as the bank's) to a new building at a major university.
    d. Community project to attract new industry in three large, abandoned factory buildings (town of 10,000 people).
    e. Five-year overhaul of a nuclear submarine.
    f. Implementing MRP in a manufacturing company of 1,000 employees.
    g. New-product development testing (including market research) for a major food company.
    h. Moving an army division from one closed-down post to a new one in another state.
    i. Planning a national sports championship event.
    j. Building a 500-room hotel in Lincoln, Nebraska.
    k. Building a 500-room hotel in Manhattan.

17. The accompanying network segments are all part of the same home-construction project. Where is a dummy activity needed, and why?

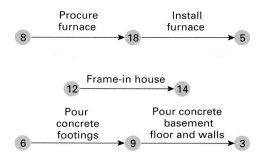

18. Exhibit 15–16 shows a simulation of a simple network with equally possible activity times of 4, 5, or 6. In discussing the figure, it was stated that expected project duration increases to 5.8 for the five equally probable activity times, 3, 4, 5, 6, and 7. Verify the figure 5.8.

19. A network consists of two activities that occur at the same time. Each is expected to take one, two, or three weeks to complete, and the probabilities of each possible time are $\frac{1}{3}$, $\frac{1}{3}$, and $\frac{1}{3}$. What is the expected project duration based on the critical path? What is it based on PERT simulation?

20. A network consists of two activities that occur at the same time. Each is expected to take one or two months to complete, and the probabilities of each possible time are $\frac{1}{2}$ and $\frac{1}{2}$.

    a. What is the expected project duration based on the critical path? What is it based on PERT simulation?

    b. What would the expected project duration be using PERT simulation if the network had three instead of two activities, each with equally probable activity times of one or two months?

21. Develop an example of how each of the following tools of process improvement—fishbone chart, Pareto chart, check sheet—might be used in a construction project. Focus your examples on ways to reduce project uncertainty and lateness.

For Further Reference

Books

Funk, Jeffrey L. *The Teamwork Advantage: An Inside Look at Japanese Product and Technology Development.* Portland, Ore.: Productivity Press, 1992 (HD66.F86).

Harris, Robert B. *Precedence and Arrow Networking Techniques for Construction.* New York: John Wiley & Sons, 1978 (TH438.H37).

Kerzner, Harold, and Hans Thamhain. *Project Management for Small and Medium Size Business.* New York: Van Nostrand Reinhold, 1984 (HD69.P75K491).

Meredith, Jack R., and Samuel J. Mantel Jr. *Project Management: A Managerial Approach.* New York: John Wiley & Sons, 1989.

Morris, Peter W.G. *The Management of Projects.* London: Thomas Telford, 1994.

Nicholas, J. M. *Managing Business and Engineering Projects.* Englewood Cliffs, N. J.: Prentice-Hall, 1990.

Wiest, Jerome D., and Ferdinand K. Levy. *A Management Guide to PERT/CPM.* 2nd ed. Englewood Cliffs. N.J.: Prentice-Hall, 1977 (TS158.2.W53).

Periodicals/Societies

Decision Services (Decision Sciences Institute).

Journal of Operations Management (American Production and Inventory Control Society).

IIE Transactions (Institute of Industrial Engineers).

Project Management Journal (Project Management Institute).

Source: © Walter Hodges/Tony Stone Images

OM Resources: Measurement, Management, Improvement

V

Most topics in the previous 15 chapters involve human and physical resources—the potential energy of operations management—in one way or another. In Part V they receive special attention: the human resources in Chapter 16, the physical in Chapter 17, and how *you* fit in in Chapter 18.

One overlapping issue is stress. It is natural to wonder, or to assert, that the drive in OM for continuous improvement might make work more stressful.[1] Throw in high technology, which can massively fail (e.g., extended regional power-grid blackouts) and leave us humans helpless, and stress levels elevate some more.

In their research report, "Sources of Stress in an Automated Plant," however, Karuppan and Schniederjans suggest ways that stresses might be alleviated. They suggest that operators may gain control over technology and their environments when they keep and analyze breakdown records, devise plans for quality control, and contribute to selection, testing, and programming of new equipment. They also allude to the benefits of operator cross-training and job rotation to relieve boredom.[2] These points are in keeping with good OM practices, which are brought out in earlier chapters and those remaining as well.

Stress, however, is not all bad. Athletes deliberately stress their bodies and minds in order to gain the satisfaction of bettering themselves. Should organizations and workforces do less? We revisit this matter in Chapter 18.

16 PRODUCTIVITY AND PEOPLE

Chapter Outline

"When geese fly in their characteristic 'V' formation, the flapping motion of each member of the flock creates an aerodynamic lift for the bird immediately behind. When the lead bird tires, it falls back and another one moves up to take its place at the point. This collaborative effort increases the flying range of the geese by at least 70 percent over what it would be if they flew alone or in random formation.

"Everyone here knows that story," says Mike Simms, plant manager for Wainwright Industries, 1994 winner of a Baldrige Award. "It's an important emotional lesson about teamwork."[1]

To businesspeople, the word *productivity* means productivity of labor. More properly, productivity applies to all assets, including facilities, materials, information. But labor productivity gets the most attention. Most companies measure it, analyze it, and fret over it. Sometimes, the quest for higher labor productivity can foster a climate of mutual distrust and enmity, a matter we take up later in the chapter. In addition, companies too often fail to capitalize on the beneficial effects of teams on productivity: Wainwright Industries' metaphor of a flock of geese.

Part of the problem is that the usual measures of labor productivity are flawed. They really do not fairly measure what they purport to measure.

If labor productivity is low, that does not necessarily mean the labor resource is under-performing. More likely, the management system is deficient. Managing people as individuals instead of teams is one deficiency. There are many others, such as failing to provide any of the following: high-quality and timely information, training, designs, equipment, materials, technical support, strategic guidance, and proper motivational climate. The quality and productivity of labor depends on all of these factors. A few of these are topics in this chapter, but most have to do with resources and processes discussed in each of the other chapters.

Thus, this chapter's scope is necessarily narrow. The first half focuses on broad managerial concerns: historical roots; fairness issues; cost management issues; simple, noncost approaches; and operator-centered maintenance. The last half is technique oriented; it provides formulas, metrics, and procedures for productivity management and includes a supplement.

We are restricting the issue to productivity management within the firm and excluding productivity of nations.

Roots: Productivity and Scientific Management

The first organized approach to improving the productivity of labor arose in the United States at the turn of the century from the work of the pioneers of **scientific management.** Prominent among them were Frederick W. Taylor, Frank and Lillian Gilbreth, and others, including Harrington Emerson, who specialized in office processes. Their approach was to standardize the labor element of operations: standard methods and standard times. Nonstandard labor practices were simply too expensive and wasteful.

Scientific management, so named by U.S. Supreme Court Justice Louis Brandeis, was born in a period of transition and could be thought of as the last phase of the Industrial Revolution. Earlier phases concerned invention, mechanization, standardization of parts, division of labor, and the factory system. Machines and parts were standardized, and labor was divided into narrow specialties. Prior to scientific management, however, labor productivity was controlled more by supervisors' skill than by design. Taylor's and the Gilbreths' techniques for methods study (or motion study) and time study extended science into the realm of the line employee.

Briefly stated (and paraphrasing Taylor), the four principles of scientific management are

1. Develop a science for each element of a person's work, which replaces the old rule-of-thumb method.
2. Scientifically select and then train, teach, and develop the work force, instead of—as in the past—having employees choose their own work and having them train themselves as best as they can.

3. Heartily cooperate with the employees so as to ensure all of the work being done is in accordance with the principles of science.

4. Ensure that there is an almost equal division of work and responsibility between the management and the employee. The management takes over all work for which they are better fitted than the employees, while in the past almost all of the work and the greater part of the responsibility were thrown upon the employees.[2]

Impact of Scientific Management

While putting the finishing touches on the Industrial Revolution, scientific management ushered in the beginnings of the modern manufacturing era. Since the United States was the birthplace of scientific management, it enjoyed the first benefits. Methods and standards programs spread rapidly in U.S. manufacturing firms between 1900 and 1950, which may help explain the phenomenal growth of industrial output in the United States in the first half of the century.

Beginning in the 1940s, comparable programs found their way into hospitals, food service, hotels, transportation, and other services. So carefully industrially engineered is the McDonald's hamburger that Levitt calls it "the technocratic hamburger."[3] By the early 1980s, the industrial engineering department at United Parcel Service (UPS) had grown to 3,000 people and "had so perfected manual package handling that UPS had the industry's lowest costs."[4] In many industries, it has been hard to compete without good methods design and labor standards.

Scientific management is not without its critics. Labor unions often have resisted time standards. Some believe that under work measurement a person is treated like a microcomputer memory chip. At the first sign of performance deterioration, discard or replace the chip; it's just not cost-effective to attempt to repair or recycle it. Often the ultimate plan is to replace the entire memory system, and even the computer itself, with faster memory and more powerful equipment.

Some of the criticisms focus more on "Taylorism" (referring to Frederick W. Taylor, the "father" of scientific management) than on the movement itself. One of Taylor's ideas was that each function should have its own specialist-managers, so that a production associate might have one boss for training, another for quality, another for scheduling, and so forth. After decades of building up separate functional entities, companies in the 1980s began to see the folly: little communication or cooperation across the functions. Re-engineering would be required to re-unite the firm.

Whether Taylor, who died in 1915, should be held responsible for the excesses of seven or more decades is debatable. There is, however, no question about Taylor's central role in the development of methods study and time standards, which, as was noted in Chapter 1, have been instrumental in providing the documentation for training. Time standards have been maligned, but nevertheless they have a valued role in time-based competition. Moreover, the methods study techniques have been absorbed into modern-day total quality management and process improvement, considered next.

Process Improvement and Productivity

Modern improvement tools, presented in Chapter 5, are a mixture of old and new: process flowcharting from the Taylor/Gilbreth era, plus several newer tools that originated in connection with quality improvement (see the 11 tools for process improvement, Exhibit 5–8). Here we take a second look, from a productivity angle.

Systematic productivity improvement, as developed by Taylor, the Gilbreths, and other pioneers of scientific management, involved **methods study,** with **flow-charting** at the core. Methods study always has been aimed at improving not only productivity but also safety and ease of performing the work. Making the work easier to do safely increasingly gets into issues of human physiology, stress, and bodily limitations, and has spawned a subfield of process improvement called **ergonomics.** Because of escalating worker's compensation and litigation costs, interest in ergonomics has never been higher.

Methods study takes place at the job level and at the process level. As Exhibit 16–1 shows, each application has a different set of before-and-after flowcharts.

One type of analysis at the job level is **motion study,** which is limited to the work of an immobile employee at a desk or work bench. The analyst flowcharts what the left and right hands are doing. The other type of job-level study is for a mobile employee tending more than one machine; the analyst flowcharts both the person's and the machine's activities.

Both kinds of job-level analyses use standard flowcharting symbols and may also employ a flowcharting form with time units on the vertical. The flowcharting analysis steps are as follows:

- Flowchart the present method (*before* chart).
- Move, combine, or eliminate steps.
- Flowchart the proposed new method (*after* chart).
- Immediately determine the resulting productivity improvement by comparing cycle time on the *before* and *after* charts.

Job-level methods study pertains to the productivity and ergonomic conditions of direct labor, but not to overall productivity, which includes typically out-of-control overhead costs. Improvement teams may use process-level analysis in directly attacking the high overhead costs and wastes, along with some direct-labor wastes.

Unlike job-level flowcharts, process flowcharts do not have a time scale and thus do not readily reveal how much productivity improvement is achieved. If it is really important to know, a cost analyst could be called in to estimate and compare the costs of the old and new processes. Industrial engineers, who've used process flowcharts for decades, have rarely found it necessary to translate improvements into before and after costs. It is clear that productivity improves with the elimination of non-value-adding steps, which are visually portrayed by flowcharting symbols: arrow (transport), upside-down triangle (storage), big D (delay), and square (inspection).

While these process improvement techniques have generally been effective when administered by specialists such as industrial engineers, they can be even

"A single case of carpal tunnel syndrome, a painful condition involving compression of the wrist's median nerve, costs up to $30,000. . . . Eliminating this type of ergonomics problem sometimes requires less than $1,000."[5]

Type	Application	Flowchart
Job level:		
Motion study	Manual task at work bench or desk	Left-and-right-hand time chart
Operator-machine analysis	Operator tending machines	Operator-machine time chart
Process level:	Mobile employee, product, or customer	Process flowchart

Exhibit 16–1

Methods Study: Job and Process Improvement

more so in the hands of empowered front-line employees. We take up this matter as part of an overall critique of scientific management next.

Humanity and Fairness Issues

Scientific management is a two-edged sword, one edge sharp and the other dull. The sharp edge raises productivity; the dull one leaves wounds and scars (see Into Practice, "Cracking . . . ").

Employers have long sought solutions to the human problems associated with the application of methods and time standards. The most promising approaches, past and present, lie in putting variety and meaning back into the task or job. Closely related is the need to make sure that the reward system will recognize task differences and the many ways in which employees can serve their employers and customers. Those issues—tasks, jobs, customer-service effects, and the reward system—are considered next.

Tasks and Jobs

The design of work and work systems has evolved through three phases. First was scientific management, which focuses on the task itself. Next came job design, which aims at improving the job and therefore the life of a jobholder. Today's approach, emphasized throughout this book, is on service to the next and final customer and related feelings of satisfaction by the server. A review of the three phases follows.

Into Practice

Cracking the Electronic Whip

America's is a post-industrial service economy, runs the conventional wisdom; it's an economy wherein the product is information and work occurs in a clean, well-lighted place. It's the age of the telemarketer, the customer-service rep, and the flight reservationist—all of whom rely on computer technology to do their jobs. Abuse of workers in this new economy would seem unlikely, but it's here, with age-old cruelty. Twenty-six million employees nationwide, from telephone operators to elevator mechanics, have their work tracked electronically. For ten million of these men and women, computer-generated statistical evaluations are used to judge job performance and, it is held, to increase productivity. But the computer can't measure the physical and mental toll exacted by the stress of second-by-second surveillance.

Examples, from a supervisor's hand-written comments on a computer printout showing performance of one airline reservation agent:

- Agent is "reprimanded for taking 0.39 minutes" (about 23 seconds) "to complete her paperwork for each call."
- Agent's "percent utilization," 93.55 percent, is below this airline's 96.5-percent minimum standard. Agent must do better or will get a warning "or even unpaid suspension."
- Agent's UNM ("unmanned") time, "almost always time spent in the bathroom," adds up on the printout to 22 minutes—unacceptably high.
- Total number of calls handled, 79 for the day, is way below the airline's expectation of 150 to 200 calls a day. "Raw totals, and not customer needs, are what management is concerned with."

Source: Adapted from Sharon Danann, "Cracking the Electronic Whip." Harper's Magazine, August 1990 pp. 58–59.

Tasks   Division of labor, performed scientifically using methods-study techniques, yields a well-engineered task. Consider the task of scraping food leavings off a stainless steel tray into a garbage can. Is that task also a job; that is, can the firm define it as a job and hire someone to do just that task over and over? The answer is yes. Such narrow tasks are sometimes treated as a whole job.

Jobs.   If all jobs were developed like the plate-scraping one, wouldn't work life be intolerable? A collection of concepts called **job design** attempts to avoid such a fate for working people.

Best known among the job-design ideas are job enlargement and job enrichment. Job enlargement dates back to the 1950s, when Thomas Watson, founder of IBM, promoted the effort out of his strong belief in providing people with meaningful work. Job enlargement means expanding the number of tasks included in a person's job—for example, cooking, serving, and scraping plates; it offers horizontal variety. Job enrichment, a later development with roots at Texas Instruments and AT&T, expands on the job enlargement idea. Enlargement means more tasks; enrichment means more meaningful, satisfying, and fulfilling tasks or responsibilities; for example, an enriched job may entail use of mental and interpersonal skill—scraping plates and teaming up with others to select new dishes, scrapers, and dishwashing equipment.

The liberating effects of enlargement/enrichment are not necessarily in conflict with the restrictions of prescribed methods and time standards. In fact, one could argue that without standards, an enlarged/enriched job might be poorly defined, exposing the employee to frustration and criticism. Existence of job standards offers a guidepath for avoiding problems, thereby offering more freedom for the associate to work on process improvements, which translate into still better job standards.

Customers, Internal and External

Enlargement and enrichment, as originally conceived, were oriented to the individual, not to the team and not to the next or final customer. The following corrects this deficiency:

- Ensure that enlargement is directed toward mastery of the jobs of fellow team members—that is, cross-training. Exhibit 16–2 shows a display of employee cross-training attainments for a company in Ireland.
- Ensure that enrichment is customer oriented. Specifically, this calls for associates to acquire the data collection, analysis, problem-solving, and teamwork skills and responsibilities required in total quality management.

*𝒫*RINCIPLE 7:

Cross-train for mastery of multiple skills.

An obstacle in the way of learning more skills is the job classification system, or work rules.

How could the Buick division of General Motors have turned itself around so dramatically, from among GM's sickest divisions in the mid-1980s to having car models in the J. D. Powers top-10 auto quality listing by 1990? Perhaps this had something to do with it: A cooperative agreement between Buick management and the United Auto Workers union that reduced the number of job classifications from hundreds to just three. Pay for skills, replacing the seniority pay system, also was part of the deal.[6] **Skill-based pay** fits with the new requirement for associates to master multiple skills. It is often palatable to the employee, union or nonunion,

EXHIBIT 16–2

Cross-Training Display, Upright-Ireland

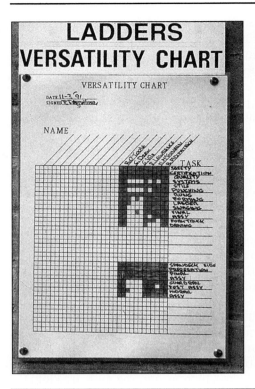

Visual display of employee cross-training at Upright-Ireland. As a manufacturer of special-order aluminum scaffolding in Ireland, Upright needs a high degree of labor flexibility in order to cope with the large variety of orders. (For example, Upright was the producer of scaffolding used by artisans restoring the Sistine Chapel, The Vatican, Rome.)

because the common concern has shifted somewhat from job security to work-life security; each new skill mastered becomes another line on the employee's résumé, should a résumé be needed sometime.

Pay and Other Motivators

The concept of skill-based pay, also called pay for knowledge, emerged in connection with TQM and JIT: TQM calls for all employees to get involved in data collection, analysis, and improvement; assume process ownership; and take first responsibility for quality. Both TQM and just-in-time require that associates become cross-trained, able to move to where the work is, and fix things that go wrong on the spot; otherwise, there will be delays, and work will not get done just in time.

If associates assume all these new skills and duties, shouldn't they be paid more? Of course. It's only fair, though some companies cannot immediately afford it. This concept of fair pay (pay for skills) does not easily replace other fair-pay ideas, however. Exhibit 16–3 lists six popular views on fair pay, skill-based pay being the sixth.

*P*RINCIPLE 14:

Front-line teams: first line of attack on problems.

Concepts of Fair Pay.   One concept of fair pay is that everyone should be paid the same; minimum-wage laws are a means of bringing that about. Pay by time worked is a second fair-pay concept, and a popular one. Pay by job content also

E XHIBIT 16–3   **Concepts of Fair Pay**

What Is Fair Pay?	*Who Subscribes to This?*
1. Everyone Paid the Same. Rationale: We are all created equal; we are all products of our environments and partners in society. Means: High minimum wage applied equally to all.	Organized labor Socialists
2. Pay by the Hour (or Week, Month, Year). Rationale: Though we are products of our environment, society's work must be done, and work is most easily measured in time units. Means: Have employees punch time clocks, and reprimand them for tardiness.	Supervisors (easy to figure out pay) Organized labor (employees like to "put in their time"—or their time and a half)
3. Pay According to Job Content. Rationale: It is not the person who should be paid but the position; "heavy" positions should be paid heavily, "light" positions lightly. Means: Job evaluation, using job ranking/classification, point plan, factor comparison.	Personnel managers (requires a large pay-and-classification staff) Bureaucrats (seems rational and impersonal; fits concept of rank or hierarchy)
4. Pay According to Output. Rationale: Though we are products of our environment, society's work must be done, and work should be measured in output (not merely time on the job). Output efficiency is based on a count of actual units produced as compared with a standard. Means: Piecework, incentive pay, gain sharing.	Industrial engineers Economists
5. Pay According to Supply and Demand. Rationale: Society's messiest jobs must be done too, and more pay for less desirable jobs is necessary to attract employees. Means: Let the labor market function (or list jobs needing to be done, and set pay according to willingness to do each job—the *Walden II* method).	Some economists (e.g., those advocating below-minimum wages for teenagers) B. F. Skinner (see his book *Walden II*)
6. Pay for Skills. Rationale: Pay system should encourage learning so employees can take "ownership" of their processes and can quickly fix problems. Means: Extra pay for passing tests of mastery of more skills and knowledge.	A growing number of some of the best-known companies

seems fair, especially in large organizations where unequal pay for the same work would be a visible problem; evaluating job content has been a major function in larger human-resources departments. A fourth concept of fair is pay based on output against standards, often called **incentive pay.** A pure incentive is simply a piece rate; for example, a store coupon counter's piece rate might be $1 per hundred. But laws, such as the United States wage-and-hour laws, require that piece-rate earnings not fall below the minimum wage, based on hours worked.

Another popular system is **measured daywork,** which is only nominally an incentive-pay system. In measured daywork, standard output serves as a target that trainers and supervisors help the employee attain. The employee who cannot attain it is moved to another position or advised to seek work elsewhere.

Reward and Recognition.   Pay, of course, is not the only effective motivator; it may not even be the strongest. To complete our discussion of productivity, we must note the impact of low-cost and no-cost rewards, recognition, celebration, and personal pride.

- *Suggestions.* Companies that win Baldrige or Deming quality awards generally have high rates of employee suggestions. Until recently, one suggestion per employee per year would have been impressive among Western companies. Now, a growing number of Western companies are in double digits—for example, Globe Metallurgical, winner of a 1988 Baldrige Quality Prize and a winner of a 1989 Shingo Prize. Moreover, at least two, Milliken & Co., 1989 Baldrige prize winner, and Wainwright Industries, 1994 Baldrige winner, have achieved the suggestion-rate level of top Japanese firms (see Exhibit 16–4), and Milliken showers praise and recognition upon everyone who contributes. While most firms pay something for even small suggestions, others bestow only praise and recognition, which has similar effects.
- *Personal, team, and group awards.* Companies are devising numerous awards to help sustain continuous improvement momentum: Friday afternoon pizza parties, cookouts, and keggers; a day off, with the supervisor filling in; a next-to-the-door parking place; T-shirts, mugs, and plaques; theater or sports-event tickets; dinner for two at a fancy restaurant; all-expense-paid

Company	Number of Suggestions	Number of Employees	Per Employee
Japanese*			
Tohoku Oki	734,044	881	833.2
Mazda	3,025,853	23,929	126.5
Fuji Electric	1,022,340	10,226	99.6
Matsushita	6,446,935	81,000	79.6
Canon	1,076,356	13,788	78.1
Toyota	2,648,710	55,578	47.6
Nippondenso	1,393,745	48,849	38.5
North American			
Milliken, 1991			52.0
Wainwright, 1994			65.0

EXHIBIT 16–4

Employee Suggestion Rates for Selected Leading Companies

*Source: "The Power of Suggestions," Japan Human Relations Association, April 1988, cited in Min Basadur, "Managing Creativity: A Japanese Model," *The Executive*, May 1992, pp. 29–42.

trip to Hawaii; and trips for the whole team to a fine hotel to present its improvement at the annual management conference. While standard reinforcement theory does not distinguish particularly between private and public praise, today's leading companies tend toward a strong preference for making it public: wall charts, ceremonies, company and public news media, and so forth.

- *Meet the customer and supplier.* Superior companies, especially in North America, are sending their front-line employees to visit customers and suppliers, who are sometimes out of town or even out of the country. Reorganization into cells has the effect of putting individuals into continuous contact with their next-process customer and prior-process supplier. Whether in the next state or at the next desk, being in contact with one's customer or supplier may offer the chance of genuine satisfaction; being denied this opportunity tends to reduce the possibilities for feeling real pride of service.

When the individual feels fairly paid, is justly praised in a public manner, and can personally see the impact of good work on the customer's face, the productivity loop is effectively complete. (See the Contrast box, "A Fair Day's . . . .")

We have examined some dominant human issues in productivity management and a few ways that superior companies deal with them. Related issues that companies must address include ways of measuring productivity, including cost-based metrics, considered next.

Twenty-two finalist teams, pared from over 3,000 worldwide, gathered at the Marriott-O'Hare for Motorola's "Total Customer Satisfaction Team Competition." Using comedy, statistics, scatter diagrams, and fishbone charts, the teams presented their projects and top management manned the scoring tables.[7]

Productivity and Cost

As colorful center for the Los Angeles Lakers, Shaquille O'Neal scores some 30 points per game. He is productive per number of minutes played and, probably, per dollar that he is paid: a quality asset, a bottom-line player. Sports fans judge a basketball player's productivity according to O'Neal's kind of output units (points, rebounds) but are savvy enough also to weigh input units such as game minutes and salary. The National Basketball Association might prefer to judge the productivity of a "Shaq" in number of fans per game who come to see him and his team; Shaq's team fills arenas all around the league.

*C*ontrast

A Fair Day's . . .

Nineteenth Century: A Fair Day's Grog*	Twentieth Century: A Fair Day's Work	Twenty-First Century: A Fair Day's Improvement
Company A: "All hands drunk; Jacob Ventling hunting; molders all agree to quit work and went to the beach. Peter Cox very drunk and gone to bed."	Standard methods and standard times provide a basis for uniform measurement of human performance and, therefore, control of it.	Broad array of tools of data collection, analysis, problem solving, measurement, customer focus, teamwork, reward, and recognition make continuous improvement a normal and satisfying part of everyone's job.
Company B: "Men worked no more than two or three hours a day; spent the remainder in the beer saloon playing pinochle."		*Source: Shoshana Zuboff, In the Age of the Smart Machine, New York: Basic Books, 1988, p. 32.

Whether you consider the din of shouting fans, clanking factory machines, humming office equipment, or babbling customers, the bottom line for operations management is usually output units compared with input units. The measures are used for performance appraisal, recognition, reward, and motivation for continual improvement. Therefore, getting the units right is important to every department, team, and associate. Experts, such as cost and time analysts, have usually been in charge. Let's take a look at the measurement experts' handiwork: the classic cost-variance system.

Cost Variance

cost variance
Standard cost minus actual cost.

For years, best business practice has called for use of periodic cost variances as a control on productivity. The system sums up standard cost and actual cost for all work completed in a period. Standard cost represents what the output for the period should cost using normal amounts of direct labor, materials, and so forth; the actual cost is made up of actual payroll, material, and other expenditures. Periodic reports, sent out to each operating manager, list cost variances. If actual cost is higher than standard cost, a negative cost variance results, and the pressure is on operations to do better.

More specifically, the cost-variance report is segmented into subcategories, including labor cost variance and material cost variance. A negative labor variance suggests that the direct-labor force should work more diligently; a negative material variance means it should work more carefully so as not to scrap so much material, and it also sends a message to purchasing to seek better prices and better quality.

Misplaced Blame

In manufacturing, direct labor now averages less than 15 percent of operating cost.

A modern view is that far too much blame—for cost, scrap, rework, delays, and so forth—has been heaped on front-line employees. A century ago, when direct labor amounted to over 50 percent of operating cost on average, emphasis on labor variance made more sense. Today, overhead costs are commonly over five times the cost of direct labor. While a complete cost-variance system includes overhead cost, overhead includes too many diverse elements for an overhead variance to have much impact; managers therefore have fixed their attention on the labor-variance data.

There are other reasons, besides the shrinking direct-labor cost component, for questioning the classic cost-variance measurement system. One is the realization that quality, not just output, is a key to competitive advantage. Another is the wholesale reorganization of resources (re-engineering) that has been taking place in many businesses: away from fragmented and toward product- or customer-focused. This paves the way to simpler, more meaningful measures of performance. A third is overlapping job responsibilities: Front-liners are assuming first responsibility for quality, good workplace organization, upkeep of equipment, data collection and diagnosis, problem solving, and, sometimes, interviewing and training new employees. Formerly, those activities were treated as indirect labor, supervision, and overhead.

Data Collection

Still another disadvantage of conventional productivity systems is the extensive data required to feed them. For example, some systems require expenses to be assigned to minute budgetary codes. Others require data on when an associate starts and completes work for a given client or job, and commonly the associate works for several clients or jobs every day. This system thereby captures time working and time not working—for reasons such as stoppages for approvals, lack of material, breakdowns. These data allow computation of direct-labor productivity or efficiency. To collect all that data, some companies have been persuaded to install data-entry terminals all over the operating area, not for value-adding services but just to monitor them.

An alternative outlook favors lumping together all labor costs, not tracking labor job by job, or separating direct labor from other payroll costs. As front-line associates team up with experts and managers, dividing lines blur, and so do the old labor-cost categories. For example, a Westinghouse plant in North Carolina was reorganized into several product-focused miniplants, each of which became a new, smaller, more-focused cost center. Employees' pay is automatically charged to the miniplants to which each is assigned; once a week supervisors simply turn in an exception report noting any absenteeism or overtime hours.[8] The output of each miniplant is known and so is the miniplant's share of the payroll; no detailed payroll assignment is needed. One use of the data is to provide a supervisor with a report on a miniplant's labor productivity. The greater purpose is to track full costs (labor, material, and overhead) of end products, costs that are mostly contained within each miniplant (see "New Productivity" in the Contrast box).

Effective Measures

While productivity measurement has often become cumbersome, costly, and ineffective, there are plenty of examples of simple, useful ones:

• *Retailers.* A widely used measure is sales per square foot. Stu Leonard's food stores and Circuit City electronic stores rate exceptionally high on this scale. Under this measure, store managers and sales associates become more attuned to

Contrast

Productivity

Old Productivity

Narrow, fractionated: On the output side, emphasis is on operations (rather than whole products). On the input side, focus is on direct-labor cost, charged to operations and departments (not to products or customers).

New Productivity

Broad, integrated: On the output side, focus is on whole products or subproducts. On the input side, all human-resource and other operating costs are included and related to whole products or specific customers.

---

customer needs—for example, for quality, quick service, and attentiveness—because these factors bring in business. On the other hand, if stores are rated on sales per salesperson, managers might tend to cut staff, resulting in declining service and, finally, less business.

• *Accounting, legal, and consultancy firms.* A common measure is billable hours (an hour of time billable to the client) per professional associate. This measure, again, reflects ability to attract customers. Moreover, it gives managers and professionals room to be real operations managers, that is, to weigh the value of different types of staffing, equipment, training, thoroughness, after-sale service, and so forth.

• *Manufacturers.* Harley-Davidson, the motorcycle manufacturer, is among the vanguard of producers shifting toward new, team-oriented productivity and quality measures. Two of the company's new measures are motorcycles per employee and total conversion cost per bike.[9] Formerly, like most other manufacturers, Harley computed productivity separately for each of its many work centers and departments. The new, simple, overall measures encourage these units to work together, and they support Harley's extensive efforts to eliminate inventories between departments and to merge the formerly separated processes into product-focused cells. Effects of these improvements show up clearly and directly in the new measures of performance for a whole motorcycle.

These examples illustrate measures that are effective, unifying, and simple:

• *Effective.* The measures are directed toward business activity, customers, and the products or services themselves. Less effective are measures of resource activity instead of business activity, and functions rather than products and customer allegiance.

• *Unifying.* The aim is to include not just front-line labor but all operations and operating costs.

• *Simple.* The new thinking: Complex data collection, person by person, job by job, function by function, is out; using already-available data is in.

Even the best single measures of performance, however, are insufficient. In superior companies, the expectation is that each employee will contribute in many more ways than just "doing the job." The idea is to directly control the causes of cost, rather than monitor costs after the fact.

Controlling Causes of Cost

When a company abandons detailed, period-cost measures, aren't there some risks? Won't it be all too easy for shirkers to escape detection, for poor performance to be hidden? Perhaps so, if the company has no better way to deal with costs and wastes. A better way, however, has proven itself. It is a multifaceted system of eliminating the causes of cost, poor quality, delays, and other undesirables.

*P*RINCIPLE 15:

Cut reporting; control causes.

Seven Deadly Wastes

This system introduces additional, detailed process improvement measures, and it takes aim at the so-called **seven deadly wastes.** Originally formulated for factories,[10] the seven wastes are adapted for any organization as follows:

1. *Waste of doing more than the customer wants or needs.* In an office, this includes too many reports issued too often, too many meetings, too many interruptions. At retail it would include badgering the customer and demonstrating products and models that go beyond the customer's interests. In a factory it is, simply, overproduction.

2. *Waste of waiting.* This is wasting the time of clients, suppliers, or the workforce.

3. *Transport waste.* Ill-planned layouts of facilities can mean long travel distances from process to process for customers, suppliers, the workforce, materials, supplies, mail, tools, and equipment.

4. *Processing waste.* In the value-adding operations themselves, processing wastes can add up: Files are not properly cross-referenced. Procedures are not kept up-to-date. The task sequence is cumbersome or difficult to do.

5. *Inventory waste.* This includes all of the extra costs of holding and monitoring inventories, such as outdated catalogs and records, obsolete materials, and items bought or produced in excessive quantities too early for use.

6. *Waste of motion or energy.* Mere motion or consumption of energy do not equal useful work. The test is, Does it add value to the product? If not, it wastes motion or energy.

7. *Waste of defects and mishaps.* Any defect, any mishap creates a chain reaction of other wastes—potentially all of the preceding six wastes—to "make it right." Included are wasting time, adding transport distance (e.g., return and do it over), inserting extra processing, requiring more inventories, and wasting motions or energy. Poor quality affects nearly everything negatively.

In effectively attacking these wastes, teams of associates apply a full array of problem-solving tools (e.g., the seven basic tools, which were presented in Chapter 5). They display what they are doing and the results visually on wall charts, ideally big ones that are hard not to notice. The visual measurement data fall into three categories:

1. *Product, service, component, or customer specific.* Rework, returns, claims, scrap, mishaps, nonconformities, yield, on-time completions, cycle time, flow distance, space, and idle inventory.

2. *Process specific.* Process changeover and get-ready time, response ratios, check sheets, and control charts.

3. *Activities, recognition, rewards, celebration.* Present improvement projects, present training programs, completed projects, completed training, number of suggestions, appreciation letters from customers, awards won, plaques, photos of recognition ceremonies, and so forth.

Visual Controls[11]

This system is visual, located where the work is performed, usually owned by operating people, and up-to-date. Controlling causes in this way is, in the words of H. Thomas Johnson, "unlike the distant, often distorted financial echoes of those causes that appear in traditional cost and performance reports."[12] The full system of visual measures emphasizes all of the factors listed in Chapter 1 (Exhibit 1–5) as "customer requirements"—namely, quality, flexibility, service, cost, response time, and variability.

Examples of the visual system are shown in the photographs in Exhibit 16–5, which come from Milliken & Co. A large, privately held textile and chemical producer, Milliken has charts of these kinds throughout its offices and plants.

PRINCIPLE 14:

Record data at the workplace.

The improvement charts have several purposes. If there really is progress, the people involved can take pride in the visible display of improvements.[13] Further, improvement trends silently call for more of the same, a motivational benefit. Finally, a good assortment of wall charts can be an excellent tool for communication among operations, support people, management, and visiting customers or suppliers. The charts may even help draw timid managers and others out of their offices to the source of problems. While it is not natural for a manager to carry a computer report to the floor to use in discussing problems, performance charts in the workplace are a natural focal point for discussion.

In the cause-control system, cost ceases to be used for controlling productivity. The on-the-spot visual signboard system controls the causes, and productivity improvement (as well as improvement in quality, cycle time, etc.) follows.

EXHIBIT 16–5   Visual Management at Milliken and Company

An "alcove of excellence" in a main trafficway.

A "wall of fame" with data and photos of award winners.

Cost and Other Conventional Measures

That does not mean that cost data and other conventional measures have no importance in operations management. Some of the valued uses of cost data are

- *Target costing.* As used in product development, target costing (discussed in Chapter 4) aims at killing a bad project early if the cost target cannot be met.
- *Budget watching.* Some companies (e.g., Miller Brewing Company's brewery in Trenton, Ohio) teach the fundamentals of budgeting to all associates so that everyone can help find ways to stay within the budget.
- *Careful usage of purchased materials.* Some organizations (e.g., Boeing's Door Center in Renton, Washington) label bins of purchased materials with the unit costs of the materials, which instills cost consciousness; production associates are less likely to use materials carelessly and more likely to focus their improvement activities on issues dealing with high-cost items.
- *Regulatory requirements.* Regulatory agencies require reports on the value of inventories and statements of profit and loss, but those reports require only a fraction of the data needed for a full-blown cost-variance system.

Besides these uses of cost data, many companies are looking for ways to salvage some of their traditional productivity measures by correcting some of their weaknesses. One weakness, the fixation on front-line labor, is reduced when associates assume responsibility for quality, data collection, and other duties usually handled by large staffs of overhead people. This brings more of the productivity equation under the control of front-liners, and the size of the overhead group and its cost shrink.

Another weakness is the tendency to count any output as productivity, even customer-rejected goods and services. Helping to correct for this tendency are shortened cycle times, which tie operations more closely in time to real customer needs. Related to this is the shift toward product-focused organization, which helps make any measure of productivity more focused on what the customer is paying for.

Despite these improvements, the old productivity system retains the weaknesses of being periodic, delayed, staff directed, and not cause oriented. The traditional system of determining product costs has these deficiencies and others. But new cost-accounting methods offer help.

Cost of Goods and Services

> *Insurance Agent A:* "How can the company be making money on these individual policies? Those clients are a pain to sell to and a headache when they've got a claim."
>
> *Agent B:* "Who cares, as long as you get your commission?"

This scenario repeats itself in nearly all large businesses, where costs are not easily tied to the actual service, customer, or product. While front-line people—managers and cost accountants, too—have long asked these kinds of questions, only recently has the truth emerged. And the truth often is that the low-volume specials (individual insurance policies, perhaps) are not profitable. They are not priced high enough to make money because they are not assigned their fair share of company costs. By company costs we mean, especially, overhead costs, which usually dwarf direct-labor costs. High-volume commodity items (e.g., group insurance policies), on the other hand, usually receive more than their share of overhead cost. As a result, they are often overpriced or inaccurately judged to be financial losers.

By now, hundreds of articles and many books have cited this systematic bias in company costing systems. While cost accounting, pricing, and profit management are a bit beyond the scope of operations management studies, we nevertheless must note how the cost-bias problem can adversely affect OM decisions. Consider the following problem scenarios for a catering business:

- An improvement team of buyers, cooks, helpers, and drivers has come up with several productivity improvement ideas for high-volume catering customers (e.g., an airline), but at the same time a management group decides to abandon the high-volume business because the biased cost system falsely shows it to be losing money.
- Low-volume catering (weddings, etc.) actually is the money-losing business segment, but aided by biased costing, it looks profitable (in fact, the sales manager for that segment has received a hefty pay hike). No one has had an incentive to improve it, service quality is barely adequate, and before long this segment is losing customers and—now, clearly—money.

Costs are important, as well, for a few other common operations management activities, including evaluating process, method, and equipment alternatives, and making make-or-buy and sourcing decisions.

According to one line of critical thought, several major businesses that American manufacturers abandoned as losers in the 1970s and early 1980s, such as commodity memory chips, actually may have been profitable.[14] Operations managers, not seeing any way to cut costs enough, would have been party to decisions to abandon such commodity product lines. Companies in the world's largest mass market shedding highest-, instead of lowest-, volume products even sounds illogical.

Activity-based costing (ABC) directly addresses the bias in overhead cost allocation. ABC methods attempt to assign overhead costs to a product or service only where there is actual overhead activity related to the item. Briefly, in the ABC method a team, consisting of an accountant and representatives of an overhead activity such as scheduling or maintenance, forms to search for simple activity cost drivers. For example, operating overhead costs could be allocated to a product based on a single driver, cycle time. The reasoning is that if a product is active for five days (cycle time = 5), the product probably actually receives five days of overhead cost; if another product zips through in just one day, it is scarcely seen or handled by overhead people and therefore should receive proportionately less overhead cost—by this method only one-fifth as much.

Cost, like dust, settles on items that move too slowly.

Since its development in the mid–1960s, activity-based costing has spread quickly. It is widely valued for use in making critical operating and competitive decisions, which require accurate costs.

The same accuracy-enhanced cost data could also be used for correcting the inaccuracies in cost-variance reporting. Some believe, however, that the cost-variance system has outlived its usefulness. A number of other measures are available and are more effective and less costly to administer, so the reasoning goes. In the remainder of the chapter, we present some of the other measures and motivators.

Busy and Productive Resources

Walk into a drugstore when it is moderately busy, and what do you see? A clerk in the cameras and film department flitting back and forth taking care of three customers; one cashier up front ringing up a customer's purchases, and another cashier trying hard not to look idle and bored; customers bumping into each other in the cold remedies aisle while most other aisles are empty. The cameras and film clerk is busy, and working very efficiently. One cashier is busy, the other idle. The space around cold remedies is highly utilized, whereas most of the rest of the store isn't even justifying the power to keep the lights on.

We have identified some common, noncost ways of evaluating the productivity of various resources. Terms like *efficiency, busyness* and *idleness,* and *utilization* can be used loosely; they also have precise meanings and can be measured numerically. Examples follow, first for equipment and other nonhuman resources; then for people.

Equipment Utilization

A general formula for **utilization** of labor or equipment is:

$$\text{Utilization} = \frac{\text{Time in use}}{\text{Time available}} \qquad (16\text{--}1)$$

Equipment utilization reports, expressing equation 16–1 as a percentage, are common in larger companies. For some equipment, 40 hours (one shift operation) is used as available hours per week. Sometimes two or more shifts are the basis. Data for the reports sometimes can be collected automatically by timers in the vehicle, conveyor line, data terminal, medical device, or other equipment.

The machine utilization report has at least three purposes. First, it serves as a check on how well the plant and the company plan in advance for the right capacity. Second, trends in utilization suggest when more capacity will be needed so that equipment can be ordered in advance. Third, when the report shows decreasing utilization, that suggests the need for sales promotions or for rethinking the purpose for having the unutilized capacity.

Exhibit 16–6 shows a machine utilized over 100 percent on a one-shift basis; that means the machine is run on overtime, extra shifts, or weekends, which may require payment of overtime wages. The company might have seen the trend months earlier so that another machine or a larger machine was put on order and is due in soon.

With today's mood of questioning virtually everything in operations management, the utilization report has come under fire. Harley-Davidson has simply eliminated equipment utilization reports. Why? Because the reports can cover up certain faults and result in treating symptoms, not causes. The next list points out potential weaknesses in equipment utilization reports or the way the reports are used:

Exhibit 16–6

**Equipment
Utilization Trend
Report**

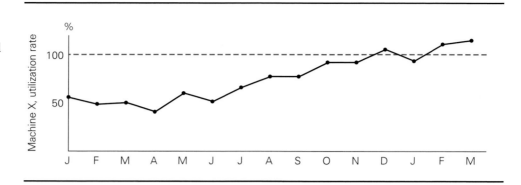

- High utilization can be achieved by disposing of slow equipment and running all jobs on new, fast machines. But old, slow equipment can be valuable when considering moving equipment into cells or other focused zones within a building.
- Utilization may include bad time (e.g., a copier making blank or wrinkled copies) or get-ready and setup times. If the firm adds capacity when equipment is engaged in such ineffective activities, poor habits set in.
- High utilization may be achieved by running very large lots, which produce unneeded inventories and lengthen cycle times.
- Utilization reports can encourage dabbling in peripheral services to keep equipment busy; over time, the facility becomes unfocused.
- Utilization is usually measured in hours, when the real concern should be utilization of capital (return on investment).
- Finally, and perhaps most important, 100-percent utilization is not even desirable. For example, no computer center wants its mainframe to be 100-percent utilized, because the effect would be long backlogs, interminable delays in getting jobs run, and anxious customers squabbling for priority.

*P*RINCIPLES 11 AND 13:

Cut flow time, inventory, and lot size.

Utilization of Space, Information, Materials, and Tools

Besides equipment utilization, some firms, especially larger ones, measure and report on space utilization. The reports express space in use as a percentage of total space, which may be broken down by type of space or type of use. Colleges and universities generally report based on several room-use categories, which in the United States are specified by the Department of Education.

Use of information resources can also be measured. Typically the measure is frequency of use rather than percentage of time in use. For example, an organization may archive records and files based on a certain standard of use or nonuse and dispose of them completely in the next phase of records/file control. (*Migration* is a common records-management term for moving information from active storage to archives to disposal.) Internet page "visits" and file download requests are other indicators of information utilization.

Measures of materials utilization might include scrap, theft, deterioration, obsolescence, and misplacement, all of which hinder productive use of materials and supplies. Approximately the same utilization measures may be applied to tools.

Labor Utilization

For the labor resource, it is common to keep track of absences resulting from illness, jury duty, military duty, labor-union activities, tardiness, and so forth. Each of these eats into productive time.

More specifically, the utilization formula, Equation 16–1, also works for the human resource.

Assume, for example, that a five-person office group spends 2,000 minutes at work on an assortment of 38 jobs (such as letters and reports) in an eight-hour day, which for five people is 2,400 minutes (8 × 60 × 5). The utilization, from equation 16–1, is

$$\text{Utilization} = \frac{\text{Time working}}{\text{Time available for work}}$$

$$= \frac{2{,}000}{2{,}400} = 0.83, \text{ or 83 percent}$$

And what about the other 400 minutes of the 2,400-minute day? We should not be too quick to label it idleness. The five office associates might use that time for worthwhile activities such as cross-training or teaming up on improvement projects.

The utilization formula is simple, but it requires data on time working. An efficient, proven approach for getting those data is work sampling.

Work Sampling

A **work-sampling study** yields data on percentage of time working, idled, or delayed. Further, the study team can subdivide the idleness into categories, thereby showing process bottlenecks. Example 16–1 illustrates.

EXAMPLE 16–1   WORK SAMPLING—PATHOLOGY LAB

The director of Midtown Pathological Labs is concerned. Costs are going up rapidly; the staff has plenty to do, yet is often idled by assorted problems. The director decides to probe the sources of delay by conducting a one-week work-sampling study. Of special interest are lab equipment failures, supply shortages, delays waiting for instructions, excessive coffee breaks, and lab technicians absent from the work area. The director prepares a work-sampling data sheet that includes those five categories of delay (plus an *other* category); she also works up a schedule for taking 100 sample observations (20 per day).

The schedule and completed form are shown in Exhibit 16–7. The results, the staff not working 35 percent of the time, confirm the director's impression of serious delay problems. The breakdown into categories of delay yields insight as to causes.

The management system can be blamed for the first 18 percent of nonworking time. Equipment failure (3 percent), supply shortages (6 percent), and wait for instructions (9 percent) are management failures to provide technicians with resources for keeping busy.

The 13 percent of delay for coffee breaks is an employee problem. Authorized coffee breaks are a 15-minute morning break and a 15-minute afternoon break. This amounts to 30 minutes or, in percent of an eight-hour day:

$$\frac{30 \text{ min}}{8 \text{ hr.} \times 60 \text{ mins./hr.}} = 0.0625 \approx 6 \text{ percent}$$

EXHIBIT 16–7
Work-Sampling Data Sheets—Midtown Pathological Labs

SCHEDULE OF OBSERVATION TIMES

Mon. Tues. Wed. Thurs. Fri.

8:01
8:13
9:47
9:59
10:12
10:59
11:16
11:32
1:00
1:15
1:19
2:52
2:55
2:56
2:57
3:02
3:29
3:37
4:07
4:32

WORK-SAMPLING FORM

Category of activity	Observations (tallies)	Percentages
Working	𝍸 𝍸 𝍸 𝍸 𝍸 𝍸 𝍸 𝍸 𝍸 𝍸 𝍸 𝍸 𝍸 (65)	65%
Not working:		
• Equipment failure	||| (3)	3%
• Supplies shortage	𝍸 | (6)	6%
• Wait for instructions	𝍸 |||| (9)	9%
• Coffee break	𝍸 𝍸 ||| (13)	13%
• Out of area	|| (2)	2%
• Other	|| (2)	2%
Total	100	100%

The coffee-break abuses may be dealt with immediately. The data on resource shortages do not offer a solution, but they do tip off the director on where to look.

Besides delay statistics, work sampling yields the complement, utilization rate. As we have seen, utilization (65 percent in the example) means busyness—hours busy divided by hours available. But most of us are very busy at times and not so busy at others. To avoid bias, the analyst doing work sampling must take care to do the study in a representative time period—representative of average conditions, if that is the goal, or representative of very busy conditions if peak periods are being examined. Ways of avoiding other types of bias, including insufficient sample size, can be found in basic industrial engineering books.

Labor Efficiency

Human labor is a unique resource that is not merely utilized. Unlike the nonhuman kind (e.g., equipment and materials), the human resource has a will; it can choose to work at a normal pace or much faster or slower than that. Later, we shall see how to find out what normal, or standard, pace is. For now, we'll examine one of the uses of standard time—determining **labor efficiency,** which is done in one of two ways:

standard time
The time a fully-qualified person is expected to need to complete a task under normal conditions.

$$\text{Efficiency} = \frac{\text{Standard time per unit}}{\text{Actual time per unit}} \text{ or, simply, } \frac{\text{Standard time}}{\text{Actual time}} \qquad (16\text{–}2)$$

$$\text{Efficiency} = \frac{\text{Actual units per time period}}{\text{Standard units per time period}} \text{ or, simply, } \frac{\text{Actual units}}{\text{Standard units}} \quad (16\text{–}3)$$

Note that the two versions are mathematically equivalent; each is an inversion of the other.

Efficiency for Nonuniform and Uniform Products.   We may illustrate by returning to our five-person office team, which turned out 38 jobs yesterday. Assume that 34 is the standard output per day (for five people). According to equation 16–3,

$$\text{Efficiency} = \frac{38 \text{ actual units/day}}{34 \text{ standard units/day}}$$

$$= 1.12, \text{ or } 112 \text{ percent}$$

To use equation 16–2, the data must be converted to time per unit. Say that in their 2,400 minutes, the office staff actually spends 1,900 minutes at work on the 38 completed jobs. The other 500 minutes include coffee breaks, cleanup, improvement meetings, and time off for someone to visit a dentist. Then,

$$\text{Standard time} = \frac{1,900 \text{ minutes/day}}{34 \text{ standard units/day}}$$

$$= 55.9 \text{ minutes/unit}$$

and

$$\text{Actual time} = \frac{1,900 \text{ minutes/day}}{38 \text{ actual units/day}}$$

$$= 50.0 \text{ minutes/unit}$$

Then, by equation 16–2,

$$\text{Efficiency} = \frac{55.9 \text{ minutes/unit}}{50.0 \text{ minutes/unit}}$$

$$= 1.12 \text{ or } 112 \text{ percent}$$

In this example, the 38 jobs (letters, reports, etc.) are not uniform. Thus, the standard time of 55.9 minutes represents an average job, but of course some jobs could take all day and others just a few minutes. With such a nonuniform product, an efficiency measure still can be meaningful, but only if it covers a sufficiently long time period, in which the mix of complex and simple jobs would tend to even out. One day and 38 jobs are not enough for a fair efficiency reading. Monthly reporting would be more acceptable. (See other examples for nonuniform operations in the Into Practice box, "Efficiency . . .")

Fairness becomes less of an issue when the output units are high in volume and uniform, or nearly so, such as stuffing envelopes in a mass political mailing. A fair efficiency rating, using equations 16–2 or 16–3, could even be turned out daily (although it is hard to think of reasons for doing so that often).

The matter of uniformity or type of output is itself a productivity measurement issue.

Measures of Output.   Measuring productive output is not always just a matter of counting envelopes or completed letters and reports. A few other output measures

$$\mathcal{I}nto \ \mathcal{P}ractice$$

Efficiency and Time Standards for Nonuniform Operations

Example: The U.S. Air Force Logistics Command, which operates very large job-shops for aircraft repair, compares accumulated standard times against accumulated clock hours for most of its repair-shop crews (and calculates efficiency using equation 16–3). The reporting period of two weeks is long enough to include perhaps hundreds of task time standards.

Example: Most college libraries use computers to produce catalog cards. A cataloging aide with book in hand enters data about a new book at a terminal, and the data are transmitted to a central library cataloging service center. The center's computer database is searched to find (in the United States) a Library of Congress catalog number for the book. For the search to be successful,

the cataloging aide must enter the right data. This can be difficult, for example, for foreign-language books, musical compositions, and government documents.

Managers at one college library set a monthly standard rate (historical) of 300 books per cataloging aide. Aides deeply resented the standard rate because some aides arrived early in the morning in order to fill their carts with easy books, which allowed them to easily exceed 300 books per month. Other aides who liked the challenge of the tough books actually looked worse when the monthly report came out. The solution: distribute books to cataloging aides at random each morning. That way, each receives about the same variety of types of books over a period of months.

are commonly used in other kinds of operations. Exhibit 16–8 summarizes the measures for the three basic types of operation.

As the exhibit shows, in repetitive or continuous operations measuring output simply requires counting completed units that meet minimum quality standards. The count may be in units per day, and the unit of measurement may be pieces, gallons, yards, or numbers of clients. The count may be transformed into yield (good units completed divided by total units started) or variance from (amount short of) quantity scheduled.

In job production, output measurement can be costly and difficult. A parts order may be routed through multiple work centers, with output measured at each. As is shown in Exhibit 16–8, the measurement may include a unit count of clients or documents processed or parts successfully produced (not scrapped). Time of completion is also reported so priorities may be recomputed for upcoming work centers. Periodically, perhaps every two weeks, a report may summarize work moved out after successful completion as compared with work moved into each work center. Another report may show job-order due dates met, which measures the success for all the work centers put together. Due dates met is also a suitable output measure in simpler job operations involving perhaps only one unit and one work center. Examples are repairing a pair of shoes, papering the walls of a room, performing a lab test, and cooking a meal. Percent of completion is a suitable measure where processing time at a given work center is long (days or weeks) and the output is not readily countable. Examples are major overhauls and renovations.

Three kinds of output measures listed in Exhibit 16–8 for project operations are percent of completion, milestones completed on time, and events completed on time. Those measures are discussed in connection with project management and the PERT/CPM technique in Chapter 15.

Type of Operation	Output Measures
Continuous or repetitive	Unit count
Job	Unit count (work center) Due dates met (job orders) Percent of completion
Project	Percent of completion Milestones completed on time Events completed on time

EXHIBIT 16–8

Output Measures, by Type of Operations

Productivity Reporting in Perspective

Reports on resource productivity tend to proliferate and get out of hand, sometimes to the point where as much is spent on reporting as on paying for the resources. This happened at a Tektronix plant producing portable oscilloscopes. A study revealed that the labor reporting, including data entry, computer processing, error correction, and other steps, was costing as much as the total payroll the labor reports were supposed to control! Needless to say, Tektronix canceled the labor reporting, which eliminated about 35,000 computer transactions per month.[15]

It is staff organizations, such as purchasing, human resources, and accounting, that generate resource reports. Those organizations are input oriented, but they exist only for serving line operations, which are output oriented and customer oriented. But preservation, growth, and power instincts can conflict with the ideal of providing only the resources necessary for use in serving customers. Those instincts tend to result in too much resource management and too many reports. When large organizations fall on hard times, regaining economic health may include cutting staff employees and many of their reports. The tens of thousands of jobs lost in industries such as financial services in recent years serve as a reminder.

Thus far, we have considered cost and noncost approaches to productivity management. Next we examine the time standard, a key source of data for these approaches.

Time Standards and Their Uses

Work is simply a form of exertion. But a unit of work (such as a job, task, or project) is defined more specifically, including the time taken to perform it.

Sometimes work time is estimated in advance. For example, in a two-person operation, if person B must wait for person A to finish a job, B will want an advance estimate of how long A's job will take. A and B as an improvement team may want to time their operations as part of a process-improvement project. Others may want time estimates in order to judge whether A and B can handle the work or will need help (more staff). Still others may use these times in preparing an estimate or bid. In addition, the existence of time estimates is likely to have motivational value—a target for A and B to shoot for.

To summarize, we have identified five purposes of time standards (time estimates): coordination and scheduling, process improvement, staffing, estimating and bidding, and motivation. In the remainder of this section, we examine these five topics.

Coordination and Scheduling

The primary use of time standards is in coordination and scheduling. Actually, by definition, a schedule is a time standard, with proper adjustments for efficiency and utilization; that is, the time between the scheduled start and the scheduled finish of a task equals standard time—the time it should take under normal assumptions:

1. Adjusted downward for a fast employee or upward for a slow employee.
2. Adjusted downward for less than 100-percent labor utilization (i.e., for expected idleness).

Mathematically, scheduled output for a given time period is

$$\text{Scheduled output} = \frac{\text{Efficiency} \times \text{Utilization}}{\text{Standard time per unit}} \tag{16–4}$$

or

$$\text{Scheduled output} = \frac{\text{Standard units}}{\text{per time period}} \times \text{Efficiency} \times \text{Utilization} \tag{16–5}$$

where (from equation 16–1)

$$\text{Utilization} = \frac{\text{Time working}}{\text{Time available for work}}$$

A useful inversion of equation 16–4 is

$$\text{Scheduled time} = \frac{\text{Standard time per unit}}{\text{Efficiency} \times \text{Utilization}} \tag{16–6}$$

As equation 16–6 shows, when efficiency or utilization improve (denominator), scheduled time is reduced.

Where coordination demands are light, formal scheduling of work units may be unnecessary. But there is nearly always at least a vague time plan for starting and finishing an upcoming task.

Analysis, Planning, and Motivation

A second set of uses of time standards includes

- *Analysis of alternative methods and equipment.* Improvement teams may use time standards in estimating amount of labor required for each alternative.
- *Staffing.* Staff(labor) needed is the product of units forecast times standard time per unit. Labor budgeting goes a step further. Labor budget equals staff needed times average wage. (See the Into Practice box, "Time Standards . . . .")
- *Estimating and bidding.* The staff component of an estimate or bid is computed the same way as the staff budget. Accurate bidding is critical to profitability in project work. Estimates or bids are also important in many kinds of services such as medicine, law, consultancy, and automotive repair.
- *Motivation.* Without a deadline, people tend to put things off. A time standard acts like a deadline, helping to keep people motivated to meet the standard. A weakness is that the time standard may not seem like a real need to employees. People are more likely to respond to a known, valid

$\mathscr{I}$*nto* $\mathscr{P}$*ractice*

Time Standards for Staffing Attorney's Offices

In one effort to set time standards on lawyers' tasks, the sole purpose was to straighten out a staffing mess. The lawyers worked in 36 program offices of the U.S. Department of the Interior, and it was hard to assign the proper number of lawyers to each office.

The department hired a consultant to help define work units and set standards. The basic work unit was a *matter* (not a case, because matters often did not result in cases). Secretaries kept records on the time lawyers spent on fifty-nine varieties of matters. The results were fairly consistent throughout the United States, and the average times served as historical (nonengineered) standards for use in staffing decisions; that is, in a given office demand for each

matter could be forecast (by trend projection, etc.) and multiplied by standard time to yield labor hours, which converted into staff needs.

Professional work like that of a lawyer is not only variable but often seen as something of an art and resistant to standardization. The lawyers cooperated because the limited purpose—better staffing—was made clear. Probably there would have been no cooperation had the purpose been to judge efficiency or even to schedule lawyers' tasks.

Source: Part of the consultant's story is told in Marvin E. Mundel, *Motion and Time Study: Improving Productivity*, 5th ed. (Englewood Cliffs, N.J.: Prentice-Hall, 1978), pp. 485–94 (T60.7.M86).

customer need date or quantity, which itself could be based on a time standard. The motivational value of a time standard also depends on whether people believe it is valid, which depends on the techniques used in developing the standard, our next topic.

Time Standards Techniques

Exhibit 16–9 lists six ways of developing a time standard. The first four are engineered, which means rigorously developed to a high level of validity. The last two are nonengineered. In this section we consider the differences and go through the details for time study, the most prevalent technique. Discussion of the remaining five techniques is reserved for the chapter supplement.

Engineered and Nonengineered Standards

Four techniques may result in engineered time standards. Engineered standards are prepared at some expense following the scientific methods of the industrial engineer. The expense of an engineered time standard may be worthwhile if precision is needed, for example, in highly repetitive processes, where small gains add up fast. The following steps lead to an engineered standard:

1. Clearly specify the method.
2. Obtain time values via a proper sampling procedure or from validated tables.
3. Adjust for employee pace.
4. Include allowances for personal, rest, and delay time.

Each step adds precision. A precise time standard is associated with a known standard, preferably improved, method. One way to get precise time values is to

EXHIBIT 16–9 **Techniques for Setting Time Standards**

Technique	Source of Times	Timing Role of Analyst
Engineered:		
1. Time study	Stopwatch (or film)	Direct observation: Record times for several cycles of the task; judge and record pace.
2. Work sampling	Percent of study period busy at given task divided by number of units produced	Direct observation: Randomly check employee status; keep tallies of employee activities and pace; obtain production count.
3. Predetermined	Table lookup	Define task in basic body motions; look up time values in basic motion tables.
4. Standard data	Table lookup	Define task in small, common elements (e.g., pound nail); look up time value in standard-data tables.
Nonengineered:		
5. Historical (statistical)	Past records on actual task times	Determine arithmetic mean and/or other useful statistics.
6. Technical estimate (guesstimate)	Experienced judgment	Experienced person estimates times, preferably after breaking task into operations.

use direct observation and a proper sampling procedure; direct observation is avoided by use of a synthetic time value from validated tables. Where direct observation is used, the time value should be adjusted for employee pace, but validated tables for time values have built-in pace adjustments. Finally, the pace-adjusted time is further adjusted by adding reasonable allowances for employees' personal and rest time and for unavoidable delay.

guesstimate Also known as WAG or SWAG, common abbreviations for slightly salty phrases some readers may be familiar with.

The nonengineered techniques, based on history or guesstimates, control none of the above four factors of precision. Even the first four techniques in Exhibit 16–9 are worthy of the term *engineered* only if they are precisely developed following the four steps. In the following discussions, we see how the steps apply for each technique.

Time Study

World War II was the heyday of film analysis. Almost anything that might help the war effort received funding.

The most direct approach to time standards is timing an employee who is performing the task. A stopwatch is the usual timing device, but motion picture film or videotape also works. **Time study** is best for shorter-cycle tasks. The cost of having an analyst at the worksite and timing a proper number of cycles of the task tends to rule out time study for longer-cycle tasks. The four time-study steps are explained next and illustrated in Solved Problem 3 in this chapter.

1. *Select task and define method.* There are choices to be made here. For example, packing and crating a large refrigeration unit consists of packing the unit into a carton, placing the carton on a pallet, building a wooden crate around the carton and pallet, stenciling, and steelstrapping. A single time study of the whole series

of tasks is one possibility. Alternatively, analysts could separately time-study each major task, but each of those involves lesser tasks, which could be separately time-studied. Pounding a single nail into a crate could be the task chosen for study.

Once the task has been chosen, the analyst defines the method and its elements. The definition must clearly specify the actions that constitute the start and the end of each element, which is how the analyst knows when to take each stop-watch reading.

2. *Elemental time.* Tools of the time-study analyst include a clipboard, a preprinted time-study data sheet, and a stopwatch. The watch is mounted on the clipboard. Before timing, the analyst observes for a while to be sure the operator is following the prescribed method.

In the timing phase, the analyst records a stopwatch reading for each element. Several cycles of the task should be timed so that effects of early or late readings can be averaged out. Multiple cycles also provide a better basis for judging pace and observing unavoidable delays and irregular activities. Comments on irregularities are entered in a remarks section on the data sheet.

The number of cycles to time could be calculated based on the statistical dispersion of individual element readings. However, most firms pay more attention to the cost of multiple cycles than to the statistical dispersion of readings. For example, General Electric has established a table as a guide to the number of cycles.[16] The table calls for timing only 3 cycles if the cycle time is 40 minutes or more, but it calls for timing 200 cycles if the cycle time is as short as 0.1 minutes. Since 200 cycles at 0.1 minutes adds up to only 20 minutes of observer time, the 200-cycle study may cost less to do than the 3-cycle study of a 40-minute task.

The result of timing is an average **elemental time (ET),** a raw time value.

3. *Pace rating.* If the analyst times a slow person, the average cycle time will be excessive—*loose* is the term usually used; if a faster person is timed, the ET will be tight. To avoid loose or tight standards, the analyst judges the employee's pace during the study. The *pace rating* is then used mathematically to adjust ET to yield a *normal time.* This is called *normalizing.* The normal pace is 100 percent, a 125-percent pace is 25 percent faster, and so on.

Pace rating is the most judgmental part of setting time standards, but it need not be pure guesswork. Films from the American Management Association and other sources provide training in pace rating. The films show a variety of factory and office tasks. The same task is shown at different speeds, and the viewer writes down the apparent pace for each speed. Then, with the projector shut off, the viewer's ratings are compared with an answer key. Correct answers have been decided upon by experts or measured by film speed.

Most people can become good enough at pace rating to be able to come within ± 5 percent of the correct ratings. It is easier to rate a person who is close to normal than one who is very slow or fast. Because of this, it is a good idea for the analyst to try to find a normal employee to observe in doing a time study (or work-sampling study). Sometimes pace rating is omitted by preselecting an employee who is performing at normal; the omission is illusory since the rating is done in the employee selection step.

4. *Personal, rest, and delay (PR&D).* The normalized time per unit is not the standard time, because we can't expect a person to produce at that normal rate hour after hour without stopping. Personal time allowances (rest room, etc.) and rest allowances (e.g., coffee breaks) may be set by company policy or union contract. In industrial shops, the rest allowance may be for more than coffee; it may go as high as 50 percent for tasks performed in a freezer or near a furnace.

Common benchmarks of normal (100-percent) pace:
• Hand motions: Deal four hands of 13 cards in 30 seconds.
• Walking, normal person, unloaded, level surface: three miles an hour.

Strictly speaking, unavoidable delay—for example, difficulty in meeting tight tolerances or small variations in materials or equipment—is inherent in the method. Some companies also include certain delays that are beyond the method, such as unbalanced work flows, lack of work, or breakdowns. Unavoidable delays are sometimes determined by a work-sampling study in which occurrences of various types of delay are tallied.

The allowances are usually combined as a percentage, referred to as the *personal, rest, and delay (PR&D) allowance.* The combined allowance is then added to the normalized time, resulting in a standard time.

In the chapter supplement, we briefly discuss four other approaches to determining a time standard: work sampling, predetermined, standard data, and historical. The four basic steps—obtain method, obtain time values, adjust for pace, and add allowances—are common to all the approaches. The main difference is in the way of obtaining the time values.

Summary

Productivity is in a state of change, except for the basic components of measuring it: outputs compared with inputs. The traditions of productivity measurement date back to scientific management, which emerged at the turn of the century as a final phase of the Industrial Revolution. Its main ingredients are methods study, process design, and time standards.

Care must be taken to ensure that productivity improvement does not dehumanize jobs, for this could lead to longer-term degradation of performance. Fortunately, an assortment of techniques that focus on meeting customer needs (e.g., JIT and TQM) also show promise for putting meaning back into people's work lives. For example, skill-based pay provides employees with new opportunities to develop, grow, and make themselves more valuable to present or future employers.

One use of time standards is determination of standard labor cost, which when compared with actual labor cost yields labor variance. Labor variance, material variance, and total cost variance are the core of periodic accounting-based productivity measurement, which is entrenched in much of industry. A weakness has been too much emphasis on direct labor productivity; too much also on mere outputs, as opposed to meeting customers' needs.

Companies are addressing the weaknesses by moving resources into groups focused on whole products provided just in time with total quality, costing the outputs of the whole rather than the parts, putting up cause-control charts throughout the operating areas, and extensively training employees to become multiskilled problem solvers. Inasmuch as most operating costs become contained in the focused groups, complex operation-by-operation cost collection may no longer be needed.

To judge effectiveness, operations people need measures of results that are business-, customer-, and product-oriented, such as retail sales per square foot or total conversion cost per unit of output. The best ways to reduce costs are to control the causes of cost through cutting out wasteful delays and transactions, employing process controls, and motivating improvement teams by making improvement activities and results visible. Improvement takes aim at the "seven deadly wastes": doing too much, waiting, transport waste, processing waste, inventory waste, motion or energy waste, and defects and mishaps.

Still, cost data have value in OM, especially for target costing, budget watching, careful usage of purchased materials, and meeting regulatory requirements. Still another need in regard to cost data is finding out unit cost of products for use in product-line decisions, such as make or buy. While product costing has been fraught with error in the past, improvements are forthcoming through use of activity-based costing (ABC) techniques.

The newer productivity and costing methods are still far from dominant. Traditional methods improvement and time standards are still in wide use and likely to continue to play several important roles. Current emphasis on total quality and process control breathes new life into one of the old techniques, process flowcharting, which may be done at the bench level, the operator-machine level, or the whole-process level.

Utilization rate (for equipment, labor, or other resources) is time in use over time available. A weakness is that this measure merely focuses on busyness, not on whether the resource is busy doing something that customers want. Work sampling studies can generate utilization data broken down by category of delay.

Labor efficiency goes beyond utilization; it gets at amount of output while working (speed), as compared with an output standard. Output measures themselves include unit counts; due dates, events, or milestones met; and percent of completion.

Time standards are necessary for coordinating and scheduling, analyzing operations, and motivating employees for improvement. Accurate time standards, for example, facilitate undercapacity labor scheduling, which allows time for important indirect work activities. Time standards also play key roles in determination of efficiency, utilization, and productivity values. They also may foster self-motivation among employees.

There are six basic techniques for setting time standards: stopwatch time study, work sampling, predetermined standards, standard-data time standards, historical standards, and technical estimates. Engineered (high-precision) standards require controls on methods, time measurement, employee pace, and allowances for personal, rest, and delay time.

Solved Problems

Problem 1

At Metro Gas and Electric, the productivity of each of five functional departments involved in billing (for power consumption and other sales to commercial, industrial, and residential customers) is reported monthly. The main measure in the report is cost variance, which is based on cost of billings processed as compared with standard cost. An improvement team has concluded that the variance system generally fails to lead to improved performance. What changes should they recommend?

Solution 1

The first step is to re-engineer the five departments into a few focused cells; for example, separate cells for commercial, industrial, and residential customers—and perhaps separate cells for power usage and for other sales. That will contain most of the operating costs within each focused cell.

Other steps include posting cause-control charts in every cell, upgrading the skill levels of every employee, perhaps including pay for skills, and using activity-based costing to more accurately find the costs and track cost trends for processing bills in each cell.

Problem 2   Gate City Tire sells and installs tires, some by appointment and the rest to drop-in customers. Appointments are carefully scheduled so that (1) the customer may be told when
the car will be ready and (2) installers are kept busy. The manager knows that under normal
conditions a four-tire installation takes about 20 minutes. The time varies depending on the
installer's speed (efficiency) and the delay (utilization) encountered. Gate City follows the
concept of under-capacity scheduling: For an 8-hour paid shift, the company schedules 7.3
hours of tire installing.

During the 7.3 hours of assigned work, efficiency has been found to be 90 percent; it is
low because the present crew lacks experience. Utilization, again during the 7.3 assigned
hours, is 80 percent. Delays arise from tool breakdowns, parts shortages, special customer
requests, and two authorized 15-minute coffee breaks; these, plus miscellaneous delays, account for the 20-percent nonutilization time.

Regardless of expected daily output, each daily job may be separately scheduled. For example, the third job of the day, a phoned appointment, is assigned to Jeff, who has been only
80 percent efficient. But, the manager expects no delays for lack of materials, tool breakdowns, or other problems, and it is not near coffee-break time; thus, he expects utilization
on this job to be 100 percent.

  a. Calculate the current scheduled daily output.
  b. What is the scheduled installation time of the third job of the day, assuming
      Jeff is given the job?

Solution 2   *a.* From equation 16–5,

$$\text{Scheduled output} = \frac{7.3 \text{ hours} \times 60 \text{ minutes/hour}}{20 \text{ minutes/installation}} \times \frac{90 \text{ percent}}{\text{efficiency}} \times \frac{80 \text{ percent}}{\text{utilization}}$$

$$= 15.768, \text{ or approximately 16 installations per day}$$

  b. The scheduled installation time, from equation 16–6 is

$$\text{Scheduled time} = \frac{20 \text{ minutes/installation}}{80 \text{ percent} \times 100 \text{ percent}} = 25 \text{ minutes}$$

Problem 3   A proposed bolt-washer-nut assembly method was approved, and a time-study analyst
was assigned to develop a time standard for the task. After observation, the analyst has reduced the task to four timable elements. Six cycles are timed by the continuous stopwatch
method, and each element is pace rated. Calculate the standard time. (For a short-cycle task
like bolt-washer-nut assembly, it would take less than an hour to time, say, 30 cycles, but our
six-cycle example is sufficient to illustrate the procedure.)

Solution 3   The time-study data sheet is shown in Exhibit 16–10. The analyst reads the stopwatch in
hundredths of a minute and does not insert decimal points until after the last computation.
The stopwatch begins at zero and runs continuously for 7.55 minutes. The analyst enters
continuous readings below the diagonal line, and then computes elemental times by successive subtraction.

Average elemental time (ET) is the sum of elemental times divided by 6; for element 2,
ET is divided by 5 because one irregular elemental time was thrown out. The average goes
below the diagonal line in the ET column. The analyst judges pace and enters pace ratings
in the rating factor (RF) column, with decimal points not included. Normalized time (NT)
equals ET times RF. The NT column adds up to 110, or 1.10 minutes per cycle.

The analyst adds a PR&D allowance, which has been negotiated with the labor union. It
provides 3-percent personal time (e.g., blow nose), two 15-minute rest (coffee) breaks, and
2-percent unavoidable delay allowance. These are minimum allowances; the contract allows rest time to be set higher for highly fatiguing work, and the delay allowance may be
set higher for tasks involving abnormal delays.

EXHIBIT 16–10 Time-Study Data Sheet-Bolt—Washer-Nut Assembly

Element	Cycles						ET	RF	NT	Remarks
	1	2	3	4	5	6				
1. Get bolts and place in fixture.	12 — 12	10 — 116	13 — 240	11 — 349	16 — 468	10 — 656	72 — 12	110	13.2	
2. Get Washers and place on bolts.	14 — 26	16 — 132	15 — 255	14 — 363	93 — 561	14 — 670	73 — 14.6	100	14.6	5th cycle: Blew nose
3. Get nuts and assemble onto bolts.	75 — 101	86 — 218	77 — 332	82 — 445	79 — 640	78 — 748	477 — 79.5	95	75.5	
4. Drop assemblies down chutes.	05 — 106	09 — 227	06 — 338	07 — 452	06 — 646	07 — 755	40 — 6.7	100	6.7	

Calculations	Total normalized time × (PR&D allowance + 100%):	110.0 × 111.25%
	Standard time	122.375, or 1.22 minutes/unit

The two 15-minute breaks convert to percentage of an eight-hour, or 480-minute, day by

$$\frac{30 \text{ minutes}}{480 \text{ minutes}} = 0.0625, \text{ or } 6.25\%$$

$$\text{Total PR\&D allowance} = 3\% + 6.25\% + 2\%$$

$$= 11.25\%$$

In a final computation, the analyst multiplies the total normalized time by the PR&D allowance of 11.25 percent plus 100 percent (which is mathematically the same as adding 11.25 percent of the total normalized time). The result is the standard time of 1.22 minutes per unit.

Review Questions

1. What is the primary method of measuring productivity?
2. How can job enlargement/job enrichment be applied to enhance teamwork instead of being oriented to the individual?
3. Is it fair to pay based on amount of work produced? Why or why not?
4. How does skill-based pay help drive productivity improvement? What are some other good motivators?
5. Why have some managers and accountants questioned the value of the cost-variance system?
6. What is meant by the phrase *control causes of cost*?

7. Explain the visual controls concept.

8. How should organizations deal with the seven deadly wastes?

9. What operating decisions rely on product/service cost data? How can bias be avoided in arriving at those cost data?

10. In methods study, what information is included in a before-and-after comparison?

11. Which flowcharting symbols are used in each of the three types of methods study? Explain.

12. How do work-sampling studies reveal deficiencies in the management system?

13. How can labor efficiency and utilization be allowed for in scheduling?

14. How can wages be based on time standards given minimum-wage laws?

15. When is a nonengineered time standard not good enough?

16. Why isn't the ET the time standard?

17. Which of the PR&D factors are task dependent? Explain.

18. In what sense is pace rating unfair? Fair?

19. How can labor standards be fair if tasks are variable?

Exercises

1. The president of Universal Service Corp. is concerned. His company is in serious financial trouble, even though its cost system (roughly the same system most other firms use) shows that labor costs have been going down significantly for months. How would you advise the president?

2. Name the four most important visual performance charts for control of causes in each of the following cases:
   a. A movie theater chain.
   b. A long-running play.
   c. A home-building construction company.
   d. A custom spray-painting plant.

3. Laws in many countries require division of company employees into management and labor, with different employment laws for each. For decision-making purposes, however, some companies have abolished these categories. Hewlett-Packard, for example, considers everyone overhead, with no separate category called direct labor.
   a. What is the effect of this practice on measuring labor productivity?
   b. Discuss the advantages and/or disadvantages of this practice.

4. "Equal pay for equal work" was the hot pay issue in an earlier era. Next came "Equal pay for comparable work." With which concept(s) of fair pay (from Exhibit 16–3) does the comparable-work idea seem most consistent? Explain.

5. Jim Talbot, supervisor at Florida Power and Light (first non-Japanese winner of Japan's Deming quality prize), has been quoted as saying, "I can, literally, look at a wall and see what is going on in my department."
   a. What does this statement suggest about the type of measures and controls in place in Talbot's department?
   b. Discuss what things should be on Mr. Talbot's walls for his visual system to be effective and complete.

6. Thumb's Tax Service has grown by 45 percent per year for the last three years, and now has 42 tax offices supported by a company headquarters of 13 people (tax specialists, computer programmers, marketers, etc.) along with a range of computer equipment. Thumb's profits, however, have been weak to nonexistent. Everyone suspects the reason is Thumb's costing, which leads to pricing in which difficult

private and commercial clients pay an average of only 35 percent more than easy ones.

    a. What operating decisions at a tax service like Thumb's require good cost data? In your answer, explain what costs are needed.

    b. How can Thumb's management team resolve the costing problem?

7. At International Express Company, professionals and technicians from the industrial engineering, (IE) department and the quality assurance (QA) department are engaged in a turf battle. The IEs are claiming that they are the experts in flowcharting and methods improvement and should retain that responsibility. The QA specialists are claiming they should now have the responsibility. Who is right? Explain.

8. Three key monthly reports reviewed by officers at Nanosoft Inc., a software development firm, are (1) utilization of Nanosoft's six copying machines; (2) utilization of labor, including clerical, machine operators, analysts, and programmers, based on work sampling studies covering a different office area each month; and (3) utilization of books, reports, and documents in the Nanosoft library. Discuss the probable effectiveness of these reports. Should anything be changed in this reporting system? Explain.

9. (See MTM discussion in this chapter supplement.) A salesperson has an order for 1,000 candles in the shape of an athletic team's mascot. Production control assembles the following data from the candlemaking shop, to be used in setting a price (direct cost and overhead plus markup):

Elemental time	20,000 TMUs
Allowance for personal time and unavoidable delay	9%
Authorized break time	20 minutes per day

Recent candlemaking statistics are

Total clock hours for candlemakers	350 hours
Standard hours' worth of candles produced	380 hours

    a. What standard time should be used in computing standard cost?

    b. If there are two employees in candlemaking, how many hours should be scheduled for them to complete the order for the 1,000 special candles?

    c. Assume the candle order has been finished and took 190 hours to complete. What rate of efficiency did a crew attain?

10. The director of a social agency is preparing next year's budget. The agency's caseload averaged 42 clients per day last year, but it has been increasing at an annual rate of 15 percent. The director and caseworkers agree that it takes 3.5 hours on average to handle each client properly.

    a. How many caseworkers should be requested as the staff component of next year's budget assuming the 15-percent increase in caseload? Assume that caseworkers work an average 250 days per year (which allows for vacation days, sick days, etc.) at eight hours per workday.

    b. What kind of time standard is the agency using? Is there any way to improve this?

    c. What other reasonable uses exist for the time standard?

11. Assume your boss is supervisor of the packing and crating department and has just sent you the following memo: "The president wants all shops, including ours, covered by time standards. I'd like you to do a preliminary study to see if reasonable time standards can be set for our type of work. Everything we pack is of a different size. So how can we have standard times?"

    a. Respond to the boss's memo.

    b. What technique for setting time standards is best for this type of work? Explain.

12. In an automobile plant, a time-standards analyst finds that the average elemental time for mounting tires onto rims is 3.6 minutes. If the personal, rest, and delay allowance is 14 percent and the pace rating 105 percent, what is the standard time?

13. An MTM analyst predicts that installing a cord on a proposed new telephone set will take 4,250 TMUs.
    a. What is the standard time in minutes if the shop allows a 20-percent PR&D allowance? (See MTM discussion in chapter supplement.)
    b. How can the analyst set a standard on a proposed telephone set? Doesn't the item have to actually exist? Discuss.

14. An employee in an electronics plant is using a lugging machine to attach a connector onto the end of a wire. (The machine automatically kicks the wire into a chute once the connector has been attached.) The following data are provided by a time-study analyst. Stopwatch readings are in hundredths of a minute and cumulative from element to element and cycle to cycle.

		Cycle			
Job Element	*1*	*2*	*3*	*4*	*Pace Rating*
Cut length of wire	21	48	74	103	100
Insert into lugger and press start button	30	58	86	112	90

   a. What is the standard time? Assume a personal time allowance of 5 percent, a delay allowance of 3 percent, and two 20-minute coffee breaks per eight-hour day.
   b. What would be the advantage in using methods-time-measurement (MTM) instead of stopwatch time study? (See MTM discussion in chapter supplement.)

15. A work sampling study has been conducted for the job of spray-painting a set of parts. The job consists of mounting the parts on hangers, then spraying them. The PR&D allowance is 20 percent. The analyst's tally sheet is shown below:

Job: Spray painting   Time period: Five 8-hour days

Activities Sampled	*Tallies*	*Total*	*Work Count*	*Pace Rating*
1. Mount	ЖЖ ЖЖ ЖЖ ЖЖ ЖЖ ЖЖ	30	20	110
2. Spray	ЖЖ ЖЖ ЖЖ ЖЖ ЖЖ ЖЖ ЖЖ ЖЖ ЖЖ ЖЖ	50	20	120
3. Nonwork	ЖЖ ЖЖ ЖЖ ЖЖ	20		
Total		100		

   a. What is the elemental time for each task? (See work-sampling discussion in chapter supplement.)
   b. What is the rated time for each task?
   c. What is the standard time for each task?
   d. What is the value of the data on nonwork time? How could the data be improved to make them more useful?

16. A supervisor has done a work-sampling study of a subordinate, a clerk-typist. The purpose was to set time standards for typing letters and retrieving letters on file. Therefore, those two tasks were tallied on the work-sampling tally sheet, along with a miscellaneous category for all other clerk-typist activities. The complete tally sheet is as follows:

Subject: Typist			Tasks: Typing letters and retrieving letters on file			
Dates: November 29–December 10 (10 working days)			Analyst: Clerical supervisor			

Activities Sampled	Tallies	Total Count	Percentage Rating	Work Count	Pace Rating
1. Type letters	卌 卌 卌 卌 卌 卌 卌 卌 卌 卌 卌 卌 卌 卌 卌 卌	80	40%	60	90
2. Retrieve letters	卌 卌 卌 卌 卌 卌	30	15	150	80
3. Miscellaneous	卌 卌 卌 卌 卌 卌 卌 卌 卌 卌 卌 卌 卌 卌 卌 卌 卌 卌	90	45	—	—
Totals		200	100%		

a. PR&D allowance is 12 percent. Compute elemental time, rated time, and standard time for each task. (See work-sampling discussion in chapter supplement.)

b. Discuss the possible uses of these time standards.

c. Comment on the fairness and/or validity of these time standards. Are they engineered?

17. Mailroom associates at an insurance company prepare all of the company's premiums and letters for mailing. A time study has been done on the job of enclosing premium statements in envelopes. Continuous stopwatch data are given below; the readings are in hundredths of minutes:

Job Element	Cycle							Performance Rating
	1	2	3	4	5	6	7	
Get two envelopes	11		55		105		151	105
Get and fold premium	22	41	65	83	116	135	162	115
Enclose in envelope and seal	29	48	73	97	123	143	169	95

a. Develop a time standard and calculate standard output per 480-minute day, providing 15 percent for allowances.

b. Assume that the premiums and letters are of various sizes and shapes. The get-and-fold element takes much longer if the item is large and requires several more folds than are needed if the item is small. Therefore, the time standard could be unfair to some of the associates it covers. Suggest some situations in which the standard would be unfair. Suggest some options for making it fair.

c. Assume an infrequent element: At every 25th envelope, an associate wraps 25 envelopes with a rubber band and places them in a box. This element was timed once, and the elemental time was 15 with a performance rating of 90. With this added factor, recompute the time standard and output from question a.

18. At Wabash Airways analysts have calculated that a flight attendant needs two minutes to fully serve a meal to a passenger on one of its aircraft; that is, the standard time is two attendant-minutes per meal.

a. If two flight attendants are assigned to an aircraft with 80 passengers on board and serve all of them in a flight having one hour of serving time, what is their efficiency?

b. If a new jumbo aircraft seats 600 passengers, how many flight attendants are needed for a flight with 100 minutes of serving time?

19. At the Transcona Plating Company, all metal-plating jobs are covered by time standards. Last week the company did 850 standard hours' worth of plating jobs. Total clock time for production employees was 1,000 hours that week, and their actual hours of direct labor (hours allocated to actual plating jobs) was 800.
    a. What is the efficiency rate?
    b. What is the utilization rate?

20. Following is a list of tasks on which time standards/estimates may be set. Suggest a suitable technique or techniques for setting a time standard for each task, and explain your choice.

    a. Mowing grass.
    b. Soldering connections in small electronic components.
    c. Drafting (design drawing).
    d. Typing and filing.
    e. Overhauling or adjusting carburetors.
    f. Cooking in fast-food restaurant.
    g. Computer programming.
    h. Installing auto bumpers on car assembly line.

CASE STUDY

LAND AND SKY WATERBED COMPANY

Land and Sky Waterbed Company of Lincoln, Nebraska, was the fourth-largest waterbed company in the United States and the largest in the Midwest. Land and Sky (L&S) was founded in 1972 by two brothers, Ron and Lynn Larson. They remain as co-owner/managers. One of the brothers is responsible for research and development. (Outside R&D consultants are called on for assistance sometimes.)

The total workforce, including office staff, is 67. The oldest employee is the vice president, Jim Wood, a psychology graduate in his mid-30s. Wood has played a major role in developing the scheduling, inventory, quality, and employee payment system at L&S.

The Product Line

L&S produces two lines of waterbed mattresses and liners in standard sizes (king, queen, double, super single, and twin). L&S also manufactures special made-to-order mattresses for other frame manufacturers. The Land and Sky label goes on the higher-quality gold and bronze bed sold exclusively to franchised dealers. L&S produces another brand called the Daymaker. It is sold without advertising as a commodity product. The Daymaker is available to any dealer.

A trade group for the waterbed industry has not yet achieved consensus on standard dimensions for king size, queen size, and so forth, for the soft-sided foam frame. Therefore, the L&S product line includes more than 60 sizes, built to order. Also, some customers make beds to their own dimensions before checking to see what mattress size they can readily obtain. L&S will accept special orders for such unusual sizes, but the price will be high and the order will take 30 days to be filled.

L&S also makes two kinds of soft-sided frames, which make a waterbed look like a conventional bed with box spring and ordinary mattress ("a waterbed that appeals to older

Case topics: Self-discovery of JIT; make-to-order JIT; offline subassembly; pay for knowledge/multifunctional employees; pay incentive for quality; frequency of deliveries from key suppliers; evolving from a small to a large business.

Source: Adapted from the *World Class Manufacturing Casebook: Implementing JIT and TQC.* Copyright © 1987 by Richard J. Schonberger. Reproduced by permission of The Free Press, a Division of Simon & Schuster.

people," according to Jim Wood). One kind is made of rigid foam and is cheap and easy to make. The other kind, L&S's own unique design, has a plastic rim built in and is called Naturalizer 2000; the rim keeps the foam from breaking down.

Competitive Climate

Since waterbed manufacturing is not highly technical and is quite labor intensive, competitors spring up all over. Low-wage countries like Taiwan are becoming tough competitors.

L&S markets its product line throughout the United States and Canada. An Australian producer makes to L&S's specifications under a licensing agreement. (Jim Wood now wishes that L&S had set up its own Australian subsidiary, rather than licensing the Australian manufacturer.) The European market for waterbeds is still too small to bother with.

There are two main market outlets. The older outlet is the small waterbed retailer, many of whom tend to be less experienced in the ways of the business world and therefore unstable. Later waterbeds became popular enough for a second major market outlet to emerge: old-line furniture stores. The two market types place very different demands on the waterbed manufacturer, the small waterbed retailer wanting instant delivery response.

L&S has developed a quick-response production system aimed at filling these orders faster than the competition. Most orders can be shipped within 48 hours, and same-day production and shipment is possible though not cost-effective. Some inventory of finished waterbeds is kept in bonded public warehouses in different regions of the country, which further speeds up order filling in those regions.

One complicating factor is that a few retailers are unsophisticated in their ordering. For example, one retailer phoned in a large order specifying the quantity but not which models he wanted. When asked which models, he said, "Just send about what I have ordered before." That was not of much help because prior orders had come in at different times for different models.

The old-line furniture stores order more conventionally. They plan orders carefully in advance and do not expect delivery right away, but do drive a hard bargain on price. In response to that price-conscious market, L&S has instituted procedures that tightly control material storage costs, labor costs, and costs of scrap and defects.

The Plant

L&S is in an industrial park, housed in three noncustom metal buildings arranged in a U-shaped configuration. Building 1, at one leg of the U, houses the sales and administrative offices with a shipping and receiving warehouse in the back. Building 2, forming the bottom of the U, is the main manufacturing and quality-check area. Building 3, the other leg of the U, is for fiber baffle production and assembly, liner production, and injection molding and assembly of soft-sided frames. A parking lot in the center of the U is also used for vinyl storage.

Assembly

Producing the Waterbed.   *Vinyl processes.* The waterbed begins as a roll of vinyl. At first operation, an associate cuts it to size by hand. (A $20,000 cutting machine had been used, but it broke down often and yielded too much scrap.) The next steps are to install valves and corner seam panels using special machines. Then the vinyl sheets go to machines that fuse the corners together by high-frequency radio waves. Last, the ends and sides are sealed (see Exhibit CS16–1).

Baffle installation. High-quality waterbeds contain a fiber baffle that keeps the water from making waves when in use. Research and development at L&S has come up with a baffle made of polyurethane fiber that reduces the wave time from 25 to 3 seconds. L&S considers fusing of the side and end seams on the mattress especially important, and the best operators are assigned that operation. One outside observer watching the job estimated that the two operators were working at about 140 percent of normal pace.

Responsiveness.   Total throughout time for these steps in making the waterbed is 35 minutes. The daily output is about 450 waterbed units.

One way that L&S holds down production-cycle time is by performing early stages of manufacture, such as cutting the vinyl, installing valves, and fusing corners, before knowing exactly what the model mix is. Later the same day, late-arriving orders are totaled by product type, and final model-mix instructions go out to the shop floor. Some of the options that are determined at the last minute are (1) the number that are to be top-of-the-line beds with fiber baffles and (2) the number that are to have the L&S label or the Daymaker commodity label.

Question 1. In what sense do the assembly operations sound like just-in-time production? (No one at L&S had ever heard of JIT at the time of the case.) What JIT improvements do you suggest for assembly?

Subassemblies and Accessories

Baffles (a subassembly) and frames and liners (accessories) are scheduled so as to avoid stockouts. The items are made as follows:

Fiber baffles. Baffles are machine-cut on the cutting machine originally bought for $20,000 to cut vinyl. Then holes are drilled around the edges of a stack of fiber sheets, and vinyl ties are threaded through the holes to hold the stack together for storage and transport; the idea for vinyl ties was developed after glue and plastic hooks failed.

Soft-sided frames. Frames are injection-molded and assembled. L&S has patented a plastic rim insert, for which it spent $250,000 on research and development, which lends support and adds life to the foam in the frame.

Exhibit CS16-1
Sealing Ends and Sides

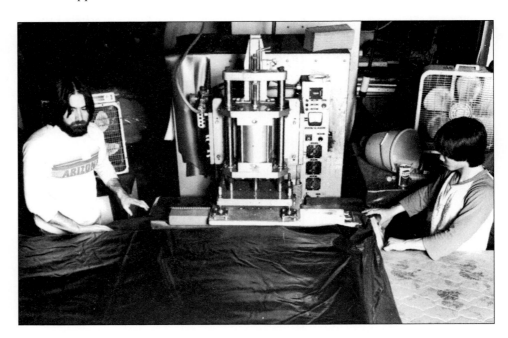

Cardboard-reinforced bottom liner. The bottom liners were developed by L&S to make it faster and easier for the customer to set up the waterbed; the liners cut setup time by about 20 percent and have been on the market for about seven months. Retailers love this feature because the liner is reusable, a good sales point. The bottom liners sell for $16 to $20 at retail.

Question 2. What could be done about subassembly and accessories manufacture to mold them into more of a JIT relationship with their customers (assembly and final pack and ship)?

Pay System

In July 1982, L&S converted from a straight hourly pay plan to a piece-rate system having the following features:

Base piece rate. The base piece rate depends on the assigned job (e.g., $0.20 per bed).

Achievement raise. An operator gets a 5-percent bonus on top of a base rate for each additional machine that the operator learns to run. A few operators have learned to run 10 or 12 machines and therefore get 50–60 percent more than the base piece rate. The bonus buys flexibility for the company. Typically an operator who can run just 2 or 3 machines averages $5–$7 per hour, while one who can run 12 machines might earn $9–$11 per hour. Jim Wood stated that other companies send people home when a machine is down; here "we put them on another machine."

Quality bonus. Operators get a bonus of 25 percent of total pay per period for zero errors. The bonus decreases for each error found: one or two errors, 20 percent; three errors, 15 percent; four errors, 10 percent; five errors, 5 percent, and six or more errors, 0 percent. The owners were initially dubious about the 25 percent bonus (Jim Wood's idea). Previously the bonus was 15 percent. Their feeling was, "Why pay a large bonus for what the employees are supposed to do anyway?" But they agreed to give the plan a try and were very pleased with the results. The error rate had been about 5 percent (5 out of 100 beds). It was down to about 0.5 percent by October. Some of the better operators were achieving zero-error rates.

Error penalty. The operator has to pay a penalty of $0.65 for every error discovered by quality control inspectors. Errors are easily traced back to the operator responsible, because each operator has an employee number that is attached to the bed when the operator is working on it. If the operator notifies quality control of an error by marking it, then the penalty is only $0.25. Plans are in motion to make the penalty zero for an admitted error; that way there will be no temptation to try to sneak one by the inspector. Inspection is much more efficient and valid when operators mark their own errors.

Quality control (QC) does the bookkeeping for the entire piece-rate and quality-incentive system. QC people record daily production and quality performance data for each employee. All information is maintained on the computer.

Labor Policies

Waterbeds are a somewhat seasonal product, which makes staffing difficult. The peak seasons are March-April-May and August-September-October. L&S will not build inventory just to keep operators busy. Competition from other waterbed manufacturers is fierce, especially the Taiwanese manufacturers of liners, which makes low-cost, low-inventory policy a competitive necessity. Therefore, in the slack season operators are laid off—strictly by productivity, not seniority.

Since bed materials are too large for one person to handle easily, operators usually work in pairs; pairings are generally by comparable skill levels. If one operator is tardy or absent, the partner must keep busy on lower-pay work and forgo the chance for piece-rate bonuses—a sacrifice the operator is sure to complain about. Therefore, policies on absenteeism and tardiness are rigid: Absenteeism usually means automatic termination.

Question 3. In what ways does the pay and labor system stand in the way of, or further, quicker response?

Quality Control and Warranties

Quality-control inspectors visually check each bed, inspecting surfaces for blemishes, seams, valves, and so forth. Once in a while the inspector will blow up a bed with air like a balloon in a more thorough leak check. Water is not used to test beds because it leaves a residual odor.

If no blemishes or defects are found, L&S ships the bed to the retailer with a five-year warranty. Beds with a flaw are sold as blems at a lower cost with a three-year warranty.

Question 4. Critique the L&S approach to quality control.

Purchasing and Inventory Control

In the waterbed business, material costs are a good deal higher than payroll costs. Thus, materials are tightly controlled.

There are few manufacturers of vinyl, a key raw material, and vinyl suppliers require a 30-day lead time. Vinyl suppliers ship to L&S by a regular purchase-order schedule, and any schedule changes require about 30 to 60 days' advance notice. Therefore, demand forecasting is important for L&S. One of the owners does the forecasting, which is based on seasonal factors and past sales.

Other materials are recorded by a visual reorder-point method. When stock looks low based on the projected manufacturing schedule, an order is placed. The safety stock is typically about two-and-a-half days' supply.

Average raw material inventory is typically two to three weeks' worth. In other words, inventory turns 20 times a year or more. That is partly a matter of necessity. Fiber must be stored indoors, but since it is bulky and there simply is not space to store more, it is maintained at a two-and-a-half-day inventory level. Fiber orders are delivered twice a week in semitrailer loads of 8,000 pounds.

The main purchased material is vinyl in large rolls. Since vinyl is waterproof and may be stored cheaply outdoors, L&S orders larger lots of vinyl than it does for other materials. Vinyl is received about three times a month, 40,000 pounds at a time.

Purchasing and traffic (shipping) are under the management of a single individual, Mr. Bergman. He buys from at least two sources, which provides protection in case one supplier should shut down, a serious matter since L&S's inventories are kept so low. On occasion, purchased parts have been delayed to the point where vinyl rolls are gone; then the operators do what they can with scrap materials, after which they perform other duties or shut down and go home.

Finished goods are stored in the warehouse for a short time prior to loading onto an outbound truck.

A complete physical inventory of finished goods and raw materials is taken every four weeks.

Question 5. What are some ways to improve purchasing procedures?

Question 6. How can L&S protect itself from the miseries that plague most Western companies as they grow large?

For Further Reference

Books

Caruth, Donald L. *Work Measurement in Banking.* 2nd ed. Boston: Bankers Publishing, 1984 (HG1616,W6C37).

Greif, Michel. *The Visual Factory: Building Participation through Shared Information.* Portland, Ore.: Productivity Press, 1991 (originally published in French, 1989) (HD30.3.G7413).

Hirano, Hiroyuki, ed.-in-chief, and J. T. Black, ed. English edition. *JIT Factory Revolution: A Pictorial Guide to Factory Design of the Future.* Portland, Ore.: Productivity Press, 1991 (TS155.H49).

Johnson, H. Thomas. *Relevance Regained: From Top-Down Control to Bottom-Up Empowerment.* New York: Free Press, 1992 (HD31.J555).

Kazarian, Edward A. *Work Analysis and Design for Hotels, Restaurants, and Institutions,* 2nd ed. Westport, Conn.: AVI Publications, 1979 (TX911.K36).

Konz, Stephan A. *Work Design: Industrial Ergonomics.* 2nd ed. Columbus, Ohio: Grid, 1983 (T60.8K66).

Krick, Edward V. *Methods Engineering: Design and Measurement of Work Methods.* New York: John Wiley & Sons, 1962 (T56.K7).

Maynard, Harold B.; G. T. Stegemerten; and John L. Schwab. *Methods-Time Measurement.* New York: McGraw-Hill, 1948 (T60.T5M3).

Niebel, Benjamin W. *Motion and Time Study.* 9th ed. Burr Ridge, Ill.: Richard D. Irwin, 1993 (T60.7.N54).

Salvendy, Gavriel, *Handbook of Human Factors.* New York: John Wiley & Sons, 1987.

Periodicals/Societies

Industrial Engineering Solutions (Institute of Industrial Engineering).

Journal of Systems Management (Association for Systems Management) (paperwork management and systems analysis).

SUPPLEMENT

FOUR METHODS OF DEVELOPING TIME STANDARDS: WORK SAMPLING, PREDETERMINED, STANDARD DATA, AND HISTORICAL

Work Sampling Standards

In Example 16–1 we looked at work sampling as a technique for determining labor utilization and delay rates. Work sampling for setting a time standard requires one extra piece of data: a production count, that is, a count of units produced or customers served during the study period. Elemental time (ET), then, is

$$\text{Elemental time} = \frac{\text{Percent of time on task} \times \text{Total minutes in study period}}{\text{Production count}} \quad (16\text{–}7)$$

As in time study, the analyst transforms elemental time (ET) into standard time by normalizing for employee pace (rating factor, RF) and adding a PR&D allowance:

$$\text{Standard time} = \text{ET} \times \text{RF} \times (100 \text{ percent} + \text{PR\&D}) \quad (16\text{–}8)$$

The following example illustrates the method and also discusses some issues that might arise in its application.

Example S16–1:   Developing Time Standards by Work Sampling at Midtown Pathological Labs

The director of Midtown Pathological Labs conducted a one-week work-sampling study of the lab staff. The results were that the staff was working 65 percent of the time. The director also tallied the type of work task observed. The lab performs two major types of analysis and a host of miscellaneous analyses. The director found that the 65-percent work time was divided as follows:

Serum-blood tests (standard tests) in chemistry lab	30%
Whole-blood tests (complete blood count) in hematology lab	25
Miscellaneous tests in either lab	10
Total work time	65%

There are two lab technicians in the chemistry lab and one in hematology.

At the end of the study, the director found that 48 serum tests and 32 whole-blood tests had been performed. Her estimates of operator pace are 90 percent for serum and 105 percent for whole-blood tests. Midtown uses a PR&D allowance of 13 percent.

With these data, calculate a time standard for both the serum test and the whole-blood test. Discuss the precision and fairness of the resulting standards and any effects on capacity planning.

Solution

Serum test:
From equation 16–7:

$$\text{Elemental time} = \frac{0.30 \times 5 \text{ days} \times 480 \text{ minutes/technician-day} \times 2 \text{ technicians}}{48 \text{ tests}}$$

$$= 30 \text{ minutes per test}$$

From equation 16–8:

$$\text{Standard time} = \text{ET} \times \text{RF} \times (100 \text{ percent} + \text{PR\&D})$$

$$= 30 \times 90 \text{ percent} \times 113 \text{ percent}$$

$$= 30.51 \text{ minutes per test (per technician)}$$

Whole-blood test:

$$\text{Elemental time} = \frac{0.25 \times 5 \text{ days} \times 480 \text{ minutes/technician-day}}{32 \text{ tests}}$$

$$= 18.75 \text{ minutes}$$

$$\text{Standard time} = \text{ET} \times \text{RF} \times (100 \text{ percent} + \text{PR\&D})$$

$$= 18.75 \times 105 \text{ percent} \times 113 \text{ percent}$$

$$= 22.25 \text{ minutes per test}$$

Are these precise (engineered) time standards? The technicians in the chemistry lab don't think theirs is. They point out to the director that their method is to run the serum tests in batches and as a two-person team. There could be one or many samples in a batch, but the time to run a batch does not directly depend on the number of samples in it. The time standard for serum testing is imprecise, indeed, invalid, because the work-sampling study was not precise as to method.

The hematology technician has a milder objection: A mere 25 observations of the whole-blood testing were extrapolated into an assumed 600 minutes of testing time during the week. While the sample size seems rather small, the technician and the director decide that the standard time of 22.25 minutes per test is usable for short-term capacity adjustments. These include scheduling overtime, using part-time help, and subcontracting to other labs.

For example, on a given day, perhaps 30 blood samples will arrive and require testing in hematology. At 22.25 minutes per test, the workload is $22.25 \times 30 = 667.5$ minutes of testing. Since an eight-hour day is only 480 minutes, the director had better tell the technician to plan on some overtime that evening. Part-time help and subcontracting are other options.

Predetermined Standards

Predetermined time standards really are only partially predetermined. The predetermined part is the tables of time values for basic motions. The other part is properly selecting basic-motion time values in order to build a time standard for a larger task.

Basic-motion tables were Frank Gilbreth's idea, but it took some 35 years of effort by many researchers to develop them, mostly through film analysis. The best-known tables are those of the MTM (Methods-Time Measurement) Association.[17] Our limited discussion focuses on **methods-time measurement (MTM).** MTM and other synthetic techniques have several advantages:

1. No need to time; the data are in tables.

2. No need to observe; the standard may be set before the job is ever performed and without disrupting the employee.

3. No need to rate pace; the time data in the tables were normalized when the tables were created.

A disadvantage of MTM is the great amount of detail involved in building a standard from the tables. Basic MTM motions are tiny; motions are measured in *time measurement units (TMUs),* and one TMU is only 0.0006 minutes. A 1.0-minute cycle time equals 1,667 TMUs. One MTM motion usually takes 10 to 20 TMUs; thus, about 80 to 160 basic motions would be identified in the 1.0-minute period. Although much training is required of the analyst to achieve that detail, MTM is preceived as a fair approach to time standards and is widely used.

Other predetermined time systems not requiring so much detail:

- Work-Factor.
- MODAPTS.

The MTM Association has developed tables for the following types of basic motions: reach; move; turn and apply pressure; grasp; position; release; disengage; eye travel and eye focus; body, leg, and foot motions; and simultaneous motions. Again, most times were developed by film analysis.

One of the tables, the reach table, is shown in Exhibit S16–1. From the table we see, for example, that reaching 16 inches to an "object jumbled with other objects in a group so that search and select occur" takes 17 TMUs. That motion, abbreviated as an *RC16* motion, takes about 0.01 minutes or less than a second.

In an MTM study, the analyst enters each motion on a simultaneous motion (SIMO) chart, which is a left-and-right-hand chart. The total TMUs on the chart are converted to minutes. The total is the rated (leveled) time, not the elemental time, because 100-percent pace is built into the tables. Add a PR&D allowance, and you have the standard time.

Standard Data

Standard-data standards, like predetermined (e.g., MTM) standards, are synthetically produced from tables. But standard-data tables are for larger units of work. An example is the flat-rate manuals used in the auto-repair industry. Flat-rate tables list times for repair tasks such as "replace spark plugs" and "change oil." Auto manufacturers produce such

EXHIBIT S16–1   **Reach Table for MTM Analysis**

Length of Reach in Inches	Time in TMUs*				Hand in Motion (TMU)		Case and Description
	Case A	Case B	Case C or D	Case E	A	B	
¾ or less	2.0	2.0	2.0	2.0	1.6	1.6	*A*—Reach to object in a fixed location or to object in other hand or on which the other hand rests.
1	2.5	2.5	3.6	2.4	2.3	2.3	
2	4.0	4.0	5.9	3.8	3.5	2.7	
3	5.3	5.3	7.3	5.3	4.5	3.6	*B*—Reach to single object in location that may vary slightly from cycle to cycle.
4	6.1	6.4	8.4	6.8	4.9	4.3	
5	6.5	7.8	9.4	7.4	5.3	5.0	*C*—Reach to object jumbled with other objects in a group so that search and select occur.
6	7.0	8.6	10.1	8.0	5.7	5.7	
7	7.4	9.3	10.8	8.7	6.1	6.5	
8	7.9	10.1	11.5	9.3	6.5	7.2	
9	8.3	10.8	12.2	9.9	6.9	7.9	*D*—Reach to a very small object or where accurate grasp is required.
10	8.7	11.5	12.9	10.5	7.3	8.6	
12	9.6	12.9	14.2	11.8	8.1	10.1	*E*—Reach to indefinite position to get hand in position for body balance, next motion, or out of way.
14	10.5	14.4	15.6	13.0	8.9	11.5	
16	11.4	15.8	17.0	14.2	9.7	12.9	
18	12.3	17.2	18.4	15.5	10.5	14.4	
20	13.1	18.6	19.8	16.7	11.3	15.8	
22	14.0	20.1	21.2	18.0	12.1	17.3	
24	14.9	21.5	22.5	19.2	12.9	18.8	
26	15.8	22.9	23.9	20.4	13.7	20.2	
28	16.7	24.4	25.3	21.7	14.5	21.7	
30	17.5	25.8	26.7	22.9	15.3	23.2	

*One time measurement unit (TMU) represents 0.00001 hour.

Source: MTM Association for Standards and Research. Copyrighted by the MTM Association for Standards and Research. No reprint permission without written consent from the MTM Association, 16–01 Broadway, Fair Lawn, New Jersey 07410.

tables for repairs on new cars. Flat-rate manuals for older cars, which take more time to repair, are available from independent companies. Best known are the Chilton manuals.

If precise time study, work sampling, or MTM is the basis for the tables, the standard data may be considered to be engineered. It is normal for a firm to keep time standards on file, and it is just one more step to assemble standards from the files into standard-data tables. The next step is to assemble standard data for a whole trade or industry. This has been done in auto repair and other common trades, notably machining and maintenance trades.

The standard-data tables come in several levels. Basic motions (e.g., MTM) are the most detailed level. Next come combinations of basic data (e.g., MTM Association's general-purpose data), such as a joint time for reach-grasp-release. Then come elemental standard data for common elements, like gauging and marking. Standard data for still larger units of work are at the level of whole tasks, such as those of auto repair mechanics or electricians.

Variable working conditions and lack of common methods from firm to firm may compromise the built-in precision of standard data. Still, standard data are efficient in that they bring time standards down to the level of the planner, the supervisor, and the operator. Experts create the tables, but we all can use them.

Historical Standards and Technical Estimates

Nonengineered techniques—historical and technical estimates—are far more widely used than engineered techniques, and rightly so. Most of our work (or play) is variable, and the cost to measure it with precision is prohibitive. Still, explicit time estimates help improve management, and nonengineered techniques serve the purpose. Historical standards and technical estimates are simple to develop and need not be explained further.

FACILITIES MANAGEMENT 17

Chapter Outline

Positioning along the
Provider–Customer Chain
Facility Requirements Pyramid
Location and Its Economics
Location Rating System
Preemptive Strategy

Maintaining Quality of Physical
Resources
Total Preventive Maintenance
Quality through Readiness
Facility Management for the
  Environment

Maintenance Organization: People
and Procedures
Types of Maintenance

Employees, Teams, and Functions
5 S's, Plus Safety Management
Dedicated Maintenance
Maintenance Database
Maintenance Inventories
PM Time

Handling and Transportation
Unit Load versus Piece by Piece
Distance–Quantity Analysis
Containerization

Case Study: Swanbank Frozen Foods

On the phone to your Fidelity Investments advisor, you ask about the firm's global-growth fund. "I'd be happy to send you our brochure, which gives the fund's performance and other details," your advisor says.

But the prospectus doesn't come from your advisor. There are more efficient ways to serve Fidelity's customers, who request some millions of "kits" of informational materials and statements annually. To do this well, Fidelity has opened a huge printing and mailing facility in Covington, Kentucky. Using tracking and storage techniques perfected by manufacturers, "the nation's largest mutual-fund company has tried to reinvent the inglorious task of sorting, stuffing, and stamping mail . . . Fidelity promises that when a customer calls seeking written information, it will be in the mail the next day. Each day's requests are sent electronically to Covington the following morning at 2 AM E.S.T. Fidelity has already pulled often-requested materials. For much of the mail, the company downloads the names and addresses into machines that 'ink-jet' the data on the cover and apply metered postage. The machines then optically read the ZIP Code, spray on a Postal Service bar code, sort the letters and spit them into different trays. About 90 percent of the shipments never see the inside of a post office [but are] hauled away by Postal Service trucks and taken directly to the airport."[1]

Realtors say the three important factors in buying a house are location, location, and location. Our shopping patterns suggest the location of stores is similarly important. And transportation economics often make location a key success factor for processors of physical goods, though, as we've just seen for Fidelity Investments, technology and air freight can alter those economics.

Regardless of location, once inside the facility, our concern shifts to facility condition and efficiency. Is the property run down and ugly or sparkling clean and attractive? And does traffic within the facility flow smoothly, or are handling and transport congested and difficult?

These facility management matters—location, maintenance, and handling—are the main topics of this chapter. (Layout within the facility, another aspect of facility management, was included in Chapter 12.) Human issues are especially important in determining location and in keeping facilities in a high state of maintenance. We take up those matters first and handling last.

Positioning along the Provider–Customer Chain

Care to do most of your wardrobe shopping from your home by catalog? Companies such as Spiegel, L. L. Bean, and Lands' End are ready for your business. Their aim is to provide rapid-response, trouble-free home shopping service. A key facility need is a warehouse full of goods to ship. Saks Fifth Avenue, on the other hand, caters to the walk-in shopper with a hushed, nicely appointed decor. Its strategy is to operate a modest number of fine stores and to retain a sense of exclusivity.

$\mathcal{P}$RINCIPLE 6:

Organize resources to focus on a product, service, or customer family.

A carpeted showroom floor might be part of the desired image for a Porsche dealer, but it might be considered inappropriate at a dealership for construction or agricultural vehicles. Likewise, a health club catering to young people might build more aerobics and weight-training rooms, while a club seeking older members might favor pools and walking tracks. And Anita, the photographer from Chapter 7, will not need studio facilities if she elects not to do portrait work.

Thus, distinctive competencies, desired image, and market niche are determinants of facility needs. However, although the above examples are familiar retail ones, facilities positioning issues are present along the entire supply and distribution chain.

Facility Requirements Pyramid

Regardless of position in the supply chain, where the using organization does not have the needed facilities itself, it must rely on those of suppliers. Every organization does so to some extent. Furthermore, the company and its chain of suppliers depend on infrastructure, which consists of facilities for communication, transportation, and intermediate storage; utilities; and protective systems such as dams and environmental controls.

In partnering up with a supplier, it is important to certify that the supplier has the right facilities and that they are in good condition.

Exhibit 17–1 illustrates this dependency in the form of a facilities pyramid. Usually a company's own facilities are the first order of business, but failure of a supplier's facilities or infrastructure problems can weaken the pyramid's base. To maintain a high level of customer service, a company might have to provide more facility support than anticipated. For example, firms that move plants into low-cost, perhaps rural, locations sometimes have to build roads, drill wells, or pay to expand sewer systems—public facilities. Lack of infrastructure is often a problem

EXHIBIT 17–1

The Facility Requirements Pyramid

in less-developed countries, while crumbling infrastructure might be the concern in developed ones.

We can illustrate the facilities pyramid by considering a catalog shopping business like L. L. Bean. First, it needs its own facilities for processing orders. A mail-order business has its own warehousing and shipping facilities, and it might also have facilities to design, produce, and mail catalogs. But it probably would rely on suppliers' facilities for manufacturing of products advertised in its catalogs.

Beyond that, the mail-order business would have to rely considerably on public facilities, or infrastructure. Order conveyance depends on the mail and communication systems. Goods would arrive and be shipped via streets, highways, rails, bridges, airports, ports, and navigable waterways. Inadequate public water systems, sewage treatment plants, and flood-control facilities in the business's zone of operations could greatly increase costs for the mail-order house or any of its suppliers.

Let's summarize by drawing attention to the top of the pyramid in Exhibit 17–1: When a company answers the question What facilities are needed? it must include those required for planning and design, production, transportation, marketing, service, and the communications and information links that tie them all together and connect the company with its customers. Cutting across all of these facilities elements are concerns for safety and protection of the environment. Clearly, facilities-related decisions need cross-functional, team-based expertise, for the effects can extend throughout an organization and into its environment. Of those facilities-positioning decisions, however, the most far-reaching one is usually location.

Location and Its Economics

As the last century ended, daring individuals accomplished spectacular feats of travel, circling the globe in less than 70 days, making real the fiction of Jules Verne's 1872 classic, *Around the World in 80 Days.* As this century ends, the ordinary citizen could make the trip in less than 70 hours. Rather than guessing what lies another century ahead, we will simply note that it takes little time to move people or things from one spot on the globe to another. Communications advances are equally impressive. Satellites, microwave links, fiber-optic cables, and so on, make nearly immediate voice and facsimile transmission a global reality. The Into Practice box, "Locating 'Next Door' … ," illustrates a highly customer-oriented example of location strategy.

Any official of a city that has gained or lost a major business or government facility will be able to point out the economic impact on the community. Location is far-reaching because where the jobs go, the money goes. Payrolls, along with

Locating "Next Door" to Million-Dollar Customers

Among the 40,000-odd custom plastic molders in the world, Nypro, headquartered in an old former textile mill in Clinton, Massachusetts, stands out in several respects. Of primary importance is its plant location strategy. Nypro wants very strong ties to just a few large customers, rather than weak, sporadic business with hundreds of customers. To this end, it reduced its customer base from a one-time total of over 600 to 31. Its strategy is to seek customers having a potential of at least a million dollars of sales within two years. To serve its customers exceptionally, it locates its plants, numbering about 20, "next door" where possible and otherwise within 100 miles of the customer.

Source: Leslie Gabriele, Robert McInturff, and Michael Perview, "Nypro's Team Efforts Put the Customer First," *Target*, November–December 1993, pp. 45–48.

the jobs and tax revenues generated as payrolls are spent, separate the haves among cities, states, and nations, from the have-nots. Communities recognize this and keep increasing what they are willing to spend to attract businesses and jobs. According to Robert Reich, U.S. Secretary of Labor, "In 1980 Tennessee paid the equivalent of $11,000 per job to entice Nissan" to locate in the state, and "by 1986 Indiana had to spend $50,000 per job to induce Subaru-Isuzu to set up shop" there. South Carolina's tab for bringing in BMW "is the equivalent of about $100,000 per job."[2]

Until recently, research, design, and management jobs generally stayed in highly developed countries, and lower-skilled jobs were relegated to underdeveloped or emerging nations. But look at some recent examples of who's doing what:[3]

- Hewlett-Packard's new portable inkjet printer business is run from Singapore. The design, manufacture, and profit responsibility are all Singapore based.
- In the village of Fermoy, County Cork, Ireland, 150 Metropolitan Life Insurance Company employees analyze medical insurance claims to determine eligibility for reimbursement in the United States. The work requires knowledge of medicine, the American medical system, and the insurance business.
- In 1990, General Electric bought Tungsram, the Budapest, Hungary, light bulb manufacturer. In the bargain, GE got a workforce that turned out to be among the world's best at designing and making advanced lighting systems.

The migration of work to new locales usually is preceded by extensive analysis of alternatives, sometimes including a systematic rating procedure. We discuss one such system, in use at United Technologies, Inc., a large industrial corporation, next.

Location Rating System

The first of three steps is to comparatively rate the importance of a large number of location factors. Exhibit 17–2 is an abbreviated example (many more factors could be included in a location study).

The figure shows that each of 14 factors (A through N) is compared with each other one; ratings are inserted on the matrix. Take, for example, the intersection of factors G and K, "other technology-related companies in area" and "access to suppliers." The rating in the diamond-shaped box is 3G. Checking the "importance" scale, we see that 3 means "medium preference," in this case, a medium preference of G over K.

The bottom row in Exhibit 17–2 contains total weighting raw scores: the sums of the times each letter appears in the matrix. By studying the scores, we might be able to guess what kind of facility this matrix represents. Availability of higher education (F) is number one in importance; nearness to customer (C) and access to suppliers (K) are near the bottom. Could the facility be a design center?

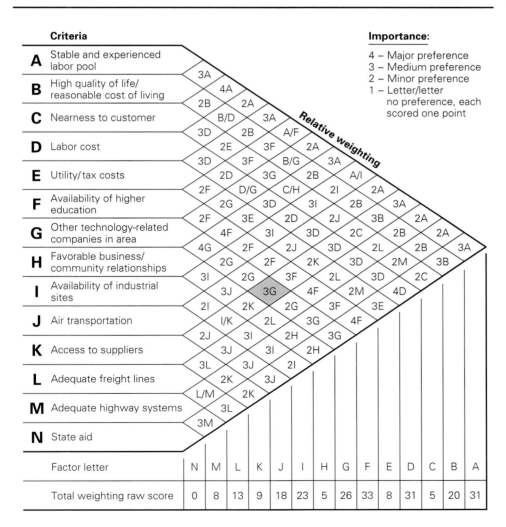

EXHIBIT 17–2

Evaluation Matrix for Relative Weighting of Location Factors*

Importance:

4 – Major preference
3 – Medium preference
2 – Minor preference
1 – Letter/letter
no preference, each scored one point

Factor letter	N	M	L	K	J	I	H	G	F	E	D	C	B	A
Total weighting raw score	0	8	13	9	18	23	5	26	33	8	31	5	20	31

*Not a comprehensive list.

Source: Adapted from Eugene Bauchner, "Making the Most of Your Company's Resources," *Expansion Management*. 1989 Directory. pp. 20–25.

EXHIBIT 17–3
Rating Prospective Locations

A. Rating Locations by Factors				Locations			
Factor	*Red*	*Yellow*	*Green*	*Orange*	*Blue*	*Purple*	*White*
F. Higher education	10	5	4	7	8	6	9
G. Other technology-related companies	6	5	4	7	8	9	10
A. Stable, experienced labor pool	6	5	4	7	8	9	7
D. Labor cost	9	6	7	4	8	10	5
E. Utility/tax cost	7	6	5	3	8	10	9
J. Air transportation	10	6	5	8	9	7	4

B. Weighted Location Scores				Locations			
Factor	*Red*	*Yellow*	*Green*	*Orange*	*Blue*	*Purple*	*White*
F. Higher education (33)	330	165	132	231	264	198	297
G. Other technology-related companies (26)	156	130	104	182	208	234	260
A. Stable, experienced labor (31)	186	155	124	217	248	279	217
D. Labor cost (31)	279	186	217	124	248	310	155
E. Utility/tax cost (8)	56	48	40	24	64	80	72
J. Air transportation (18)	180	108	90	144	162	126	72
Total weighted score	1,187	792	707	922	1,194	1,227	1,073
Ranking	3	6	7	5	2	1	4

Source: Adapted from Eugene Bauchner, "Making the most of Your Company's Resources," *Expansion Management,* 1989 Directory, pp. 20–25.

Step 2 in United Technologies' system is to rate the locations under consideration against the location factors, A through N in this case. Exhibit 17–3A is a partial matrix (listing just 6 of the 14 factors) showing the site ratings on a ten-point scale for seven locations; in a real study, place names rather than colors would be on the matrix. We see that location Red gets the highest rating, 10, on factor F, higher education. In fact, all of location Red's ratings (for the factors shown) are fairly high. But these are not the final ratings. A third stage is needed.

The third matrix, Exhibit 17–3B, combines ratings from the first and second steps. Location Red got 10 points for higher education, and higher education was rated 33 in importance; 10 times 33 is 330, which goes into the upper-left corner in Exhibit 17–3B. The rest of the matrix gets the same treatment, column totals are added, and total weighted scores are compared. Location Purple is the winner with 1,227 points; locations Blue and Red are not far behind.

Intangibles, such as the whim of a CEO, could change the decision, or politics could intervene. In any case, systematic analysis is valuable because it reduces a lot of data to a few numbers, which can be used to influence the final decision. As we see next, however, gamesmanship also can figure into location strategies.

Preemptive Strategy

If you are a bridge player, you know that a preemptive bid is a very high opening bid made when one has few points. The purpose is to raise the stakes enough to discourage competitors from making their own bids, even though they may have more points. A similar strategy occurs in locating a business or adding productive capacity. A grocery chain, hotel, or pizza franchise may decide to open its next facility in a sparsely populated location in the hope of discouraging competitors. Manufacturers also sometimes follow facility strategies aimed partly at deterring competition. Sometimes just an announcement (which itself can be a bluff) of an intent to add capacity somewhere may convince a competitor not to do likewise because overcapacity, with resulting lower profit expectations, might result. The practice is called a **preemptive strategy** in business just as it is in the game of bridge.

The location decision, while high on importance, is low on frequency. On the other hand, keeping the facilities in high-quality condition requires ongoing maintenance, our next topic.

Maintaining Quality of Physical Resources

Suppose one of the following occurs at your computer terminal at work:

- As you are working, your screen suddenly goes blank. When you call computer operations you are told, "Sorry, the system failed again. We're fixing it now."
- As you log on one morning, a message warns you that the system will be shut down for a specified time period that day for periodic maintenance. This happens four or five times a month, seemingly at random and for varying lengths of downtime.
- During log-on, the system maintenance downtime schedule for the next several months is displayed, showing short downtime periods that occur on the same date and at the same time each month.

The three events describe different levels of performance and thus quality of service to customers. Quality is worst in the first example, and it improves as we move from one to another. In the third example, except for a short downtime maintenance period that occurs regularly and predictably, the network should be ready whenever you need to use it.

In Chapter 5, we learned that process performance depends on how well the process has been designed, built or installed, operated, and maintained. Here, we examine maintenance, whose goal is to keep operating resources in good working order, safe, and ready for use when needed. Part of meeting that goal is prevention: Stop trouble before it happens. Doing this well requires a broad-based attack on causes—a program of total preventive maintenance, which is the facility-maintenance counterpart of total quality control.

Total Preventive Maintenance

When you take your car in for complete service, you get an oil change and lubrication, vacuumed interior, cleaned windows, and a sticker applied to the door frame or window corner reminding you when to return for the next service. Beyond that, the mechanics rotate tires or tune up the engine—if the maintenance schedule calls for it—and replace key components or overhaul certain systems if necessary to avoid failure or unsafe operation. In combination, these services include the three main elements of total preventive maintenance (TPM):

Total productive maintenance is the term often used in manufacturing; we use total preventive maintenance, which is more type-of-business neutral.

- Regular preventive maintenance, including housekeeping.
- Periodic prefailure replacement or overhauls.

- Intolerance for breakdowns or unsafe conditions (see Into Practice, ". . . La Victoria Foods").

Intolerance for facility deficiencies, the third goal, is a hallmark of the Walt Disney culture. Every Disney amusement park employee must continually maintain and clean the premises as well as write up and call in problems requiring maintenance expertise. Disney World in Florida has become a popular destination not only for vacationers but also for benchmarking teams wanting to study Disney's fault-intolerant total maintenance program.

Another example of ardent attention to TPM is the aircraft industry: In aircraft maintenance, prevention is everything; waiting for failure to identify a maintenance need is unacceptable. The Air Force bomber B–52 is a good example of the payoff: decades of continued flight. Even more remarkable is the 65-year-old DC–3; the military version, the C–47, is affectionately known as the "Gooney Bird." A few hundred of these venerable aircraft are still logging miles, thanks to good design and thorough preventive maintenance practices.

On a lesser scale, the conscientious automobile owner also follows the TPM philosophy seriously: Commit a little time and money for regular oil changes and less-frequent but necessary overhauls in order to prevent having to spend even greater amounts of time and money on a breakdown. By giving a little, we gain a lot: a resource that remains in a high state of readiness.

Maintainability at La Victoria Foods

"KISS—Keep It Simple Son—that is what I tell myself," grins Wes Guthrie, purchasing expediter at La Victoria Foods. The company's single plant, in Industry, California, produces salsas, jalapeños, nachos, and tomatillo entero.

"The simpler it is in a food plant, the better efficiency you have because there is less to break down . . . . When the chilis are here and when the tomatoes are here, we have to run. We cannot have breakdowns—none of this produce keeps."

Maintenance superintendent Andy Zamberlin notes that when he came to La Victoria 13 years before, the place was a nightmare. It had "too much complicated machinery such as stop/starts [switches], electric motors, and electric eyes that just did not run right." Some component was always breaking down and it often took hours to determine what had broken.

Zamberlin and his staff eliminated much of the assorted conventional electromechanical controls. Today, "almost all of La Victoria's equipment is run by PLC's [programmable logic controllers, a type of computer]. Several PLCs control the batching process. Some control the steam process, which is the 'breaking' or peeling of the tomatoes. Others control the fillers themselves . . . . These are programmed so that the drive motors are in step with the capping machines so they do not speed one up and slow one down." There are few parts on the food-processing equipment to break, and when a fault does occur, computers quickly identify the program.

But, as Guthrie points out, this kind of process control requires a good deal of human involvement. "We've got tomatoes of different sizes and textures. They might be mushy, they might be hard, they might not peel . . . . There are so many variables." He adds, "These PLCs have to be user-controllable. You program parameters, but the operator has to be able to control it."

Source: Adapted from Blake Svenson, "Keeping It Simple to Reduce Spoiled Efficiency in the Food Industry," *Industrial Engineering,* June 1992, pp. 29–32.

Quality through Readiness

A facility that is safe and ready for use when needed prevents many problems. The salesperson leaving the office to serve an important customer, for example, has no time for a car that won't start—nor does the customer. The total quality movement thus depends on its handmaiden, total preventive maintenance, for meeting its customer-centered objectives.

Unfortunately, maintenance is short on both glamour and visibility; too often maintenance has been high on the budget-cutter's list when financial problems arise. Years of neglect take their toll. On the one hand are outright failures: batteries that die, tires that blow, and engines that freeze up. On the other are failures to meet customer expectations or exacting specifications, from dirty premises to broken-off adjustment cranks and knobs to machine surfaces pocked from a thousand hammer blows.

Consider, also, how often customers have to wait for a service provider to find a pen, pencil, stapler, or proper form or tool. Inability to find a needed resource due to a cluttered or poorly organized or labeled workplace is an obvious sign of poor upkeep. So too are scattered piles of repair parts and their identifying forms, broken fixtures, dirty equipment or work areas, and sloppy personal appearances. More subtly, overflowing in-baskets and disorganized files—even if hidden in cabinets, desks, or on computer disks—reflect poor maintenance too. Unavailable or improperly trained human resources can also be delay-causing culprits. In short, if it impedes timely and responsive high-quality customer service, it is a target for better maintenance.

> *Search time* is *delay time* which lengthens *response time* to the customer.

Facility Management for the Environment

Increasingly, companies are finding ways to make facilities management environmentally friendly: Offices recycle paper and other wastes, use refillable ink cartridges, have precious metals extracted from obsolete electronic equipment, and design buildings for low energy use. Factories do the same, plus install smokestack scrubbers, scrap recovery, waste-water recycling, and so on.

Usually these measures provide income or reduce costs as well as contributing to corporate citizenship. However, they are largely voluntary or, in limited cases, required by a regulatory agency. Henceforth, however, companies will have an additional incentive to manage for the environment: The International Organization for Standardization, well known for its ISO 9000 series of quality standards, has been at work developing the ISO 14000 series of management-for-the-environment standards.

In 1992, the ISO formed Technical Committee 207 to draft the ISO 14000 series. ISO 14001 sets the minimum, basic provisions. Using this standard, companies will either self-declare conformance or will seek third-party registration. ISO 14004 provides guidelines for developing an environmental management system. Other standards in the series will involve such matters as auditing, labeling, and life-cycle analysis.[4]

Much of environmental management is likely to be the responsibility of the facilities management organization. In some cases that responsibility may be treated as an enlargement of the firm's total preventive maintenance mission. Carrying out that mission revolves around people and procedures.

Maintenance Organization: People and Procedures

The centerpiece of total preventive maintenance is operator ownership backed up by special maintenance expertise to handle nonroutine problems. The wisdom of this approach becomes apparent as we consider traditional types of maintenance-related procedures in the following sections.

Types of Maintenance

We classify maintenance operations into two general categories:

> **periodic maintenance** Discretionary regular-interval maintenance aimed at forestalling breakdowns and ensuing work stoppages; sometimes is *preventive* periodic maintenance.
> **irregular maintenance** Maintenance necessary because of a breakdown or a facility alteration.

- *Periodic maintenance.* Periodic maintenance occurs at some regular interval (e.g., custodial activities are often performed daily). Of course, periodic maintenance forms the core of a preventive maintenance (PM) program. There are three popular versions of PM:

  1. PM based on calendar or clock time—maintenance at regular intervals. An example is the hourly change of a filter on a clean room's air-conditioning unit.
  2. PM based on time of usage, perhaps based on number of cycles. For example, change the cartridge in a laser printer after every 4,000 pages of print. This is often called **predictive maintenance**; the idea is to do maintenance before the predicted time of failure.
  3. PM based on regular inspection. A maintenance requirement may be revealed by planned (perhaps daily or weekly) inspections. The U.S. Air Force refers to this as IRAN (*i*nspect and *r*epair *a*s *n*ecessary) maintenance.

- *Irregular maintenance.* This includes repairs, overhauls, irregular custodial work (e.g., cleaning up spills), irregular PM (e. g., prefailure replacement of components based on control-chart deviations, tests, unusual equipment noises, etc.), installation and relocation of equipment, and minor construction.

Maintenance work has traditionally been assigned to associates housed in a central maintenance department, perhaps called plant or facilities maintenance, or (as in many hospitals) in a unit within the facilities engineering group. Typical types of maintenance associates include

- *Millwrights.* These are skilled people who move and install equipment (e.g., in a mill), an irregular, hard-to-manage maintenance activity.
- *Repair technicians.* These are skilled, well-paid troubleshooters who have sharp diagnostic skills. Since they specialize in fixing problems, appropriate staffing levels are hard to predict.
- *Custodians.* Typically, these people are charged with housekeeping and perhaps minor repairs, light painting, and so forth. Staffing without costly idleness is fairly easy.
- *Preventive maintenance associates.* This category is hardest to define, for in addition to associates regularly scheduled for PM duties (perhaps on a special maintenance shift), available millwrights and repair personnel also perform PM duties, though typically at higher labor costs. The traditional idea was that skilled operators should not have to bother with chores like

lubrication, nor should they be trained to clean equipment, change a filter or V-belt, and so forth. Let maintenance people do it.

Now that we have a basic grasp of what maintenance is supposed to do, we can consider how this might better be accomplished. Effective maintenance management focuses on

1. Achieving the right mix of periodic and irregular maintenance.
2. Improving planning, scheduling, and staffing of irregular maintenance, and improving the effectiveness of periodic maintenance.

Flexibility, regularity, and simplification—possible when maintenance becomes a front-line operator's responsibility—help to meet these ends.

Employees, Teams, and Functions

The phrase *employee ownership* refers to the associates believing that equipment condition is their responsibility and that maintenance, engineering, and outside service representatives are backups. This parallels the shift in responsibility for quality from quality professionals to front-line associates. TPM and TQM are cut from the same cloth. Exhibit 17–4 shows one manner of dispersing the maintenance function. As earlier chapters have noted, in the product- or customer-focused organization associates not only perform value-adding transformations, but they are also cross-trained to perform some of their own operations support. Maintenance specialists and other experts are often assigned to the group to provide on-the-spot training and technical support.

> *P*RINCIPLE 7:
>
> Cross-train for mastery of multiple skills.

The case for employee-centered maintenance is multifaceted. Front-line associates learn their equipment better, gain fuller control over their own processes, and take greater pride in their workplace when they assume cleanup tasks and responsibility for minor repairs. This cuts repair time since there is

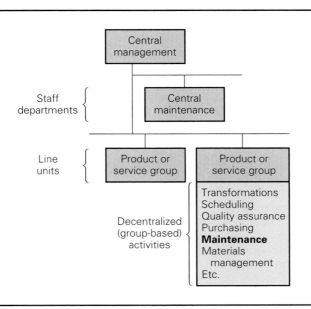

EXHIBIT 17–4

Modern Maintenance Organization

$\mathscr{P}_{\text{RINCIPLE}}$ 9:

Look for flexible, movable equipment.

less waiting around for someone from maintenance to come and change a bulb, for instance. Furthermore, the trend toward multiple, smaller, more mobile equipment and furnishings makes front-line associates less dependent on mill-wright availability; they can perform much of the relocation and installation themselves.

In addition, the involved employee is more likely to develop ideas for fail-safing, which is a superior form of failure prevention (see discussion in Chapter 5). Finally, workforce scheduling is easier because maintenance can often be performed at times when scheduled work has been completed early; this is true at least under JIT, which calls for associates to perform maintenance and other improvements rather than overproducing.

The backup role, however, is still important. While well-trained operators become the first line of defense against breakdowns, special expertise is needed to handle nonroutine trouble or direct maintenance-related training and other projects. That expertise might come from a central maintenance department or, especially in more recent years, from cross-functional teams dispersed throughout the organization.

Shifting primary maintenance responsibility to front-line associates doesn't put the maintenance department out of business; in fact, its responsibilities can become more focused and better defined; see the Contrast box. In addition to providing training and auditing of the TPM program, the maintenance department typically has plantwide responsibilities for buildings and grounds, utilities, environmental control, health and safety, facility design and improvement, and overall facility economics. As responsibilities shift, it is important that front-line associates acquire more than how-to maintenance skills; they also need the support of a stimulating, disciplined environment to ensure that critical activities get carried out. The 5 S's provide some of this support.

5 S's Plus Safety Management

The 5-S concept, originated in Japan, calls for regularly scoring each area within a facility on five characteristics related to good housekeeping and organization of work space. The S's stand for five Japanese words, but Western companies seem to be choosing their own meanings. Boeing's version of the S's is as follows: *sorting,*

$\mathscr{C}$ontrast

Maintenance Responsibilities

Traditional

- Maintenance is a functional support activity; employees rely on specialists (typically) in the central maintenance department for custodial services, preventive and repair maintenance, and millwright work.

Employee Ownership/TPM

- Front-line associates have first responsibility for maintenance in their workplaces.
- Specialists from a maintenance department or on cross-functional teams have backup responsibility to handle difficult or unusual problems.

sweeping, simplifying, standardizing, and *self-discipline.* Other companies' S's generally are similar. While the S's may seem to deal with rather trivial matters, they tend to add up to big problems if not controlled. As an example, the fourth Boeing "S" is *standardizing,* which includes ensuring that every team member follows the standard, prescribed method. If in a hospital every nurse has a different way of hooking up an IV to a patient, the results could endanger some patients' lives. The consequences of salespeople who all write up orders differently include added cost and confusion in processing the orders and occasional foul-ups that lead to defection of a customer.

The 5-S system usually entails some kind of public display of scoring against the S's. At Boeing's welded duct plant in Auburn, Washington, display boards in every work area extol the S's and show photo examples of good and bad practices. The lower photo in Exhibit 17–5 is an example.

Some companies and hospitals employ **spider diagrams** as the display device. Exhibit 17–6 is an example. The raw diagram is five arms extending outward from a central point, each arm representing one of the S's and scaled off

---

Exhibit 17–5   **5 S's at Boeing's Welded Duct Facility, Auburn, Washington**

Top left: Typical plant scene before the 5 S's—disorderly, jumbled, undisciplined.

*Top right: Scene from Welded Duct plant after implementation of the 5 S's showing everything well **s**orted (designated locations are marked off by white and yellow lines on floor), **s**wept, **s**implified, and **s**tandardized, all of which facilitate **s**elf-discipline by team members.*

*Right: Total preventive maintenance communication board; facilitates the 5 S's, especially **s**tandardizing and **s**elf-discipline.*

Photos courtesy of Boeing.

Exhibit 17–6

Spider Diagram Displaying Scores against the 5 S's

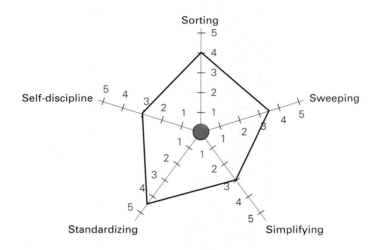

from zero to five points, where zero at the center is the target of perfection. Periodically—commonly once a week—a designated outside rater scores each unit. The rater could be a higher-level manager (e.g., a head nurse or department head) or perhaps a maintenance manager or quality engineer. The scores plot as dots on the arms, and the rater connects the dots to look like a simple web. Next week the web had better be smaller—scores closer to the zero target at the center.

A sixth S, *safety*, may easily be added to the spider diagram, and it easily deserves that kind of intensive management. In some industrialized states, high worker's compensation insurance costs steadily drive away new businesses and send away existing ones. Other costs include potential law suits, interrupted production, and loss of key people and costs of hiring and training a replacement.

Roy Harmon observes that large companies do a much better job of providing safe working conditions than small ones. This he attributes to their having "the resources to devote to safety engineering and . . . the Occupational Safety and Health Administration policing them." Larger companies' accidental death rate per thousand employees is just one-fifth of a percent of the rate of the smallest companies.[5]

Along with the discipline of the S's, it is often a good idea to dedicate certain people as responsible for certain facilities.

Dedicated Maintenance

A company much admired for its commitment to maintenance is United Parcel Service, which keeps most of its over-the-road and delivery vehicles operating and looking as good as new for 20 years or more (see Exhibit 17–7). A feature of the UPS program is dedicated mechanics and drivers. A driver operates the same vehicle every day, and a mechanic maintains the same group of vehicles. Many military aircraft maintenance programs also use dedicated operator/mechanic programs. Sometimes the names of both the pilot and the maintenance crew chief are painted on the aircraft. Both individuals proudly claim ownership and are responsible for the performance of the aircraft.

EXHIBIT 17–7   **Maintenance at United Parcel Serivce**

Exceptional maintenance of tractors, trailers, delivery trucks, planes, and sorting equipment is the basis for UPS's advertising slogan: "The Tightest Ship in the Shipping Business."

Photos reprinted courtesy of United Parcel Service.

At UPS, mechanics work at night on delivery vehicles driven mostly during the day, but drivers and mechanics stay closely in touch. Drivers complete a post-trip vehicle inspection report every day, noting any problems. The mechanic goes to work on those problems that evening, and records completed work on the form. Then, the driver uses the form in conducting a pretrip inspection every morning. Thank-yous and other personal comments between driver and mechanic are common. Similar interactions and documentation between pilots and maintenance crew chiefs have long been standard in military and, in some cases, commercial aircraft maintenance programs.

The interdependency of driver, vehicles, and mechanic keeps responsibilities focused and avoids blaming. In the more typical situation of changing mechanics, operators, and equipment, any of the individuals can become lax, fail to keep good records, and leave problems for the next person or shift.

*P*RINCIPLE 6:

Organize resources into focused family groupings.

Maintenance Database

Clearly, a vital aspect of aircraft and UPS vehicle maintenance programs is thorough record keeping. Everything that happens to a vehicle or plane is recorded, every problem and every maintenance action. A complete history of engine, chassis, and all other major components is available.

A complete database permits computer calculation of failure rates, necessary for determining prefailure replacement schedules; mean times to repair, useful in scheduling maintenance people's time; and component reliabilities, which designers use to improve next-generation components.

As an added service to regular customers, some automotive service garages maintain computerized records of automobile maintenance. Customers are freed from some record-keeping worry, but the garage also benefits: Mechanics know when to call and suggest appointments, what parts are likely to need replacement, and what, if any, warranty time remains. Like aircraft and UPS vehicles,

Into Practice

A Midnight Crisis

Midnight: Taking their regular break, the leader and another member of the third-shift production team at a large, highly automated factory are drinking coffee and shooting the breeze. Their duties really are monitoring and keeping all facilities humming, since the equipment largely runs itself. Just then, the team leader's beeper interrupts the conversation.

12:01: A teammate reports that a major piece of production equipment has failed. Leaving their half-drunk coffee cups in place, the two colleagues head for the trouble spot on the double. Upon arrival, the team runs the machine's self-diagnostic program and finds a controller failure of unprecedented nature. No one has any idea why or how this failure occurred or how to fix it.

12:27 AM The team leader aims the infrared transmitter on his notebook-sized computer/personal digital assistant at one of the many receivers mounted on columns throughout the factory, thus connecting to the Internet through the company's host computer. He searches for the "home page" of the equipment manufacturer and finds it in seconds. Quickly scanning down the menu, he clicks onto the troubleshooters' user-group forum. Previously identified equipment problems are neatly categorized by primary subsystems, and he locates the proper one. After reviewing about 20 titles, he finds one labeled "Mysterious Problems."

12:31 AM Lo and behold, a mysterious problem identical to the one in his plant is detailed, along with a solution: replacing a major component of the control system, one far too expensive to stock in maintenance stores. The team leader quickly returns to the home page and finds the equipment maker's hotline number and clicks on it. Within seconds he is connected to the customer-service system. Because it is so late, no one is in the office to help him, so he clicks on the "dire emergency" selection, sending a beeper signal to the supervisor of the firm's distribution center—which works around the clock, seven days a week.

12:34 AM Aware that an emergency order is coming in by E-mail, the supervisor heads for her nearest terminal and logs on. Meanwhile, the production team leader has entered the serial number of the equipment that failed and has selected the controller he needs from the parts-list menu. The information is transmitted instantaneously. At the distribution cen-

ter, the supervisor transfers the E-mail message to a search query file and checks on availability of the needed controller. Several are in stock and the locations are listed. With a couple of keystrokes, the warehouse retrieval system is alerted over a radio-frequency transmitter system. An order-picking robot transports the controller to the shipping area.

12:40 AM Since the production team's company has a close working partnership with the equipment supplier, it has an "open account" for buying repair and accessory items. The E-mail message is copied to an order file, and emergency shipping noted. The computer system in the shipping area sends a message to the production team's computer, which is on standby, confirming that the required controller is available and asks how "hot" the need is. The team leader sends an E-mail response: "Immediate." This triggers a message to the equipment maker's carrier partner to pick up for same-day delivery.

12:50 AM The parcel delivery company, whose sorting center also works 24 hours a day, dispatches one of its flex associates to pick up the controller from the manufacturer, located about 30 minutes away. Traffic at 1 AM is light and the pickup is made, the bar code scanned into the parcel company's computer system for tracking, and returned to the sorting center—where the driver is told to continue on to the airport, 10 minutes away, taking along the normal 2 AM parcel shipment.

2:10 AM The controller is loaded on the Same Day Air flight to the airport nearest the manufacturer's plant. Flight time is one hour and 35 minutes, including the time needed to log on to the air-traffic-control computers and record the flight plan.

3:45 AM Wheels touch down at an airport about 25 minutes' drive from the manufacturer's plant. The parcels are unloaded and scanned to record arrival, and a driver is dispatched to deliver them. The controller arrives at the manufacturer's receiving dock at 4:30 AM. The bar code on the carton is scanned and the manufacturer's computer recognizes this as a part shipment from the equipment supplier. Since the two companies are linked for electronic funds transfer, no receiving report or invoice is needed. Payment is made instantaneously—electronically—and recorded on the log of transactions that will be generated at the end of the quarter.

(continued)

$$\mathcal{I}\!nto\ \mathcal{P}\!ractice$$

(concluded)

4:45 AM The malfunctioning controller is un-plugged and the new one is installed in its place. Diagnostics are run, and the problem is cleared up. The machine is restarted. Test parts are run satisfactorily. Production begins flowing again.

5:07 AM The team leader and his teammates head for the cafeteria to complete their interrupted coffee break. One notices the morning newspaper lying on the table revealing a headline in the second section:

"Communications Technology Changes the World of Production." After scanning the article, he says sarcastically. "I wish they'd quit writing all this stuff about the coming of electronic miracles. When my whole family knows how to program the VCR, *then* we'll have an electronic miracle!"

Source: Adapted from John Mariotti, "A Midnight Crisis," *Industry Week*, September 18, 1995, pp. 41–43.

well-designed and well-maintained automobiles can have long operating lifetimes, and an automobile's value is enhanced if it is accompanied by a thorough set of maintenance records. The Into Practice box, "A Midnight Crisis," describes a not-very-distant maintenance scenario employing extensive maintenance-facilitating databases plus other information technologies.

Maintenance Inventories

While the Midnight Crisis involved failure of a major component, it is the many lesser, or MRO (maintenance, repair, and operating), parts that cause most of the maintenance headaches. Recall from Chapter 9 that MRO inventory is classified as a class B item, indicating that it is not typically among the most costly inventory (class A items), but that neither is it considered part of the "trivial many" (class C items). In a TPM environment, with the focus on increased operator involvement and rapid response, location and care of MRO inventories deserve careful attention. Also, in JIT operations distances must shrink. This includes MRO inventory storage space, which must be close to the action and efficiently used.

It is common for even a medium-sized plant to have hundreds, even thousands, of MRO items, despite standardization and component-part reduction programs. Many are like household hardware items we buy, small and available only in quantities of 10s or even 100s. Exhibit 17–8 shows how people at the Macomb, Illinois, plant of NTN–Bower Corporation contain the parts. Drawer cabinets located near the point of usage (Exhibit 17–8A) consume less than half the space of shelving and facilitate storage of small items like brackets, sleeves, and pins (see Exhibit 17–8B). Adjacent part-location records and clear labeling on drawers make retrieval of even the most obscure item easy. The results? Lower failure rates and less downtime.

PM Time

Referring again to the Midnight Crisis, we might wonder if the failure could have been prevented rather than swiftly reacted to. The trouble is, when equipment runs day and night, people may not be able to get at it to perform necessary maintenance, and breakdowns follow. TPM's solution calls for setting aside time each day for PM. The following are two examples of how this may be done, even in continuous operations.

EXHIBIT 17–8   The Little Parts–Managing MRO Items

A.   Small-part storage drawer cabinets

B.   Open storage cabinet drawer

Source: Courtesy of NTN-Bower Corporation. Used with permission.

- As noted in Chapter 3 in an Into Practice box, Miller Brewing Company in Trenton, Ohio, operates three shifts, 24 hours a day, which seems not to allow time for preventive maintenance. The plant's unique staffing plan overcomes this apparent deficiency: All production associates work nine-hour shifts instead of the usual eight. Part of the extra hour per shift is for preventive maintenance, renovating canning lines (millwright work), and housekeeping. In addition, the nine-hour shifts create a one-hour overlap during which crews from each shift meet together. This provides shift-to-shift continuity—usually missing in multishift operations—and opportunity to inform next-shift people of maintenance or other problems.

- At a U.S. particle-board plant, the large mix-mold-bake-cool line was run 24 hours a day, seven days a week, except for 1 hour of maintenance per week. For lack of regular PM, the line produced much scrap and defective particle board. When asked why there was no daily maintenance shutdown, the reply was, "We have startup problems." The general manager of several Brazilian particle-board plants heard that story and offered this comment: "We *do* shut down for maintenance every day, and we *don't* have startup problems." By having to face startup each day, they had learned how to make it an easy routine.

Perhaps a carryover from old accounting logic creates a tendency to want to run very expensive machines continuously. But the enlightened view asks, Don't our most expensive machines deserve our best care rather than our worst? This view is gaining ground in industry, especially as total quality and JIT success elevate the importance of reliability, availability, and maintainability.

The final kind of facilities taken up in the chapter, handling and transportation systems, are included as objects needing TPM-level care. Beyond that are other more specific management issues, taken up next.

Handling and Transportation

Transportation and handling facilities add cost but not value, yet they are needed for work to move through operations and out into customers' hands. In this section we examine handling concepts and analysis, and containerization, one of the techniques for reducing handling while goods are being moved.

Unit Load versus Piece by Piece

A well-established practice that is supposed to hold down handling cost is the **unit-load concept.** The idea is simple: Avoid moving piece by piece; instead, accumulate enough pieces to move them as a unit load. Examples are truckloads and rail-car loads between sites, and a loaded pallet, skid, drum, tote box, hand truck, and carton within a facility.

While the unit-load idea has long been popular, it can conflict with such customer-focused objectives as speedier, more flexible response. The latter can call for moving items piece by piece with no extra stock in a state of idleness and no delay for building up a load.

PRINCIPLE 13:

Decrease cycle interval and lot size.

Actually, the unit-load concept and piece-by-piece viewpoints can converge. If functional layouts are broken up and work centers grouped into work cells, handling distances collapse. Without distance to span, the economical unit-load size is pushed downward and may approach one piece. This course of action is easiest to accomplish when the processing equipment consists of multiple smaller machines, each of which can be a member of a different cell. A single, high-cost, high-capacity machine, on the other hand, usually requires its own work center some distance away from preceding and succeeding processes, thus suggesting larger transport loads. In any event, handling and transport are continuous costs in most organizations, and they warrant careful analysis to minimize those costs.

PRINCIPLE 11:

Decrease flow distances

PRINCIPLE 9:

Install multiple copies of small, simple machines.

Distance–Quantity

Handling analysis requires two steps: (1) analyzing resource flows (materials and other resources that require handling, e.g., tools and mail), and (2) prescribing handling methods. If the first step is done well, the second is relatively easy.

Data collected on each product or resource can be plotted on a distance–quantity (DQ) chart or, if products/resources are dissimilar, on a distance–intensity (DI) chart. Intensity of flow, a measure developed by Muther, equals quantity times transportability. Transportability is an artificial measure that may include size, density or bulk, shape, risk of damage, condition, and sometimes value of the given item.[6]

The DQ or DI chart helps show the types of handling methods needed. Exhibit 17–9, serving as a guide, has four quadrants. A low-distance, high-volume product would plot in the first quadrant, which suggests complex handling equipment such as conveyors. Low-distance, low-volume calls for simple handling (second quadrant) such as hand-carry. High distance, low-volume calls for simple transport equipment (any of the vehicle types in the third quadrant). High-distance, high-volume (fourth quadrant) suggests poor layout; handling distances are too great. If re-layout is impractical right away, the need is for complex transport equipment, such as a railroad.

EXHIBIT 17–9
DQ or DI Chart Indicating Preferred Handling Methods

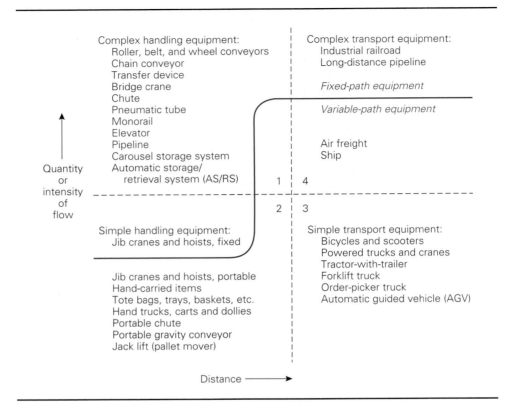

The solid line cutting through the chart makes another distinction. Above the line are fixed-path types of handling equipment; below it are variable-path types. It is well to be cautious about investing in the fixed-path variety; it may be too costly to relocate or modify fixed equipment when needs change. It is common to enter a plant of average age and see unused remnants of an overhead conveyor or pneumatic tube system up in the rafters. Automatically guided vehicles and self-guiding order pickers were something of a breakthrough in the 1960s. They have fixed-path advantages, but it is cheap to change their route: Simply paint a new white line on the floor for those that optically follow a line, or embed a new wire in the floor for those that sense a magnetic field generated by a current-carrying wire.

Some equipment has both handling and storage functions. One example is carousel systems, which are rotatable racks holding small parts, tools, documents, dry cleaning, and so forth. Another example, the automatic storage/retrieval system (AS/RS) consists of rows of racks with automated, computer-controlled, devices to put away and later select baskets or pallets of stock. Both types of equipment were widely installed in North America in the late 1970s and the 1980s. Recently, many companies have been figuring out ways to dismantle some of them; the racks conflict with the goal of avoiding storage. The AS/RS is fine in distribution centers, but when used for storing work-in-process inventories, it is usually a symptom of coordination problems. An exception is a newer type of "mini" AS/RS, which is small enough to be placed at the location where parts or tools are made or used (see Exhibit 17–10).

EXHIBIT 17–10

**Mini AS/RS—
Installed at Point
of Use**

*Mini automatic storage/retrieval system installed next to plastic injection molding machine in
South Korean factory. With mini AS/RS, the owner of the inventory is the machine operator, not a
central stock room.*

Courtesy of Dorner Mfg. Corp., Hartland, Wisconsin.

Forklift trucks have also lost some of their popularity as a means of handling
in-process materials. If machines are close together, as in cells or product layout,
materials may be moved by hand, conveyor, transfer device (transfer between adjacent stations), robot, or chute.

After the analyst identifies general types of handling equipment, it is time for
detailed consideration of cost, reliability, maintainability, and adaptability.
Suppliers of material-handling equipment may help with the detailed design and
then submit bids.

The equipment in quadrant 4 and some of the equipment in quadrant 3 of
Exhibit 17–9 serve a transportation as well as a handling function. Such equipment
tends to be costly enough to warrant special cost analyses.

Containerization

Container design, though usually neglected, can be an essential element of effective handling and transportation. The goals are to protect the goods, ensure exact
counts, and simplify loading and unloading.

The Automotive Industry Action Group's containerization task force has developed standard reusable collapsible containers for auto parts (see Exhibit 17–11),
usable by competing suppliers and auto assembly plants. The containers avoid
throw-away materials, especially cardboard, which cuts costs by a surprisingly
large amount—over $50 per car already, according to the manager of one auto as-
sembly plant. Other industries are also plunging into containerization, but mostly
with each firm doing its own.

The new containers often are designed to hold an exact, easily verifiable quantity, perhaps through use of partitions or "egg-crate" molded bottoms or inserts.
That helps solve a chronic problem. Outside suppliers would deliberately ship too
much, hoping to be paid for the excess, or, where the supplier had a stock shortage, ship less than the ordered quantity. Over-and undershipment led to costly delays (to count every piece upon receipt) and generated ill will. The new designs

Exhibit 17–11

**Reusable
Collapsible
Container**

Courtesy Perstorp Xytec, Inc.

allow for counting containers, not pieces; or not counting at all, except on an audit basis. Containerization is all the more necessary in just-in-time operations; JIT lowers inventories and available storage space to the point where receipt of too little or too much can't be tolerated.

On a larger scale, containerization includes semitrailers or large seagoing cargo containers that can also move by rail or be trucked. Cargo containers avoid costly handling of diverse small crates and boxes.

JIT shippers load the cargo boxes with small amounts of multiple components, called kits, rather than loading a huge lot of just one item into the container. Some plants use the transport-kit technique to receive just one day's supply of mixed parts every day from across an ocean.

Summary

Facilities management includes facilities location, maintenance, and handling systems—plus layout within the site, which was included in Chapter 12. In positioning a facility—that is, the physical site—the first concern is that the facilities support the organization's market niche, special competencies, and image. A second concern is the facility under the control of suppliers, and a third is the infrastructure, including transportation and storage, utilities, and environmental systems. The three concerns form a facilities requirements pyramid, with infrastructure as the foundation.

The economics of physical location are complicated by rapid advances in worldwide transportation and communication, which sometimes make it feasible to site a business unit in a low-wage country across an ocean. Many of the issues in selecting a location can be evaluated using location rating models. Most such models allow the selection team to consider a broad set of factors such as labor, education, markets, taxes, supply sources, infrastructure, and transportation expense. The models include numerically weighting each factor for its importance.

The alternate sites are scored on each factor, and a composite score points to the model's best choice, which could easily be overruled for other reasons not included in the model. For example, a preemptive strategy is to announce a pending capacity addition in a certain location in order to discourage a competitor from locating there.

Once a site is established, the facility management issue turns to its maintenance. While maintenance can seem mundane, it actually is a vital factor in the quality, customer-service, and safety equation. A high form of this, called total preventive maintenance (TPM), involves broad participation in maintenance activities rather than their being relegated to a plant maintenance department. The three main elements of TPM are regular preventive maintenance, periodic prefailure correction, and intolerance for breakdowns or unsafe conditions.

The housekeeping side of TPM ensures that the many little deficiencies will not add up to major failures or customer defections. A spider diagram, which looks like a simple spider web, is a useful way of displaying an outside rater's scores on the so-called 5 S's: sorting, sweeping, simplifying, standardizing, and self-discipline.

There are two general classes of maintenance operations: periodic and irregular. Periodic maintenance occurs regularly and forms the core of TPM. Variations may be a function of calendar or clock time, time (or amount) of usage, or inspection results. Irregular maintenance includes repairs, overhauls, and work performed as the result of a special test, unusual noise, and so forth.

The key to successful TPM is operator ownership, where the front-line associate assumes first-level responsibility for maintaining equipment and the workplace. A central maintenance department or cross-functional teams dispersed throughout the organization provide backup, especially for difficult jobs. Advantages of such an approach include greater operator familiarity with equipment, better equipment care, faster repairs, process fail-safing, and a fuller utilization of work time—essential especially in JIT environments.

Dedicated maintenance, long a key part of aircraft care, is emerging in organizations outside the aircraft industry. United Parcel Service, for example, has a specific driver and mechanic permanently assigned to each of its vehicles. Successful PM depends on a good database, properly locating and storing maintenance-related inventories and ensuring that sufficient time for PM is inserted into the schedule.

A dominant aim of site-to-site and within-site handling analysis is to reduce handling cost. Discrete move quantities called units loads and sophisticated handling systems are conventional approaches; under just-in-time, however, the view is that the best handling is no handling, since handling represents delay. Although zero handling is impossible, some companies have dismantled automated storage and handling systems in favor of simpler handling of smaller lots over shorter distances.

An approach called systematic handling analysis starts with distance–quantity (or distance–intensity) data that suggest the type of handling equipment: simple or complex handling, simple or complex transport. Finally, specific handling equipment is selected. Variable-path equipment is more adaptable than fixed-path equipment.

The use of collapsible, resusable containers designed to hold an exact quantity is increasing. Containerization reduces losses and amount of handling. The precise quantities per container eliminate time-consuming receiving counts and foster the precision called for in JIT purchasing.

Review Questions

1. What is facilities positioning? Is the positioning process over after locations are chosen? Explain.
2. What three sets of facilities must positioning teams consider? Discuss each.
3. Identify factors that might be considered in location decisions.
4. What might a community, state, or nation do to attract business and industry? How do new location economics affect these efforts?
5. Given their facilities deficiencies, how might small, underdeveloped countries hope to benefit from global commerce?
6. Multiple variables could be important to facilities positioning teams. How might a team evaluate them all systematically?
7. What is a preemptive positioning strategy? How might such a strategy affect competition?
8. What is total preventive maintenance?
9. How does a TPM program support total quality?
10. What is the role of housekeeping and the 5 S's in an overall maintenance program?
11. How are spider diagrams used in a maintenance program?
12. What is the role of cleanliness in the assessment of an overall maintenance program?
13. Give examples of periodic and irregular maintenance.
14. What are the three popular versions of PM?
15. How might maintenance activity responsibility be assigned in a TPM-oriented company?
16. What is operator-centered maintenance? What are its advantages?
17. How do maintenance improvement teams augment other components of a TPM program?
18. What should be the role of a central maintenance department?
19. What is dedicated maintenance? How does it support the TPM idea?
20. What role do maintenance records play in TPM programs?
21. What is the controversy about making time in the schedule for maintenance?
22. It is a good idea to transport in unit loads? Explain.
23. What are the advantages of variable-path handling equipment?
24. Explain the role of containerization in modern operations management.

Exercises

1. Find out what you can about current location strategies for the following industries:

Carpeting.	Furniture.
Movie theaters.	Bottling.
Petroleum refining.	Electric power generation.

Boxing and packing materials.   Plastic molding.

Data entry.   Credit-rating services.

 a. How does the overall strategy serve various customers?

 b. Of the many variables that might affect location decisions, which seems to predominate?

2. Find out what you can about the U.S. Motor Carrier Deregulation Act of 1980. How has it affected handling or location strategies (or both) in North American industry? Discuss.

3. "Our approach to the labor union is to run from it." That is one auto parts executive's explanation of why they had nonunion plants in small, remote rural towns around the country. How do you think that strategy will be affected by the automakers' determination to get daily deliveries from their suppliers? Discuss.

4. Stuart Reeves, senior vice president for EDS, which manages information and technology, says:

> If you're hiring college types, there isn't a lot of difference among quality across nations. The difference among college graduates by countries is a lot less than the difference among day laborers and high schoolers. And there's a lot of pent-up talent out there.[7]

 a. If Mr. Reeves is correct, how might his assessment affect location decisions?

 b. If Mr. Reeves is correct, how would you use this information if you were a consultant retained to help an emerging nation become more attractive to foreign investors?

5. To what extent do commercial semitrailer tractor drivers get involved in PM and repairs to their equipment? (You may need to interview someone.) Do you think their involvement is enough?

6. To what extent do copy-machine operators get involved in cleaning and maintaining their own machines (clean glass, clean rollers, resupply with fluids and papers, etc.)? In repairing their machines? (You may need to interview someone.) Is their involvement adequate?

7. Every maintenance operation requires some degree of facilities analysis, planning, and control. Ten maintenance operations are listed below:

Replace ceramic tiles in a floor.

Mop floors.

Repair power outage.

Change oil and grease equipment.

Change extrusion heads (simply unscrew dirty one and screw on clean one) as they randomly clog up (in a factory full of plastics extrusion lines, each with an extrusion head to form the plastic).

Replace drive belts, bearings, and so on as they fail (among large group of various machines on factory floor).

Repaint walls.

Maintain spare motors for bank of spinning machines.

Remodel president's office.

Repair shoes (shoe repair shop).

 a. Name one or more analysis techniques (if any) that apply to each maintenance operation.

  b. List the data inputs necessary for conducting the analysis. (Note: Some of the analysis methods are presented in other chapters.) Two completed examples follow:

Maintenance Operation	Analysis Technique	Data Inputs
Rearrange office equipment	Layout analysis (Chapter 12)	Flow data (types and volume) Relationship data
Prepare platform with utility hookups for new equipment	Design guidelines (Chapter 4)	Customer needs and process requirements

  c. Fit each of the maintenance operations into one of the 5 S's (Boeing's S's) and briefly explain why it fits. If any of the maintenance operations do not fit any of the S's, explain why and suggest an alternate method of controlling performance.

8. Devise a way that you, or you and your partner or living or working associates, might use a version of the spider diagram and 5 S's to eliminate small aggravations that sometimes expand into big ones. Discuss your plan.

9. With computers (microprocessors) now in common use as automobile control devices, they sometimes serve a preventive maintenance purpose. A dash panel could be used to input into a computer every maintenance operation performed on the car, and mileage data could be entered into the computer automatically. A screen could then recommend preventive maintenance whenever a program determines a need.

  a. To what extent is this idea in use right now? What are some obstacles in the way of implementing or improving on such a PM system?

  b. What are some important items of historical data that would need to be programmed into the auto's computer? Where would such data come from? Explain.

  c. Large numbers of nearly identical autos are sold, which provides a sizable potential database for gathering failure and wear-out data. For almost any type of factory machine, there is a smaller potential database; that is, there are far fewer copies of the same machine. Yet good factory PM is based on good failure records. How can a good database be developed for factory machines?

10. Joe Black is head of the maintenance operations division of the plant engineering department at Wexco, Inc. Rumors have been flying around his division. The buzzing is regarding the company's plan to launch a new program called Operator Ownership. The program is aimed at the problem of machine undependability and would place more responsibility for machine performance on the machine operators—a step backwards, in the minds of Black and his subordinates.

  Part of the worry is that operator ownership is budget cutting (slashing the maintenance budget) in disguise, which equals losses of jobs in maintenance operations. Black also harbors natural concerns regarding losses of personal prestige and power.

  Are those worries really justified? Discuss.

11. Hewlett-Packard pays its janitors, guards, and food service associates the same wage as its product assembly people, yet the product assembly people have higher status. At one H-P division, the division manager intends to begin rotating assembly people into the lower-status positions, and vice versa. But she wonders how the assemblers will react when asked to "push a broom." From what you have learned about responsibility for maintenance, do you think that this rotation plan is a step in the right direction? Explain. What else might be done?

12. Captain Henry Harrison has spent much of his career in navy shipyards. In the last 10 years, he has held three positions of authority over shops that build and repair ships. He has been a firm believer in conducting frequent inspections of shop

facilities and is a stickler for having everything neat, clean, and painted. Some people think Captain Harrison spends too much time on this. What do you think?

13. Acme Corporation has invested $5 million in storage and handling gear: $1 million in pallet racks, $1 million in an operatorless wire-guided vehicle delivery system, $1 million in carousel storage (three carousels), $1 million in an AS/RS, and $1 million in a transporter (moving parts from person to person in production cells and lines).

   Evaluate these five handling/storage systems. Rank them in worst-to-best order for a plant pursuing just-in-time production with continual improvement. Explain.

14. Examine the "Principles of Operations Management" (Exhibit 2–3). Which seem most directly affected by handling and transportation issues? Discuss.

15. The chapter suggests that wise customers choose supplier partners that have facilities in good condition. Does it work in the other direction as well? Should suppliers be concerned about their customers' facilities? Discuss.

16. The next drawing shows a "JIT pack" devised by engineers at Texas Instruments' Automotive Electronics unit, which conveys sets of parts between TI and major automotive customers. When filled, the box weighs not more than 40 pounds. Its flexible, built-in spacers hold tubes, trays, and reels of semiconductors or other electronic components; on average, 95 percent of the materials are recyclable and/or reusable.

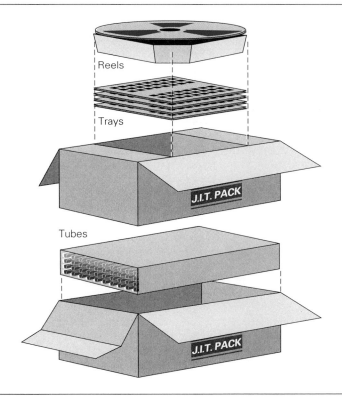

Source: Elizabeth Franklin, "Environment: Thinking 'Outside the Box,' " *Semisphere,* June 1995, pp. 8–9. Courtesy, Texas Instruments Semiconductor Group.

   a. Based on what you've learned about just-in-time, how does this container support JIT objectives?
   b. What other benefits can be derived from the JIT pack?
   c. Which principles of operations management does the JIT pack relate to?

SWANBANK FROZEN FOODS

Swanbank is a major North American frozen food producer. Its Forbes, North Carolina, plant produces between 280,000 and 320,000 frozen dinners per day. Each year the schedule is cut back in the spring, in advance of reduced summer sales, and raised again in the fall.

In 1983 Jerry Hanks, plant manager at Forbes, inaugurated a just-in-time effort. Hank's JIT task force has progressed to goal setting, and one goal was to set a daily production rate for each product (type of dinner) and meet it every day.

At that time, setting even a modest rate and hitting it daily was not remotely possible. The normal problems of undependable deliveries of ingredients and packaging materials could perhaps be resolved. Internal problems in food preparation, mixing, cooking, aluminum tray stamping, and material handling also seemed solvable. The big problems were in final assembly and packaging. This case study concerns only that stage of production.

Fill and Pack

Final assembly and packaging consisted of three high-speed fill-and-pack lines located side by side in a large area stretching lengthwise from the main factory area through two plant additions. The lines were 600 to 850 feet long and conveyor driven. Filling nozzles, chutes, gravity drop devices, and mechanical pushers deposited cooked food items into aluminum tray compartments at early work stations along the line. Automatic cartoners, corrugated box packers, and palletizers were at the end of the line.

The lines were by no means fully automated. A crew of 50 to 60 people, classified as direct labor and supervision, tended a line. Their normal jobs were to load trays and kettles of cooked ingredients into hoppers. Their abnormal jobs were to keep production going manually whenever nozzles clogged up and jam-ups occurred on the line.

The company had always taken pride in the high speed at which its tray-filling lines were designed to run, about 270 trays per minute. However, with trays moving at that speed past many fill stations, through long and not always straight and level lengths of conveyor, and into temperamental cartoning and packing equipment, slight misalignments could result in spectacular jam-ups. Trays and their contents could fly into the air and quickly litter the floor and cover the equipment with gravy, peas, and apple cobbler. In such instances, the nearest line crew member would rush to hit the stop button. Then crew members would roll in trash barrels, push carts, and other apparatus so they could manually fill and forward stalled trays and dispose of ruined ones.

A line stop could also sometimes summon technicians from maintenance. Their job was to fix the cause. Often the cause was minor and fixable within a few minutes by a line supervisor or maintenance technician already present at lineside. Filling equipment was also frequently adjusted to correct for spilling of food portions into the wrong tray compartment, which tended to happen frequently because of the fast line speeds. Those adjustments often could be done on the fly.

Records kept by line supervisors revealed that the mean stoppage time per shift was three hours and the mean number of stops per shift was 26. Exhibit CS17–1 is a distribution of the duration of stoppages per shift. The distribution summarizes a sample of stoppages over 50 shifts. It shows that the vast majority of stoppages were short; in fact, 58 percent

---

Case Topics: total preventive maintenance; just in time; linearity; operator ownership; breakdowns; failure rates; line speed (production rate); material handling; buffer stock; crew staffing; shift scheduling; facility layout; job assignments/labor flexibility; line changeover/cleanup; preventive maintenance; equipment design for operations.

were 12 minutes or less. Just 13 percent were over 30 minutes, and these incorporated just one instance each of several different stoppage durations, such as 39, 41, . . . , 93, 171, . . . minutes. The longest stoppage in the 50 shifts sampled was 3 hours 17 minutes.

The high incidence of stoppages affected design of the line. Between each pair of fill stations, the conveyor length usually was long enough to hold a few dozen trays. Then, whenever the line stopped, the extra trays could be processed manually. Over the years, the conveyors lengthened as line speeds were increased.

When a line stoppage incident included under- or overfilling, spillover, or damaged containers, the bad product went into trash barrels. The average trash rate had been 5 percent.

Unfortunately, although the trash contained food, no one—company people, local charities, welfare agencies, or farm groups—could come up with an economical way to salvage the good food. The waste was bulldozed under at the local landfill. The average cost of one trashed unit was $0.38, of which $0.015 was container and packaging material (usually just an aluminum tray, since most stoppages came before cartoning).

Work Pace

When the line was running full speed, line crew members were not hard-pressed to keep up. Most people who watched the line would estimate that perhaps half the crew size, say, 30 people, could keep up with the line. With half a crew, each person would have to tend two geographically separated stations, but even with walk time from one to the next, it appeared that they should have been able to keep up; for example, dump a fresh kettle of gravy into a feeder tank, walk to the next station, load a tray of veal cutlets into the magazine of a feeder machine, walk back to gravy, and repeat.

Hanks summed up the crew size and work pace issue this way: "Half of the line crew are on hand because the equipment doesn't run right." Indeed, the leisurely pace of the line crew could swiftly change to frenzy, and it often did whenever the line stopped. Manual processing around the bottleneck was fast and furious. During longer stoppages—say, 20 minutes or more—line crews would run out of partially filled trays and then have to stop. They stayed idle until maintenance technicians and line supervisors could fix the problem and restart the line.

The unionized labor force was accustomed to this hurry-and-then-wait work life. Hanks and the JIT team anticipated the need for an education effort, but not big problems with labor, in the upcoming JIT conversion effort.

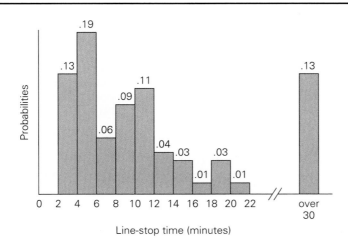

Distribution of Durations of Stop Times

Work Shifts and Practices

Most of the year the Forbes plant operated five days a week with two work shifts per day. A 2½ hour changeover and cleanup shift followed each work shift. Product changes, chicken to beef or ravioli to lasagna, for example, generally occurred at the end of each shift. The shift schedule was as follows:

First work shift	5:30 AM–2:00 PM
Changeover/cleanup	2:00 PM–4:30 PM
Second work shift	4:30 PM–1:00 AM
Changeover/cleanup	1:00 AM–3:30 AM

Average line output per shift varied, depending partly on what product the line was producing. Some products, such as spaghetti dinners, were run at a slower speed than, say, fried shrimp dinners. The main cause of variable line output, however, was amount of line stoppage during a shift. Over one three-week period, output on line 3 was as shown in Exhibit CS17–2.

Cleanup and Line Changeover

A five-person maintenance crew performed cleanups. About half the crew worked on disengaging filling equipment from the chain conveyor and reengaging equipment for use on the next shift. The other half began the task of shoveling, scraping, and push-brooming the litter of food and containers. Large piles went into garbage cans; smaller scatterings near the conveyor were pushed into a trough centered below the conveyor.

The crew started with fill-and-pack line 1, then went to line 2, then 3. As soon as line 1 was torn down and prep-cleaned, part of the crew, in rubber hip boots, began hosing down everything on that line. Hosing was in the direction of the central trough, where it drained into a filtering system. The filtered matter was recovered, containered, and sold as feed to chicken growers.

As hosers moved to line 2, technicians wheeled the next set of filling machines to line 1 and attached and adjusted them for the next production run. The hose crew moved to line 3 and the setup technicians to line 2. Filling equipment to be used from one shift to the next stayed connected but was flushed in place. Hosing included detergent wash-down after the late shift but water only following the first shift.

As production lines started up, the maintenance crew moved to other areas. One remaining task was to completely flush and steam-clean the filling equipment just removed from the three lines. That was done in a separate steam room.

Equipment Maintenance

The filling machines were about 20 years old but had been ingeniously designed for quick and easy attach/detach from the rotary conveyor line shaft, and they were built to last. A strong corporate manufacturing engineering group (in another city) that had designed the equipment had dwindled to just a few people over the years.

EXHIBIT CS17–2   Output on Line 3 over Three-Week Period

Day	1	2	3	4	5	6	7	8	9	10	11	12	13	14	15
Output (000 trays packed)	95	102	123	100	87	103	57	85	113	103	68	107	60	102	108

The filling equipment in the steam room was cleaned—and that was all. There was no time for mechanical checking or other maintenance. In fact, throughout the Forbes plant there was a notable lack of preventive maintenance (PM). Lines were lubricated daily by someone from maintenance, but not thoroughly. Old-timers recalled when there had been good PM in the Forbes plant and throughout the company, but PM programs had been pruned by company budget cutters. As PM dwindled, the plant's mode of operation evolved to, in Jerry Hanks's words, "run until it breaks."

The JIT task force was very much aware of the need to reinstall PM. The challenge was to do it without appreciably increasing payroll and other costs.

Questions

1. Is the equipment maintenance problem severe? Support your answer with data and facts, if available. Consider possible causes of problems other than equipment troubles.

2. What are the Forbes plant's three biggest problems, in rank order? Are they interrelated or mostly independent? Discuss.

3. Devise a PM plan, including tasks, schedules, and labor needs, that will not appreciably raise costs. Discuss the benefits of the plan and its prospects for working.

For Further Reference

Books

Apple, James M. *Plant Layout and Material Handling.* 3rd ed. New York: Ronald Press, 1977 (TS155.A58).

Cordero, S.T. *Maintenance Management Handbook.* Englewood Cliffs, N.J.: Fairmont Press, 1987.

Coyle, John J.; Edward J. Bardi; and Joseph L. Cavinato. *Transportation.* 3rd ed. St. Paul, Minn.: West Publishing. 1990 (HE151.C88).

Hirano, Hiroyuki. *The Five Pillars of the Visual Workplace.* Portland, Ore.: Productivity Press, 1995 (originally published in Japanese in 1990) (TS155.H48513).

Kulwiec, Raymond: A., ed.-in-chief. *Materials Handling Handbook.* 2nd ed. New York: John Wiley & Sons, 1985 (TS180.M315).

Mobley, R. Keith. *An Introduction to Predictive Maintenance.* New York: Van Nostrand Reinhold, 1990 (TS192.M624).

Molnar, John. *Facilities Management Handbook.* New York: Van Nostrand Reinhold, 1983 (TH151.M59).

Nakajima, Seiichi. *Introduction to TPM: Total Productive Maintenance.* Portland Ore.: Productivity Press, 1988 (originally published in Japanese in 1984) (TS192.N3513).

Steele, Frits. *Making and Managing High-Quality Workplaces: An Organizational Ecology.* New York: Teachers College Press, 1986 (HF5547.2.S74).

Taff, Charles A. *Management of Physical Distribution and Transportation.* 7th ed. Burr Ridge, Ill.: Richard D. Irwin, 1984.

Tomlingson, Paul D. *Industrial Maintenance Management.* 8th ed. Chicago: McLean Hunter, 1989.

Tsuchiya, Seiji. *Quality Maintenance: Zero Defects through Equipment Management.* Portland, Ore.: Productivity Press, 1992.

Wireman, Terry. *Total Productive Maintenance: An American Approach.* New York: Industrial Press, 1991.

Periodicals/Societies

AITPM Action Line (American Institute for Total Productive Maintenance).

Factory Management.

Industrial Engineering Solutions (Institute of Industrial Engineers).

Maintenance Technology

Material Management Pacesetter (International Materials Management Society).

Modern Materials Handling.

Office.

Plant Engineering (includes plant maintenance).

Today's Office.

18 WHAT'S NEXT—FOR YOU AND FOR OM?

Chapter Outline

People, Teams, Jobs, and Careers
  Employee Factor—OM Experience
  Employer Factors—Customer Service and Career Paths

Change
  Manufacturing in the Lead
  Services Close Behind

Quality of Work Life and the Environment

Improvement Scenario
TQM in Less-Developed Countries
Environmental Protection

Currents and Countercurrents

First to Know

Case Study: Becoming World Class at K2 Corporation

> Colleen Barrett is the No. 2 executive at Southwest Airlines and the highest-ranking woman in the airline industry. Her chief role is as keeper of the airline's unique and acclaimed corporate culture. As a news story put it, "Long before 'empowerment' became a management buzz word, Ms. Barrett was giving employees freedom from centralized policies. She constantly reinforces the company's message that employees should be treated like customers. . . .
>
> Hal F. Rosenbluth, CEO of Rosenbluth Travel thinks along the same lines. His book, *The Customer Comes Second*, explains the "secrets of exceptional service," as practiced at Rosenbluth Travel, which was featured in *The 100 Best Companies to Work for in America*. Who does he say comes first? His employees.[2]
>
> And, to reiterate from Chapter 1, Scott Adams, creator of the Dilbert cartoon series, says who comes first: "You, personally, are No. 1—you!—and then your family and then your co-workers. And somewhere after that is the customer and the stockholder.[3]

Are Colleen Barrett, Hal Rosenbluth, and Scott Adams on to something? Elevating employees to the vaunted stature of customers? The world's workforces, battered by layoffs and advanced cases of insecurity, might hope so.

We raise the issue of the employee for two reasons: (1) You now are or are likely to become one; and (2) the still-evolving field of operations management, in which most employed people work, may under-represent the employee in its enthusiasm for teams and customers. In this final chapter, we note some of the ways in which people can take care of themselves and their private interests, while still advancing the cause of improved operations and success in the greater organization and society as a whole. In the process, we discuss the impact of contemporary OM on job diversity, individual career management, keeping up, and staying relevant.

People, Teams, Jobs, and Careers

The first 17 chapters have focused on a few closely integrated new and evolving goals:

- Total quality.
- Data-based continuous improvement.
- Customer- and product-focused organization and performance measurement.
- Cross-functional teams.
- Streamlined, seamless flow of people, goods, and information.
- Flexibility.
- Simplicity.

Despite their cohesiveness, these aims do not describe a single profession. Rather, they suggest that operations management includes an assortment of jobs and people, and that operations management is a part of every person's job. Coordinating this diversity is itself a major OM issue. This diversity may also raise personal issues for you; for example, how you and your career might fit in. We address those questions next and expand on them in remaining sections of the chapter.

Employee Factor—OM Experience

If it hasn't already, your career will include considerable OM experience, which typically occurs in one of four ways: working in an OM department, providing offline OM support, serving on cross-functional teams, and participating in career-broadening assignments. (Of course, combinations of these factors are also possible.)

- *OM departments.* You may work in an operations department, managed by a vice president or director of operations, in a health care organization, welfare agency, military unit, information-processing firm, transportation company, or manufacturer. This is the operating end of the business— where products are made, campaigns are carried out, passengers and freight are moved, services are delivered, selling is done, information is processed, and so on.
- *OM support.* As we have seen, a lot of operations management takes place offline, before, while, and after operations themselves are performed. Examples include setting strategy and forecasting, designing and planning, buying and hiring, training and maintaining, scheduling and dispatching, locating and moving, and monitoring and controlling. Sometimes these activities are clearly in supporting roles, and sometimes distinctions between front-line and offline operations become blurred. What's important—for effective customer service—is that these activities blend seamlessly.
- *Cross-functional teams.* In nearly every chapter of this book, we have noted the growing reliance that first-rank organizations place on cross-functional

teams for solving problems and improving processes. The team may
involve both professionals and front-line employees (see Exhibit 18–1).
Regardless of your profession, your membership on such teams will
involve you in operations management issues and improvement
techniques presented in this text.

- *Career-broadening assignments.* If your career path begins in a non-OM
  specialty, you may gain OM experience by serving for a time in an
  operations department; the reverse also applies, of course.

Some companies have devised cross-careering policies that make career-broadening
assignments easier and more attractive. For example,

- Becton Dickinson, a medical devices company, has initiated what it calls
  horizontal promotion, a promotion and pay increase for moving to another
  specialty, say, from accounting to purchasing or from order entry to first-
  line supervision.

- Knighton Optical, a chain of retail optical shops with its own optical
  manufacturing plant, has cross-trained its accountants as opticians who
  can fit glasses for customers, and has trained its retail clerks to grind lenses
  and finish glasses in manufacturing.

- Calcomp, a maker of computer-driven plotters, moves senior development
  engineers to line supervisory positions.

- Corning Inc.'s Celcor division in Blacksburg, SC, screened 18,000 job
  applications to select 150 associates capable of learning the plant's high-
  tech skills and working in a team setting; most of the new hires had some
  college and several had four-year degrees. By the end of two years, all the
  associates must have mastered three families of skills.[4]

Thus, whether you are based in operations or not, you should consider the
value of broadening your understanding of other specialties. Increasingly, em-

---

EXHIBIT 18–1

Cross-functional Team—Bearing Manufacturer

*Representatives from throughout the plant meet to solve problems at NTN-Bower's bearing plant
in Macomb, Illinois.*

Courtesy of NTN-Bower Corporation. Used with permission.

ployers will be attracted to people who build breadth of skills. In fact, in studying operations management, you have improved your preparation for a variety of careers, specialties, and professions. See Exhibit 18–2.

Employer Factors—Customer Service and Career Paths

When employees participate in career-broadening experiences, employers also gain. An obvious example is workforce flexibility. Flexibility breeds responsiveness, reducing the time customers must wait while providers get the right mix of human resources together. In addition, as Edward Lawler puts it, a "broad perspective helps employees to be innovative in improving operations. Thus, they become more effective in a quality circle, or any other problem-solving group."[5] For example, a buyer with receiving or stockroom experience will be not only a better buyer but also better able to work with receiving and stockroom associates on work-flow improvement projects. Similarly, a salesperson who takes an inside operations job is likely to bring to the job an outside customer view and total business success vision.

Lawler makes the related point that since high-performance organizations have been flattening their organization structures, they need to create "new career tracks that do not depend on upward mobility" and that provide "a new 'nonlinear' way for people to grow and to succeed in their careers."[6]

The large baby-boom population exerts pressures in the same direction: many associates seeking few vertical advancement openings. Since the baby boomers will remain in the labor force for nearly two more decades, employers will not soon escape from the need for policy changes such as horizontal promotions.

Other human resource trends (besides population cycles and employee cross-training) will surely cause further changes in operations management and in management broadly. We will examine some of these forces and speculate on their effects in the remainder of this chapter.

$\mathscr{P}$RINCIPLE 7:

Cross-train for mastery of multiple skills

Over 150 years ago, Ralph Waldo Emerson wrote his classic essay, "Self Reliance." His theme, "trust thyself," is perhaps the best advice available today as individuals cope with new rules of employment. The future belongs to those who try to control their own destinies, who commit to a lifetime of learning. Richard Nelson Bolles (author of the job-hunter's bible, *What Color Is Your Parachute?*) advises everyone to inventory his or her skills, add to them every single year, and always have a ready answer to the question, what would you do if you lost your job tomorrow?

Experts agree that "the most employable people will be flexible folk who can move easily from one function to another, integrating diverse disciplines and perspectives." Competitive businesses know this. Although many have undergone deep downsizing, they are taking steps to ensure they keep the employees they want. There is also the hope that after a period of perhaps painful demolition of outdated workplace structures and ideas, jobholders will have more respect, responsibility, challenge, and fun.

Anyone who wants to be retained should start adapting now. Abraham Zaleznik, psychoanalyst and professor emeritus at the Harvard business school, feels that "the theme of the dawning era is greater accountability on the part of individuals and corporations." He says, "We're all up against a relentless, impersonal reality called the marketplace, which will reward those who do good jobs and punish those who don't."

Source: Adapted from Stratford Sherman, "A Brave New Darwinian Workplace," *Fortune*, January 25, 1993, pp. 51–56.

EXHIBIT 18–2

"Self-Reliance" Revisited

Change

Change in operations management has been so extensive that many concepts treated in this book were unknown before the 1980s. The future is unpredictable, and the present, which contains the roots of future directions, is hard to assess. Even so, we can suggest at least a few desirable changes, such as those that improve people's work lives, the environment, and standards of living. We would also like to see the benefits of today's best OM practices spreading from leading companies and industries to the rest, and we would like to see people in minimum-wage jobs and economically depressed countries helped by these practices as well.

Manufacturing in the Lead

Most of the new concepts we have discussed originated in the manufacturing sector. Still, the majority of manufacturers retain older, less effective approaches and have not yet seriously embraced the new. Those that have done so set an impressive example that is hard to ignore. Ford Motor Company, for example, sold about the same number of vehicles in 1978 and 1988, but in 1988 they did it with half as many production associates. According to *The Wall Street Journal*, "Industry observers largely credit an employee involvement program [that Ford introduced] in the early 1980s."[7] That program has focused on the techniques of statistical process control, just-in-time, design for manufacture and assembly, and total preventive maintenance.

We believe that many manufacturers will adopt these techniques before too long because, simply, they will be noncompetitive without them. The specter of extinction can be a powerful stimulus. In addition, it is becoming easier for manufacturers to change and adapt, especially since the necessary information is so widely available. Quality councils have sprung up in many cities and regions: most states and provinces sponsor quality awards; most of the 1,600-odd community and technical colleges in the United States and Canada offer subsidized instruction in statistical process control; and books and articles on quality and continuous improvement are flooding the market.

At one time, a good product (perhaps patented), a hard-to-copy technology, or superior marketing could make up for weak operations management. Moreover, weak OM usually was not so serious as to cause bankruptcy. Today, we think all that has changed: Superior OM blends with superior design, marketing, accounting, supplier relations, human-resource management, and business strategy as essential components of success. Weak OM, on the other hand, tends to coincide with many other management weaknesses.

For these reasons, we may be approaching a golden age of manufacturing in which the majority of firms will improve their operations management dramatically. Those that don't will probably fail quickly, and their valuable assets will be acquired cheaply by strong companies. The wave of business mergers and acquisitions in the 1970s and early 1980s was driven mostly by financial objectives, but the new wave, seemingly upon us, should be aimed at creating successful companies through management excellence, with lean effective operations management leading the way.

Exhibit 18–3 summarizes these points for manufacturing and postulates similar developments in three service environments. In the next section, we elaborate on those service-sector developments.

Manufacturing:	Unprecedented OM-based advantages of superior companies should induce average companies to change.
Retailing:	OM-based quick-response and total-quality partnerships may push other retailers to adapt.
Information services:	Adoption of remote processing (to tap special skills or low wages) may be followed by adoption of world-class operations management concepts to maintain a competitive edge.
Public service:	Lacking profit and sales targets, public servants may employ service and productivity targets as a way to have an impact, and total quality management might be the tool of choice.

EXHIBIT 18–3
Exploiting Gaps and Opportunities through Advanced Operations Management

Services Close Behind

At the end of the 1980s and into the 1990s, leading providers of a variety of services caught TQM fever. Although it is too early to make definitive evaluations (or suggest that a golden age of services is on the horizon), we can note two essential changes:

1. We had believed that many services, such as health care, sales, and teaching, were resistant to productivity improvement, and we had failed to realize how much rework, waste, delay, returns, and customer dissatisfaction is typically embedded in these services. We now realize that room for improvement is a Grand Canyon.

2. We also realize that most of the concepts and techniques of continuous improvement are effective in all lines of work.

However, the pace of improvement in services may be mixed. Service organizations in highly competitive businesses may be forced to change quickly; more insulated organizations may be able to avoid this necessity for the time being. The following are examples of service businesses that are more competitively exposed:

Retailing.   The opening of Toys 'R' Us stores in Japan sent shock waves through Japan's creaky distribution system. Japanese laws have been changed to accommodate high-volume, low-price retailers because consumers demanded it; many mom-and-pop toy shops have been put out of business. Wal-Mart has been doing the same thing in North America, forcing smaller retailers into niches or out of business.

Toys 'R' Us and Wal-Mart are two very successful chain retailers. (Examples could also be cited from specialty goods and general merchandise.) Central in their success formulas is partnering up with suppliers and freight carriers to minimize total inventories while still keeping the shelves stocked. These just-in-time partnerships eliminate intermediate warehousing and slash ordering and shipping transactions. In addition, project teams with members drawn from the retailer, freight carrier, producer, and even the producer's supplier are at work solving all sorts of intercompany problems.

A *Business Week* cover story featured Wal-Mart, Toys 'R' Us, Home Depot, and Circuit City, along with the cover-story title, "Clout!" These retailers are using their power and influence in transforming the supply chain and "revolutionizing the way consumer products are bought and sold."[8] However, Sears, Roebuck & Co.,

*P*RINCIPLE 13:

Operate at the customer's rate of use.

along with Hudson Bay stores in Canada and Marks and Spencer in the United Kingdom, had equal clout in the pre-Wal-Mart era. They were famous for using it, too, for driving a hard bargain on price. But in that era, concepts such as JIT, supplier partnership, and cross-functional problem-solving teams were not taught and were largely unknown in Western enterprise.

Today, these ideas are common knowledge. They have become part of the mainstream of business studies and are finding their way into textbooks in government, education, and other fields as well. Retailers achieve competitive advantage by using these techniques, and when a retailer has a blind spot, a knowledgeable supplier may take its just-in-time proposal to the retailer, pointing out ways to jointly cut costs and improve service. Milliken & Company's textile managers have taken such proposals not only to their customers in the apparel and upholstered furniture business and transport companies, but all the way to clothing and furniture retailers.

Many high-performance retail–supplier partnerships are partially founded on TQM concepts, but the situation seems a bit different in information services.

Information Services.   Increasingly, companies are farming out computer software development and heavy-duty data-entry jobs to information service companies in India. Grocery chains fly sacks of merchandise coupons to Caribbean Islands for counting. Designers scattered around the globe jointly develop new products for Texas Instruments and the Gap. Omaha has become a center for telephone services such as airline reservations and credit checking. Satellite communications, the Internet and its many services, computer-aided design, rapid prototyping, air freight, and other technologies make these arrangements possible. Thus, the lowering of trade barriers that is occurring around the world is in some ways incidental; data and information already move from country to country without customs inspections.

So far, these outsourcing arrangements generally do not promote total quality management or continuous improvement. Just-in-time is not managed in; real-time speed simply seems to be a part of the technology. Management wants to harness special skills (e.g., pattern makers in Hong Kong, liquid-emitting diode designers in the Netherlands, or a neutral English accent for telephone answerers in Omaha), or to find useful skills at a very low wage (e.g., computer programmers in India).

Although any firm can use communications technology to outsource information services, it seems inevitable that firms will have to do more than just chase low wages or special skills to be competitive. Superior companies will gain an edge by employing TQM-based techniques to improve quality and flexibility, eliminate waste, and continuously improve.

Public Services.   Denied the option of global outsourcing, public agencies have even more reason to implement total quality management. TQM is now a dominant subject of employee training in public services. Results include, for example, substantial error reductions in the U.S. Internal Revenue Service, many times faster repair of city vehicles in Madison, Wisconsin, and elimination of chronic misplacement of X-rays in the San Diego Naval Hospital system.

Doubters may say that TQM in government is just a fad and that the government's customer is not clearly enough defined for customer-focused TQM to be effective. However, a more significant factor is that government often has less incentive to measure success than profit-making firms have. This can be frus-

*𝒫*RINCIPLE 6:

Organize chains of customers.

trating to dedicated public servants, who may see TQM as a way to finally make a noticeable impact. Moreover, concepts that greatly improve an agency's ability to provide quick, accurate response and increase productivity may help make government service more personally fulfilling.

Quality of Work Life and the Environment

Personal fulfillment can be a powerful motivator, at least for those whose basic personal needs are taken care of. But what about people working at the minimum wage, in a clerical, fast-food, data-entry, janitorial, or general labor capacity? To be competitive, their employers may deliberately encourage high turnover to reduce the pressure to grant pay raises. They may also offer mainly part-time work to avoid paying benefits, and call in extra part-timers to avoid paying overtime. Jobholders in these businesses may fall below the poverty line; be unable to pay for proper medical care, housing, and food; and have many unmet physiological and security needs.

Here we refer to Abraham Maslow's hierarchy of needs: Physiological, security, love, esteem, and, at the top, fulfillment.

Improvement Scenario

Nevertheless, there may be a role for TQM in these businesses. Here is a possible scenario:

- Burgers, Inc., launches a "word-class services" program via a two-day training course for every employee, including office support and managerial associates.
- Baseline performance measures, such as customer wait time, food and packaging waste, store cleanliness index, inventories, and invoice processing time, are plotted on large charts.
- Project teams, both spontaneous and assigned, are formed to improve performance, which they record on the wall charts. The teams capture and deal with root causes, then plot new points on the charts.
- Team members who are enthusiastic leaders, communicators, or innovators stand out. Supervisors and store managers don't want to lose these employees, so they are given more hours, benefits, and pay raises.
- The overall level of competence and motivation of the workforce rises, and increasing numbers of associates rise up through the ranks to become supervisors, store managers, and executives. Other employees move on to other careers but with impressive problem-solving credentials.
- Better pay brings some of these standout associates up out of poverty, so that their physiological needs can be met. Burgers, Inc., values their continued employment, which meets their security needs. These associates are better fixed to pursue higher-level needs. Later on in life, some of these people may be at the level of high personal fulfillment, but meanwhile they see learning, innovation, and continuous process improvement as a path out of poverty and a way to improve their credentials and résumés.
- Burgers, Inc., enjoys a reputation for the best quality and service in its industry at competitive prices. Though it offers pay raises, benefits, and security, the improvement teams drive out costly wastes so that its costs are no higher than those of its less-capable competitors.

*𝒫*RINCIPLE 14:

Record quality, process, and problem data at the workplace.

Does this scenario sound familiar? It should. The Kentucky Fried Chicken example in Chapter 5 partially follows this improvement sequence. The same scenario could help uplift people in underdeveloped countries from poverty and no-hope existence.

TQM in Less-Developed Countries

The world will remain a tinder box of discontent if weak economic systems cannot be strengthened; the security of wealthy industrialized countries thus is tied to economic improvement in less-developed countries. In previous chapters, we reviewed a few examples of companies in less-developed countries that pay low wages (very low by Western standards) but still achieve world-class results:

- We noted the extensive implementation of TQM and JIT at Eicher Tractor Co, in India (Chapter 2).
- The Rio Bravo IV case study detailed the many JIT and continuous improvement achievements at a Packard Electric plant in Juarez, Mexico (Chapter 8).

In each case, company officers committed significant resources for employee training; TQM-literate managers and associates took it from there. Many similar examples exist in less-developed economies throughout South America and Asia. In many firms, world-class operations management and global competitiveness occur amid poverty, primitive infrastructure, stifling bureaucratic red tape, and unstable governments. The success formula should work at least as well in low-wage firms in developed countries, which face far fewer difficulties.

Environmental Protection

Improvement teams will devote some of their time to job and environmental health and safety. They will do so in their own self-interest and because insurance policies and governmental regulations may require certain levels of protection. Moreover, companies will encounter increasing pressure from customers and the public to achieve certification under ISO–14000, the international standard for environmental management (see Exhibit 18–4). Environmental activists also press the issue and sometimes prove that strong safety and environmental policies pay. Companies known for their vigorous safety programs, such as Du Pont, have much lower workers' compensation payment rates.

EXHIBIT 18–4

ISO–14000 at a Glance

ISO–14000 is a series of generic environmental standards developed by the International Organization for Standardization. Begun in 1992, initial portions of ISO–14000 were released in 1996. Key components include ISO–14004, the guiding standard for creating and maintaining an environmental management system (EMX), and

ISO–14001, the specification standard which sets the minimum requirements for registration to ISO–14000. Other parts of the series contain specific provisions that address environmental audits, environmental labeling, environmental performance evaluation, life-cycle analysis, and the environmental aspects of product standards.[9]

International trade pacts also appear to be moving companies in this direction. For example, although the North American Free Trade Agreement encourages expansive trade between Mexico and its northern neighbors, political leaders in the United States and Canada press for Mexico to upgrade and enforce antipollution and employment standards. The European Community is at least as firm about incorporating tough environmental and labor standards into its internal and external trade pacts. The United Nations also regularly debates these issues. Although international environmental, safety, health, and labor standards are being developed, implementation must occur at a much lower level. Front-line and cross-functional process-improvement teams seem to be the natural instrument for implementation.

*𝒫*RINCIPLE 7:

Continually invest in improved health, safety, and security.

Currents and Countercurrents

Globalism affects operations management in many ways, but especially in the phenomenal growth of market size as trade barriers fall. A Coke now is available almost everywhere, a potential market of over five billion people. But a few years ago, Coca-Cola was excluded from most of the Soviet bloc, China, and India. The company's businesses strategy is simple: Build focused factories that produce economies of scale and meet its quality standards, and form supplier and distribution partnerships of all kinds. The nine success factors for process industries presented in Chapter 13 (Exhibit 13–2) set forth the operations management practices that carry out that strategy.

McDonald's, Gillette, Bank of America, Metropolitan Life, and other high-volume businesses may follow similar strategies. The vast world market offers relief from the limited strategy of just fighting Burger King, Schick, Citibank, and Prudential for local market share.

As these companies expand around the world, local companies are often swallowed up or go broke. For instance, James River Corp., a large American paper company, acquired joint ownership of 13 paper companies in 10 European countries. The European venture, called Jamont, then had the task of sorting out different countries' preferences. Regarding toilet tissue, the conventional wisdom said: "German-speaking countries. . . buy strength. The French want soft. And the Americans crave very soft."[10] But Jamont managers found that consumers want softness and strength regardless of nationality. Gradually, Jamont managers are developing similar world-class practices for all its plants: Low quality-standards are raised, equipment is upgraded, and volume drives costs down. For example, all 13 plants formerly made their own deep-colored napkins, a time-consuming process involving costly dye changing. Now a single specialized Jamont plant in Finland makes deep-colored napkins for all 10 countries. Such opportunities arise from doing business in a mass market instead of a fractionated one.

*𝒫*RINCIPLE 6:

Organize resources for product focus.

But there is a countercurrent: While the big get bigger in new and massive markets, opportunities are growing for agile suppliers of speciality goods and services in those same mass markets. Unfortunately, however, while the Coca Colas and Citibanks of the world have always offered fairly good quality and high efficiency, most specialty companies have been woeful performers by today's standards. Customers may wait interminably and have little input or feedback; when the product or service is finally delivered, it's often wrong and needs to be redone.

As noted in Chapter 12, providers of custom or specialty goods and services have lower volumes and higher variety, factors that partially explain their poor performance.

This description could apply to a printer, a tailor, a foundry, a bridge builder, a doctor, a lawyer, or a city agency.

The nine-point list of Exhibit 13–2 summarizes world-class OM for the high-volume processor, but a world-class formula for the specialty company must be significantly longer and more complex. In fact, we have included ways to improve low-volume specialty operations in almost every chapter, in part because specialty operations are so complex and nonroutine. Modular design (Chapter 4), queue limitation (Chapter 10), quick-change flexibility (Chapter 11), total preventive maintenance (Chapter 17) and cells (Chapter 12) are just some of the concepts important to improving specialty operations.

First to Know

In studying operations management, we have been exposed to several major evolutions in strategy. In the early 1980s, quality consciousness began to sink in and quality as competitive advantage became the dominant new strategy. A few years later, the focus was on time-based competition, then globalization, and lately, flexibility.

These ideas were developed as an integrated whole in certain pioneering books of the late 1970s and early 1980s, and they gained extra prominence after being blessed in prestigious business periodicals such as the *Harvard Business Review*. Moreover, each of these strategies tends to move like an avalanche through the adopting business, especially affecting operations management. People wonder, Is there more? If so, what's next?

We don't know. Rather than trying to guess, we would rather make this point: What's important is being the first to know and, therefore, having the first chance to implement and gain the advantage. It seems likely that the first to know will be organizations having strong benchmarking and competitive analysis, supplier and customer partnerships, a global presence, extensive continuous training, ethnic variety, and highly involved employees skilled at getting things done right the first time. In your own career, taking charge of building these first-to-know capabilities can be your best protection.

Summary

Operations management is in a period of renaissance, drawing upon diverse specialties, professions, and departments. A full OM career will include time in front-line operations and in a few OM support specialties as well. Each career step, however, should involve teaming up for problem solving with specialists in other career tracks. Flatter organization structures make horizontal movements attractive for people's careers and good for the firm's human resource development.

Organizations in all sectors are being competitively driven to implement total quality management, just-in-time, and related newer OM concepts.

- In manufacturing, these concepts have made weak companies strong. Visible examples (e.g., Ford Motor Co.) may help convince other manufacturers that they can no longer get by without wholesale changes in their operations management.

- In retailing, successful firms like Toys 'R' Us and Wal-Mart are forging quick-response, waste-eliminating partnerships with their supply chains. Manufacturers like Milliken & Co. are pressing for the same OM-based solutions with their chains of customers. Old-line retailers may have to adapt, retreat into niche retailing, or expire.

- In information services, technology permits locating a service center almost anywhere. Western companies are setting up operations in geographically remote areas, sometimes to tap special talents but often to cut wages. Since any firm may set up remote data services, gaining an edge may require using advanced OM concepts at the remote site.

- In nonprofit organizations, especially government, managers may be attracted to TQM-related ideas as a way to make an impact. Knowledge and training resources on how to do it are widely available and affordable.

It may seem that low-wage employees would be too concerned about their survival to worry about continuous improvement. However, if the employer provides the training and gets TQM going, some low-wage associates may be able to contribute innovative solutions that improve their employer's competitiveness. The employer may value this contribution sufficiently to begin treating the associate better, with better pay and job security. In this scenario, low-wage employees see problem-solving skills and behaviors as a path upward, and act accordingly. There is partial evidence that this scenario has worked in, for example, fast-food restaurants.

A popular topic for improvement teams is enhancing their own job safety and health, in part because it is sensible to do so and in part in response to government regulations and environmentalist pressure. In addition, international trade pacts are including environmental standards for both pact members and outsiders. Global and political mandates to preserve the environment can be supported by TQM teams.

As trade barriers fall, superior companies, which often include advanced OM concepts in their success formulas, begin to tap massive new markets. High-volume producers or service providers standardize and adopt a short list of OM improvement concepts (see Exhibit 13–2). By contrast, specialty firms have a much more complex range of operations to manage and thus must employ a larger range of OM improvements (concepts found in nearly every chapter).

As operations management continues to evolve, companies—and OM associates—will want to be the first to know about the next development. The best ways of staying current include continuous benchmarking, training, global involvement, and participation on improvement projects with diverse other people.

Review Questions

1. If you're employed in a job or profession other than operations, how can you put these operations management studies to use?

2. What socioeconomic trend is behind the development of what Becton Dickinson calls horizontal promotion?

3. Will TQM, JIT, and related concepts continue to expand in use in manufacturing companies? Explain.

4. What OM-related factors contribute to the success of retailers like Wal-Mart and Circuit City?

5. What can a manufacturer do to make its chain of customers, extending all the way to the retailer, more successful?

6. When remote partnerships for information services become established, can OM-related concepts play a useful role? If so, which concepts, and how?

7. Does TQM appeal to public servants? Explain.

8. Are people at the bottom level of Maslow's hierarchy of needs likely to take an interest in continuous improvement? Explain.

9. Is continuous improvement likely to interest low-wage people in less-developed countries? Explain.

10. Governments and international bodies keep tightening environmental and labor standards. Will this cause affected companies' costs to rise, competitiveness to decline, and associates to resist? Explain.

11. Who will be best able to benefit from the enormous markets created by trade pacts? Explain.

12. How can you and your employer benefit from the continuing renaissance in operations management?

Exercises

1. If your family owned a store selling clothing, variety goods, or consumer electronics and a competitor like Home Depot or Circuit City opened a store in the same area, what would you advise your family to do? Explain.

2. Could medical opinions be delivered routinely from one country to another? If so, would TQM have any special value in such an arrangement? Answer the same question with regard to legal services and public accounting.

3. Bright Hope, Inc., operates a chain of private hospitals. A team of its managers benchmarked Wal-Mart and Toys 'R' Us, and team members are excited about what they've learned. The next step is to develop a plan to implement the relevant parts of the Wal-Mart and Toys 'R' Us success formula. What should this plan consist of? Explain.

4. You serve meals in a university cafeteria, but with little enthusiasm for the work even though food service is your intended career. Your supervisor and upper managers are very receptive to suggestions. Develop an OM-based plan that will (a) make your present job more satisfying, (b) be received reasonably well by your front-line associates, (c) be welcomed by your bosses, and (d) be helpful to your career development.

5. Find out what you can about ISO–14000.
    a. What kinds of organizations are most likely to feel pressure and derive value from adopting this standard?
    b. What is the current status of ISO–14000? (For example, what percentages of companies have embraced the standard in your country and internationally? Is the standard relatively stable or rapidly changing?)

6. In this chapter's speculations about future directions for operations management, little was said about emerging technologies. If you can, develop a logical scenario of significant OM changes that are based mainly on new technologies. If you think that technologies will have little impact, or that technological changes and effects are completely unpredictable, explain why.

BECOMING WORD-CLASS AT K2 CORPORATION

Scott Doss had just described the rapid progress he and his fellow maintenance technicians had made over the last three months in lowering setup times on the mold presses used in forming ski bottoms. He went on to speculate on further improvements:

> Everyone on the team is looking ahead to the day when we can have a mold prestaged, maybe with removable plates—whatever—with molds already on; slide this one out and slide in the next one that's already been plugged in and preheated and is ready to go. What we've concentrated on, so far, are things where we don't have to remove the bolts—where we just change the profile. In the future basically anything is possible.

With faster mold changeovers, schedulers were starting to plan smaller lots that could be run more often with better response to the customer. Lot sizes on the presses had been weeks' or months' worth in the past, but Doss expressed the hope that "in the next couple of years, we get to the point where we could change day to day if we had to."

Doss's employer is K2 Corporation, a manufacturer of high-quality snow skis. K2, which has been in the ski-manufacturing business for nearly three decades, became a subsidiary of Anthony Industries Co. in 1986. K2's main plant and headquarters is located on Vashon Island, across Puget Sound from Seattle. K2's current annual sales volume is $60 million, which is about 10 percent of the world market for skis. The company employs 500 people.

Spotlight on Manufacturing

In the fall of 1987, K2 hired consultant Peter Scontrino to study K2's compensation plan for hourly employees. At that time, about 35 percent of the company's hourly workers were paid on a piece-based incentive system. Mr. Scontrino learned that K2 managers favored extending that plan to cover more job classifications. Scontrino, however, believed that the company should shelve the incentive system and move toward a gain-sharing plan. He recommended Richard J. Schonberger's book, *World-Class Manufacturing*, as background reading for K2 managers.

Before long, the K2 management team had developed plans for its own "world-class manufacturing" system, which included gain sharing, just-in-time production, total quality control, employee involvement, and total preventive maintenance. Implementation of the plan was swift, including the following improvements by late summer 1988:

- The former inventory of plastic top-edge strips was about 150,000 pieces, a $2\frac{1}{2}$ weeks' supply. Still, with 22 different size/color combinations, it was common to be out of one that was needed. Now the inventory is about 20,000 and there are no stockouts. The machine operator runs a kanban quantity of 300 strips only when a green card is in one of the 22 slots in a nearby rack; otherwise the slot holds a red card. Material control people insert the green or red kanbans each morning based on how much of each part is on hand in the mold-press room. The operator, who has duties elsewhere, runs the strip cutter only when green cards are present. (The operator had to quit producing for six weeks in order to whittle down the large inventory.)
- The steel-edge crew (which bends and welds "cracked" steel to metal tail protectors to form a one-piece steel-edge assembly) has reduced its flow time from four days to six hours, its lot size from 450 to 150 pieces, and its inventory from 50 carts (20,000 pieces) to a maximum of 11 carts. The maximum is controlled by 11 kanban squares among the machines on the floor. Each operator has line-stop authority.

_____

This case is based on research conducted by Richard J. Schonberger in August 1988.

EXHIBIT S18–1   Skis in Rough Base Finishing at K2 Corp.

A. Three to four weeks' worth of skis—before world-class manufacturing emphasis

B. Three to four hours' worth of skis—after world-class manufacturing emphasis

Implementation was done in one day, but it took almost a week to work the steel inventory down by halting receipts from the local supplier (who provides the material already punched).

- Setup time on mold presses making K2's foam-core type of ski bottom has been reduced from 30 minutes to as little as 5 minutes.
- Setup time on mold presses for K2's premier braided-fiber ski bottom has been reduced from two weeks to as little as 10 hours at zero capital cost. The setup reduction effort included providing each operator with a set of the right tools; rewiring electrical panels; checking first skis at the bench instead of in the lab; using uniform, easy-to-adjust, shorter bolts (requiring fewer turns); installing setting rails; using air equipment with Allen socket heads; putting T-handles on Allen wrenches; using stacked shims; and painting each machine as it was converted. Ten of the 50 presses were converted during summer 1988, with the rest due for conversion by year's end.
- In rough-base finishing, molded ski bottoms go through seven wet-sanders and four grinders, which had been grouped into three separate work centers; now they are merged into a flow line operated by an 11-person team. Formerly 60 to 90 carts (three or four weeks' worth) of skis were crammed into the rough-finishing room. Now carts come directly from molding for nearly immediate processing (no work orders); the buffer stock is about 10 carts, or three to four hours' worth, so feedback to molding on quality problems is fast. See the before and after photos in Exhibit S18–1.
- Lead time to produce a set of graphics (designs that go on the tops of the skis) has been cut from one week to one shift or less.
- Changeover time on the five silk-screening lines has been reduced from 25 minutes to as little as 5 minutes.
- There used to be a queue of about 150 carts in front of the room housing the large piece of equipment (designed in-house) that joins ski tops to bottoms; it is now more like 7 carts (a typical cart holds 150 skis).
- Skis formerly spent about three weeks in finishing; now they zip through in one shift.

- Rework in finishing had been 50–60 percent; it is now down to about 0.5 percent. At the same time, attainable plant capacity has increased from under 2,000 good pairs per day to about 2,500 per day. The quality and capacity improvements occurred during the turmoil of hiring 100 new people and bringing them up to proper skill level.
- Inventory of the basic raw material (uniglass) has been reduced from $225,000 to $41,000.
- In 1986, there were 300 carts (about 50,000 skis) on the floor; now it is perhaps 20 carts.
- In many parts of the plant, work orders and completion reporting by bar-code scanning have been eliminated, along with sending material into stock and performing storekeeping on it. Jeff Bardsley, production and inventory control planner, states that he had been spending up to eight hours a day on the computer. "Now I'm out on the floor, and I can see what the real problems are." Lead times on some items were reduced from three weeks to four days.
- At Vashon for meetings in August 1988, K2's sales representatives from all over the world were excited by what they saw in the factory. Some expressed the view that K2 is now the standard against which the best in the industry would have to be measured.

What's next?

With such a string of impressive—and quick—accomplishments, a nagging notion in the back of some people's minds at K2 is, What's next? And how do we keep up the enthusiasm and create a sustained work culture of continuous improvement?

Case Questions

1. Is it reasonable for K2 people to expect much more improvement? Sustained improvement?
2. Outline a strategic plan for operations management at K2 for the next five years.

For Further Reference

Books

Berry, Leonard L.; David R. Bennett; and Carter W. Brown, *Service Quality: A Profit Strategy for Financial Institutions.* Burr Ridge, Ill.: Dow Jones-Irwin, 1989 (HG1616.C87B47).

Naisbitt, John, and Patricia Aburdene, *Megatrends 2000: Ten New Directions for the 1990s.* New York: Wm. Morrow, 1990 (HN59.2.N343).

Ohmae, Kenichi. *The Borderless World: Management Lessons in the New Logic of the Global Marketplace.* Harper Business and McKinsey & Company, Inc., 1990.

Plossl, George W. *Managing in the New World of Manufacturing.* Englewood Cliffs, N.J.: Prentice-Hall, 1991 (HD9720.5.P56).

Porter, Michael E. *The Competitive Advantage of Nations.* New York: The Free Press, 1990 (HD3611.P654).

Schonberger, Richard J. *Building a Chain of Customers: Linking Business Functions to Create the World-Class Company.* New York: The Free Press, 1990 (HD58.9.S36).

Periodicals

Looking to the future is a popular activity. Many reputable business, economic, and scientific periodicals publish articles on it.

Areas under the Normal Curve

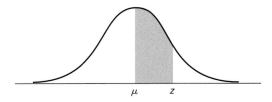

Example

The area between the mean (μ) and the point one standard deviation above the mean (z = 1.00) is 0.3413, or 34.13 percent of the total area under the curve. The area between z = −1.00 and z = 1.00 is 0.3413 + 0.3413 = 0.6826.

TABLE A–1 Areas of Standard Normal Distribution

Z	0.00	0.01	0.02	0.03	0.04	0.05	0.06	0.07	0.08	0.09
0.0	0.0000	0.0040	0.0080	0.0120	0.0160	0.0199	0.0239	0.0279	0.0319	0.0359
0.1	0.0398	0.0438	0.0478	0.0517	0.0557	0.0596	0.0636	0.0675	0.0714	0.0753
0.2	0.0793	0.0832	0.0871	0.0910	0.0948	0.0987	0.1026	0.1064	0.1103	0.1141
0.3	0.1179	0.1217	0.1255	0.1293	0.1331	0.1368	0.1406	0.1443	0.1480	0.1517
0.4	0.1554	0.1591	0.1628	0.1664	0.1700	0.1736	0.1772	0.1808	0.1844	0.1879
0.5	0.1915	0.1950	0.1985	0.2019	0.2054	0.2088	0.2123	0.2157	0.2190	0.2224
0.6	0.2257	0.2291	0.2324	0.2357	0.2389	0.2422	0.2454	0.2486	0.2518	0.2549
0.7	0.2580	0.2612	0.2642	0.2673	0.2704	0.2734	0.2764	0.2794	0.2823	0.2852
0.8	0.2881	0.2910	0.2939	0.2967	0.2995	0.3023	0.3051	0.3078	0.3106	0.3133
0.9	0.3159	0.3186	0.3212	0.3238	0.3264	0.3289	0.3315	0.3340	0.3365	0.3389
1.0	0.3413	0.3438	0.3461	0.3485	0.3508	0.3531	0.3554	0.3577	0.3599	0.3621
1.1	0.3643	0.3665	0.3686	0.3708	0.3729	0.3749	0.3770	0.3790	0.3810	0.3830
1.2	0.3849	0.3869	0.3888	0.3907	0.3925	0.3944	0.3962	0.3980	0.3997	0.4015
1.3	0.4032	0.4049	0.4066	0.4082	0.4099	0.4115	0.4131	0.4147	0.4162	0.4177
1.4	0.4192	0.4207	0.4222	0.4236	0.4251	0.4265	0.4279	0.4292	0.4306	0.4319
1.5	0.4332	0.4345	0.4357	0.4370	0.4382	0.4394	0.4406	0.4418	0.4429	0.4441
1.6	0.4452	0.4463	0.4474	0.4484	0.4495	0.4505	0.4515	0.4525	0.4535	0.4545
1.7	0.4554	0.4564	0.4573	0.4582	0.4591	0.4599	0.4608	0.4616	0.4625	0.4633
1.8	0.4641	0.4649	0.4656	0.4664	0.4671	0.4678	0.4686	0.4693	0.4699	0.4706
1.9	0.4713	0.4719	0.4726	0.4732	0.4738	0.4744	0.4750	0.4756	0.4761	0.4767
2.0	0.4772	0.4778	0.4783	0.4788	0.4793	0.4798	0.4803	0.4808	0.4812	0.4817
2.1	0.4821	0.4826	0.4830	0.4834	0.4838	0.4842	0.4846	0.4850	0.4854	0.4857
2.2	0.4861	0.4864	0.4868	0.4871	0.4875	0.4878	0.4881	0.4884	0.4887	0.4890
2.3	0.4893	0.4896	0.4898	0.4901	0.4904	0.4906	0.4909	0.4911	0.4913	0.4916
2.4	0.4918	0.4920	0.4922	0.4925	0.4927	0.4929	0.4931	0.4932	0.4934	0.4936
2.5	0.4938	0.4940	0.4941	0.4943	0.4945	0.4946	0.4948	0.4949	0.4951	0.4952
2.6	0.4953	0.4955	0.4956	0.4957	0.4959	0.4960	0.4961	0.4962	0.4963	0.4964
2.7	0.4965	0.4966	0.4967	0.4968	0.4969	0.4970	0.4971	0.4972	0.4973	0.4974
2.8	0.4974	0.4975	0.4976	0.4977	0.4977	0.4978	0.4979	0.4979	0.4980	0.4981
2.9	0.4981	0.4982	0.4982	0.4983	0.4984	0.4984	0.4985	0.4985	0.4986	0.4986
3.0	0.4986	0.4987	0.4987	0.4988	0.4988	0.4989	0.4989	0.4989	0.4990	0.4990
3.1	0.4990	0.4991	0.4991	0.4991	0.4992	0.4992	0.4992	0.4992	0.4993	0.4993
3.2	0.4993	0.4993	0.4994	0.4994	0.4994	0.4994	0.4994	0.4995	0.4995	0.4995
3.3	0.4995	0.4995	0.4995	0.4996	0.4996	0.4996	0.4996	0.4996	0.4996	0.4997
3.4	0.4997	0.4997	0.4997	0.4997	0.4997	0.4997	0.4997	0.4997	0.4998	0.4998
3.5	0.4998	0.4998	0.4998	0.4998	0.4998	0.4998	0.4998	0.4998	0.4998	0.4998
3.6	0.4998	0.4998	0.4999	0.4999	0.4999	0.4999	0.4999	0.4999	0.4999	0.4999
3.7	0.4999	0.4999	0.4999	0.4999	0.4999	0.4999	0.4999	0.4999	0.4999	0.4999
3.8	0.4999	0.4999	0.4999	0.4999	0.4999	0.4999	0.4999	0.5000	0.5000	0.5000
3.9	0.5000	0.5000	0.5000	0.5000	0.5000	0.5000	0.5000	0.5000	0.5000	0.5000

APPENDIX B
Two-Digit Random Numbers

TABLE B–1   **Two-Digit Random Numbers—Uniform Distribution**

42	27	11	61	64	20
55	39	37	71	35	78
24	42	25	60	61	78
82	70	68	68	28	08
56	38	62	42	05	47
48	15	21	40	25	78
95	76	15	43	63	18
86	86	96	50	43	17
49	47	10	94	14	22
41	74	33	33	28	76
95	47	92	56	95	95
78	31	27	77	66	63
84	18	88	65	46	81
40	00	61	17	82	53
80	00	85	42	64	44
12	55	13	20	74	16
84	27	50	45	97	19
01	22	40	81	36	10
25	12	07	98	82	74
46	12	83	52	30	42
83	02	73	53	18	07
69	18	16	09	93	65
78	22	36	94	45	32
43	18	05	33	44	45
07	34	46	30	49	10
00	50	31	12	42	88
55	34	73	61	96	44
17	39	51	92	64	44
22	81	84	00	95	32
57	00	21	12	36	96
02	20	12	50	71	82
70	15	52	75	67	60
28	36	84	20	73	23
86	60	52	37	46	79
04	34	33	73	42	91
95	35	13	16	75	03
89	14	24	19	29	82
92	46	72	35	17	81
30	28	74	35	87	67
86	31	84	29	75	89
13	21	48	73	40	73
38	87	98	23	72	43
02	42	81	84	08	38
72	22	79	60	26	26
16	05	14	42	74	74
70	03	63	58	32	12
45	45	96	64	49	83
05	38	40	89	75	32
29	24	05	17	03	53
20	87	26	88	06	18

APPENDIX C
Answers to Selected Problems and Exercises

The authors' intent is to guide your thought processes and provide brief feedback. Generally, answers given here are "check answers" to about half of the exercises. When a quantitative response is required, we supply only the final value along with its units. When the exercise requires discussion or multiple responses, we offer examples of some acceptable answers. A brief parenthetical identifier begins each item.

Chapter 1

2. (Operations and other functions)
   (Line functions)
   > Stock (investments) brokerage—operations encompasses money management
   > Advertising agency—operations encompasses marketing or demand management

   (Staff function)
   > Employment agency—operations encompasses human-resources management function

4. (Nonprofit organizations)
   Example: U.S. Postal Service:

   - Money: A traditional accounting function.
   - Design: New products/services such as 2nd-Day delivery, Express mail, and stamps-by-mail.
   - Demand: The postal service advertises, sets prices, conducts market research, and makes sales contracts with commercial customers.
   - Operations: Receiving, sorting, and delivering mail are primary operations activities.

6. (Six basic customer wants)

   > Example: Airline travelers: One passenger who has to make a connecting flight at the destination airport might attach a higher priority to on-time arrival at the gate than another passenger who terminates travel at the destination. The second passenger may be more concerned with the speed at which luggage is available at the luggage claim carousel. A third passenger might value low fares most, and a fourth might seek out friendly service from gate and flight attendants.

   > Example: Patrons at a busy lunch counter: One patron places greatest priority on fast

   service, another on menu variety (a quality dimension), a third on low cost, and a fourth on consistently being able to get raspberry pie for dessert (no variability).

   > Example: Clothing manufacturing: When purchasing cloth, one manufacturer might give highest priority to cloth quality, another to cost, a third to short delivery times, and a fourth to flexibility of delivery scheduling.

8. (American Customer Satisfaction Index (ACSI))
   - For a summary of initial ACSI results, see "The Quality Forum X: Quality 2000—The Next Decade of Progress," *Quality Progress,* December 1994, pp. 31–34.
   - Explanation of purpose, measurement details, and target industries/sectors for the ASCI may be found in Jon Brecka, "The American Customer Satisfaction Index," *Quality Progress,* October 1994, pp. 41–44.
   - An exploratory critique of the ACSI by a panel of American Society for Quality Control (ASQC) Fellows appears in "The ASQC Fellows Project," *Quality Progress,* May 1995, pp. 49–54.

10. (Business news magazine reports) Stories about productivity, a crisis in North American industry, began to appear in the late 1970s and were relatively common by the early 1980s. *Business Week* carried a special report entitled "The Hollow Corporation" in its March 3, 1986, issue. The "hollowing of industry" has been viewed as an attempt by manufacturers to enhance productivity by outsourcing production of key components, and to some extent delivery of key services, that had historically been done in-house. Some, though not all, view outsourcing as a way of pushing inventory "issues" back on suppliers rather than tackling the source of problems (e.g., better quality, shorter cycle times, flexibility, etc.).

Chapter 2

2. (Professor Wickham Skinner's views) One example: Skinner, "Implementation of Operations Strategy," *Operations Management Review,* Winter 1996, pp. 2–4, which traces OM strategy to Skinner's student days. His professor cited research about flip-flopping performance of a few

manufacturers over time, which stimulated thoughts about strategies as possible determining factors.

4. (Fidelity Investments and Charles Schwab— strategies) Briefly, Charles Schwab aimed at becoming a discount (low-cost) broker. Fidelity's unusual strategy is selling *both* its own funds *and* distributing them through brokers.

6. (Competition and operations management) Competition fosters continuous improvement. As one customer need is met by one provider, others scramble to catch up and then forge ahead.

8. (North American Bearing Company)
   a. Principle 8: Maintain present equipment before thinking about acquiring new.
   b. Principle 10 (In this case, make it easy to perform maintenance right the first time) and Principle 14 (Here, give front-line teams responsibility and commensurate authority to perform appropriate maintenance) should be major components of the long-term strategy.

10. (Classic Wooden Toy Company) Generally, all of the implementation principles (numbers 5 through 15) serve to improve responsiveness. Specific examples include Principle 12 (cut setup and changeover times on woodworking equipment), Principle 11 (cut flow and wait time), Principle 15 (cut transactions and reporting), and Principle 7 (cross-train employees).

12. (John Deere) The up-to-date policy supports service to the customer. It directly supports Principle 7 and indirectly supports others, especially Principles 1, 2, 7, and 15.

14. (Seagate) Principle 14 stresses recording and ownership of process data at the workplace to help ensure that line people get first crack at using those data for problem solving (Principle 15).

Chapter 3

2. (Zero defects) As you move down the list, pause to consider the potential effects of a mistake from each of the providers. None of us wants to be on the receiving end of defects. Our aim should be to avoid providing any. The last item helps pinpoint how that aim might be addressed now.

4. (Price versus quality) The perception that higher price denotes higher-quality service is the issue. Although challenged in recent years by

numerous cost-effective, high-quality providers, that perception still permeates some sectors.

6. (PDCA cycle) Example for combating meeting tardiness and absenteeism:
   • Plan around attendance barriers by comparing members' schedules, and discuss causes.
   • Do implement a meeting schedule that is acceptable to all.
   • Check attendance and tardiness records.
   • Act by making the meeting schedule permanent or revising it if appropriate.

8. (Acme motor-generator set) It is an expense (arguably an investment) for quality and for productivity, better service, lower operating costs, and perhaps safety.

10. (Ace Auto Repair)
   a. Yes. Front-liners should take responsibility for quality; also, before the job leaves the work area is the best time to make corrections if needed.
   b. Yes. It is a part of appraisal and prevention of subsequent defects.
   c. Yes. Even though mechanic will attempt to do the job right the first time, the extra time spent to perform the check adds value to the job.
   d. Yes. To continue with the logic in (c), inspection of the work is a part of doing the job right the first time. And, if properly designed, the inspection check and test procedure will be quick.
   e. No change. The consequences of careful inspection just become more obvious.

12. (Sandwiches-Are-We) The idea of using benchmarking is a good one, but a better starting point (arguably the first part of the benchmarking procedure) is a thorough study of the process by which sandwiches are made and delivered. Such a study often reveals possibilities for quick and cheap improvements.

14. (Malcolm Baldrige National Quality Award winners) You will find considerable variation in post-Baldrige award performances—from increasing financial success to bankruptcy, for instance. Overall, however, winners have enjoyed higher levels of success across a wide range of organizational performance indicators.

16. (Tuition increase study group)
   a. This group is probably not a team as defined in your text. With sustained effort, as well as growing membership and power, however, it could evolve into one.

b. Customers, providers, and those empowered to enact changes ought to be represented.

18. (Bank tellers) It is a poorly designed circle since all participants are from the same work area and, in this case, all have the same job title.

Chapter 4

2. (*Business Week* annual R&D scoreboard) *Business Week* no longer prints the annual scoreboard in its June or July issues, but it is available through its home page on the America Online (AOL) Internet service. [http://www.aol.com]

4. (Chess clock—design improvements) Suggestions might include reduction in the number of screws (Guideline 7) and replace the special fasteners with standard ones (Guideline 9).

6. (Electrical outlet and switch plates—design improvements) Design for snap-in installation: Mold the plates with a lip at each end and design the inner box with receiving lips. Benefits include elimination of millions of screw-downs each year by highly paid construction and paint crews. Possible disadvantage: Unless the snap is tight, unwatched children might be able to unsnap and get shocked. (Older, metal electrical boxes that had to be screwed to wall studs have already been replaced with plastic boxes that carpenters quickly nail to studs.)

8. (Monitor Manufacturing Company—improved design) Follow the design guidelines, notably number 6 (modular designs).

10. (UPS—design changes) In addition to vehicle redesigns needed to accommodate the natural-gas fuel systems, other factors that might require new designs include maintenance training, fuel purchase and delivery systems, and possibly even route layouts.

12. (TRI-CON—specifications) Minimal specifications promote producibility; the practice also encourages customers' designers to work closely with supplier.

14. (Modular car assembly—design guidelines) Relevant guidelines: 2, minimize parts: 6, use modules: 7, ease of assembly; 8, one-way assembly; 9, avoid special fasteners.

16. (Reducing number of operations) Example: Many service establishments (video rentals, automobile quick-lube outlets, etc.) use terminals/cash registers where customer's phone number or vehicle license number pulls up complete customer identification data, account status, last service date, and other information. There's no need for clerk to re-enter on each visit.

18. (Security system timer—reliability) For example, at 200 hours, the reliability of the timer is about 0.9. Depending on what is being secured, of course, that figure may be all the risk that the user is willing to bear.

20. (Fuel system control valve—reliability)
    a. At two weeks, $R = 0.98$
    b. Reliability can be enhanced through redundancy—have a parallel backup control valve.

22. (Furnace thermostat—reliability and availability)
    a. $R = 0.72$; $R = 0.51$; $R = 0.37$
    b. $A = 0.99992$ if we assume that there are 720 hours per month.
    c. Probably not. The two-hour repair time might cause slight personal discomfort for a few minutes and cause personnel to grab a sweater, but unless there are special circumstances that the problem omits, the mean repair time is not extreme.

24. (Coolant line sensor—system reliability)
    a. $R = 0.9936$
    b. $R = 0.9995$

Chapter 5

2. (Jostens Diplomas or Ampex—improvements)

Jostens: Responsibility for quality was transferred to front-line associates (including the recently relocated former inspectors). Requisite tools (e.g., computers) and necessary information were placed under front-line control, and cross-training programs were implemented. In short, OM Principles 2, 7, and 14 were followed.

Ampex: Direct effort went into cutting cycle time and reducing flow distance (OM Principles 11 and 13). Scrap was cut (Principle 10), as were setup times (Principle 12). Ampex invested in employee training (Principle 7) and front-line associates assumed responsibility for purchasing (Principle 14). As with Jostens, Ampex improvements stem from following OM principles.

4. (Office furniture manufacturer—improvements)

Major changes that ought to be made:

- Review and revise furniture designs using criteria explained in Chapter 4. Quality begins with product design.

- Focus on process design as well; specific efforts should follow Exhibit 5–1. Emphasis should be on building quality in rather than on after-the-fact inspection.
- Since producers will assume first responsibility for quality, they should receive training in SPC and other tools of process improvement.
- Establish partnership relationships with a few good suppliers, visit their plants and certify their processes, and ask for their inputs; cease reliance on receiving inspections.
- Cross-train employees so they can help one another if problems arise; lean more toward group-based incentives; ensure that process improvement time is provided; make sure that the focus shifts from output to good output all along the production chain.

6. (Travel authorization flowchart) Response should replace initial portion of Exhibit 5–10B with a manual-based travel request and response loop.

8. (AmPen—fishbone chart and Pareto diagram)
    a. Fishbone chart categorizes causes of error, alerts people to cause–effect relationships.
    b. Pareto chart shows relative importance of problems or defects; here, the impurity problem dramatically overshadows the others, and it should be the first problem attacked.

10. (Mathematics SAT scores—fishbone chart)
    a. The fishbone chart skeleton contains five major categories of process variables that could cause low SAT scores; four remain for you to complete. You might, for example, begin with METHODS and consider how methods problems might be caused, in turn, by problems in the schedule and in the curriculum. Work backward toward root causes for each schedule and curriculum problem. Repeat for each major category.
    b. Brainstorm to discover which secondary "bones" are most likely causes. Further data collection might be taken to reveal the scope of problems (e.g., Just how many computers does the school have? What software is needed?). Other schools might be benchmarked. Experiments on instructional methods might be in order.

12. (Fail-safing approach to common problems)
    a. Forgetting to set alarm: Use bedtime checklist.
    b. Missing appointments: Get watch or computer notepad with appointment beeper.

    c. Running out of gas: Fill by odometer reading, say every 350 miles.
    d. No tollway booth change: Quit smoking and carry change in auto ashtray; dump pocket change there each evening.
    e. Losing one of a pair: Never separate the pair (of socks, earrings, gloves, etc.).

14. (Oil Can Store—run diagram and histogram)
    a. First, plot the run diagram. The plot is simple and helps with the next two actions. Next, before we use this (or any other) process data as a basis for analysis or improvement, we need to question the data and discover what it tells us. Can we assume that these 25 times constitute a fair and accurate representation of the time required to perform the oil change and lube job? If so, what do the data say? Here, the run diagram shows a slight upward drift (end-of-day fatigue).
    b. Next, create trial spec limits. Specs must represent what the process is capable of providing and what the customer will tolerate. In this situation, you have some options. For example:

       (1) Since 12 minutes is about the middle of the data set, you might somewhat arbitrarily decide to set trial spec limits at 7 and 17 minutes (that is, 12 ± 5 minutes). Obviously, you would want to investigate what factors led to the four "outliers" (6, 18, 18, and 19 minutes).

       (2) You might have reason to believe that the smaller "hump" in the histogram reflects rushed jobs, and decide to focus on just the larger "hump." You might set 15 minutes as the target time, but allow 3 minutes more or less as a reasonable variation, Thus, your spec would be 15 ± 3 minutes.

    c. The histogram reveals more about the process. There are two "bumps," the larger centered at 15 minutes and the smaller centered at 9 minutes. Is there an explanation for this? Perhaps compact cars require about a third less time? Or maybe a certain mechanic is noticeably faster than the others?
    d. The run diagram and histogram might be used to assist with employee training. Explain that any service job that exceeds the "spec limits" should be the subject for discussion as to cause. Avoid the word blame; the idea is to learn why some jobs go much faster or slower than the

norm. Remember, some of the jobs will fall outside the newly established spec limits, so there will be opportunity to study process variations.

16. (Choice of process-control charting method)

Beer: mean and range, since we take an actual measurement of alcohol content (variable data). Billiard balls: mean and range, since we measure actual breakage force.
Motor vibration: Run diagram, plot vibration after each adjustment.
Electronic component: Run diagram for piece-by-piece measure of electrical property, shift to proportion-defective chart during early production.
Fans: Proportion-defective chart; take samples from production batches and plot proportion of each sample that does not operate, or perhaps number-of-defects chart if each fan is inspected as to number of defects.
Lenses: Proportion-defective chart, take samples and plot proportion defective.
Table surface: Number-of-defectives chart, plot number of defects (scratches, blemishes, and other marks) on each.

18. (Spark-O-Plenty—mean and range charts)
    a. X-bar chart: $\bar{X} \approx 0.500$; UCL = 0.511; LCL = 0.489
       Range chart: $\bar{R}$ = 0.023; UCL = 0.046; LCL = 0
    b. The process is out of control. Find and eliminate assignable cause(s) and start over.

20. (OK-Mart & Electro Corp.—process control chart)
    a. Center line on the proportion-defective chart should be drawn at 0.2 percent ($\bar{p}$ = 0.002).
    b. Process improvements are needed; find and correct cause of defects, then sample again for a new chart.

22. (Rescue Services Training—number-of-defects chart)
    a. $\bar{c}$ = 4.2 UCL_c = 10.35 LCL_c = 0
    b. The process is not in control.
    c. Example recommendation: As one of its initial steps, the training group should develop a check sheet (similar to the one shown in Solved Problem 3) that classifies errors. Recording during SERE training would then not only count mistakes but also reveal the most frequently occurring ones.

24. (Food processing company—process capability)
    a. Total tolerance band is 0.16 oz.; supplier's inherent capability (0.20 oz.) is not good enough, so don't buy.
    b. No change. The supplier's problem is excess variation in process output; a change in location and process control can't change that fact.
    c. Advise both to work together to determine and remove cause of excess variability.

26. (Plug-N-Go—process capability)
    a. C_{pk} = 0.833
    b. About 0.62 percent of the valve covers are out of spec.
    c. Two actions: First, always strive to reduce variation in process output; second, shift process downward toward target specification of 0.50 cm.

28. (Variation stackup—services provider)
    Example: Classes meet on the hour and last for 50 minutes; marketing professors hold classes over into the 10-minute break and accounting professors start classes early.
    Example: An airline ticket agent books a traveler for a flight that will allow 30 minutes—according to the airline's schedule—to make a connecting flight at the next airport, but the first flight runs between 20 and 40 minutes late most of the time.

Chapter 6

2. (Forecasting in organizational types) Examples: type 1, highway construction; type 2, air-conditioning contractor; type 3, tractor manufacturer; type 4, small appliance manufacturer.

4. (County Hospital) Group totals: actual, 2,729; forecast, 2,580; error, + 149, or 5.8 percent. Item error, 25.6 percent.

6. (Metro Auto Sales) Examples: Rolling forecast mode and group forecasting mode.

8. (Television/radio station—forecasting) All managers should forecast. The manager needs to know market area demand for program types (e.g., sports, music, news, local versus network specials, etc.). Also, forecasts of economic sector strength could help attract advertisers.

10. (Lawngirl Manufacturing Company—demand for service parts)
  a. The greater the time span, the greater the smoothing effects.
  b. One-week MA forecast = 800
  Three-week MA forecast = 793
  Nine-week MA forecast = 776
  c. Longer time spans are better for stable products with widely dispersed markets—the case for lawnmower replacement (service) parts.

12. (Forecasting —seasonality)
  a. $130 \div 133 = 0.98$
  b. $168 \times 0.98 = 165$
  c. The forecast should be 154, the latest calculated MA value.

14. (Citrus Life and Casualty Company— exponential smoothing) Forecast for next week is 11.2 boxes.

16. (Huckleberry Farms, Inc.—forecasting)
  a. Six-month MA forecast is 501.5 cases; it is applicable to the next future period.
  b. The nine-month MA forecast is best; its MAD value, 30.7 cases, is lowest.
  c. Exponential smoothing forecast is 509.1 cases and is applicable to January next year.
  d. Best smoothing coefficient: $\alpha = 0.5$ with an MAD of 36.4 cases.
  e. Three-quarter MA forecast = 1,546 cases, applicable to first quarter. (Jan.-Feb.-Mar.) next year. Three-quarter MA forecast = 5,952 cases, applicable to next year. Quarterly exponential smoothing forecast = 1,574 cases, applicable to next quarter. Annual exponential smoothing forecast = 6,079 cases, applicable to next year.
  f. Computer-calculated straight trend line: $Y = 473.3 + 0.924 (t)$; your eyeball forecast will appear nearly flat.
  g. Seasonality is expected; data plots reveal peaks in winter months (except February) with dips in summer (except for June).
  h. Example seasonal indexes:
     January   1.10
     February 0.98
     March   1.08
  i. (Unadjusted trend) × (Seasonal index) = Seasonally adjusted forecast.
  Example: for January, $507 \times 1.10 = 558$ cases

17. (Custom Draperies—MAD and tracking signal)
  a. MAD = $24 \div 4 = 6$ orders
  b. Tracking signal = $-24 \div 6 = -4$. The forecasting model is tending toward bias; α should be adjusted.

19. (North American Hotels, Inc.—correlation)
  a. There is fair negative correlation with no lead.
  b. There is a good positive correlation with no lead.

21. (Anderson Theaters—correlation)
  a. $r = 0.539$
  b. A correlation of 0.539 is quite good. But a correlation without a lead is useful only to the extent that the correlate variable may be predicted better or easier than the demand. Here, the theater chain can obtain the college calendar and develop fairly accurate student population figures.

Chapter 7

2. (HP) Retraining and reassignment are major tools. That is easier when very talented people are hired in the first place. Aggressive development of new products and services ensures that there will be a place to go when older lines fade away.

6. (Bright Way) With a chase-demand strategy, Bright Way becomes more like a typical janitorial service. It would rely more on a transient workforce for adjustable capacity, so there would be less need to plan capacity far ahead. New management problems would be in the labor area; hiring/firing, scheduling, and supervisor concerns.

8. (Windward Sportswear)
  a. Response may vary, depending on logic. Examples:
    • No. Demand surges above 130 per week in two of the five weeks, suggesting that customers won't be adequately served.
    • Yes. By assuming that overtime is used or additional capacity is available (say, from the director and other cross-trained associates), customers can be served.
  b. Example response: Windward purchasers could staff at 130 per week and, with cross-training and flexible cell assignments, have a ready reserve of additional purchasing talent for weeks with heavy demand. In slower weeks, people have TQ meetings, train, and so forth.

c. Example: Streamline with flow lines focused on various types of POs.

10. (Computer software)
  - Recent standard: 1,400 packages/30 labor hours = 46.67 packages per hour.
  - With new demand: 1,200 packages/46.67 packages per hour = 25.7 labor hours needed at full capacity.
  - So at 90-percent undercapacity scheduling, assign 25.7 ÷ 0.9 = 28.6 labor hours per day.

12. (Concrete Products, Inc.)
  a. Have six operators and use shortened workweeks as needed. If contracts prevent that, use part-time personnel.
  b. Have five operators and use overtime (or subcontracting if reliable concrete specialists can be found) as required.

14. (Gulf Tube and Pipe Company: production and capacity plans)
  a. Chase demand (in millions of lineal feet):

Week	1	2	3	4
Production plan	5.5	5.3	4.9	4.1

  b. Level-capacity:

Week	1	2	3	4
Production plan	4.9	4.9	4.9	4.9

  c. Capacity plans (number of operators):

Week	1	2	3	4
Chase-demand	11.0	10.6	9.8	8.2
Level-capacity	9.8	9.8	9.8	9.8

  d. Inventories absorb demand swings under level-capacity strategy and thus vary more.

19. (Piney Woods Furniture Company) Order calls for 1,000 cabinets, or 1,000/50 = 20 minimum order equivalents, due in week 6:
  a. Cabinet order loads for load-profile weeks − 4, − 3, and − 2 translate into MPS requirements (in cubic yards) as follows: 800 for week 2, 200 for week 3, and 400 for week 4. Added to other load yields, total kiln load is shown in the table below.

Chapter 8

2. (Iota Company) Increase the risk. Raise the reorder point.

4. (Hewlett-Packard)
  a. The computer transactions added no value to goods and services destined for customers. Excess documentation, like the work orders here, is a hidden cost associated with having inventories.
  b. Student exercise.

6. (Ivy Memorial Hospital) Example items: Involve suppliers early; inform them of the QR effort and explain the demand elements that will be "pulling the string" for hospital services and thus supplier goods and services. Next, try to separate those demands into independent and dependent items; they'll help determine how much lead time the hospital will be able to give suppliers. And, of course, all parties along the supply channels need to streamline processes.

8. (QR examples)
  a. The Luxottica eyeware and apparel examples deal with consumer goods, but the chapter-opening example extends QR concepts into the durable goods sector.
  b. Probably so for billing and funds transfer. And eventually, EDI may prove superior to the fax-based linkups.
  c. Fax first since the equipment is cheaper and widely available to all members (even the smallest of businesses) in the supply chain. Later, EDI can be implemented as the supplier–customer partnerships strengthen. EDI proves superior for sharing MPS data for large end items.

10. (MRP, for an industrial thermostat producer) Cycle time is still very bad. The company has not attacked and reduced non-value-adding delays.

11. (Complex, delay-prone inter-sector material flows—improvements)
  a. Eliminate most distributors; ship direct from the few remaining distribution centers to

b. Week 4 shows a 200 cubic yard-hour overload.
c. Move the delivery date to week 5.

For Exercise 7–19a

Week	1	2	3	4	5	6
Load (cubic yard-hours)	5,000	6,000	5,500	6,200	5,700	6,000

stores, and ship directly from the factory to nearby stores.

    b. Test the markets by opening new West-Coast and European distribution centers; if the markets are indeed good, open new manufacturing plants there and avoid the high costs of moving heavy furniture long distances.

    c. Adopt quick response based on bar-code scanning in retail stores. Resulting data drives dress-making schedules in local plants.

12. (Bottlenecks at paint facility)
    a. TOC recommends longer production runs, for example, several weeks' worth on the press and paint lines. Also, as with basic JIT, TOC calls for smaller transfer batch sizes.
    b. JIT advises cutting setup times (quick paint color and press die changes) to justify small process lots; high machine maintenance at frequent intervals to eliminate breakdowns; and quality control to avoid lost machine time and rework.

13. (Queues at a campus testing service) Examples: Split large batch (say, from a large class) of papers into smaller transfer batches (between order entry and scanner). Work during lull times to reduce setups, and perform preventive maintenance so that breakdowns are minimized.

14. (Inventory turnover, Elmo's Burger Shoppe)

Annual sales:	$50,000 per month x 12 months = $600,000
Annual CGS:	CGS + (0.10 x CGS) = $600,000; so CGS = $545,454 per year
Inventory turnover:	T = $545,454 ÷ $12,000 = 45.5 turns per year

    No, Elmo's should not calculate partial turns, because it has no WIP and no finished goods.

15. (ABC Specialities, Inc.)
    $T_{RM} = 6$; $T_{WIP} = 7$; $T_{FG} = 0.33$; $T_{TOT} = 3.33$

16. (Variabilities and Taguchi's social loss concept) Both messages: "On-target" performance is the goal. Deviations detract from customer service and loss to *some* segment of society.

Chapter 9

2. (Buyer–Supplier Relationships) Example responses:
    a. Aerospace company.
        Quality. Extremely high component reliability/quality is needed in view of the high costs of failure and the high risks present in complex systems comprising many components; quality at the source is a must.
        Design. The buying company cannot be expert in all advanced technologies, thus must (and does) rely heavily on suppliers' designers.
        Order conveyance. High volume of engineering changes makes electronic data interchange (EDI) attractive.

    d. Major accounting firm.
        Type of agreement, number of sources, and delivery frequency/order size. Exclusive, single supplier for each family of purchased services (e.g., health care, pension/profit-sharing, investment counseling, office equipment repair, and perhaps data processing) and each major category of supplies increases business volume per supplier, making more-frequent contact economical.

4. (CalComp, Inc.) A design goal is fewer parts (see Chapter 3), but the other two items directly support principles of supplier–customer partnerships. All would serve to improve quality and delivery of incoming materials and thus help cut the plant's operating costs.

6. (Home Remodeling)
    a. Breakeven = 40 patios.

8. (Travel department) Breakeven is 2,353 tickets/year. Travel department should buy rather than make.

10. (ABC uses) Example: Make or buy analysis/decisions: A items, done by executive committee; B items, done by product or materials manager; C items, done by inventory planner.

12. (ABC classes)

Item Number	Dollar Usage Last Year	Class
030	$30,000	A
109	6,000	B
All others		C

14. (THIS Company) As conditions stand, loss of THIS Company's business could well be the death of the uniform supplier. One critical issue facing Adam, however, is time: THIS must be responsive to its customers; does Adam have enough time to bring the current uniform supplier up to quick-response partnership status?

16. (Organizational purchasing) Examples:
    b. The city is heavily involved in buying intangibles; examples include consultants' services and software.

c. Approved supplier lists: all except liquor wholesaler. Bid solicitation: city government and larger manufacturers (for selected items). Blanket orders: high-volume standard items going into fashions, home appliances, electric power, glass, plastics, computers, ships, aerospace.

18. (VA in JIT companies) JIT requires on-the-spot problem solving, including any design changes. For value analysis to be done on the fly, specifications should be held to a minimum, or focus just on performance specs.

20. (Jane Doe, standardization) Bad. Shows a lack of standardization.

Chapter 10

2. (Sentrol Inc., telephone answering) Strategy is practical. Call arrival distributions suggest times to staff the telephone system with extra personnel, cross-trained in customer service, of course.

4. (X-ray machines)
   a. Push: Components are pushed onto final assembly.
   b. Convert to pull system, perhaps using kanban squares.

6. (Partial MRP data for FOQ) The fixed-order quantity is 160. Scheduled receipts are due in weeks 1 and 5, and a planned order release is scheduled for week 2.

10. (Tape dispenser)
    b. Planned order release schedule: Roll of tape, 5,000 in week 3 and 5,000 in week 6; Spool, 2,000 in week 1 and 5,000 in week 4.
    c. Planned receipts for rolls of tape are due in weeks 4 and 7, and for spools in weeks 3 and 6. Planned receipts do not become scheduled receipts, however, until orders are placed.

14. (Kitchen knives)
    a. Order 2,400 rivets in week 2.
    b. Order 2,400 blocks in week 3.
    c. Order 130 wood bars in week 3.

16. (Hospital safety stock factors) Example: for X-ray film, safety stock factors are high cost and obsolescence, so keep safety stock low. (But need rapid replenishment from medical supply company or other medical facilities in case of urgent high demand.)

18. (Brown Instrument Co. *ROP*)
    a. $ROP = 81.4$
    b. Both *DLT* and *SS* would increase.

20. (Service level and safety stock)
    a. $SS = 51$
    b. All three factors should lower the safety stock.

22. (Fuel oil *ROP*)
    a. About 3.75 orders per winter.
    b. $DLT = 3,000$ gallons; $SS = 3,400$ gallons.

Chapter 11

2. (Quick Setup at KFC and at General Mills) Example responses:
   - At the KFC restaurants, materials were positioned closer to window (Guideline 3) and packer box sizes were standardized (Guideline 7).
   - Addition of handles to avoid having to find, grasp, and position a tool when an adjustment must be made (Guideline 6) and doing as much as possible before the setup (pit stop) is needed—away from the ongoing action (Guideline 2).

4. (Die handling)
   a. Guidelines 3, 4, 5, and 6 are clear, others possible.
   b. Guidelines 7 and 8; more standardization and simplification.

6. (Lot-for-lot versus batch) Yes, the comparison also makes sense for processing when clients are people.

8. (Provincial government)
   a. $EOQ = 600$ boxes
   b. The *EOQ* is a zone that takes in the extra 10 percent. But OM Principle 13 calls for seeking ways to justify smaller lots.

10. (Maple Tree Insurance)
    At $3.00, $EOQ = 258$ boxes (not feasible)
    At $2.60, $EOQ = 277$ boxes (feasible)

12. (Cannery) At $0.60, $EPQ = 3,266$ (feasible; total annual costs = $24,490); at $0.50, $EPQ = 3,577$ (not feasible). Total annual costs at order quantity of 4,000 are $20,450. The correct order quantity (4,000) will last about 1.2 months and is $2,000 worth.

15. (Ordinaire, Inc.—*EOQ* savings) Smaller order quantities will cause a decrease in stockroom costs within a few months. Processing the increased number of orders could create countervailing costs (e.g., for stockouts, and higher prices if volume discounts are lost). However, closer monitoring and supplier partnerships could, over time, eliminate these cost increases.

The direct material stockroom might not have space for the larger lots, leading to poor storage practices, higher handling costs, and various losses. Also, the larger lots will tie up more capital.

17. (Federal Time Corporation)
    a. $EOQ = 6,532$ lenses.
    b. Single-digit setup: Equip molding machines with tables to hold molds at usage height; use rollers or air cushions to make it easier to slide molds into position.

18. (Semiconductors in small lots) By always running in small lots; cut setup times to make that easier.

Chapter 12

2. (Operations management development) in repetitive operations, long runs of very nearly identical operations mean that OM development costs may be amortized over a large number of output units; thus, unit cost is smaller.

4. (Operations environments) Example: Construction crew foreman for builder of large, one-of-a-kind bridges. Project environment: industry is oligopolistic (few firms can handle such jobs) and each job is bid; volume is very low and each bridge is unique (high variety). Tools and equipment are flexible and include land-based and barge-mounted piling drivers, cranes, and other heavy construction equipment. Tools for steel and concrete placement and working are also required. Layout is fixed position; the bridge stays put while people, materials, and equipment move around it.

6. (College layout) Although your school may certainly differ, many use the traditional functional layout: Within the university, each college is grouped together in one or a few buildings, and within each college, the department faculty are grouped together. Common business college groupings include Departments of Accounting, Economics, Finance, Management, Marketing, and so forth.
    Traditional advantages included sharing of resources such as typists and office equipment. Today, with the trend toward self-contained work sites (often away from the office) some of these advantages have disappeared. Disadvantages include the same problems with any functional organization—cross-fertilization of ideas can be stymied.

7. (State University—musical presentation layout)
    a. Layout at each site is fixed position, but repetition of activities exists.
    b. Increased variety (from one show to four) makes each presentation more like a project.
    c. Streamlining might include quick setups and set changeovers.

8. (Bailey & Benson—streamlining in a CPA firm) Creative movement downward along the diagonal from custom to commodity and from intermittent to continuous operations mode—made possible by well-planned streamlining efforts—does not necessitate a severance of close customer connections.

10. (Layout types—examples)
    • Auto assembly: product.
    • Shipbuilding: fixed position.
    • Shoe repair: process.
    • Hospital: mixed.

17. (Principles of OM—related to layout and re-layout) Principles 6, 9, and 11 are closely related to layout and re-layout issues.

Chapter 13

2. (Continuous versus repetitive processing) Examples:
    a. Soft drinks: Syrup processing (flavoring, sweetening, coloring, etc.) is continuous; bottling or canning is repetitive.
    b. Nursing care: Electronic monitoring of patient's heartbeat is continuous; hourly charting of temperature is repetitive.

4. (Detergent manufacturing)
    • Process design and capital investment; much automation and extensive process engineering.
    • Reliability of supply; firm, long-term contracts with suppliers and dependable transportation (e.g., an owned, or controlled pipeline).

6. (Synchronized mixed-model schedule) Not quite. Building A should strive for mixed-model schedules.

8. (Faiko Time Co.) Faiko should regularize mechanism assembly to about seven per day (for example, four of type A, two of B. and one of C); check demand every two weeks and adjust schedule as required. Enclosures are less amenable to regularizing. Still, perhaps there is dominant demand for one type and it should get regularized production.

10. (Product wheel—production examples) Example responses:

- Process industry products such as chemicals that have relatively low, intermittent demand individually but are collectively enough to keep facility busy.
- Families of parts with near-identical processing steps but with variations in color or shape, such as a family of different types of plastic containers.

12. (Line balancing analysis)
   a. Sum of the task times: $\sum t = 100 \times 0.01 = 1.00$ minutes.

   To produce 500 units in a 430-minute day, the required cycle time is

   Cycle time = 430 minutes ÷ 500 units = 0.86 minutes per unit

   Minimum required stations = Total work content time ÷ Cycle time

   Thus, Minimum stations = 1.00 minutes ÷ 0.86 minutes = 1.16, but since we must have an integral number of stations, we round up to 2.
   b. One balance (not necessarily the best) uses two stations with a cycle time of 0.55 minutes. Task assignments, with longest operation time as the criterion for assignment, in order of assignment are
   Station 1: A, F, E, C, D, I, B for a total work content time of 0.55 minutes (zero delay).
   Station 2: K, G, H, J, L for a total work content time of 0.45 minutes (0.10 minutes delay).

   Balance delay

   $$d = \frac{nc - \sum t}{nc} = \frac{(2)(55) - 100}{(2)(55)} = 0.091;$$

   that is, 9.1 percent

   In this balance, all delay occurs at the second station. We could move task B to Station 2, thus making work content time equal 0.52 minutes at Station 1 and 0.48 minutes at Station 2. Cycle time could then be lowered to 0.52 minutes, and balance delay would be reduced to

   $$d = \frac{0.04}{1.04} = 0.0385; \text{ about 3.9 percent}$$

13. (Worker's compensation claim processing—line balancing)

   Available time = 440 minutes/day × 5 days/week = 2,200 minutes per week.

   If 50 claims must be processed, the maximum cycle time must be 2,200 ÷ 50 = 44 minutes.

Since total work content time $(\sum t) = 234$ minutes, the minimum number of stations is

234 ÷ 44 = 5.32, which rounds up to 6

Since minimum cycle time is 40 minutes (unless task L can be split), we have a very narrow range of desirable cycle times as the job exists now. An initial balance using six stations and 45 minutes' cycle time yields a balance delay of 13.3 percent and provides the following task assignments:

Station	Tasks	Delay
1	C, B, A	0
2	H	10
3	D, I	4
4	F, G, E, K	2
5	J	15
6	L	5

Although the cycle time is slightly larger than it needs to be, perhaps a portion of task A can be left over for personnel at Station 2, thus effectively speeding up the process a bit. Actually, a close balance such as this is often the best attainable until process redesign occurs.

15. (Zeus, Inc., mixed models) Full cycle (10 minutes) production ratio L:M:S equals 1:2:4.
   a. Ten-minute cycle SMSMSLS challenges supplier to match it, possibly with simpler dedicated equipment.
   b. Supplier should slow down as Zeus slows down, and use excess labor for training and improvement projects.
   c. Zeus's schedule is too full. A policy of undercapacity scheduling is needed so targets can be met almost every day; for example, try L:M:S = 44:88:172 units per day.

17. (Heat treating mixed models) Mixed-model sequence is AAAB; five hours will be required.

19. (Computer table mixed model) Model ratio D:E:F:G equals 1:3:2:4. The most repetitive mixed-model sequence is GEFGEFGEDG, six times/day.

21. (Repetitive scheduling in bank) Yes, check and deposit processing are examples.

Chapter 14

2. (Advertising agency) Three examples: Create flow lines or cells dedicated to handling major categories of job types. Adopt queue limitation

and flow-control simplification, and, on a grander scale, consider focusing the business on a few types of jobs to reduce variety.

4. (Gantt charts) Student exercises.

6. (Gantt chart project task)
   a. Date is day 11. The task is 83 percent complete and is two days ahead of schedule.
   b. Chart should show three days ahead of schedule.
   c. Saturdays, Sundays, and holidays are skipped.

8. (Work-center load imbalance)
   a. If the work center is a gateway, leveling techniques can be used, perhaps firm planned orders. In extreme cases, the master scheduler can be asked to adjust the MPS.
   b. Computer processes open order file, accumulating loads by time bucket for each work center. Next, the same thing is done for the planned orders via CRP software. The combination produces the load report.

10. (Jerrybuilt Machines, Inc.) The order list is
    916 slack = − 1
    889 slack = + 1
    901 slack = + 4

12. (Job release sequence—prioritizing rules)
    a. FCFS: A, B, C, D, E
    b. SPT: E, C, A, D, B
    c. EDD: E, A, D, C, B
    d. LS: E, A or D, B, C

14. (Blanking center—job priority list) The order list is
    444 slack = − 1
    222 slack = + 1
    333 slack = + 2

15. (Applications) Example response: Getting a driver's license:
    • Scheduling: Walk-in, first come, first served, or by-appointment system
    • Dispatching: Queue control at each station, first come, first served.
    • Expediting: Probably limited need. However, if tests had been passed but applicant needed to leave for some reason (e.g., forgot checkbook), then applicant could move directly to the fourth station upon return.

17. (City Planning Department—computerized order tracking) The assistant administrator has a point; tracking orders might tell where in the system they are, but it does nothing to speed up their processing. Computerized record maintenance can be quite valuable, for it permits information sharing and rapid movement of need-to-know details. But, if the sole purpose is to track orders, the money will be better spent if used for additional resources at bottleneck spots.

Chapter 15

4. (Dummy activity) Dummy activity 16–13 assures that both 12–16 and 10–13 precede 13–18 but that only 12–16 precedes 16–18.

7. (Antenna system)
   b. Critical path: 1–3–7 = 9 days.
   c.

Activity	Slack
1–3	0
3–7	0
All others	1

   d. Critical path: 1–2–4–6–7 = 11.

9. (Network crashing)
   b. 1–2–3–4–5, 15 days; $1,240.
   c. May be crashed to 11 days at a project cost of $1,730.

11. (Path analysis)
    a. 1–2–5–3–4, 17 days. 1–2–3–4, 16 days.
    b. Two days.

13. (Slack calculations)
    a. + 7.
    b. − 1.

15. (Time–cost trade-off analysis)
    a. To reduce by one day, $185 (hint: requires shortening two activities).
    b. Days = 13

17. (Dummy activity) Dummy needed from 3 to 12,

19. (Critical path and network simulation) Critical path time is 2 weeks; PERT simulation time is 2 4/9 weeks.

Chapter 16

2. (Visual Performance Charts)
   a. Queue length.
   b. Check sheet.
   c. Check sheet.
   d. Color-change time.

4. (Comparable Work and Fair Pay) Comparable work requires that work content be measured, so the pay-according-to-job-content concept applies—item 3 in Exhibit 16–2.

5. (Florida Power and Light) Operations-oriented measures appear on charts easily seen by all.

Controls are suggested by the processes; associates monitor performance and act on results.

7. (International Express Company) Neither should have it. Promote front-line responsibility.

10. (Social service agency)
    a. 22 employees (rounded).
    b. Historical.

12. (Auto plant time standards) $3.6 \times 1.14 \times 1.05 = 4.31$ minute/wheel.

14. (Lugging machine standard time)
    a. S.T. = 0.314 minute/piece.
    b. MTM data are already normalized, so pace rating is unnecessary.

16. (Typing work sampling) Assuming a 480-minute workday:
    a. Typing: ET = 32.00 minutes; RT = 28.80 minutes; ST = 32.26 minutes. Retrieving: ET = 4.80 minutes; RT = 3.84 minutes; ST = 4.30 minutes
    b. Uses include staffing, scheduling, and evaluating equipment and methods.
    c. Yes, they are engineered. If biases (such as easy versus hard job assignments) are controlled, the standards could be used for personnel evaluation.

18. (Wabash Airways)
    a. Efficiency = 133 percent.
    b. 12 attendants.

20. (Setting time standards) Examples:
    • Soldering connections: time-study or predetermined standards.
    • Computer programmers: historical standards.

Chapter 17

2. (Motor carriers) JIT operations have caused more carriers to offer as-requested delivery times and other services. This willingness to serve customers' needs may slow the movement to locate supplier plants adjacent to customers.

4. (EDS hiring and location) If employers perceive equal talent is available around the globe, then the labor skill-factor ceases to be as important in location decisions.

6. (Copy machines) Operators do a considerable amount of maintenance and minor repair work; cleaning glass and rollers, adding toner and other fluids, and clearing paper jams. Major repairs and PM (usually predictive) are performed by service technicians, especially for large models.

8. (Spider diagram—problem solving) Though this is meant to be an individualistic response, your plan should include the aim of having the diagram shrink each week or whenever you and your associates get together to review progress. Initial problem levels are reflected by points far from the center, and the "perfect web" happens when all dots are at the center.

10. (Wexco, Inc.—operator ownership) Loss of staff size need not equate to loss of prestige. Black and his personnel may find their knowledge in greater demand, thus increasing their prestige in the company.

12. (Captain Henry Harrison) The captain's approach is sound. A clean workplace reduces search time, prevents accidents, improves machine operation, and improves morale of personnel.

14. (Principles of OM—Handling and transportation issues) Principle 11 is especially relevant. Principles 6 and 9 also relate in more indirect ways.

15. (Supplier concern about customers' facilities) Probably so. The customers' competitiveness depends on facilities.

Chapter 18

2. (Global medical opinions) Yes, and to some extent this is being done now. Language and communication network barriers are crumbling, making the task easier. TQM still has value; the provider–customer relationship still exists.

4. (University cafeteria) (Hint: Draw from the principles of operations management.) Consider, for example, Principles 6 and 9: Can you set up flow lines or cells dedicated to a family of meal types? Can you equip them?

Part I

[1]Stephen Kreider Yoder, "How H-P Used Tactics of the Japanese to Beat Them at Their Game," *The Wall Street Journal,* September 8, 1994, p. A1.

Chapter 1

[1]Chetan S. Sankar, William R. Boulton, Nancy W. Davidson, and Charles A. Snyder, "Building a World-Class Alliance: The Universal Card—TSYS Case," *Academy of Management Executive* 9, no. 2 (1995), pp. 20–29.

[2]Claude S. George, Jr., *The History of Management Thought* (Englewood Cliffs, N.J.: Prentice-Hall, 1968), pp. 86–99.

[3]Peter F. Drucker, *Post-Capitalist Society* (New York: HarperCollins, 1993), pp. 36–39.

[4]George, op. cit., pp. 129–30.

[5]One of the more thorough and coherent compendia of O.R.'s history and scope is a rather obscure source: Norman Gaither, "The Origins & Historical Development of Operations Research-Management Science," Working Paper No. 42 (Norman, Okla.: University of Oklahoma, Bureau for Business & Economic Research, August 1973).

[6]Barbara B. Flynn, Sadao Sakakibara, and Roger G. Schroeder, "Relationship between JIT and TQM: Practices and Performance," *Academy of Management Journal* 38, no. 5 (1995), pp. 1325–60.

[7]Gabriel A. Pall, *Quality Process Management* (Englewood Cliffs, N.J.: Prentice-Hall, 1987), pp. 18–19.

[8]Tom Brown, "Decoding the 'Clueless' Manager," an interview with Scott Adams, *Industry Week,* July 3, 1995, pp. 14–18.

[9]*Statistical Abstract of the United States,* U.S. Department of Commerce, Bureau of the Census, September, 1995, no. 670. "Productivity and Related Measures: 1970 to 1994," p. 430.

[10]Jon Brecka, "The American Customer Satisfaction Index," *Quality Progress,* October 1994, pp. 41–44.

[11]Ronald E. Yates, "New Way to Gauge Economy," *Chicago Tribune,* September 18, 1994, p. 1ff.

[12]Robert W. Hall, *Attaining Manufacturing Excellence: Just In Time, Total Quality, Total People Involvement* (Burr Ridge, Ill.: Dow Jones-Irwin, 1987), p. 24.

[13]M. Scott Myers, *Every Employee a Manager,* 3rd ed. (San Diego: University Associates, 1991).

Chapter 2

[1]Alex Taylor, "GM's $11,000,000,000 Turnaround," *Fortune,* October 17, 1994, pp. 54–74.

[2]Thomas A. Stewart, "3M Fights Back," *Fortune,* February 6, 1996, pp. 94–99.

[3]*Thorndike-Barnhart Comprehensive Desk Dictionary* (Garden City, N.Y.: The Country Life Press, 1951); in the same source, *strategic* is "pertaining to raw material necessary for warfare . . . [and] of an air force or bombing . . . " *The New Encyclopedia Britannica* (Chicago: Encyclopedia Britannica, Inc.: 1989) still lists only military references to *strategy* and related words—an entire column of them in the index.

[4]Kenichi Ohmae, *The Mind of the Strategist: Business Planning for Competitive Advantage* (New York: Penguin Books, 1983), chap. 8 (HD31.0485).

[5]Wickham Skinner, "Manufacturing—Missing Link in Corporate Strategy," *Harvard Business Review,* May–June 1969, pp. 136–45.

[6]Under the topic "industrial productivity" the *Business Periodicals Index* lists 203 articles in the period 1979 through 1981; a decade later, 1989 through 1991, the number had fallen to only 68 articles. Two examples of 1979-81 articles: "America the Sluggish," *Economist,* July 26, 1980, pp. 14+; "Why It Won't Be Easy to Boost Productivity," *Business Week,* October 1, 1979, pp. 49-50.

[7]"The Hollow Corporation," special report, *Business Week,* March 3, 1986.

[8]George Stalk, Jr., "Time—The Next Source of Competitive Advantage," *Harvard Business Review,* July–August 1988, pp. 41–51.

[9]"Inventing Eurocleaning," in "The Tough New Consumer," *Fortune,* special issue, Autumn/Winter 1993, pp. 30–31.

[10]Cited in Bruce D. Henderson, "The Origin of Strategy," *Harvard Business Review,* November–December 1989, pp. 139–43.

[11]William H. Davidow and Bro Uttal, "Service Companies: Focus or Falter," *Harvard Business Review,* July–August 1989, pp. 77–85.

[12]Wickham Skinner, "The Focused Factory," *Harvard Business Review,* May–June 1974, pp. 113–21.

[13]David J. Collins and Cynthia A. Montgomery, "Competing on Resources: Strategy in the 1990s," *Harvard Business Review,* July–August 1995, pp. 118–28.

[14]C. K. Prahalad and Gary Hamel, "The Core Competencies of the Corporation," *Harvard Business Review,* May–June 1990, pp. 79–91.

[15]Michael E. Porter, *The Competitive Advantage of Nations* (New York: The Free Press, 1990), p. 3.

[16]Ibid., p. 10.

[17]Jack Sheinkman, "Amalgamated Clothing and Textile Workers Union," *Quality Progress,* September 1993, pp. 57–58.

[18]James P. Womack, Daniel T. Jones, and Daniel Roos, *The Machine That Changed the World* (New York: Rawson Associates, 1990), p. 13.

[19]Ibid.

[20]Michael E. Porter, *Competitive Strategy: Techniques for Analyzing Industries and Competitors* (New York: The Free Press, 1980), pp. 35–40.

[21]Aleda V. Roth, "World Class Operations: A Paradigm for OM Research in the Strategic Management of Health Care Services," *Decision Line,* July 1995, pp. 5–7.

[22]*Random House Unabridged Dictionary,* 2nd ed. (New York: Random House, 1993).

[23]Karen Bemowski, "Three Electronics Firms Win 1991 Baldrige Award," *Quality Progress,* November 1991, pp. 39–41.

Chapter 3

[1]Karen Bemowski, "Quality Is Helping Canadian Airlines International Get off the Ground," *Quality Progress,* October 1995, pp. 33–35.

[2]See *The Quality Imperative* (New York: McGraw-Hill, 1994) [HF5415.157.B87]. This *Business Week* guide, a collaborative work of more than 100 *Business Week* reporters, is an outgrowth of the classic October 1991 issue with the same title.

[3]J.M. Juran, "The Upcoming Century of Quality," *Quality Progress* 27, no. 8 (August 1994), pp. 29–37.

[4]Ibid., p. 32.

[5]Barbara B. Flynn, Roger Schroeder, and Sadao Sakakibara, "Determinants of Quality Performance in High- and Low-Quality Plants," *Quality Management Journal* 2, no. 2., (Winter 1995), pp. 8–25.

[6]Samuel Feinberg, "Overcoming the Real Issues of TQM Implementation," *Quality Progress* 28, no. 5 (July 1995), pp. 79–81.

[7]H. Gitlow, S. Gitlow, A. Oppenheim, and R. Oppenheim, *Tools and Methods for the Improvement of Quality* (Burr Ridge, Ill.: Richard D. Irwin, Inc., 1989), chap. 1.

[8]J.M. Juran and Frank Gryna, *Quality Planning and Analysis,* 2nd ed. (New York: McGraw-Hill, 1980), p. 13.

[9]U.S. General Accounting Office, *Management Practices: U.S. Companies Improve Performance through Quality Efforts* (Gaithersburg, Md: U.S. General Accounting Office, Report GAO/NSIAD–91–190, 1991).

[10]Robert D. Buzzell and Bradley T. Gale, *The PIMS Principles: Linking Strategy to Performance* (New York: The Free Press, 1987), pp. 107–11.

[11]B. Ray Helton, "The Baldie Play," *Quality Progress* 28, no. 2 (February 1995), pp. 43–45.

[12]James L. Heskett, Thomas O. Jones, Gary W. Loveman, W. Earl Sasser, Jr., and Leonard A. Schlesinger, "Putting the Service-Profit Chain to Work," *Harvard Business Review* 72, no. 2 (March–April 1994), pp. 164–74.

[13]Robert C. Camp, *Benchmarking: The Search for Industry Best Practices That Lead to Superior Performance* (Milwaukee: ASQC Quality Press, 1989).

[14]Ronald E. Yates, "Lawyers Not Exempt from Quality Crusade," *Chicago Tribune,* December 1, 1991.

[15]Robert C. Camp, *Business Process Benchmarking* (Milwaukee: ASQC Quality Press, 1995).

[16]James L. Lamprecht, *ISO 9000 and the Services Sector* (Milwaukee: ASQC Quality Press, 1994).

[17]"ISO 9002: A Good Investment," *Quality Digest,* December 1995, p. 14.

[18]George Q. Lofgren, "Quality System Registration: A Guide to Q90/ISO 9000 Series Registration," *Quality Progress,* May 1991, p. 37.

[19]Davis S. Huyink and Craig Westover, *ISO 9000: Motivating People, Mastering the Process, and Achieving Registration!* (Burr Ridge, Ill.: Irwin Professional Publishing, 1994), p. 34.

[20]Joao S. Neves and Behnam Nakhai, "The Evolution of the Baldrige Award," *Quality Progress* 27, no. 6 (June 1994), pp. 65–70.

[21]Juran, "The Upcoming Century of Quality," p. 32.

[22]Richard D. Dobbins, "A Failure of Methods, Not Philosophy," *Quality Progress,* July 1995, pp. 31–33.

[23]"The Second Lean Enterprise Report: Executive Summary," Torrance, Calif: Anderson Consulting, 1994.

[24]Harry V. Roberts and Bernard F. Sergesketter, *Quality Is Personal: A Foundation for Total Quality Management* (New York: The Free Press, 1993).

[25]*The Quality Imperative. A Business Week* guide. The Editors of *Business Week* with Cynthia Green. New York: McGraw-Hill, 1994 (HF5415.157.B87).

[26]America's discovery of Deming has been traced to Clare Crawford-Mason, a television producer. Working on a documentary on the decline of American industry in the 1970s. Crawford-Mason heard of Deming's work in Japan and pursued her journalistic instincts. See Mary Walton, *The Deming Management Method* (New York: Dodd, Mead, 1986), chap. 1 (HD38.W36). Also, a series of articles on Deming and the impact of his contribution appears in *Quality Progress,* December 1995.

[27]W. Edwards Deming, *Quality, Productivity, and Competitive Position* (Cambridge, Mass.: MIT Center for Advanced Engineering Study, 1982), p. 316.

[28]J. M. Juran, *Managerial Breakthrough* (New York: McGraw-Hill, 1964).

[29]For a detailed presentation of this sequence, see J. M. Juran and Frank M. Gryna, Jr., *Quality Planning and Analysis,* 2nd ed. (New York: McGraw-Hill, 1980), chap. 5 (TS156.J86).

[30]J. M. Juran, "The Quality Trilogy," *Quality Progress* 19, no. 8 (August 1986), pp. 19–24.

[31]Armand V. Feigenbaum, *Total Quality Control,* 3rd ed. (New York: McGraw-Hill, 1983), p. 11 (TS156.F44).

[32]Philip B. Crosby, *Quality Is Free: The Art of Making Quality Certain* (New York: McGraw-Hill, 1979), p. 146 (TS156.6.C76).

[33]Philip B. Crosby, *Let's Talk Quality* (New York: McGraw-Hill, 1989), p. 181.

[34]Ranjit Roy, *A Primer on the Taguchi Method* (New York: Van Nostrand Reinhold, 1990), pp. 31–32.

[35]Robert H. Lochner, "Pros and Cons of Taguchi," *Quality Engineering* 3, no. 4 (1991), pp. 537–49.

[36]Genichi Taguchi, Elsayed A. Elsayed, and Thomas Hsiang, *Quality Engineering in Production Systems* (New York: McGraw-Hill, 1989), chap. 2.

Chapter 4

[1]Gary Hoover, Alta Campbell, and Patrick J. Spain, eds. *Hoover's Handbook of American Business* (Austin, TX: The Reference Press, 1995).

[2]"The Fortune 500," *Fortune,* May 15, 1995.

[3]Joseph Weber, "A Better Grip on Hawking Tools," *Business Week,* June 5, 1995, p. 99.

[4]Ibid.

[5]Karl T. Ulrich and Steven D. Epplinger, *Product Design and Development* (New York: McGraw-Hill, 1995), p. 154.

[6]C. Merle Crawford, *New Products Management* (Burr Ridge, Ill.: Irwin, 1994), p. 80.

[7]Ulrich and Eppinger, *Product Design and Development,* chap. 5.

[8]Cited in presentation materials by International TechneGroup, Inc., Spring 1991.

[9]James P. Womack, Daniel T. Jones, and Daniel Roos, *The Machine That Changed the World* (New York: Rawson Associates, 1990), p. 63.

[10]David E. Bowen and Edward E. Lawler III, "Total Quality-Oriented Human Resources Management," *Academy of Management Executive,* Spring 1992, pp. 29–41.

[11]Bruce Nussbaum, "What Works for One Works for All," *Business Week,* April 20, 1992, pp. 112–13.

[12]For a critique of QFD, see Edward M. Knod, Jr., and Ann Dietzel, "Quality Function Deployment: Potential Pitfalls," *P/OM Proceedings,* Midwest Business Administration Association, March 1992, pp. 33–40.

[13]Detailed matrices are discussed in Bob King, *Better Designs in Half the Time: Implementing QFD, Quality Function Deployment in America* (Methuen, MA: GOAL/QPC, 1987).

[14]Charles A. Cox, "Keys to Success in Quality Function Deployment," *APICS—The Performance Advantage,* April 1992, pp. 25–28.

[15]"Growth versus the Environment" (cover story), *Business Week,* May 11, 1992, pp. 66–75.

[16]Geoffrey Boothroyd and Peter Dewhurst, *Design for Assembly* (Wakefield, R.I.: Boothroyd Dewhurst, Inc., 1987).

[17]Yutaka Kato, Germain Boër, and Chee W. Chow, "Target Costing: An Integrative Management Process," *Journal of Cost Management,* Spring 1995, pp. 39–50.

[18]Ranjit Roy, *A Primer on the Taguchi Method.* New York: Van Nostrand Reinhold, 1990), chap. 7.

[19]Thomas B. Barker. *Engineering Quality by Design: Interpreting the Taguchi Approach* (New York: Marcel Dekker, Inc., 1990), chap. 1.

[20]Gary Jacobson and John Hillkirk, *Xerox: American Samurai* (New York: MacMillan, 1986), pp. 178–79.

[21]Robin Yale Bergstrom, "The Quality/Environment Curve," *Production,* June 1995, pp. 62–63.

[22]Susan Moffat, "Japan's New Personalized Production," *Fortune,* October 22, 1990, pp. 132–35.

[23]Joseph F. McKenna, "From JIT, with Love," *Industry Week,* August 17, 1992, pp. 45–51.

[24]"IBM Discovers Simple Pleasures," *Fortune,* May 21, 1991, p. 64.

[25]"Winners: The Best Product Designs of the Year," *Business Week,* June 5, 1995, p. 88.

[26]Mehran Sepehri, "IBM's Automated Lexington Factory Focuses on Quality and Cost Effectiveness," *Industrial Engineering,* February 1987, pp. 66–74.

[27]Jerome Goldstein, "What's a Matchmaker Doing at a TV Assembly Plant?" *In Business* 16, no. 3, May–June, 1994.

Chapter 5

[1]Dirk Dusharme, "An Interview with Richard L. Chitty," *Quality Digest,* December 1995, pp. 50–51.

[2]A. V. Feigenbaum, *Total Quality Control: Engineering and Management* (New York: McGraw-Hill, 1961).

[3]Frank M. Gryna, "The Quality Director of the '90s," *Quality Progress,* April 1991, p. 37.

[4]"When You Discover Things You Don't Like to Hear About," *Industry Week,* April 17, 1989, p. 54.

[5]*Oliver Wight Operations Consulting and Education,* a newsletter, February 1995.

[6]Lloyd Dobyns and Clare Crawford-Mason, *Quality or Else: The Revolution in World Business* (Boston: Houghton Mifflin, 1991), p. 139.

[7]*Statistical Quality Control Handbook,* 2nd ed. (Indianapolis: AT&T Technologies, 1956), p. 217.

[8]Ron Winslow, "Hospitals' Weak Systems Hurt Patients, Study Says," *The Wall Street Journal,* July 5, 1995, pp. B1 and B5.

[9]Adapted from Ross Johnson and William O. Winchell, *Production and Quality* (Milwaukee: American Society for Quality Control Press, 1989), p. 10.

[10]Uday M. Apte and Charles C. Reynolds, "Quality Management at Kentucky Fried Chicken," *Interfaces,* May–June 1995, pp. 6–21.

[11]Ibid.

[12]This is an actual case, with data slightly modified: Cort Dondero, "SPC Hits the Road," *Quality Progress,* January 1991, pp. 43–44.

[13]Ibid.

[14]Connie R. Faylor, "Pennsylvania Builds Tomorrow's Work Force," *Quality Progress,* June 1995, pp. 71–73.

Chapter 6

[1]Chuck Murray, "Robots Roll from Plant to Kitchen," *Chicago Tribune,* October 17, 1993.

[2]Nada R. Sanders and Karl B. Manrodt, "Forecasting Practices in US Corporations: Survey Results," *Interfaces,* 24, no. 2 March–April 1994, pp. 92–100.

[3]William J. Carroll and Richard C. Grimes, "Evolutionary Change in Product Management: Experiences in the Car Rental Industry," *Interfaces,* September–October 1995, pp. 84–104.

[4]Al Ries and Jack Trout, *Bottom-Up Marketing* (New York: McGraw-Hill, 1989), p. xii.

[5]Robert Goodell Brown, *Smoothing, Forecasting, and Prediction of Discrete Time Series* (Englewood Cliffs, N.J.: Prentice-Hall, 1963), p. 102 (TA168.B68).

[6]Nada R. Sanders, "The Dollar Considerations of Forecasting with Technique Combinations," *Production and Inventory Management Journal* 33, no. 2 (1992), pp. 47–50.

[7]Bernard T. Smith, *Focus Forecasting: Computer Techniques for Inventory Control* (Boston: CBI Publishing, 1978) (HD55.S48).

[8]Virginia Cowles, *The Rothschilds: A Family of Fortune* (New York: Alfred A. Knopf, 1973), pp. 47–50 (HG1552.R8C66).

Chapter 7

[1]Alexander M. Blanton, "Capital Goods Notes" (financial analyst's research report). New York: Ingalls & Snyder, September 15, 1995.

[2]Brian Schaenzer, "Beyond Quality and Price: Time-Based Competition," *APICS—The Performance Advantage,* July 1995, pp. 32–37.

[3]Adapted from W. Earl Sasser, R. Paul Olsen, and D. Daryl Wychoff, *Management of Service Operations* (Boston: Allyn and Bacon, 1978), pp. 303–05 (HD9981.5.S27).

[4]Gary S. Vasilash and Robin Yale Bergstrom, "Customer Obsession at Solectron," *Production* (May 1995), pp. 56–58.

[5]John F. Proud, "Master Scheduling: More Art than Science," *Industrial Engineering Solutions*, September 1995, pp. 38–42.

[6]John F. Proud, "Rough Cut Capacity Planning: The 'How To' of It," *APICS—The Performance Advantage*, February 1992, pp. 46–49.

Chapter 8

[1]Jon Van, "Firms Tool Up with Information," *Chicago Tribune,* Tuesday, November 5, 1991.

[2]"A Letter from Ted," *GW2k Gateway Magazine*, Fall 1995, p. 2.

[3]Jeffrey G. Miller and Thomas E. Vollmann, "The Hidden Factory," *Harvard Business Review,* September–October 1985, pp. 142–50.

[4]For some 10 years Richard Schonberger has been asking his seminar audiences what their companies use as a carrying-cost rate. Twenty-five percent is still a common response (among those who can even answer the question), but a few are citing much higher numbers (e.g., 65 percent and 75 percent).

[5]Jon Van, "Retail and Apparel Trades Tailor New Technology, Systems," *Chicago Tribune,* Monday, March 16, 1992.

[6]"Automatic Data Collection," promotional brochure for the automatic identification industry providing technology for quick-response partners, undated, un-numbered (circa 1993).

[7]Jon Van, "Retail and Apparel Trades Tailor New Technology," March 16, 1992.

[8]"Cutting Out the Middleman," *Forbes,* January 6, 1992, p. 169.

[9]Myron Magnet, "Meet the New Revolutionaries," *Fortune* (February 24, 1992), pp. 94–101.

[10]Alex Taylor III, "GM: Some Gain, Much Pain," *Fortune,* May 29, 1995, pp. 78–84.

[11]David Young, "Logistics Revolution Spreads Stealthily," *Chicago Tribune,* November 12, 1995, pp. 5–1, 6.

[12]Jon Bigness, "In Today's Economy, There Is Big Money to Be Made in Logistics," *The Wall Street Journal,* September 6, 1995, pp. A1 and A9.

[13]Myron Magnet, "Meet the New Revolutionaries," pp. 94–101.

[14]Per Ola and Emily d'Aulaire, "Freight Trains Are Back and They're on a Roll," *Smithsonian,* June 1995, pp. 36–49.

[15]Ibid.

[16]Barry Lopez, "On the Wings of Commerce," *Harper's Magazine,* October 1995, pp. 39–54.

[17]Interview with Ed Stenger, August 1994.

[18]Jim Treece, "The Supplier Is Sometimes Right," *Production,* May 1995, p. 16.

[19]Leslie Gabriele, Robert McInturff, and Michael Pervier, "Nypro's Team Efforts Put the Customer First," *Target,* November–December 1993, pp. 45–48.

[20]Jim Treece, "The Supplier Is Sometimes Right," p. 16.

[21]Steven A. Melnyk, moderator of debate between Julie Fraser and Phil Moen, "Finite Capacity Scheduling versus Infinite Capacity Scheduling," *APICS—The Performance Advantage,* August 1995, pp. 42–47.

[22]An elaboration of the theory of constraints, called synchronous manufacturing, is described in M. Michael Umble and M. L. Srikanth, *Synchronous Manufacturing* (Cincinnati: South-Western Publishing Co., 1990) (TS155.U48).

[23]Examples of use of photos and schematic drawings, as well as more on the response-ratio technique, may be found in Richard J. Schonberger, *World-Class Manufacturing Casebook: Implementing JIT and TQC* (New York: Free Press, 1987).

[24]Richard J. Schonberger, *World-Class Manufacturing: The Next Decade* (New York: Free Press, 1996), Chap. 1.

Chapter 9

[1]Hau L. Lee and Corey Billington, "The Evolution of Supply-Chain-Management Models and Practice at Hewlett-Packard," *Interfaces,* September–October 1995, pp. 42–63.

[2]Stan Crock, "The Pentagon Goes to B-School," *Business Week,* December 11, 1995, pp. 98–100.

[3]Keki R. Bhote, *Strategic Supply Management: A Blueprint for Revitalizing the Manufacturing–Supplier Partnership* (New York: American Management Association, 1989), p. 13.

[4]James P. Womack, Daniel T. Jones, and Daniel Roos, *The Machine That Changed the World* (New York: Rawson Associates, 1990), chap. 6.

[5]Larry C. Giunipero, "AME Survey Report: A Survey of JIT Purchasing in American Industry," *Target,* Winter 1988, pp. 25–28.

[6]Roy L. Harmon, *Reinventing the Factory II* (New York: The Free Press, 1992), p. 126.

[7]Michael Barrier, "Overcoming Adversity," *Nation's Business,* June 1991, pp. 25–29.

[8]Leonard L. Berry and A. Parasuraman, *Marketing Services: Competing through Quality* (New York: The Free Press, 1991), p. 141.

[9]Chester Placek, "GM, Ford, and Chrysler Get Together to Develop Uniform SPC Procedures for Suppliers," *Quality,* December 1991, p. 13.

[10]"Building Buyer–Seller Partnerships," *Management Accounting Guideline* 32, Hamilton, Ontario, Canada: The Society of Management Accountants of Canada, 1995, p. 33.

[11]Robert H. Hayes and William J. Abernathy, "Managing Our Way to Economic Decline," *Harvard Business Review,* July–August 1980, pp. 67–77.

[12]Michael Allen, "Bottom Fishing: Developing New Line of Low-Priced PCs Shakes Up Compaq," *The Wall Street Journal,* June 15, 1992.

[13]Edmund Faltermayer, "U.S. Companies Come Back Home," *Fortune,* December 30, 1991, pp. 106–12.

[14]Lamar Lee, Jr., and Donald W. Dobler, *Purchasing and Materials Management: Text and Cases,* 3rd ed. (New York: McGraw-Hill, 1977), pp. 54–55 (HD52.5.L4).

[15]"In Failed Bid for UAL, Lawyers and Bankers Didn't Fail to Get Fees," *The Wall Street Journal,* November 30, 1989, p. A1.

[16]Based on Arthur E. Mudge, *Value Engineering: A Systematic Approach* (New York: McGraw-Hill, 1971), pp. 263–64 (TS168.M83).

[17]*Reduce Costs and Improve Equipment through Value Engineering,* Directorate of Value Engineering, Office of the Assistant Secretary of Defense for Installations and Logistics, Washington, D.C., January 1967 (TS168.U5).

Chapter 10

[1]For details on kanban variations and rules of use, see Yasuhiro Monden, *Toyota Production System* (Norcross, Ga.: Industrial Engineering and Management Press, 1983).

[2]A. Ansari and Batoul Modarress, "Wireless Kanban," *Production and Inventory Management Journal*, First Quarter 1995, pp. 60–64.

[3]"America's Best Plants," *Industry Week*, October 20, 1990.

[4]Joseph C. Quinlan, "The Remaking of Baldor Electric," *Quality in Manufacturing*, September–October 1995, pp. 36–37.

[5]See Joseph Orlicky, *Material Requirements Planning* (New York: McGraw-Hill, 1975), Chapter 10, "Product Definition" [TS155–8.O74].

[6]David A. Turbide, "MRP II: Still Number One!" *IIE Solutions*, July 1995, pp. 28–31.

[7]Paul Hoy, "Client/Server MRP II Comes of Age," *APICS—The Performance Advantage*, June 1995, pp. 38–41.

[8]Himanshu Kumar and Ram Rachamadugu, "Is MRP II Dead?" *APICS—The Performance Advantage*, September 1995, pp. 24–27.

[9]Ronald A. Hicks and Kathryn E. Stecke, "The ERP Maze," *IIE Solutions*, August 1995, pp. 12–16.

[10]Aleda V. Roth and Roland van Dierdonck, "Hospital Resource Planning: Concepts, Feasibility, and Framework," *Production and Operations Management*, Winter 1995, pp. 2–29.

[11]Data on MRP/MRP II gains are drawn from two sources: Wight, *MRP II*, Chapter 4, and Roger G. Schroeder, John C. Anderson, Sharon E. Tupy, and Edna M. White, "A Study of MRP Benefits and Costs" (Working Paper, Graduate School of Business Administration, University of Minnesota, May 1980).

[12]Oliver W. Wight, *MRP II: Unlocking America's Productivity Potential* (Williston, VT: Oliver Wight Limited Publications, 1981), p. 58 [TS161.W5x].

[13]George W. Plossl, *Managing in the New World of Manufacturing* (Englewood Cliffs, NJ: Prentice Hall, 1991), p. 177 [HD9720.5.P56].

[14]Thomas J. Peters and Robert H. Waterman, *In Search of Excellence* (New York: Harper & Row, 1982), pp. 164–65 [HD70.U5P424].

[15]The use of queue limits in an engineering department is the subject of a case study (company name disguised) by William A. Wheeler, Boston: Coopers and Lybrand, 1984.

Chapter 11

[1]Robert C. Camp. *Business Process Benchmarking: Finding and Implementing Best Practices* (Milwaukee, ASQC Quality Press, 1995), Chapter 11 [HD62.15.C345].

[2]A basic reference for manufacturing processes is Shigeo Shingo, *A Revolution in Manufacturing: The SMED [Single-Minute Exchange of Die] System* (Portland, Ore.: Productivity Press, 1985).

[3]Shigeo Shingo, *Non-Stock Production: The Shingo System for Continuous Improvement* (Portland, Ore.: Productivity Press, 1988), p. 9.

[4]While EOQ and ROP are sometimes studied as a set, we prefer to point out that EOQ may be used with a variety of order-timing methods and ROP may be used with a variety of lot-sizing methods.

[5]Jorge Haddock and Donald E. Hubricki, "Which Lot-Sizing Techniques Are Used in Material Requirements Planning?" *Production and Inventory Management*, Third Quarter 1989, pp. 53–56.

[6]Gene Woolsey, well known in the management science community for his colorful "reality check" writings, wrote an editorial attacking the EOQ model's unrealistic assumptions: "A Requiem for the EOQ: An Editorial," *Production and Inventory Management*, Third Quarter 1988, pp. 68–72.

[7]This algorithm may not be the most efficient in all cases, but it works quite well for situations with a relatively small number of price breaks.

Part IV

[1]John Hoerr, "Work Teams Can Rev Up Paper-Pushers, Too," *Business Week*, November 28, 1988, pp. 64–72.

Chapter 12

[1]Pierre Pean, "How to Get Rich off Perestroika," *Fortune*, May 8, 1989, pp. 145–50.

[2]Henry Ford, *Today and Tomorrow* (Garden City, N.Y.: Doubleday, 1926), p. 115.

[3]This description is from Pero Tafur, *Travels and Adventures* (London: G. Routledge & Sons, Ltd., 1926) p. 1435, cited in R. Burlingame, *Backgrounds of Power* (New York: Charles Scribner's Sons, 1949).

[4]Richard R. Muther, *Systematic Layout Planning* (Boston: Cahners, 1973), pp. 3–1–3–8 (TS178.M87).

[5]Copies of the programs are available as follows: CORELAP from Engineering Management Associates of Boston, and CRAFT from the IBM Share Library System. Enhanced versions of these programs are announced frequently.

[6]Jon Van, "Factory Remedies Help Hospital Cut Woes," *Chicago Tribune*, December 2, 1991, p. 1ff.

[7]Problem adapted from materials developed for Material Handling Analysis, a course developed by Richard Muther & Associates and sponsored by the University of Kansas Extension Center, 1965.

[8]Reprinted from Brian Fynes and Sean Ennis, "From Lean Production to Lean Logistics: The Case of Microsoft Ireland," *European Management Journal* 12, no. 3 (September 1994), pp. 322–30, with permission from Elsevier Science Ltd., Pergamon Imprint, The Boulevard, Langford Lane, Kidlington OX5 1GB, U.K. Adapted and amended.

[9]J. A. Crowley, "1992 and the Transport Sector," Dublin: EUROPEN Bureau of the Department of the Taoiseach, 1992.

[10]Wickam Skinner, "The Focused Factory," *Harvard Business Review*, May–June, 1974, pp. 113–21.

[11]L. W. Stern, F. D. Sturdivant, and G. A. Getz, "Accomplishing Marketing Channel Change: Paths and Pitfalls," *European Management Journal* 11, no. 1 (1993), pp. 1–8.

[12]B. J. La Londe, and R. F. Powers, "Disintegration and Reintegration: Logistics of the Twenty-First Century," *International Journal of Logistics Management* 4, no. 2 (1993), pp. 1–12.

Chapter 13

[1]"A Smart Cookie at Pepperidge," *Fortune,* December 22, 1986, pp. 67–74.

[2]This description of Milliken's Cypress plant was supplied by Mr. Sam P. Gambrell, director of Milliken Industrial Engineering Services, in a personal correspondence, December 1990.

[3]Tupper Cawsey, "The Sarnia Polymers Department, Esso Chemical Canada," in *Case Studies in Accountability,* vol. I of monograph series, January 1991 (Hamilton, Ontario: The Society of Management Accountants of Canada), pp. 52–60.

[4]The method and the example are adapted from Wayne K. Smith, James L. Ingraham, and David M. Rurak, "Time and Pull: A DuPont Case History," *Target,* January/February 1993, pp. 27–42.

[5]Adapted from Gary R. LaPerle, "Letter to the Editor," *Target,* July–August 1995, p. 51.

[6]The linearity index was devised by Hewlett-Packard Company.

[7]This example is a segment of a case study prepared by Richard Schonberger, June 1994, with the assistance of Patrick O'Malley, vice president for Deposit Services at First Chicago.

[8]Adapted from Theodore O. Prenting and Nicholas T. Thomopoulos, *Humanism and Technology in Assembly Line Systems* (Rochelle Park, N.J.: Spartan Books, 1974), pp. 131–32 (TS178.4P73).

Chapter 14

[1]Scott McCartney, "How to Make an Airline Run on Schedule," *The Wall Street Journal,* December 22, 1995, pp. B1 and B7.

[2]For example, see J. F. Cox III, J. H. Blackstone, Jr., and M. S. Spencer, eds. *APICS Dictionary,* 8th ed. (Falls Church, Va.: American Production and Inventory Control Society, 1995). The dictionary contains 16 entries relating to *job,* 8 entries relating to *batch,* and 15 entries relating to *lot.*

[3]Joseph Orlicky, *Material Requirements Planning* (New York: McGraw-Hill, 1975), p. 83 (TS155.8.O74).

[4]See, for example, O. Kermit Hobbs, Jr., "Application of JIT Techniques in a Discrete Batch Job Shop," *Production and Inventory Management Journal* 35, no. 1 (First Quarter), 1994. [This article won the *Production and Inventory Management Journal*'s Romey Everdell Best Article Award for 1994.]

[5]The original purpose was to display variances from planned production rates in repetitive production.

[6]Adapted from Oliver W. Wight, *Production and Inventory Management and the Computer Age.* (Boston: CBI Publishing, 1974), pp. 81–82 (TS155.W533). Note that operation lead times are detailed, whereas job-order lead times, discussed earlier for computing planned order releases, are gross.

[7]See Cases 2 and 3 in Richard J. Schonberger, *World-Class Manufacturing Casebook: Implementing JIT and TQC* (New York: The Free Press, 1987).

Chapter 15

[1]Peter W. G. Morris, *The Management of Projects* (London: Thomas Telford, 1994), pp. 90–92.

[2]Ibid., p. viii.

[3]Ibid., p. 217.

[4]Robert C. Camp, *Business Process Benchmarking* (Milwaukee: ASQC Quality Press, 1995), chap. 1.

[5]Ibid., p. 137.

[6]Morris, *The Management of Projects,* p. 78.

[7]Ibid., p. 104.

[8]John F. Love, *McDonald's: Behind the Arches* (Toronto: Bantam Books, 1986).

[9]Jeffrey L. Funk, "Case Study: Managing the Organizational Complexity of Applying CIM to Semiconductor Manufacturing in the Mitsubishi Corporation," *Manufacturing Review,* March 1991, pp. 5–17.

[10]Marvin L. Patterson, *Accelerating Innovation: Improving the Process of Product Development* (New York: Van Nostrand Reinhold, 1993), pp. 149–50 (TS176.P367).

[11]Morris, *The Management of Projects,* p. 249.

[12]Often the listing is event oriented rather than activity oriented; for example, instead of earliest- and latest-start activity times (ES and LS), there will be time-earliest and time-latest event times (T_E and T_L).

[13]An explanation is given in A. R. Klingel, Jr., "Bias in PERT Project Completion Time Calculations for a Real Network," *Management Science* 13, no. 4 (December 1966), pp. B–194–201.

[14]Adapted from J. S. Sayer, J. E. Kelly, Jr., and M. R. Walker, "Critical Path Scheduling," *Factory,* July 1960.

Part V

[1]Janice Klein, "The Human Costs of Manufacturing Reform," *Harvard Business Review,* March–April 1989, pp. 60–66.

[2]Corinne M. Kaufman and Marc J. Schneiderjans, "Sources of Stress in an Automated Plant," *Production and Operations Management,* Spring 1995, pp. 108–26.

Chapter 16

[1]Les Landes, "Leading the Duck at Mission Control," *Quality Progress,* July 1995, pp. 43–48.

[2]F. W. Taylor, *The Principles of Scientific Management* (New York: Harper & Row, 1911), pp. 36–37.

[3]Theodore Levitt, "Production-Line Approach to Service," *Harvard Business Review,* September–October 1972, pp. 41–52.

[4]Peter Coy and Chuck Hawkins, "UPS: Up from the Stone Age," *Business Week,* June 15, 1992, p. 132.

[5]Paula M. Noaker, "Ergonomics on Site," *Manufacturing Engineering,* June 1992, pp. 63–66.

[6]Brian S. Moskal, "The Wizards of Buick City," *Industry Week*, May 7, 1990, pp. 22–27.

[7]Ronald E. Yates, "For Motorola, Quality an Olympian Effort," *Chicago Tribune*, January 27, 1992

[8]S. S. Cherukuri, "Westinghouse Electric Corporation Asheville's Focused Factories Make a Difference—the 'Village' Concept," *Target*, Fall 1988, pp. 30–32.

[9]John A. Saathoff, "Maintaining Excellence through Change," *Target*, Spring 1989, pp. 13–20.

[10]Kiyoshi Suzaki, *The New Manufacturing Challenge: Techniques for Continuous Improvement* (New York: Free Press, 1987), pp. 12–18.

[11]See Michel Greif, *The Visual Factory: Building Participation through Shared Information* (Portland, Ore.: Productivity Press, 1991); Hiroyuki Hirano and J. T. Black, eds., *JIT Factory Revolution: A Pictorial Guide to Factory Design of the Future* (Productivity Press, 1988).

[12]H. Thomas Johnson, "A Blueprint for World-Class Management Accounting," *Management Accounting*, June 1988, pp. 23–30.

[13]A description of the use of visible performance graphs in a plant assembling minicomputers can be found in Richard C. Walleigh, "What's Your Excuse for Not Using JIT?" *Harvard Business Review*, March–April 1986, pp. 38–54.

[14]H. Thomas Johnson, "Managing Costs: An Outmoded Philosophy," *Manufacturing Engineering*, May 1989, p. 44.

[15]Peter B. B. Turney and Bruce Anderson, "Accounting for Continuous Improvement," *Sloan Management Review*, Winter 1989, pp. 37–47.

[16]Benjamin W. Niebel, *Motion and Time Study*, 9th ed. (Burr Ridge, Ill.: Richard D. Irwin, 1993), p. 389; also see a more elaborate table from Westinghouse on the same page (T60.N54).

[17]The tables were originally developed by H. B. Maynard and associates. See Harold B. Maynard, G. J. Stegemerten, and John L. Schwab, *Methods-Time Measurement* (New York: McGraw-Hill, 1948), (T60.T5M3).

Chapter 17

[1]James S. Hirsch, "A High-Tech System for Sending the Mail Unfolds at Fidelity," *The Wall Street Journal*, March 20, 1996, pp. A1, A6.

[2]Robert B. Reich, "Toward a New Economic Development," *Industry Week*, October 5, 1992, pp. 37–44.

[3]Brian O'Reilly, "Your New Global Workforce," *Fortune*, December 14, 1992, pp. 52–66.

[4]Forsyth Alexander, "ISO 14001: What Does It Mean for IEs?" *Industrial Engineering Solutions*, January 1995, pp. 14–18.

[5]Roy L. Harmon, *Reinventing the Business: Preparing Today's Enterprise for Tomorrow's Technology* (New York: Free Press, 1996), pp. 170–71. Also, cited in the same source, Barbara Marsh, "Chance of Getting Hurt Is Generally Far Higher at Smaller Companies," *The Wall Street Journal*, February 3, 1994.

[6]A method for determining transportability may be found in Richard Muther, *Systematic Handling Analysis* (Management and Industrial Research Publications, 1969) (TS180.M8).

[7]Brian O'Reilly, "Your New Global Workforce," *Fortune*, December 14, 1992, pp. 52–66.

Chapter 18

[1]Scott McCartney, "Airline Industry's Top-Ranked Woman Keeps Southwest's Small-Fry Spirit Alive," *The Wall Street Journal*, November 30, 1995, pp. B1, B12.

[2]Hal F. Rosenbluth, *The Customer Comes Second: And Other Secrets of Exceptional Service* (New York: Quill, 1992).

[3]Tom Brown, "Decoding the 'Clueless' Manager," an interview with Scott Adams, *Industry Week*, July 3, 1995, pp. 14–18.

[4]Fess Green, "College Grads on the Factory Floor: A Case of High Commitment Work Teams," *Production and Inventory Management Journal*, First Quarter 1994, pp. 8–12.

[5]Edward E. Lawler III, "Pay the Person, Not the Job," *Industry Week*, December 7, 1992, pp. 19–24.

[6]Ibid.

[7]Neal Templin, "Team Spirit: A Decisive Response to Crisis Brought Ford Enhanced Productivity," *The Wall Street Journal*, December 15, 1992.

[8]See *Business Week*, December 21, 1992.

[9]For additional details on ISO 14000, see Forsyth Alexander, "ISO 14001," *IIE Solutions*, January 1996, pp. 14–18; and Laura Struebing, "9000 Standards?" *Quality Progress*, January 1996, pp. 23–28.

[10]Janet Guyon, "A Joint-Venture Papermaker Casts Net across Europe," *The Wall Street Journal*, December 12, 1992.

ABC (inventory) analysis Materials classification system in which all stocked items are classified by annual dollar volume. The high-value A items receive close control; medium-value B items get intermediate control; low-value C items receive lowest priority.

Acceptance sampling Quality inspection technique in which a sample is taken from a completed production lot and tested. If the sample passes, the lot is assumed good, if the sample fails, the entire lot is inspected.

Activity Basic unit of work in a project.

Activity-based costing (ABC) A method of costing whereby a job, product, or service is assigned overhead costs only if overhead activity is actually expended to support it; replaces the old methods of allocating overhead costs, typically in proportion to direct labor costs.

Activity control Term usually meant to include dispatching along with input control of work releases into either gateway or bottleneck work centers.

Activity-on-arrow network A PERT/CPM network form in which activities are shown as arrows.

Activity-on-node network A PERT/CPM network form in which activities are shown as nodes.

Adaptive smoothing Technique for automatic adjustment of time-series smoothing coefficients based on some function of forecast error, commonly the tracking signal.

Agile manufacturing Streamlined, flexible approach that shortens the supply chain between manufacturing and the final consumer; responsiveness enhanced by information system linkages from retail setting to manufacturing cell.

Aggregate demand Long- and medium-range demand expressed in collective terms rather than broken down by type of product or service or specific model.

Aggregate demand forecast Forecast for whole-product or capacity groups; long- or medium-term focus.

American Customer Satisfaction Index (ACSI) A quarterly index that measures customer satisfaction, initially in seven economic sectors made up of 40 industries that are, in turn, represented by 200 organizations.

Appointment book A master schedule for the provision of services; a statement of the services to be provided.

Approved supplier A supplier given preferential treatment in purchasing decisions by earning high ratings on quality, delivery, price, and service.

Assignable-cause variation See **Special-cause variation.**

Attribute inspection Inspection requiring only a yes–no, pass–fail, or good–bad judgment.

Attributes data Data obtained through a classifying judgment (e.g., yes/no, go/no-go, pass/fail) as to the nature of the quality characteristic in question.

Automatic storage and retrieval system (AS/RS) Automated equipment, such as racks, bins, forklifts, and computerized location records, collectively designed to hold and retrieve inventory.

Autonomous operations The assignment of all work in certain products to a single work station; work is not passed from station to station.

Availability Proportion of time a resource is ready for use. Time over which the proportion is determined may exclude planned time for maintenance.

Backflush A post-deduction method of accounting for component stock usage at the time of end-product completion. Uses **BOM** explosion to identify quantity of components to deduct from inventory record balances.

Backlog Collection of orders awaiting processing.

Backorder An order accepted when stock is out; usually filled when stock arrives.

Backscheduling Subtracting lead time (or throughput time) from the due date to find the time to start processing or to place an order with a supplier; a basic MRP calculation.

Backward integration Setting up to provide goods or services formerly purchased; (sometimes) buying a supplier company, making it a subsidiary.

Backward scheduling See **Backscheduling.**

Balance delay Ratio of waiting or idle time to total available time per cycle in an assembly line.

Batch A large quantity (a lot) of a single item.

Batch processing A type of operations in which multiple units of a single item are treated as one processing unit (batch).

Benchmarking Investigating best practices anywhere in the world for a given process; basis for comparing benchmarked practice with that of one's own organization in order to inspire improvement.

Bill of labor Labor requirements (type and quantity) to produce a product or provide a service; analogous to a **BOM.**

Bill of materials (BOM) Product structure for an assembly; shows required components and their quantity at each level of fabrication and assembly.

Bill of materials (BOM) explosion Breaking down an order for end products into major, secondary, tertiary, and so forth, components for the purpose of finding gross requirements for all component items.

Blanket orders A contract covering purchase of relatively low-cost items for which there is continuous but varying need; specifies price and other matters, but delivery is usually triggered by simple release orders issued as required.

Bottleneck Work station or facility for which demand exceeds service capacity; same as a constraint.

Buffer stock Inventory maintained to provide customer service in the face of demand and production uncertainty; also known as safety stock. See also **Offline buffer stock.**

Buying down Attempting to buy an item with historical price swings at a time when the price is down.

Capacity The ability to accommodate.

Capacity control Keeping work centers busy but not overloaded; takes place after work-center loading and may include expediting.

Capacity planning Planning for adjustable resources such as labor, equipment usage, and aggregate inventory, typically over a medium-term (a few weeks to about 18 months) planning horizon.

Capacity planning team The master planning team charged with balancing the company's capacity policies with aggregate customer demand.

Capacity requirements planning (CRP) A computer-based method of revealing work-center loads; determines labor and machine resources needed to achieve planned outputs.

Capital cost Cost (e.g., interest rate) of acquiring money; a component of **Inventory carrying cost.**

Carrying cost The cost, above and beyond unit price, to carry or hold an inventory item in a state of idleness.

Catalog buying Purchasing from current supplier catalogs; the common purchasing procedure, for example, for off-the-shelf maintenance, repair, and operating (MRO) items.

Cause–effect diagram See **Fishbone diagram.**

Cell A linkage of maker–customer pairs, created by drawing people and machines from functional areas and placing them in the same work area to reduce movement distances, inventory, and throughput time and to improve coordination.

Cellular layout A layout in which work stations and machines are arranged into cells that provide families of goods or services that follow similar flow paths; very similar to product layout.

Certification Formal approval of a supplier as a source for purchased goods and services; typically bestowed after a supplier exhibits process control,

design and delivery standards, and other desirable traits. See **supplier certification.**

Changeover Changing the setup on a machine, production line, or process in order to produce a new product or service; also called **setup.**

Chase demand (strategy) A capacity management strategy in which sufficient capacity is maintained to meet current demand; capacity levels chase (respond to) demand fluctuations.

Check sheet A simple data-recording tool on which the user records observations with a check or tic mark. Over time, the marks reveal the underlying frequency distribution.

Closed-loop MRP An MRP system with feedback loops aimed at maintaining valid schedules; includes file control, rescheduling actions, and production activity control.

Commodity product An undifferentiated product.

Common cause Cause for common variation in process output (after specific or assignable causes have been removed).

Common variation Variation remaining in process output after all special variation has been removed; may be thought of as the natural variation in a process that is in statistical control.

Competitor A rival seeking the same objectives that you seek; a person or another organization vying with you or your company for sales and customers, or perhaps for employees, permits, funding, partnership with good suppliers, and so on.

Competitive analysis Thorough study ("reverse engineering") of a competitor's product or service; aimed at generating usable ideas and, sometimes, for lowering complacency about competitors.

Complete physical inventory An actual count of all inventory items.

Component item An item that goes into the assembly of the parent item; for example, a bulb is a component of a flashlight.

Composition of demand Refers to the varying degree of importance of each order in a group awaiting processing; of interest to a master planning committee, especially when demand exceeds capacity, so that more important demands (for preferred customers, or earning higher profit) can receive priority.

Computer-integrated manufacturing (CIM) Computer assistance or direct control of manufacturing from product and process design to scheduling to production and material handling; may include FMS, CAD, and CAM.

Concurrency Technique for reducing cycle times in projects by doing design and production of later stages at the same time as, and coordinated with, earlier activities.

Concurrent design Design strategy based on simultaneous rather than sequential design; employs multifunctional teams to simultaneously design outputs along with processes that will produce, deliver, and service those outputs.

Constraint See **Bottleneck**

Continuous operations Perpetual production of goods that flow; may include production of one batch after another.

Continuous process See **Continuous operations**

Core competencies Key business outputs or processes through which an organization distinguishes itself positively. See **Distinctive competency.**

Correlation coefficient A measure of the degree of association between two or more variables.

Cost variance Productivity measure computed by subtracting actual costs of inputs from standard costs of outputs for a given operating unit or job.

Crash (crashing) Reducing an activity's time by adding resources; crashing critical activities reduces project time.

Critical path The path (activity sequence) through a project network that is estimated to consume the most time.

Critical path method (CPM) A network-based project management technique initially used on construction projects; about the same as **PERT.**

Cross-docking Technique for improving responsiveness by skipping storage time at distribution centers. Material from suppliers' vehicles is moved directly into customers' vehicles for (sometimes) immediate delivery to final consumer.

Cross-functional team See **Multi-functional team.**

Custom product A highly differentiated, unique, special-purpose, or one-of-a-kind product.

Customer The next process (where the work goes next); also, the end user or consumer.

Cycle counting An inventory counting plan in which a small fraction of items are counted each day; an alternative to complete physical inventory.

Cycle interval The time interval (minutes, hours, days, or weeks) between when a certain product or service is made or delivered until the next time it is made or delivered.

Cycle time (1) Raw average time between completion of two successive units of output; for example, an ice maker that dumps six trays of ice per hour operates at a cycle time of 10 minutes. (2) Length of time, including delays, required for materials or a customer to move through a defined value-adding process. Synonym: **Throughput time.**

Cyclical pattern Recurring pattern in a time series; generally, each occurrence spans several years.

Daily priority report (Also called **dispatch list**) Job priority listing for a given shift or day; lists jobs in the order they are to be released into a work center.

Delayed differentiation Retaining standard forms or parts further along the assembly sequence; waiting as long as possible to transform common- or general-purpose items into special-purpose parts. Synonym: Postponement.

Demand forecasting Estimating future demand for goods and services.

Demand management Recognizing and managing all demands for products and services in accordance with the master plan.

Deming Prize Japan's most prestigious award for individual or organizational achievement in the field of quality; named after the late W. Edwards Deming.

Dependent-demand item An item for which demand results from demand for a parent item; for example, demand for mower blades is dependent on demand for mowers.

Derating Running a machine or production line at less than rated (maximum) capacity to forestall breakdowns, deteriorating quality, and early wear-out.

Design concept A combination of verbal and prototype forms telling what is going to change, how it is going to be changed, and how the customer will be affected by the change.

Design-build team Team consisting of product-design and process-development people, whose aim is a producible product design.

Design for operations (DFO) Concept of designing a product or service to be easy to produce or provide; a manufacturing version is design for manufacture and assembly (DFMA).

Design of experiments (DOE) A family of techniques used to plan and conduct experiments. In OM, the term is often used in reference to quality improvement activities.

Design review A check on engineering designs to ensure satisfaction of customers' requirements and producibility.

Destructive testing Product inspection that destroys the product's usefulness, rendering it unfit for sale; may be used, for example, in inspecting a sample of flashbulbs.

Dispatcher A person whose responsibility is to release jobs into work centers or, sometimes, resources to jobs.

Distinctive competency A strength that sets an organization apart from its competition.

Distribution requirements planning (DRP) Incorporation of distribution requirements into master production schedules; requirements are based on actual forecast needs, not just shelf replacement.

Dummy activity A PERT/CPM network activity that consumes no time or resources; used to clarify a network diagram.

Earliest finish (EF) The earliest possible time when a project activity may be completed; *EF* equals *ES* plus activity duration (*t*).

Earliest start (ES) The earliest possible starting time for a project activity; if an activity has multiple predecessors, its *ES* is equal to the latest predecessors' *EF*.

Early-life failure Mortality upon startup for a component or product; often caused by improper assembly or rough handling.

Early supplier involvement A program for getting a supplier's personnel involved early in new development or changes affecting items the supplier provides.

Economic order quantity (EOQ) The (fixed) quantity to be ordered in each order cycle that will minimize total inventory costs.

Efficiency Standard time divided by actual time or actual output (units) divided by standard output (units).

Efficient customer response (ECR) Advanced form of quick response designed to speed up replenishment, assortment selection, promotion, and product introduction.

Electronic data interchange (EDI) A standardized computer-to-computer messaging system used to transmit orders, billing information, and perhaps funds among organizations.

Elemental time In time study, the average observed job element time before performance rating and allowance adjustments are included.

Engineering change orders (ECOs) Formal changes in product or process design that alter bills of materials, routing, or production technique.

Enterprise resource planning (ERP) A term coined by the Gartner Group of Stamford, Connecticut; generally refers to extension of manufacturing resource planning concepts to both upstream and downstream members of the supply chain.

Ergonomics Study of a work environment with emphasis on human physiological concerns; efforts to "fit the job to the person" are examples of ergonomics in practice.

Event (node) Point signifying completion of one or more project activities and sometimes the beginning of others; consumes no time or resources but merely marks a point in time.

Expediting (Expediter) Actions aimed at pulling urgent jobs, purchases, or customers through more quickly; expediters also called parts chasers.

Exponential smoothing A form of weighted moving-average forecasting that uses a smoothing coefficient to assign an aged weight to each period of historical data.

Facilitator An individual with overall responsibility for formation, training, and leadership of improvement teams.

Facilities Plant and equipment that are generally fixed and unalterable for months to years.

Fail-safing Equipping or designing a process to be incapable of (*a*) allowing an error to be passed on to the next process, or (*b*) allowing an error at all.

Failure rate Average number of failures in a given time period; the inverse of **Mean time between failures.**

Finite-capacity planning Workload planning methods that consider the limited (finite) capacity of work stations in each scheduling period and assign work to scheduling periods accordingly.

Firm planned order An MRP tool for overriding the automatic rescheduling feature of MRP; useful for getting a job into a gateway work center at a convenient time, even if different from the calculated order due date.

Fishbone chart A chart resembling the skeleton of a fish in which the spine bone represents the major cause of quality problems and connecting bones, contributing causes; reveals cause–effect linkages. (Also known as **cause–effect diagram** and **Ishikawa diagram.**)

Fixed-period quantity Lot-sizing order quantity equal to projected net requirements for a specific time period.

Fixed-position layout A facility layout in which the product is kept in one place and facilities come to it; examples include construction and production of very large items.

Flowcharts A family of charts showing work sequence; used in data collection and analysis in an improvement study.

Flow-control system Interrelated set of activities, equipment, and software used to plan and regulate movement of materials, information, and/or customers through a processing sequence.

Focus forecasting A form of simulation-based forecasting; involves selection of the most accurate of several forecasting models as the basis for the next forecast.

Focused factory Concept that stresses doing one or a few things well at a given plant.

Forecast error For a given time period, actual demand minus forecast demand.

Forward scheduling Beginning with current date or expected start date, adding throughput (lead) time, thus arriving at a scheduled order completion date.

Functional layout A form of layout in which similar facilities and functions are grouped together in one place, usually meaning that all people working within each functional area are also grouped together.

Gain sharing An incentive pay system in which everyone receives a share of the value of productivity increases.

Gantt chart A widely used scheduling chart, with horizontal rows representing jobs or resources to be scheduled and vertical divisions representing time periods.

Gantt control chart A chart used to control certain types of jobs with stable priorities—for example, renovation and major maintenance.

Gross requirements The total amount of each component needed to produce the ordered quantity of the parent item.

Group-based capacity planning Creating aggregate capacity plans with product and service groups or families as core requirement components and a cross-trained labor force available for assignment.

Hedging A form of purchasing that offers some protection from price changes; applies especially to commodities and includes trading on futures markets.

Histogram A graphical data summary tool for recording and displaying data into predefined categories; used to study location and dispersion of observations.

Holding cost An element of inventory carrying cost; generally associated with stockroom costs, insurance, inventory taxes, and damage or shrinkage during storage.

Hot-list jobs Jobs involving parts not available but needed immediately for open orders currently in progress.

House of quality Name given to the basic QFD matrix, which includes a house-like roof showing correlations between process factors. See also **Quality function deployment.**

Idleness rate Percentage of time that a facility is idle; computed as 1 minus the utilization rate.

Incentive pay Pay based on work output; in its purest form, a piece rate.

Independent-demand item An item that does not go into a parent item.

Infinite-capacity planning A workload planning system that assumes the availability of resources required to provide needed parts and services in each scheduling period and assigns work accordingly; relies on an activity control subroutine to adjust priorities when bottlenecks arise.

Input control Control of work releases to gateway or bottleneck work centers.

Inventory carrying cost See **Carrying cost.**

Inventory turnover Annual cost of goods sold divided by value of average inventory.

Irregular maintenance Unscheduled repairs, machine installations (millwright work), and minor construction.

Ishikawa diagram See **Fishbone diagram.**

ISO 9000 Standards Series of quality systems standards developed and maintained by Geneva-based International Organization for Standardization. The ISO 9000 family is intended to provide a generic core of quality systems standards applicable across a broad range of industry and economic sectors.

ISO 14000 Standards Series of standards that provide guidance on the development and implementation of environmental management systems and principles, and on their coordination with other management systems; developed and maintained by the Geneva-based International Organization for Standardization.

Item demand Demand broken down into specific types or models of products or services.

Item master file An inventory file containing records for each component and assembly; holds on-hand balances, planning factors, and independent-demand data.

Job A task of limited size and complexity, usually resulting in something tangible; the whole work activity required to fill a service order or produce a component.

Job design The function of fitting tasks together to form a job that can be assigned to a person; emphasis is on creating useful jobs that people can and want to do. Job enlargement, job enrichment, and cross-training are associated with theories of job design.

Job operations Intermittent processing, frequently one at a time; characterized by extreme variation in output and process; type of operations in a job shop.

Just-in-time (JIT) operations A system of managing operations with little or no delay time or idle inventories between one process and the next.

Kanban A communication or signal from the user to the maker (or supplier) for more work; from the Japanese word for "card" or "visible record"; a queue-limitation device.

Labor efficiency The ratio of standard time allowed to actual time consumed per unit of work; alternatively, the ratio of actual units completed per time period to standard units for that time period.

Latest finish (LF) The latest possible completion time for a project activity to avoid project delay; if the activity has multiple successor activities, its *LF* equals the successors' earliest *LS.*

Latest start (LS) The latest possible starting time for a project activity to avoid project delay; $LS = LF -$ Activity duration (t).

Layout The physical organization or geography found in a facility. Basic types include product, cellular, functional, and fixed-position.

Lead time See **Cycle time.**

Leading indicator A variable that correlates with demand one or more periods later, giving some signal of magnitude and direction of pending demand change.

Lean production See **Toyota production system.**

Learning curve Graphical representation of the economy-of-scale concept: greater volume yields lower unit cost; the curve plots resource consumption as a function of lot quantity.

Level-by-level MRP processing The MRP way of calculating planned order release quantities and dates, top (zero) level of the BOM first, then subsequent lower levels; ensures complete capture of all requirements.

Level capacity (strategy) A capacity management strategy that seeks to retain a stable or constant amount of capacity, especially labor.

Leveling (normalizing) In setting time standards, adjusting the elemental time to reflect the pace (level of effort) of the person observed, which yields the leveled (normalized) time.

Line balancing A procedure for dividing tasks evenly among employees or work stations in a product or cellular layout; also known as assembly-line balancing.

Linear output Production of the same quantity, sometimes in the same mix, each time period; also may mean meeting a variable schedule every day.

Linearity index A measure of the success in attaining targeted production or processing quantities; mathematically, it is 100 percent minus the mean percent deviation from scheduled production quantity.

Load leveling Scheduler's attempt to release a mix of orders that neither overloads nor underloads work centers.

Load profile Future work-center capacity requirements for open and planned orders.

Loading (load, workload) Assigning workload to a work center.

Logistics Activities associated with the management of freight and distribution systems.

Lot Large purchase or production quantity of the same item; often has its own identifying number.

Lot delay Delay incurred in sequential processing settings when a piece sits idle during the processing of other pieces in the lot.

Lot-for-lot processing The simplest approach to lot sizing; the exact order quantity required by the parent item or ordered by the customer.

Lot size Quantity of an item produced, serviced, or transported at one time.

Lot sizing Planning order quantities.

Lot splitting Splitting a lot quantity into multiple sublots, traditionally for expediting reasons: stop (split up) a current lot already on a machine so a hot job can replace it. Under JIT, lot splitting is fairly normal practice (not expediting), especially if a lot can be split among several of the same type of machine or work station.

Lumpy workload (demand) Highly variable pattern of workload (demand).

Maintainability Features that make equipment or products easy to maintain.

Malcolm Baldrige National Quality Award (MBNQA) The United States' most prestigious award for organizational achievement in the field of quality; named after the late Secretary of Commerce Malcolm Baldrige.

Manufacturability See **Producibility.**

Manufacturing resource planning (MRPII) A comprehensive planning and control system that uses the master production schedule as a basis for scheduling production, capacity, shipments, tool changes, design work, and cash flow.

Master planning Broadly, matching aggregate demand with capacity; narrowly, steering the firm's capacity toward actual item demands that materialize over time.

Master production schedule (MPS) Master schedule for a goods-producing company.

Master schedule A statement of what the firm plans to produce (goods) and/or provide (services), broken down by product model or service type.

Master scheduling team The master planning team with responsibility for steering the firm's capacity toward actual demand items and toward specific, budgeted, process-improvement activities.

Material requirements planning (MRP) A computer-based system of planning orders to meet the requirements of an MPS, and of tracking inventory flows.

Mean absolute deviation (MAD) A measure of forecast model accuracy; the sum of absolute values of forecast errors over a number of periods divided by the number of periods.

Mean chart A process control chart for variables inspection showing the sample averages for a number of samples or subgroups and thus revealing between-sample variations.

Mean time between failures (MTBF) Average time elapsing between failure of a repairable item, or average time to first failure of a nonrepairable item; the inverse of **Failure rate.**

Mean time to repair (MTTR) Average time to effect repair or replacement.

Measured daywork A nominal incentive-wage system in which standard output serves as a target for an employee.

Methods study Procedure for improving the way work is done; follows the scientific method of inquiry.

Methods-time measurement (MTM) Procedure for developing synthetic time standards by referring to tables of standards for basic motions.

Milestone A key event in a project; one type of upper management–oriented network consists solely of milestone events.

Mixed-model assembly lines Assembly lines on which more than one model of a product is made.

Mixed-model processing Production schedule that is repetitive in short cycles; conducive to supplying some of each needed model each day closely in line with customer requirements.

Model A likeness (mental, graphic, mathematical, or procedural) of a reality.

Modular design Design strategy that relies on relatively few universal components which may be assembled in various configurations in order to provide flexibility (e.g., different models or types) to customers.

Motion study Methods-improvement approach focusing on basic hand and body motions called **Therbligs.**

Moving average In forecasting, the mean or average of a given number of the most recent demand amounts, which becomes the forecast for the next (first future) period; the procedure repeats each period by dropping the oldest, and adding the newest, demand.

Multi-functional team Team consisting of individuals drawn from across a spectrum of functional disciplines. Synonym: **Cross-functional team.**

Multiple regression/correlation A mathematical model allowing for investigation of a number of causal variables in order to determine their simultaneous effect on a predicted variable such as demand.

Negotiation A form of purchasing without competitive bidding, typically in a stable supply situation; usually applies to high-dollar-volume items produced to a buyer's specs.

Net requirement For an item, its gross requirement minus current or projected stock on hand.

Netting A procedure for determining the net requirement for an item; a basic MRP calculation.

Network In project management, a diagram showing sequencing of activities that constitute the project.

Non-value-adding (NVA) Having the quality of adding cost but no value to goods or services.

Normal time Time for accomplishment of a work task after the elemental time has been adjusted to reflect pace rating. See also **Pace rating.**

Number-of-defects chart A process control chart for attributes inspection based on the number of defective items in each sample.

Offline buffer stock Buffer stock that is kept out of active storage and handling; its purpose is to provide low-cost protection against infrequent, unpredictable process stoppages or surges in demand without consuming throughput time.

Open-office concept An office arrangement plan that eliminates most floor-to-ceiling walls; stresses use of modular furniture and movable, partial-height partitions; and deemphasizes compartmentalization of people.

Open order An order that has been placed but not completed.

Operation Part of a job; one step or task that requires a new setup, often at a different work center.

Operations The operating end of the business, where resources are transformed into goods and services.

Operations management Direction and control of operations; includes self-management, expert management, team management, and formal manager management; aims are improvement of transformations and allied processes.

Operations strategy Component of overall business or organizational strategy that governs and guides transformation activities that, in turn, create output goods and services.

Order A request from a customer accepted for fulfillment by a provider.

Order entry Organizational acceptance of an order into the order-processing system; includes credit checks, customer documentation, translation into operations terms, stock queries, and order number assignment.

Order fulfillment Broad set of activities that collectively ensure delivery of goods or services in response to a specific customer order.

Order promising Making a commitment to a customer to ship or deliver an order.

Outsourcing Finding an outside source of a good or service, instead of making or providing it internally.

Overlapped production Condition in which a lot is in production at two or more work centers at the same time, typically because some of the lot is rushed forward on a hot basis; normal practice within work cells.

Pace rating Judging the pace of the subject of a time-standards study, where 100 percent is considered normal; yields a factor used in normalizing or leveling the elemental time.

Parent item For a component, its next higher level assembly; the part into which a component goes.

Pareto chart A chart showing items in any population grouped by category from most to least frequently occurring; useful in categorizing data in order to set priorities for process improvement.

Pay for skills Remuneration system in which employees are paid more for acquiring additional skills and greater knowledge; also known as skill-based pay, or pay for knowledge.

Periodic maintenance Regularly scheduled custodial services and preventive maintenance.

Perpetual inventory system A system in which every issue from inventory triggers a check of on-hand stock to see if the reorder point has been reached.

Personal, rest, and delay (PR&D) allowance Amount of time added to normal time to yield standard time; accommodates personal needs and unavoidable delay when setting time standards.

Planned order (planned order release) Anticipated order placement; indicated by item, date, and quantity.

Planning horizon Period of time covered by a certain type of plan; for example, a long-range forecast might, in a certain kind of business, have a planning horizon of five years.

Pokayoke See **Fail-safing.**

Policy Directive used to guide implementation of strategy.

Precedence diagram A chart showing a repetitive job broken into sequenced flow lines; used in assembly-line balancing.

Predictive maintenance Maintenance in advance of failure or wear out, based on predicted life of the component to be maintained.

Preventive maintenance (PM) Any actions, including adjustments, replacements, and basic cleanliness, that forestall equipment failure; may be based on calendar time, time of usage, or faults revealed in an inspection.

Priority report A (typically) daily list of job priorities sent to a work center; also called a dispatch list.

Process A unique set of interrelated elements that act together to determine performance; categories from which the specific elements are taken include labor, materials, methods, machines, measurement, maintenance, and management.

Process capability In general, a statement of the ability of process output to meet specifications; inherent capability is the width (approximately six standard deviations) of the distribution of process output.

Process capability index A numerical expression of the degree to which a process output meets a given specification. The C_{pk} index is a commonly used process capability index.

Process control A condition signifying that all special or assignable variation has been removed from process output; only common or chance variation remains. Also known as statistical control.

Process control chart Statistical control chart on which to record samples of measured process outputs; the purpose is to note whether the process is statistically stable or changing, so that adjustments can be made as needed.

Process delay Delay incurred as a result of a bottleneck; for example, an entire lot is stalled due to insufficient capacity at the next work center in the job routing.

Process flowchart See **Flowcharts.**

Process industry An industry that produces goods that flow, pour, or mix together; also called continuous-flow process industry.

Process lot A number of units treated as one lot for processing; may be subdivided or combined with other lots into a different-sized transfer lot for handling and transport.

Producible or **producibility** Easy to make without error and undue cost with present or planned equipment and people; a desirable product design characteristic; also, manufacturability or operability.

Product layout A type of layout in which facilities are placed along product flow lines, with the customer (next process) next to the provider.

Product planning Developing lines of goods and services.

Product structure See **Bill of materials (BOM).**

Production activity control Keeping work on schedule on the shop floor, using progress information (feedback), which is compared with schedules; sometimes employs daily priority report, which gives priority based on relative lateness.

Production control Directing or regulating the flow of work through the production cycle, from purchase of materials to delivery of finished items; flow control. A production control department may include operations planning, scheduling, dispatching, and expediting.

Production line Multiple sequential processes arranged into one grand process to produce a product or narrow family of products.

Production/operations management (POM) See **Operations management.**

Production plan Total planned production, or production rate; unspecific as to product model or type of service.

Production rate Pace of production output, expressed in units per time period.

Productivity In general, output divided by input; in various forms, may apply to labor, materials, or other resources.

Program evaluation and review technique (PERT) A network-based project management technique originally developed for R&D projects; about the same as CPM.

Progressive operations Production in which material being worked on is passed from work station to work station; alternative to autonomous production.

Project A large-scale, one-of-a-kind endeavor; generally employs large amounts of diverse resources.

Project manager A manager or management team having responsibility for a project, not a function. Various project manager types include project manager, commodity manager, project coordinator, project engineer, and brand manager, each having a different degree of authority over the project.

Project team Multi-functional team assembled to plan and carry out a project.

Proportion-defective chart A process control chart for attributes, which shows the proportion or fraction defective in each sample.

Pull system/pull-mode operations A system in which the user pulls work from the maker or provider by some kind of signal (called kanban); pull signals should be issued at rate of actual usage.

Push system A system in which the maker pushes work forward into storage or onto the next process with little regard for rate of use; rate of pushing out the work often is preset by schedule.

Quality Perception of value in the eyes of the customer.

Quality action cycle Iterative program for ensuring quality that places primary emphasis on defect prevention but also incorporates detection as a back-up. Steps include design, self-inspection and correction, defect discovery, process analysis, and continuous improvement.

Quality assurance In general, the activities associated with making sure that the customer receives quality goods and services; often, the name given to a department charged with carrying out these responsibilities.

Quality characteristic A process performance (output) property of a product or service deemed important enough to control.

Quality control circle (quality circle) A small work group that meets periodically to discuss ways to improve quality, productivity, or the work environment.

Quality cost (1) *Traditional.* Costs directly attributable to activities performed to prevent and/or detect defective output, and to correct and/or recover

from the effects of defective output. (2) *Modern.* Cost or loss to society of any deviation from target.

Quality function deployment (QFD) Matrix-based procedure for displaying customers' requirements, processes for meeting them, and competitors' versus one's own company's capabilities on each process; basic QFD matrix may be supplemented with other, more detailed process matrices. See also **House of quality.**

Quality value Competitive benefits of quality outputs; they may accrue through marketing advantages and through reduced costs of operations.

Queue limiter (queue limitation) Device that places an upper limit on number of units waiting (or time waiting) for processing. See also **Kanban.**

Quick response (QR) System of linking final retail sales with production and shipping schedules back through the chain of supply; usually employs point-of-sale scanning plus electronic communication and may employ direct shipment from a factory, thus avoiding distribution warehousing.

Random events In a time series, patternless occurrences, such as jumps or drops in demand, for which there is no apparent cause.

Range chart A process control chart for variables; shows range of each sample—that is, within-sample variation.

Regularized schedule A schedule in which certain items are produced at regular intervals.

Reliability Probability that an item will work at a given time.

Reorder point (ROP) Quantity of on-hand inventory that serves as a trigger for placing an order for more.

Repetitive operations Producing the same item or providing the same service over and over.

Requisition An internal request to have something purchased; usually goes to a purchasing department, which uses it in preparing a purchase order.

Rescheduling notice A notice (usually from an MRP system) that an order for a component part needs to be rescheduled; stems from a change in due dates or quantities for one or more parent items.

Residual inventory Inventory left over when an order is canceled or reduced in quantity.

Resource requirements planning A gross check to see if items in the master schedule will overload a scarce resource; also known as rough-cut capacity planning on the trial master schedule.

Response ratio A measure of idle work in work centers using ratios of lead time to work content, process speed to use rate, and pieces to work stations or operators; process improvements are reflected in smaller ratios.

Robust design Design that is able to withstand unfavorable operating conditions and hostile operating environments.

Rolling forecast A forecast that is redone at intervals, typically dropping oldest data and replacing it with most recent data.

Rough-cut capacity planning Conversion of an operations plan into capacity needs for key resources. The purpose is to evaluate a plan before trying to implement it.

Routings Path from work center to work center that work follows in its transformation into a finished item or complete service; standard routings may be kept in records.

Run diagram A running plot of measurements of some process or quality characteristic, piece by piece as a process continues.

Scatter (correlation) diagram A plot of effects (e.g., quality changes) against experimental changes in process inputs.

Scientific management School of management developed in the late nineteenth century by Frederick Winslow Taylor and contemporaries; incorporates close regimentation and measurement of work, ergonomics, training as to prescribed procedures, and reliance on standard methods and times.

Seasonal index Ratio of demand for a particular season to demand for the average season.

Seasonal variation (seasonality) Recurring pattern in a time series; occurring within one year and repeating annually.

Service level Percentage of orders filled from stock on hand.

Service parts Parts or components produced to supply the after-sales service market.

Service–profit chain A series of causal links suggesting that profit and growth flow from customer loyalty, which is a result of customer satisfaction. Customer satisfaction stems from perceived value of goods and services received. That value is created by satisfied, loyal, and productive employees. Employee satisfaction, in turn, flows from high-quality support services and policies that empower employees. See also **Value chain.**

Serviceability Degree to which an item may be maintained—either kept in service through preventive maintenance or restored to service after a breakdown.

Setup See **Changeover.**

Seven deadly wastes Basic or root categories of undesirable outcomes (wastes) due to poor process design or faulty operations. Wastes stem from overproduction, waiting, transport, processing, inventory, motion, and poor quality.

Shop calendar A scheduling calendar with workdays as sequentially numbered days; sometimes numbered 000 to 999.

Shop floor control See **Activity control.**

Simultaneous engineering Inclusion of supplier, process, and manufacturing engineers early in product design stages; aims for shorter lead times, better quality, and better coordination. See also **Concurrent design.**

Skill-based pay Compensation system in which employees are paid primarily for attainment of skills. Also called **Pay for knowledge.**

Slack (slack time) (1) In project management, slack is the amount of time an activity may be delayed without delaying the project schedule; usually changes as the project progresses. (2) In job scheduling and dispatching, slack is available time (time until job is due) minus required time (time needed to perform the job).

Social loss (of bad quality) A concept introduced by Genichi Taguchi stating that there is a cost imparted to society whenever process output deviates from the target.

Soliciting competitive bids Inviting prospective suppliers to bid (offer a price) on a contract to provide goods or services according to specifications.

Special-cause variation A type of variation in process output that can be traced to a specific cause such as a fault or malfunction, removal of which removes the variation.

Specification Process output description commonly in two parts: the target (nominal) and the tolerances.

Speculation (speculative) buying Purchasing to get an attractive price rather than because of need.

Spider diagram Graphical display used to portray changing status of selected group performance factors which are depicted as lines radiating outward from a central point; better performance is reflected as a plot closer to the center.

Standard data Tables of time-standard values used to construct synthetic standards.

Standard deviation (SD) A measure of dispersion in a distribution; equal to the square root of the variance; in forecasting, defined as the square root of the mean-square error.

Standard time The time a qualified person is expected to take to complete a task; the normal time plus an allowance factor.

Standardization Settling on a few, rather than many, variations of a given part, product, or service.

Statistical process control (SPC) Collection of process analysis techniques including process flowchart,

Pareto analysis, fishbone chart, run diagram, control chart, and scatter diagram.

Stockkeeping unit (SKU) An item of inventory at a particular geographic location. For example, if six packs of canned Classic Coca Cola are in a special display near the checkout counters and also stocked with the other soft drinks, that constitutes two SKUs.

Stockout Failure to deliver from stock upon receipt of a customer order.

Strategy A basic type of plan with far-reaching effects; a foundation for more specific plans.

Streamlined operations Steady-flow operations with few delays, stops, starts, or storages.

Supplier certification See **Certification.**

Synchronized scheduling (synchronized processing) Processing with schedules in which the timing of delivery or production of a component is meshed with the use rate of the parent item.

Systematic layout planning (SLP) A multistep approach to layout planning based on flow and relationship data.

Systems contract A contract with a supplier for a defined set of items, often allowing orders to be placed by line managers without going through the purchasing department.

Technical estimate A nonengineered, experience-based, time standard.

Theory of constraints Approach to operations that attempts to schedule and feed work so as to maximize work-flow rate (and therefore cash flow as well) through bottlenecks and constraints.

Throughput time See **Cycle time.**

Time fence A point on a company's planning horizon that separates the firm portion (typically, the near future) from the tentative portion (more distant future).

Time measurement unit (TMU) A time unit in MTM analysis: 1 TMU = 0.0006 minutes, or 0.00001 hours.

Time-phased order point (TPOP) A subset of MRP for handling independent-demand items.

Time series A sequential set of observations of a variable taken at regular intervals over time.

Time standard See **Standard time.**

Time study A direct approach for obtaining the cycle time to be used in setting a time standard; obtained by stopwatch or film analysis.

Tolerance stackup See **Variation stackup.**

Total preventive maintenance (TPM) A full agenda of procedures that improve dependability of equipment, with emphasis on maintaining equipment before it breaks down; bestows primary responsibility for PM on equipment operator.

Total quality (TQ) Comprehensive management approach to ensure quality throughout an organization; includes planning and design, supplier and user/processor interface, self-inspection for control, and continual improvement in customer service through process monitoring and feedback; places primary responsibility for quality at the source (i.e., the maker or provider).

Total quality control (TQC) See **Total quality.**

Total quality management (TQM) Deliberate actions taken to ensure total quality.

Toyota production system A system of management first perfected at Toyota Motor Company. Key characteristics include total quality, just-in-time operations, total preventive maintenance, minimization of wastes, empowerment of cross-trained employees, and great emphasis on continuous improvement throughout all facets of company operations.

Tracking signal Typically, the cumulative forecast error in a time series divided by the MAD; used as a limit to trigger adjustment in smoothing coefficients in adaptive smoothing models.

Transfer lot A number of units treated as one lot for transport; may be larger or smaller than lots sized for processing (**process lots**).

Trend A long-term shift, positive or negative, in the value of a time series; also known as slope.

Undercapacity (labor) scheduling Scheduling labor output at less than full capacity; allows schedule to be met on most days and allows times for operators to work on quality and maintenance.

Unit-load concept A concept calling for accumulation of enough pieces to make a "full load" before moving any pieces.

Universal design A design that is flexible enough to appeal to a broad cross-section of the market.

U-shaped layout A popular variant of product or cellular layout; improves flexibility, teamwork, equipment and tool use, and work flow by arranging work stations into a semi-circular or U-shaped pattern.

Utilization Ratio of time in use to time available.

Value-adding activities Activities in which value is added to the resource undergoing transformation; does not include non-value-adding transactions, inspections, handling, delays, and so on.

Value analysis (VA) Examination of existing product design specifications with the aim of lowering cost; typically centered in the purchasing department.

Value chain Series of transformation processes that move a good or service from inception to final consumer; major activity groups include funding, design, testing, production, distribution, marketing, and delivery. Ideally, each step increases the worth (or, value) of the item in the eyes of the next customer. See also **Service–profit chain.**

Value engineering (VE) Same as **value analysis,** but typically centered in the engineering organization.

Variables data Data obtained through measurement of some underlying (usually) continuous distribution (e.g., physical dimensions, weight, time).

Variables inspection A test in which measurements of an output (quality) characteristic are taken.

Variation stackup The output that results when two or more components at extreme edges within tolerance (specification) limits are assembled or mixed together; often the result is an assembly, batch, or service that performs poorly or is out of specification limits.

Vendor-managed inventory (VMI) An advanced version of quick response in which customers confer to their suppliers those activities necessary to manage customers' inventory.

Work breakdown structure (WBS) Product-oriented list and definition of major modules and secondary components in a project.

Work cell See **Cell.**

Work content time Time required to make a complete assembly or perform a job; usually the sum of the times of all tasks needed.

Work in process (WIP) Partly completed work that is either waiting between processes or is in process.

Work-sampling study Work measurement technique in which the analyst makes random, direct observations of subject employee's activity, records output volume, and uses these data to create an engineered time standard.

Zero defects (ZD) Proposed as the proper goal of a quality program; an alternative to the past practice of setting an acceptable quality (defect) level.

I N T E R N E T   E X E R C I S E S

Chapter 1

1. Visit the home page your authors have constructed to support your use of this text through http://www.irwin.com/management/pom. Add this page to your web "bookmarks" or "frequent sites" file. You might take a few minutes to explore this site to familiarize yourself with its features.

2. Professor John Grout, Southern Methodist University, has assembled a list of acronyms frequently used in production and operations management and has posted his list on the World Wide Web (http://www.cox.smu.cdu/jgrout/acronym.html). During this course, you might wish to make use of Prof. Grout's list, so add his page to your web "bookmarks" or "frequent sites" file. While you are there, you might also take a quick look at the list.

Chapter 2

1. A cornerstone of the *Principles of Operations Management* is a high level of confidence in the human component. The mission statement of the U.S. Department of Labor's Employment and Training Administration also addresses the issue of human capabilities in the workplace. Visit the ETA's Web site (http://www.doleta.gov) and review its mission statement, paying particular attention to the assumptions about the human at work. Is it consistent with the principles of OM? Discuss.

2. Cranfield University in the United Kingdom hosts the Manufacturing Strategy Home Page. Visit the site (http://www.cranfield.ac.uk/public/mn/mr940715/). What are the current issues in manufacturing strategy?

3. *Team exercise.* Conduct an Internet search for just-in-time (JIT). Prepare a report on the degree to which JIT is embedded as strategy around the globe. (Hint: The Curtin University of Technology in Perth, Australia, maintains a World Wide Web page devoted to just-in-time.)

Chapter 3

1. *Team exercise.* Several states have quality awards. Prepare a report on the general nature, criteria, administration, and recent winners of some of these awards. You might begin with a visit to the Internet home page for the American Society for Quality Control (ASQC) (http://www.asqc.org).

2. The American Society for Quality Control (ASQC) experienced explosive membership growth during the 1980s and 1990s. What steps has the Society taken to improve the quality of its services to members even as the demand for these services has increased dramatically? To what extent might other service providers employ similar steps? Explain.

3. *Team exercise.* Visit the home page for the International Organization for Standardization (http://www.iso.ch/welcome.html). Prepare a report on the process used to develop and implement international standards.

4. Visit the web site for the American National Standards Institute (http://www.ansi.org). What services does ANSI provide through this site? How might the Institute assist an organization in meeting the quality expectations of customers?

5. The National Institute for Standards and Technology (NIST) is responsible for administration of the Malcolm Baldrige National Quality Award (MBNQA). Visit the NIST site (http://www.nist.gov) and summarize information about the MBNQA and recent winners.

Chapter 4

1. Visit the home page for the Quality Function Deployment Institute (http://qfdi.org/www/qfdi/). Prepare a brief report on current Institute activities and publications.

2. *Team exercise.* Numerous Internet sites contain information about simultaneous (or concurrent) design or engineering. Visit some of those sites and prepare a report of your findings; pay particular attention to:
   a. The industry in which the application takes place.
   b. Benefits claimed and difficulties encountered.

3. The University of Wisconsin maintains a web site containing information about design-for-disassembly. Visit that site (http://smartcad.me.wisc.edu/~kyonghum/kh.html) and report on your findings.

Chapter 5

1. *Team exercise.* Prepare a report that describes examples of Pareto analysis applications in services. An Internet search is a good first step.

2. Clemson University maintains a server dedicated to global continuous quality improvement (CQI). Visit the site (http://deming.eng.clemson.edu) and prepare a report detailing its purpose, offerings, and other services.

3. Conduct an Internet search for "total quality management." (Note: We put the words in quotes to indicate that you should have them included as a string in your search.) What do the results of your search reveal about the current state of TQM? Be as specific as to industries, nations, tools, sectors (e.g., public, nonprofit) as you can.

Chapter 6

1. Conduct an Internet search for the term "demand forecasting." You are likely to get more than 1,000 matches. Modify your search by inquiring about demand forecasting in selected industries. Report on your findings.

Chapter 7

1. The American Production and Inventory Control Society (APICS) has been the sponsoring organization for much of the body of knowledge on capacity planning and master scheduling. Visit the APICS site (http://www.apics.org) along with any other related Internet sites you might discover, and prepare a report on current projects that addresses these topics.

2. Use "master planning" coupled with "manufacturing" as targets in an Internet search. How many matches did you obtain? What is the general nature of the top 10 (according to